CAMBRIDGE CLASSICAL
COMMENTAR

39

ANTIPHON THE SOPHIST: THE FRAGMENTS

ANTIPHON THE SOPHIST

THE FRAGMENTS

EDITED WITH INTRODUCTION,
TRANSLATION, AND COMMENTARY

BY
GERARD J. PENDRICK

CAMBRIDGE
UNIVERSITY PRESS

CAMBRIDGE UNIVERSITY PRESS
Cambridge, New York, Melbourne, Madrid, Cape Town, Singapore,
São Paulo, Delhi, Dubai, Tokyo

Cambridge University Press
The Edinburgh Building, Cambridge CB2 8RU, UK

Published in the United States of America by Cambridge University Press, New York

www.cambridge.org
Information on this title: www.cambridge.org/9780521126120

First published 2002
Third printing 2004
This digitally printed version 2009

A catalogue record for this publication is available from the British Library

Library of Congress Cataloguing in Publication data

Antiphon, of Athens.
The fragments / Antiphon the Sophist ; edited with introduction,
translation and commentary by Gerard J. Pendrick.
p. cm. — (Cambridge classical texts and commentaries ; 39)
Includes bibliographical references and indexes.
ISBN 0 521 65161 1
1. Sophists (Greek philosophy) 2. Philosophy, Ancient. I. Title:
Antiphon the Sophist. II. Pendrick, Gerard J. III. Title. IV. Series.
PA3870. A2 2001
183′.1—dc21 2001035690

ISBN 978-0-521-65161-5 Hardback
ISBN 978-0-521-12612-0 Paperback

For the members of my family, living and dead

CONTENTS

PREFACE

This work aims to present a complete collection and discussion of the evidence for the life and writings of the fifth-century BC sophist Antiphon. For the texts of ancient authors who quote or discuss Antiphon, I am entirely dependent on the editions listed in Works Cited at the end of this volume. For the Oxyrhynchus papyri of Antiphon's treatise *On Truth*, I have relied on existing collations, those of the original editors of the papyri (Grenfell and Hunt and M. S. Funghi) as well as the new collation of all the papyrus texts by G. Bastianini in the *Corpus dei papiri filosofici*. Where the reports of these editors differ, this has been noted in the critical apparatus. Although I offer no new readings in these papyri, I have suggested a few new supplements and criticized the various restorations proposed. In no case, however, are my suggestions or criticisms dependent on paleographical considerations (in which I have and claim no expertise). For the new fragment deriving from Diogenes of Oenoanda's Epicurean inscription (F80(b)), I am dependent on Martin Smith's edition. For the fragment from Galen preserved in Arabic (F29A), I translated the German version of the Arabic offered by the original editors Meyerhof and Schacht, and my translation was subsequently checked against the Arabic by Professor Fritz Zimmermann.

Although I have added new material to that collected by prior editors, for the sake of convenience I have attempted to adhere as closely as possible to the numeration employed by Diels and Kranz in *Fragmente der Vorsokratiker* and Mario Untersteiner in the fourth volume of his *Sofisti*. One difference from their practice, however, should be noted: texts designated with a number and capital letter (e.g. F24A, F29A) represent independent fragments, while those designated with a number followed by a lower-case letter in parentheses (e.g. F13(a), F80(b)) represent component parts of a single fragment. The new material includes several additional texts pertaining to Antiphon's activity as a dream-interpreter (T11–12, F81B); numerous passages from the Aristotelian commentators and other ancient and medieval writers pertaining to Antiphon's quadrature attempt and argument about the buried bed (F13, F15); the new papyrus *P.Oxy.* 3647, supplementing *P.Oxy.* 1364 (F44(b)); the new text from Diogenes of Oenoanda, supplementing the evidence of Cicero (F80(b)); and in the case of many fragments preserved in the lexicographical tradition, fuller citations of the evidence than previous editors have offered.

Ancient authors (other than Antiphon) are cited from the editions listed in Works Cited, and my references to page-, line-, and fragment-numbers reflect those editions.

This book began life (longer ago than I care to remember) as a Columbia University doctoral dissertation. I would like to acknowledge support received during the initial stages of work on the dissertation from a Whiting Foundation Fellowship. I would further like to express my thanks to all my teachers at Columbia, particularly James Coulter, who first interested me in the sophists, and Richard Janko, whose extensive and helpful comments on the dissertation guided me in its subsequent reworking. My greatest scholarly debt is to Leonardo Tarán, who served as adviser on the dissertation and read a penultimate draft of the commentary on several key fragments. More generally, Professor Tarán's encouragement, support, and friendship have sustained me throughout my work. Everything I know about ancient philosophy I have learned, directly or indirectly, from him.

Professors Michael Reeve and David Sedley read the entire manuscript for the Cambridge Classical Texts and Commentaries series. Their comments and corrections saved me from many errors and improved the book at many points. Professor Reeve also gave me extensive help with the critical apparatus and the Conspectus Siglorum. I am deeply indebted and grateful to both of them. Additional help on the Conspectus was provided by Professor James Diggle. I would also like to express my sincere thanks to Professor Fritz Zimmermann, who generously marked the original Arabic of F29A, checked and corrected my translation against it, and further corresponded with me concerning the meaning of Arabic terms. I am indebted to my Cambridge editors, Pauline Hire and now Michael Sharp, for their patience and support at every stage of the production of this book. They have made my experience as a Cambridge author a pleasure.

A final and different sort of debt is owed to my parents, to Nathalie, and to my children Danielle, Denis, Matthew, and Alan for their patience, support, and endurance through the long years of this book's genesis. Without them, I would never have had the strength to complete it. To them, and to all of my family, I owe more than I can ever express in words.

Decatur, Georgia
6 April 2001

INTRODUCTION

I THE IDENTITY OF ANTIPHON

Among the plethora of Antiphons known from the later fifth and the fourth centuries BC, particularly at Athens, are several who have often been confused, in antiquity as well as in modern scholarship. These include Antiphon son of Sophilus, of the deme Rhamnus, the famous Athenian logographer and politician who was an originator of the oligarchic coup of 411;[1] Antiphon ὁ σοφιστής, who disputes with Socrates in Xenophon's *Memorabilia*;[2] and Antiphon the tragic poet, who is cited several times by Aristotle. The poet Antiphon is certainly to be distinguished from Antiphon of Rhamnus. For while the latter was tried and executed at Athens in 411 on a charge of treason, a widespread ancient tradition puts the former's death in Syracuse, at the hands of the elder Dionysius. Cf. Aristotle, *Rhetoric* 1385a9–10; Plutarch, *De Stoicorum repugnantiis* 1051C–D, *Quomodo adulator* 68A–B; [Plut.], *Vitae X or.* 833B–C; Philostratus, *Vitae sophistarum* 499–500.[3] Joël (1893–1901), 2.649 with n. 1 rejected this ancient tradition and identified all the above-mentioned Antiphons, as does the author of the pseudo-Plutarchan *Vit. X or.*[4] (Philostratus

[1] *PA* 1304; Fraser and Matthews (1994), s.v. Ἀντιφῶν (57); Thucydides, 8.68.

[2] *PA* 1278; Fraser and Matthews (1994), s.v. Ἀντιφῶν (4); *Memorabilia* 1.6.1–15 = T1.

[3] Cf. Narcy (1989), 225, 240.

[4] To the confusion of Antiphons [Plut.] adds the figure of Antiphon son of Lysonides (*PA* 1283; Fraser and Matthews [1994], s.v. Ἀντιφῶν (5)). Avery (1982), 153 n. 32 and Edwards (1998) sought to defend the credibility of [Plut.]. The former argued that the confusions result from conflation of different sources, each of which offers reliable information about the particular Antiphon it deals with; the latter interpreted expressions such as λέγεται, ὥς φασι, δοκεῖ, and ὥς τινες as disclaimers by which [Plut.] sought to avoid responsibility for

also confuses the poet with Antiphon of Rhamnus.) But the credibility of [Plut.] is non-existent, and the chronological grounds for distinguishing the poet Antiphon and the Rhamnusian are convincing.[5] Chronological and other considerations also seem to rule out identification of the poet with Xenophon's Antiphon.[6] In the past, this identification was supported by Joël, Luria, and others; more recently, Narcy has defended it as at least possible.[7] Narcy points out that the encounters of Antiphon and Socrates depicted by Xenophon are mentioned in Aristotle's Περὶ ποιητῶν, a work on poets (cf. T5 with commentary); he suggests this may imply that Xenophon's Antiphon was himself a poet. But the suggestion is fanciful; and the parallels Narcy tries to draw between F44(a)I.13–23 (from the sophist Antiphon's Περὶ ἀληθείας) and the anecdotes about the poet are unconvincing. The real problem of identity concerns not the poet Antiphon, but the relationship between Xenophon's Antiphon "the sophist" and Antiphon of Rhamnus. Modern commentators more often than not have identified these two – the so-called unitarian position.[8] But according to Hermogenes of Tarsus (*De ideis* 399.18–400.6 = T2(a), ll. 1–10), Didymus of Alexandria and many others distinguished the Rhamnusian Antiphon

information he considered dubious. These arguments amount to special pleading.

5 On the unreliability of [Plut.] cf. Taylor (1772), 268–73; van Spaan (1773), 825; Sauppe (1896), 512–13; Andrewes in Gomme et al. (1981), 170; Cuvigny (1981), 27–31.

6 Cf. van Spaan (1773), 827; Sauppe (1896), 513; Nestle (1942), 389–90; Schmid (1940), 99; Untersteiner (1954), 228 n. 7 = (1967), 2.45 n. 7.

7 Cf. Luria (1924b), 330, (1927b), 1065; Joël (n. 1 above); Narcy (1989), 225–26, 240–41. Wilamowitz (1959), 1.61 n. 1 also considered the identification possible.

8 Cf. Joël (1893–1901), 2.638–73 and (1921), 663 n. 3; Croiset (1917); Aly (1929), 105–77; Hommel (1941); Morrison (1961) and (1972), 108–11; Avery (1982); Decleva Caizzi (1969), 71–83, (1984), (1985), 69, (1986b); Gagarin (1990), (1997), 5–6. Narcy (1989) offers a lengthy survey of the modern debate.

from the "other" Antiphon who was author of Περὶ ἀληθείας and similar philosophical works. Since Hermogenes' "other" Antiphon is plausibly identified with the Antiphon depicted by Xenophon, there arises the possibility of distinguishing a "sophist" Antiphon from the Rhamnusian politician and logographer – the so-called separatist position.[9] Morrison (1961), 54; Narcy (1989), 230, and others have objected to the use of the term "sophist" in this context (cf. below). But its use is no mere modern custom (as these commentators pretend): it goes back at least to Xenophon, and is repeated in later ancient authors.[10] Three types of evidence have been brought to bear in the discussion on the identity of Antiphon: the ancient testimonia; the linguistic and stylistic characteristics of the various works current in antiquity under the name of Antiphon; and the ethical, political, and religious ideas these works have been thought to reveal. The ancient testimonia, which offer the surest support for the separatist position, will be considered first.

The earliest and best evidence for the existence of a sophist Antiphon distinct from Antiphon of Rhamnus is provided by Xenophon's account of a series of conversations between Socrates and Antiphon ὁ σοφιστής (cf. T1).[11] Antiphon's purpose in all three conversations is to discredit Socrates as a teacher, in order to win over some of his followers (cf. commentary on T1). Two interrelated characteristics of the Antiphon in the *Memorabilia* are cru-

[9] Cf. van Spaan (1773), 824–27; Blass (1887–98), 1.93–94; Bignone (1938), 161–215; Schmid (1940), 98–100; Untersteiner (1954), 228–30 = (1967), 2.45–47; Pendrick (1987), (1993).

[10] Cf. below, and commentary on T1, l. 1; T3, ll. 1–2.

[11] On the importance of Xenophon's evidence cf. Seeliger (1924), 15; Schmid (1940), 100. Schmid contended that Xenophon's Antiphon could not be the Rhamnusian because all datable conversations in the *Memorabilia* fall in the last decade of the fifth century (after his execution). But the contention is untenable; cf. Avery (1982), 151 n. 26, with references.

cial to the question of his identity. The first is his status as a professional, paid educator and rival of Socrates (something which is implied by the entire episode). This characteristic almost certainly distinguishes Xenophon's man from Antiphon of Rhamnus. For despite many claims to the contrary, there is no conclusive evidence that Antiphon of Rhamnus was a professional teacher of the kind implied by Xenophon's portrait of Antiphon. The later ancient tradition that made Thucydides the pupil of Antiphon of Rhamnus rests on mere inference and can be dismissed (cf. commentary on T2(a), ll. 15–17, with references). Nor does Socrates' joke at *Menexenus* 236A (ἀλλὰ καὶ ὅστις ἐμοῦ κάκιον ἐπαιδεύθη, μουσικὴν μὲν ὑπὸ Λάμπρου[12] παιδευθείς, ῥητορικὴν δὲ ὑπ' Ἀντιφῶντος τοῦ Ῥαμνουσίου, ὅμως κἂν οὗτος οἷός τ' εἴη Ἀθηναίους γε ἐν Ἀθηναίοις ἐπαινῶν εὐδοκιμεῖν) prove that the Rhamnusian taught rhetoric. Most likely Antiphon owes his mention here to his reputation as one of the outstanding *practitioners* of oratory in the late fifth century. His identification as a teacher (ἐπαιδεύθη) is probably no more than an accommodation to the context, in which he and Lamprus are ironically juxtaposed with Aspasia and Connus, the supposed teachers of Socrates.[13] Plutarch, *De gloria Atheniensium* 350C speaks of the Rhamnusian as the head of a school: τοὺς ἐν ταῖς σχολαῖς τὰ μειράκια προδιδάσκοντας τοὺς Ἰσοκράτεις καὶ Ἀντιφῶντας καὶ Ἰσαίους. But such evidence (despite Morrison [1961], 49 n. 3, [1972], 123–24) is late and unreliable. In this context it is worth recalling that at the Rhamnusian's trial on the charge of treason, the prosecution evidently mentioned his activity as a paid logographer: ἀλλὰ μὲν δὴ λέγουσιν οἱ κατήγοροι ὡς συνέγραφόν τε δίκας ἄλλοις καὶ ὡς [ὡς Crönert: τὸ ε ed. pr.]

[12] On Lamprus cf. Abert (1924), 586–87.

[13] On the *Menexenus* passage cf. Pohlenz (1913), 262 n. 1; Méridier (1931), 79; de Vries (1949), 257, and especially Clavaud (1982), 76, 263–77.

ἐκέρδαινον ἀπὸ τούτου (*De rerum mutatione* fr. 1a, II.14–22; cf. Thucydides, 8.68). Yet while the prosecution called attention to Antiphon's practice of *writing* speeches for pay, there is nothing here about *teaching* oratory for pay. Xenophon's Antiphon, by contrast, is a paid, professional educator (cf. below). Many critics point to the *Tetralogies* as evidence that Antiphon of Rhamnus did in fact teach rhetoric.[14] But there are serious grounds for doubting that the *Tetralogies* were written, or could appropriately serve, as models for the use of students (as is usually supposed). Other motives for their composition and "publication" are readily conceivable, and they do not by themselves prove that their author was a professional teacher of rhetoric (cf. Dover [1950], 59). In sum, the case for regarding Antiphon of Rhamnus as a professional teacher is very weak (cf. Andrewes in Gomme et al. [1981], 173–74). Gagarin (1990), 30 contended that Antiphon of Rhamnus' intellectual interests and wide influence entitle him to "be considered a teacher in some sense," but this is irrelevant to the question at hand. For Xenophon depicts a sophist and professional rival of Socrates who is a teacher in much more than the vague sense indicated.

The second feature of Xenophon's Antiphon serving to distinguish him from the Rhamnusian is the epithet τὸν σοφιστήν which Xenophon attaches to him (cf. van Spaan [1773], 825; Gernet [1923], 175 with n. 2). It is often argued to the contrary that this epithet could not serve to differentiate Xenophon's man from the Rhamnusian, who as a teacher and practitioner of rhetoric would quite naturally be designated a sophist.[15] As was argued above, however, the evidence that Antiphon of Rhamnus taught rhetoric is

[14] Cf. Bignone (1938), 166 n. 1; Nestle (1942), 391 with n. 89; Morrison (1961), 49 n. 3; Avery (1982), 156 with n. 39; Gagarin (1990), 30 n. 13.

[15] Cf. Gomperz (1912), 58; Croiset (1917), 15–16; Bignone (1938), 162; von der Mühll (1948), 1; Morrison (1961), 51 with n. 3; Guthrie (1971a), 286; Avery (1982), 151 n. 26; Gagarin (1990), 31–33.

far from compelling. The epithet σοφιστής could certainly be applied to a logographer like Antiphon, particularly in a hostile context. Cf. Aeschines, *or.* 1.175; Demosthenes, *or.* 59.21; von der Mühll (1948), 1 n. 3; Gagarin (1990), 31–32. But the real issue is not whether Xenophon *could* have referred to the Rhamnusian as a sophist, but whether he would have done so, and why. As Gagarin (1990) has shown, Antiphon of Rhamnus is usually identified in ancient texts by name alone, or by name and demotic, or by name together with the epithet ῥήτωρ, which in this context means "politician" (cf. Dodds [1959], 194). If Xenophon's epithet τὸν σοφιστήν referred to the Rhamnusian, it would represent an unusual designation requiring some sort of explanation. Croiset (1917), 15 and Gagarin (1990), 32–33 attempted to provide one by suggesting that Xenophon added the epithet to avoid confusion and to distinguish his man from others of the same name. Croiset thought of possible confusion with the poet Antiphon; Gagarin, with the Antiphon killed by the Thirty (cf. Xenophon, *Hellenica* 2.3.40). But it is difficult to see why Xenophon would have felt the need to distinguish his Antiphon from either of these men, neither of whom could easily be confused with a professional teacher and rival and contemporary of Socrates (cf. Avery [1982], 151 n. 26). More important, these suggestions fail to account for the specific designation "sophist," in particular its pejorative tone and note of hostility. (Gagarin [1990], 33 acknowledged the tone but did not try to explain it.) There is an element of truth in Gigon's contention that τὸν σοφιστήν serves to identify Antiphon "von vornherein" as an opponent of Socrates (cf. Gigon [1953], 152; Avery [1982], 151 n. 26). Yet this too fails to come to grips with the fundamental issues. Those who would identify the Antiphon in the *Memorabilia* with Antiphon of Rhamnus do not even attempt to explain Xenophon's choice of the Rhamnusian (of all people) to exemplify Socrates' sophistic rivals or his adoption of such a hostile attitude toward a man with whose politics (at least) he might be thought to have sympathized. Once it is granted that Xenophon's Antiphon is a professional educator distinct from the Rhamnusian, then the epithet "sophist" (with its pejorative overtones) and the professional rivalry with Socrates fall into place.[16] Gagarin (1990), 31–32 objected that Xenophon could not have distinguished a "sophist" Antiphon from Antiphon of Rhamnus unless such a figure had been well known; and even then would have added a demotic, patronymic, or ethnic designation (rather than τὸν σοφιστήν) in order to do so. Now, the fact that other references to a "sophist" Antiphon are much later than Xenophon does not by itself prove (*pace* Gagarin) that such a figure was unknown in the fourth century. On the contrary, Xenophon's use of the tag τὸν σοφιστήν seems to presuppose some familiarity with the identity of the man so (briefly) designated. The suggestion that Xenophon would have used an ethnic, demotic, or patronymic ignores the fact that he seldom employs additional means of identification beyond the bare name, and in particular eschews demotics in the identification of Athenians. As Whitehead (1988), 146 concluded: "Xenophon took no *systematic* care, either with Athenians or in general, to distinguish between *homonyms* in his narrative by providing them with patronymics or other marks of additional identification."[17] Xenophon sometimes employs patronymics in connection with non-Athenian sophists (cf. *Memorabilia* 4.4.5, *Symposium* 4.62, *Anabasis* 2.6.17; but contrast *Symposium* 1.5, *Memorabilia* 3.1.1). His failure to

[16] On Xenophon's Antiphon as a "type" of the sophist hostile to Socrates cf. Wilamowitz (1931–32), 2.217 n. 1; Gigon (1953), 152, 165.

[17] Cf. Whitehead (1988), 145–47. But examples such as Callistratus ὁ δημηγόρος (*Hellenica* 6.2.39, 6.3.3) and Nicostratus ὁ καλὸς ἐπικαλούμενος (*Hellenica* 2.4.6) show that the conditions Gagarin (1990), 32 laid down for the use of supplementary designations in Xenophon are too rigid. Cf. Whitehead (1988), 146.

do so in Antiphon's case may well indicate that the latter was in fact an Athenian (cf. below).

Two further features of Xenophon's portrait of the sophist Antiphon have led critics to identify him with Antiphon of Rhamnus.[18] One is Antiphon's evident greed or φιλαργυρία (cf. T1 with commentary). This is a characteristic for which Antiphon of Rhamnus is known to have been attacked in comedy. Cf. [Plut.] *Vitae X or.* 833C (= Plato, fr. 110): κεκωμῴδηται δ' εἰς φιλαργυρίαν ὑπὸ Πλάτωνος ἐν Πεισάνδρῳ. As Philostratus and others make clear, however, Antiphon of Rhamnus' reputation for greed arose from his practice of writing speeches for money. Cf. Philostratus, *Vitae sophistarum* 499 (= Plato, fr. 110): καθάπτεται δὲ ἡ κωμῳδία τοῦ Ἀντιφῶντος ὡς δεινοῦ τὰ δικανικὰ καὶ λόγους κατὰ τοῦ δικαίου ξυγκειμένους ἀποδιδομένου πολλῶν χρημάτων αὐτοῖς μάλιστα τοῖς κινδυνεύουσιν; Antiphon, *De rerum mutatione* fr. 1a, II.14–22 (quoted above); Diodorus Siculus *apud* Clement of Alexandria, *Stromata* 1.16.79.3; Ammianus Marcellinus, 30.4.5. The greed which characterizes Xenophon's Antiphon should be related instead to his status as a professional educator or sophist. The sophists' practice of charging fees for instruction opened them generally to accusations of greed (cf. Blank [1985], 3–6 and *passim*); and Xenophon in particular often mentions this practice (cf. *Symposium* 1.5, 4.62; *Anabasis* 2.6.16; T1, ll. 81–83). The second feature concerns the matter of politics. In his third and final exchange with Socrates (T1, ll. 97–102), Antiphon criticizes the latter for undertaking to teach the art of politics without practicing it. This line of attack has suggested to many that Xenophon's Antiphon must himself be a professional politician, and therefore identical with Antiphon

[18] Cf. Croiset (1917), 16; Aly (1929), 110; von der Mühll (1948), 1; Morrison (1961), 57; Avery (1982), 152–55.

of Rhamnus.[19] (Others agree with the inference that Xenophon's Antiphon practiced politics, but deny that he ought for this reason to be identified with the Rhamnusian.) However, it does not follow from Antiphon's criticism that he himself practiced politics. For one thing, Antiphon does not so much urge Socrates to engage in politics (as is usually supposed) as bring out an alleged contradiction between Socrates' teaching on the one hand, and his practice on the other. Nothing is said (or implied) about Antiphon himself teaching politics, and so nothing follows about him practicing politics. Moreover, Antiphon's criticism (as Leonardo Tarán points out to me) is a topos or commonplace, comparable to Aristotle's remark that while the sophists profess to teach politics, it is not they but the politicians who practice it (*Nicomachean Ethics* 1180b35–1181a2), and to Plato's comments on the discrepancy between Homer's poetic representations of war and politics and his lack of practical experience in such matters (*Republic* 599C–600E).[20] These considerations undermine the inference that Xenophon's Antiphon is himself a practicing politician, and therefore identical with the Rhamnusian.

The identity of Xenophon's Antiphon was a matter for disagreement already in later antiquity. In the list of rivalries involving famous poets and philosophers cited by Diogenes Laertius from the third book of Aristotle's Περὶ ποιητῶν (2.46 = T5), Antiphon ὁ τερατοσκόπος is said to have contended eristically (ἐφιλονείκει) with Socrates. This refers in all probability to the encounters in the *Memorabilia*. Whoever was responsible for the designation

[19] So Croiset (1917), 16; Aly (1929), 110; Morrison (1961), 58; Avery (1982), 151.

[20] Cf. Tarán (1981), 4 n. 11. Nestle (1940), 47 with n. 45 argued that *Memorabilia* 1.6.15 is derived from Plato (cf. *Apology* 31Cff.; *Gorgias* 521D) and as such reveals nothing about Antiphon.

τερατοσκόπος seems not to have identified Xenophon's Antiphon with the Rhamnusian, to whom he would hardly have referred with this epithet.[21] On the other hand, the author of the pseudo-Plutarchan *Vitae X or.* (or his source) identified the Antiphon in the *Memorabilia* with Antiphon of Rhamnus.[22] Speaking of the Rhamnusian, he remarks: διατριβὴν δὲ συνέστησε καὶ Σωκράτει τῷ φιλοσόφῳ διεφέρετο τὴν ὑπὲρ τῶν λόγων διαφορὰν οὐ φιλονείκως ἀλλ' ἐλεγκτικῶς, ὡς Ξενοφῶν ἱστόρηκεν ἐν τοῖς Ἀπομνημονεύμασιν (*Vit. X or.* 832C).[23] Additional evidence of interest in the identity of Xenophon's Antiphon is provided by Athenaeus, who mentions a monograph entitled *On the Antiphon in Xenophon's Memorabilia* written by a certain Hephaestion (cf. *Dipnosophistae* 15 673D–F = T4, with commentary). According to Athenaeus, Hephaestion plagiarized the material for his monograph from an earlier monograph by Adrastus of Aphrodisias, who had discussed both Antiphon the tragic poet and the character Plexippus from the latter's tragedy *Meleager*. Hephaestion's and Adrastus' interest in the Xenophontic Antiphon almost certainly extended to the question of his identity *vis-à-vis* other personages of the same name (cf. Sauppe [1896], 509; von der Mühll [1948], 1 n. 2; commentary on T4). This inference is rejected by Avery (1982), 151 n. 24 and Gagarin (1990), 41–42, the latter of whom suggested that Adrastus discussed the moral character of the poet Antiphon and of the *dramatis persona* Plexippus, while Hephaestion discussed the Xenophontic Antiphon's manner of

[21] The epithet is usually ascribed to Aristotle; but cf. commentary on T5. Gagarin (1990), 41 n. 50 rejected the inference, on the grounds that we do not know who added the epithet or why it was added. But our ignorance on these points does not really affect the issue.

[22] On the unreliability of [Plut.] cf. nn. 4–5 above.

[23] Similarly Photius, *Bibliotheca* 486a (8.42) and the anonymous *Vita Antiphontis* 7. According to Blass (1887–98), 1.93, these depend on [Plut.]; but others disagree (cf. commentary on T6).

arguing with Socrates.[24] But this suggestion does not do justice to the available evidence concerning Adrastus' work, which indicates that he offered detailed discussions of literary-historical problems of all kinds (cf. Moraux [1973–84], 2.323–30).[25] In addition, Athenaeus specifies that Adrastus discussed the person of Antiphon the poet at considerable length (καὶ πλεῖστα ὅσα καὶ περὶ αὐτοῦ τοῦ Ἀντιφῶντος εἰπόντος). It is difficult to avoid the inference that Adrastus dealt with the question of the identity of the poet Antiphon *vis-à-vis* others of the same name, including the Antiphon in the *Memorabilia*; and Hephaestion will have followed suit.

Xenophon's evidence for the existence of a sophist Antiphon distinct from Antiphon of Rhamnus is confirmed by the opinion of Didymus of Alexandria (and others) as reported by Hermogenes of Tarsus. By way of preface to his stylistic analysis of the works current under the name of Antiphon (T2(a), ll. 1–10), Hermogenes reports that from among the many men named Antiphon, Didymus singled out two in particular, referred to as σοφιστεύσαντες (on the meaning of this term cf. commentary on T2(a), l. 4). One of these two is identified as Antiphon ὁ ῥήτωρ – that is, the Rhamnusian (cf. *De ideis* 400.22 ὁ τοίνυν Ῥαμνούσιος Ἀντιφῶν) – author of the *Tetralogies* and similar legal speeches. From the Rhamnusian Didymus distinguished "the other" (ἕτερος) Antiphon, author of Περὶ ἀληθείας and similar philosophical works, who is said also to have been a dream-interpreter.[26] Hermogenes neglects to report the reasons which led Didymus (and others) to

[24] Gagarin (1990), 41 argued that the title of Hephaestion's work does not suggest that it concerned the question of identity. But still less does it suggest the contents Gagarin proposed for it.

[25] On Adrastus' philological interests and knowledge generally cf. Moraux (1973–84), 2.314–17, 323–32.

[26] On the division of works between the two Antiphons cf. section II below.

these conclusions. Despite this, many commentators have inferred that Didymus based his distinction between the Rhamnusian and "the other" Antiphon on perceived stylistic differences within the *corpus Antiphonteum*. Hence these commentators have felt free to reject Didymus' distinction, in the belief (correct in itself) that stylistic considerations do not suffice to establish his separatist conclusions.[27] The inference regarding Didymus' rationale rests solely on Hermogenes' silence, however, and is quite unjustified.[28] In the first place, Hermogenes himself was a critic of style, and his focus on stylistic criteria reflects his own preoccupations rather than those of Didymus (cf. Bignone [1938], 166 n. 4). This point applies equally to the argument Hermogenes offers against Didymus' distinction as to the disparities of style he cites in favor of it. Gagarin (1990), 36 overlooked this when he noted that Hermogenes cites evidence against the distinction from Plato and others and concluded that Hermogenes "investigated carefully the matter of identity." For the "evidence" in question reduces to a stylistic argument (cf. T2(a), ll. 14–20, with commentary). In the second place, it is possible and even likely that Hermogenes encountered Didymus' views on the problem of Antiphon at second hand and/or in abbreviated form. Didymus' prodigious output suffered the usual fate of scholarly literature in antiquity, and was frequently excerpted (cf. Cohn [1903], 446). This might help to explain Hermogenes' failure to record Didymus'

[27] Cf. Drerup (1901), 301–6 (but contrast the doubts expressed at 306); Croiset (1917), 17; Altwegg (1908), 8; Joël (1893–1901), 2.639, 642, (1921), 663 n. 3; Aly (1929), 114, 168–69; Nestle (1942), 372; Hommel (1941), 2; Morrison (1961), 55; Decleva Caizzi (1984), 97–98; Gagarin (1990), 36–37, 43.

[28] Narcy (1989), 228 seems to regard it as a matter of significance that Hermogenes' information on the "other" Antiphon "est dépourvue d'éléments biographiques." But he failed to point out that the same holds for Hermogenes' information on Antiphon of Rhamnus.

rationale for the distinction. Nevertheless, it is important to note that Hermogenes does at least allude to evidence (other than that of style) in support of the distinction, in his remark on ἱστορία: πρὸς δὲ καὶ ἀπὸ ἱστορίας φαίνεται κτλ. (T2(a), l. 3). What exactly Hermogenes means by ἱστορία is uncertain (cf. commentary ad loc.). But on any interpretation, his remark seems to allude to some sort of factual information supporting Didymus' distinction. And it is entirely reasonable to assume that Didymus himself was acquainted with such information (cf. Bignone [1938], 166 n. 4). In sum, it is quite unjustified to infer that Didymus based his distinction on stylistic considerations alone, and to reject the distinction for this reason. Exploiting the ambiguity of Hermognes' term εἶδος, which can mean "genre" as well as "style," Cassin (1985), 67–71 tried to move the discussion from the question of literary style to the notion of what she called "compétence." Cassin suggested that Didymus and his modern followers have distinguished the Antiphons out of a conviction that rhetorical works should belong to an "orator," and philosophical works to a "sophist" (cf. Decleva Caizzi [1984], 97). But there is simply no evidence that such a consideration influenced Didymus, Hermogenes, or any other ancient author concerned with the problem of Antiphon. Some modern commentators have objected that Didymus' distinction represents merely an isolated or even unique view in antiquity.[29] But this ignores Hermogenes' explicit information to the contrary, that "many others" (ἄλλοι τέ φασιν οὐκ ὀλίγοι, T2(a), l. 2) shared Didymus' opinion. Our ignorance of the identity of these others does not diminish the value of Hermogenes' information.

In contrast to the authors discussed above, the vast majority of ancient and medieval writers who refer to

[29] Cf. Aly (1929), 114; Hommel (1941), 1–2; Gagarin (1990), 43–44 and *passim*.

"Antiphon" show no awareness of the problem of identity and do not attempt to distinguish a sophist from Antiphon of Rhamnus. In the works of Aristotle, for example, the name Antiphon appears eleven times. In *Physics* 185a17 (= F13(a)), 193a9–28 (= F15(b)), and *Sophistici elenchi* 172a7 (= F13(b)), Aristotle refers to the (sophist) Antiphon three times by bare name, without a distinguishing epithet. Antiphon of Rhamnus is likewise referred to three times by bare name (Ἀθηναίων πολιτεία 32.2; *Ethica Eudemia* 1232b6–9; fr. 624). Antiphon the tragic poet is referred to twice with the epithet "poet" (*Rhetoric* 1385a10; *Mechanics* 847a20), but three times without it (*Ethica Eudemia* 1239a37; *Rhetoric* 1379b15, 1399b27). Such lack of concern to identify the particular Antiphon in question has led some commentators to infer that Aristotle (and his imitators) did not distinguish the author of the philosophical works from Antiphon of Rhamnus.[30] But the inference does not follow. It is necessary to keep in mind the peculiar nature of the *corpus Aristotelicum* and the specialized and knowledgeable audience to which works such as the *Physics* and *Sophistici elenchi* were addressed. If Aristotle could take for granted his audience's familiarity with such things as the details of the sophist Antiphon's quadrature attempt, it should cause no surprise if he neglects to supply more elementary information such as the identity of Antiphon in question. Furthermore, in most cases the context would suffice to make clear which Antiphon he had in mind. In the *Rhetoric*, for example, Aristotle twice omits a distinguishing epithet when citing the poet Antiphon in connection with the drama *Meleager* (*Rhetoric* 1379b15, 1399b27). Yet when the same man is cited in the same work for an anecdote in connection with his death at the hands of the tyrant Dio-

[30] Cf. Joël (1893–1901), 663 n. 3; Morrison (1961), 51–55; Gagarin (1990), 33. For a different analysis of Aristotle's testimony on Antiphon cf. Narcy (1989), 225–27, 240–41.

nysius, Aristotle adds the tag "poet," presumably because he did not think it immediately obvious from the context which Antiphon was meant (*Rhetoric* 1385a10). These considerations go far to account for Aristotle's apparent nonchalance in citing "Antiphon."[31]

Later authors who quote from or refer to the sophist Antiphon without distinguishing him from the Rhamnusian include the doxographer Aëtius (F9, F26–28, F32); Galen (F1–2, F29–29A); Christian authors such as Clement of Alexandria (F66) and Origen (F12); Athenaeus (T4, F73); Philostratus (T2(b)); the anthologist Stobaeus (F49–51, F53–54, F57–62), and lexicographers from Aelius Dionysius and Pollux to Photius and the *Suda*. Among all these, Gagarin (1990), 39–40 attached special significance to the case of Valerius Harpocration, who preserves a large number of fragments from the sophist Antiphon in his *Lexicon* of Attic orators. Harpocration quotes by title from the sophist Antiphon's Περὶ ἀληθείας, Περὶ ὁμονοίας, and Πολιτικός, as well as from numerous speeches of Antiphon of Rhamnus. Yet he never indicates any awareness that these various works might belong to different authors. Gagarin inferred that Harpocration must have known, and rejected, Didymus' rationale for distinguishing the Antiphons. Not only this, Harpocration (in Gagarin's words) must have been unaware of "any significant scholarly opinion favoring a separatist view." Such inferences, however, go far beyond the evidence. Harpocration cites sev-

[31] Compare how Aristotle refers to "Plato," without a distinguishing epithet, in *Topics* 140a3–5 in connection with the rare words ὀφρυόσκιος (of the eye), σηψιδακές (of a kind of spider), and ὀστεογενές (of marrow). Both the general context and the frequent use of Platonic material in this work might lead the unwary to suppose that the philosopher is meant (as some modern commentators have in fact done). Yet the reference is certainly to Plato the comic poet, whom Aristotle refers to again without a distinguishing epithet in *Rhetoric* 1376a10. Cf. Cherniss (1944), 23 n. 18.

eral of Didymus' commentaries on the Attic orators, and utilized some of his lexicographical works. But it is not known where Didymus expressed his views on Antiphon, and uncertain whether Harpocration even knew of them.[32] On two occasions, Harpocration questions the authenticity of speeches ascribed to "Antiphon" (s.v. δημοτευόμενος, δ 32, on the Πρὸς Φίλιππον ἀπολογία; s.vv. ῥητορικὴ γραφή, ρ 3, on the Κατὰ πρυτάνεως). Again, however, it is not known what source or sources Harpocration depended on for information about issues of ascription in the *corpus Antiphonteum*. None of Harpocration's thirty-nine citations of Didymus concerns a problem of ascription. The only authorities he cites by name on questions of ascription are Dionysius of Halicarnassus and Callimachus, on the authenticity of the speech Πρὸς Κριτίαν περὶ τοῦ ἐνεπισκήμματος attributed to Demosthenes (s.vv. ἐνεπίσκημμα καὶ ἐνεπισκήψασθαι, ε 51). There is reason to believe that Harpocration utilized Dionysius' views on the ascription of speeches in the Lysianic corpus as well (cf. Dover [1968b], 15–19).[33] But there is no evidence that Dionysius concerned himself with problems of ascription in the *corpus Antiphonteum*. The outstanding ancient authority in this area was Caecilius of Calacte, but Harpocration cites him only once, and not on a problem of ascription (s.v. ἐξούλης, ε 72).[34] Despite this, both Blass (1887–98), I.102–3 and Aly (1929), 113 assumed that Harpocration reflects the views of Caecilius on questions of ascription in the *corpus Antiphonteum*. This is possible, of course, but is unsupported by evidence. (Aly further assumed, without any justification whatsoever, that all information on Anti-

[32] On Harpocration's use of Didymus cf. Cohn (1903), 458–59 and commentary on T2(a), ll. 2–3.

[33] On the occasional inconsistencies in Harpocration's ascriptions cf. Pendrick (1993), 11 n. 40.

[34] Cf. [Plut.], *Vitae X or.* 833C = Caecilius, fr. 100; Blass (1887–98), I.102–7; Brzoska (1897), 1181–82.

phon in the later lexicographical tradition goes back to Caecilius.[35]) Papyrus discoveries which have made it possible to compare Harpocration's work with the sources available to him suggest that he offers but a small selection from the learning at his disposal (cf. Schultz [1912], 2413–14, with references). Moreover, the *Lexicon* as extant is abridged (cf. Dindorf [1853], XXII–XXIII; Keaney [1991], XXV). In the circumstances, it is hazardous to draw inferences from silence regarding Harpocration's possible knowledge or opinion of Didymus' distinction.

From the way in which Harpocration and other late ancient authors cite the sophist Antiphon's Περὶ ἀληθείας, Περὶ ὁμονοίας, and Πολιτικός, it can safely be inferred that these works were regularly included in copies of the *corpus Antiphonteum* circulating in later antiquity.[36] When and how they came to be incorporated in it is not known; it is possible that Callimachus catalogued them among the works of the Rhamnusian in his πίναξ of orators.[37] After Callimachus, Caecilius of Calacte exercised great influence on the shape of the *corpus Antiphonteum* (cf. above). Aly (1929), 113 supposed that Caecilius identified the sophist Antiphon and the Rhamnusian; Blass (1887–98), 1.102–3 thought that he did not, and assumed that the sophist's works were among the twenty-five speeches designated by Caecilius as inauthentic. The difficulty then is to explain why Harpocration and other authorities appear to ignore Caecilius' conclusions. Blass suggested that because the sophist's works stemmed from *an* Antiphon (though not from the Rhamnusian), their authenticity is not questioned in Harpocration and others. But the suggestion is less than

35 Harpocration (for one) seems not to have used Caecilius' lexicographical work on the orators, at least directly. Cf. Brzoska (1897), 1186.

36 But Antiphon the sophist's dream-book probably was not (cf. below).

37 On Callimachus' Πίνακες cf. Pfeiffer (1968), 127–31, 278, and *passim*. For the ῥητορικά cf. Callimachus, frr. 430–32, 443–48.

completely convincing. In any case, the views of Didymus (and others) on the problem of the Antiphons had no discernible effect on the form of the *corpus Antiphonteum*, which continued to include Περὶ ἀληθείας, Περὶ ὁμονοίας, and Πολιτικός. The bare fact of their inclusion, however, no more proves their author identical to Antiphon of Rhamnus than the inclusion of speeches by Apollodorus son of Pasion in the Demosthenic corpus proves that Apollodorus was the same person as Demosthenes.[38] But it does help to explain why Galen, Harpocration, and other ancient authorities could cite these works (without apparent scruple) as belonging to "Antiphon" or even "Antiphon of Rhamnus." The *corpus Platonicum* provides an instructive parallel. Late writers clearly felt free to cite as Plato's even works they knew or suspected to be spurious, on the principle that anything included in available editions of Plato could be cited as Plato's (cf. Tarán [1975], 7 with n. 23). It is at least conceivable that some of the authors who cite the works of the sophist Antiphon as if they belonged to the Rhamnusian may similarly have known or suspected otherwise. Other late writers – including Philostratus and the author of the pseudo-Plutarchan *Vitae X or.* – certainly did not. But the essential point is that the form of the *corpus Antiphonteum* undoubtedly contributed to the widespread confusion of the sophist Antiphon with Antiphon of Rhamnus in later antiquity. In this context, it is worth emphasizing that ancient authorities from Thucydides (8.68) and Lysias (*or.* 12.67) on who refer to the Rhamnusian Antiphon without distinguishing him from the sophist represent a different case. Antiphon of Rhamnus was a famous politician and orator familiar to anyone acquainted with

[38] On Apollodorus and the *corpus Demosthenicum* cf. (e.g.) Lesky (1971), 671. On the uncertainties involved in the ascription of works of Attic orators in general, and the value of Callimachus' ascriptions in particular, cf. Dover (1968b), 23–26.

the history of rhetoric or of fifth-century Athens. Later writers referring to him would scarcely have felt it necessary to distinguish him from the much less familiar sophist (even if they were aware of the distinction). Modern commentators who have analyzed the ancient tradition on "Antiphon" have unjustifiably ignored this consideration.[39]

The ancient testimonia, then, offer probable (though not certain) evidence for the existence in the late fifth century of a sophist Antiphon distinct from Antiphon of Rhamnus. Some supporters of the separatist position have attempted to reinforce this conclusion with arguments drawn from an analysis of language and style.[40] Luria (1926c), for example, argued that the distinction is proved by simple orthography, since the sophist Antiphon consistently used spellings in –ττ– and –ξυν–, the Rhamnusian in –σσ– and –συν–. But Luria's own collection of the evidence shows that neither author is consistent on these points (cf. Rosenkranz [1930], 144–45, 170, 173; Bignone [1938], 215 n. 1). Bignone (1938), 175–215 offered a detailed stylistic comparison between the works of the sophist Antiphon and the extant speeches of the Rhamnusian. This analysis, while subtle and not without interest, falls far short of demonstrating his separatist conclusions, and is open to the fundamental objection of failing to take account of the generic distinction between dicanic oratory and philosophical treatises.[41] The fragmentary character of the sophist's writings, and the difficulty of dating them, further exacerbate the uncertainties attaching to stylistic analysis in this case (cf. Dover [1950], 60). Linguistic and stylistic differences between the fragments of the sophist Antiphon and the speeches of the Rhamnusian undoubtedly exist. For exam-

[39] So Altwegg (1908), 6–12; Aly (1929), 109–13; Morrison (1961); Narcy (1989), 225–30; Gagarin (1990).

[40] Cf. Bignone (1938), 175–215; Luria (1926c); Gomperz (1912), 59.

[41] Cf. Aly (1929); Hommel (1941); Morrison (1961), 55–56.

ple, periphrastic expressions combining ἐστι with a verbal noun are common in the Rhamnusian but relatively infrequent in the philosophical fragments, while the contracted comparative forms in –ω attested in one passage of Περὶ ἀληθείας are completely absent from the Rhamnusian (and exceedingly rare in other Attic orators).[42] Nevertheless, it seems prudent to follow the judgment of Hermogenes, who acknowledges stylistic disparities among the works ascribed to Antiphon, but refuses to rule out the possibility of a single author deploying even such divergent styles (cf. T2(a), ll. 20–22, with commentary).

The contents of the writings ascribed to Antiphon have also been scoured for evidence in support either of the unitarian or of the separatist position on the problem of identity. The pious utterances about the gods in the speeches of the Rhamnusian seemed to Luria (1963) to conflict with the sophist Antiphon's supposed denial of divine providence (cf. F12 with commentary). Yet Decleva Caizzi (1984), 97 n. 11, (1986b), 299–300 claimed to detect the same rational and secular attitude toward religion in the speeches as in the fragments of Περὶ ἀληθείας. A much more serious argument is offered by Bignone (1938), 172–73, Luria (1963), 64–66, and others who claim that the hostile attitude toward νόμος visible everywhere in the papyrus fragments of Περὶ ἀληθείας is simply incompatible with the oft-repeated praise of established laws in the speeches of the Rhamnusian, and more generally with the latter's conservative politics. Supporters of the unitarian position sensibly counter that it is naive to treat statements in court speeches written for the use of litigants (whether real or imaginary) as unequivocal expressions of Antiphon of Rhamnus' own personal views.[43] More recent commen-

[42] Cf. F44(a)v.20–22, 27–29; Rosenkranz (1930), 151, 162, 173.

[43] Cf. Morrison (1972), 110; Avery (1982), 150–51; Nestle (1942), 399.

tators turn this separatist argument on its head, contending that the critique of νόμος in the papyrus fragments of Περὶ ἀληθείας amounts to an attack on Athenian *democratic* law and so points to the Rhamnusian as its author, who tried to overthrow the democratic government of Athens.[44] Schmid (1940), 162 with n. 1, 166 also thought that the attitude towards law in the papyrus fragments originated in oligarchic circles, although he did not infer that Περὶ ἀληθείας was written by the Rhamnusian. Dreher (1983), 75–76 agreed that the criticism is anti-democratic in spirit, but rejected the unitarian position on the ground that the sophist Antiphon was no friend of oligarchy, but rather a critic of all government. This last position – with substitution of νόμος for "government" – perhaps comes closest to the truth. For it is plainly mistaken to interpret the argument of the papyrus fragments in terms of Athenian party politics. The discussion in F44(a) is avowedly general in scope (cf. I.6–10: δικαιοσύνη [δ᾽ οὖ]ν τὰ τῆς πόλεως νόμιμα, ἐν ᾗ ἂν πολιτεύηταί τις, μὴ παραβαίνειν); and the critique of law and legal procedures developed there and in F44(c) would apply under any form of government, democratic, oligarchic, or monarchical. Wiesner (1994), 230–35 and *passim* attempted to reconcile the differing attitudes towards law in Περὶ ἀληθείας and the speeches of the Rhamnusian by arguing that the critique of νόμος in the former is not absolute but admits of exceptions. Wiesner pointed to the qualification "most" in the phrase τὰ πολλὰ τῶν κατὰ νόμον δικαίων πολεμίως τῇ φύσει νενομοθέτηται (F44(a)II.26–31), which he interpreted as an admission that some laws at least are in accord with nature. As examples of such laws Wiesner instanced the laws against homicide, which are praised by the speakers

[44] So Mazzarino (1966), 1.321 with n. 285; Isnardi Parente (1975), 22; Decleva Caizzi (1984), 99–100, (1986a), 69; Wiesner (1994), 237–38; Luginbill (1997).

of Antiphon of Rhamnus, *or.* 5.14–15 and 6.2 as the best of all laws. But the papyrus fragments of Περὶ ἀληθείας give no indication about which laws their author thought were in accord with nature, and Wiesner's identification of these with the laws against homicide lauded in the Rhamnusian's speeches is purely arbitrary. In the first place, the qualities for which homicide laws are praised in the speeches – their antiquity (ἀρχαιοτάτοις) and their endurance without change (τοὺς αὐτοὺς ἀεὶ περὶ τῶν αὐτῶν) – have nothing to do with anything said about νόμος in the papyrus fragments. Secondly, as even Wiesner (1994), 234 admitted, the speeches do not in fact attribute to homicide laws the characteristics Wiesner himself identified as necessary (on the argument of the papyrus fragments) for laws to accord with nature: universal validity and the quality of furthering life instead of restricting it. It is difficult to see how homicide laws are immune from the objections raised in the papyrus fragments against νόμοι of all kinds: of being conventional (ὁμολογηθέντα) rather than natural (φύντα), imposed on nature (ἐπίθετα), incapable of preventing and/or punishing would-be offenders (cf. F44(a)v.25–vi.33), etc. Isnardi Parente (1975), 14–16 and Decleva Caizzi (1985), 193 n. 8, 205, (1986b), 301 contended that the papyrus fragments' emphasis on individual advantage is at odds with Athenian democratic ideology, which privileged the good of the many over the interests of the few, but in accord with the anti-democratic sentiments of the Rhamnusian, who on this argument will be the author of Περὶ ἀληθείας. Yet surely advocates of oligarchic government in Athens as elsewhere claimed (like their democratic opponents) to uphold the common good against the selfish interests of individuals. In any case, as the speaker of Lysias, *or.* 25.8 shrewdly notes, the pursuit of self-interest knows no political boundaries: πρῶτον μὲν οὖν ἐνθυμηθῆναι χρὴ ὅτι οὐδείς ἐστιν ἀνθρώπων φύσει οὔτε ὀλιγαρχικὸς οὔτε δημοκρατικός, ἀλλ' ἥτις ἂν ἑκάστῳ πολιτεία συμφέρῃ, ταύτην προθυμεῖται καθεστάναι.

The fragility of all attempts to bolster conclusions about the identity of Antiphon through analysis of the contents of the *corpus Antiphonteum* is well illustrated by the case of F44(b) of Περὶ ἀληθείας. Formerly, this fragment was widely interpreted as a critique of class-distinctions, and its author thought to hold radical egalitarian views incompatible with Antiphon of Rhamnus' conservative politics.[45] This interpretation was questioned by a number of commentators,[46] and has now been decisively refuted by the evidence of the new fragment *P.Oxy.* 3647, which demonstrates that the argument has nothing to do with class-distinctions (cf. commentary on F44(b)). In its new form, however, the very same fragment has become the centerpiece of an elaborate argument by Decleva Caizzi (1986a), 67–69, (1986b), 294–96 in support of the unitarian position. Following up an idea first suggested by Isnardi Parente (1975), 20 and later elaborated by Funghi (1984), 5, Decleva Caizzi compared F44(b) with the views on law and nature expressed in the funeral oration delivered by Socrates in Plato's *Menexenus*. In the encomium to Athenian democracy in *Menexenus* 238B–239A, for example, "nature" is understood (in literal fashion) as birth at Athens, which unites all Athenians but at the same time sets them apart from other peoples. Nature in this sense is not opposed to νόμος but linked inseparably with it. Cf. *Menexenus* 239A: ἀλλ' ἡ ἰσογονία ἡμᾶς ἡ κατὰ φύσιν ἰσονομίαν ἀναγκάζει ζητεῖν κατὰ νόμον. For Antiphon, by contrast, nature is the same in all people, and is antithetical to law. Again, in *Menexenus* 245C–D Socrates stresses the natural (φύσει) en-

[45] Cf. Bignone (1938), 68–70, 170–72; Luria (1963); Nestle (1942), 399.

[46] Cf. Mazzarino (1966), 1.317 n. 281; Moulton (1972), 344–45; Isnardi Parente (1975), 17–26; Avery (1982), 148–49; Decleva Caizzi (1984), 101.

mity obtaining between barbarians and Greeks, especially Athenians – an idea far removed (Decleva Caizzi supposes) from Antiphon's conception of the natural similarity between Greeks and foreigners. Decleva Caizzi concluded from the comparison that Plato meant to caricature the views expressed in F44(b). Since Antiphon of Rhamnus is mentioned by name at *Menexenus* 236A alongside Aspasia (to whom Socrates ascribes the funeral oration he delivers), Decleva Caizzi inferred that the Rhamnusian is the source of the ideas subsequently caricatured, and thus is the author of Περὶ ἀληθείας. But it is hard to see how Plato's mention of the Rhamnusian at *Menexenus* 236A implicates him in the views expressed later in Socrates' speech. It is much more plausible to interpret the funeral oration as a parody of rhetoric and of Athenian ideology and propaganda in general than as an attack on the views of any specific individual – let alone the author of F44(b).

It is unsafe to try to extrapolate Antiphon of Rhamnus' general views on law, morality, and society (if he had any) from courtroom speeches written for the use of others or from his own practical political activities. And the views of the sophist Antiphon are but imperfectly known from fragmentary evidence preserved without a larger context to guide its interpretation. In these circumstances, attempts to bring the evidence of intellectual attitudes to bear on the problem of the identity of Antiphon seem likely to remain inconclusive.

According to Hermogenes, Didymus' "other" Antiphon was also a diviner and dream-interpreter. This identification seems to confirm the sophist Antiphon as author of the dream-book current in antiquity under the name of Antiphon (cf. sections II and V below, and T3 with commentary).[47] Curiously, the dream-book itself does not ap-

[47] Cf. Sauppe (1896), 513; Bignone (1938), 173–74; Stenzel (1924), 34, 42; Luria (1927b), 461–66; Schmid (1940), 167–68.

pear in Hermogenes' list of the sophist's works; presumably this is because it was not included in the standard *corpus Antiphonteum* (cf. below). Wilamowitz (1959), 1.61 n. 1 and Heinimann (1945), 134 n. 34, however, doubted the identification of the sophist Antiphon with the dream-interpreter, and Nestle (1942), 388–89 rejected it. Nestle pointed to evidence which he considered incompatible with the identification, including the supposed "radical rationalism" of Περὶ ἀληθείας and the sophist's alleged denial of divine providence and hostility to divination (cf. T8–9 and F12). But Nestle's interpretation of the import of the anecdotes which comprise T8–9 is demonstrably mistaken; and it is far from certain that Antiphon really denied divine providence (cf. commentary on T8–9 and F12). For the rest, Nestle's arguments have little force and can be safely dismissed (cf. Luria [1927b], 462, 464–65). A potentially more serious argument against the identification was offered by Dodds (1951), 119 n. 100, (1954), who claimed that Socrates' use of the phrase παρ' ἡμῖν at *Memorabilia* 1.6.13 (= T1, l. 75) implies that the sophist was not an Athenian. If so, then he could not be identical with the dream-interpreter, who is identified as an Athenian by Artemidorus (F78) as well as in the *Suda* (T3). Dodds' view of the implications of παρ' ἡμῖν, however, is most likely mistaken (cf. commentary on T1, ll. 75–76). And there are good reasons for believing that the sophist Antiphon was in fact an Athenian (cf. below). John Tzetzes' claim (T11(b)) that Antiphon the diviner was a contemporary of Alexander the Great would constitute a decisive chronological objection to identifying him with the sophist. But the claim appears to be based solely on the (wholly unreliable) evidence of the Alexander-romance (cf. commentary on T11(b)). The identification of the sophist with the author of the dream-book would be put beyond doubt if it were certain that the epithet τερατοσκόπος in Diogenes Laertius, 2.46 (= T5) goes back to Aristotle. But unfortunately this is uncertain (cf. above, and commentary on T5). The complete absence of citations from the dream-book in the lexicographical sources which preserve so many fragments of the sophist Antiphon's writings strongly suggests that the work did not form part of the standard *corpus Antiphonteum*. (Presumably it circulated separately, perhaps with other dream-books.) But this does not constitute a reason to doubt the identification of its author with the sophist.

Of the sophist Antiphon's life but little is known. From the evidence of Xenophon it appears that he was a professional educator or sophist, was active in Athens, and was an approximate contemporary of Socrates.[48] The *Suda* identifies him as an Athenian. The strict Attic dialect of the papyrus and other fragments (cf. Rosenkranz [1930], 145) supports this, as does the sophist's likely identification with the author of the dream-book (cf. above). In addition, Xenophon's use of the epithet "sophist" may perhaps imply that his Antiphon was an Athenian; otherwise, he could have used an ethnic designation to distinguish his man from the Rhamnusian (cf. above). The dearth of biographical data on the sophist Antiphon (which Gagarin [1990], 36–37, 43 and others treat as support for the unitarian position) probably results in part from his widespread confusion in later antiquity with Antiphon of Rhamnus.

II DIVISION OF WORKS

Hermogenes provides the main evidence for the attribution of the writings of the sophist Antiphon:

[48] For σοφιστής in the sense of "professional educator" cf. Plato, *Protagoras* 317B (καὶ ὁμολογῶ τε σοφιστὴς εἶναι καὶ παιδεύειν), *Apology* 19E; Aeschines, *or.* 1.173 (ὑμεῖς, ὦ ἄνδρες Ἀθηναῖοι, Σωκράτην ... τὸν σοφιστὴν ἀπεκτείνατε, ὅτι Κριτίαν ἐφάνη πεπαιδευκώς); Zeller in Zeller and Nestle (1920), 1335–36.

ὧν εἷς μέν ἐστιν ὁ ῥήτωρ, οὗπερ οἱ φονικοὶ φέρονται λόγοι καὶ ⟨οἱ⟩ δημηγορικοὶ καὶ ὅσοι τούτοις ὅμοιοι, ἕτερος δὲ ὁ καὶ τερατοσκόπος καὶ ὀνειροκρίτης λεγόμενος γενέσθαι, οὗπερ οἵ τε Περὶ τῆς ἀληθείας εἶναι λέγονται λόγοι καὶ ὁ Περὶ ὁμονοίας [καὶ οἱ δημηγορικοὶ] καὶ ὁ Πολιτικός (= T2(a), ll. 5–10).

Hermogenes' form of expression (οὗπερ ... εἶναι λέγονται) indicates that the ascription of Περὶ ἀληθείας κτλ. does not rest solely on his own authority. Wilamowitz (1876), 296 identified Caecilius of Calacte as his source. This is not impossible; but nothing in the context suggests it, and Caecilius' views on the identity of Antiphon are otherwise unknown (cf. section 1 above). More likely the ascription goes back to Didymus, like the distinction of the two Antiphons itself, which forms the larger context of the division of works here reported.

In the text as transmitted, public speeches (δημηγορικοὶ λόγοι) are attributed to both Antiphon of Rhamnus and the sophist Antiphon. Joël (1893–1901), 2.639 suggested that this reflects disagreement among Hermogenes' sources regarding the attribution of the public speeches, but most critics agree in assuming a textual corruption. Aly (1929), 156 and Drerup (1901), 302 defended the ascription of public speeches to the sophist, citing Πολιτικός as an example of one. But this work hardly qualifies as a public speech in the sense intended. (For the type of work Hermogenes has in mind cf. commentary on T2(a), l. 6.) Taylor (1772), 269 proposed to delete Πολιτικός as well as the δημηγορικοί from the list of the sophist's works, and to insert the former into the list of the Rhamnusian's works.[49] His proposal found favor with van Spaan (1773), 805 and Buresch (1886), 75. Spengel (1828), 115 went even

[49] Diels and Kranz (*FVS* 2.334 n.) as well as Narcy (1989), 228 claim that the words καὶ ὁ Πολιτικός are inserted after δημηγορικοὶ in the list of the Rhamnusian's works in cod. Vaticanus 107 (= Va). But Rabe reports this reading only from printed editions.

further, transposing the words καὶ ὁ Περὶ ὁμονοίας καὶ οἱ δημηγορικοὶ καὶ ὁ Πολιτικός from the list of the sophist's works to the list of the Rhamnusian's works. He has been followed by Walz (1832–36), 3.386; Schmidt (1854), 310; Grossmann (1950), 44 n. 49, and others. In support of this drastic revision of the text, Spengel pointed to subsequent passages in which Hermogenes refers to Περὶ ἀληθείας alone, without mentioning Περὶ ὁμονοίας and Πολιτικός.[50] But these certainly do not prove that Hermogenes ascribed Περὶ ἀληθείας alone to the sophist (cf. commentary on T2(a), ll. 12–14). Furthermore, as Sauppe (1850), 146, (1896), 510–11 rightly pointed out, the τε in the list of the sophist's writings (οἵ τε Περὶ τῆς ἀληθείας κτλ.) is presumptive evidence against Spengel's proposal, since this particle is unlikely to have been added by a copyist. (Sauppe also objected to the word-order produced by the changes suggested by Spengel and Taylor.) Even Spengel himself seems later to have backed away from his earlier proposal.[51] The easiest and most plausible solution to the textual difficulty is Sauppe's simple deletion of the words καὶ οἱ δημηγορικοὶ from the list of the sophist's works. Sauppe plausibly suggested that after the (second) οἱ in the list of the Rhamnusian's works had been accidentally omitted, the correct text καὶ ⟨οἱ⟩ δημηγορικοί was written in the margin and subsequently inserted in the wrong place. This explanation seems to be confirmed by the evidence of cod. Laurentianus 60.27 (= Lb), where the words

[50] Cf. T2(a), ll. 12–14 (πολὺ γὰρ ὡς ὄντως τὸ παραλλάττον τῶν ἐπιγραφομένων τῆς Ἀληθείας λόγων πρὸς τοὺς λοιπούς); ibid. ll. 18–20 (τὸν Θουκυδίδην δὲ πολλῷ κεχωρισμένον καὶ κεκοινωνηκότα τῷ εἴδει τῶν τῆς Ἀληθείας λόγων); ibid. ll. 25–26 (οὗπερ οἱ τῆς Ἀληθείας εἰσὶ λεγόμενοι λόγοι).

[51] Cf. Spengel (1853–56), 2.XVIII, 414.9–13. Unfortunately, the relevant passage in Spengel's text of Hermogenes is marred by printer's errors (cf. Sauppe [1896], 510–11; Buresch [1886], 75) – a fact of which Narcy (1989), 229 seems to be unaware.

καὶ οἱ δημηγορικοὶ have been mistakenly transposed to follow Περὶ τῆς ἀληθείας εἶναι λέγονται λόγοι. This strongly suggests that they were a marginal correction, inserted in the wrong place by the scribe of Lb or of his exemplar (so Diels, *FVS* 2.334 n.). Sauppe's solution has been adopted by Rabe as well as by Diels and Kranz, Untersteiner, and most other editors and commentators on Antiphon. With it, the sophist Antiphon is credited with Περὶ ἀληθείας, Περὶ ὁμονοίας, and Πολιτικός, to which should be added the dream-book current in antiquity under the name of Antiphon (cf. sections I above and V below).

Not all commentators have been satisfied with the division of works reported by Hermogenes. The undeniable differences of style and content between Περὶ ἀληθείας and Περὶ ὁμονοίας led Heinimann (1945), 134 to doubt the sophist's authorship of Περὶ ὁμονοίας, and Wilamowitz (1931–32), 2.217 n. 1 and Grossmann (1950), 44 n. 49, 125 to reject it. (Note the different view taken in Wilamowitz [1893], 1.173 n. 77, [1959], 1.62; cf. section IV below.) Nestle (1942), 385–88, 396–97 with nn. 114–16, 399 with n. 130 also doubted the sophist's authorship of Περὶ ὁμονοίας, which he would attribute instead to Antiphon of Rhamnus. (For a different view cf. Nestle [1940], 47.) Nestle supported this position by pointing to the work's supposed parallels with Thucydides, whose teacher he believed the Rhamnusian to have been. (Cf. *contra* section I above, and commentary on T2(a), ll. 15–17.) As if to compensate the sophist Antiphon for the loss of Περὶ ὁμονοίας, Nestle (1942), 394 with n. 103 proposed to ascribe to him both the *Tetralogies* and the Προοίμια καὶ ἐπίλογοι (frr. 68–70) customarily attributed to the Rhamnusian. (Buresch [1886], 133–35 also attributed the *Tetralogies* to the sophist.) Nestle conjectured that both works formed part of the rhetorical handbook (Τέχναι ῥητορικαί) current in antiquity under the name of Antiphon (frr. 71–76), which he would attribute accordingly to the sophist (cf. Nestle [1942], 390–91, 394). But there is no reason whatsoever to suppose that either the *Tetralogies* or the Προοίμια καὶ ἐπίλογοι belonged to the Τέχναι ῥητορικαί, which seems in any case to be spurious (cf. F3 with commentary; Norden [1918], vol. 1 "Nachträge," 7). More worthy of serious consideration is Wilamowitz's theory that the Πολιτικός ascribed to the sophist by Hermogenes is identical with Antiphon of Rhamnus' political tract against Alcibiades entitled Ἀλκιβιάδου λοιδορίαι. This theory will be discussed in section v below. Suffice it to say here that Hermogenes' division of works remains the only objective evidence for the attribution of the sophist's *œuvre*, and none of the proposals to modify it carries any real conviction.

From the anecdote about Antiphon's "grief-clinic" reported in [Plut.], *Vitae X or.* and elsewhere (cf. T6), Dümmler (1901), 178 n. 1, Buresch (1886), 76–84, and other commentators inferred the existence of a written Τέχνη ἀλυπίας or "Art of removing grief," which they ascribed to the sophist Antiphon. No such work is quoted by any ancient or medieval authority, however, and Hermogenes seems unaware of its existence. Moreover, the anecdote as recounted in all the sources clearly envisages *oral* instruction rather than a written work. Cf. T6(a), ll. 6–7: πυνθανόμενος τὰς αἰτίας; T6(b), l. 2: εἰς ὑποδοχὴν ἀκροατῶν; T6(d), ll. 2–3: νηπενθεῖς ἀκροάσεις. Untersteiner (1962), 29; Morrison (1972), 117, and others interpret the phrase τέχνην ἀλυπίας συνεστήσατο in [Plut.] to mean "composed a manual." But as Guthrie (1971a), 290 n. 1 rightly pointed out, the phrase means rather "contrived a technique," just as the similar phrase συνέστησεν τὴν ἡμετέραν τέχνην in Plato, *Symposium* 186E refers to the establishment of the art of medicine rather than the composition of a medical treatise. The wording of Photius, T6(c), l. 2 (τέχνην . . . ἐξευρεῖν) points in the same direction. There is absolutely no basis, therefore, for postulating a written

Τέχνη ἀλυπίας.[52] Altwegg (1908), 40 suggested that Antiphon's Περὶ ὁμονοίας was referred to in antiquity as a τέχνη ἀλυπίας and inspired the anecdote about the grief-clinic. Aly (1929), 113 strangely suggested that the Τέχνη ἀλυπίας may be identical with the dream-book current in antiquity under the name of Antiphon (cf. section VI below). Neither suggestion is supported by any evidence.

Luria (1924a), (1927b), 1066, (1928c) proposed to attribute to the sophist Antiphon a fragmentary text on the ethical value of studying poetry preserved in *P.Oxy.* 3.414. The attribution (surprisingly) has received the endorsement of Wilamowitz (1927), 288 n. 1; Untersteiner (1962), 101–7, (1954), 229 n. 17 = (1967), 2.46 n. 17; Lanata (1963), 214–17, and others. Luria's arguments in support of it, however, are entirely arbitrary and were rightly rejected by Burkert (1964), 142–43 (cf. Decleva Caizzi and Bastianini [1989], 236). Other works current in antiquity under the name of Antiphon have no claim to be considered as the sophist's. [Plut.], *Vitae X or.* 833D reports that some people attributed to "Antiphon" the work entitled Περὶ τῶν ἀρχαίων ποιητῶν καὶ μουσικῶν ascribed elsewhere to Glaucus of Rhegium.[53] The origin and basis of the attribution to Antiphon are totally unknown (cf. Jacoby [1910], 1418). Sauppe (1896), 526 conjectured a confusion arising from the names of Plato's brother and half-brother, Glaucon and Antiphon; but this seems far-fetched. Equally uncertain is the identity of the Antiphon in question. Jacoby (1910), 1418 confidently asserted that the sophist alone could be meant. But the widespread confusion surrounding the name of Antiphon (which is particularly evident in [Plut.]) urges caution.[54] Athenaeus (*Dipnosophistae*

[52] Cf. Diels, *FVS* 2.336–37 n.; Nestle (1942), 379 n. 40.

[53] On Glaucus' work cf. Jacoby (1910).

[54] Cf. Sauppe (1896), 526; Gomperz (1891), 49 n. 3; commentary on T10. On the unreliability of [Plut.] cf. section I and nn. 4–5 above.

14 650E = *FVS* 87 B 118) cites "Antiphon" in connection with a work on farming: Ἀντιφῶν ἐν τῷ Περὶ γεωργικῶν. As Kaibel long ago recognized, however, Antiphon's name here is almost certainly a mistake for "Androtion."[55]

III *ON TRUTH*

The treatise variously entitled Περὶ (τῆς) ἀληθείας[56] or (ἡ) Ἀλήθεια[57] was Antiphon the sophist's longest and most important work. Many fragments are cited explicitly from the first book (F1–2, F4–5, F10–11, F14–15, F17–21) or the second (F22–23, F24A, F25, F29–30, F33), so it may be safely inferred that the work consisted of two books. Untersteiner (1954), 229 = (1967), 2.46 and Decleva Caizzi and Bastianini (1989), 182 spoke of "at least" two books ("almeno due libri"), and Greene (1944), 236 suggested the possibility of a third. But Galen's phrase ἐν τῷ προτέρῳ τῆς Ἀληθείας (*In Hippocratis De officina medici* = F1, ll. 3–4) appears to rule out more than two (cf. Mewaldt [1929], 79 n. 14). Early Greek prose works as a rule lacked formal titles, and the title Περὶ ἀληθείας (or Ἀλήθεια) need not go back to Antiphon himself.[58] Περὶ ἀληθείας (or Ἀλήθεια) seems to represent a standard type of title, one given to prose treatises

[55] Cf. Jacoby, *FGrHist* IIIB 1.108; Diels, *FVS* 2.370 note. Untersteiner (1962), 176–77 missed the correction (as Kerferd [1965], 33 pointed out).

[56] So Hermogenes, T2(a), ll. 8–9; Pollux, 6.143 (= F3); Origen, *Contra Celsum* 4.25 (= F12), etc.

[57] So Hermogenes, T2(a), ll. 13, 19–20, 25; Galen, *In Hippocratis Epidemiarum librum* III 3.33 (= F29); Harpocration, s.v. ἄοπτα (= F4); *Suda* s.v. διάθεσις (= F24A), etc.

[58] Cf. Aly (1929), 115; Schmalzriedt (1970), 126 n. 21. On the problem of titles of early works in general cf. Nachmanson (1941); Schmalzriedt (1970). David Sedley suggests that an author like Antiphon who wrote more than one work must have had some way of referring to them and is therefore much more likely to have given them titles. But the example of Plato shows that this is not necessarily true even for a fourth-century author.

by Protagoras, Antisthenes, and Simmias of Thebes as well as to the first half of Parmenides' poem.[59] Some commentators have suggested that Antiphon entitled his Περὶ ἀληθείας in deliberate polemical allusion to Protagoras' similarly-named Ἀλήθεια. It is not certain, however, that Antiphon knew Protagoras' work by its now-familiar title, which may not be earlier than the time of Plato.[60] More important, the case for anti-Protagorean polemic in Antiphon is extremely weak (cf. section v below and commentary on F1, F13, F44(a), F44(b), and F48).

Ancient and medieval sources preserve twenty-seven verbatim citations from Περὶ ἀληθείας, many of which consist of but single words. Other fragments, cited from Antiphon but without a book-title, are plausibly attributed to Περὶ ἀληθείας on grounds of content (cf. F24, F31, and F34–39, with commentary). By far the most extensive and important remains of the work are preserved on papyrus, specifically *P.Oxy.* 1364, fr. 1 (= F44(a)); *P.Oxy.* 1364, fr. 2 + *P.Oxy.* 3647 (= F44(b)); and *P.Oxy.* 1797 (= F44(c)). The fortunate coincidence (first noticed by Wilamowitz) of a brief citation in Harpocration with three lines from *P.Oxy.* 1364, fr. 1 (= F44(a)1.18–20) guarantees the attribution to Περὶ ἀληθείας of this text and the physically related *P.Oxy.* 1364, fr. 2 + 3647 (= F44(b)). The close similarities in style and content between these fragments and *P.Oxy.* 1797 (= F44(c)) make the attribution of the latter in turn all but certain (cf. commentary ad loc.). Taken together, the papyrus fragments contribute more than four hundred lines of text to our knowledge of what is arguably the earliest

[59] For the works of Simmias and Antisthenes cf. Diogenes Laertius, 6.16, 2.124; Sauppe (1896), 514; Schmalzriedt (1970), 126 n. 21.

[60] On the title of Protagoras' work cf. Zeller in Zeller and Nestle (1920), 1354 n. 2; Nachmanson (1941), 9–10; Untersteiner (1961), 72; Schmalzriedt (1970), 64–71. The latter argued that Protagoras' Ἀλήθεια is the earliest example of an actual title in the modern sense, one deliberately chosen by the author.

surviving example of philosophical prose written in the Attic dialect. In addition to the verbatim fragments, ancient and medieval sources preserve important doxographical information about Antiphon which almost certainly pertains to doctrines expounded in Περὶ ἀληθείας (cf. F9, F12, F13, F15, F26–28, and F32, all with commentary).[61] To the fragments and reports attributed to Περὶ ἀληθείας with certainty or a high degree of probability, Diels and subsequent editors added a number of fragments whose provenance is much more uncertain (cf. F6–8, F16, F34–35, and F40–42, all with commentary). Blass (1889a) long ago identified a number of passages from the twentieth chapter of Iamblichus' *Protrepticus* as fragments from the work of a fifth-century sophist. Blass originally suggested that these texts derive from the sophist Antiphon, and in particular from Περὶ ἀληθείας. This attribution was justly criticized by Töpfer (1902), and definitively refuted by the evidence of the papyrus fragments of Περὶ ἀληθείας (cf. Grenfell and Hunt [1915], 94–95; Nestle in Zeller and Nestle [1920], 1328 with n. 3). Their unknown author has long since come to be known as the "Anonymus Iamblichi."

The remains of Περὶ ἀληθείας cover an extraordinarily diverse range of subjects, including epistemology or psychology (F1–5); physical sciences such as cosmology (F22–25), astronomy and meteorology (F26–29), and geology (F30–32); geometry (F13); and human institutions and conduct (F44(a)–(c)). Many of the specific problems addressed were staples of Presocratic and sophistic speculation, such as the nature and πάθη of the heavenly bodies (F26–28); the formation and salinity of the sea (F32); the quadrature of the circle (F13); the reliability of sense-perception (F1, F4–5); and the relation between law and nature (F44(a)–

[61] Although not fragments in the strict sense, the doxographical texts were printed by Diels and Kranz together with the fragments proper. All subsequent editors follow suit.

(b)). Other fragments demonstrate that Περὶ ἀληθείας dealt also with medical and physiological subjects such as the aetiology of disease and embryology (F29A and F33–39, with commentary). Presocratic interest in embryology is well known and widely attested.[62] But the Presocratic philosophers' wider concern with the subject of medicine is not as familiar, despite Aristotle's explicit testimony that many of his predecessors concerned themselves with the principles of health and disease: φυσικοῦ δὲ καὶ περὶ ὑγιείας καὶ νόσου τὰς πρώτας ἰδεῖν ἀρχάς· οὔτε γὰρ ὑγίειαν οὔτε νόσον οἷόν τε γίγνεσθαι τοῖς ἐστερημένοις ζωῆς διὸ σχεδὸν τῶν περὶ φύσεως οἱ πλεῖστοι καὶ τῶν ἰατρῶν οἱ φιλοσοφωτέρως τὴν τέχνην μετιόντες, οἱ μὲν τελευτῶσιν εἰς τὰ περὶ ἰατρικῆς, οἱ δὲ ἐκ τῶν περὶ φύσεως ἄρχονται περὶ τῆς ἰατρικῆς (*De sensu* 436a17–b1).[63] His testimony is corroborated by the extant evidence on Alcmaeon, Philolaus, and others,[64] and also by the extensive treatment of physiological and medical topics (including the aetiology of disease) in Plato's *Timaeus*, a work which emulates the range and scope of the Presocratic "inquiry about nature," ἱστορία περὶ φύσεως.

The great variety of subject-matter treated in Περὶ ἀληθείας has puzzled critics. Bignone (1938), 79 was reduced to characterizing the work as a kind of encyclopedia ("una specia di enciclopedia"), while Heinimann (1945), 133–34 suggested that it was constructed posthumously from several different λόγοι on different subjects. It is

[62] Cf. Parmenides, *FVS* 28 A 52–54, B 17–18; Alcmaeon, *FVS* 24 A 13–17, B 3; Empedocles, *FVS* 31 A 81–84, B 65, B 67–68; Anaxagoras, *FVS* 59 A 107–11; Democritus, *FVS* 68 A 140–44, A 149, B 148; Diogenes of Apollonia, *FVS* 64 A 25–28, B 9.

[63] The same point is made in *De respiratione* 480b23–30; cf. Mansfeld (1990a), 3058–59 with n. 3.

[64] Cf. Alcmaeon, *FVS* 24 A 1, B 4; Philolaus, *FVS* 44 A 27–28; Democritus, *FVS* 68 A 159; Anaxagoras, *FVS* 59 A 105, and commentary on F29A.

worth recalling, however, that the books of Presocratics such as Anaximander and Anaxagoras (for example) seem to have covered a comparably wide range of subject-matter (cf. Cherniss [1951], 323–24 = [1977], 66–67; Heidel [1921] = [1980], 239–88). It is not easy to find a parallel for Antiphon's particular combination of natural philosophy and ethics in a single work. But too little is known about the books of Antiphon's Presocratic and sophistic predecessors and contemporaries to conclude that Περὶ ἀληθείας was unique in this respect. (For a possible parallel in Archelaus cf. commentary on F44(b).) The structure or arrangement of topics in Περὶ ἀληθείας is but imperfectly known. Fragments assigned explicitly to the first book concern sense-perception and thought (F1, F3–5); desire (F17, F21); the argument about the buried bed (F15); and other subjects of uncertain nature (F10, F14). Fragments from the second book deal with diverse scientific and medical questions (F22–23, F24A, F25, F29–29A, F30, F33–39). Unfortunately, several of the most important fragments cannot be certainly located, among them F13 (the squaring of the circle) and the papyrus fragments (on justice, law, and nature).

Whether the seemingly disparate contents of Περὶ ἀληθείας were united by a consistent theme or common thread of argument are matters for conjecture. Some commentators, comparing the work with the poem of Parmenides and with Protagoras' Ἀλήθεια, have proposed that it dealt with the general theme of truth or reality as contrasted with appearance.[65] In Antiphon's case, this will have taken the form of a contrast between φύσις (identified, or at least associated, with truth) and νόμος (associated with appearance). It is interesting, and perhaps

[65] So Schmid (1940), 159–62; Nestle (1942), 372, 379; Decleva Caizzi and Bastianini (1989), 82–83.

significant, that this contrast reappears in quite different contexts in F15, F44(a), and F44(b) (cf. commentary ad locc.). Yet there are many fragments that seemingly have nothing to do with this theme. Other commentators have proposed more specific variations on this same general type of interpretation. Aly (1929), 141–47, for example, identified the central theme of the work as the search for an essence or true reality (οὐσία) underlying the flux of appearances, whether in the realm of physical bodies (F15), mathematical objects (F13), or ethical concepts (F44(a)–(c)). Morrison (1963), (1972), 212 considered the main subject to be the problematic relationship between names and the things to which they refer. Untersteiner (1954), 233–71 = (1967), 2.55–107 saw the work as a polemical attempt to re-establish against the destructive arguments of Gorgias the unity of what Untersteiner calls "experiences" (cf. Kerferd [1965], 32–33, and section VII below). According to Romeyer-Dherbey (1985), 96–115, the basic subject of the work (as of Antiphon's whole philosophy) is the quest for the metaphysical entity he terms the "ἀρρύθμιστον," or that which is without structure (cf. commentary on F10 and F15). Luginbill (1997) took a completely different approach, interpreting the work as (literally) pro-oligarchic propaganda designed to undermine prevailing Athenian democratic conceptions of justice and law in the service of his aristocratic political faction. Luginbill's interpretation of Περὶ ἀληθείας in crude political terms distorts the argument of the papyrus fragments (cf. commentary on F44(a)) and fails to do justice to the other extant evidence for the work. These fundamental weaknesses are shared by the attempts of other commentators to identify a single, unifying theme underlying the remains of Περὶ ἀληθείας, all of which rest on doubtful or uncertain interpretations of a few fragments only and ignore much of the surviving evidence for the work (especially that pertaining to the second book). In addition, all assume in advance what ought rather to be demonstrated: that (in the words of Nestle [1942], 372) "Antiphon *muss*, ähnlich wie Protagoras, *eine nach systematischer Einheitlichkeit der Weltanschauung strebende Natur gewesen sein* [my italics]."

Internal evidence offers no firm criteria for dating Περὶ ἀληθείας. Most commentators settle for a date somewhere in the last three decades of the fifth century.[66] Such a dating is defensible, though by no means demonstrable, on grounds of both style and content. Stylistically, the relatively simple periodic structure perhaps points to a period anterior to the full development of Attic prose style. With regard to content, there is no trace of the influence of Socrates or Plato. Also, Antiphon's treatment of the antithesis of law and nature seems in several respects to fall short of the most mature stage in the development of this famous antithesis (cf. Heinimann [1945], 142 with n. 62 and *passim*). Some critics have contended that Περὶ ἀληθείας was parodied by Aristophanes in the *Clouds*, and so must be dated before 423 (or 418, if the parody derives from the revised edition).[67] But the contention is unpersuasive.[68] The many parallels with the works of Antiphon's predecessors and contemporaries which commentators have sought to identify in the remains of Περὶ ἀληθείας (with varying degrees of success) contribute nothing to the dating of the work.

On the style of Περὶ ἀληθείας cf. commentary on T2(a), F29, F44(c), and introductory note on F44.

[66] Cf. Aly (1929), 140–41; Schmid (1940), 162, 169; Heinimann (1945), 141–42; Untersteiner (1954), 229 n. 16 = (1967), 2.46 n. 16 (whose reference to Altwegg is mistaken); Guthrie (1971a), 286 n. 2 (who misrepresents the remarks of Schmid [1940], 159).

[67] Cf. Luria (1924a), 380, (1924b), 326, (1926d), (1927b), 1062, (1928b), 220–25; Nestle (1942), 381 with n. 44. Dümmler (1889), 85 was the first to suggest that Aristophanes parodied Antiphon.

[68] Cf. Heinimann (1945), 141; Moulton (1972), 357–60; commentary on F44(a)v.4–8.

IV *ON CONCORD*

Ancient and medieval lexicographical sources preserve fourteen brief quotations from Antiphon's Περὶ ὁμονοίας.[69] The fact that no book-number is attached to any of them implies that the work consisted of only one book. Hermogenes' use of the singular ὁ Περὶ ὁμονοίας (*sc.* λόγος, T2(a), l. 9) agrees with this. Although most of these quotations are quite brief, as a group they manifest several of the characteristics mentioned by Philostratus in his description of the style of Περὶ ὁμονοίας (*Vitae sophistarum* 500 = T2(b)), for example the use of *sententiae* (cf. F52) and poetic or metaphorical diction (cf. F68–70).

The anthologist Stobaeus has preserved a further group of eleven fragments, several of substantial length, attributed to "Antiphon" but without a book-title (F49–51, F53–53A, F54, F58–62). The fact that Stobaeus elsewhere quotes from Antiphon of Rhamnus without mentioning a title (cf. 3.20.43; 4.5.19, 65, all from *or.* 5) suggests the possibility that some or all of these Stobaeus fragments may derive from a lost speech or speeches of the Rhamnusian. Yet the contents and style of most of them obviously preclude an origin in dicanic (or demegoric) oratory. It is much more plausible, therefore, to attribute them as a group to the sophist Antiphon. Commentators have disagreed, however, about the work or works to which they should be assigned.[70] Sauppe (1896), 523 ascribed them all to Πολιτικός. Blass (1881), 139 n., 144 n., (1887–98), 1.111–13, 3.2.361–62 assigned F60–61 to Πολιτικός, but the re-

[69] Photius, *Lexicon* s.v. ἵνα (ι 133, 2.326) = F55 adds the article (Περὶ τῆς ὁμονοίας). Philostratus, *Vitae sophistarum* 500 = T2(b), ll. 2–3 cites the work as ὁ ὑπὲρ τῆς ὁμονοίας – an example of the frequent confusion of περί and ὑπέρ in later Greek, on which cf. Dover (1968b), 14 n. 13.

[70] No evidence whatsoever supports Joël's bizarre theory that the Stobaeus fragments derive from a dialogue of Antisthenes in which Antiphon figured as a *dramatis persona*.

mainder to Περὶ ὁμονοίας. Croiset (1883), 151–52 attributed F57, F59, and F60–61 to Πολιτικός, and the rest to Περὶ ὁμονοίας. (Luria [1926b] also assigned F60–61 to Πολιτικός, on the assumption that this work is identical with Antiphon of Rhamnus' Ἀλκιβιάδου λοιδορίαι; cf. sections II above and V below.) But Wilamowitz (1876), 296, (1893), I.173 n. 77 assigned them all to Περὶ ὁμονοίας, and Diels and Kranz, Untersteiner, and most other editors and commentators have followed suit. Stylistic considerations support the attribution, since most of the fragments display the features mentioned by Philostratus (T2(b)), including poetic or lofty diction; a prolix manner of expression; and an abundance of γνῶμαι.[71] The stylistic argument failed to impress Guthrie (1971a), 287, who interpreted Philostratus' term γνωμολογίαι to mean "collections of maxims," and concluded that even if they do derive from Περὶ ὁμονοίας, the Stobaeus fragments probably do not express Antiphon's own thought. γνωμολογίαι, however, may refer rather to the "sententious style" of Περὶ ὁμονοίας (cf. LSJ, s.v.). But even if it is interpreted as Guthrie suggested, his conclusion that the γνῶμαι do not express Antiphon's own thought does not follow. Quite apart from the question of style, many of the Stobaeus fragments can be linked thematically with fragments cited explicitly from Περὶ ὁμονοίας: F53–53A and F54, for example, with F52; F58 with F55; and F49, F51, and F60–61 with F67A. It is reasonable therefore to accept Wilamowitz's assignment of the Stobaeus fragments to Περὶ ὁμονοίας, with the understanding that one or another of them might well have a different origin. To the fragments so far enumerated Diels and subsequent editors have added F56, F64, and F66, with differing degrees of plausibility (cf. commentary ad locc.).

[71] Cf. Blass (1887–98), I.111–12; Altwegg (1908), 52; Schmid (1940), 163 n. 1.

Efforts to reconstruct the theme and contents of Περὶ ὁμονοίας usually begin from the title, where the term ὁμόνοια has been variously interpreted. The majority of critics have understood it as referring to civic or social concord, and interpreted Περὶ ὁμονοίας accordingly as an exhortation to harmony directed at the warring political factions in Athens.[72] In favor of this view is the simple fact that "civic concord" is the commonest (though not the only) meaning of the word ὁμόνοια in Antiphon's time. Furthermore, the pervasiveness of factional strife in the later fifth century provides a plausible historical context for a work on this theme.[73] The major stumbling-block to this type of interpretation, however, is the notorious absence of both the term ὁμόνοια and the idea of civic concord from extant fragments of the work. For the numerous attempts that have been made to read the theme of civic concord into F54, F58, F61–62, F64–65, and other fragments must be pronounced a failure (cf. commentary ad locc.). Despite the attempts of Jacoby (1908), 9 and Krämer (1915), 54 to explain away this absence, it remains very difficult for supporters of the civic concord interpretation to account for. Other commentators have interpreted ὁμόνοια rather differently, in terms of the "psychic" concord or harmony of the individual with himself.[74]

72 So Sauppe (1896), 521; Croiset (1883), 150–52; Wilamowitz (1893), 1.173 n. 77; Bignone (1938), 86–97, 109–39; Krämer (1915), 14–16, 54–59; Mewaldt (1929), 81–84; Aly (1929), 149–50; Nestle (1942), 381–82; Schmid (1940), 163–65. Dümmler (1889), 79, (1901), 182 thought the work presented Antiphon's ideal of state and society.

73 Cf. Thucydides, 3.82; Democritus, *FVS* 68 B 250, B 249, B 255; Thrasymachus, *FVS* 85 B 1; Gorgias, *FVS* 82 A 1, B 8a; Jacoby (1908), 9–11; Krämer (1915), 13–27, 38–40; Nestle (1938), 14–18; de Romilly (1972).

74 Cf. Altwegg (1908), 59–60; Jacoby (1908), 21–25; Goebel (1910), 384; Stenzel (1924), 40–42; Pfister (1925), 204; Altheim (1926), 268–69; Ueberweg and Praechter (1926), 129; Regenbogen (1940a), 100; Untersteiner (1962), 108, (1954), 254–55 = (1967), 2.78–79; Höistad (1948), 108–10, some of whom combine this with the civic concord interpretation, supposing that Antiphon dealt with ὁμόνοια in both senses.

This sort of interpretation, however, is even less plausible than the civic concord alternative. There is no support whatsoever for it in the fragments themselves (cf. commentary on F54 and F58–59). Blass (1889a), 12–13 suggested the possibility of a connection between Antiphon's Περὶ ὁμονοίας and a fragment from Iamblichus' *Epistle on Concord* preserved by Stobaeus (2.33.15) which relates "psychic" concord to other varieties of ὁμόνοια. Diels and Kranz (followed by Untersteiner) went so far as to prefix this text to the remains of Περὶ ὁμονοίας (cf. *FVS* 87 B 44a). The Iamblichus passage has no demonstrable connection with Antiphon, however, and proves nothing about his conception of ὁμόνοια.[75] Significantly, the very notion of "psychic" concord is not attested before Plato, whose tripartite psychology and conception of virtue as the harmonious cooperation of different psychic faculties it seems in fact to presuppose.[76] Even as committed a supporter of the psychic concord interpretation as Altwegg (1908), 59 admitted he could find no early instance of ὁμόνοια in the sense required. Luginbill (1997), 165–69 combined the psychic and social concord interpretations in a novel way. He suggested that Περὶ ὁμονοίας was intended as oligarchic propaganda which used the example of a balanced individual who achieves personal ὁμόνοια and avoids personal anarchy in order to argue the need for states governed on the same principles of right thinking, orderliness, intelligent decision-making, etc. Luginbill's construct puts an implausible partisan spin on the ostensibly apolitical (not to say banal) ethical commonplaces of the Stobaeus fragments,

[75] Cf. Altwegg (1908), 58–59 (whose view is misrepresented by Luria [1927b], 1071); commentary on F59.

[76] Cf. Plato, *Republic* 351E–352A, 432A, 554D, *Phaedrus* 237E; [Plato], *Definitions* 411; Krämer (1915), 53–54; Schmid (1940), 164 n. 17; Nestle (1942), 381 n. 48; commentary on F59. For a different view cf. Jacoby (1908), 23–24.

and is furthermore open to all of the objections raised above against the psychic and civic concord interpretations.

It is imprudent to try to draw inferences about the theme and contents of Antiphon's Περὶ ὁμονοίας from the title alone. Early Greek prose works as a rule lacked formal titles, and the title Περὶ ὁμονοίας need not go back to Antiphon himself. (Cf. the remarks on the title Περὶ ἀληθείας in section III above.) Furthermore, the titles subsequently attached to originally untitled works were often adapted from a work's opening words, or given with a view to only one portion of a work's contents. Hence, such titles can give an incomplete or misleading idea of the actual subject-matter in the case of works of heterogeneous content. (For illuminating examples of this phenomenon cf. Nachmanson [1941], 49–52.) It is perfectly conceivable that the title Περὶ ὁμονοίας derives from a portion of Antiphon's work no longer extant which dealt with the subject of civic concord. But it is equally conceivable that it derives from parts of the work concerned with marriage and the family (cf. F49) or with friendship (cf. F62, F64–65), since ὁμόνοια and related terms are well attested in these contexts also.[77] There is simply no way of knowing, on the limited evidence at our disposal, exactly how the title relates to the contents of Antiphon's work.

An examination of the remains of Περὶ ὁμονοίας without recourse to conjecture based on the title reveals a variety of themes. A number of fragments emphasize the brevity and difficulties inherent in human life (cf. F49, F50, F51, F66). The opening words of F49 (προελθέτω ὁ βίος εἰς τὸ πρόσθεν), taken together with the evidence of other fragments, suggests that Antiphon reviewed the successive stages of life from youth to old age, highlighting the hard-

[77] Cf. Blass (1887–98), 3.2.359–60; Krämer (1915), 9, 11, 45–49, 52; Lycurgus, fr. 64 (ὅταν γυνὴ ὁμονοίας τῆς πρὸς ⟨τὸν Blass⟩ ἄνδρα στερεθῇ, ἀβίωτος ὁ καταλειπόμενος γίγνεται βίος.

ships of each.[78] The misery of human life is a commonplace of Greek literature and thought from Homer on. Cf. *Iliad* 24.525–26; Hesiod, *Works and Days* 90–104; Semonides, fr. 1.20–22; Bacchylides, 5.160–62 with Maehler (1982), 2.116–17; Empedocles, *FVS* 31 B 121; Democritus, *FVS* 68 B 285; etc. And the hardships of life's successive stages are enumerated in a fashion comparable to that of Περὶ ὁμονοίας in the pseudo-Platonic *Epinomis* 973D–974A and *Axiochus* 366D, as well as in the Cynic Teles' argument against hedonism (Stobaeus, 4.34.7 = fr. V, Hense [1909], 49–51).[79] Some commentators would relate this theme to the alleged τέχνη ἀλυπίας and/or the topic of consolation familiar from the later genre of consolation-literature.[80] The anecdote about the grief-clinic implies oral instruction rather than a written work, however, and there is no reason whatsoever to connect it with Περὶ ὁμονοίας (cf. section II above and commentary on T6). The theme of the misery of human life has in and of itself no necessary connection with the topic of consolation; and the fragments of Περὶ ὁμονοίας in which the theme appears fail to establish one. Another important theme discernible in a number of fragments concerns the failure of human beings to make adequate or proper use of their lives and material resources (cf. F52, F53–53A, and F54–55, all with commentary). Other fragments deal with the subjects of σωφροσύνη (F58–59); education (F60–61); friendship (F62, F64–65); and legendary or fabulous peoples (F45–47). Several fragments consist of single words and cannot be securely placed in any thematic context (F67, F68–71). It does not seem possible to unite these disparate themes and topics in

[78] Cf. F49, F51, and F66, all with commentary; Sauppe (1896), 522–23; Altwegg (1908), 22–23, 29; Jacoby (1908), 30, 37; Aly (1929), 150; Schmid (1940), 164 with n. 1.

[79] On the *Epinomis* passage cf. Tarán (1975), 210–11, with the many parallels there cited.

[80] So Buresch (1886), 72–83; Kassel (1958), 9–10.

the framework of a coherent argument. Altwegg (1908), 14–60, 95–98 and Jacoby (1908), 9–47 labored diligently to do so, offering detailed reconstructions of the work; but their efforts must be pronounced unsuccessful.[81] The problem may be simply the scarcity of our evidence; but it is at least conceivable that Antiphon's work was never much more than a string of sententious utterances on diverse topics of ethical interest.[82]

The style of Περὶ ὁμονοίας is succinctly and accurately described by Philostratus (T2(b); cf. above). Its main features are an abundant use of rare and/or poetic vocabulary, synonyms, rhetorical figures, similes, bold metaphors, and γνῶμαι or ethical maxims.[83] Jacoby (1908), 63 aptly compared Plato's description of the style of the sophist Polus of Acragas (*Phaedrus* 267B–C = *AS* B XIV 10): τὰ δὲ Πώλου πῶς φράσωμεν αὖ μουσεῖα λόγων, ὡς διπλασιολογίαν καὶ γνωμολογίαν καὶ εἰκονολογίαν, ὀνομάτων τε Λικυμνίων, ἃ ἐκείνῳ ἐδωρήσατο πρὸς ποίησιν εὐεπείας.[84] The elevated style and sententious contents of Περὶ ὁμονοίας emulate the characteristics of serious poetry, and identify the work as an example of sophistic popular ἐπίδειξις.[85] Schmid (1940), 166 with n. 2 suggested a different generic affiliation, contending that Περὶ ὁμονοίας is the earliest extant example of popular-philosophical diatribe. In support of this contention Schmid referred to Clement of Alexandria, *Stromata* 1.16.79.3: φασὶ δὲ καὶ τοὺς κατὰ

[81] Cf. the reviews of their respective efforts in Kalinka (1910) and Cahen (1910). Cf. also Wilamowitz (1893), 1.173 n. 77; Schmid (1940), 164–65; Nestle (1942), 382–84.

[82] Cf. von Arnim (1898), 13–14, especially 14: "Aneinanderreihung von Gnomen, nicht zusammenhängende Gedankenentwicklung war bis auf Sokrates die übliche Form ethischer Darstellungen."

[83] Cf. Aly (1929), 153–55; Bignone (1938), 193–213; Schmid (1940), 165–66; Jacoby (1908), 48–69, and commentary on F45–71 *passim*.

[84] On the meaning of the underlined terms cf. Thompson (1868), 115.

[85] Cf. Aly (1929), 154. On sophistic epideixis cf. Schmid (1907); Kroll (1940), 1045; Nestle (1942), 259–60; Guthrie (1971a), 41–44.

διατριβὴν λόγους καὶ τὰ ῥητορικὰ ἰδιώματα εὑρεῖν ... Ἀντιφῶντα ⟨Σω⟩φίλου Ῥαμνούσιον. The words τοὺς κατὰ διατριβὴν λόγους have nothing to do with Περὶ ὁμονοίας or with diatribe, however, but refer instead to Antiphon of Rhamnus' *Tetralogies*. Sophistic epideixis and the later Stoic-Cynic diatribe share certain characteristics, but it is a mistake to conflate these distinct literary genres.

There is no internal or external evidence for the chronology of Περὶ ὁμονοίας, which has been variously dated. Schmid (1940), 166 placed it in the politically troubled period after 408 and considered it later than Περὶ ἀληθείας. But most commentators reverse the chronological relationship and place Περὶ ὁμονοίας much earlier, in the late 440s or the 430s.[86] The main grounds for such an early dating are the parallels with Attic tragedy to which critics have never wearied of calling attention.[87] But none of the alleged borrowings is conclusive one way or the other, and attempts to date the work on this basis seem doomed to failure. (Cf. further commentary on F49, F60, and F61.) The mature Attic prose-style of the fragments has seemed to some commentators a stumbling-block to an early dating, especially if the influence of Gorgias is admitted.[88] But Gorgianic influence is disputed (cf. commentary on F49). And in any case, too little is known about the evolution of Attic prose in the last decades of the fifth century to warrant any firm conclusions on this score. The chronology of Περὶ ὁμονοίας, both absolutely and in relation to Περὶ ἀληθείας, remains an open question.

[86] Cf. Altwegg (1908), 60–76; Aly (1929), 153; Finley (1939), 65–68; Greene (1944), 232; Nestle (1942), 399 n. 130.

[87] Cf. Dümmler (1901), 174–79; Nestle (1901), 563 (Stellenregister s.v. "Antiphon sophista"); Altwegg (1908), 60–76; Jacoby (1908), 33–37; Bignone (1938), 139–52, 198–201; Moulton (1972), 350 n. 46, with references.

[88] Cf. Jacoby (1908), 35; Schmid (1940), 166 n. 1. Even such an advocate of early dating as Nestle (1942), 399 n. 130 felt this as a difficulty.

V *POLITICUS*

Ancient sources preserve five brief citations from Antiphon's Πολιτικός (F72–76), which evidently consisted of but one book. The title is of a conventional type. Besides the Platonic Πολιτικός, a work entitled Τί τὸ ἐπιτήδειον ἢ Πολιτικός is ascribed to Crito, and works entitled Πολιτικόν to Antisthenes and Pythagoras. Cf. Diogenes Laertius, 2.121, 6.15, 8.7; *Suda* s.v. Πυθαγόρας (π 3120, 4.262); Sauppe (1896), 522. In the case of Antiphon's work, the title may be interpreted as "politician" (so Nestle [1942], 372, 388) or as "discourse on politics" (so LSJ, s.v. πολιτικός III; von Arnim [1916], 8; Kranz, *FVS* 2.367). It is impossible to gain any clear idea of the work's form or contents from the title and the few short fragments preserved.

It was the lifelong contention of Wilamowitz that Πολιτικός is identical with the political pamphlet against Alcibiades entitled Ἀλκιβιάδου λοιδορίαι or Κατ' Ἀλκιβιάδου λοιδορίας ascribed to Antiphon of Rhamnus (frr. 66–67).[89] The identification has been approved by Susemihl (1877), 798 n. 39; Buresch (1886), 75–76; Krämer (1915), 58–59; Aly (1929), 156; Nestle (1942), 388; Dover (1950), 55 n. 2, and others. Luria (1926b) also accepted it, but conceived the work – implausibly – as a theoretical treatise on education rather than a personal invective against Alcibiades (cf. commentary on F61). Wilamowitz's case for identifying the two works begins from the metaphor of "lunching" on possessions (F73), which he contended must envisage a specific individual. Wilamowitz cited a series of ancient texts (including Pliny, *Natural History* 14.143; Eupolis, frr. 76, 99.13–14, 385; Pherecrates, fr. 34) in which he thought to discover allusions to Alcibiades' alleged habit of imbibing alcohol early in the day. Wilamowitz concluded that

[89] Cf. Wilamowitz (1876), 295–98, (1893), 1.170 n. 71, (1931–32), 2.217 n. 1.

F73 as well as F76 derive from the context of an invective and refer to none other than Alcibiades. Since these fragments are ascribed to Πολιτικός, this work must be identical with Antiphon of Rhamnus' Ἀλκιβιάδου λοιδορίαι. (Wilamowitz explained that the latter title is the author's original one, while Πολιτικός stems from later writers.) Wilamowitz's whole construct was rejected by Blass (1887–98), 1.113–14, 3.2.359–60, who pointed out that F73 is formulated in the third person, whereas the only extant verbatim citation from Ἀλκιβιάδου λοιδορίαι is an apostrophe to Alcibiades in the second person. Blass further argued that F73 looks more like a general statement than abuse directed at an individual, and that the habit of squandering resources could just as well have been mentioned by the sophist Antiphon as by the Rhamnusian. Goossens (1942) contended against Wilamowitz that F76 refers rather to Cimon than to Alcibiades. In support of this contention, Goossens cited the famous fragment of Eupolis' Πόλεις quoted by Plutarch, *Cimon* 15 (= fr. 221): κακὸς μὲν οὐκ ἦν, φιλοπότης δὲ κἀμελής· κἀνίοτ' ⟨ἂν⟩ ἀπεκοιμᾶτ' ἂν ἐν Λακεδαίμονι κἂν Ἐλπινίκην τῇδε καταλιπὼν μόνην. But accusations of φιλοποσία are common in ancient literature (cf. commentary on F76). And even if the wording of F76 is a deliberate reminiscence of Eupolis' lines, it would not follow that Cimon is the subject. Certainly it is not difficult to imagine F73 and F76 belonging to the context of an invective, and this lends an air of plausibility to the identification of Πολιτικός with the Rhamnusian's Ἀλκιβιάδου λοιδορίαι. But despite Wilamowitz's claim to the contrary, the metaphor of "lunching" on possessions is by no means so unusual as to compel the conclusion that a particular individual, let alone Alcibiades, must be envisaged (cf. commentary on F73). It is worth noting that Athenaeus quotes from both Πολιτικός and Ἀλκιβιάδου λοιδορίαι, by title, without any hint that they may be one and the same work (cf. *Dipnosophistae* 12

525B = Antiphon of Rhamnus, fr. 66; 10 423A = F73).[90] The arguments for identifying Πολιτικός with Ἀλκιβιάδου λοιδορίαι are insufficient to overturn the division of works reported by Hermogenes.

VI DREAM-BOOK

Antiphon the sophist's dream-book is not cited (at least by name) in any of the lexicographical sources to which we owe so much of our knowledge of his other works. Presumably this is because it was not included in regular editions of the *corpus Antiphonteum* (cf. section I above). The *Suda* refers to it with the phrase περὶ κρίσεως ὀνείρων, which is more likely a description than an actual title. The existence of dream-books or dream-tablets (πινάκια) is well attested in the later fifth and the early fourth centuries BC.[91] The profession of dream-interpreter is of course older still, being attested already in the *Iliad*.[92] Antiphon's distinction lies in the fact that his book was apparently the first *literary* work written on the subject of dream-interpretation – or at least the first to have achieved wide circulation (cf. Kaiser in Krauss and Kaiser [1965], 154 n. 1). The fourth book of the Hippocratic *De victu* (which Rehm showed must be dated no earlier than circa 370 BC) is almost certainly later (cf. van Lieshout [1980], 187–88, with references). Other early examples of literary dream-books are those ascribed to Panyasis the younger (cf. Del Corno [1969], 34–36, 121–22; van Lieshout [1980], 190–92) and to Aristander of Telmessus, the court-diviner of

90 It is only fair to add that Athenaeus occasionally refers to the same work under different titles (cf. Nachmanson [1941], 19, 31).

91 Cf. Isocrates, *or.* 19.5; Xenophon, *Anabasis* 7.8.1; Plutarch, *Aristides* 27; Wilamowitz (1919), 65–66; Bouché-Leclercq (1879–82), 1.295–96; van Lieshout (1980), 174–75, 181–82.

92 Cf. *Iliad* 1.63, 5.149–50; Hopfner (1937), 2235; Dodds (1951), 106 with n. 22; van Lieshout (1980), 165–67.

Philip and Alexander (cf. Del Corno [1969], 7–23, 105–8; van Lieshout [1980], 192–95; commentary on T11(a)). Most of our knowledge about the contents of Antiphon's dream-book derives from Cicero, whose information is now supplemented in an important fashion by a new fragment from Diogenes of Oenoanda's Epicurean inscription (fr. 24 = F80(b)). Antiphon's dream-book is also mentioned briefly by Artemidorus, *Onirocritica* 2.14 (= F78).[93] Other references to Antiphon as a diviner or dream-interpreter testify to his continuing notoriety, but do not supply reliable information about the contents of his book (cf. T7–9, T11–12, F81, F81A, and F81B, all with commentary). Sauppe (1896), 525 and others have suggested that Antiphon's book gave separate treatment to the subject of portents (τέρατα). Portents and omens occur frequently in dreams, however, and their interpretation is an integral part of the art of dream-interpretation itself (cf. Bouché-Leclercq [1879–82], 1.291–92; Del Corno [1969], 130 n. 1). It is therefore unnecessary to assume a special section devoted to portents.

In a series of publications, the Russian scholar S. Luria sought to extract from the pages of Artemidorus a systematic theory of dream-interpretation which he proposed to ascribe to Antiphon (cf. Luria [1926a], [1927b], [1928a]). More specifically, Luria attributed to Antiphon the substance of *Onirocritica* 1.8 and 4.2, in which Artemidorus sets out a system of six elements (στοιχεῖα) in accordance with which dreams are to be interpreted: φύσις, νόμος, ἔθος, τέχνη, ὀνόματα, and χρόνος. (Dietrich [1927] would ex-

[93] Kaiser in Krauss and Kaiser (1965), 13 would ascribe to Antiphon the dream about being struck by lightning and its differential interpretation according to whether the dreamer is rich or poor (*Onirocritica* 2.9, 110–11). But the mere fact that Artemidorus ascribes this interpretation to οἱ πάνυ παλαιοί does not justify the attribution to Antiphon. As Del Corno (1969), n. 4 pointed out, other referents are conceivable, for example "Phemonoe" (cf. *Onirocritica* 2.9, 114).

tend the material supposedly borrowed from Antiphon even further than Luria had proposed.) Luria believed that he had discovered in these passages a complete system of sophistic thought (including, but not limited to, the field of dream-interpretation) which exalted nature in opposition to law and custom. Combining this "discovery" with the Stoic distinction between natural (ἄτεχνος, *naturalis*) and artificial (τεχνικός, *artificiosus*) divination,[94] Luria argued that in the fifth century there existed two opposing schools of dream-interpretation, one conservative and religious, the other radical and (pseudo-)scientific, and identified Antiphon as the founder, theoretician, and most famous exponent of the latter. Dietrich (1927) and Untersteiner (1962), 196–211, (1954), 256–57 = (1967), 2.80–82 embraced Luria's theory, and Del Corno (1962), 339 n. 8, (1969), 131 considered it at least possible. Latte (1929) = (1968), 218–24, however, supplied a devastating critique of the whole construct. Latte convincingly rejected Luria's source-critical speculations about Artemidorus' classification of "elements" (στοιχεῖα) and showed the implausibility of deriving *Onirocritica* 4.2 from Antiphon. As Latte pointed out, by Artemidorus' time the antithesis of law and nature had become so familiar a commonplace that it is utterly superfluous to seek out a fifth-century sophistic source for it. Latte furthermore demolished Luria's reconstruction of two opposing schools of dream-interpretation by pointing out that the Stoic distinction between "natural" and "artificial" concerns modes of *divination* rather than *methods* of dream-interpretation. *All* dream-interpretation is artificial according to the sense of this distinction, depending as it does on the application of human interpretative procedures to the ambiguous subject-matter of allegorematic dreams. Latte's conclusions were accepted by Kranz (*FVS* 2.367 n.) and further reinforced by Blum (1936), 72–80,

[94] Cf. Cicero, *De divinatione* 1.11, 34, 72, 109–110, 2.26–27, and below.

who plausibly argued that Artemidorus' discussion of elements combines a Sceptic source with logical principles of division derived ultimately from the tradition of rhetorical instruction.

To judge from the limited evidence at our disposal, it appears that Antiphon's dream-book did not present a systematic theory of dream-interpretation, but rather a collection of individual dreams and their explanations.[95] From the examples reported by Cicero, Aly (1929), 100–1 and Del Corno (1962), 349–52 plausibly inferred that Antiphon offered two different and opposing interpretations for each dream. Van Lieshout (1980), 223 noted that this procedure seems to be reflected also in the anecdote about Antiphon related by Clement of Alexandria (*Stromata* 7.4.24.4 = T8). Aly proposed to connect the procedure with the well-known sophistic practice of ἀντιλογία, of which (he suggested) the dream-book was intended to be an ironic and witty example. Del Corno interpreted it more seriously, as an application of Antiphon's thoroughgoing philosophical relativism to the special field of dream-interpretation.[96] But a careful reading of Cicero's report suggests that in the case of the examples discussed there, the opposing interpretations are not equally valid, but those of Antiphon superior (cf. van Lieshout [1980], 223). And the suggestion is confirmed by the new evidence from Diogenes (cf. commentary on F80(b)), which indicates that Antiphon's interpretation proved to be correct. If so, then the opposing interpretations were probably not intended as demonstrations of relativism or of Antiphon's ability to construct contradictory but equally valid expla-

[95] Cf. Fischer (1899), 4; Latte (1929), 159 = (1968), 222–23; Blum (1936), 78; Kaiser in Krauss and Kaiser (1965), 13. For the preponderance of example over theory Kaiser compared the case of the *Ars rhetorica* of Anaximenes of Lampsacus.

[96] Del Corno later abandoned this interpretation; cf. Del Corno (1969), 130 n. 2.

nations. Rather, they will have served to show off Antiphon's ingenuity in besting rival interpreters and discovering the less obvious, but correct meaning of the dream symbolism. Van Lieshout (1980), 224–25, 226–28 argued for a different sort of connection between the methods of the dream-book and Antiphon's larger philosophical concerns. He contended that into the traditional εἰκασμός-procedure[97] of dream-interpretation Antiphon introduced a wholly new element: the analysis of dream-items as *verbal* phenomena. Van Lieshout related this type of analysis to the "linguistic approach to truth" which (following Morrison [1963]) he identified as a central preoccupation of Περὶ ἀληθείας (cf. section III above). As van Lieshout himself admitted, however, there is no support whatsoever for this theory in the extant evidence for the dream-book. Moreover, the interpretation of Περὶ ἀληθείας defended by Morrison and van Lieshout is at best dubious (cf. section III above, and commentary on F1, F13, and F15).

The fact that Antiphon composed a dream-book does not by itself prove that he was a professional diviner or dream-interpreter. Admittedly he appears as one in the examples from the dream-book reported by Cicero and Diogenes (cf. F80(a), F80(b)). But as Del Corno (1962), 351 n. 36, (1969), 130 n. 3 pointed out, this is probably just a narrative device designed to increase the vivacity of the presentation. The other evidence for his having been one is anecdotal and tenuous.[98]

VII ANTIPHON'S THOUGHT IN ITS FIFTH-CENTURY CONTEXT

By its very nature, the fragmentary and incomplete evidence for the writings of the sophist Antiphon steadfastly

[97] Cf. van Lieshout (1980), 207–12.

[98] Cf. Del Corno (1962), 350 (but contrast the apparently different view taken in Del Corno [1969], 130 with nn. 2–3).

resists attempts to impose on him a unified and consistent philosophical system. This applies, in the first instance, to the many scholarly attempts to reconcile the differences between Περὶ ἀληθείας and Περὶ ὁμονοίας – differences both real and apparent and embracing style as well as content. Περὶ ἀληθείας, on the one hand, covered a wide range of subjects both scientific and ethical in a reasoned expository style largely (though not wholly) devoid of rhetorical ornament. Περὶ ὁμονοίας on the other seems to have dealt exclusively with ethical topics in a style that is rhetorically ornate, consciously poetic, more emotional and affective than argumentative.[99] In particular, the antithesis of law and nature so prominent in the remains of Περὶ ἀληθείας is completely absent from the fragments of Περὶ ὁμονοίας. More specifically still, the praise of self-control (σωφροσύνη) and deprecation of disobedience (ἀναρχία) in F58 and F61 of Περὶ ὁμονοίας seem to some commentators impossible to reconcile with the attitude toward law and justice in the papyrus fragments of Περὶ ἀληθείας (cf. further commentary on F58 and F61). For some critics the differences between the two works are so great as to exclude common authorship (cf. section II above). Others accommodate them by postulating a chronological development in Antiphon's thought – a thesis unsupported by any evidence.[100] Yet another approach seeks to view the two works as complementary rather than contradictory, and to pinpoint the unity in doctrine or viewpoint underlying them.[101] The most elaborate effort along these lines

[99] For stylistic comparison of the two works cf. Bignone (1938), 193–95; Wilamowitz (1959), 1.62; Aly (1929), 154–55, 173–74; Schmid (1940), 165–66.

[100] For the developmental thesis cf. Theander (1920), 2 n. 2; Hommel (1941), 2–3; Wilamowitz (1959), 1.84; Momigliano (1969), 143–44.

[101] Cf. Pfister (1925), 204–5; Altheim (1926), 268–69; Aly (1929), 150–53; Mewaldt (1929), 79 n. 15; Untersteiner (1962), 107–8, (1954), 254–55 = (1967), 2.78–79; Wiesner (1994).

was made by Bignone (1938), 79–97, 109–39, who tried to show that Antiphon *identified* justice as defined in Περὶ ἀληθείας with the civic concord commended in Περὶ ὁμονοίας. Bignone's argument, however, rests on the shakiest of foundations. In the first place, Antiphon's own ideal of justice (*pace* Bignone) is almost certainly not to be found in F44(c) or elsewhere among the remains of Περὶ ἀληθείας (cf. commentary on F44(c)). Secondly, that Antiphon even dealt with civic concord in Περὶ ὁμονοίας (let alone identified it with justice) is no more than a guess (cf. section IV above). In fact, none of the evidence cited by Bignone proves that anyone ever identified justice and concord.[102] The very same objections apply (*ceteris paribus*) to efforts by other commentators to reconcile Περὶ ἀληθείας and Περὶ ὁμονοίας, to the extent that such efforts begin from the twin presuppositions that Antiphon espoused a theory of justice and preached civic or psychic concord. Nill (1985), 69–73 attempted a reconciliation between the ethical viewpoints of the two works on the more promising basis of the concept of self-interest. Wiesner (1994), 238, 242–43, and *passim* explained that the two works engage different domains. Περὶ ἀληθείας as a theoretical treatise deals with the sphere of the necessary, Περὶ ὁμονοίας with the human realm of the contingent, where the egoistic orientation towards nature and perfect self-interest on display in Περὶ ἀληθείας is restrained by the need to make concessions for the sake of community and the interests of others. Whatever degree of plausibility one assigns to the various attempts to reconcile Περὶ ἀληθείας and Περὶ ὁμονοίας, the question inevitably arises whether it is perhaps not mistaken in principle (as a few commentators have been bold enough to suggest) to expect doctrinal consistency

[102] Cf. Regenbogen (1940a), 99–100; La Face (1969), 33–34; Guthrie (1971a), 150 n. 1; Slings (1981), 206–12, especially 212 n. 4, (1999), 185 n. 331.

from a sophist like Antiphon, who may have espoused different views in different works in the course of defending now one thesis, now another.[103] In any case, in the present state of our evidence it must suffice to recognize without explaining them the very real differences of style and subject-matter between the two works, and the perhaps more apparent than real inconsistencies in doctrine.

The ambitious attempt of Mario Untersteiner to impose a unified system of thought on the remains of Antiphon's writings merits separate consideration.[104] In general terms, Untersteiner interpreted Antiphon's entire philosophy as a reaction against what he understood as the nihilism and irrationalism of the sophist Gorgias. Dümmler (1889), 82–85 and Luria (1927b), 1064–67 had claimed to find echoes of Antiphon's thought in Plato's famous summary of atheistic materialism in *Laws* 888E–889E. Untersteiner went much further, treating the passage as a virtual doxography of Antiphon.[105] Combining the contents of this passage with the thesis of anti-Gorgian polemic, Untersteiner constructed for Antiphon a systematic philosophy which affirms against Gorgias the validity of what Untersteiner called "experiences" and dissolves all ontological and epistemological contradictions in the unity of nature (φύσις), truth (ἀλήθεια), and concord (ὁμόνοια). Burkert (1964), 143–44 and Kerferd (1965) have adequately exposed the purely arbitrary character of Untersteiner's theory of anti-Gorgian polemic. As for the *Laws* passage, it cannot safely

[103] Cf. Nestle (1940), 47; Mazzarino (1966), 1.317–18, 321 with n. 287; Isnardi Parente (1975), 16–17. (Grossmann [1950], 44 n. 49 considered this possibility, but preferred to adopt Spengel's rewriting of the text of Hermogenes; cf. section II above.) Gomperz (1927), 64 with n. 2 suggested that Περὶ ἀληθείας may have been meant as an exhibition of its author's cleverness in making the novel and surprising plausible.

[104] Cf. Untersteiner (1954), 233–71 = (1967), 2.55–107.

[105] Cf. Funghi (1984), 4; Decleva Caizzi (1986b).

be used as evidence for Antiphon's thought. The passage's combination of natural philosophy with an ethical standpoint devaluing law and exalting nature is admittedly reminiscent of Antiphon's Περὶ ἀληθείας. More specifically, the passage sketches an opposition between νόμος or τέχνη and φύσις which recalls Antiphon's argument about the buried bed (see F15 with commentary). Nevertheless, the fact that commentators have connected this passage of the *Laws* with thinkers as diverse as Empedocles, the atomists, Archelaus and his followers, Protagoras, Prodicus, Critias, and even the young Aristotle[106] hints at its eclectic character, and suggests that Plato did not have the doctrine of any one individual in mind.[107] For the rest, Untersteiner's interpretation of Antiphon is built upon many arbitrary readings of individual fragments and is not even remotely plausible.[108]

None of the attempts to impose a consistent philosophical system on the remains of Antiphon's writings succeeds in inspiring conviction. Nevertheless, it is possible at least to situate him in the philosophical context and traditions of his time. The fragments themselves offer numerous points of contact with the concepts, concerns, and theories of Antiphon's predecessors and contemporaries (cf. commentary *passsim*). In Περὶ ἀληθείας, for example, Antiphon dealt with many of the standard problems of Presocratic speculation in the areas of cosmology, meteorology, embryology, and other branches of what Plato (*Phaedo* 96A) calls the "inquiry concerning nature," περὶ φύσεως ἱστορία

[106] For references cf. Untersteiner (1962), 180–83 and Cherniss (1959–60), 112–13.

[107] Cf. Beardslee (1918), 100–1; England (1921), 2.453; Bignone (1938), 70 n. 1; Heinimann (1945), 119 n. 24; Burkert (1964), 143; Kerferd (1965), 33; Guthrie (1971a), 116.

[108] For a penetrating exposition and critique of Untersteiner's method of interpreting philosophical fragments (though without reference to Antiphon) cf. Holland (1956).

(cf. section III above). The conventional character of Antiphon's interests is equally visible in the remains of Περὶ ὁμονοίας, which abound in the maxims and commonplaces of didactic poetry and popular ethics (cf. commentary on F45–71 *passim*). Moving beyond these generalities, commentators have endeavored to link Antiphon with a range of specific sophistic and Presocratic philosophers. Thus Diels and many others claimed to discern the influence of the Eleatics in a number of fragments from Περὶ ἀληθείας. But in the same places where Diels and others saw Eleatic ideas, Gomperz (1912), 64–68 detected the influence of Empedocles, and Diès, Momigliano, and others that of Anaxagoras.[109] Luria (1927b), 1066 with n. 3, (1928b), 208–32, (1933), 127, Moulton (1974), and others have argued for pervasive Democritean influence on Antiphon, while Gomperz (1927), 66 with n. 1, 75 would reverse the direction of influence. Yet Mewaldt (1929), 85 n. 36 and others have rejected any direct connection between the two (cf. commentary on F51). Bignone and others have interpreted F44(a) (from Περὶ ἀληθείας) as a refutation of Protagoras' conception of justice, while Funghi and Decleva Caizzi detected anti-Protagorean polemic in F44(b) as well (cf. commentary ad locc.). Untersteiner's views on the supposed relations between Antiphon and Gorgias have been discussed earlier. The influence of Hippias has been detected in Antiphon's views on the antithesis of law and nature and the relations between Greeks and barbarians (cf. commentary on F44(b)). In a very few cases, it is plausible to explain a doctrine attested in the fragments as a direct borrowing from one of Antiphon's predecessors or contemporaries. The peculiar theories of the sun and lunar eclipses in F26 and F28 of Περὶ ἀληθείας, for example, are most likely adopted from Heraclitus (cf. commentary ad locc.). But for the most part, the efforts of commentators

[109] Cf. F1, F4–5, and F10, with commentary.

to identify borrowings and allusions (polemical or otherwise) in the fragments are speculative and unconvincing. The same conclusion applies in regard to Antiphon's relationship to Attic tragedy and comedy, where direct borrowing (in either direction) has often been asserted but never convincingly demonstrated (cf. commentary on F44(a), F49, and F61). What remains is a general picture of Antiphon's eclecticism, a tendency which is paralleled in many of his contemporaries and is one of the defining characteristics of late fifth-century thought.[110]

Of far greater interest and importance for the history of thought than the eclectic science of Περὶ ἀληθείας and ethical commonplaces of Περὶ ὁμονοίας are the views on justice, law, and nature found in the papyrus fragments of Περὶ ἀληθείας (F44(a)–(c)). These fragments provide the most extensive surviving discussion of the νόμος–φύσις antithesis in fifth-century literature.[111] As such they invite comparison with the treatments of this topic to be found in several of Plato's dialogues, in particular the *Gorgias* and the *Republic*.[112] In the *Gorgias*, Callicles forcefully asserts the fundamental opposition of law and nature in a manner reminiscent of Antiphon (cf. *Gorgias* 482E–484C). His summary statement of their relationship (*Gorgias* 482E: ὡς τὰ πολλὰ δὲ ταῦτα ἐναντί' ἀλλήλοις ἐστίν, ἥ τε φύσις καὶ ὁ νόμος) closely recalls Antiphon's similar pronouncement (F44(a)II.26–30: ὅτι τὰ πολλὰ τῶν κατὰ νόμον δικαίων πολεμίως τῇ φύσει κεῖται). (Cf. commentary ad loc.) Both Antiphon and Callicles identify the demands of nature with self-interest, the individual's pursuit of his own advan-

110 Cf. Burnet (1930), 350–61; Fredrich (1899), 130–41; Cherniss (1951), 344 = (1977), 87.

111 On the antithesis of νόμος and φύσις cf. Beardslee (1918), 68–81; Heinimann (1945).

112 For the Platonic evidence and its relationship to Antiphon cf. Menzel (1922), 13–51, 59–64.

tage.[113] Cf. *Gorgias* 482c–d (ἡ δέ γε οἶμαι φύσις αὐτὴ ἀποφαίνει αὐτό, ὅτι δίκαιόν ἐστιν τὸν ἀμείνω τοῦ χείρονος πλέον ἔχειν καὶ τὸν δυνατώτερον τοῦ ἀδυνατωτέρου) with F44(a)I.12ff. and *passim.* Both regard the restraints imposed by law as "chains" or "bonds" on nature. Cf. F44(a)IV.3–6 (τὰ δὲ ξυμφέροντα τὰ μὲν ὑπὸ τῶν νόμων κείμενα δεσμοὶ τῆς φύσεώς ἐστι) with Callicles' image of the chained lion (*Gorgias* 483E–484A), which Dodds (1959), 268–69 thought may have been inspired in part by Antiphon. Like Polus in the discussion before him, Callicles contends that being wronged (τὸ ἀδικεῖσθαι) is worse (κάκιον) – that is to say, less beneficial for an individual – than doing wrong (τὸ ἀδικεῖν).[114] That Antiphon held a similar view is strongly suggested by the argument of F44(a)V.1–24 taken in conjunction with the equation of harming (βλάπτειν) and wronging (ἀδικεῖν) attested in F44(c) (cf. commentary ad locc.).

Yet the differences between Antiphon and Callicles are at least as significant as the similarities. It is of fundamental importance that Callicles regards the "natural" morality he formulates as normative or prescriptive in character: he speaks repeatedly of "natural justice." Cf. *Gorgias* 483c–d (quoted above); 483D (ὅτι οὕτω τὸ δίκαιον κέκριται, τὸν κρείττω τοῦ ἥττονος ἄρχειν καὶ πλέον ἔχειν); 483E (ἀλλ' οἶμαι οὗτοι κατὰ φύσιν τὴν τοῦ δικαίου ταῦτα πράττουσιν κτλ.); 484A–B (καὶ ἐνταῦθα ἐξέλαμψεν τὸ τῆς φύσεως δίκαιον); 490A; 491D; Dodds (1959), 266. The papyrus fragments, by contrast, offer no indication that Antiphon defended any normative conception of justice. Unlike Callicles, he nowhere applies the label "just" to behavior in accord with nature but contrary to law and convention. This crucial point is rightly insisted upon by Furley (1981), against the consensus view which credits

[113] Cf. von Arnim (1916), 8; Menzel (1922), 64.

[114] Cf. Plato, *Gorgias* 469B, 473A, 474cff., 483A; Dodds (1959), 249.

Antiphon with a doctrine of natural justice (φύσει δίκαιον) in contradistinction to legal or conventional justice (νόμῳ δίκαιον).[115] This basic and important difference in doctrine helps to explain the divergent rhetorical *tones* of Callicles' great ῥῆσις in the *Gorgias* (482C–486D) and Antiphon's discussion in the papyri. The former represents an impassioned defense and advocacy of an ideal of justice, albeit a highly unconventional one (cf. Dodds [1959], 266–67). Antiphon's treatment of the same issues, by contrast, is detached and theoretical. As Barnes (1982), 513–14; Nill (1985), 54, and other recent critics have justly asserted, it contains no explicit recommendations or injunctions. Many older commentators took the opposite view, for example Luria (1963) and von Arnim (1916), 7, the latter of whom speaks of "der *Rat* Antiphons, vor Zeugen dem Gesetze treu zu bleiben usw. [my italics]." The force of this observation is only slightly diminished by the consideration that if Antiphon genuinely believed it is sometimes in an individual's best interests to transgress the laws, he probably also supposed (as Greeks generally did) that the individual would *act* in accordance with those interests.

Another important point of difference between Antiphon and Callicles is the ideal of the "strongman" which the latter proclaims. Such a man aims to acquire political power in order to be able to satisfy the demands of the limitless desire for gain (πλεονεξία) to which he gives full rein. Cf. *Gorgias* 483C–D; 490A (τοῦτο γὰρ οἶμαι ἐγὼ τὸ δίκαιον εἶναι φύσει, τὸ βελτίω ὄντα καὶ φρονιμώτερον καὶ ἄρχειν καὶ πλέον ἔχειν τῶν φαυλοτέρων); 491E (ἀλλὰ τοῦτ' ἐστὶν τὸ κατὰ φύσιν καλὸν καὶ δίκαιον . . . ὅτι δεῖ τὸν ὀρθῶς βιωσόμενον τὰς μὲν ἐπιθυμίας τὰς ἑαυτοῦ ἐᾶν ὡς μεγίστας εἶναι καὶ μὴ κολάζειν, ταύταις δὲ ὡς

[115] For the conventional view cf. Aly (1929), 142; Diels (1917); Philippson (1918), 123; Pfister (1925), 202–3; Nestle (1942), 375; Wilamowitz (1931–32), 2.217; Saunders (1977–78), 226–30; La Face (1969), 43–88.

μεγίσταις οὔσαις ἱκανὸν εἶναι ὑπηρετεῖν δι' ἀνδρείαν καὶ φρόνησιν κτλ.); Dodds (1959), 264, 291. (The doctrine of the strongman is alluded to in *Laws* 890A: τὸν κατὰ φύσιν ὀρθὸν βίον, ὅς ἐστιν τῇ ἀληθείᾳ κρατοῦντα ζῆν τῶν ἄλλων καὶ μὴ δουλεύοντα ἑτέροισι κατὰ νόμον.) Antiphon seems not to have envisaged the possibility of such a figure, who is capable of trampling the norms of society underfoot by brute force, nor of such unbridled πλεονεξία. On the contrary, he emphasizes the oppressive restrictions imposed upon individuals by laws and customs (cf. F44(a)II.30–III.18). Those who would maximize their own advantage by transgressing the laws, he contends, will do so only in secret and when unobserved (cf. F44(a)I.12–20). In the presence of witnesses, the calculus of relative advantage (not unbridled πλεονεξία) counsels obedience rather than transgression, so as to avoid shame and loss (cf. F44(a)I.20–23, II.3–10, with commentary). Menzel (1922), 64 formulated the differences concisely with his statement that the Calliclean strongman aims at pre-eminence in the state, Antiphon's individual at freedom from the state. This is in accord with the differing ends or goals envisaged by each: limitless πλεονεξία in the case of Callicles, relative best advantage in Antiphon's. The absence of the notion of rule by the stronger differentiates Antiphon's discussion also from the argument put forward by the Athenians in the Melian dialogue (and echoed elsewhere in Thucydides).[116] On the other hand, Thucydides' portrait of a universal human inclination to act from motives of self-interest rather than of morality and justice is in close agreement with the presuppositions of Antiphon's argu-

[116] Cf. Thucydides, 5.105: ἡγούμεθα γὰρ τό τε θεῖον δόξῃ τὸ ἀνθρώπειόν τε σαφῶς διὰ παντὸς ὑπὸ φύσεως ἀναγκαίας, οὗ ἂν κρατῇ, ἄρχειν. Cf. also 1.76; 3.82, 84; 4.61; and the careful analysis of Menzel (1922), 54–58.

ment.[117] Heinimann (1945), 135; Furley (1981), 84–85, and others have suggested that Antiphon's use of the concept of advantage or self-interest (τὸ ξυμφέρον) was influenced by contemporary medical thought. This is possible. But the concept is ubiquitous in late fifth-century thought and literature (cf. Nill [1985]), and it seems superfluous to seek a particular source. One last difference between Antiphon and Callicles appears in the latter's appeal to the behavior of animals as a standard of "natural" conduct; cf. *Gorgias* 483D (δηλοῖ δὲ ταῦτα πολλαχοῦ ὅτι οὕτως ἔχει, καὶ ἐν τοῖς ἄλλοις ζῴοις κτλ.). This type of argument can be paralleled in fifth-century texts.[118] But (*pace* Heinimann and others) there is no reason to impute it to Antiphon.

The views put forward by Thrasymachus in the first book of the *Republic* are in many respects comparable to those of Callicles (cf. Menzel [1922], 45–47). But his position differs essentially from that of Antiphon.[119] For example, Thrasymachus (like Callicles but unlike Antiphon) consistently defends the ideal of πλεονεξία and the advantage of the stronger (cf. *Republic* 343D–344A: λέγω γὰρ ὅνπερ νυνδὴ ἔλεγον, τὸν μεγάλα δυνάμενον πλεονεκτεῖν), whether he calls this justice or injustice.[120] More importantly, the antithesis of law and nature is conspicuously absent from Thrasymachus' argument. But the situation is quite different with Glaucon's restatement of the immoralist thesis in the second book of the *Republic* (358B–361D), which has a great deal in common with Antiphon's argu-

[117] Cf. Thucydides, 1.76, 3.40, 3.44, 3.82, 5.89–90; Guthrie (1971a), 84–88.

[118] Cf. Aristophanes, *Clouds* 1427–29; Dodds (1959), 267; Heinimann (1945), 146–47.

[119] Luginbill (1997), 175–77 contended that the arguments of Thrasymachus and Antiphon are closer to each other than either is to Callicles' argument, with its doctrine of natural justice.

[120] For Thrasymachus' inconsistency cf. *Republic* 338C, 343B–344C with Tarán (1985), 101–4.

ment.[121] Like Antiphon – but unlike Thrasymachus – Glaucon frames his discussion of justice, advantage, and their opposites in terms of the antithesis of law and nature. Cf. *Republic* 358E (πεφυκέναι γὰρ δή φασιν κτλ.); 359C (ὃ πᾶσα φύσις διώκειν πέφυκεν ὡς ἀγαθόν, νόμῳ δὲ κτλ.). Glaucon adds another antithesis, that of appearance and reality (cf. *Republic* 361B–362A, 365C). Antiphon does likewise (cf. F44(a)II.21–23 οὐ γὰρ διὰ δόξαν ... ἀλλὰ δι' ἀλήθειαν). Glaucon identifies justice with law, δίκαιον with νόμιμον (cf. *Republic* 359A: καὶ ὀνομάσαι τὸ ὑπὸ τοῦ νόμου ἐπίταγμα νόμιμόν τε καὶ δίκαιον). Antiphon's argument begins from the same (conventional) conception of justice (cf. F44(a)I.6–11, with commentary). Both Glaucon and Antiphon stress the *conventional* nature of justice. Cf. *Republic* 359A (συνθέσθαι ἀλλήλοις μήτ' ἀδικεῖν μήτ' ἀδικεῖσθαι κτλ.) with F44(a)I.27–31 (καὶ τὰ μὲν τῶν νόμων ὁμολογηθέντα οὐ φύντα). Glaucon characterizes the practice of justice as a compromise between the greater good of committing injustice and the greater evil of suffering it (cf. *Republic* 358B–359A). He furthermore avers that injustice is universally considered more advantageous than justice (cf. *Republic* 360C: λυσιτελεῖν γὰρ δὴ οἴεται πᾶς ἀνὴρ πολὺ μᾶλλον ἰδίᾳ τὴν ἀδικίαν τῆς δικαιοσύνης; 364A; 367E). A similar assumption about the relative advantages of justice and its opposite underlies the argument of F44(a). Antiphon differs from Glaucon, however, in his consistent and conspicuous avoidance of the term ἀδικία, "injustice." He speaks instead of "transgressing" (παραβαίνειν) the laws (cf. F44(a)II.3–5) and of not "submitting" (προσίεσθαι) to them (cf. F44(a)V.25–33). The precise significance of this (seemingly deliberate) maneuver is difficult to gauge. Glaucon contends that justice is less advantageous than injustice, and is practiced only

[121] Cf. von Arnim (1916), 7; Kuiper (1920), 50.

under compulsion (cf. *Republic* 360C: οὐδεὶς ἑκὼν δίκαιος ἀλλ' ἀναγκαζόμενος, ὡς οὐκ ἀγαθοῦ ἰδίᾳ ὄντος). He illustrates this contention with the famous story of Gyges' ring (*Republic* 359C–360C). The story's cynical presumption that human beings will commit injustice whenever they can get away with it is in perfect agreement with Antiphon's argument that self-interest is best served by obeying the law in the presence of witnesses, but ignoring it in their absence. Like Callicles and Thrasymachus, however, Glaucon presupposes a deep-seated human impulse toward πλεονεξία. Cf. *Republic* 359C (ἐπ' αὐτοφώρῳ οὖν λάβοιμεν ἂν τὸν δίκαιον τῷ ἀδίκῳ εἰς ταὐτὸν ἰόντα διὰ τὴν πλεονεξίαν, ὃ πᾶσα φύσις διώκειν πέφυκεν ὡς ἀγαθόν, νόμῳ δὲ βίᾳ παράγεται ἐπὶ τὴν τοῦ ἴσου τιμήν). And though Glaucon does not emphasize the figure of the strongman (as Callicles does), the possibility of such a figure is not entirely lost sight of. Cf. *Republic* 359B (ἐπεὶ τὸν δυνάμενον αὐτὸ ποιεῖν καὶ ὡς ἀληθῶς ἄνδρα οὐδ' ἂν ἑνί ποτε συνθέσθαι τὸ μήτε ἀδικεῖν μήτε ἀδικεῖσθαι· μαίνεσθαι γὰρ ἄν) and Menzel (1922), 50. Antiphon, by contrast, envisages a more limited potential for the pursuit of self-interest in a world where the constraints of law and custom seem all-embracing (cf. F44(a)II.30–III.18).

The discussion thus far has centered on the relations between nature, law, justice, and self-interest in F44(a) of Περὶ ἀληθείας. In F44(b), Antiphon uses the antithesis of law and nature in the rather different context of an argument about the natural similarity of all human beings. Not surprisingly, this argument has attracted comparison with Hippias' brief disquisition on law and nature in Plato, *Protagoras* 337C–D: Ὦ ἄνδρες, ἔφη, οἱ παρόντες, ἡγοῦμαι ἐγὼ ὑμᾶς συγγενεῖς τε καὶ οἰκείους καὶ πολίτας ἅπαντας εἶναι – φύσει, οὐ νόμῳ· τὸ γὰρ ὅμοιον τῷ ὁμοίῳ φύσει συγγενές ἐστιν, ὁ δὲ νόμος, τύραννος ὢν τῶν ἀνθρώπων, πολλὰ τὴν φύσιν βιάζεται κτλ. While the majority of commentators have supposed that Antiphon is dependent on Hippias,[122] Heinimann (1945), 142–43 argued that Hippias was a mere popularizer of doctrines originally developed by Antiphon and others. Comparison between the two is complicated by the question of the precise import of Hippias' remarks. The consensus view would credit Hippias with a full-blown theory of cosmopolitanism.[123] There seems to be little justification for such a view, however, and his remarks are more plausibly interpreted as advocating a form of Panhellenism, based on the kinship of wise men.[124] Be that as it may, Hippias employs the antithesis of law and nature in the context of an attempt to demonstrate the natural kinship of individuals whom law and convention wrongly divide – and this much at least is reminiscent of Antiphon's argument. Antiphon goes much further, however, broadening the notion of natural similarity to include all human beings, Greek and barbarian alike. To "nature" thus broadly conceived Antiphon opposes not conventional opinion in the abstract (νόμῳ, as in *Protagoras* 337D), but the laws and customs of different peoples (cf. F44(b)II.3–4 with commentary). Whatever the similarities between Antiphon's argument and the remarks of Hippias, the possibility of establishing a connection between the two sophists depends on the prior question of whether the *Protagoras* passage can be treated as reliable evidence for the views of the historical Hippias. And this is a question without an answer.

Although the antithesis of law and nature does not appear in F44(c), the subject of conventional justice does. In this fragment, Antiphon attempts to show that conventional notions regarding just or right action are inconsistent, even contradictory. His argumentative procedure re-

[122] So Diels (1917), 100–1; Stenzel (1924), 38; Regenbogen (1940a), 99, 102; Nestle (1942), 380.

[123] Cf. the authorities cited in Schütrumpf (1972), 5 nn. 3–4.

[124] Cf. Schütrumpf (1972), 12 with n. 4, 17–24; Hall (1989), 215–17.

calls the dialectical method pioneered by Zeno, and later used by Gorgias in the treatise Περὶ τοῦ μὴ ὄντος ἢ περὶ φύσεως (cf. *FVS* 82 B 3).[125] Antiphon's application of the method to the subject of justice seems to be without parallel, either in the extant remains of sophistic literature or in the discussions put in the mouths of sophists by Plato. The closest analogue is perhaps to be found in the conversation between Alcibiades and Pericles in Xenophon, *Memorabilia* 1.2.40–46 (cf. Menzel [1922], 51–53). There, Alcibiades attempts to reduce the conventional conception of law to absurdity – which may have been Antiphon's goal as well.

[125] For a good brief description of the method cf. Lee (1936), 111–23.

TEXTS AND TRANSLATIONS

CONSPECTUS SIGLORUM ET SYMBOLORUM

1. SIGLA

Note: Dates of manuscripts given here that differ from those supplied by the original editors come from more recent publications that I take to be more authoritative; but it would have been hard to carry out a thorough check. Consistency in designations of manuscripts has been sought but not (perhaps) everywhere achieved.

Aëtius, *Placita*, ed. Diels (1879):
  Stob. = Stobaei *Anthologium* (ed. Wachsmuth and Hense [1884–1912]):
    F = Neapolitanus III D 15, saec. XIV
    P = Parisinus gr. 2129, saec. XV
    Aug. = Monacensis 396 (olim Augustanus), saec. XV
  [Plut.] = [Plut.], *De placitis philosophorum* (ed. Lachenaud [1993]):
    M = Mosquensis gr. 352 (olim 339), saec. XI/XII
    m = Marcianus gr. 521, saec. XIII
    α = Ambrosianus C 126 inf., paulo ante 1296
    A = Parisinus gr. 1671, anni 1296
    E = Parisinus gr. 1672, saec. XIV
    Voss. = Leidensis Vossianus gr. Q 2, saec. XV/XVI
    pap. = *P. Antin.* 2.85, fr. 3 (a) + (b) verso (ed. Barns and Zilliacus [1960], 74–83)
    Euseb. = excerpta Eusebii (ed. Mras [1954–56])
    Ar = versio Arabica (ed. Daiber [1980]; cf. Mansfeld and Runia [1997], 152–61)
Alexander of Aphrodisias, *In Aristotelis Metaphysica*, ed. Hayduck (1891):
  A = Parisinus gr. 1876, saec. XIII/XIV

L = Laurentianus 87.12, saec. XI/XII
F = Ambrosianus F 113 sup., saec. XV
Sepulved. = interpretatio Latina Sepulvedae (Paris 1536)

[Alexander], *In Aristotelis Sophisticos elenchos*, ed. Wallies (1898):
I = Laurentianus 85.1, saec. XIV
a = editio Aldina (Venice 1520)

Anecdota Graeca, ed. Bachmann (1828):
Coisl. = Parisinus Coislin. 345, saec. X

Anonymus, *In Aristotelis Sophisticos elenchos paraphrasis*, ed. Hayduck (1884):
L = Laurentianus 71.32, saec. XIV
N = Neapolitanus III E 12, saec. XV
M = Monacensis gr. 38, saec. XVI

Anonymus, *Vita Antiphontis*, ed. Thalheim (1914):
A = Crippsianus sive Burneianus 95, saec. XIV
N = Oxoniensis Bodl. Auct. T.2.8, saec. XIV

Aristotle, *Metaphysics*, ed. Jaeger (1957), Ross (1924):
E = Parisinus gr. 1853, saec. X
J = Vindobonensis phil. gr. 100, saec. X
A^b = Laurentianus 87.12, saec. XI/XII
Al^c = Alexandri citatio

Aristotle, *Physics*, ed. Ross (1936), (1950):
E = Parisinus gr. 1853, saec. X ineuntis
F = Laurentianus 87.7, saec. XIV
I = Vaticanus gr. 241, saec. XIII
J = Vindobonensis phil. gr. 100 (olim 34), saec. X
Phil. = Philoponi commentaria
Simpl. = Simplicii commentaria
Them. = Themistii paraphrasis
vers. = versio Arabo-Latina

Aristotle, *Sophistici elenchi*, ed. Ross (1958):
A = Vaticanus Urbinas gr. 35, saec. IX vel X ineuntis
B = Marcianus gr. 201, anni 955
C = Parisinus Coislin. 330, saec. XI
D = Parisinus gr. 1843, saec. XIII

u = Basileensis 54 (F II 21), saec. XII
Boeth. = Boethii translatio
Mich.^{c,p} = Michaelis Ephesii citatio, paraphrasis
Soph. = Sophoniae paraphrasis

Artemidorus, *Onirocritica*, ed. Pack (1963):
L = Laurentianus 87.8, saec. XI
V = Marcianus gr. 268, saec. XV

Athenaeus, *Dipnosophistae*, ed. Kaibel (1887–90):
A = Marcianus gr. 447, saec. X ineuntis

Cicero, *De divinatione*, ed. Ax (1938), Pease (1920–23):
A = Leidensis Vossianus lat. Fol. 84, saec. IX
V = Vindobonensis lat. 189, saec. IX
B = Leidensis Vossianus lat. Fol. 86, saec. IX
Erlang. = Erlangensis 618, saec. XV
Asc. = editio Ascensiana altera (Paris 1521)
Ald. = editio Aldina (Venice 1523)

Clement of Alexandria, *Stromata*, ed. Stählin–Früchtel (1960–70):
L = Laurentianus 5.3, saec. XI

Diogenes Laertius, ed. Long (1964):
B = Neapolitanus III B 29, saec. XII
F = Laurentianus 69.13, saec. XIII
P = Parisinus gr. 1759, saec. XIII ineuntis

Eutocius, *In Archimedis Dimensionem circuli*, ed. Heiberg (1910–15):
A = the lost codex of G. Valla, which is reconstructed from codices:
D = Laurentianus 28.4, saec. XV
E = Marcianus gr. 305, saec. XV
G = Parisinus gr. 2360, saec. XVI
H = Parisinus gr. 2361, anni 1544
Basil. = editio princeps T. G. Venatorii (Basel 1544)

Excerpta Vindobonensia, ed. Meineke (1855–57), 4.290–96:
cod. = Vindobonensis theol. gr. 128, saec. XIV

Fulgentius, *Mitologiae*, ed. Helm (1898):
R = Vaticanus Reginensis lat. 1462, saec. XI
T = Trevericus VI.3, saec. X

H = Bibl. Brit. Harleianus 2685, saec. IX
M = Montepessulanus 334, saec. IX
D = Guelferbytanus Gudianus 333, saec. XII
E = Vaticanus Reginensis lat. 1567, saec. XII
G = Guelferbytanus Gudianus 331, saec. XI
Bern = Bernensis 427, saec. X

Galen, *In Hippocratis Epidemiarum librum* III, ed. Wenkebach (1936):
L = Laurentianus 74.25, saec. XIV
M = Monacensis gr. 231, saec. XV/XVI
Q = Parisinus gr. 2174, saec. XVI
V = Marcianus App. class. v.5, saec. XV
Hun. = versio Arabica Hunaini (Scorialensis arab. 804, saec. XIII)

Galen, *In Hippocratis librum De officina medici commentarii iii*, ed. Kühn (1821–33), 18.2.629–925; cf. Diels, *FVS* 2.337–39:
P = Parisinus gr. 1849, saec. XIV
M = Marcianus gr. 279, saec. XV (M is derived from P)

Gnomologium Vindobonense, ed. Wachsmuth (1882):
cod. = Vindobonensis theol. gr. 149, saec. XIV

Gnomologium Vaticanum, ed. Sternbach (1888):
cod. = Vaticanus gr. 743, saec. XIV

Harpocration, *Lexicon decem oratorum*, ed. Keaney (1991), Dindorf (1853):
D = Parisinus gr. 2552, anni 1496 (Epit. Harp.)
E = Heidelbergensis Palat. 375, saec. XII (Epit. Harp.)
Q = Cantabrigiensis Dd. IV.63, ca. 1330
K = Marcianus gr. 444, saec. XIV
M = Vaticanus gr. 871, saec. XV
N = Darmstadtiensis 2773, saec. XIV/XV
P = Cantabrigiensis Trin. Coll. O.I.5 (olim 1029), saec. XVI
Ald. = editio Aldina (Venice 1503)
Epit. Harp. = Epitome Harpocrationis (cf. Keaney [1991], XXIII–XXV, Dindorf [1853], XV–XX)

Hermogenes, *De ideis*, ed. Rabe (1913):

Pa = Parisinus gr. 1983, saec. XI
Pc = Parisinus gr. 2977, saec. XI
Vc = Vaticanus Urbinas gr. 130, saec. XI
Ac = Ambrosianus 523, saec. XI
Ba = Basileensis 70, saec. XI
Og = Oxoniensis Novi Coll. 258, anni 1308
Va = Vaticanus gr. 107, saec. XII
Lb = Laurentianus 60.27, saec. XIV
Md = Marcianus gr. 430, anni 1338/9
Pl = Parisinus gr. 2986, saec. XIV, XV
Pt = Parisinus gr. 2985, saec. XV
Sf = Scorialensis T. III.10, saec. XII

Hesychius, *Lexicon*, ed. Latte (1953–66), Schmidt (1858–68):
H = Marcianus gr. 622, saec. XV

Lucian, *Verae historiae* 2, ed. Macleod (1972):
witnesses of the γ tradition:
Γ = Vaticanus gr. 90, saec. X
ω = Marciani gr. 840 (olim 434) pars vetusta, saec. X/XI
S = Mutinensis α. V. 8.15, saec. XI
witness of the β tradition:
P = Vaticanus gr. 76, saec. XIV

Melampus, Περὶ παλμῶν μαντική, ed. Diels (1907):
B = Parisinus gr. 2118, saec. XVI
R = editio princeps C. Perusci (Rome 1545)
N = versio Latina A. Niphi (Basel 1534)

Philoponus, *In Aristotelis Physica*, ed. Vitelli (1887):
K = Marcianus gr. 220, saec. XV
L = Vaticanus gr. 1028, saec. XIV
M = Marcianus gr. 230, saec. XIV
R = Parisinus gr. 2063, saec. XIV
t = editio V. Trincavelli (Venice 1535)

Φιλοσόφων λόγοι, ed. Schenkl (1888):
Par. = Parisinus gr. 1166, saec. XI/XII
Pal. = Heidelbergensis Palat. 356, saec. XIV

flor. Vind. = gnomologium ineditum (cod. Vindobonensis theol. gr. 167)
Photius, *Bibliotheca*, ed. Henry (1959–77):
A = Marcianus gr. 450, saec. X
M = Marcianus gr. 451, saec. XII
Photius, *Lexicon*, ed. Theodoridis (1982–98), Porson (1822):
b = Berolinensis gr. oct. 22, saec. XIII
g = Galeanus, Cantabrigiensis Trin. Coll. o.3.9 (olim 306), saec. XII
z = Zavordensis 95, saec. XIII/XIV
[Plut.], *Vitae X or.*, ed. M. Cuvigny (1981):
E = Parisinus gr. 1672, paulo post 1302
α = Ambrosianus C 126 inf., paulo ante 1296
Pollux, *Onomasticon*, ed. Bethe (1900–37):
M = Ambrosianus D 34 sup., saec. X
F = Parisinus gr. 2646, saec. XV
S = Salmanticensis I 2.3, saec. XV
A = Parisinus gr. 2670, saec. XV
V = Marcianus gr. 520, saec. XV
C = Heidelbergensis Palat. 375, saec. XII
L = Laurentianus 56.1, saec. XIV
B = Parisinus gr. 2647, saec. XIII
Priscian, *Institutiones*, ed. Hertz (1855–59):
R = Parisinus lat. 7496, saec. IX
V = Leidensis Vossianus lat. O 12, saec. IX/X
M = Monacensis lat. 280 A, saec. XI
O = Parisinus lat. 7499, saec. IX
D = Bernensis Bongarsianus 109, saec. X
N = Vindobonensis phil. lat. 348, saec. X
Pseudo-Callisthenes, *Historia Alexandri Magni*, ed. Kroll (1926); cf. Calderan and Rosellini (1993):
A = Parisinus gr. 1711, saec. XI
L = Leidensis Vulc. 93, saec. XV
β = recensio β
Arm = versio Armeniaca, saec. V
Val = versio Latina Iulii Valerii, saec. IV

(My apparatus offers selected readings only; for a fuller report cf. Kroll [1926].)

Seneca, *Controversiae*, ed. Håkanson (1989):

A = Antverpiensis 411, saec. X/XI

B = Bruxellensis 9581–9595, saec. IX

V = Vaticanus lat. 3872, saec. IX

Simplicius, *In Aristotelis Physica*, ed. Diels (1882):

D = Laurentianus 85.2, saec. XII/XIII

E = Marcianus gr. 229, saec. XIII exeuntis

E^b = lectiones in E ex alio libro suppletae in particula primo omissa (cf. Diels [1882], VII)

F = Marcianus gr. 227, saec. XIII exeuntis

a = editio Aldina (Venice 1526)

Stobaeus, *Anthologium*, ed. Wachsmuth and Hense (1884–1912):

F = Neapolitanus III D 15, saec. XIV

P = Parisinus gr. 2129, saec. XV

Aug. = Monacensis 396 (olim Augustanus), saec. XV

L = Laurentianus 8.22, saec. XIV

A = Parisinus gr. 1984, saec. XIV

M = Scorialensis 90 (Σ II 14), saec. XII ineuntis

M^d = cod. Scorialensis collatio Dindorfiana (cf. Hense in Wachsmuth and Hense [1884–1912], 3.XXIX)

S = Vindobonensis philol. gr. 67, saec. XI ineuntis

Br = Bruxellensis miscell. 11360, saec. XIV/XV

Voss = Leidensis Vossianus gr. O 9, saec. XV

Tr. = editio V. Trincavelli (Venice 1536)

Mac. = Macarii Chrysocephali rosetum (cod. Marcianus gr. 452, saec. XIV)

corp. Par. = corpus Parisinum gnomologicum (cod. Parisinus gr. 1168, saec. XIII; cf. Hense in Wachsmuth and Hense [1884–1912], 3.XXXVIII–XXXIX)

gnomol. Par. = gnomologium Parisinum (cod. Parisinus suppl. gr. 134, saec. XIV, ed. Sternbach [1893]; cf. Hense in Wachsmuth and Hense [1884–1912], 3.L–LII)

[Max.] = the florilegium falsely ascribed to Maximus the Confessor (cited from the Latin translation of Jean Ribit published in Gesner [1546])

Apostol. = Apostolius (ed. Leutsch and Schneidewin [1839–51], 2.233–744)

Suda, ed. Adler (1928–38):

A = Parisinus gr. 2625 (litt. Α–Θ), saec. XIII–XIV et Parisinus gr. 2626 (litt. Κ–Ψ), saec. XII–XV

A² = pars recentior Paris. gr. 2625, saec. XIV

B = Parisinus gr. 2622, saec. XIII

G = Parisinus gr. 2623, saec. XV

I = Angelicanus 75, saec. XV

M = Marcianus gr. 448, saec. XIII

S = Vaticanus gr. 1296, anni 1205

T = Vaticanus gr. 881, anni 1434

F = Laurentianus 55.1, anni 1422

V = Leidensis Vossianus gr. F 2, saec. XII

ed. pr. = editio Demetrii Chalcondylis (Milan 1499)

Tertullian, *De anima*, ed. Waszink (1947):

A = Parisinus lat. 1622, saec. IX

B = editio M. Mesnartii (Paris 1545)

Gel. = editio S. Gelenii (Basel 1550)

Themistius, *In Aristotelis Physica paraphrasis*, ed. Schenkl (1900):

B = Vratislaviensis Magdalenaeus 1442, saec. XIV ineuntis

L = Parisinus gr. 1891, saec. XVI

M = Mutinensis gr. 4 (II A 4), saec. XIV ineuntis

W = Marcianus gr. 205, saec. XV ineuntis

a = editio Aldina (Venice 1534)

Xenophon, *Memorabilia*, ed. Marchant (1921), Hude (1934):

A = Parisinus gr. 1302, saec. XIII

B = Parisinus gr. 1740, saec. XIII/XIV

M = Marcianus gr. 511, saec. XIV

O = Marcianus gr. 368, saec. XV

C = Parisinus gr. 1642, saec. XV

D = Parisinus gr. 1643, saec. XV
V = Leidensis Vossianus alter
Stob. = citationes Stobaei (ed. Wachsmuth and Hense [1884–1912]):
A = Parisinus gr. 1984, saec. XIV
M = Scorialensis 90 (Σ II 14), saec. XII ineuntis
M^d = cod. Scorialensis collatio Dindorfiana (cf. Hense in Wachsmuth and Hense [1884–1912], 3.XXIX)
S = Vindobonensis philol. gr. 67, saec. XI ineuntis
Br = Bruxellensis miscell. 11360, saec. XIV/XV

2. SYMBOLA

In manuscripts:

[ ]	excision of word(s) or letter(s) extant in the manuscript(s)
***	lacuna
⟨ ⟩	supplement of word(s) or letter(s) missing in the manuscript(s)

In papyri:

⟨ ⟩	supplement of letter(s) omitted by the scribe
α̣α̣α̣	imperfectly preserved letters
⟦ ⟧	excision of letter(s) extant in the papyrus
[ ]	supplement of letter(s) now unreadable or not extant in the papyrus
. . .	missing letters, each dot representing one letter
⌊ ⌋	letter(s) not extant in the papyrus but restored from another source

In the Epicurean inscription (F80(b)):

[ ]	letter(s) restored by the modern editor, where the text is damaged
α̣α̣α̣	imperfectly preserved letters

___ missing letters, where the exact length of the lacuna is uncertain

vvv blank spaces left by the stonemason, each *v* representing a space sufficient for one letter

Testimonia

T1 Xenophon, *Memorabilia* 1.6.1–15

ἄξιον δ' αὐτοῦ καὶ ἃ πρὸς Ἀντιφῶντα τὸν σοφιστὴν διελέχθη μὴ παραλιπεῖν. ὁ γὰρ Ἀντιφῶν ποτε βουλόμενος τοὺς συνουσιαστὰς αὐτοῦ παρελέσθαι προσελθὼν τῷ Σωκράτει παρόντων αὐτῶν ἔλεξε τάδε· Ὦ Σώκρατες, ἐγὼ μὲν ᾤμην τοὺς φιλοσοφοῦντας εὐδαιμονεστέρους χρῆναι γίγνεσθαι· σὺ δέ μοι δοκεῖς τἀναντία τῆς φιλοσοφίας ἀπολελαυκέναι. ζῇς γοῦν οὕτως ὡς οὐδ' ἂν εἷς δοῦλος ὑπὸ δεσπότῃ διαιτώμενος μείνειε· σῖτά τε σιτῇ καὶ ποτὰ πίνεις τὰ φαυλότατα, καὶ ἱμάτιον ἠμφίεσαι οὐ μόνον φαῦλον, ἀλλὰ τὸ αὐτὸ θέρους τε καὶ χειμῶνος, ἀνυπόδητός τε καὶ ἀχίτων διατελεῖς. καὶ μὴν χρήματά γε οὐ λαμβάνεις, ἃ καὶ κτωμένους εὐφραίνει καὶ κεκτημένους ἐλευθεριώτερόν τε καὶ ἥδιον ποιεῖ ζῆν. εἰ οὖν ὥσπερ καὶ τῶν ἄλλων ἔργων οἱ διδάσκαλοι τοὺς μαθητὰς μιμητὰς ἑαυτῶν ἀποδεικνύουσιν, οὕτω καὶ σὺ τοὺς συνόντας διαθήσεις, νόμιζε κακοδαιμονίας διδάσκαλος εἶναι. καὶ ὁ Σωκράτης πρὸς ταῦτα εἶπε· Δοκεῖς μοι, ὦ Ἀντιφῶν, ὑπειληφέναι με οὕτως ἀνιαρῶς ζῆν, ὥστε πέπεισμαι σὲ μᾶλλον ἀποθανεῖν ἂν ἑλέσθαι ἢ ζῆν ὥσπερ ἐγώ. ἴθι οὖν ἐπισκεψώμεθα τί χαλεπὸν ᾔσθησαι τοῦ ἐμοῦ βίου. πότερον ὅτι τοῖς μὲν λαμβάνουσιν ἀργύριον ἀναγκαῖόν ἐστιν ἀπεργάζεσθαι τοῦτο ἐφ' ᾧ ἂν μισθὸν λάβωσιν, ἐμοὶ δὲ μὴ λαμβάνοντι οὐκ ἀνάγκη διαλέγεσθαι ᾧ ἂν μὴ βούλωμαι; ἢ τὴν δίαιτάν μου φαυλίζεις ὡς ἧττον μὲν ὑγιεινὰ ἐσθίοντος ἐμοῦ ἢ σοῦ, ἧττον δὲ ἰσχὺν παρέχοντα; ἢ ὡς χαλεπώτερα πορίσασθαι τὰ ἐμὰ διαιτήματα τῶν σῶν διὰ

T1 codd. = A B M O C D V et Stob. (codd. S M A Br) 6 γίνεσθαι A M: γενέσθαι O 6 σοφίας M O 7 γοῦν] γὰρ A 7 οὐδὲ εἷς A 8 σῖτα A: σιτεῖα B: σιτία alii 8 τε ⟨γὰρ⟩ Heindorf 12 εὐφραίνῃ B 19 ἂν om. A 22 ἐφ' οἷς A λάβωσιν A B: λαμβάνωσιν C M O

TESTIMONIA

T1 Socrates' conversations with Antiphon the sophist deserve not to be omitted. Once, when Antiphon wanted to take away Socrates' companions, he approached Socrates in their presence and said: "Socrates, I thought that those who practice philosophy ought to become happier. But you seem to me to have derived the opposite benefit from philosophy. You live, at any rate, as no slave would endure living under a master: you eat the cheapest foods and drink the cheapest drinks; you wear not only a cheap coat, but the same one summer and winter; you constantly go without shoes or a shirt. Furthermore, you do not take money, which gladdens people as they acquire it, and makes them live more freely and more pleasantly when they have it. So, if (like teachers of other subjects) you are going to make your companions imitators of yourself, consider yourself a teacher of misfortune." Socrates said in reply: "Antiphon, I think you have supposed me to live so painfully that I am convinced you would prefer to die than to live as I do. Very well, let us examine what hardship you perceive in my life. Is it the fact that, if I do not take money, I do not have to converse with anyone I don't want to, whereas those who do take money have to finish what they have taken payment for? Or do you consider my lifestyle cheap because I eat less healthy and strength-giving foods than you? Or because my foods are harder to pro-

τὸ σπανιώτερά τε καὶ πολυτελέστερα εἶναι; ἢ ὡς ἡδίω σοι ἃ σὺ παρασκευάζῃ ὄντα ἢ ἐμοὶ ἃ ἐγώ; οὐκ οἶσθ᾽ ὅτι ὁ μὲν ἥδιστα ἐσθίων ἥκιστα ὄψου δεῖται, ὁ δὲ ἥδιστα πίνων ἥκιστα τοῦ μὴ παρόντος ἐπιθυμεῖ ποτοῦ; τά γε μὴν ἱμάτια οἶσθ᾽ ὅτι οἱ μεταβαλλόμενοι ψύχους καὶ θάλπους ἕνεκα μεταβάλλονται, καὶ ὑποδήματα ὑποδοῦνται, ὅπως μὴ διὰ τὰ λυποῦντα τοὺς πόδας κωλύωνται πορεύεσθαι· ἤδη οὖν ποτε ᾔσθου ἐμὲ ἢ διὰ ψῦχος μᾶλλόν του ἔνδον μένοντα, ἢ διὰ θάλπος μαχόμενόν τῳ περὶ σκιᾶς, ἢ διὰ τὸ ἀλγεῖν τοὺς πόδας οὐ βαδίζοντα ὅπου ἂν βούλωμαι; οὐκ οἶσθ᾽ ὅτι οἱ φύσει ἀσθενέστατοι τῷ σώματι μελετήσαντες τῶν ἰσχυροτάτων ἀμελησάντων κρείττους τε γίγνονται πρὸς ἃ ἂν μελετῶσι καὶ ῥᾷον αὐτὰ φέρουσιν; ἐμὲ δὲ ἄρα οὐκ οἴει, τῷ σώματι ἀεὶ τὰ συντυγχάνοντα μελετῶντα καρτερεῖν, πάντα ῥᾷον φέρειν σοῦ μὴ μελετῶντος; τοῦ δὲ μὴ δουλεύειν γαστρὶ μηδ᾽ ὕπνῳ καὶ λαγνείᾳ οἴει τι ἄλλο αἰτιώτερον εἶναι ἢ τὸ ἕτερα ἔχειν τούτων ἡδίω, ἃ οὐ μόνον ἐν χρείᾳ ὄντα εὐφραίνει, ἀλλὰ καὶ ἐλπίδας παρέχοντα ὠφελήσειν ἀεί; καὶ μὴν τοῦτό γε οἶσθα, ὅτι οἱ μὲν οἰόμενοι μηδὲν εὖ πράττειν οὐκ εὐφραίνονται, οἱ δὲ ἡγούμενοι καλῶς προχωρεῖν ἑαυτοῖς ἢ γεωργίαν ἢ ναυκληρίαν ἢ ἄλλ᾽ ὅτι ἂν τυγχάνωσιν ἐργαζόμενοι ὡς εὖ πράττοντες εὐφραίνονται. οἴει οὖν ἀπὸ πάντων τούτων τοσαύτην ἡδονὴν εἶναι ὅσην ἀπὸ τοῦ ἑαυτόν τε ἡγεῖσθαι βελτίω γίγνεσθαι καὶ φίλους ἀμείνους κτᾶσθαι; ἐγὼ τοίνυν διατελῶ ταῦτα νομίζων. ἐὰν δὲ δὴ φίλους ἢ πόλιν ὠφελεῖν δέῃ, ποτέρῳ ἡ πλείων σχολὴ τούτων ἐπιμελεῖσθαι, τῷ ὡς ἐγὼ νῦν ἢ τῷ ὡς σὺ μακα-

28 ὄντα om. A   ἃ ἐγώ| λέγω A M O   31 οὐκ οἶσθ᾽ A M ante corr.   33 κωλύονται A ante corr. B   33–34 τοῦ πορεύεσθαι Stob. M[d] Br   36 ὅποι Dindorf   36–37 βούλομαι (ἂν omisso) A   38 τε om. A Stob. A: γε Stob. M[d]   39 μελετήσωσι Stob.   40–41 ἐμὲ . . . μελετῶντα M O: ἐμοὶ . . . μελετῶντι cet. codd.   42 μήθ᾽ A   47 καλῷ B ante corr.   48 ἄλλο ὅτι A B   51 τε om. A   52 δὴ| μὴ B Stob. A ante corr.   53 εἰ προτέρω B ante corr.   ἡ A: ἢ B ante corr. C: ἢ B post corr.: om. Stob.   πλέον Stob. S M[d] Br   54 τῷ om. O   σὺ| εὖ B

cure than yours, owing to their greater rarity and cost? Or because the foods you provide yourself are more pleasurable to you than mine are to me? Don't you know that whoever eats most pleasurably has the least need of sauce? And that whoever drinks most pleasurably has the least desire for a drink he does not have? As for coats, you know that those who change them do so because of cold and heat, and put on shoes so as not to be prevented from walking by things that hurt their feet. Now, have you ever noticed me staying indoors more than anybody else because of the cold, or fighting with anyone for shade because of the heat, or not walking wherever I want to because my feet hurt? Don't you know that, if they exercise, those who naturally have the weakest bodies become better at what they train for and endure it more easily than those who are very strong but do not exercise? Then don't you think that I, who train my body to endure whatever happens to it at any given time, can bear all things more easily than you can, if you do not exercise? Do you think anything is more responsible for a person's not being enslaved to the belly, or to sleep, or to sex, than the possession of other things more pleasurable than these? Things that not only give pleasure when they are in use, but also provide the hope that they will always be beneficial? Furthermore, you know that those who think they are not succeeding are not happy; whereas those who think that their farming, or ship-owning, or whatever else they happen to do is going well for them, are happy, in the belief that they are succeeding. Now do you think the pleasure from all these things is as great as that which comes from the belief that you are yourself becoming better, and acquiring better friends? I go through life with this belief. And if it proves necessary to help friends or city, who will have greater leisure to take care of this: someone who lives as I do, or one

ῥίζεις διαιτωμένῳ; στρατεύοιτο δὲ πότερος ἂν ῥᾷον, ὁ μὴ δυνάμενος ἄνευ πολυτελοῦς διαίτης ζῆν ἢ ᾧ τὸ παρὸν ἀρκοίη; ἐκπολιορκηθείη δὲ πότερος ἂν θᾶττον, ὁ τῶν χαλεπωτάτων εὑρεῖν δεόμενος ἢ ὁ τοῖς ῥᾴστοις ἐντυγχάνειν ἀρκούντως χρώμενος; ἔοικας, ὦ Ἀντιφῶν, τὴν εὐδαιμονίαν οἰομένῳ τρυφὴν καὶ πολυτέλειαν εἶναι· ἐγὼ δ' ἐνόμιζον τὸ μὲν μηδενὸς δεῖσθαι θεῖον εἶναι, τὸ δ' ὡς ἐλαχίστων ἐγγυτάτω τοῦ θείου, καὶ τὸ μὲν θεῖον κράτιστον, τὸ δ' ἐγγυτάτω τοῦ θείου ἐγγυτάτω τοῦ κρατίστου.

πάλιν δέ ποτε ὁ Ἀντιφῶν διαλεγόμενος τῷ Σωκράτει εἶπεν· Ὦ Σώκρατες, ἐγώ τοί σε δίκαιον μὲν νομίζω, σοφὸν δὲ οὐδ' ὁπωστιοῦν· δοκεῖς δέ μοι καὶ αὐτὸς τοῦτο γιγνώσκειν· οὐδένα γοῦν τῆς συνουσίας ἀργύριον πράττῃ. καίτοι τό γε ἱμάτιον ἢ τὴν οἰκίαν ἢ ἄλλο τι ὧν κέκτησαι νομίζων ἀργυρίου ἄξιον εἶναι οὐδενὶ ἂν μὴ ὅτι προῖκα δοίης, ἀλλ' οὐδ' ἔλαττον τῆς ἀξίας λαβών. δῆλον δὴ ὅτι εἰ καὶ τὴν συνουσίαν ᾤου τινὸς ἀξίαν εἶναι, καὶ ταύτης ἂν οὐκ ἔλαττον τῆς ἀξίας ἀργύριον ἐπράττου. δίκαιος μὲν οὖν ἂν εἴης, ὅτι οὐκ ἐξαπατᾷς ἐπὶ πλεονεξίᾳ, σοφὸς δὲ οὐκ ἄν, μηδενός γε ἄξια ἐπιστάμενος. ὁ δὲ Σωκράτης πρὸς ταῦτα εἶπε· Ὦ Ἀντιφῶν, παρ' ἡμῖν νομίζεται τὴν ὥραν καὶ τὴν σοφίαν ὁμοίως μὲν καλόν, ὁμοίως δὲ αἰσχρὸν διατίθεσθαι εἶναι. τήν τε γὰρ ὥραν ἐὰν μέν τις ἀργυρίου πωλῇ τῷ βουλομένῳ, πόρνον αὐτὸν ἀποκαλοῦσιν, ἐὰν δέ τις, ὃν ἂν γνῷ καλόν τε κἀγαθὸν ἐραστὴν ὄντα, τοῦτον φίλον ἑαυτῷ ποιῆται, σώφρονα νομίζομεν·

57 ἀρκείη O ante corr. ὅτι τῶν M O 58 εὑρεῖν om. M O δυνάμενος Stob. Br μᾶλλον ἢ M O ῥᾴστοις V Stob.: ῥᾴστοις ῥᾴστως cet. codd. 59 τὴν] τῶ A post corr. 60 εἶναι τρυφὴν καὶ πολυτέλειαν οἰομένῳ B 60–61 δ' ἐνόμιζον A B: δὲ νομίζω cet. codd. Stob. 61 δεῖσθαι M O: δέεσθαι cet. codd. Stob. 65 μὲν δίκαιον M O 67 γοῦν] γὰρ A 68 τό om. B 69 νομίζων post εἶναι B 72 ἔλαττον B: ἐλάττω cet. codd. εἰσεπράττου A 73 ἐξαπατᾶ A: ἐξαπατᾶσε B ἐπὶ om. B 75 ὑμῖν M O 76–77 καλῶς ... αἰσχρῶς Richards 79 καὶ ἀγαθὸν B 80 τοῦτον post ποιῆται transp. Schenkl ποιεῖται Stob. A

who lives in the way you deem happy? Who would have an easier time on a military expedition, someone who cannot live apart from an extravagant way of life, or one who is satisfied with whatever is at hand? Who would be forced to surrender more quickly, someone who requires what is hardest to find, or one who is satisfied with using what is easiest to find? You are like someone who thinks that happiness is luxury and extravagance, Antiphon. But I thought that needing nothing is divine, and needing the fewest things possible is closest to the divine; and that the divine is best, and what is closest to the divine is closest to the best."

Again another time, when Antiphon was conversing with Socrates, he said: "Socrates, I consider you just, you know, but in no way wise; and I think that you yourself recognize this. At least, you do not charge any money for your company. Yet you would not give anyone your coat, or house, or any other of your possessions you think is worth money, for less than its value, let alone for free. It is clear, then, that if you thought your company were worth anything, you would not charge less for it than it was worth. Just, then, you may be, since you do not deceive for your own advantage; but wise you are not, since what you know is worthless." Socrates said in reply: "Antiphon, among us it is considered both admirable and disgraceful to dispose of one's beauty and wisdom. If someone sells his beauty for money to whoever wants it, he is called a prostitute. But if someone befriends one he recognizes as a fine and noble lover, we consider him chaste and temperate. In

καὶ τὴν σοφίαν ὡσαύτως τοὺς μὲν ἀργυρίου τῷ βουλομένῳ πωλοῦντας σοφιστὰς [ὥσπερ πόρνους] ἀποκαλοῦσιν, ὅστις δὲ ὃν ἂν γνῷ εὐφυᾶ ὄντα διδάσκων ὅτι ἂν ἔχῃ ἀγαθὸν φίλον ποιεῖται, τοῦτον νομίζομεν, ἃ τῷ καλῷ κἀγαθῷ πολίτῃ προσήκει, ταῦτα ποιεῖν. ἐγὼ δ' οὖν καὶ αὐτός, ὦ Ἀντιφῶν, ὥσπερ ἄλλος τις ἢ ἵππῳ ἀγαθῷ ἢ κυνὶ ἢ ὄρνιθι ἥδεται, οὕτω καὶ ἔτι μᾶλλον ἥδομαι φίλοις ἀγαθοῖς, καὶ ἐάν τι ἔχω ἀγαθόν, διδάσκω, καὶ ἄλλοις συνίστημι παρ' ὧν ἂν ἡγῶμαι ὠφελήσεσθαί τι αὐτοὺς εἰς ἀρετήν· καὶ τοὺς θησαυροὺς τῶν πάλαι σοφῶν ἀνδρῶν, οὓς ἐκεῖνοι κατέλιπον ἐν βιβλίοις γράψαντες, ἀνελίττων κοινῇ σὺν τοῖς φίλοις διέρχομαι, καὶ ἄν τι ὁρῶμεν ἀγαθὸν ἐκλεγόμεθα· καὶ μέγα νομίζομεν κέρδος, ἐὰν ἀλλήλοις φίλοι γιγνώμεθα. ἐμοὶ μὲν δὴ ταῦτα ἀκούοντι ἐδόκει αὐτός τε μακάριος εἶναι καὶ τοὺς ἀκούοντας ἐπὶ καλοκἀγαθίαν ἄγειν.

καὶ πάλιν ποτὲ τοῦ Ἀντιφῶντος ἐρομένου αὐτόν, πῶς ἄλλους μὲν ἡγεῖται πολιτικοὺς ποιεῖν, αὐτὸς δ' οὐ πράττει τὰ πολιτικά, εἴπερ ἐπίσταται· Ποτέρως δ' ἄν, ἔφη, ὦ Ἀντιφῶν, μᾶλλον τὰ πολιτικὰ πράττοιμι, εἰ μόνος αὐτὰ πράττοιμι ἢ εἰ ἐπιμελοίμην τοῦ ὡς πλείστους ἱκανοὺς εἶναι πράττειν αὐτά;

T2(a) Hermogenes, *De ideis* 2.11 (399.18–400.21, 401.12–23 Rabe)

περὶ δὲ Ἀντιφῶντος λέγοντας ἀνάγκη προειπεῖν ὅτι, καθάπερ ἄλλοι τέ φασιν οὐκ ὀλίγοι καὶ Δίδυμος ὁ γραμ-

81 ἀργυρίῳ A Stob. A 82 ὥσπερ πόρνους del. Ruhnken 83 εὐφυῆ A B M O: εὐφυῆς Stob. M[d] A: εὐφυᾶ D ἔχοι B O 84 φίλον ἑαυτῷ A ποιῆται A B Stob. M[d] 85 προσήκοι A 88 ἂν Stob. σχῶ M O 89 ὠφεληθήσεσθαι A αὐτὸς Naber 90 πάλ A 91 βίβλοις B ἀνειλίττων B 93–94 φίλοις O: ὠφέλιμοι V 94 γενώμεθα Stob. M[d] A 98–99 ἡγεῖται ... πράττει ... ἐπίσταται codd. inter indic. et optat. variant 99 ἐπίστατο Stob. A: ἠπίστατο B post corr. ἂν om. A 100–101 εἰ ... πράττοιμι om. B **T2(a)** codd. = Pa Pc Vc Ac Ba Og Va Lb Md Pl Pt Sf 1 τοῦ ἀντιφῶντος Ac

the same way, those who sell their wisdom for money to whoever wants it are called sophists. But whoever befriends one he recognizes to be naturally talented – and teaches him whatever good thing he has – this man, we think, does what a fine and noble citizen should do. I, at any rate, Antiphon, take pleasure in good friends the way others do in a good horse, or dog, or bird – and even more so. If I have anything good, I teach it to them, and commit them to the care of others from whom I think they will derive some benefit in regard to virtue. Together with my friends, I unroll and go through the treasures of the wise men of old, which they wrote down and left behind in books; and if we see anything good, we pick it out. We consider it a great gain if we become one another's friends." I thought, as I heard this, that Socrates was happy himself, and led his listeners to nobility.

Again another time, Antiphon asked Socrates how he thought he could make others proficient in the art of politics when he did not practice it himself – if indeed he knew it. Socrates replied: "Would I be practicing the art of politics more if I were to practice it by myself, or if I were to take care that as many men as possible are competent to practice it?"

T2(a) When speaking about Antiphon, it is necessary to say in advance that – as not a few others say, particularly Didymus the grammarian,

ματικός, πρὸς δὲ καὶ ἀπὸ ἱστορίας φαίνεται, πλείους μὲν γεγόνασιν Ἀντιφῶντες, δύο δὲ οἱ σοφιστεύσαντες, ὧν καὶ λόγον ἀνάγκη ποιήσασθαι· ὧν εἷς μέν ἐστιν ὁ ῥήτωρ, οὗπερ οἱ φονικοὶ φέρονται λόγοι καὶ ⟨οἱ⟩ δημηγορικοὶ καὶ ὅσοι τούτοις ὅμοιοι, ἕτερος δὲ ὁ καὶ τερατοσκόπος καὶ ὀνειροκρίτης λεγόμενος γενέσθαι, οὗπερ οἵ τε Περὶ τῆς ἀληθείας εἶναι λέγονται λόγοι καὶ ὁ Περὶ ὁμονοίας [καὶ οἱ δημηγορικοὶ] καὶ ὁ Πολιτικός. ἐγὼ δὲ ἕνεκα μὲν τοῦ διαφόρου τῶν ἐν τοῖς λόγοις τούτοις ἰδεῶν πείθομαι δύο τοὺς Ἀντιφῶντας γενέσθαι – πολὺ γὰρ ὡς ὄντως τὸ παραλλάττον τῶν ἐπιγραφομένων τῆς Ἀληθείας λόγων πρὸς τοὺς λοιπούς – ἕνεκα δὲ τοῦ καὶ παρὰ Πλάτωνι καὶ παρ᾽ ἄλλοις ἱστορουμένου πάλιν οὐ πείθομαι· Θουκυδίδην γὰρ Ἀντιφῶντος εἶναι τοῦ Ῥαμνουσίου μαθητὴν ἀκούω πολλῶν λεγόντων, καὶ τὸν μὲν Ῥαμνούσιον εἰδὼς ἐκεῖνον, οὗπερ εἰσὶν οἱ φονικοί, τὸν Θουκυδίδην δὲ πολλῷ κεχωρισμένον καὶ κεκοινωνηκότα τῷ εἴδει τῶν τῆς Ἀληθείας λόγων, πάλιν οὐ πείθομαι. οὐ μὴν ἀλλ᾽ εἴτε εἷς ὁ Ἀντιφῶν ἐγένετο, δύο λόγων εἴδεσι τοσοῦτον ἀλλήλων διεστηκόσι χρησάμενος, εἴτε καὶ δύο, χωρὶς ἑκάτερος ὁ μὲν τοῦτο ὁ δὲ ἐκεῖνο μετελθών, ἀνάγκη χωρὶς περὶ ἑκατέρου διελθεῖν· πλεῖστον γάρ, ὡς ἔφαμεν, τὸ μεταξύ . . .

ὁ δ᾽ ἕτερος Ἀντιφῶν, οὗπερ οἱ τῆς Ἀληθείας εἰσὶ λεγόμενοι λόγοι, πολιτικὸς μὲν ἥκιστά ἐστι, σεμνὸς δὲ καὶ ὑπέρογκος τοῖς τε ἄλλοις καὶ τῷ δι᾽ ἀποφάνσεων περαίνειν τὸ πᾶν, ὃ δὴ τοῦ ἀξιωματικοῦ τε λόγου ἐστὶ καὶ πρὸς

3 τῆς ἱστορίας Vc Ba μὲν γὰρ Ac 6 φονικοὶ] σοφιστικοὶ Og οἱ add. Walz et Spengel post δημηγορικοὶ add. καὶ ὁ πολιτικός Walz Spengel 9 ὁ Pa Vc Ac Ba: οἱ Pc: om. Va 9–10 καὶ οἱ δημηγορικοὶ post λόγοι (l. 9) transp. Lb: del. Sauppe 10 καὶ οἱ πολιτικοί Md 11 τῶν Pa Pc Ac: τοῦ Vc Ba τῶν ἰδεῶν Lb 14 ἕνεκεν Vc Ba τοῦ ex τούτου Vc Ba 19 ⟨τούτου⟩ κεχωρισμένον Blass τῶν om. Ba Vc ante corr. 20 εἴτε om. Vc ante corr. ὁ om. Pl Pt 22 διεστηκόσι Blass: διεστηκότων codd. 24 ἔφημεν Sf 25–26 εἰσὶ λόγοι ⟨οὕτως add. Pc⟩ λεγόμενοι Pc Vc Ba 27 τε Pc Vc Ac Ba: δὲ Pa τῷ] τὸ Vc Ba ἀποφάσεων Vc Ac Ba 28 τε Pa Vc Ac Ba: om. Pc

and as appears from inquiry as well – there have been a great number of Antiphons, but two who were sophists, of whom account must be taken. One of these is the rhetor, whose homicide and public speeches, and all those similar to these, are current. The other Antiphon is the one said to have been a diviner and dream-interpreter, to whom are said to belong the discourse *On Truth* and that *On Concord* and the *Politicus*. Because of the difference of style among these works, I am inclined to believe that there were two Antiphons; for the difference between the work entitled *Truth* and the rest is really large. Then again, because of the information in Plato and others, I am inclined not to believe it. For I have read many people who say that Thucydides was the student of Antiphon of Rhamnus. And I know that it is the Rhamnusian to whom the murder speeches belong, and that Thucydides is far apart from these and shares the style of the work *Truth*. So I am inclined not to believe there were two Antiphons. However, whether there was one Antiphon (employing two styles so different from each other) or in fact two (each employing a different style), it is necessary to discuss each separately. For as we said, the difference is very great . . .

The other Antiphon, to whom the discourse called *Truth* belongs, is anything but political. Rather, he is dignified and weighty, particularly because he accomplishes every-

μέγεθος ὁρῶντος, ὑψηλὸς δὲ τῇ λέξει καὶ τραχύς, ὥστε καὶ μὴ πόρρω σκληρότητος εἶναι. καὶ περιβάλλει δὲ χωρὶς εὐκρινείας· διὸ καὶ συγχεῖ τὸν λόγον καὶ ἔστιν ἀσαφὴς τὰ πολλά. καὶ ἐπιμελὴς δὲ κατὰ τὴν συνθήκην καὶ ταῖς παρισώσεσι χαίρων. οὐ μὴν ἤθους γέ τι οὐδ' ἀληθινοῦ τύπου μέτεστι τῷ ἀνδρί, φαίην δ' ἂν ὡς οὐδὲ δεινότητος πλὴν τῆς φαινομένης μέν, οὐ μὴν οὔσης γε ὡς ἀληθῶς.

T2(b) Philostratus, *Vitae sophistarum* 1.15 (2.17 Kayser = 500 Olearius)

λόγοι δ' αὐτοῦ [*sc*. Ἀντιφῶντος] δικανικοὶ μὲν πλείους, ἐν οἷς ἡ δεινότης καὶ πᾶν τὸ ἐκ τέχνης ἔγκειται, σοφιστικοὶ δὲ καὶ ἕτεροι μέν, σοφιστικώτερος δὲ ὁ ὑπὲρ τῆς ὁμονοίας, ἐν ᾧ γνωμολογίαι τε λαμπραὶ καὶ φιλόσοφοι σεμνή τε ἀπαγγελία καὶ ἐπηνθισμένη ποιητικοῖς ὀνόμασι καὶ τὰ ἀποτάδην ἑρμηνευόμενα παραπλήσια τῶν πεδίων τοῖς λείοις.

T3 *Suda* s.v. Ἀντιφῶν (α 2744–46, 1.245 Adler)

Ἀντιφῶν, Ἀθηναῖος, τερατοσκόπος καὶ ἐποποιὸς καὶ σοφιστής. ἐκαλεῖτο δὲ Λογομάγειρος.

Ἀντιφῶν, Σοφίλου, Ἀθηναῖος, τῶν δήμων Ῥαμνούσιος· διδάσκαλος δὲ αὐτοῦ οὐδεὶς προγινώσκεται· ἀλλ' ὅμως ἦρξε τοῦ δικανικοῦ χαρακτῆρος μετὰ Γοργίαν. λέγεται δὲ καὶ Θουκυδίδου γενέσθαι διδάσκαλος. ἐκαλεῖτο δὲ Νέστωρ.

Ἀντιφῶν, Ἀθηναῖος, ὀνειροκρίτης. περὶ κρίσεως ὀνείρων ἔγραψεν.

30 pr. καὶ om. Ac   τῆς σκληρότητος Pc   **T2(b)** 3 σοφιστικώτερος] σοφιστικώτατος Sauppe   **T3** codd. = A G I T S M B   3 Σοφίλου] Φίλου S   τὸν δῆμον T M   5–6 λέγεται δὲ καί om. S   6 Θουκυδίδου M: Θουκυδίδης G S (compendium dubium habent A I T)   γενέσθαι om. S

thing through categorical assertions – which is characteristic of discourse that is dignified and looks toward magnitude. He is lofty and rugged in his diction, so as to be not far from harshness. He amplifies without clarity, and so confuses his discourse and is unclear in most respects. He is careful in his composition and delights in balanced clauses. The man has no share in character or sincerity, however, nor (I would affirm) in impressiveness, except that which is apparent, but unreal.

T2(b) The majority of Antiphon's works are court-speeches, in which are present skill and everything which comes from art. Others again are sophistic, and very sophistic is the work *On Concord*, in which there are brilliant philosophical maxims, impressive diction adorned with poetic vocabulary, and prolix exposition like smooth plains.

T3 Antiphon, an Athenian, diviner and epic poet and sophist. He was called "speech-cook."

Antiphon, son of Sophilus, an Athenian, from the deme Rhamnus. No teacher of his is known; nevertheless, he started the dicanic form of discourse, after Gorgias. He is also said to have been the teacher of Thucydides. He was called "Nestor."

Antiphon, an Athenian, dream-interpreter. He wrote on the interpretation of dreams.

T4 Athenaeus, 15 673D–F (3.488–89 Kaibel)

ταῦτα ἴσασιν οἱ θεοὶ ὡς πρῶτος αὐτὸς ἐν τῇ καλῇ Ἀλεξανδρείᾳ εὗρον κτησάμενος τὸ τοῦ Μηνοδότου συγγραμμάτιον καὶ ἐπιδείξας πολλοῖς ἐξ αὐτοῦ τὸ παρὰ τῷ Ἀνακρέοντι ζητούμενον. λαβὼν δὲ παρ' ἐμοῦ ὁ πᾶσιν κλοπὴν ὀνειδίζων Ἡφαιστίων ἐξιδιοποιήσατο τὴν λύσιν καὶ σύγγραμμα ἐξέδωκεν ἐπιγράψας Περὶ τοῦ παρ' Ἀνακρέοντι λυγίνου στεφάνου· ὅπερ νῦν ἐν τῇ Ῥώμῃ εὕρομεν παρὰ †τῇ ἀντικοττυραι Δημητρίῳ†. τοιοῦτος δέ τις καὶ [ὁ Ἡφαιστίων συγγραφεὺς καὶ] περὶ τὸν καλὸν ἡμῶν Ἄδραστον ἐγένετο. ἐκδόντος γὰρ τούτου πέντε μὲν βιβλία Περὶ τῶν παρὰ Θεοφράστῳ ἐν τοῖς περὶ Ἠθῶν καθ' ἱστορίαν καὶ λέξιν ζητουμένων, ἕκτον δὲ περὶ τῶν ἐν τοῖς Ἠθικοῖς Νικομαχείοις Ἀριστοτέλους, ἐννοίας ἀμφιλαφῶς παραθεμένου περὶ τοῦ παρὰ Ἀντιφῶντι τῷ τραγῳδιοποιῷ Πληξίππου καὶ πλεῖστα ὅσα καὶ περὶ αὐτοῦ τοῦ Ἀντιφῶντος εἰπόντος, σφετερισάμενος καὶ ταῦτα ἐπέγραψέν τι βιβλίον Περὶ τοῦ παρὰ Ξενοφῶντι ἐν τοῖς Ἀπομνημονεύμασιν Ἀντιφῶντος, οὐδὲν ἴδιον προσεξευρών, ὥσπερ κἀν τῷ Περὶ τοῦ λυγίνου στεφάνου.

T5 Diogenes Laertius, 2.46 (1.76 Long) = Aristotle, fr. 75 Rose

τούτῳ [*sc.* Σωκράτει] τις, καθά φησιν Ἀριστοτέλης ἐν τρίτῳ Περὶ ποιητικῆς, ἐφιλονείκει Ἀντίλοχος Λήμνιος καὶ Ἀντιφῶν ὁ τερατοσκόπος, ὡς Πυθαγόρᾳ Κύλων Κροτωνιάτης· καὶ Σύαγρος Ὁμήρῳ ζῶντι, ἀποθανόντι δὲ Ξενοφάνης ὁ Κολοφώνιος· καὶ Κέρκωψ Ἡσιόδῳ ζῶντι, τελευτήσαντι δὲ ὁ προειρημένος Ξενοφάνης· καὶ Πινδάρῳ

T4 cod. = A 6 Περὶ Musurus: παρὰ A 8 τῇ ἀντικοττυραι Δημητρίῳ A: παρὰ τῇ ἐν οὐίκῳ Τυραρίῳ Δήμητρι Kaibel (coll. Hor., *Epist.* II 1.269); sed cf. Gulick (1941) ad loc. 9 ὁ Ἡφαιστίων συγγραφεὺς καὶ del. Casaubon 10 ἄδραντον A: corr. Casaubon 13 νικομαχίοις A ἀμφιλαφεῖς Kaibel **T5** codd. = B F P 2 ποιητικῆς] ποιητῶν Castelvetro 3–4 Κύλων Κροτωνιάτης Menagius: κύδων καὶ ὀνάτας F P 4 Σύαγρος Lilius Gyraldus: σάγαρις codd.

T4 "The gods know that I myself first discovered this in our beautiful Alexandria, after I acquired the little treatise of Menodotus, and from it showed many people the problem in Anacreon. But Hephaestion, who accuses everyone of plagiarism, appropriated the solution from me and published a treatise entitled *On the Crown of Withes in Anacreon*, which we found in Rome just now at . . . He did the same with our fair Adrastus. For after Adrastus had published five books on problems of content and style in Theophrastus' *On Characters*, and a sixth on problems in Aristotle's *Nicomachean Ethics* – mentioning an abundance of ideas about the Plexippus in Antiphon the tragic poet, and saying a great number of things about Antiphon himself as well – Hephaestion appropriated this too (just like in the *On the Crown of Withes*), and wrote a book entitled *On the Antiphon in Xenophon's Memorabilia*, although he had made no additional discoveries of his own."

T5 As Aristotle says in the third book of *On Poetry*, a certain Antilochus of Lemnos and Antiphon the diviner argued contentiously with Socrates, as Cylon of Croton did with Pythagoras; as Syagrus did with Homer in his lifetime, and Xenophanes of Colophon after his death; as Cercops did with Hesiod in his lifetime, and the aforesaid Xenophanes after his death;

Ἀμφιμένης ὁ Κῷος· Θάλητι δὲ Φερεκύδης καὶ Βίαντι Σάλαρος Πριηνεύς· Πιττακῷ Ἀντιμενίδας καὶ Ἀλκαῖος, Ἀναξαγόρᾳ Σωσίβιος, καὶ Σιμωνίδῃ Τιμοκρέων.

T6(a) [Plut.], *Vitae X or.* 833C–D

λέγεται δὲ τραγῳδίας συνθεῖναι καὶ ἰδίᾳ καὶ σὺν Διονυσίῳ τῷ τυράννῳ. ἔτι δ' ὢν πρὸς τῇ ποιήσει τέχνην ἀλυπίας συνεστήσατο, ὥσπερ τοῖς νοσοῦσιν ἡ παρὰ τῶν ἰατρῶν θεραπεία ὑπάρχει· ἐν Κορίνθῳ τε κατεσκευασμένος οἴκημά τι παρὰ τὴν ἀγορὰν προέγραψεν ὅτι δύναται τοὺς λυπουμένους διὰ λόγων θεραπεύειν· καὶ πυνθανόμενος τὰς αἰτίας παρεμυθεῖτο τοὺς κάμνοντας. νομίζων δὲ τὴν τέχνην ἐλάττω ἢ καθ' αὑτὸν εἶναι ἐπὶ ῥητορικὴν ἀπετράπη.

T6(b) Anonymus, *Vita Antiphontis* 5–7 (XVI–XVII Thalheim)

τοῦ πολιτεύεσθαι δὲ ἀποστὰς νέος ὢν ἐν Κορίνθῳ παρὰ τὴν ἀγορὰν οἴκημα εἰς ὑποδοχὴν ἀκροατῶν ποιήσας καὶ ἔξωθεν ἐπιγράψας ὅτι τοὺς λυπουμένους παραμυθεῖται, εἶτα φιλοχρήματος ὢν καὶ οὐ πολλὰ ἐκ τούτου κερδαίνων τραγῳδίας ἐποίει. ἀποστὰς δὲ καὶ τούτων ἐπὶ ῥητορικὴν ἐτράπετο . . .

T6(c) Photius, *Bibliotheca* 486a Bekker (8.42–43 Henry)

λόγος δὲ αὐτὸν καὶ τραγῳδίας συνθεῖναι, ἰδίᾳ τε καὶ Διονυσίῳ συνδιατρίβοντα τῷ τυράννῳ. σχολάζοντα δὲ πρότερον τῇ ποιήσει τέχνην φασὶν αὐτὸν ἐξευρεῖν ἀλυπίας, καὶ κατὰ τὴν ἀγορὰν ἐν Κορίνθῳ οἰκημάτιόν τι οἰκοδομησάμενον ἐπιγράψαι δύνασθαι αὐτὸν τοὺς λυπουμένους διὰ λόγων θεραπεύειν· καὶ δὴ καὶ πυνθανόμενος

T6(a) codd. = E α 1–2 Διονυσίῳ E: Διονύσῳ α **T6(b)** cod. = A N 2 ἀποδοχὴν A 3 post παραμυθεῖται lacunam statuerunt quidam 5 καὶ ante τούτων om. A ante corr. **T6(c)** codd. = A M 2 συνδιατρίβοντα A: διατρίβοντα M 4 οἰκημάτιόν τι A post corr.: οἰκήματι ὄντι A ante corr. M

as Amphimenes of Cos did with Pindar; as Pherecydes did with Thales, and Salarus of Priene with Bias; as Antimenidas and Alcaeus did with Pittacus, and as Sosibius did with Anaxagoras, and Timocreon with Simonides.

T6(a) Antiphon is said to have composed tragedies both by himself and with the tyrant Dionysius. While he was still involved with poetry, he contrived an art of removing grief, like the treatment of doctors for the sick. He procured a workshop in Corinth beside the agora, and put out a notice that he was able to treat the grief-stricken through words. He assuaged the sick, inquiring into the causes. But thinking the art to be beneath him, he turned to rhetoric.

T6(b) Staying away from politics when he was young, he made a workshop in Corinth beside the agora for the reception of listeners, and put up a notice outside that he could assuage the grief-stricken. Then, because he was greedy and was not making much from this, he composed tragedies. But he abandoned this too and turned to rhetoric.

T6(c) There is a tradition that he also composed tragedies, both by himself and while staying with the tyrant Dionysius. They say that earlier, while he was devoting himself to poetry, he discovered an art of removing grief; and that, after building a workshop in the agora in Corinth, he advertised his ability to treat the grief-stricken through words. He

τὰς αἰτίας τῆς λύπης τοὺς ἀνιωμένους παρεμυθεῖτο. τοῦτο δὲ τὸ ἐπιτήδευμα ἧττον εἶναι νομίσας τῆς ἑαυτοῦ μεγαλονοίας ἐπὶ ῥητορικὴν ἐτράπη.

T6(d) Philostratus, *Vitae sophistarum* 1.15 (2.15–16 Kayser = 498 Olearius)

πιθανώτατος δὲ ὁ Ἀντιφῶν γενόμενος καὶ προσρηθεὶς Νέστωρ ἐπὶ τῷ περὶ παντὸς εἰπὼν ἂν πεῖσαι νηπενθεῖς ἀκροάσεις ἐπήγγειλεν, ὡς οὐδὲν οὕτω δεινὸν ἐρούντων ἄχος, ὃ μὴ ἐξελεῖν τῆς γνώμης.

T7 Lucian, *Verae historiae* 2, 33

ἐν μέσῃ δὲ τῇ ἀγορᾷ πηγή τίς ἐστιν, ἣν καλοῦσι Καρεῶτιν· καὶ πλησίον ναοὶ δύο, Ἀπάτης καὶ Ἀληθείας· ἔνθα καὶ τὸ ἄδυτόν ἐστιν αὐτοῖς καὶ τὸ μαντεῖον, οὗ προεστήκει προφητεύων Ἀντιφῶν ὁ τῶν ὀνείρων ὑποκριτής, ταύτης παρὰ τοῦ Ὕπνου λαχὼν τῆς τιμῆς.

T8 Clement of Alexandria, *Stromata* 7.4.24.4 (2.17 Stählin–Früchtel); cf. Theodoretus, *Graecarum affectionum curatio* 6.18 (155 Raeder)

χαρίεν τὸ τοῦ Ἀντιφῶντος· οἰωνισαμένου τινός, ὅτι κατέφαγεν ὗς τὰ δελφάκια, θεασάμενος αὐτὴν ὑπὸ λιμοῦ διὰ μικροψυχίαν τοῦ τρέφοντος κατισχναμένην, Χαῖρε, εἶπεν, ἐπὶ τῷ σημείῳ, ὅτι οὕτω πεινῶσα τὰ σὰ οὐκ ἔφαγεν τέκνα.

T9 *Gnomologium Vindobonense* 50 (14 Wachsmuth) = *Gnomologium Vaticanum* 71 (1 Sternbach)

Ἀντιφῶν ἐρωτηθεὶς τί ἐστι μαντικὴ εἶπεν· ἀνθρώπου φρονίμου εἰκασμός.

T7 codd. = Γ Ω S P 1 τίς om. P 3–4 προειστήκει P **T8** 1–5 similia ex Clemente derivata habet Theodoretus

assuaged the distressed, inquiring into the causes of their grief. But thinking this pursuit to be beneath his lofty mentality, he turned to rhetoric.

T6(d) Antiphon, being very persuasive, and nicknamed "Nestor" because of his ability to persuade when speaking on any subject, announced pain-removing lectures, in the belief that people would tell no grief so terrible that he could not remove it from their mind.

T7 In the middle of the agora there is a spring, which people call Careotis. Nearby are two temples, of Deception and of Truth. There also is their sanctuary and their oracle, in front of which Antiphon the dream-interpreter stood prophesying, who had received this office from Sleep.

T8 Antiphon's response is clever. When someone took the fact that a sow had devoured its piglets as an omen, he observed that the sow was emaciated from hunger because of its keeper's meanness, and said: "Rejoice at the omen, since the sow, despite being so hungry, did not eat *your* children."

T9 When asked what the art of divination is, Antiphon said: "The conjecture of an intelligent man."

T10 Philodemus, *De poematis*, *P.Herc.* 994, XXXVIII.14–23 (*VH*^{2} VI.187 = 49 Gomperz = 113 Sbordone)

εὔδηλος ἡ τῶν ἄλλων φληνạφ[ία φ]αίνεται ṭῷν ἢ ταὐṭạ̀ τẹ́ρπειν καὶ ὀχλεῖν ἢ διάφορα κατηξιωκότọν, ὡς καί τινος τῶν ἀρχαίων Ἀντιφῶντος, εἴτ' οὖν ῥητορικὸς εἴτε καὶ φιλọ́ṣοφος ἠβούλετ' εἶναι.

T11(a) Pseudo-Callisthenes, *Historia Alexandri Magni* (recensio vetusta) II.1–4 (II.6–21 Kroll)

μετ' ὀλίγας δὲ παντελῶς ἡμέρας ἔν τινι συμφύτῳ τόπῳ τῶν βασιλείων καθεζομένου τοῦ Φιλίππου, παντοίων ὄρνεων παρ' αὐτοῦ τρεφομένων καὶ ἐν τῷ χωρίῳ νεμομένων, πρὸς τὴν ἡσυχίαν ἐν φιλολόγοις βιβλίοις γενομένου αὐτοῦ ὄρνις ἥμερος νεοττὸς εἰς τοὺς κόλπους αὐτοῦ ἁλλομένη ἔτεκεν ᾠόν, ὃ κατακυλισθὲν ἐπὶ τῆς γῆς ἐρράγη. ἀφ' οὗ ἐξεπήδησε μικρὸν δρακόντιον· κυκλεῦσαν δὲ τὸ ᾠόν, ὅθεν ἐξῆλθε, καὶ εἰσελθεῖν βουλόμενον, πρὶν βαλεῖν ἔσω τὴν κεφαλὴν ἐτελεύτησεν. τούτου γεναμένου ταραχθεὶς οὐ μετρίως ὁ Φίλιππος μετεπέμψατο τὸν κατὰ ἐκεῖνον τὸν καιρὸν ἐπίσημον σημειολύτην Ἀντιφῶντα καὶ ὑφηγεῖται αὐτῷ τὸ γενόμενον. ὁ δὲ πρὸς τοῦτο εἶπεν· Υἱός σοι ἔσται, ὃς βασιλεύσει καὶ περιελεύσεται τὸν ὅλον κόσμον, τῇ ἰδίą̣ δυνάμει πάντας ὑποτάσσων· οὗτος δὲ

T10 3 ῥητορικους **T11(a)** codd. = A L et β Arm Val (lectiones selectae tantum; notitiam pleniorem praebet Kroll [1926]) 1 μετὰ δὲ ἡμέρας τινὰς L ὀλίγου A 1–2 τινι τῶν βασιλικῶν τόπων συμφύτω L: τινι συγχύτῳ τῷ βασιλεῖ A 2 sqq. hinc L cum β fere consentit nec iam notatur 3–4 νεμομένου A 4–5 γινομένου cum ε suprascr. A 5 ὄρνις ἥμερος] οὖν ἰσήμερος A νεοττὸς Müller: νόθος A 6 ante κατακυλισθὲν add. καὶ A 7 κυκλεῦον A: corr. ex β 8 καὶ εἰσελθεῖν] κατεισελθεῖν A 8–9 *priusquam cupitum ageret* Val 9 βάλλει A: καὶ βαλὸν (πάλιν add. Arm) β Arm 12 γεννώμενον A post γενόμενον add. τὴν ὄρνιν, τὸ ᾠόν, τὸν δράκοντα, τὸ κυκλοῦν, τὴν τελευτήν Arm (similia habet Val) ὁ καὶ πρὸς τοῦτο Ἀντιφῶν εἶπεν A post εἶπεν add. *ad incrementum peritiae suae dei adminiculo inspiratus* Val (similia habent β Arm) 13 βασιλεύσει καὶ A: om. cett. 14 post ὑποτάσσων add. αὐτὸς δὲ οὐδενὶ ὑποταχθήσεται Arm

T10 ... the babbling of the others appears manifest: those who have maintained that either the same sounds, or different ones, give pleasure and pain, as Antiphon did also, one of the ancients, whether he professed to be a philosopher or a rhetorician.

T11(a) Quite a few days later, when Philip was sitting in a wooded area of the palace, with birds of all sorts kept by him feeding in the place, a tame young bird jumped into his lap while he was at rest and engaged with learned books, and laid an egg, which rolled to the ground and broke. From it leaped a small serpent, which encircled the egg it had come out of and wanted to go back in, but died before it could put its head in. Philip was quite upset when this happened, and sent for the then-famous diviner Antiphon, and told him what had happened. Antiphon said in reply: "You shall have a son, who will be king and will encompass the whole world, subjugating everyone to his authority. But

εἰς τὰ ἴδια συστρέφων ὀλιγοχρόνιος τελευτήσει. ὁ γὰρ δράκων βασιλικόν ἐστι ζῷον, τὸ δὲ ᾠὸν παραπλήσιον κόσμῳ, ὅθεν ὁ δράκων ἐξῄει. κυκλεύσας δὲ τὸ ᾠὸν καὶ συστρέψαι βουλόμενος, πρὶν βάλῃ τὴν κεφαλὴν εἰς τὴν γεγεννηκυῖαν αὐτὸν πατρίδα, ἔξωθεν τετελεύτηκεν. οὗτος μὲν οὖν ἐπιλύσας τὸ σημεῖον δωνατισθεὶς ἐξῄει.

T11(b) John Tzetzes, Scholium on Hermogenes' *De ideis* 400.3 Rabe (*apud* van Spaan [1773], 804)

τερατοσκόπος· ὀνείρους τε καὶ τέρατα πολλοῖς ἐφερμηνεύων. ὁ τερατοσκόπος Ἀντιφῶν ἦν Ἀλεξάνδρου χρόνοις.

T12 Tertullian, *De anima* 46.10 (64 Waszink)

quanti autem commentatores et affirmatores in hanc rem? Artemon Antiphon Strato Philochorus Epicharmus Serapion Cratippus Dionysius Rhodius Hermippus, tota saeculi litteratura.

15 ὑποστρέφων β 17 κόσμου A τὸ ᾠὸν A (*ovum* Val): τὸν κόσμον β Arm 18 βάλλη A 19 τετελευτηκέναι A: οὐκ ἔφθασεν ἀλλ' ἐτελεύτησεν β Arm: πατρίδα ἔφθασε τετελευτηκώς Müller 20 δονατισθεὶς A: δωματισθεὶς L: δῶρα λαβὼν β Arm: δοκιμασθεὶς Val **T12** *codd.* = *A B Gel.* 1 et affirmatores *om. A* 2 arthemon *A* 3 diony * sius *ex* dioni * sius *A*: et Dionysius *B Gel.* rodius *cum* h *suprascr. A*

after a short life he will die while returning home. For the serpent is a kingly creature, and the egg, from which it came out, is like the world. When the serpent had encircled the egg and wanted to go back, it died outside, before it could put its head into the fatherland that had given it birth." After explaining the omen, Antiphon went away endowed with gifts.

T11(b) Diviner: interpreting dreams and portents for many. Antiphon the diviner lived in the time of Alexander.

T12 How many interpreters and guarantors of this thing [*sc.* revelatory dreams] are there? Artemon, Antiphon, Strato, Philochorus, Epicharmus, Serapion, Cratippus, Dionysius of Rhodes, Hermippus – the whole literature of an age.

Fragments

1–44: ΠΕΡΙ ΑΛΗΘΕΙΑΣ

F1 Galen, *In Hippocratis librum De officina medici commentarii iii* (18.2.656 Kühn) (speaking of Critias)

καὶ πολλάκις ἐν τῷ αὐτῷ [*sc.* ἐν Ὁμιλιῶν προτέρῳ] καὶ ἐν τῷ δευτέρῳ τῶν Ὁμιλιῶν ἀντιδιαιρῶν ταῖς αἰσθήσεσι τὴν γνώμην, πολλάκις εἴρηκεν, ὥσπερ καὶ ὁ Ἀντιφῶν ἐν τῷ προτέρῳ τῆς Ἀληθείας οὕτω λέγων· **ταῦτα δὲ γνοὺς εἴσ⟨ῃ⟩ ἕν τι οὐδὲν αὐτῶν, οὔτε ὧν ὄψει ὁρᾷ ⟨ὁ ὁρῶν⟩ μακρότατα οὔτε ὧν γνώμῃ γιγνώσκει ὁ μακρότατα γιγνώσκων.**

F2 Galen, *In Hippocratis librum De officina medici commentarii iii* (18.2.656 Kühn) (immediately after F1)

καὶ· **πᾶσι γὰρ ἀνθρώποις ἡ γνώμη τοῦ σώματος ἡγεῖται καὶ εἰς ὑγίειαν καὶ νόσον καὶ εἰς τὰ ἄλλα πάντα.**

F3 Pollux, 6.143 (2.38 Bethe)

ἀπαρασκεύῳ γνώμῃ ἐν τοῖς Περὶ ἀληθείας Ἀντιφῶν εἶπεν, ἀπαρασκεύαστον δ' ἐν ταῖς ῥητορικαῖς τέχναις – δοκοῦσι δ' οὐ γνήσιαι.

F1 codd. = P M 3–7 ἐν τῷ προτέρῳ τῆς Ἀληθείας οὕτω λέγων· ταῦτα δὲ γνοὺς εἴσῃ ἕν τι οὐδὲν ⟨ὂν⟩ αὐτῷ (vel αὐτῶν) οὔτε ὧν ὄψει ὁρᾷ ⟨ὁ ὁρῶν⟩ μακρότατα οὔτε ὧν γνώμῃ γιγνώσκει ὁ μακρότατα γιγνώσκων Diels: ἐν τῷ προτέρω τῆς ἀληθείας ἐν τῷ λέγον (λεγ̈ P) τοῦ τάδε γνοὺς εἰς ἕν τε οὐδὲν αὐτῶ οὐτέων ὄψει (vel ὄψι) ὁρᾶν μακροττ′ (ττ′ suprascr.) οὐτέων γνώμη γιγνώσκει ὁ μακροττ′ (ττ′ suprascr.) γιγνώσκων P M: ἐν τῷ πρώτῳ περὶ τῆς ἀληθείας ἐν τῷ λόγῳ ταῦτα δὲ γνοὺς εἰς ἕν τε οὐδὲν αὐτῶ οὐτέων ὄψει ὁρᾷ μακρότητα οὐτέην γνώμῃ γιγνώσκει ὁ μακρότητα γιγνώσκων Chartier: alii alia (cf. comm.) **F2** codd. = P M 1 ἡγεῖται] ἡρεῖται M: αιειται P 2 ὑγείαν P **F3** codd. = F S A C B 1 καὶ παρασκεύῳ γνώμῃ F S: ἀπαρασκευαστῷ γνώμῃ B C 2–3 ἐν ταῖς … γνήσιαι om. B C

FRAGMENTS

1–44: ΠΕΡΙ ΑΛΗΘΕΙΑΣ

F1 Many times in that same first book of *Homiliae*, and in the second, Critias has used the word "mind" [*gnome*], distinguishing it from the senses, as Antiphon too does in the first book of *Truth*: **perceiving these things, you will know absolutely none of them, neither the things which he who sees farthest sees with sight, nor the things which he who perceives farthest perceives with the mind**.

F2 And: **since for all human beings the mind leads the body, both in sickness and health, and in all other things**.

F3 In *On Truth* Antiphon said **with an unprepared** [*aparaskeuos*] **mind**, but in the treatise on rhetoric "unprepared" [*aparaskeuaston*] (but the treatise is thought not to be genuine).

F4 Harpocration, s.v. ἄοπτα (α 167, 31 Keaney); cf. *Anecdota Graeca* s.v. (109 Bachmann), Photius, *Lexicon* s.v. (α 2196, 1.211 Theodoridis), *Suda* s.v. (α 2843, 1.256 Adler)

ἄοπτα· ἀντὶ τοῦ ἀόρατα καὶ οὐκ ὀφθέντα, ἀλλὰ δόξαντα ὁρᾶσθαι. Ἀντιφῶν Ἀληθείας α′.

Cf. also Pollux, 2.57–58 (1.100 Bethe) Ἀντιφῶν ... καὶ **ἄοπτα** [= F7] ... καὶ **ἄοπτα** ὡς Ἀντιφῶν.

F5 Harpocration, s.v. ἀπαθῆ (α 170, 32 Keaney); cf. *Anecdota Graeca* s.v. (109 Bachmann), *Suda* s.v. (α 2873, 1.259–60 Adler)

ἀπαθῆ· ἀντὶ τοῦ τὰ μὴ ὡς ἀληθῶς γεγονότα πάθη. Ἀντιφῶν Ἀληθείας α′.

F6 Pollux, 2.58 (1.101 Bethe)

καὶ **διοπτεύειν** Κριτίας καὶ Ἀντιφῶν, Ἀντιφῶν δὲ καὶ **εἴσοπτοι**.

F7 Pollux, 2.57 (1.100 Bethe)

Ἀντιφῶν δὲ καὶ **τὸ ὀψόμενον** εἶπε, καὶ τῇ ὄψει οἷον τοῖς ὀφθαλμοῖς, καὶ ὀπτήρ [= Antiphon, *or.* 5.27], καὶ ἄοπτα [= F4].

F8 Pollux, 2.76 (1.106 Bethe)

ἡ γὰρ ὀδμὴ καὶ εὐοδμία δοκεῖ μὲν τοῖς πολλοῖς εἶναι καλὰ

F4 1–2 ante ἀντὶ transp. Ἀντιφῶν (Ἀληθείας α′ omissis) Epit. Harp. *Anecd.* Phot. *Sud.* **F5** 1 ἀντὶ τοῦ Harp.: ὁ δὲ Ἀντιφῶν ἀπαθῆ πληθυντικῶς *Sud.*: Ἀντιφῶν Epit. Harp.: om. *Anecd.* 1–2 Ἀντιφῶν Ἀληθείας α′ om. Epit. Harp. *Anecd. Sud.* **F6** codd. = M F S A C B 1–2 καὶ διοπτεύειν ... εἴσοπτοι om. B C 1 διοκριτίας A (sine lacunae signo) 1–2 Κριτίας ... εἴσοπτοι om. M **F7** codd. = M F S A C B 1 Ἀντιφῶν ... εἶπε] ὀψώμενον δὲ παρὰ Ἀντιφῶντι M ὀψόμενος Sauppe 1–2 καὶ τῇ ὄψει ... ὀφθαλμοῖς om. M 1 οἷον] οἵως S: ἧκουν A **F8** codd. = M F S A C B 1–4 ἡ γὰρ ὀδμὴ ... τις ἂν om. B 1 ὀσμή M ἐυοσμία A M 1–2 δοκεῖ ... ἔστι δὲ om. C

F4 Unseen for "invisible" and not seen but seeming to be seen. Antiphon in the first book of *Truth*.

F5 Not experienced for experiences which did not really occur. Antiphon in the first book of *Truth*.

F6 To look into, Antiphon and Critias; and Antiphon also **visible**.

F7 Antiphon also said **that which will see**, and "with the sight" like "with the eyes," and "eyewitness," and "unseen" [= F4].

F8 "Scent" and "fragrance" seem fine words to most

τὰ ὀνόματα, ἔστι δὲ ποιητικά, ἐν δὲ τοῖς καταλογάδην Ἰωνικὰ καὶ Αἰολικά· παρὰ μόνῳ δ' Ἀντιφῶντι **ὀδμὰς** καὶ **εὐοδμίαν** εὕροι τις ἄν.

F9 Aëtius, 1.22.6 (318 Diels) [Περὶ οὐσίας χρόνου]

Ἀντιφῶν καὶ Κριτόλαος [= Critolaus, fr. 14 Wehrli] νόημα ἢ μέτρον τὸν χρόνον, οὐδ' ὑπόστασιν.

F10(a) *Suda* s.v. ἀδέητος (α 435, 1.46 Adler); cf. *Anecdota Graeca* s.v. (183 Bekker)

ἀδέητος· ὁ μηδενὸς δεόμενος καὶ πάντα ἔχων. Ἀντιφῶν ἐν α' Ἀληθείας· **διὰ τοῦτο οὐδενὸς δεῖται οὐδὲ προσδέχεται οὐδενός τι, ἀλλ' ἄπειρος καὶ ἀδέητος.**

F10(b) Harpocration, s.v. ἀδέητος (α 26, 5–6 Keaney); cf. *Anecdota Graeca* s.v. (27 Bachmann), Photius, *Lexicon* s.v. (α 329, 1.39 Theodoridis), Hesychius, s.v. (α 1031, 1.39 Latte)

ἀδέητος· ἀντὶ τοῦ ἀνενδεὴς παρ' Ἀντιφῶντι Ἀληθείας α'.

F11 Harpocration, s.v. δεήσεις (δ 8, 67 Keaney); cf. Photius, *Lexicon* s.v. (δ 98, 1.380 Theodoridis), *Anecdota Graeca Oxoniensia* s.v. (2.492 Cramer), *Suda* s.v. (δ 170, 2.16 Adler)

δεήσεις· ἀντὶ τοῦ ἐνδείας. Ἀντιφῶν Ἀληθείας α'.

Cf. also cod. Marcianus gr. 444 (saec. XIV), fol. 130r

2–4 ἐν δὲ τοῖς . . . τις ἄν om. C   2 τῇ καταλογάδην F S   3–4 καὶ Αἰολικὰ . . . τις ἄν om. M   3 μόνον A   3–4 ὀσμὰς καὶ εὐοσμίαν A   4 εὐοδμίας F S   **F9** Stob. 1.8.40[b] (codd. = F P Aug.) lemm. Ἀντιφάνης κριτόλαος add. F in marg.: ἀντιφάνης καὶ κριτόλαος P in textu   1 ἀριστοφάνης P   2 ἢ μέτρον P: ἡμέτερον F   οὐδ' F P: οὐχ Aug.   **F10(a)** codd. = A G I T S M   1–3 Ἀντιφῶν . . . ἀδέητος om. *Anecd.*   2 οὐδὲ Bernhardy: οὔτε codd.   3 ἄπηρος Sauppe: εὔπορος van Spaan   **F10(b)** 1 ante ἀντὶ add. Ἀντιφῶν Epit. Harp. *Anecd.* Phot.   ἀντὶ τοῦ om. Hesych.   παρ' Ἀντιφῶντι Ἀληθείας α' om. Epit. Harp. *Anecd.* Phot. Hesych.   **F11** 1 Ἀληθείας α': Ἀληθείας πρώτῳ *Sud.*: om. *Anecd. Oxon.*

people, but they are poetic, and in prose-writers Ionic and Aeolic. Only in Antiphon would you find **scents** and **fragrance**.

F9 Antiphon and Critolaus say that time is a thought or measure and not a substance.

F10(a) "Without needs": he who needs nothing and has everything. Antiphon in the first book of *Truth*: **for this reason he needs nothing nor accepts anything from anyone, but is without limits and without needs**.

F10(b) **Without needs** for "lacking nothing." In Antiphon in the first book of *Truth*.

F11 **Wants** for "needs." Antiphon in the first book of *Truth*.

(Keaney [1967], 212) Ἀντιφῶν δὲ **δεήσεις** ἀντὶ τοῦ ἐνδείας εἶπεν Ἀληθείας α′.

F12 Origen, *Contra Celsum* 4.25 (2.242 Borret)

εἰ δὲ τὴν τοῦ ἀνθρώπου μικρότητα οὐ διὰ τὸ σῶμα ἐξευτελίζετε ἀλλὰ διὰ τὴν ψυχήν, ὡς οὖσαν ὑποδεεστέραν τῶν λοιπῶν λογικῶν καὶ μάλιστα σπουδαίων καὶ διὰ τοῦθ' ὑποδεεστέραν, ἐπείπερ ἡ κακία ἐστὶν ἐν αὐτῇ, τί μᾶλλον οἱ ἐν Χριστιανοῖς φαῦλοι καὶ οἱ ἐν Ἰουδαίοις κακῶς βιοῦντες ὁρμαθός εἰσι νυκτερίδων ἢ μύρμηκες ἢ σκώληκες ἢ βάτραχοι, ἢ οἱ ἐν τοῖς λοιποῖς ἔθνεσι μοχθηροί; ὡς κατὰ τοῦτο πάνθ' ὁντιναοῦν μάλιστα κεχυμένῃ τῇ κακίᾳ χρώμενον νυκτερίδα καὶ σκώληκα καὶ βάτραχον καὶ μύρμηκα εἶναι ὡς πρὸς τοὺς λοιποὺς ἀνθρώπους. κἂν Δημοσθένης τις οὖν ὁ ῥήτωρ ᾖ μετὰ τῆς παραπλησίας ἐκείνῳ κακίας καὶ τῶν ἀπὸ κακίας αὐτῷ πεπραγμένων, κἂν Ἀντιφῶν ἄλλος ῥήτωρ νομιζόμενος εἶναι καὶ τὴν πρόνοιαν ἀναιρῶν ἐν τοῖς ἐπιγεγραμμένοις Περὶ ἀληθείας παραπλησίως τῇ Κέλσου ἐπιγραφῇ· οὐδὲν ἧττόν εἰσιν οὗτοι σκώληκες ἐν βορβόρου γωνίᾳ τοῦ τῆς ἀμαθίας καὶ ἀγνοίας καλινδούμενοι.

F13(a) Aristotle, *Physics* 185a14–17

ἅμα δ' οὐδὲ λύειν ἅπαντα προσήκει, ἀλλ' ἢ ὅσα ἐκ τῶν ἀρχῶν τις ἐπιδεικνὺς ψεύδεται, ὅσα δὲ μή, οὔ, οἷον τὸν τετραγωνισμὸν τὸν μὲν διὰ τῶν τμημάτων γεωμετρικοῦ διαλῦσαι, τὸν δὲ Ἀντιφῶντος οὐ γεωμετρικοῦ.

F13(b) Aristotle, *Sophistici elenchi* 171b34–172a7

ὁ δ' ἐριστικός ἐστί πως οὕτως ἔχων πρὸς τὸν διαλεκτικὸν ὡς ὁ ψευδογράφος πρὸς τὸν γεωμετρικόν· ἐκ γὰρ τῶν

F12 8 ὁντιναοῦν φαῦλον Koetschau 13 ῥήτωρ] τοῦ ῥήτορος Norden **F13(a)** codd. = E F I J et Phil. 3 post τετραγωνισμὸν add. τοῦ κύκλου I J post corr. Phil. διὰ om. I γεωμέτρου I **F13(b)** codd. = A B C D u et Boeth. Soph. Mich.^{c,p} 2 γεωμετρικόν codd. Boeth.: γεωμέτρην Mich.^{c} Soph.

F12 If you disparage a man's meanness on account not of his body but of his soul, on the grounds that it is inferior to the souls of other rational beings (especially those that are good), and inferior for this reason, because there is vice in it – why, then, are bad Christians and bad-living Jews a cluster of bats, ants, worms, or frogs any more than evil men of other races? So that on this view, anyone at all who practices vice in special profusion is a bat, worm, frog or ant in comparison with the rest of men. Whether one is a Demosthenes, the orator, with vice like his and the vicious actions performed by him; or an Antiphon, thought to be another orator, who did away with divine providence in his work entitled *On Truth* (like Celsus' title) – no less are people like these worms, wallowing in a muddy corner of folly and ignorance.

F13(a) At the same time, it is not actually necessary to solve all difficulties, but only those that are falsely arrived at from the principles; those that are not, it is not necessary to solve. It is a geometer's task, for example, to refute the quadrature by means of segments. But the quadrature of Antiphon it is not a geometer's task to refute.

F13(b) The eristic argument is related to the dialectical argument somewhat as the drawer of false diagrams is

αὐτῶν τῷ διαλεκτικῷ παραλογίζεται, καὶ ὁ ψευδογράφος τῷ γεωμέτρῃ. ἀλλ᾽ ὁ μὲν οὐκ ἐριστικός, ὅτι ἐκ τῶν ἀρχῶν καὶ συμπερασμάτων τῶν ὑπὸ τὴν τέχνην ψευδογραφεῖ· ὁ δ᾽ ὑπὸ τὴν διαλεκτικὴν περὶ τἆλλα ὅτι ἐριστικὸς ἔσται δῆλον. οἷον ὁ τετραγωνισμὸς ὁ μὲν διὰ τῶν μηνίσκων οὐκ ἐριστικός, ὁ δὲ Βρύσωνος ἐριστικός· καὶ τὸν μὲν οὐκ ἔστι μετενεγκεῖν ἀλλ᾽ ἢ πρὸς γεωμετρίαν μόνον, διὰ τὸ ἐκ τῶν ἰδίων εἶναι ἀρχῶν, τὸν δὲ πρὸς πολλούς, ὅσοι μὴ ἴσασι τὸ δυνατὸν ἐν ἑκάστῳ καὶ τὸ ἀδύνατον· ἁρμόσει γάρ. ἢ ὡς Ἀντιφῶν ἐτετραγώνιζεν.

F13(c) Themistius, *In Aristotelis Physica paraphrasis* 3.27–4.8 Schenkl

εἰ μὲν οὖν τηροῦντες τὰς ἀρχὰς ἐν τοῖς ἑξῆς τι παρελογίζοντο, ἀκόλουθον ἦν ἐπιδεικνύναι τῷ φυσικῷ, πῇ φενακίζουσιν· εἰ δὲ δι᾽ ὧν παρακρούονται τὰς ἀρχὰς αὐτὰς ἀναιροῦσιν, οὐκ οἰκεῖον τὸ λύειν τοὺς λόγους αὐτῶν τοῦ μετιόντος τὴν ἐπιστήμην, ἐπεὶ καὶ τὰ ψευδογραφήματα ὅσα μὲν σῴζει τὰς γεωμετρικὰς ὑποθέσεις λυτέον τῷ γεωμετρῇ, ὅσα δὲ μάχεται πρὸς ἐκείνας, παραιτητέον, οἷον δύο τινὲς κύκλον ἐπιχειρήσαντες τετραγωνίζειν Ἱπποκράτης τε ὁ Χῖος καὶ ὁ Ἀντιφῶν. τὸν μὲν οὖν Ἱπποκράτους λυτέον· τὰς γὰρ ἀρχὰς φυλάττων παραλογίζεται τῷ μόνον μὲν ἐκεῖνον τὸν μηνίσκον τε-

3 τῷ διαλεκτικῷ Wallies: τῇ διαλεκτικῇ codd. Mich.[c] Soph. Boeth. παραλογίζεται A B D Boeth. Mich.[c] Soph.: παραλογίζονται C u καὶ] καθάπερ (παραλογίζεται add. C D) καὶ C u D Boeth.: καθάπερ Soph.: ὥσπερ καὶ Mich.[p] 4 τῷ γεωμέτρῃ Poste: τὸν γεωμέτρην A B D u Soph.: τὸν γεωμετρικόν C: τῇ γεωμετρίᾳ Mich.[p] 6 περὶ μὲν A B C D Boeth. τἆλλα μαθήματα D 9 ἔσται u ἄλλη ἢ Soph. μόνην γεωμετρίαν Soph. 10 πολλούς codd. Mich.[c] Boeth.: πολλά Mich.[p] Soph. 12 ἁρμόζει u **F13(c)** codd. = B L M W a 2 δεικνύναι W 3–4 τὰς αὐτὰς ἀρχὰς L 6 μὲν om. W 7 ἐκείνας W post corr. L: ἐκείνους M W ante corr.: ἐκεῖνα B 8–9 τετραγωνίζειν ἐπιχειρήσαντες W: ἐπεχείρησαν τετραγωνίζειν L 9 τε] δὲ B ante corr. ὁ alt. om. B post corr. L 11 τῷ L: τὸ M W B

related to the geometer. For the eristic argument draws false conclusions from the same principles as the dialectical one, and the drawer of false diagrams draws conclusions from the same principles as the geometer. Yet the drawer of false diagrams is not eristic, because he draws his false diagrams in accordance with the principles and conclusions that fall under the art of geometry. But the argument that falls under the art of dialectic will clearly be eristic in the case of other subjects. For example, the quadrature by means of lunes is not eristic, but that of Bryson is. The former cannot be transposed to any subject outside geometry, since it proceeds from peculiar principles. But the latter can be transposed against many people, namely all who do not know what is possible and impossible in each subject – for it will fit. Or as Antiphon tried to square the circle.

F13(c) Now if they preserved the principles but drew some false inference in the conclusions, it would be the natural philosopher's task to show where they cheat. But if by their fallacies they do away with the very principles, the refutation of their arguments does not belong to the practitioner of science. For in the case of false diagrams too, the geometer should refute those that preserve the assumptions of geometry, but decline to refute those that conflict with them. A certain pair, for instance, tried to square the circle – Hippocrates of Chios and Antiphon. The quadrature of Hippocrates should be refuted, for it preserves the principles and is fallacious by reason of the fact that it squares only the lune inscribed about the side

τραγωνίσαι ὃς γράφεται περὶ τὴν τοῦ τετραγώνου πλευρὰν τοῦ εἰς τὸν κύκλον ἐγγραφομένου, * * * ἀπόδειξιν· πρὸς Ἀντιφῶντα δὲ οὐκέτ᾽ ἂν ἔχοι λέγειν ὁ γεωμέτρης, ὃς ἐγγράφων τρίγωνον ἰσόπλευρον εἰς τὸν κύκλον καὶ ἐφ᾽ ἑκάστης τῶν πλευρῶν ἕτερον ἰσοσκελὲς συνιστὰς πρὸς τῇ περιφερείᾳ τοῦ κύκλου καὶ τοῦτο ἐφεξῆς ποιῶν ᾤετό ποτε ἐφαρμόσειν τοῦ τελευταίου τριγώνου τὴν πλευρὰν εὐθεῖαν οὖσαν τῇ περιφερείᾳ. τοῦτο δὲ τὴν ἐπ᾽ ἄπειρον τομὴν ἀναιροῦντος ἣν ὑπόθεσιν ὁ γεωμέτρης λαμβάνει.

F13(d) Philoponus, *In Aristotelis Physica* 31.9–24, 27–32.3 Vitelli

ὁ δὲ Ἀντιφῶν καὶ αὐτὸς ἐπεχείρησε τετραγωνίσαι τὸν κύκλον, ἀλλ᾽ οὐ σῴζων τὰς γεωμετρικὰς ἀρχάς. ἐπεχείρησε δὲ οὕτως. ἐάν, φησί, ποιήσω κύκλον καὶ γράψω ἐντὸς τετράγωνον, τέμω δὲ τὰ τμήματα τοῦ κύκλου τὰ γενόμενα ἐκ τοῦ τετραγώνου δίχα, εἶτα ἀγάγω εὐθείας ἀπὸ τῆς τομῆς ἑκατέρωθεν ἐπὶ τὰ πέρατα τοῦ τμήματος, ποιῶ ὀκτάγωνον σχῆμα. ἐὰν δὲ πάλιν τὰ περιέχοντα τὰς γωνίας τμήματα τέμωμεν δίχα, καὶ πάλιν ἀγάγωμεν ἀπὸ τῶν τομῶν εὐθείας ἑκατέρωθεν ἐπὶ τὰ πέρατα τῶν τμημάτων, ποιοῦμεν πολύγωνον σχῆμα. ἐὰν οὖν ἐπὶ πολὺ τοῦτο ποιῶμεν, γίνεται πολυγωνότατον σχῆμα μικρὰς πάνυ ἔχον τὰς γωνίας, ἃς αἱ περιέχουσαι εὐθεῖαι διὰ τὸ σμικρὰς πάνυ εἶναι ἐφαρμόσουσι τῷ κύκλῳ. ἐπεὶ οὖν δέδοται πᾶν τὸ δοθὲν εὐθύγραμμον σχῆμα τετραγωνίσαι, ἐὰν τετραγωνίσω τὸ πολύγωνον τοῦτο, ἐπειδὴ

12 παρὰ M   13 lacuna in L expleta est his verbis insertis: πάντα δὲ μηνίσκον οἷόν τε τετραγωνίζειν λαβεῖν εἰς (ex Simpl., *In Arist. Phys.* 58.16)   15 τὸ B   16 ἑκάστῃ L   17 συνιστὰς B post corr. L (compendium habet B ante corr.): συνιστᾶ M W   20 δὲ M: δὲ ἣν W B: δ᾽ ἣν L: δὲ ἣν ⟨τοῦ⟩ Diels   **F13(d)** codd. = K L M R t   1 τὸν] τὴν t   6 τὰ πέρατα τοῦ (πέρατα τοῦ add. in marg. L) τμήματος K L: τὰ τοῦ τμήματος πέρατα M t   8 τέμω L   11 ποιῶμεν τοῦτο L   12 ἔχοντα L   15–16 ἐὰν . . . τετραγωνίσας om. K sed add. in marg.

of a square inscribed in a circle ... demonstration. But to Antiphon the geometer would no longer be able to reply. He inscribed an equilateral triangle in a circle, and on each of the triangle's sides constructed another, equilateral triangle with its vertex on the circumference of the circle. And continuing this process, he supposed that at some point the side of the final triangle, though a straight line, would coincide with the circumference. But this is the mark of one who does away with infinite divisibility, which the geometer takes as an assumption.

F13(d) Antiphon too tried to square the circle, but without preserving the principles of geometry. This is how he did it: if (he says) I construct a circle and inscribe a square in it, and divide in two the circle-segments produced by the square, and then draw straight lines on each side from the point of division to the end-points of the segment, I produce an octagon. If we again divide in half the segments enclosing the angles, and again draw straight lines on each side from the points of division to the end-points of the segments, we produce a polygonal figure. Now if we do this for a long time, a figure with very many sides and very small angles is produced; and the straight lines enclosing these angles will coincide with the circle, since they are very small. Granted, then, that any given rectilinear figure can be squared, if I square this polygon, I shall have

ἐφαρμόζει τῷ κύκλῳ, τετραγωνίσας ἔσομαι καὶ τὸν κύκλον. οὗτος οὖν ἀναιρεῖ τὰς γεωμετρικὰς ἀρχάς· ἀρχὴ γάρ ἐστι γεωμετρικὴ μηδέποτε ἐφαρμόζειν εὐθεῖαν περιφερείᾳ, οὗτος δὲ δίδωσι, διὰ σμικρότητα, τινὰ εὐθεῖαν ἐφαρμόζειν τινὶ περιφερείᾳ ... ὁ μέντοι Ἀντιφῶν ἀνελὼν τὰς γεωμετρικὰς ἀρχάς, τὸ μηδέποτε περιφερείᾳ εὐθεῖαν ἐφαρμόζειν, οὕτω τὸ ἑξῆς συνεπέρανεν. φησὶν οὖν ὅτι τὸν τετραγωνισμὸν τοῦ κύκλου ἐλέγξαι ψευδῆ ὄντα τὸν μὲν Ἱπποκράτους γεωμετρικοῦ ἐστι διαλῦσαι, ὡς φυλάττοντος τοῦ Ἱπποκράτους τὰς γεωμετρικὰς ἀρχάς, τὸν δὲ Ἀντιφῶντος οὐκέτι διαλύσει ὁ γεωμέτρης, ἐπεὶ ἀνῃρημένων τῶν γεωμετρικῶν ἀρχῶν οὕτω συνῆκται.

Cf. *In Aristotelis Analytica posteriora* 149.10–14 Wallies οἷον ζητεῖται παρὰ τοῖς γεωμέτραις ὁ τοῦ κύκλου τετραγωνισμός· καὶ τοῦτον [μὲν] Ἀντιφῶν μὲν καὶ Βρύσων ἔδοξαν εὑρηκέναι, κακῶς αἰτοῦντες δοθῆναι αὐτοῖς οἷς μὴ συγχωρήσαιεν ἂν γεωμέτραι, ὁ μὲν εὐθεῖαν ἐφαρμόζειν περιφερείᾳ, ὁ δὲ οὗ ἔστι μεῖζον καὶ ἔλαττον ἀνομογενές, τούτου εἶναι καὶ ἴσον.

Cf. also *In Aristotelis Physica* 206.20–25 Vitelli ἀνάγκη γὰρ τὸν τοιοῦτον διὰ τῶν ἀσαφῶν τὰ σαφῆ κατασκευάζειν, οἷος ἦν Αντιφῶν πειραθεὶς δι᾽ ἀποδείξεως δεῖξαι ὅτι τὰ τῷ αὐτῷ ἴσα καὶ ἀλλήλοις ἐστὶν ἴσα, ὃς καὶ ἐν τῷ τετραγωνισμῷ τοῦ κύκλου ἑαυτὸν παρελογίσατο· τὰ γὰρ τῷ αὐτῷ, φησίν, ἴσα τὸν αὐτὸν τόπον κατέχει, τὰ τὸν αὐτὸν τόπον κατέχοντα καὶ ἀλλήλοις ἴσα, τὰ τῷ αὐτῷ ἄρα ἴσα καὶ ἀλλήλοις ἐστὶν ἴσα.

18–19 εὐθεῖαν περιφερεία L: εὐθεῖα περιφερεία K: εὐθείᾳ περιφέρειαν M t   19–20 οὗτος δὲ ... περιφερείᾳ om. M t   20 τινὶ περιφερεία L: περιφερεία τινί K   20–22 ὁ μέντοι ... τὸ ἑξῆς om. L M t   22 οὖν M t: δὲ K: om. L   24 ἱπποκράτους t: ἱππκτ′ (κτ′ suprascr.) K: ἱπποκράτην L M   εἶναι K   24–25 φυλάσσοντος L   27 οὗτος R

squared the circle as well, since the polygon coincides with it. Antiphon, then, does away with the principles of geometry. For it is a geometrical principle that a straight line never coincides with an arc of a circle, whereas he allows a certain straight line to coincide with a certain arc, on account of its smallness.... Antiphon, however, concluded in this fashion, doing away with the principles of geometry (that a straight line never coincides with a circle-arc). Now Aristotle says that it is the geometer's task to prove Hippocrates' circle-quadrature false, since Hippocrates preserves the principles of geometry. But Antiphon's quadrature the geometer will not refute, since it was brought to such a conclusion, with the principles of geometry done away with.

For instance, among the geometers the quadrature of the circle is sought. Antiphon and Bryson thought that they had discovered it, wrongly asking that assumptions be granted which geometers would not assent to: in the case of the former, that a straight line coincide with a circumference; in the case of the latter, that to something than which there exists a greater and a smaller of a different kind, there exist also an equal.

This sort of person necessarily establishes the evident through what is not evident, just as Antiphon tried to demonstrate that things equal to the same thing are equal to each other, who also misled himself by fallacious reasoning in the squaring of the circle. For, he says, things that are equal to the same thing occupy the same place; things that occupy the same place are also equal to each other; therefore, things that are equal to the same thing are also equal to each other.

F13(e) Simplicius, *In Aristotelis Physica* 54.12–55.24 Diels

τὸν γὰρ τετραγωνισμὸν τοῦ κύκλου πολλῶν ζητούντων (τοῦτο δὲ ἦν τὸ κύκλῳ ἴσον τετράγωνον θέσθαι) καὶ Ἀντιφῶν ἐνόμισεν εὑρίσκειν καὶ Ἱπποκράτης ὁ Χῖος, ψευσθέντες. ἀλλὰ τὸ μὲν Ἀντιφῶντος ψεῦδος διὰ τὸ μὴ ἀπὸ γεωμετρικῶν ἀρχῶν ὡρμῆσθαι ὡς μαθησόμεθα οὐκ ἔστι γεωμετρικοῦ λύειν, τὸ δὲ Ἱπποκράτους, ἐπειδὴ τὰς ἀρχὰς φυλάξας τὰς γεωμετρικὰς ἐψεύσθη, γεωμετρικοῦ λύειν. ἐκείνους γὰρ δεῖ λύειν μόνους τοὺς λόγους ὅσοι τηροῦντες τὰς οἰκείας ἀρχὰς τῆς μεθόδου οὕτως παραλογίζονται, τοὺς δὲ δι᾽ ὧν παρακρούονται ἀναιροῦντας τὰς ἀρχὰς οὐ λυτέον.

ὁ δὲ Ἀντιφῶν γράψας κύκλον ἐνέγραψέ τι χωρίον εἰς αὐτὸν πολύγωνον τῶν ἐγγράφεσθαι δυναμένων. ἔστω δὲ εἰ τύχοι τετράγωνον τὸ ἐγγεγραμμένον. ἔπειτα ἑκάστην τῶν τοῦ τετραγώνου πλευρῶν δίχα τέμνων ἀπὸ τῆς τομῆς ἐπὶ τὰς περιφερείας πρὸς ὀρθὰς ἦγε γραμμάς, αἳ δηλονότι δίχα ἔτεμνον ἑκάστη τὸ καθ᾽ αὑτὴν τμῆμα τοῦ κύκλου. ἔπειτα ἀπὸ τῆς τομῆς ἐπεζεύγνυεν ἐπὶ τὰ πέρατα τῶν γραμμῶν τοῦ τετραγώνου εὐθείας, ὡς γίνεσθαι τέτταρα τρίγωνα τὰ ἀπὸ τῶν εὐθειῶν, τὸ δὲ ὅλον σχῆμα τὸ ἐγγεγραμμένον ὀκτάγωνον. καὶ οὕτως πάλιν κατὰ τὴν αὐτὴν μέθοδον, ἑκάστην τῶν τοῦ ὀκταγώνου πλευρῶν δίχα τέμνων, ἀπὸ τῆς τομῆς ἐπὶ τὴν περιφέρειαν πρὸς ὀρθὰς ἄγων καὶ ἐπιζευγνὺς ἀπὸ τῶν σημείων, καθ᾽ ἃ αἱ πρὸς ὀρθὰς ἀχθεῖσαι ἐφήπτοντο τῶν περιφερειῶν, εὐθείας ἐπὶ τὰ πέρατα τῶν διῃρημένων εὐθειῶν, ἑκκαιδεκάγωνον ἐποίει τὸ ἐγγραφόμενον. καὶ κατὰ τὸν αὐτὸν πάλιν λόγον τέμνων τὰς πλευρὰς τοῦ

F13(e) codd. = D E E^b F a   2 τὸ τῷ κύκλῳ a   5 ὡρμᾶσθαι E^b 8 δεῖ om. F   9 παρασυλλογίζονται a   10 ἀναιροῦντας D E^b F (in rasura): ἀναιροῦντες a   16 τὴν περιφέρειαν Torstrik   18 ἀπὸ a: ἐπὶ D E^b F   20–21 τὸ ἐγγεγραμμένον σχῆμα a F   22 τὴν om. E^b ἑκάστην τὴν τοῦ F   25 καθὰ D   26 τὰ πέρατα om. D   διειρημένων E^b ante corr.   27–28 ἑκκαιδεκάγωνον . . . πλευρὰς τοῦ om. E^b 28 πάλιν λόγον D: λόγον πάλιν a F

F13(e) While many sought the quadrature of the circle (this was the construction of a square equal to a circle), Antiphon and Hippocrates of Chios both believed that they found it – falsely so. But Antiphon's fallacy it is not the geometer's task to solve, on account of the fact that it is not based on geometric principles (as we shall learn), whereas Hippocrates' fallacy is for the geometer to solve, since he committed it while preserving the principles of geometry. For only those arguments that preserve the principles proper to the method of investigation while drawing false conclusions should be refuted. Those that violate the principles through their fallacies need not be refuted.

Antiphon drew a circle, and inscribed in it one of the polygonal figures that can be inscribed. Let the inscribed figure be (say) a square. Then, dividing each of the square's sides in two, he drew lines at right angles from the point(s) of division to the arcs of the circle, each line obviously dividing its own circle-segment in half. Then, from the point(s) of division on the arcs he connected straight lines to the end-points of the square's sides, so as to produce four triangles from the straight lines and make the whole inscribed figure an octagon. So again by the same procedure – dividing each of the octagon's sides in half, drawing lines at right angles to the arc from the point(s) of division, and connecting straight lines to the end-points of the octagon's divided sides from the points at which the lines drawn at right angles touched the arc of the circle – he made the inscribed figure a polygon of sixteen sides. Dividing the sides of the inscribed sixteen-sided polygon in

ἑκκαιδεκαγώνου τοῦ ἐγγεγραμμένου καὶ ἐπιζευγνὺς εὐθείας καὶ διπλασιάζων τὸ ἐγγραφόμενον πολύγωνον καὶ τοῦτο ἀεὶ ποιῶν ᾤετο ποτὲ δαπανωμένου τοῦ ἐπιπέδου ἐγγραφήσεσθαί τι πολύγωνον τούτῳ τῷ τρόπῳ ἐν τῷ κύκλῳ, οὗ αἱ πλευραὶ διὰ σμικρότητα ἐφαρμόσουσι τῇ τοῦ κύκλου περιφερείᾳ. παντὶ δὲ πολυγώνῳ ἴσον τετράγωνον δυνάμενοι θέσθαι, ὡς ἐν τοῖς Στοιχείοις παρελάβομεν, διὰ τὸ ἴσον ὑποκεῖσθαι τὸ πολύγωνον τῷ κύκλῳ ἐφαρμόζον αὐτῷ, ἐσόμεθα καὶ κύκλῳ ἴσον τιθέντες τετράγωνον.

καὶ δῆλον ὅτι ἡ συναγωγὴ παρὰ τὰς γεωμετρικὰς ἀρχὰς γέγονεν οὐχ ὡς ὁ Ἀλέξανδρός φησιν, Ὅτι ὑποτίθεται μὲν ὁ γεωμέτρης τὸ τὸν κύκλον τῆς εὐθείας κατὰ σημεῖον ἅπτεσθαι ὡς ἀρχήν, ὁ δὲ Ἀντιφῶν ἀναιρεῖ τοῦτο. οὐ γὰρ ὑποτίθεται ὁ γεωμέτρης τοῦτο, ἀλλ' ἀποδείκνυσιν αὐτὸ ἐν τῷ τρίτῳ βιβλίῳ. ἄμεινον οὖν λέγειν ἀρχὴν εἶναι τὸ ἀδύνατον εἶναι εὐθεῖαν ἐφαρμόσαι περιφερείᾳ, ἀλλ' ἡ μὲν ἐκτὸς κατὰ ἓν σημεῖον ἐφάψεται τοῦ κύκλου, ἡ δὲ ἐντὸς κατὰ δύο μόνον καὶ οὐ πλείω, καὶ ἡ ἐπαφὴ κατὰ σημεῖον γίνεται. καὶ μέντοι τέμνων ἀεὶ τὸ μεταξὺ τῆς εὐθείας καὶ τῆς τοῦ κύκλου περιφερείας ἐπίπεδον οὐ δαπανήσει αὐτὸ οὐδὲ καταλήψεταί ποτε τὴν τοῦ κύκλου περιφέρειαν, εἴπερ ἐπ' ἄπειρόν ἐστι διαιρετὸν τὸ ἐπίπεδον. εἰ δὲ καταλαμβάνει, ἀνῄρηταί τις ἀρχὴ γεωμετρικὴ ἡ λέγουσα ἐπ' ἄπειρον εἶναι τὰ μεγέθη διαιρετά. καὶ ταύτην καὶ ὁ Εὐ-

30 ἐγγεγραφόμενον a 31 ἐποίει Torstrik: ποιῶν ⟨τὸ ἐπίπεδον τὸ μεταξὺ τοῦ πολυγώνου καὶ τῆς περιφερείας ἔλαττον ἐποίει⟩ Usener ᾤετο ποτὲ Diels: ὥστε ποτὲ E^b (obl. D): ὡς τὸ ποτὲ F: ἕως οὗ a post δαπανωμένου add. ταύτῃ a post ἐπιπέδου add. ἔμελλεν a 33 μικρότητα a 35 δυνάμεθα a 35–36 παρέλαβον F 36 διὰ D E^b: ὡς διὰ F: ὥστε διὰ a 37–38 ἐφαρμόζοντες τετράγωνον (αὐτῷ ... τιθέντες interceptis) F: ἐφαρμόζοντες τετράγωνον ἴσον αὐτῷ, ἐσόμεθα κτλ. a 40 δέ φησιν a 41 τὸ om. a F τὸν om. D 43 ἀλλὰ δείκνυσιν (ὰ δείκν in rasura) F 44 τῷ τρίτῳ] τῶ ιγ D F: τῷ ὀγδόῳ a E^b εἶναι ἀρχὴν λέγειν a 44–45 ἀδύνατον τὸ [εἶναι] Schmidt Rudio 46 ἐφάψεται E^b F: ἐφάπτεται a D 47 κατὰ ⟨ἓν⟩ σημεῖον Tannery 48 ante τὸ spatium quattuor litterarum habet D 51 διαιρεῖν a

the same way again, connecting straight lines, and doubling the inscribed polygon, and doing this continually, he thought that at some point, with the area of the circle progressively exhausted, a polygon would be inscribed whose sides would coincide with the circumference of the circle, on account of their smallness. Since (as we learned in the *Elements*) we are able to construct a square equal to any polygon, we will have constructed as well a square equal to a circle, because the polygon coinciding with the circle is assumed to be equal to it.

Clearly the conclusion is against the principles of geometry not (as Alexander claims) "because the geometer assumes as a principle that a circle touches a straight line at a point, and Antiphon does away with this." For the geometer does not assume this, but proves it in the third book [*sc.* of the *Elements*]. It is better, then, to say it is a principle that a straight line cannot coincide with an arc, and that a line outside a circle will touch it at one point, one inside will touch it at two points only and not more, and that the contact takes place at a point. He will not exhaust the area between the straight line and the arc of the circle by continually dividing it, of course, nor will he ever reach the circumference of the circle, since the area is infinitely divisible. If he does reach it, a geometrical principle has been violated: the one which says that magnitudes are infinitely divisible. This is the principle that Eudemus too

δημος [= fr. 140 Wehrli] τὴν ἀρχὴν ἀναιρεῖσθαί φησιν ὑπὸ τοῦ Ἀντιφῶντος.

F13(f) Eutocius, *In Archimedis Dimensionem circuli* (3.228 Heiberg)

εἴη δ᾽ ἂν ὡς πρὸς τὸ προκείμενον ἐφεξῆς τὸ γεγραμμένον Ἀρχιμήδει βιβλίδιον Κύκλου μέτρησιν τὴν ἐπιγραφὴν ἔχον, ἐν ᾧ τὴν πρόθεσιν τἀνδρὸς ἐξ αὐτῆς τῆς ἐπιγραφῆς γνωρίζομεν· βούλεται γὰρ ἐπιδεῖξαι, τίνι χωρίῳ εὐθυγράμμῳ ἴσος ἂν εἴη κύκλος, πρᾶγμα πάλαι πρὸς τῶν πρὸ αὐτοῦ κλεινῶν φιλοσόφων ἐζητημένον. δῆλον γὰρ ὅτι τουτὶ ἂν εἴη τὸ ζητούμενον ὅπερ Ἱπποκράτης τε Χῖος καὶ Ἀντιφῶν ζητήσαντες ἐπιμελῶς ἐκείνους ἡμῖν τοὺς παραλογισμοὺς εὑρήκασιν, οὓς ἀκριβῶς εἰδέναι νομίζω τούς τε τὴν Εὐδήμου Γεωμετρικὴν ἱστορίαν ἐπεσκεμμένους καὶ τῶν Ἀριστοτελικῶν μετασχόντας κηρίων.

F13(g) [Alexander], *In Aristotelis Sophisticos elenchos* 90.6–10 Wallies

οὐκ ἐριστικὰ οὖν τὰ ψευδογραφήματα, ὅτι ἀπὸ τῶν οἰκείων ἀρχῶν παραλογίζονται, οὐδὲ εἴ τί ἐστι ψευδογράφημα περὶ ἀληθές, ἐριστικὸν ἔσται, οἷος ὁ τοῦ Ἱπποκράτους καὶ ὁ διὰ τῶν μηνίσκων τοῦ Ἀντιφῶντος τοῦ κύκλου τετραγωνισμός· οὐ γάρ εἰσιν ἐριστικοί, ὅτι τηροῦσι τὰς οἰκείας ἀρχὰς τῆς γεωμετρίας.

Cf. ibid. 92.22–24 Wallies ἢ καὶ οὕτως συμβιβάσεις τὸ ἀπορούμενον ὡδὶ λέγων· τὸν μὲν τοῦ Ἀντιφῶντος [*sc.* τετραγωνισόν], δηλονότι τὸν διὰ τῶν μηνίσκων, οὐκ ἔστι μετενεγκεῖν κτλ.

F13(h) [Alexander-2] = Michael of Ephesus, *In Sophisticos elenchos* 171b11 (3.235 Ebbesen)

54 τὴν ἀρχὴν post φησιν transp. F: om. a **F13(f)** codd. = A (D E G H) Basil. 6 ἐζητημένον Wallis: ἐζητημένων Basil.: ἐξητημενον A **F13(g)** codd. = I a 3 ἔσται a: om. I **F13(h)** cod. = Vaticanus gr. 1770 (saec. XVI): fol. 46v

claims Antiphon does away with.

F13(f) Next, in accordance with our task, is the little book written by Archimedes which has as its title *Measurement of the Circle*, in which we learn the man's intention from the title itself. For he wants to show what rectilinear figure a circle is equal to, something investigated long ago by the famous philosophers who preceded him. For clearly this is the very problem that Hippocrates of Chios and Antiphon both were carefully investigating when they discovered for us the paralogisms which those who have examined Eudemus' *History of Geometry*, and those familiar with the Aristotelian honeycomb, have (I think) a precise knowledge of.

F13(g) False diagrams, then, are not eristic, since they draw false conclusions from the principles proper to a subject. Nor will a false diagram about something true be eristic, for example Hippocrates' quadrature of the circle and Antiphon's quadrature by means of lunes. They are not eristic, since they preserve the principles proper to geometry.

τοιοῦτος καὶ ὁ τοῦ Ἱπποκράτους καὶ Ἀντιφῶντος τοῦ κύκλου τετραγωνισμός· οὐδὲ γὰρ οὗτοι ἐριστικοί, ὅτι τηροῦσι τὰς οἰκείας ἀρχὰς τῆς γεωμετρίας.

F13(i) Scholium on Aristotle, *Sophistici elenchi* 171b14–15 (2.182–83 Ebbesen)

τὸ περὶ ἀληθές, ὅτι τὰ μὲν ψευδογραφήματα περὶ ψεῦδος γίνονται· ψεῦδος γὰρ συνάγουσιν, οἷον τὸ τὰς δύο τοῦ τριγώνου πλευρὰς ἴσας τῇ μιᾷ εἶναι ἢ ἐλάττους αὐτῆς. ὁ δὲ Ἱπποκράτης ἢ ὁ Ἀντιφῶν ἢ ὁ Βρύσων ἀληθὲς συνῆγον διὰ ψευδῶν, οἱ μὲν διὰ γεωμετρικῶν, ὁ δὲ Βρύσων οὐ διὰ τοιούτων.

F13(j) "Alexander" on *Sophistici elenchi* 172a7 (2.509–10, 553 Ebbesen)

1. Anonymus Laudianus, *Commentarium in Sophisticos elenchos*

COMMENTATOR dicit probationem Antiphonis fuisse ex propriis, et tamen in margine ponit exemplum et de tribus quadratis et uno circulo et de tribus circulis et uno quadrato, cum tamen esset in his probatio ex communibus.

2. Scholium

ut id est sicut Antipho probavit quadraturum circuli, et dicit Alexander quod easdem propositiones sumpsit quas Bryso aut consimiles.

3. Scholium

[......] ratio Antiphonis modo non redditur ad memoriam propter antiquitatem, neque sciunt modo, ut GLOSSULAE dicunt ...

F13(i) codd. = Angelicanus gr. 42 (saec. XIV ineuntis): fol. 393r et Marcianus gr. 203(746) (saec. XIV): fol. 212(202)r 3 ἴσως 203 4–5 συνῆγον] -ον ex -ων 203 6 τούτων 203 **F13(j)1** *cod. = Laudianus misc. 368 (saec. XII/XIII): fol. 221rB–vA* 2 probationem] *lectio incerta* 3 ponit exemplum] *lectio incerta* **F13(j)2** *cod. = Parisinus lat. 6294 (saec. XIII exeuntis): fol. 15r in marg.* **F13(j)3** *cod. = Monacensis clm 370 (saec. XIII exeuntis): fol. 8r in marg.*

F13(h) Such also was Hippocrates' and Antiphon's quadrature of the circle. These are not eristic either, since they preserve the principles proper to geometry.

F13(i) The phrase "about something true," because false diagrams are about something false. For they draw a false conclusion, for example that two sides of a triangle are equal to the third side, or less than it. But Hippocrates or Antiphon or Bryson drew a true conclusion through false arguments: Hippocrates and Antiphon through arguments belonging to geometry, Bryson not through such arguments.

F13(j) 1. The commentator says that Antiphon's demonstration was from proper principles. Yet in the margin he puts a diagram of three squares and one circle, and of three circles and one square, though the demonstration in these was from common principles.

2. "As": that is, as Antiphon proved the quadrature of the circle. Alexander says that he adopted the same or similar premisses as Bryson.

3. Antiphon's method is not remembered on account of its antiquity, nor do they know, as the GLOSSULAE say . . .

F13(k) Anonymus, *In Aristotelis Sophisticos elenchos paraphrasis* 29.27–37 Hayduck

τοιοῦτοι δὲ οἷον τὸ τοῦ Ἱπποκράτους τοῦ Χίου ψευδογράφημα ἐπὶ τὸν τοῦ κύκλου τετραγωνισμὸν καὶ τὸ τοῦ Ἀντιφῶντος. ὁ μὲν γὰρ ἐν κύκλῳ περιγράψας τετράγωνον τὰ μέσα ἐμβαδὰ τῶν τετραγωνικῶν πλευρῶν καὶ τῆς τοῦ κύκλου περιφερείας καταναλῶσαι ᾤετο διὰ γραφῆς τριγώνων ἰσοσκελῶν, ὡς ἂν τοῦτο λαβὼν ἕξει καὶ τὸ ἐπίλοιπον τοῦ τετραγώνου (τοῦτο δ᾽ ἦν ὁ κύκλος) τῷ ὡς ἓν ἀμφότερα τὸ ὅλον εἶναι τετράγωνον. ἀλλὰ τοῦτο ἀδύνατον τῷ τὸ μέγεθος εἰς ἄπειρα εἶναι διαιρετόν. ὁ μέντοι Ἀντιφῶν ἐπεχείρει διὰ τῶν μηνίσκων ἑτέρως· ἐπεὶ δὲ πραγματειωδεστάτη ἡ τοιαύτη ἀπόδειξις τοῖς ἀγεωμετρήτως ὑμῶν ἐντυγχάνουσιν, παρεῖται. ὅμως μέντοι ἀμφότεροι ὡς ἁπλῶς ἐκ γεωμετρίας τοὺς λόγους ποιούμενοι οὐκ ἐριστικοὶ ἀλλὰ τὸ ὅλον τοῦτο πειραστικοί.

Cf. ibid. 30.35–37 Hayduck ὥστε ὁ μὲν διὰ τῶν μηνίσκων τοῦ Ἀντιφῶντος τετραγωνισμὸς καὶ ὁ τοῦ Ἱπποκράτους οὐκ ἐριστικοὶ ἐν τούτῳ κτλ.

F13(l) Scholium on Aristotle, *Posterior Analytics* 75b40 (Waitz [1844–46], 1.50)

ὅτι πολλοὶ πολλαχῶς περὶ τοῦ τετραγωνισμοῦ διέλαβον, ἀκριβῶς μέντοι οὐδεὶς ἀπεφήνατο· καὶ γὰρ οὗτος ὁ Βρύσων καὶ Ἱπποκράτης ὁ Χῖος καὶ Ἀντιφῶν ὁ σοφιστὴς καὶ ὁ μέγας Ἀρχιμήδης . . . ὁ δ᾽ Ἱπποκράτης διὰ τῶν τμημάτων ἤγουν μηνίσκων, ὁ δ᾽ Ἀντιφῶν διὰ τῆς διχοτομίας τοῦ ἐγγεγραμμένου εἰς τὸν κύκλον τετραγώνου τῶν πλευρῶν, μόνος δ᾽ ὁ μέγας Ἀρχιμήδης σχεδὸν ἀπέδειξε τοῦτο, κατ᾽ ἀκρίβειαν μέντοι οὐδείς.

F13(k) codd. = L N M 1 τοῦ κίου L: τοῦ χρου′ (ου′ suprascr.) N 2 ἐπὶ] ἐπεὶ N 6 ἕξοι M 10 Ἀντιφῶν] Ἱπποκράτης M N
F13(l) cod. = Ambrosianus 490 (olim L 93), saec. IX

F13(k) Such, for example, is Hippocrates of Chios' false diagram on the quadrature of the circle, and that of Antiphon. For the one, after circumscribing a square about a circle, thought he could exhaust the areas between the sides of the square and the circumference of the circle through the construction of isosceles triangles, believing that after he achieved this, he would also have the rest of the square (that is, the circle), by reason of the fact that both together are the whole square. But this is impossible, since the magnitude is infinitely divisible. Antiphon, however, made his attempt in a different way, through lunes. But since this sort of demonstration is very laborious for those of you who happen to be ignorant of geometry, it has been omitted. In any case, neither of them is eristic, since they make their arguments absolutely from geometry. Rather, they are for this reason wholly peirastic.

F13(l) Because many people dealt with the quadrature of the circle, in many different ways. No one, however, gave an exact account of it. For this Bryson, and Hippocrates of Chios, and Antiphon the sophist, and the great Archimedes ... Hippocrates did so through segments or lunes, Antiphon through division of the sides of a square inscribed in a circle. Only the great Archimedes almost demonstrated this; no one, however, did so exactly.

F14 Harpocration, s.v. διάθεσις (δ 42, 74 Keaney); cf. Photius, *Lexicon* s.v. (δ 319, 1.398 Theodoridis), *Anecdota Graeca Oxoniensia* s.v. (2.492 Cramer), *Suda* s.v. (δ 558, 2.56 Adler)

διάθεσις ... καὶ γὰρ τὸ ῥῆμα διαθέσθαι λέγουσιν ἐπὶ τοῦ διοικῆσαι. Ἀντιφῶν Ἀληθείας α′· **γυμνωθεῖσα δὲ ἀφορμῆς πολλὰ ἂν καὶ καλὰ κακῶς διαθεῖτο**.

F15(a) Harpocration, s.v. ἔμβιος (ε 42, 92 Keaney); cf. Photius, *Lexicon* s.v. ἔμβιον (ε 696, 2.71 Theodoridis), *Anecdota Graeca Oxoniensia* s.v. (2.493 Cramer), *Suda* s.v. (ε 946, 2.253 Adler)

ἔμβιος· Ἀντιφῶν Ἀληθείας α′· **καὶ ἡ [γῆ] σηπεδὼν τοῦ ξύλου ἔμβιος γένοιτο** ἀντὶ τοῦ ἐν τῷ ζῆν, τουτέστι ζήσειε καὶ μὴ ξηρανθείη μηδ' ἀποθάνοι.

Cf. *Anecdota Graeca* s.v. ἔμβιος (249 Bekker), *Etymologicum magnum* s.v. (334 Gaisford) ἡ σηπεδὼν τοῦ ξύλου **ἔμβιος** καλεῖται.

Cf. also Pollux, 6.196 (2.49 Bethe) καὶ ἄβιος [= F43], **ἔμβιος** ὡς Ἀντιφῶν φησί

F15(b) Aristotle, *Physics* 193a9–28

δοκεῖ δ' ἡ φύσις καὶ ἡ οὐσία τῶν φύσει ὄντων ἐνίοις εἶναι τὸ πρῶτον ἐνυπάρχον ἑκάστῳ, ἀρρύθμιστον ⟨ὂν⟩ καθ' ἑαυτό, οἷον κλίνης φύσις τὸ ξύλον, ἀνδριάντος δ' ὁ χαλ-

F14 1 γὰρ τὸ ῥῆμα et λέγουσιν om. Epit. Harp. Phot. *Anecd. Oxon. Sud.* ἐπὶ] ἀντὶ *Anecd. Oxon.* 2–3 Ἀντιφῶν ... διαθεῖτο om. Epit. Harp. Phot. *Anecd. Oxon. Sud.* **F15(a)** cod. Photii = z 1–3 sic Harp.: ἔμβιον· Ἀντιφῶν τὸ ζῶν καὶ μὴ ξηρανθὲν μηδὲ (μὴ δὲ *Anecd. Oxon.*) ἐναποθανόν (ἐναποθανών Phot. z: corr. Theodoridis) Epit. Harp. Phot. *Anecd. Oxon. Sud.* 1 γῆ del. W. Dindorf: ἐν γῇ (exempli grat.) Sedley 5–6 ante ἡ σηπεδὼν transp. καλεῖται (ἔμβιος omisso) *Et.* **F15(b)** codd. = E F I J et Phil. Simpl. Them. vers. 1 ἡ alt. om. F οὐσία E post corr. F I Phil. Simpl.: οὐσία ἡ J: E ante corr. dubium 1–2 τῶν φύσει ... ἐνυπάρχον in rasura E 1 ἐνίοις εἶναι om. F 2 ὂν add. Ross (coll. *Metaphys.* 1014b28)

F14 They use the verb "dispose" [*diathesthai*] also for "manage." Antiphon in the first book of *Truth*: **but deprived of means** (?), **it would dispose many fine things badly**.

F15(a) **And the putrefaction of the wood were to germinate** (**become alive**) for "in the state of living," that is, were to live and not dry out nor perish. Antiphon in the first book of *Truth*.

F15(b) To some people, the nature and essence of naturally existing entities seems to be the proximate material constituent present in each thing, which is in itself without form: wood, for example, is the nature of a bed, and bronze the nature of a statue.

κός. σημεῖον δέ φησιν Ἀντιφῶν ὅτι, εἴ τις κατορύξειε κλίνην καὶ λάβοι δύναμιν ἡ σηπεδὼν ὥστε ἀνεῖναι βλαστόν, οὐκ ἂν γενέσθαι κλίνην ἀλλὰ ξύλον, ὡς τὸ μὲν κατὰ συμβεβηκὸς ὑπάρχον, τὴν κατὰ νόμον διάθεσιν καὶ τὴν τέχνην, τὴν δ' οὐσίαν οὖσαν ἐκείνην ἣ καὶ διαμένει ταῦτα πάσχουσα συνεχῶς. εἰ δὲ καὶ τούτων ἕκαστον πρὸς ἕτερόν τι ταὐτὸ τοῦτο πέπονθεν (οἷον ὁ μὲν χαλκὸς καὶ ὁ χρυσὸς πρὸς ὕδωρ, τὰ δ' ὀστᾶ καὶ ξύλα πρὸς γῆν, ὁμοίως δὲ καὶ τῶν ἄλλων ὁτιοῦν), ἐκεῖνο τὴν φύσιν εἶναι καὶ τὴν οὐσίαν αὐτῶν. διόπερ οἱ μὲν πῦρ, οἱ δὲ γῆν, οἱ δ' ἀέρα φασίν, οἱ δὲ ὕδωρ, οἱ δ' ἔνια τούτων, οἱ δὲ πάντα ταῦτα τὴν φύσιν εἶναι τὴν τῶν ὄντων. ὃ γάρ τις αὐτῶν ὑπέλαβε τοιοῦτον, εἴτε ἓν εἴτε πλείω, τοῦτο καὶ τοσαῦτά φησιν εἶναι τὴν ἅπασαν οὐσίαν, τὰ δὲ ἄλλα πάντα πάθη τούτων καὶ ἕξεις καὶ διαθέσεις, καὶ τούτων μὲν ὁτιοῦν ἀΐδιον (οὐ γὰρ εἶναι μεταβολὴν αὐτοῖς ἐξ αὑτῶν), τὰ δ' ἄλλα γίγνεσθαι καὶ φθείρεσθαι ἀπειράκις.

Cf. ibid. 193b8–11 ἔτι γίγνεται ἄνθρωπος ἐξ ἀνθρώπου, ἀλλ' οὐ κλίνη ἐκ κλίνης· διὸ καί φασιν οὐ τὸ σχῆμα εἶναι τὴν φύσιν ἀλλὰ τὸ ξύλον, ὅτι γένοιτ' ἄν, εἰ βλαστάνοι, οὐ κλίνη ἀλλὰ ξύλον.

Cf. also *Metaphysics* 1014b26–35 ἔτι δὲ φύσις λέγεται ἐξ οὗ πρώτου ἢ ἔστιν ἢ γίγνεταί τι τῶν φύσει ὄντων, ἀρρυθμίστου ὄντος καὶ ἀμεταβλήτου ἐκ τῆς δυνάμεως τῆς αὑτοῦ, οἷον ἀνδριάντος καὶ τῶν σκευῶν τῶν χαλκῶν ὁ χαλκὸς ἡ φύσις λέγεται, τῶν δὲ ξυλίνων ξύλον· ὁμοίως δὲ καὶ ἐπὶ τῶν ἄλλων· ἐκ τούτων γάρ ἐστιν ἕκαστον δια-

5 ἀφεῖναι Them. 7 κατὰ E post corr. F I J Simpl.: κατὰ τὸν E ante corr. νόμον] ῥυθμὸν Simpl. et varia lectio in Them. Phil. 12 ἐκεῖνο E ante corr. Simpl.: ἐκεῖνα E post corr. F I J Them. 13 πῦρ, οἱ δὲ γῆν E vers.: γῆν, οἱ δὲ πῦρ F I J 15 τὴν alt. om. J ante corr. 16 φασιν F I J 18 καὶ ante ἕξεις E I vers.: om. F J post ὁτιοῦν add. εἶναι E post corr. F I J 20 καὶ φθείρεσθαι F I J Simpl.: om. E codd. = E J A^b et Al^c 25 δὲ om. A^b 26 φύσει E J Al^c (cf. Arist., *Phys.* 193a10): μὴ φύσει A^b (e coniectura ut vid.) 29 ἢ om. A^b

The proof of this, Antiphon claims, is the fact that if one were to bury a bed and the putrefaction were to get the power to send up a shoot, it would not be a bed but wood, since the one – the arrangement in accordance with convention and the artistic form (?) – exists accidentally, whereas the essence is that which persists, continuously undergoing these modifications. And if each of these is in the same situation in relation to some other thing (for instance bronze and gold in relation to water, bones and wood in relation to earth, and in the same way any of the others whatsoever), that thing is their nature and their essence. This is why some people claim that fire is the nature of entities, others earth, others again air, others water, others some of these, others all of them. For whatever any of them supposed is of this sort (whether one thing or more than one), this thing (or this many things) he claims is the whole of substance, while all else is affections, states, and dispositions of it; and one or another of them he claims is eternal (for they do not change out of themselves), while everything else comes into being and perishes an unlimited number of times.

Furthermore, a man is born from a man, but not a bed from a bed. This is why they say that not the shape, but the wood, is the nature of a bed, because if it were to sprout, not a bed, but wood, would come up.

"Nature," furthermore, means the proximate material constituent – without form and incapable of changing out of its own character – of which any naturally existing entity consists, or from which it comes to be; as bronze is said to be the nature of a statue and of bronze implements, wood the nature of wooden things. And similarly in the case of other things: each is made from these, while the

σωζομένης τῆς πρώτης ὕλης· τοῦτον γὰρ τὸν τρόπον καὶ τῶν φύσει ὄντων τὰ στοιχεῖά φασιν εἶναι φύσιν, οἱ μὲν πῦρ οἱ δὲ γῆν οἱ δ' ἀέρα οἱ δ' ὕδωρ οἱ δ' ἄλλο τι τοιοῦτον λέγοντες, οἱ δ' ἔνια τούτων οἱ δὲ πάντα ταῦτα.

F15(c) Alexander, *In Aristotelis Metaphysica* 357.13–21 Hayduck

τὴν δὲ ὡς τὸ ὑποκείμενον καὶ τὴν ὕλην· φύσις γὰρ καὶ ἡ ὕλη, ἐξ ἧς πρώτης ἐνυπαρχούσης τῷ γινομένῳ ἡ γένεσις· οὐ γὰρ οὕτως ἐκ τῆς ὕλης τὰ γινόμενα γίνεται ὡς ἐκ τῆς στερήσεως ἢ ἐκ τῶν ἐναντίων γίνεσθαι λέγεται· οὐ γὰρ ἐξ ἐνυπαρχόντων ἐκείνων. τὸ δὲ πρῶτον τῷ ἐνυπάρχον προσκείμενον τὴν πρώτην ὕλην δηλοῖ, οὐ τὴν ἑκάστου προσεχῆ. τὴν δὲ ὕλην φύσιν εἶπεν ἀποδειχθεῖναι Ἀντιφῶν, ὡς εἴρηκεν ἐν τῷ Α τῆς Φυσικῆς, διὰ τοῦ τὴν κλίνην, εἰ καταχωσθεῖσα δύναμιν λάβοι τοῦ βλαστῆσαι, ξύλον ἐξ αὐτῆς ἀναβλαστῆσαι, ὅπερ ἦν τὸ ὑποκείμενον, ἀλλ' οὐ τὴν κλίνην, ὃ ἦν τὸ εἶδος.

F15(d) Themistius, *In Aristotelis Physica paraphrasis* 38.1–18 Schenkl

ἐνίοις μὲν γὰρ ἡ ὕλη φύσις μᾶλλον δοκεῖ, οἷον κλίνης φύσις τὸ ξύλον, ἀνδριάντος δὲ ὁ χαλκός. κατὰ δὲ τὴν αὐτὴν αἰτίαν καὶ ὕδατος φύσις τὸ πρῶτον αὐτῷ ὑποκείμενον ἀμορφώτατόν τε καὶ ἀσχημάτιστον· σημεῖον δέ φησιν Ἀντιφῶν, ὅτι εἴ τις κατορύξειε κλίνην καὶ λάβοι δύναμιν ἡ σηπεδών, ὥστε ἀφεῖναι βλαστόν, οὐκ ἂν γενέσθαι κλίνην ἀλλὰ ξύλον, ὡς τοῦτο μὲν κατὰ συμβεβηκὸς ὑπάρχον αὐτῷ, τὴν κατὰ ῥυθμὸν διάθεσιν· ῥυθμὸν γὰρ καλεῖ τὴν μορφήν, τὴν δὲ οὐσίαν ἐκείνην οὖσαν, ἣ διαμένει ταῦτα πάσχουσα συνεχῶς. εἰ δὲ καὶ ἄλλο τι πρὸς τὸ ξύ-

F15(c) codd. = A L F et Sepulved. 5 τὸ δὲ πρῶτον τῷ L F Sepulved.: τῷ δὲ πρῶτον τὸ A 8 ἐν τῷ Α τῆς Φυσικῆς] immo B 1 193a12 10 ἀναβλαστήσειν vel ἂν βλαστῆσαι Bonitz **F15(d)** codd. = B L M W a 1 post γὰρ add. ἂν L δοκεῖ (ε in rasura) M 7 ὡς om. W 9 οὐσίαν M: οἰκείαν οὐσίαν W B L

proximate matter is preserved throughout. For the elements of naturally existing entities too they claim in this way to be 'nature,' some saying fire, others earth, others again air, others water, others something else of this sort, others some of these, others all of them.

F15(c) In another way, he speaks of nature as the substrate and the matter. For also the matter which is the primary immanent source of becoming for what becomes is nature. For things that come into being do not arise from matter in the way they are said to arise from privation or from the opposites, for they do not arise from these as immanent source. The term "first" added to "immanent" signifies prime matter, not the proximate matter of each thing. As Aristotle has said in the first book of the *Physics*, Antiphon said that matter is proved to be nature by the fact that if a buried bed were to get the power to sprout, wood (which was the substrate) would shoot up from it, not the bed (which was the form).

F15(d) Some people think rather that matter is nature: wood, for example, is the nature of a bed, bronze the nature of a statue. And for the same reason, the nature of water is the prime substrate – to the highest degree shapeless and without form – that underlies it. The proof of this, Antiphon claims, is the fact that if one were to bury a bed and the putrefaction were to get the power to put forth a shoot, it would not be a bed but wood, since the one – the arrangement according to *rhythmos* (he calls shape *rhythmos*) – belongs to it accidentally, whereas the essence is that which persists, continuously undergoing these modifications. And if something else is related to wood as

λον λόγον ἔχει, ὥσπερ τὸ ξύλον πρὸς τὴν κλίνην, οἱονεὶ ὥσπερ αὐτὸ ὑπόκειται τῇ κλίνῃ, οὕτως ὕδωρ ἢ γῆ ἢ τῶν ἄλλων ὁτιοῦν ὑπόκειται τῷ ξύλῳ, ἐκεῖνα τὴν φύσιν εἶναι τοῦ ξύλου ὥσπερ τὸ ξύλον τῆς κλίνης. διὰ τοῦτο ὅσοι μὲν πῦρ ἐνόμισαν τὴν ὕλην τῶν ὄντων, καὶ φύσιν τοῦτο ἐνόμισαν τῶν ὄντων· ὅσοι δὲ ὕδωρ ὕλην, ταὐτὸν καὶ φύσιν· ὅσοι δὲ πλείους τὰς ὕλας, πλείους καὶ τὰς φύσεις, τὰ δὲ ἄλλα πάντα πάθη τούτων καὶ ἕξεις καὶ διαθέσεις· δεῖ μὲν γὰρ ἀεὶ τὴν φύσιν σῴζεσθαι τῶν ὄντων, τοιοῦτον δὲ τὸ πρῶτον ὑποκείμενον μόνον, τὰ δὲ ἄλλα γίνεται καὶ φθείρεται ἀπειράκις. οὗτοι μὲν οὖν τοῦτον τὸν τρόπον τὴν ὕλην προσοικειοῦσι τῇ φύσει.

F15(e) Philoponus, *In Aristotelis Physica* 207.19–22, 25–208.22, 26–29 Vitelli

καί φησιν ὅτι τριχῶς λέγεται ἡ φύσις· λέγεται γὰρ καὶ τὸ πρῶτον ἑκάστῳ ὑποκείμενον φύσις, ὡς τοῖς περὶ Ἀντιφῶντα δοκεῖ καὶ τοῖς παλαιοτέροις τῶν φυσικῶν, οἵτινες τὴν ὕλην ἑκάστου φύσιν ἑκάστου εἶναι ἔλεγον . . . δοκεῖ οὖν, φησίν, ἡ ὕλη τισὶ μᾶλλον εἶναι φύσις· κατεσκεύαζε γοῦν Ἀντιφῶν τοῦτο τοῦτον τὸν τρόπον, ὅτι τὸ ἐν ἑκάστῳ ὑποκείμενον καὶ μὴ ἄλλοτε εἰς ἄλλο μεταβάλλον τοῦτό ἐστιν ἡ ἑκάστου φύσις, τὰ δὲ ἄλλα καθ' ἃ μεταβάλλει γινόμενα καὶ φθειρόμενα πάθη τούτου εἰσὶ καὶ οὐ φύσις. οὕτως οὖν τοῦ μὲν ἀνδριάντος φύσις οὐ τὸ σχῆμα, ἀλλ' ὁ χαλκός, καὶ τῆς κλίνης τὸ ξύλον, διότι τὸ μὲν σχῆμα πάθος τί ἐστι γινόμενον καὶ ἀπογινόμενον, ὁ δὲ χαλκὸς καὶ τὸ ξύλον ἀεὶ μένει. σημεῖον δὲ τοῦ τὸ ξύλον φύσιν εἶναι τῆς κλίνης ὁ Ἀντιφῶν ἔλεγεν ὅτι ἐὰν κατο-

11 οἱονεὶ M B: οἷον εἰ W L post corr.: οἷον L ante corr. a 16–17 καὶ φύσιν om. W 19 τὴν φύσιν ἀεὶ B: τὴν φύσιν αἰεὶ L 20 μόνον om. L 22 τὴν ὕλην προσοικειοῦσι M: προσοικειοῦσιν τὴν ὕλην W B L **F15(e)** codd. = K L M t 2 πρῶτον M t: α′ K: πρώτως L 5 οὖν] τε K 5–6 κατεσκεύαζε γοῦν L K: κατεσκευάζεν οὖν M t 10 μὲν ex μηδὲν L 12 τί om. K 13–14 δὲ τοῦτο ξύλον φύσις εἶναι K

wood is related to the bed – for instance, if water, or earth, or any of the others underlies wood as its substrate, just as it underlies the bed – then those things are the nature of wood as it is the nature of the bed. This is why all who thought that fire is the matter of entities thought it is their nature as well; all who thought that water is the matter of entities thought it is their nature as well, and all who thought that there are a plurality of matters thought there are a plurality of natures as well, while all else they considered to be affections, states, and dispositions of these. For the nature of entities must always be preserved, and only the prime substrate possesses this characteristic, whereas everything else comes into being and perishes an unlimited number of times. These people, then, associate matter with nature in this fashion.

F15(e) "Nature," he says, is spoken of in three ways. The prime substrate underlying each thing is called nature, as Antiphon and the older physical philosophers think, who said that the matter of each thing is its nature ... Now some people, he says, think rather that matter is nature. Antiphon, at any rate, tried in the following way to establish that the substrate in each thing (which does not change into different things at different times) is its nature, while everything else is an affection of this and not the nature, inasmuch as it undergoes change, coming into being and perishing. In this way, then, it is not the shape, but the bronze, which is the nature of the statue, and the wood which is the nature of the bed, since the shape is an affection which comes into being and perishes, whereas the bronze and the wood always abide. That wood is the nature of a bed Antiphon said is proved by the fact that if

ρύξῃς κλίνην καὶ σαπῇ, εἶτα τὴν γεννητικὴν δύναμιν ἡ σηπεδὼν λάβοι, οὐκ ἂν βλαστήσειε κλίνην, ἀλλὰ ξύλον, ὡς δὴ τοῦ μὲν σχήματος τῆς κλίνης πάθους τινὸς ὄντος, φύσεως δὲ τοῦ ξύλου, ὅπερ ἐστὶν ἡ ὕλη τῆς κλίνης· τὸ γὰρ ἐν ἑκάστῳ γεννητικὸν καὶ κινητικὸν τοῦτό ἐστιν ἡ φύσις ἑκάστου. ὃ δὲ ἐπὶ τῶν τεχνητῶν συμβαίνει, τοῦτο καὶ ἐπὶ τῶν φυσικῶν, ἐπειδὴ μιμεῖται τὴν φύσιν ἡ τέχνη. ὥσπερ οὖν ἐπὶ τῶν τεχνητῶν εὕρομεν ὅτι φύσις ἑκάστου ἐστὶν οὐ τὸ εἶδος, ἀλλ' ἡ ὕλη, διὰ τὸ τὴν μὲν ὑπομένειν, τὴν ὕλην, τὸ δὲ εἶδος οὔ, οὕτω δήπου καὶ ἐπὶ τῶν φυσικῶν ἂν εἴη ἡ μὲν ἑκάστου ὕλη φύσις, πάθος δὲ τὸ εἶδος. ὥστε εἰ καὶ ἡ τῆς κλίνης ὕλη, τὸ ξύλον λέγω, μὴ ἔστιν ἁπλοῦν τι πρᾶγμα, ἀλλὰ σύγκειται ἐξ ὑποκειμένου καὶ εἴδους, καὶ πέπονθε τὸν αὐτὸν λόγον ὅνπερ τὸ ξύλον πρὸς τὴν κλίνην, τὸ μὲν ὑποκείμενον καὶ ἡ ὕλη τοῦ ξύλου φύσις αὐτοῦ ἂν εἴη, εἴτε ὕδωρ εἴη τοῦτο εἴτε γῆ εἴτε ὁτιδήποτε ἄλλο, τὸ δὲ τοῦ ξύλου εἶδος πάθος τι τῶν γινομένων καὶ ἀπογινομένων, διότι μεταβάλλοι ἂν τὸ ὑποκείμενον, τὸ ξύλον, εἰς ἕτερον εἶδος, οἷον ἡ γῆ. ὥστε εἰ τὸ μὲν ὑπομένει, τὰ δ' εἴδη μεταβάλλουσιν εἰς ἄλληλα, τὸ δὲ ὑπομένον φύσις ἂν εἴη μᾶλλον ἢ τὸ μεταβάλλον, ἔοικε καὶ τῶν φυσικῶν ἡ ὕλη μᾶλλον εἶναι φύσις ἢ τὸ εἶδος. διὰ τοῦτο γοῦν, φησίν, ὅπερ ἑκάστῳ ἔδοξεν ὑλικὸν εἶναι αἴτιον τῶν πραγμάτων, εἴτε ἓν εἴτε πλείω, τοῦτο τὴν φύσιν εἶναι τῶν ὄντων ἔθετο, καὶ τοῦτο μὲν ὑπομένειν, τὰ δ' εἴδη ἄλλοτε ἄλλο ἐπιγίνεσθαι ... ὥστε ὅσοι μὲν ἓν τὸ ὑλικὸν αἴτιον εἰρήκασιν, εἴτε ἀέρα εἴτε ὕδωρ εἴτε ὁτιδη-

16 βλαστάσειε t   κλίνην L K: κλίνη* (η* suprascr.) M: κλίνη t   ἀλλὰ] ἢ ἄλλο K   17 τῆς κλίνης K: τῆς ὕλης L: τῆς γῆς M: om. t   19 γενητικὸν M   19–20 ἡ φύσις ἡ ἑκάστου K   23 οὐ om. L sed suprascr.   24 οὔ] οὐκ t   25 post φύσις add. αὐτοῦ ἐστὶν K   26 ἡ τῆς ὕλης κλίνης ὕλη L   32 μεταβάλοι M t   34 εἴδη] ἤδη t   34–35 δὲ ὑπομένον K: ὑποκείμενον (δὲ omisso) L M t   35 post ἔοικε add. δὲ M t   37 ἔδιξεν K   37–38 αἴτιον εἶναι M t   40 ἄλλο K t: ἄλλω M: ἄλλα L   ὅσον K   ἓν K: om. L M t   41 εἰρήκασι t   41–42 ὁτιδηποτοῦν L: ὁτιδήποτε οὖν K: ὁτιδήποτε M t

you bury a bed and it putrefies, and then the putrefaction were to get generative power, it would not produce a bed but wood, since the shape of the bed is an affection, whereas the wood – the matter of the bed – is the nature. For that which is generative in each thing, and productive of movement and change, is its nature. And what happens in the case of artifacts happens in the case of natural entities as well, since art imitates nature. So, just as we find in the case of artifacts that the nature of each thing is the matter and not the form, since the matter abides while the form does not, so also in the case of natural entities the matter of each thing will be its nature, and the form will be an affection. As a result, if the matter of the bed (I mean the wood) for its part is not something simple but is compounded of substrate and form, and is in the same relation as the wood is to the bed, then the substrate and the matter of the wood (whether water or earth or anything else whatsoever) would be its nature, while the form of the wood would be one of the affections that comes into being and perishes. For the substrate – the wood – could change into another form, for example earth. So that if the one thing abides, whereas the forms change into each other; and if that which abides (rather than that which changes) will be the nature, then it seems that in the case of natural entities as well the matter (rather than the form) is the nature. This, at any rate (he says), is why each philosopher posited as the nature of entities whatever he thought was their material cause (whether one thing or more than one), and posited that this abides, while different forms supervene at different times ... As a result, all who have said that the material cause is one (whether air or water or anything else whatsoever) have declared that this is the

ποτοῦν ἄλλο, τοῦτο εἶναι καὶ τὴν φύσιν τῶν ὄντων ἀπεφήναντο, ὅσοι δὲ πλείω, πλείονα.

F15(f) Simplicius, *In Aristotelis Physica* 273.35–274.26 Diels

σημεῖον δὲ τοῦ τὸ ὑποκείμενον ἀλλ' οὐχὶ τὸ εἶδος εἶναι τὴν φύσιν ὁ Ἀντιφῶν ὁ σοφιστὴς ἐποιεῖτο τὸ φύσιν μὲν εἶναι τὴν φύουσαν ἤτοι τὴν ἔκφυσιν καὶ διανάστασιν οὖσαν εἰς κίνησιν καὶ τοῦ ὁμοίου ἀπογέννησιν. ἐπὶ γὰρ τῶν τεχνητῶν εἴ τις κατορύξειε κλίνην καὶ λάβοι δύναμιν ἡ σηπεδὼν ὥστε ἀνεῖναι βλαστόν, οὐκ ἂν γενέσθαι κλίνην, ἀλλὰ ξύλον. τοῦτο δὲ συμβαίνει, διότι τὸ μὲν εἶδος καὶ [ἡ] κατὰ τρόπον καὶ κατὰ νόμον, τουτέστι κατὰ τὸ ταῖς τέχναις νενομισμένον καὶ πρὸς τὸ κατὰ φύσιν ἀντιδιαστελλόμενον, ὡς κατὰ συνθήκην ὂν κατὰ συμβεβηκὸς ὑπάρχον γίνεται καὶ ἀπογίνεται, ἡ δὲ ὕλη παραμένει, διότι οὐσία καὶ φύσις ἐστὶν αὕτη τοῦ πράγματος. οὐσίας γὰρ ἴδιον τὸ ἐπιμένειν. τῶν δὲ φυσικῶν κατὰ τὴν φύσιν ἐστὶν ἡ οὐσία. ὥστε καὶ συλλογίσαιο ἂν οὕτως· ἡ ὕλη καὶ τὸ ὑποκείμενον τὸ παραμένον καὶ ἀναφύον ἐν τοῖς φυσικοῖς ἐστι· τὸ τοιοῦτον οὐσία τῶν φυσικῶν ἐστιν· ἡ οὐσία τῶν φυσικῶν ἡ φύσις ἐστίν· ἡ ἄρα ὕλη ἡ φύσις ἐστὶν ἐν τοῖς φυσικοῖς, ὥστε καὶ ἡ φύσις ὕλη. ἀντιστρέφουσι γὰρ οἱ ὁρισμοί. ἐπεὶ δὲ τῶν προσεχῶν ὑποκειμένων ἕκαστον εἶδος ἔχει τι ὑποκείμενον, εἰκότως προσέθηκεν εἰ δὲ καὶ τούτων ἕκαστον πρὸς ἕτερόν τι ὑποκείμενον αὐτῷ ταὐτὸν πέπονθεν, ὥστε τὸ μὲν εἶδος μεταβάλλειν, τὸ δὲ ὑποκείμενον μένειν, οἷον εἰ ὁ μὲν χαλκὸς καὶ ὁ χρυσὸς

42 ὄντων L K: ἄλλων M t   **F15(f)** codd. = D E F a   1 οὐχὶ D E: οὐ a F   4 ὁμοίου ὥσπερ γέννησιν F   ἐπὶ γὰρ D: ἐπὶ δὲ a E: ἐπεὶ δὲ F   5 ante εἴ τις add. τῶν E   λάβη E F   6 σηπεδὸν F   ἀνεῖναι a F: ἀφεῖναι D E   8 ἡ D E F: τὸ a: del. Diels: ἡ ⟨διάθεσις ἡ⟩ Sedley   8–9 κατὰ τὸ ταῖς τέχναις D E: τὸ κατὰ ταῖς τέχναις F: τὸ κατὰ τὰς τέχνας a   12 αὑτὴ E   13 ante κατὰ add. καὶ a F   τὴν om. a   19 ἐπεὶ δὲ a E: ἐπὶ δὲ D: ἐπειδὴ F   προσεχῶς D   ὑποκειμένων] ὑπομένων (per compendium) E   21 τι a F: τι τὸ E: om. D ante corr.

nature of entities as well, and all who have said that it is more than one have declared a plurality of natures.

F15(f) The fact that nature is that which puts forth shoots, or is an outgrowth and rising-up into motion and generation of the like, Antiphon the sophist deemed to be proof that the substrate, not the form, is nature. For in the case of artificial objects, if one were to bury a bed and the putrefaction were to get the power to send up a shoot, it would not be a bed but wood. This happens because the form comes into being and perishes, since it exists accidentally according to custom and convention, that is, in accordance with what has been deemed conventional by the arts and is opposed (existing as it does by agreement) to that which is in accordance with nature. The matter, on the other hand, abides, since this is the essence and nature of the thing; for to persist is characteristic of essence. But the essence of natural things is in accordance with their nature. As the result, you could construct the following syllogism: the matter and the substrate are what abides and produces growth in natural things; this sort of thing is the essence of natural things; the essence of natural things is their nature; the matter, therefore, is the nature in the case of natural things, so that nature is matter. (For the definitions are convertible.) Since the form of each of the proximate substrates has itself some substrate, Aristotle reasonably adds "and if each of these is in the same situation in relation to something that is substrate to it," so that the form changes while the substrate abides – for example, if bronze and gold

πρὸς ὕδωρ τοῦτο πέπονθεν, τὰ δὲ ὀστᾶ καὶ ξύλα πρὸς γῆν καὶ τῶν ἄλλων ὁτιοῦν πρὸς τὸ ἐν αὐτῷ ὑποκείμενον, τὸ ὑποκείμενον ἂν εἴη ἡ φύσις καὶ ἡ οὐσία αὐτῶν. καὶ διὰ τοῦτο ὅπερ ἕκαστον ὑπέθετο τὸ πρῶτον ὑποκείμενον εἴτε ἓν εἴτε πλείω τοῦτο τὴν φύσιν καὶ τὴν οὐσίαν εἶναι τῶν ὄντων ἐνόμισεν. ὥστε ὁ μὲν Ἀντιφῶν κοινῶς ἐῴκει λέγειν τὸ ὑποκείμενον τὴν φύσιν, τῶν δὲ ἄλλων ἕκαστος ὅπερ ἔλεγε πρῶτον ὑποκείμενον, τοῦτο καὶ φύσιν ἐκάλει τῶν ὄντων εἴτε ἓν ἦν τοῦτο, ὥσπερ Θαλῆς μὲν ὕδωρ ἔλεγεν, Ἀναξιμένης δὲ ἀέρα, Ἡράκλειτος δὲ πῦρ, εἴτε πλείονα, ὡς Παρμενίδης πῦρ καὶ γῆν, εἴτε τὰ τέτταρα, ὡς Ἐμπεδόκλης· γῆν δὲ μόνην οὐδεὶς εἶπεν, ἀλλὰ τῇ συνεκδρομῇ τῶν ἄλλων καὶ ταύτην τέθεικεν ὁ Ἀριστοτέλης.

Cf. ibid. 283.14–20 Diels οὕτως οὖν καὶ ἐπὶ τοῦ παντὸς φυσικοῦ σώματος τὸ ὑπομένον ἐν ταῖς παντοίαις μεταβολαῖς τὸ αὐτὸ τοῦτο ἂν εἴη φύσις. ὑπομένει δὲ ἡ ὕλη. ὁ δὲ Ἀντιφῶν τὴν τῆς ὕλης ὑπομονὴν καὶ ἀπὸ τῆς τοῦ ὁμοίου βλαστήσεως ἐπειράθη δεικνύναι, καίτοι τῆς βλαστήσεως μᾶλλον εἶδος ἐξ εἴδους ἢ ὕλην ἐξ ὕλης γίνεσθαι δηλούσης. ἄνθρωπος γὰρ ἐξ ἀνθρώπου καὶ ξύλον ἐκ ξύλου γίνεται. εἶδος δὲ καὶ τὸ ξύλον, κἂν ὕλης ἔχῃ πρὸς τὴν κλίνην λόγον.

F15(g) Proclus, *In Platonis Timaeum* 1.10.5–13 Diehl

τῶν γὰρ παλαιῶν οἱ μὲν τὴν ὕλην φύσιν ἐκάλουν, ὡς Ἀντιφῶν, οἱ δὲ τὸ εἶδος, ὡς Ἀριστοτέλης ἐν πολλοῖς, οἱ δὲ τὸ ὅλον, ὡς τῶν πρὸ Πλάτωνός τινες, περὶ ὧν ἐν Νόμοις [892B] ἱστόρησεν, ὅτι δὴ τὰ φύσει φύσεις προσηγόρευον, οἱ δὲ τὰς φυσικὰς δυνάμεις, βαρύτητας, κουφότητας, μανώσεις, πυκνώσεις, ὥς τινες τῶν Περιπατητικῶν καὶ τῶν ἔτι ἀρχαιοτέρων φυσικῶν, οἱ δὲ

28 εἶναι om. E   28–29 τῶν ὄντων D E: τούτων a F   34 τὰ om. D   37–38 τοῦ παντὸς φυσικοῦ σώματος D: τοῦ παντὸς τοῦ φυσικοῦ σώματος F: τοῦ φυσικοῦ παντὸς σώματος φυσικοῦ E: παντὸς τοῦ φυσικοῦ σώματος a   38 τὸ ὑποκείμενον D

are in this situation in relation to water, bones and wood in relation to earth, and anything else whatsoever in relation to the substrate in it – the substrate will be their nature and their essence. This is why each philosopher considered the nature and the essence of entities to be the very thing he proposed as the primary substrate, whether one or more than one. So that Antiphon seemed to say generally that the substrate is nature, while each of the others called the "nature" of entities that which he said is their primary substrate, whether this is one thing, as Thales said it is water, Anaximenes air, Heraclitus fire; or more than one, as Parmenides said it is fire and earth; or the four elements, as Empedocles said. No one said it is earth alone; but Aristotle has put this too, by analogy with the others.

In this way then, in the case of every natural body, that which remains the same in the manifold changes will be the nature; and the matter remains. Antiphon tried to show the persistence of matter also from the sprouting of what is like, although sprouting shows that form arises from form rather than matter from matter. For a man arises from a man, and wood from wood. The wood too is form – even if it fulfills the function of matter in relation to the bed.

F15(g) Some of the ancients, Antiphon for example, called matter nature; others, for example Aristotle in many places, called form nature. Others again called the whole complex nature, for example some of those before Plato, of whom he reported in the *Laws* that they called naturally existing things "natures." Others, for example some of the Peripatetics and the even more ancient natural philosophers, called natural properties nature – heaviness, lightness, rarefaction, condensation.

τέχνην θεοῦ τὴν φύσιν προσωνόμαζον, οἱ δὲ ψυχήν, οἱ δὲ ἄλλο τι τοιοῦτον.

F15(h) [John Italus], Ἀπορίαι καὶ λύσεις (Waitz [1844–46], 1.15)

οἱ μὲν δὴ ὕλην φύσιν ἐκάλουν ὡς Ἀντιφῶν, οἱ δὲ τὸ εἶδος ὥς τινες τῶν Περιπατητικῶν.

F16 *Anecdota Graeca* s.v. ἀφήκοντος (171 Bachmann); cf. Photius, *Lexicon* s.v. (α 3336, 1.305 Theodoridis)

ἀφήκοντος· Ἀντιφῶν ἀντὶ τοῦ διήκοντος.

F17 *Anecdota Graeca* s.v. Ἀφροδίτης (173 Bachmann); cf. Photius, *Lexicon* s.v. (α 3402, 1.311 Theodoridis)

Ἀφροδίτης· ἀντὶ τοῦ ἀφροδισίων. οὕτως Ἀντιφῶν ἐν Ἀληθείας πρώτῳ.

F18 Harpocration, s.v. ἀναποδιζόμενα (α 121, 23 Keaney); cf. Photius, *Lexicon* s.v. (α 1610, 1.163 Theodoridis), *Anecdota Graeca Oxoniensia* s.v. (2.489 Cramer), *Suda* s.v. ἀναποδίζειν (α 2026, 1.182 Adler)

ἀναποδιζόμενα· ἀντὶ τοῦ ἐξεταζόμενα, ἢ ἀντὶ τοῦ ἄνωθεν τὰ αὐτὰ πολλάκις λεγόμενα ἢ πραττόμενα. Ἀντιφῶν Ἀληθείας α′.

Cf. also Pollux, 2.196 (1.143 Bethe) **ἀναποδιζόμενα** Ἀντιφῶν τὰ πάλιν ἐξεταζόμενα.

F19(a) Harpocration, s.v. ἀνήκει (α 140, 26–27 Keaney)

F16 1 post διήκοντος transp. Ἀντιφῶν Phot. **F17** cod. = Coisl. 1–2 οὕτως et ἐν Ἀληθείας πρώτῳ om. Phot. 2 πρῶτα Coisl. **F18** 1 ἀντὶ τοῦ pr. om. *Anecd. Oxon.* τοῦ ⟨πάλιν⟩ ἐξεταζόμενα Diels (cf. Pollux, 2.196) 2 πολλάκις τὰ αὐτὰ Epit. Harp. Phot. *Anecd. Oxon. Sud.* 2–3 Ἀντιφῶν Ἀληθείας α′ om. Epit. Harp. Phot. *Anecd. Oxon. Sud.*

Others called nature god's art. Others called soul nature. Others again, something else of this sort.

F15(h) Some people called matter nature, for example Antiphon; others called form nature, for example some of the Peripatetics.

F16 **Reaching** for "extending." Antiphon.

F17 **Aphrodite** for "sexual intercourse." So Antiphon in the first book of *Truth*.

F18 **Cross-examined** for "examined" or for "the same things being said or done over again many times." Antiphon in the first book of *Truth*.

ἀνήκει· παρ' Ἀντιφῶντι Ἀληθείας α' ἀντὶ ἁπλοῦ τοῦ ἥκει, ἢ οἷον ἀνεβιβάσθη καὶ προελήλυθεν.

F19(b) *Anecdota Graeca* s.v. ἀνήκει (96 Bachmann); cf. Photius, *Lexicon* s.v. (α 1917, 1.187 Theodoridis), *Suda* s.v. (α 2404, 1.215 Adler) = Aelius Dionysius, s.v. (α 138, 106 Erbse)

ἀνήκει· Ἀντιφῶν μὲν ἀντὶ τοῦ καθήκει.

F20 Harpocration, s.v. ἐπαλλάξεις (ε 77, 99 Keaney); cf. Photius, *Lexicon* s.v. (ε 1334, 2.131 Theodoridis), *Suda* s.v. (ε 1941, 2.330 Adler)

ἐπαλλάξεις· ἀντὶ τοῦ συναλλαγὰς ἢ μίξεις. Ἀντιφῶν Ἀληθείας α'.

F21 Harpocration, s.v. ὀριγνηθῆναι (ο 31, 194 Keaney); cf. Photius, *Lexicon* s.v. (1.347 Porson), *Suda* s.v. (ο 560, 3.556 Adler)

ὀριγνηθῆναι· ἀντὶ τοῦ ἐπιθυμῆσαι. Ἀντιφῶν Ἀληθείας α'.

F22 Harpocration, s.v. ἀειεστώ (α 38, 8 Keaney); cf. Photius, *Lexicon* s.v. (α 422, 1.49 Theodoridis), *Suda* s.vv. ἀεὶ ἔστω (α 618, 1.62 Adler) and αἰεὶ ἐστώ (αι 103, 2.164 Adler)

ἀειεστώ· Ἀντιφῶν τὴν ἀϊδιότητα καὶ τὸ ἐπὶ τῶν αὐτῶν ἀεὶ ἑστάναι, ὥσπερ καὶ εὐεστὼ ἡ εὐδαιμονία καλεῖται.

F19(a) 1 παρ' Ἀντιφῶντι] Ἀντιφῶν (Ἀληθείας α' omissis) Epit. Harp. ἁπλοῦ om. Epit. Harp. **F19(b)** 1 μὲν om. *Sud.* **F20** 2 Ἀληθείας α' om. Epit. Harp. Phot. *Sud.* **F21** 1 Ἀντιφῶν Ἀληθείας α' om. Epit. Harp. Phot. *Sud.* **F22** codd. = D E Q K M N P Ald. 1 ἀειεστώ Ald.: ἀειέστο Harp. cet. codd.: ἀεὶ (vel αἰεὶ) ἔστω (vel ἐστώ) divisim Epit. Harp. Phot. codd. (corr. Reitzenstein) *Sud.* post τὴν ἀϊδιότητα add. ἐν Ἀληθείας β' Phot. 2 ὥσπερ . . . καλεῖται om. Phot. εὐεστὼ Epit. Harp. *Sud.*: εὖ * * * τω Harp. post καλεῖται add. ἡ λέξις Διογενιανοῦ Phot.: ἡ λέξις Διογενιανὸς ἐν Ἀληθείᾳ δευτέρῳ *Sud.* α 618: ἡ λέξις Διογενειανοῦ ἐν Ἀληθείας δευτέρῳ τοῦ Ἀντιφῶντος *Sud.* αι 103

F19(a) Comes up for the simple "arrives," or something like "has advanced and come forward." In Antiphon in the first book of *Truth*.

F19(b) Comes up for "reaches." Antiphon.

F20 Interweavings for "interchanges" or "mixtures." Antiphon in the first book of *Truth*.

F21 Grasp at for "desire." Antiphon in the first book of *Truth*.

F22 Eternal being for "eternity" and "being always in the same state," just as happiness is called "well-being." Antiphon.

Cf. also Hesychius, s.v. ἀειεστώ (α 1266, 1.46 Latte) **ἀειεστώ·** τὴν αἰώνιον οὐσίαν, ἢ ἀϊδιότητα.

F23 Harpocration, s.v. διάστασις (δ 40, 73 Keaney); cf. Photius, *Lexicon* s.v. (δ 445, 1.408 Theodoridis), *Suda* s.v. (δ 766, 2.73 Adler)

διάστασις· Ἀντιφῶν Ἀληθείας β′· **περὶ τῆς νῦν κρατούσης διαστάσεως** ἀντὶ τοῦ διακοσμήσεως τῶν ὅλων.

F24 Harpocration, s.v. ἀδιάστατον (α 30, 6 Keaney); cf. *Anecdota Graeca* s.v. (28 Bachmann), Photius, *Lexicon* s.v. (α 354, 1.42 Theodoridis), *Suda* s.v. (α 477, 1.50 Adler)

ἀδιάστατον· τὸ μήπω διεστηκὸς μηδὲ διακεκριμένον Ἀντιφῶν εἶπεν.

Cf. also Photius, *Lexicon* s.v. ἀδιάστατον (α 359, 1.42 Theodoridis) **ἀδιάστατον·** ὡς †Ξενοφῶν†· **καὶ τὸ οἰκοδόμημα ἀδιάστατον.**

F24A *Suda* s.vv. διάθεσις καὶ διατίθεσθαι (δ 557, 2.56 Adler); cf. *Anecdota Graeca* s.v. διάθεσις (241 Bekker), *Etymologicum magnum* s.v. (267 Gaisford)

διάθεσις καὶ διατίθεσθαι· ... Ἀντιφῶν δὲ τῇ διαθέσει ἐχρήσατο ἐπὶ γνώμης ἢ διανοίας. ὁ αὐτὸς καὶ ἐπὶ τοῦ διαθεῖναι λόγον, τουτέστιν ἐπὶ τοῦ ἐξαγγεῖλαί τι. ἐν τῷ β′ τῆς Ἀληθείας ὁ αὐτὸς κέχρηται αὐτῷ καὶ ἐπὶ τῆς διακοσμήσεως.

cod. = H 4 ἀειεστον H **F23** 1 Ἀντιφῶν post διακοσμήσεως (διακόσμησις) transp. Phot. 1–2 Ἀληθείας β′ ... διαστάσεως om. Epit. Harp. Phot. *Sud.* 2 διακόσμησις Epit. Harp. Phot. *Sud.* τῶν ὅλων om. Epit. Harp. Phot. *Sud.* **F24** 4 Ξενοφῶν] Ἀντιφῶν E. Schwartz **F24A** 1–5 sic *Sud.* 1 καὶ διατίθεσθαι om. *Anecd. Et.* Ἀντιφῶν] οἱ ῥήτορες (ὁ αὐτὸς bis omissis) *Anecd. Et.* 2 post διανοίας add. τῶν δρώντων *Anecd. Et.* 3 τουτέστιν] καὶ *Anecd. Et.* 3–4 ἐν τῷ β′ ... αὐτῷ om. *Anecd. Et.* 4 τῆς alt. om. *Anecd. Et.*

F23 Concerning the now-prevailing separation [*diastasis*], for "orderly arrangement of the world." Antiphon in the second book of *Truth*.

F24 Unseparated, used by Antiphon of that which is not yet separated or distinguished.

F24A Antiphon used the word **disposition** [*diathesis*] of mind or thought. He also used it of setting forth a speech, that is, narrating something. In the second book of *Truth* he used it as well of the orderly arrangement of the world.

Cf. also Hesychius, s.v. διάθεσιν (δ 1015, 1.431 Latte) **διάθεσιν**· διακόσμησιν.

F25 Harpocration, s.v. δίνῳ (δ 12, 68 Keaney)

δίνῳ· ἀντὶ τοῦ δινήσει. Ἀντιφῶν Ἀληθείας β′.

F26 Aëtius, II.20.15 (351 Diels) [Περὶ οὐσίας ἡλίου]

Ἀντιφῶν πῦρ ἐπινεμόμενον μὲν τὸν περὶ τὴν γῆν ὑγρὸν ἀέρα, ἀνατολὰς δὲ καὶ δύσεις ποιούμενον τῷ τὸν μὲν ἐπικαιόμενον αἰεὶ προλείπειν, τοῦ δ' ὑπονοτιζομένου πάλιν ἀντέχεσθαι.

F27 Aëtius, II.28.4 (358 Diels) [Περὶ φωτισμῶν σελήνης]

Ἀντιφῶν ἰδιοφεγγῆ μὲν τὴν σελήνην, τὸ δὲ ἀποκρυπτόμενον περὶ αὐτὴν ὑπὸ τῆς προσβολῆς τοῦ ἡλίου ἀμαυροῦσθαι, πεφυκότος τοῦ ἰσχυροτέρου τὸ ἀσθενέστερον ἀμαυροῦν· ὃ δὴ συμβαίνειν καὶ περὶ τὰ ἄλλα ἄστρα.

F28 Aëtius, II.29.3 (359 Diels) [Περὶ ἐκλείψεως σελήνης]

Ἀλκμαίων, Ἡράκλειτος, Ἀντιφῶν κατὰ τὴν τοῦ σκαφοειδοῦς στροφὴν καὶ τὰς περικλίσεις.

cod. = H 6–7 -σειν (pro -σιν) bis H **F25** codd. = D E Q K M N P Ald. 1 δινbis N: δειν- bis cet. codd. (Dindorf et Keaney approbantibus) ἀντὶ τοῦ ... Ἀληθείας β′ om. E **F26** Stob. 1.25.1[f] et iterum ante 1.25.3[a] (codd. = F P) lemm. ἀντιφῶντος add. P in marg. (utroque loco) 2–3 ἐπικαιόμενον P post corr. F alt. loco P alt. loco: ἐπικειόμενον F P ante corr. 3 ὑποτονιζομένου F alt. loco **F27** Stob. 1.26.2 (codd. = F P); [Plut.] 2.28 (codd. = M m α A E et Euseb. Ar) lemm. ἀντιφῶντος add. Stob. P in marg. 1 ἰδιοφεγγῆ μὲν Stob.: ἰδίῳ φέγγει λάμπειν [Plut.] 1–2 ὑποκρυπτόμενον Euseb. 2 ἀπὸ Euseb. 2–3 ἀμαυροῦσθαι om. Ar 3 ἰσχυροτέρου πυρὸς [Plut.] M A E α Euseb. Ar: ἰσχυροτάτου φωτὸς [Plut.] m 4 δὲ [Plut.] m συμβαίνειν Stob.: συμβαίνει [Plut.] **F28** Stob. 1.26.3 (codd. = F P); [Plut.] 2.29 (codd. = M m α A E et Euseb. Ar) lemm. ἀλκμαίωνος καὶ ἑτέρων add. Stob. P in marg. 1 Ἀλκμαίων om. [Plut.] Ἀντιφῶν Heeren: Ἀντίφαντος Stob. F P: om. [Plut.] κατὰ] καὶ Stob. P ante corr. 2 στροφὴν Stob. Eus. Ar (ut vid.): συστροφὴν [Plut.] codd. καὶ τὰς περικλίσεις om. [Plut.]: καὶ ⟨σχηματίζεσθαι κατὰ⟩ τὰς περικλίσεις Ruestow

F25 **By whirl** for "by whirling." Antiphon in the second book of *Truth.*

F26 Antiphon says the sun is fire that feeds on the moist air around the earth and produces its risings and settings by continually abandoning the scorched air and clinging in turn to air which is somewhat moistened.

F27 Antiphon says the moon has its own light, and that the light that is hidden around it is obscured by the impact of the sun, since the stronger light naturally obscures the weaker. He says this happens to the other stars as well.

F28 Alcmaeon, Heraclitus, and Antiphon say the moon is eclipsed because of the turning of its bowl-shaped body, and because of the inclinations.

F29 Galen, *In Hippocratis Epidemiarum librum* III *commentaria* 3.33 (128.5–9, 129.1–8 Wenkebach)

ἄμεινον δʼ οὖν ἐστιν εἰπεῖν, εἴπερ τις ἐθέλοι καὶ περὶ τῶν τοιούτων ἀδολεσχεῖν, οὐκ ἀπὸ τῆς ἰλλώσεως γεγονέναι τὸ κατείλλουσαι νομίζειν ⟨δεῖν⟩, ἀλλʼ ἀφʼ ἑτέρου τινός, ᾧ καὶ Πλάτων φαίνεται καὶ Ἀντιφῶν κεχρημένος ... οὕτω δὲ καὶ παρʼ Ἀντιφῶντι κατὰ τὸ δεύτερον τῆς Ἀληθείας ἔστιν εὑρεῖν γεγραμμένην τὴν προσηγορίαν ἐν τῆδε τῇ ῥήσει· **ὅταν οὖν γένωνται ἐν τῷ ἀέρι ὄμβροι τε καὶ πνεύματα ὑπεναντία ἀλλήλοις, τότε συστρέφεται τὸ ὕδωρ καὶ πυκνοῦται κατὰ πολλά· ὅτι δʼ ἂν τῶν ξυμπιπτόντων †κρατήσῃ†, τοῦτʼ ἐπυκνώθη καὶ συνεστράφη ὑπό τε τοῦ πνεύματος εἰλλόμενον καὶ ὑπὸ τῆς βίας**. καὶ γὰρ καὶ οὗτος τὸ κατακλειόμενον ἢ συνειλούμενον εἰς ἑαυτὸ φαίνεται δηλῶν διὰ τῆς εἰλλόμενον φωνῆς.

F29 codd. = L M Q V et Hun. 1 εἰπεῖν om. L τις ἐθέλοι (ἐθέλει cum οι suprascr. Q) M Q V: ἄν τις ἐθέλῃ L 2 ἰλλώσεως M Q V: εἰλώσεως L 3 νομίζειν om. Hun. δεῖν add. Wenkebach 5 κατὰ om. V 6 τῆδε] δὲ L 8 ἄλλοις τό τοτε Q 9 δʼ] γὰρ Blass 10 κρατήσῃ L M Q V (quibuscum non forma, sed vi verbi congruit Hun.): κρατηθῇ Sauppe: κρυστήνῃ Wenkebach 11 εἰλλόμενον Wenkebach: εἰλόμενον M V: εἰλούμενον L Q 12 κατακλειόμενος (τὸ omisso) L 13 εἰλλόμενον Wenkebach: εἰλόμενον L: εἱλόμενον Q V: εἰλώμενον M

F29 In any case, it is better to say (should anyone wish to prattle about such things) that the word *kateillousai* must be thought to come not from "distortion" [*illosis*], but from another word which Plato and Antiphon both clearly used ... So also in Antiphon, in the second book of *Truth*, it is possible to find the name written in this passage: **whenever, then, rain-showers and contrary winds have arisen in the air, then the water is compacted and condensed, many drops at a time. Whichever of the colliding drops** (?) **is overcome** (?), **is condensed and compacted, compressed by the force of the wind**. It is clear that Antiphon too signifies by the word "compressed" [*eillomenon*] that which is confined or pressed into itself.

F29A Galen, *On Medical Names* 34.9–38 Meyerhof–Schacht

وان احتجت مني إلى شهادة استدل بها من كلام أصحاب الريطوريقي لتعلم ان اولئك أيضا إنما كانوا يريدون بقولهم حمى الحرارة النارية الخارجة عن الطبع فاسمع قول انطيفون حيث يقال: «فهذه أشياء قد أخبرتك ان المرة كانت تفعلها لانها كانت في اليدين والرجلين، واما التي كانت تتأدى إلى اللحم فانما كانت إذا كان مقدارها كثيرا احدثت حميات دائمة، لان اللحم إذا صارت إليه حدث به منها فساد في نفس جوهره وتورم فالحرارة الخارجة عن الطبع تكون من هذا الموضع فاما دوامها واطباقها فيكون من قبل المرة إذا كانت كثيرة في اللحم لم تنصب وتخف سريعا بل كانت تبقى بان تصبر عند الحرارة الخارجة عن الطبع». فأنت تجد انطيفون في كلامه هذا لم يقتصر على ان يسمى الحرارة الخارجة عن الطبع بالاسم الذي يسميها به جميع اليونانيين من أهل اللغة المعروفة بأطيقى وهي ثرمى فقال ان في جميع المحمومين حرارة تسمى بهذا الاسم دون ان اخبرك كيف تكون هذه الحرارة فنسب السبب في كونها إلى المرار. وكذلك قال أيضا في هذه المقالة الثانية بعينها من مقالاته في الحق قولا نسب فيه السبب في كون الحمى إلى المرار فقال: «واما كل شيء منها يتأدى إلى اللحم فانه يولد حميات شديدة طويلة المدة». ثم انه من بعد هذا إذا أمعن في القول قليلا يلقب الحرارة التي تكون على غير المجرى الطبيعي في النقرس بغير اللقب الذي يلقبها به جميع أصحابه فيسميها فلغمونى وحمى وهذان اسمان يدلان في هذا الموضع على اللهيب. وقد نستدل على ان القدماء كانوا يسمون كل شيء شبيه بالالتهاب فلغمونى من شرح كلامهم، فان المفسرين لكلامهم ليسوا بقليلي العدد. واما انهم كانوا يسمون ذلك أيضا حمى فأنت تستدل على ذلك من هذا القول الذي انسخه لك من قول انطيفون: «فالعروق إذا وردها أكثر مما تحتمل انفتحت وبسبب هذا يحدث بها فلغمونى، فإذا حدث بها فلغمونى وصارت توجع صاحبها وإذا استحكم ذلك سميت هذه العلة نقرسا».

F29A If you ask me for evidence from the utterances of the rhetors to serve as proof, so that you may know that these too meant by the word "fever" fiery, unnatural heat, then listen to the utterance of Antiphon where he says: **these, as I told you, are things that were caused by bile, because it was present in the hands and feet; whereas the bile which advanced to the flesh produced chronic fevers, when its mass was great. For when it advances to the flesh, there arises through it a corruption in the flesh's very substance and it swells up. The unnatural warmth therefore will come from this place; and if it lasts and becomes engrained, that will result from the bile, when it is present in abundance in the flesh and does not quickly disperse and subside, but remains, by persisting alongside the unnatural warmth**. You find, therefore, that in these words of his Antiphon does not restrict himself to calling unnatural warmth by the name by which all Greek speakers of the dialect known as Attic call it, i.e. *therme*, so as to say that in the case of all who suffer from fever there is a warmth, which is known by this name. But he also informs you how this heat will arise, and traces the cause of its genesis to varieties of bile. Again in this same second book of his discourse *On Truth*, he makes another remark in which he traces the cause of the genesis of fever to varieties of gall, by saying: **every bit of it (any one of them) which advances to the flesh produces strong, long-lasting fevers**. Thereafter, when going into it a little further, he will use for the warmth that arises in an unnatural way in connection with arthritis (gout) a designation other than that used by all his colleagues, namely *phlegmone* and fever, two names which in this context point to burning. We can show that the ancients used to call everything resembling

(continued on page 153)

F30 Harpocration, s.v. γρυπάνιον (γ 18, 64 Keaney); cf. Photius, *Lexicon* s.v. (γ 222, 1.369 Theodoridis), *Etymologicum magnum* s.v. (242 Gaisford), *Suda* s.v. (γ 468, 1.544 Adler)

γρυπάνιον· Ἀντιφῶν Ἀληθείας β′· **καῖον γὰρ τὴν γῆν καὶ συντῆκον γρυπάνιον ποιεῖ.**

F31 Photius, *Lexicon* s.v. γρυπανίζειν (γ 220, 1.369 Theodoridis); cf. *Anecdota Graeca* s.v. γυμπάνειν (228 Bekker), *Etymologicum magnum* s.vv. γρυπανίζειν and γυπάνειν (242, 244 Gaisford)

γρυπανίζειν· σείεσθαι τὴν γῆν παλλομένην καὶ ὥσπερ ⟨γ⟩ρυποῦσθαι ἀπὸ σεισμοῦ. οὕτως ἐχρήσατο Ἀντιφῶν.

F32 Aëtius, III.16.4 (381–82 Diels) [Περὶ θαλάσσης πῶς συνέστη καὶ πῶς ἐστι πικρά]

Ἀντιφῶν ἱδρῶτα †τοῦ θερμοῦ†, ἐξ οὗ τὸ περιληφθὲν ὑγρὸν ἀπεκρίθη τῷ καθεψηθῆναι †παραλυκίσασα†, ὅπερ ἐπὶ παντὸς ἱδρῶτος συμβαίνει.

F30 1 post Ἀντιφῶν add. δέ φησιν ἐν Epit. Harp. Phot. *Et. Sud.* Ἀληθείας δευτέρῳ Epit. Harp. Phot. *Sud.* 1–2 καίων . . . συντήκων Epit. Harp. Phot. *Et. Sud.* 1 post γὰρ add. ἦν *Sud.* **F31** cod. = z 1 σείεσθαι] οἴεσθαι *Anecd. Et.* (s.v γυπάνειν) παλλομένην *Anecd. Et.* (s.v γυπάνειν): βαλλομένην Phot. *Et.* (s.v. γρυπανίζειν) 2 ⟨γ⟩ρυποῦσθαι Theodoridis: ῥυποῦσθαι z: ῥυσοῦσθαι *Et.* (s.v. γρυπανίζειν): ἅλλεσθαι *Anecd. Et.* (s.v γυπάνειν) ὑπὸ *Anecd. Et.* (s.v. γυπάνειν) οὕτως . . . Ἀντιφῶν om. *Anecd. Et.* (s.v γυπάνειν): ἐχρήσατο om. *Et.* (s.v. γρυπανίζειν) **F32** [Plut.] 3.16 (codd. = M m α A E Voss. et pap. Euseb. Ar) 1 τοῦ Euseb. Ar: om. codd.: τοῦ ⟨πρώτου ὑγροῦ ἐξατμισθέντος ὑπὸ τοῦ⟩ Diels θερμόν Lachenaud περιληφθὲν A E α: περιλειφθὲν M m pap. Euseb.: om. Ar 2 ἀπεκρίθη M A E α Euseb.: ὑπεκρίθη m: ἀπεκρίθη ⟨καὶ θάλασσα ἐπωνομάσθη⟩ Diels καθεψηθῆναι pap. Euseb.: κατεψηθῆναι codd.: om. (una cum τῷ et παραλυκίσασα) Ar παραλυκίσασα M m Euseb.: παρακυλίσασα A E α: παραλυκίσαν Voss. corrector alter: παραλυκίσαντα Xylander: παραλυκισθῆναι Diels: παραλυκίσαι Lachenaud

inflammation *phlegmone* from the exegesis of what they said; for it has been explained by more than a few commentators. And that they also used to call it fever, you can show from the following remark, which I reproduce for you from the text of Antiphon: **thus when more gets into the vessels than they can bear, they open up, and because of this there arises through them (it) *phlegmone*. And when *phlegmone* arises through them (it) and starts to cause pain for the one afflicted by it, and this takes root, then one calls this disease arthritis (gout).**

(page 152)

F30 "Wrinkled," Antiphon in the second book of *Truth*: **for it** [*sc.* fire] **makes the earth wrinkled by burning it and fusing it together**.

F31 **To become wrinkled**: for the earth to quiver and quake and be bent, as it were, from an earthquake. Antiphon used the word in this way.

F32 Antiphon says the sea is sweat ... from which the enclosed moisture has been separated out and become salty (?) through boiling, something which happens in the case of all sweat.

F33(a) Harpocration, s.v. πεφοριῶσθαι (π 65, 214 Keaney); cf. Photius, *Lexicon* s.v. περιφοριῶσθαι (2.424 Porson), *Suda* s.v. (π 1342, 4.112 Adler)

πεφοριῶσθαι· ... ἐὰν δὲ γράφηται πεφορινῶσθαι, εἴη ἂν πεπαχύνθαι, ἀπὸ τῆς φορίνης· ὅτι γὰρ καὶ ἐπ' ἀνθρώπων τάσσουσι τὴν **φορίνην** δῆλον ποιεῖ Ἀντιφῶν ἐν β' Ἀληθείας.

F33(b) Harpocration, s.v. φορίνη (φ 25, 262 Keaney); cf. *Etymologicum magnum* s.v. (798 Gaisford), *Suda* s.v. (φ 597, 4.750 Adler)

φορίνη· Ἀντιφῶν Ἀληθείας β'.

F34 Pollux, 2.41 (1.94 Bethe)

καὶ καρηβαρικὸν ποτὸν ἢ βρῶμα· τὸ δὲ τοῦτο ποιεῖν **καροῦν** Ἀντιφῶν φησίν.

F35 Pollux, 2.215 (1.149 Bethe)

καὶ **ἐναιμῶδες** παρὰ Ἀντιφῶντι.

F36 Pollux, 2.223 (1.151 Bethe)

καὶ Ἀντιφῶν δ' εἴρηκεν **ἐν ᾧ τὸ ἔμβρυον αὐξάνεταί τε καὶ τρέφεται, καλεῖται χόριον.**

F33(a) 1 πεφοριῶσθαι] περιφοριῶσθαι Phot. *Sud.* 2 φορόνης *Sud.* 2–3 ὅτι γὰρ ... φορίνην] τάσσουσι (τάττουσι *Sud.*) γὰρ ἐπὶ ἀνθρώπων τὴν φορίνην (φορόνην *Sud.*) Epit. Harp. Phot. *Sud.* 3–4 δῆλον ... Ἀληθείας om. Epit. Harp. Phot. *Sud.* **F33(b)** 1 Ἀληθείας β' om. Epit. Harp. *Et. Sud.* post Ἀντιφῶν add. φησιν ὅτι ἐπ' ἀνθρωπίνου (ἀνθρωπείου *Et.*) δέρματος ἐλέγετο ἡ φορίνη Epit. Harp. *Et. Sud.* (haec ad Ἀριστομένης ἐν Γόησι [= fr. 10] recte refert Harp.) **F34** codd. = M F S A C B 1 ποτὸν] πῶμα M τὸ δὲ ... ποιεῖν om. M 1–2 τὸ δὲ ποιοῦν τὸ νόσημα καρούν B C 2 Ἀντιφῶν φησίν om. B C **F35** codd. = F S A C B 1 καὶ ... Ἀντιφῶντι om. B C **F36** codd. = F S A C B 1–2 καὶ Ἀντιφῶν ... χόριον om. B C 1 ἄντιπον F S δ' om. F S 2 χωρίον καλοῦσι F S: ὃ καλεῖται χόριον A

F33(a) "To be covered all around with skin" [*pephoriosthai*] . . . But if the word is written *pephorinosthai*, it will mean "to have become thick," from "hide" [*phorine*]. For Antiphon makes it clear in the second book of *Truth* that the word **hide** is applied to human beings as well.

F33(b) **Hide**, Antiphon in the second book of *Truth*.

F34 Food or drink that causes headache or drowsiness; and for producing this result Antiphon says **stupefy**.

F35 **Bloody**, in Antiphon.

F36 Antiphon said: **that in which the fetus grows and is nourished is called chorium**.

F37 Pollux, 2.224 (1.151–52 Bethe)

Ἀντιφῶν δ' αὐτὸν [*sc.* **ἐπίπλους**] καὶ ἀρρενικῶς καὶ οὐδετέρως καλεῖ.

F38 Pollux, 2.7 (1.82 Bethe); cf. Photius, *Lexicon* s.vv. ἄμβλωσις καὶ ἀμβλωθέντες (α 1163, 1.122 Theodoridis)

καὶ **ἄμβλωμα**, ὡς Ἀντιφῶν.

Cf. also Hesychius, s.v. ἄμβλωμα (α 3515, 1.123 Latte) **ἄμβλωμα**· ἔκτρωμα.

F39 Pollux, 2.61 (1.101 Bethe)

Ἀντιφῶν δ' ἐν τοῖς Περὶ ἀληθείας καὶ **ἀνάπηρα** εἴρηκεν.

F40 Pollux, 7.169 (2.98 Bethe)

καὶ Ἀντιφῶν **βάψιν** χαλκοῦ καὶ σιδήρου.

F41 Pollux, 7.189 (2.104 Bethe)

βιομήχανοι ὡς Ἀντιφῶν.

F42(a) Pollux, 9.53 (2.161 Bethe)

ἡ μὲν γὰρ Ἀντιφῶντος **ταλάντωσις** τὸ βάρος δηλοῖ.

F42(b) Hesychius, s.v. ταλαντώσει (τ 61, 4.125 Schmidt); cf. *Anecdota Graeca* s.v. ταλάντωσις (381 Bachmann), Photius, *Lexicon* s.v. (2.567 Porson), *Suda* s.v. (τ 36, 4.498 Adler)

ταλαντώσει· σταθμήσει, στήσει.

F38 codd. = M F S A C B 1 καὶ om. B C ὡς om. Phot.: ὡς Ἀντιφῶν om. B C **F39** codd. = M F S A C B 1 Ἀντιφῶν ... ἀληθείας et εἴρηκεν om. M Ἀντιφῶν ... καὶ om. B C περὶ ἀλήθειαν A **F40** codd. = F S A C B 1 καὶ pr. om. B βαψίναι A **F41** codd. = F S A C B 1 βιομήχανοι ... Ἀντιφῶν om. B βιομηχανία A **F42(a)** codd. = F S C L B A 1 ἡ μὲν ... δηλοῖ om. S C L A B **F42(b)** 1 -σις (pro -σει) ter *Anecd.* Phot. *Sud.*

F37 Antiphon uses **omentum** [*epiplous*] in both the masculine and neuter genders.

F38 **Aborted fetus**, as Antiphon.

F39 In *On Truth* Antiphon also said **deformed**.

F40 **Dipping** of bronze and iron, Antiphon.

F41 **Clever at getting a living**, as Antiphon said.

F42(a) For Antiphon's **balancing** [*talantosis*] signifies weight.

F42(b) **By weighing**: by measuring, by setting on the scales.

F43(a) Harpocration, s.v. ἄβιος (α 2, 1 Keaney); cf. Photius, *Lexicon* s.v. (α 38, 1.12 Theodoridis), *Suda* s.v. (α 47, 1.7 Adler)

ἄβιος· τὸν ἄβιον Ἀντιφῶν ἐπὶ τοῦ πολὺν τὸν βίον κεκτημένου ἔταξεν.

F43(b) Hesychius, s.v. ἄβιος (α 127, 1.7 Latte)

ἄβιος· πλούσιος, ὡς Ἀντιφῶν ἐν Ἀληθείᾳ.

Cf. also Pollux, 6.196 (2.49 Bethe) καὶ **ἄβιος**, ἔμβιος [= F15] ὡς Ἀντιφῶν φησί.

F44(a) *P.Oxy.* 1364, fr. 1; cf. Harpocration, s.v. ἄγοι (α 7, 2 Keaney)

I

]θ̣ου
]νοη
]ημε
] . . νευ
]μι
] δ̣ικα[ιοσ]ύνη
δ' οὖ]ν τὰ τῆς πό-
λεως̣ νόμιμα,
ἐν ᾗ̣] ἂν πολι-
τεύ]η̣ταί τις, μὴ
παρ]αβαίνειν.
χρῷ̣τ' ἂν οὖν

F43(a) 1 ἄβιος Epit. Harp. Phot. *Sud.*: om. Harp. τὸν ἄβιον post Ἀντιφῶν transp. *Sud.*: om. Epit. Harp. Phot. ἐπὶ Epit. Harp. Phot. *Sud.*: ἀντὶ Harp. τὸν alt. Epit. Harp. *Sud.*: om. Harp. Phot. 2 τάττει κεκτημένου Epit. Harp. Phot. *Sud.* **F44(a)1** ed. pr. = Grenfell et Hunt (1915); CPF = Decleva Caizzi et Bastianini (1989) 2]η ed. pr. 3]μ̣ε ed. pr. 4]ν̣ευ ed. pr. 5–6 sic ed. pr.:]νόμι-[μον·] CPF (cf. comm. ad loc.): τίθη]μι [ὅτι] Körte: alii alia 7 δ' οὖ]ν CPF: πάν]τα ⟨τὰ⟩ ed. pr.: δ' ἦ]ν H. Schöne: οὖ]ν (spatio brevius ut vid.) Diels 9]η̣ι ed. pr. 12 χρῶτ' ante corr.: ι suprascr.

F43(a) Antiphon used the word **wealthy** [*abios*] of one who possesses a livelihood [*bios*] which is substantial.

F43(b) **Wealthy**: rich, as Antiphon in *Truth*.

F44(a) ... justice, then, is not to transgress the laws of whatever city one lives in. Now a

Νόμος vs φύσις

ἄνθρωπος μά-
λιστα ἑαυτῷ
ξυμφ[ε]ρόντως
δικαιο[σ]ύνῃ, εἰ
μετὰ μὲν μαρ-
τύρων τ⸤ο⸥ὺς νό-
μους μεγά⸤λο⸥υς
ἄγοι, μονούμε-
νος δὲ μαρτύ-
ρων τὰ τῆς φύ-
σεως· τὰ μὲν γὰρ
τῶν νόμων
ἐπίθ]ετα, τὰ δὲ
τῆς] φύσεως ἀ-
ναγ]καῖα· καὶ τὰ
μὲν] τῶν νό-
μω]ν̣ ὁμολογη-
θέντ]α̣ οὐ φύν-
τα ἐστί]ν, τὰ δὲ
τῆς φύσ]εως φύν-
τα οὐχ] ὁμολογη-

II

θ̣[έ]ντα.[⟦ο]υχ[ο]⟧
⟦μολογηθεν⟧
⟦τα⟧ τὰ οὖν νόμι-
⟦——⟧
μα παραβαίνων

14 θ' post λιστα del. corr. 18–20 Ἀντιφῶν δ' ἐν τῷ Περὶ ἀληθείας φησί· τοὺς νόμους μεγάλους ἄγοι, ἀντὶ τοῦ ἡγοῖτο Harp. (cf. *Anecdota Graeca* 13 Bachmann; Photius, *Lexicon* α 223, 1.29; *Anecdota Graeca Oxoniensia* 2.488; *Suda* α 381, 1.39) 19 μεγα|λο|υς ante corr.: μεγα|λ|ως post corr. 25 ἐπίθ|ετα ed. pr.: ξύνθ|ετα (spatio longius ut vid.) Luria

F44(a)II ed. pr. = Grenfell et Hunt (1915); CPF = Decleva Caizzi et Bastianini (1989) 1–4 |ο|υχ |ο|μολογηθεντα et paragraph. del. corr.

man would make use of justice in a way most advantageous to himself if he were to regard the laws as great in the presence of witnesses, but nature as great when deprived of witnesses. For the laws are imposed, whereas nature is necessary; and the laws are not born but agreed upon, whereas nature is not agreed upon but born. When a man transgresses the laws, then,

ἐὰν λάθῃ τοὺς ὁμολογήσαντας καὶ αἰσχύνης καὶ ζημίας ἀπήλλακται· μὴ λαθὼν δ' οὔ· τῶν δὲ τῇ φύσει ξυμφύτων ἐάν τι παρὰ τὸ δυνατὸν βιάζηται, ἐάν τε πάντας ἀνθρώπους λάθῃ, οὐδὲν ἔλαττον τὸ κακόν, ἐάν τε πάντες ἴδωσιν, οὐδὲν μεῖζον· οὐ γὰρ διὰ δόξαν βλάπτεται, ἀλλὰ δι' ἀλήθειαν. ἔστι δὲ πάντων ἕνεκα τούτων ἡ σκέψις, ὅτι τὰ πολλὰ τῶν κατὰ νόμον δικαίων πολεμίως τῇ φύσ̣[ει] κ̣εῖται· νενο[μο]θ̣[έ]τηται γὰρ [ἐ]πί τε τοῖς ὀφ[θ]αλμοῖς, ἃ δεῖ

5 ἐὰν scripsi: ἢ ante corr.: ἦι post. corr.: εἰὰν Wilamowitz: εἰ ἂν CPF   αθηι ante corr.: λ suprascr.   12 εαντε: corr. ed. pr.   16 ληθηι ante corr.: α suprascr. et η del. corr.   22 βλατεται ante corr.: π suprascr.   24 τωνδε ante corr.: παντων (παν suprascr.) post. corr.: πάν⟨τως⟩ τῶνδε Diels: ⟨ἐπὶ⟩ πᾶν H. Schöne   29 τη   33 φ[θ]αλμιοις ante corr.: ι del. corr.

he is free from shame and punishment if he escapes the notice of those who agreed on them; but if he does not, he is not. If, on the other hand, he tries to do violence beyond what is possible to any of the things born with nature, the harm is no less if he escapes the notice of all men, and no greater if all see him. For he is harmed not through opinion but through reality.

The examination is being conducted for this reason: because the majority of what is just according to law and convention is hostile to nature. For laws have been established over the eyes, as to what they must

III

αὐτο[ὺ]ς ὁρᾶν καὶ ἃ οὐ [δε]ῖ· καὶ ἐπὶ τοῖς ὠσίν, ἃ δεῖ αὐτὰ ἀκούειν καὶ ἃ οὐ δεῖ· καὶ ἐπὶ τῇ γλώττῃ, ἅ τ[ε] δεῖ αὐτὴν λέγειν καὶ ἃ οὐ δεῖ· καὶ ἐπὶ ταῖς χερσίν, ἅ τε δεῖ αὐτὰς δρᾶν καὶ ἃ οὐ δεῖ· καὶ ἐπὶ τοῖς ποσίν, ἐφ' ἅ τε δεῖ αὐτοὺς ἰέναι καὶ ἐφ' ἃ οὐ δεῖ· καὶ ἐπὶ τῷ νῷ, ὧν τε δεῖ αὐτὸν ἐπιθυμεῖν καὶ ὧν μή. [ἔστι]ν οὖν οὐδὲν τ[ῇ] φύσει φιλιώτ[ερ]α οὐδ' οἰκειότε[ρα] ἀφ' ὧν οἱ νόμο[ι ἀ]ποτρέπουσι τ[οὺς] ἀν[θ]ρ̣ώπ[ους] ἢ ἐ̣φ' ἃ [προτρέ]πουσ[ιν]· τ̣[ὸ δὲ] ζῆν [ἐ]στὶ τῆς φύ̣-

F44(a)III ed. pr. = Grenfell et Hunt (1915); CPF = Decleva Caizzi et Bastianini (1989) 2 ου[δε]ι· ς ante corr.: ς del. corr. 3 ὤσιν 16 διαυτον ante corr.: ε suprascr. 18 ωμη ante corr.: ν suprascr. [ἔστι]ν ed. pr.: [οὐ μὲ]ν Diels: [οὐ]κ Wilamowitz: [ἧττο]ν CPF 19 ουδετ[ante corr.: ν suprascr. 21–25 ordinem verb. ἀφ' ὧν ... ἀποτρέπουσι et ἐφ' ἃ προτρέπουσιν invertendum suspicatur Gernet 23 αν (θρωπους om.) ante corr.: [θ]ρω[πους] inter columnas add. corr. 24 ἢ ante ἀφ' ὧν (l. 21) transp. H. Gomperz [προτρέ-] ed. pr.: [ἐπιτρέ-] H. Schöne 25 τ̣[ὸ δὲ scripsi: τ̣[ὸ γὰρ ed. pr.: τ̣[ὸ δ' αὖ Diels: π̣[άλιν τὸ Wilamowitz

and must not see; and over the ears, as to what they must and must not hear; and over the tongue, as to what it must and must not say; and over the hands, as to what they must and must not do; and over the feet, as to what they must and must not go after; and over the mind, as to what it must and must not desire. Now, the things from which the laws try to dissuade people are no more friendly or akin to nature than the things to which they encourage them. Living and dying belong to nature;

σεως κ[αὶ τ]ὸ ἀπο-
θαν[εῖ]ν̣· καὶ τὸ
μὲν̣ [ζ]ῆν αὐτ[ῇ
ἐστι[ν ἀ]πὸ τῶν
ξυμ[φερό]ντω̣[ν,
τὸ δὲ ἀ[ποθανεῖν
ἀ̣πὸ τ̣[ῶν μὴ ξυμ-

IV

φερόντω[ν. τὰ
δὲ ξυμφέρ[οντα
τὰ μὲν ὑπ[ὸ τῶν
νόμων κε[ί-
μενα δεσμ[οὶ
τῆς φύσεώς ἐ[στι,
τὰ δ᾽ ὑπὸ τῆς φύ̣-
σεως ἐλεύθερα. [οὔ-
κουν τὰ ἀλγύ-
νοντα ὀρθῷ̣ γε λ̣[ό-
γω̣ ὀνίνησιν τὴ[ν
φύσιν μᾶλλον
ἢ τὰ εὐφραίνον-
τα· οὔκουν [ἂ]ν οὐ-
δὲ ξυμφέρον-
τ᾽ εἴη τὰ λυποῦ̣[ντα
μᾶλλον ἢ τ[ὰ ἥ-
δοντ[α]· τὰ γὰρ τῷ̣

27 κ[οὖ τ]ὸ Theander 29 αὐτ[ῇ scripsi: αὐτ[οῖς ed. pr. 30–33 suppl. ed. pr. **F44(a)IV** ed. pr. = Grenfell et Hunt (1915); CPF = Decleva Caizzi et Bastianini (1989) 1 φεροντων· τα ed. pr. 2 δεξυμφεροντα· ed. pr. 3 ταμεναποτων ed. pr. ὑπὸ ed. pr. 4–5 κε[ί]μενα ed. pr.: κεκ̣[ρι]μένα von Arnim: κεκ̣[ελευσ]μένα Diels 5 δεσμ[οὶ CPF: δεσμ[ὰ ed. pr. 8 ελευθερα· ου ed. pr. 10 νουντα (α ex ο corr.): corr. ed. pr. ὀρθῷ γε ed. pr.: ορθωιλ[ante corr.: τε suprascr. 11 ονινησι ante corr.: ν suprascr. 14 όυκουν αν ed. pr. 16 τ'] γ' Theander 18 τω̣[ι: τω̣ι̣ ed. pr. 18–19 paragraph. del. corr.

and living comes to nature from what is advantageous, dying from what is not. As for advantages, those established by the laws are chains on nature, whereas those established by nature are free. Things that cause pain, at any rate, do not, in truth, benefit nature more than things that give pleasure; things that cause pain, then, are not more advantageous, either, than things that give pleasure.

⟦——⟧
ἀλη[θε]ῖ ξυμφέ-
ρ[οντ]α οὐ βλά-
π[τει]ν δεῖ ἀλ[λ' ὠ-
φ̣[ε]λεῖν. τὰ τοίνυ[ν
τῇ φύσει ξυμ-
φ̣έροντα τ[α]υτ[. .
desunt 2 vel 3 lineae
. . . . . .]ο̣τ̣ι̣ α̣[
. . . . . .]απ[. . .
. . . . . .] ανα̣[
. . . . . .]καιοι.[.
. . . . . .]ν̣ται· κα[ὶ
[οἵτινε]ς̣ ἂν πά-

V

θόν]τες ἀμύνων-
ται κ]αὶ μὴ αὐτοὶ
ἄρχ]ωσιν τοῦ δρᾶν·
καὶ ο]ἵτινε[ς] ἂ̣ν
τοὺς] γειναμέ-
νου]ς̣ καὶ κακοὺς
ὄ̣ντας εἰς αὑτοὺς
εὖ ποιῶσιν· καὶ οἱ
κατόμνυσθαι
διδόντες ἑτέ-

19 αληθ̣ε̣ι̣ ed. pr. 20 ρ[ο]ντα ed. pr. 21 π[τ]εινδει·αλλω ed. pr. 22 τοινυν ed. pr. 24 τ[α]υτ[(spatio congruentius ut vid.) CPF: τ[ο]υτ[ed. pr.: τ[ο]ῦτ[ο ἔχει ἴδιον Bignone, Regenbogen: τ[ο]ῦτ[ο ποιεῖ von Arnim: τ[ο]ύτ[ων Diels 28(27)–33(32) sic ed. pr. (fragmentum has lineas continens nunc deperditum est) 30(29) ἀνα̣ vel ανα̣ cum ε suprascr. ed. pr. 31(30) post οι legit γ, η, μ, ν, π (sed non τ) ed. pr. 31(30)–32(31) δί]καιοι [νομίζο]νται· κα[ὶ Heinimann 33(32) [οἵτινε]ς ed. pr. **F44(a)v** ed. pr. = Grenfell et Hunt (1915); CPF = Decleva Caizzi et Bastianini (1989) 1–6 suppl. ed. pr. 8 ποιωσικαι ante corr.: ν suprascr.

For things that are truly advantageous must not harm but help. Now, things which are advantageous to nature ... and those who take vengeance after suffering and do not themselves initiate the violence; and those who treat their parents well even when these have been bad to them; and those who tender an oath to others

ροις, αὐτοὶ δὲ μὴ
κατομνύμε-
νοι.] καὶ τούτων
τῶν εἰρημένων
πόλλ' ἄν τις εὕ-
ροι πολέμια τῇ
φύσει· ἔνι γε αὐ-
τοῖς ἀλγύνεσθαί
τε μᾶλλον ἐξὸν
ἧττω, καὶ ἐλάτ-
τω ἥδεσθαι ἐξὸν
πλείω, καὶ κακῶς
πάσχειν ἐξὸν
μὴ πάσχειν.
ẹἰ μὲν οὖν τις
τ]οῖς τοιαῦτα προ⟨σ-⟩
ι]ẹμένοις ἐπικού-
ρ]ησις ἐγίγνε-
το] παρὰ τῶν νό-
μ]ων, τοῖς δ̣ὲ μὴ
π]ρ̣ο⟨σ⟩ιεμένοις ἀλ-
λ' ἐ]ναντιουμέ-
ν]οις ἐλάττωσις,

VI

οὐκ ἀν[ωφελὲς ἂν
ἦν τ[ὸ τοῖς νό-

17 γε ante corr.: τ' ἐν (ν suprascr.) post corr.: δ' ἐν Regenbogen 18 τοισδ ante corr.: δ del. corr. αγυνεσθαι ante corr.: λ suprascr. 20 ηττω·ι ante corr.: ι del. corr.: ἧττον von Arnim 21 τω·ηδεσθαι ed. pr.; sed cf. CPF ad loc. 26–27 προ[ϊ]ẹμενοις: corr. ed. pr. 31 π]ρ̣οϊεμενοις: corr. ed. pr. 32]ν.αντιουμε ante corr.: . del. corr. 33 ἐλάττωσις] pr. σ ex τ (ut vid.) **F44(a)VI** ed. pr. = Grenfell et Hunt (1915); CPF = Decleva Caizzi et Bastianini (1989) 1 ἀν[ωφελὲς ἂν ed. pr.: ἀν[όνητον Diels 2 νην ante corr.: ν del. corr.

but do not swear one themselves. One would find that many of the things mentioned are hostile to nature, for there is present in them more pain, when less is possible; less pleasure, when more is possible; and suffering, when it is possible not to suffer.

Now, if there were some help from the laws for those who submit to such things, and loss for those who do not submit but resist, obeying the laws might not be unprofit-

μοις πεί[θεσθαι· νῦν
δὲ φαίνε̣[ται τοῖς
προσιεμ[ένοις
τὰ τοιαῦτα τὸ ἐ[κ
νόμου δίκαι[ον
οὐχ ἱκανὸν ἐπι-
κουρεῖν· ὅ γε πρῶ-
τον μὲν ἐπιτρέ-
πει τῷ πάσχον-
τι παθεῖν καὶ τῷ
δρῶντι δρᾶσαι·
καὶ οὔτε ἐνταῦ-
θα διεκώλυε τὸν
πάσχοντα μὴ
παθεῖν οὐδὲ τὸν
δρῶντα δρᾶσαι·
εἴς τε τὴν τιμω-
ρίαν ἀναφερό-
μενον οὐδὲν
ἰδιώτερον ἐπὶ
[τ]ῷ [π]επονθότι
Δ̄ ἢ τῷ δεδρακό-
τι·] περ̣αι γὰρ α̣[
α̣[.]τ̣ο̣ .[. .]υστ .[
ρ̣[. . . . .]ας ὡς ἔ-
παθεν[. .] δύνα-
σθαι απ[. . .]η̣ δι-

2–3 τ[οῖς νό]μοις vel τ[ὸ τοῖς νό]μοις πεί[θεσθαι· νῦν ed. pr.: τ[ὸ τοῖς νό]μοις πεῖ[σμα· νῦν Diels: τ[ὸ ἐν τοῖς νό]μοις πεῖ[σμα· νῦν CPF 4–5 suppl. ed. pr. 8 ουχ' 17 οὔτε Diels 25–26 sic ed. pr.: πεῖ[σ]αι γὰρ ἄ[ν ἕ]λ[οι]το Diels: πεῖ[σ]αι γὰρ δ[εῖ] α[ὐ]τὸν CPF post K. Schmidt et Bignone: alii alia 26–27 [το]ὺς τ[ιμω]ρ[οῦντ]ας ed. pr.: [το]ὺς τ[ιμω]ρ[ήσοντ]ας CPF post Diels 28 [καὶ] (spatio longius ut vid.) Diels: [ἢ] CPF 29 σθαι· ed. pr.; sed cf. CPF ad loc. απ̣[. . .]ε̣ι̣ ed. pr.

able. But as it is, justice in accordance with the law is manifestly incapable of coming to the aid of those who submit to such things. First, it allows the sufferer to suffer and the perpetrator to act. And just as it fails (as we saw) at the time to prevent the sufferer from suffering and the perpetrator from acting, so also when it is referred to for the purpose of punishment, it is no more peculiarly in the power of the sufferer than of the perpetrator. For ... that he suffered ...

κην[. . .]ν· ταῦ-
τα δὲ κ[α]ταλεί-
πετα[ι] ḳαὶ τῷ δρά-
σαντ[ι ἀ]ρνεῖσθαι

VII

[
[
[
[
[. . . .] . . [ἐ-
σ̣τ̣ι̣ν̣ μ̣α̣λ̣[
ὅσηπερ τ[ῷ . . κα-
τηγοροῦ[ντι ἡ τῆς
κατηγορ[ίας . . .
πειθὼ α . [. . . . .
τῷ γε πε̣[πονθό-
τι καὶ τῷ [δεδρα-
κότι· ἐ̣γίγ[
γὰρ ν[

29–30 αἰτ[ιάσ]ει vel ἀπ[αιτ]εῖ (ἀπ[αιτ]εῖ Regenbogen) δίκην [ἑλεῖ]ν Diels: ἅ γ[ε ἐρ]εῖ, δίκην [ἕξει]ν Bignone: ἀπ[άτ]ῃ δίκην [ἔχει]ν CPF 30 ταῦ- Pendrick post Janko: ν·τὰυ: ταὐ- CPF **F44(a)VII** ed. pr. = Grenfell et Hunt (1915); CPF = Decleva Caizzi et Bastianini (1989) 1 [ἑλομένῳ] (exempli grat.) Diels 4–6 sic ed. pr.: [σχολὴ δ'αὐτῷ πρὸς ἀπολογίαν ἐ]στὶν μᾶλ[λον ἢ von Arnim: [καὶ τοῦτο δεινόν ἐ]στιν μάλ[ιστα, ὅτι Bignone: [τῷ ἀπο]λ̣ο̣γ[οῦντί ἐ]σ̣τ̣ι̣ν̣ ἡ ἀπ̣[ολογία CPF: alii alia 7–10 sic ed. pr.: τ[ῷ κα]τηγοροῦν[τι ἡ τῆς] κατηγορ[ίας] πειθὼ ἀ[μύνειν Diels: τ[ῷ κα]τηγοροῦν[τι πρὸς] κατηγορ[ίαν, ἡ δὲ] πειθὼ ἀ[διαφόρως von Arnim: τ[ῷ κα]τηγοροῦ[ντι ἡ] κατηγορ[ική, ἴση] πειθὼ ἀ[μυντικὴ K. Schmidt: τ[οῖς κα]τηγοροῦ[σιν ἡ (*sc.* δύναμις) τοῦ] κατηγορ[εῖν. ἡ δὲ] πειθὼ ἀ[νώμαλος Theander: τ[ῷ γε κα]τηγοροῦ[ντι ἡ τῆς] κατηγορ[ίας ἔνι] πειθώ, ἀ[π' ἴσης Bignone: τ[ῷ κα]τηγοροῦ[ντι ἡ] κατηγορ[ία, ἡ δὲ] πειθὼ ἀν̣[τίπαλος CPF 8 τηιγορου 11 τ̣ε ed. pr. 12 τω[13 ἐ̣γίγ[νετο CPF: γ̣ίγ̣[νεται ed. pr. 13–14 γίγ[νεται·] ⟨ἡ⟩ γὰρ ν[ίκη K. Schmidt

and it is left to the perpetrator to deny these things . . .

μασι κ[
καὶ κ̣[
δυν[α-
δεσα[
οὐδ[
μα[
τευ.[
ωσε[
τωι̣[
εδ[
——
α[
τ[
θ[
⟦——⟧
⟦α[
⟦ν
⟦ασ[
η̣[
ν[
το̣[
⟦ν⟧[

F44(b) *P.Oxy.* 1364, fr. 2 + *P.Oxy.* 3647

I

]τ̣ου
] .
]ο
]λ
ἀνθ]ρ̣ώπ̣οις

13–15 γίγ[νεται] γὰρ ν[ίκη καὶ ῥή]μασι κ[αὶ Diels: ἡ] γὰρ ν[ίκη ἐν ῥή]μασι κ[εῖται vel ὁ] γὰρ ν[ικῶν ῥή]μασι κ[ρατεῖ CPF: alii alia 20–21 [ἐν]τεῦθ̣[εν ed. pr. 27–28 paragraph. del. corr. 28–30 del. corr. 34 ν del. corr. **F44(b)**I ed. pr. = Grenfell et Hunt (1915) 5 ἀνθ]ρώποις ed. pr.

FRAGMENTS

]μ̣ατα
]ητης
]ηλου· ε̣
]ωσ̣ε̣νε
τε]κμαίρε-
σθαι δὲ] παρέχει
] .[.]τας
]ειστων
]ρων⟧
]τα ε̣ -
]α̣ν
]κ̣[. .]
]
]
]
]
]
]
]
]
]
]
]
]
]
]ν̣ο
]ν
]υ̣ς⟧ουκ.[
]εν̣[

10 τε|κμαιρε ed. pr. 11 σθαι δὲ H. Schöne 13 πλ|είστων Diels 14 ρων del. corr. 33 υς del. corr. 33 ουκ (κ suprascr.) inter columnas add. corr. 34 εν̣ inter columnas add. corr. **F44(b)II** ed. pr. = Grenfell et Hunt (1915); Funghi = Funghi (1984); CPF = Decleva Caizzi et Bastianini (1989)

FRAGMENTS

II

ρων ἐπ[ιστάμε-
θά τε κ[αὶ σέβομεν·
τοὺς δὲ [τῶν τη-
λοῦ οἰκ[ούν]των
οὔτε ἐπ̣ι[στ]άμε-
θα οὔτε σέβομεν.
ἐν τ[ο]ύτῳ οὖν
πρὸς ἀλλήλους
βεβαρβαρώμε-
θα· ἐπεὶ φύσει γε
πάντ̣α̣ πάντες
ὁμοίως πεφύκ[α-
μεν καὶ βάρβα-
ροι καὶ Ἕλλην[ες
εἶναι. σκοπεῖν
δ[ὲ] παρέχει τὰ
τῶν φύσει[
ἀναγκαί[ων
πᾶσιν ἀν[θρώ-
ποις· π̣[
τε κατὰ τ[
δυνα[

1 (et praecedentia) [τῶν μὲν ἐγγυτέ]ρων vel [οἰκειοτέ]ρων Funghi: [τῶν ἡμετέ]ρων Luppe: [τῶν πατέ]ρων CPF: [τῶν ἐγχώ]ρων Pendrick: [τοὺς ἐξ Ἀθηναίων μητέ]ρων Mazzarino: [πό]ρων ed. pr.: [τοὺς ἐκ καλῶν πατέ]ρων Wilamowitz: [τοὺς μὲν ἐξ εὐπό]ρων K. Schmidt: [γενναίων πατέ]ρων Bignone 1–5 suppl. Funghi 7 τ[ο]υτω[ι] 17 [ὄντων ed. pr.: [ὁμοίως H. Fränkel 18 ἀναγκαί[ων ed. pr.: ἀναγκαῖ[α Funghi: ἀναγκαῖ[α ἐν CPF 20–24 π[ορίσαι] τε κατ[ὰ ταὐτὰ] δυνα[τὰ πᾶσι,] καὶ ἐν [πᾶσι τού]τοις Diels: π[εφύκασί] τε κατὰ τ[αῦτα] δύνα[σθαι ταὐτὸν] καὶ ἐν Wilamowitz: π[αρεῖναι ὅ]τε τὰ (vel κατὰ τὰ) [αὐτὰ] δύνα[ται τἀντὸς] καὶ ἐκ[τὸς αὐ]τοῖς Bignone: π[ρὸς βρῶσίν] τε κατὰ τα[ὐτά εἰσιν] δυνά[μεις τινὲς] καὶ ἔκ[κρισιν αὐ]τοῖς K. Schmidt: π[ᾶσι ταῖς] γε κατ[ὰ τὸ σῶμα] δυνά[μεσίν τε] καὶ ἐκ[τὸς ὁρα]τοῖς Theander: π[οριζόμενά] τε κατὰ τ[ὰς αὐτὰς] δυνά[μεις ἅπασι,] καὶ ἐν [αὐτοῖς τού]τοις CPF 21 κατ[ante corr.: τα suprascr.: κατὰ τὰ ed. pr.: alii alia (cf. supra)

F44(b) ... [the laws of those near by] we know and observe, the laws of those who live far off we neither know nor observe. Now in this we have become barbarians in one another's eyes; for by birth, at least, we are all naturally adapted in every respect to be either Greeks or barbarians. It is possible to examine ... things by nature necessary for all human beings ...

καὶ ἐṿ[
τοις οὔτε β[άρβα-
ρος ἀφώρι[σται
ἡμῶν ọ[ὐδεὶς
οὔτε Ἕλλην· ἀ-
ναπνέομέν
τε γὰρ εἰς τὸν ἀ-
έρ[α] ἅπαντες
κατὰ τὸ στόμ[α]
[κ]αὶ κατ̣[ὰ] τὰς ῥῖ-
ṿας· κ[αὶ γελῶ-
με]ν χ[αίρον-

III

τες καὶ] δακρύ-
ομε[ν] λ̣υπού-
μενọι̣· καὶ τῇ ἀ-
κοῇ τοὺς φθόγ-
γους εἰσδεχόμε-
θα· καὶ τῇ αὐγῇ
μετὰ τῆς ὄψε-
ως ὁρῶμεν· καὶ
ταῖς χερσὶν ἐρ-
γαζόμεθα· καὶ
τ̣ọῖς ποσὶν βαδ̣[ίζο-
μεν . ṿβ̣[

23 εκ̣[ed. pr. 24 τοις. 24–26 suppl. ed. pr. 26 δημων ante corr.: δ del. corr. 27 ελλην[·]α[33–34 κ[αὶ γελῶμε]ν Funghi 34 χ[αίρον- Luppe: χ[αίροντες τῷ Funghi **F44(b)III** ed. pr. = Funghi (1984) 1 τες καὶ] Luppe: νῷ ἢ] ed. pr. 3 μενọι̣[·] 6 αυτηι ante corr.: αυγηι (γ suprascr.) post corr. 11 ποσι ante corr.: ν suprascr. βαδ̣[ʹ: suppl. ed. pr. 12 μεν· (ut vid.); cf. ed. pr. ad loc.

none of us has been marked off as either barbarian or Greek. For we all breathe into the air by our mouth and nostrils; we laugh when we are happy and cry when we are sad; we take in sounds with our sense of hearing; we see with our sight with the aid of the visual ray; we work with our hands; we walk with our feet ...

IV

. [
τ̣[
. . μ̣ . [
λ̣οι̣ εἰσιν̣[
τα τὸ ἀρε[
εχωρη[
ἕκαστοι.[
καὶ το . . νομ[
το· κ.[. . ʹ
. . . . [

F44(c) *P.Oxy.* 1797

I

. . . . . .] τοῦ δικαίου
. . . . . .]. ου δοκουν-
. . . . τὸ] μαρτυρεῖν
ἀλ]λ̣ήλοις τἀληθῆ
δίκαιο]ν νομίζεται
εἶναι] καὶ χρήσιμον
οὐδὲν] ἧττον εἰς
τὰ τῶν] ἀνθρώπων
ἐπιτ]η̣δεύματα.
τοῦτο] τοίνυν οὐ δί-
καιος] ἔσται ὁ ποιῶν,
εἴπε]ρ τὸ μὴ ἀδικεῖν

F44(b)IV ed. pr. = Funghi (1984); CPF = Decleva Caizzi et Bastianini (1989) 4–6 [κα]τὰ τὸ ἀρέ[σκον συν]εχώρη[σαν] ed. pr. 5 τα-ταρέ[ante corr.: ο suprascr. 8 καινομ[ante corr.: το . . (τοῖς vel τοὺς) suprascr. 8–9 τοὺς νόμ[ους ἔθεν]το CPF **F44(c)I** ed. pr. = Grenfell et Hunt (1922); CPF = Decleva Caizzi et Bastianini (1989) 2]α̣ι̣ου vel fortasse]ν̣ου: σπουδ]α̣ί̣ου ed. pr.: ἀξιεπαί]ν̣ου (spatio longius ut vid.) Murray: ἀληθι]ν̣οῦ Bignone, K. Schmidt 3 τος τὸ] (spatio brevius ut vid.) ed. pr. 4 ἐν ἀλ]λήλοις ed. pr.: ἐπ' ἀλ]λήλοις H. Fränkel 5–7 suppl. ed. pr. 8 τὰ τῶν] ed. pr.: πάντα τ]ἀνθρώπων K. Schmidt 9–11 suppl. ed. pr. 12 εἴπε]ρ Bignone: καὶ γὰ]ρ ed. pr.: εἴπε]ρ vel ὥσπε]ρ Diels: ἐπείπε]ρ (spatio longius ut vid.) Wilamowitz

F44(c) ... bearing true witness for one another is regarded as just and no less as useful for human pursuits. Now, whoever does this will not be just, if it is just

μηδ]ένα μὴ ἀδι-
κού]μενον αὐτὸν
δίκ]αιόν ἐστιν· ἀνάγ-
κη] γὰρ τὸν μαρτυ-
ροῦ]ν̣τα, κἂν ἀλη-
θῆ μ]α̣ρτυρῇ, ὅμως
ἄλλον π]ως ἀδικεῖν·
α]ὐτὸν ἀ-
δι]κ̣ε̣ῖ̣σ̣θαι [
]νενε[
ἐ]ν ᾧ̣ διὰ τ̣[ὰ ὑπ' ἐκεί-
ν]ου μαρτ[υρηθέν-
τα ἁλίσκ[ε]ται ὁ κα-
ταμαρτυρούμενος
καὶ ἀπόλλυσιν ἢ
χρήματα ἢ αὑτὸν
δ]ιὰ τοῦτον ὃν οὐδὲν
ἀ]δικεῖ· ἐν μὲν οὖν
τ̣ούτῳ̣ τὸν κατα-
μ]αρτυρούμενον
ἀ]δ̣ικεῖ, ὅτι οὐκ ἀδι-
κο]ῦντα ἑαυτὸν ἀ-
δι]κ̣εῖ· αὐτὸς δ' ἀδικεῖ-
ται ὑ]πὸ τοῦ καταμαρ-
τυρηθ]έντος, ὅτι μι-
σεῖται] ὑ̣π' αὐτοῦ τ̣α̣-

13–17 suppl. ed. pr. 18]α̣ρτυρη. ante corr.: ι suprascr.: suppl. ed. pr. 19 ἄλλον] πῶς ed. pr. 20 εἰκὸς δὲ] ed. pr.: καὶ ἅμα] Diels: ἅμα δὲ καὶ] Wilamowitz: εἰκὸς οὖν] K. Schmidt: εἶτα δὲ] CPF]α̣υ̣τον ed. pr. 20–21 ἀ[δι]κ̣ε̣ῖ̣σθαι ed. pr.: ἃ[ν ἀδι]κ̣ε̣ῖ̣σθαι Diels: ἀ[νταδι]κ̣ε̣ῖ̣σθαι Crönert 21–22 [εἰς ὕστερο]ν· ἔνε[στί γε (ρον spatio brevius ut vid.) ed. pr.: [ὕστερον, ὧ]ν ἕνε[κα εἶπεν (ὧν spatio brevius ut vid.) Diels: [εἰς ὕστερο]ν, ἔνε[στί γ' εἰκάζειν K. Schmidt: [ἐν μίσει οὖ]ν ἐνε[χόμενος CPF 22]ν· ενε[ed. pr.; sed cf. CPF ad loc. ἔνε[στι γὰρ Crönert 23–24 suppl. ed. pr.: αὐτ]οῦ (spatio brevius ut vid.) Diels 28 αὑτὸν defendit Crönert: αὑτὸν ⟨τὸν βίον⟩ ed. pr.: αὐτὸν CPF 36–38 suppl. ed. pr. 38 τ̣α̣ [α ed. pr.

to wrong no one and not be wronged oneself. For one who bears witness, even if his testimony is true, must nevertheless somehow wrong another ... and be wronged himself ... inasmuch as the one testified against is convicted because of the testimony given by him, and loses either his money or his life because of this man to whom he does no wrong. Now in this he wrongs the one testified against, in that he harms one who is not wronging him; and he is himself wronged by the one testified against, in that he is hated by him for bearing true witness.

II

ληθῆ μαρτυ[ρή-
σας· καὶ οὐ μόν[ον
τῷ μίσει, ἀλλὰ κ[αὶ
ὅτι δεῖ αὐτὸν τ[ὸν
αἰῶνα πάντα φυ-
λάττεσθαι τοῦτο[ν
οὗ κατεμαρτύρ[η-
σεν, ὡς ὑπάρχε[ι
γ' αὐτῷ ἐχθρὸς τοιο[ῦ-
τος, οἷος καὶ λέγειν
καὶ δρᾶν εἴ τι δύν[αι-
το κακὸν αὐτόν. κα[ί-
τοι ταῦτα φαίνεται
οὐ σμικρὰ ὄντα τἀ-
δικήματα, οὔτε
ἃ αὐτὸς ἀδικεῖται
οὔτε ἃ ἀδικεῖ· οὐ γὰρ
·/. οἷόν τε ταῦτά τε δί-
καια εἶναι καὶ τὸ μη-
δ]ὲν ἀδικεῖν μη-
δὲ] αὐτὸν ἀδικεῖσθαι,
ἀλ]λ' ἀνάγκη ἐστὶν
ἢ] τὰ ἕτερα αὐτῶν
δ]ίκαια εἶναι ἢ ἀμ-
φότερα ἄδικα. φαί-
νεται δὲ καὶ τὸ δικά-
ζειν καὶ τὸ κρίνειν
καὶ τὸ διαιτᾶν, ὅπως
ἂν περαίνηται, οὐ
δίκαια ὄντα· τὸ γὰρ
ἄ]λλους ὠφελοῦν ἄλ-
λο]υς βλάπτει· ἐν δὲ

F44(c)II ed. pr. = Grenfell et Hunt (1915) 1 μαρτυρ[ed. pr. 4 το[ed. pr. 18 τὰυτα (i.e. ταὐτά): corr. ed. pr.

And he is wronged not only by the enmity, but also because he must guard himself his whole life long against this man whom he testified against, since this is the sort of enemy who would do him any harm he could in word or deed. Yet it is obvious that these are no small wrongs, neither those he suffers nor those he commits. These wrongs, and the principle of wronging no one and not being wronged onself, cannot both be just: it is necessary either that one of them be just [*sc.* and the other unjust], or that both be unjust. It is obvious as well that judging, and deciding, and arbitrating are not just, however they are accomplished. For what benefits some harms others; and in

τού]τῳ οἱ μὲν ὠφελού-
μενο]ι οὐκ ἀδικοῦ̣[ν-
ται, οἱ] δ̣ὲ βλαπτόμε[νοι
ἀδικο]ῦντα[ι......
.....]μην[........
....].ι̣νου̣[........

45–71: ΠΕΡΙ ΟΜΟΝΟΙΑΣ

F45 Harpocration, s.v. Σκιάποδες (σ 28, 237–38 Keaney); cf. Photius, *Lexicon* s.v. (2.519 Porson), *Suda* s.v. (σ 601, 4.378 Adler)

Σκιάποδες· Ἀντιφῶν ἐν τῷ Περὶ ὁμονοίας. ἔθνος ἐστὶ Λιβυκόν.

F46 Harpocration, s.v. Μακροκέφαλοι (μ 2, 169 Keaney); cf. Photius, *Lexicon* s.v. Μακροκεφάλους (μ 53, 2.534 Theodoridis), *Suda* s.v. Μακροκέφαλοι (μ 77, 3.311 Adler)

Μακροκέφαλοι· Ἀντιφῶν ἐν τῷ Περὶ ὁμονοίας. ἔθνος ἐστὶν οὕτω καλούμενον, οὗ καὶ Ἡσίοδος μέμνηται ἐν γ′ Γυναικῶν καταλόγῳ [= fr. 153 Merkelbach–West].

F47 Harpocration, s.vv. ὑπὸ γῆν οἰκοῦντες (υ 8, 256 Keaney); cf. Photius, *Lexicon* s.vv. (2.626 Porson), *Suda* s.vv. (υ 465, 4.668 Adler)

ὑπὸ γῆν οἰκοῦντες· Ἀντιφῶν ἐν τῷ Περὶ ὁμονοίας. λέγοι ἂν τοὺς ὑπὸ Σκύλακος ἐν τῷ Περίπλῳ [= *FGrHist* 709 F 6 Jacoby] λεγομένους Τρωγοδύτας καὶ τοὺς ὑπὸ Ἡσιόδου ἐν γ′ Καταλόγου [= fr. 150 Merkelbach–West] Κατουδαίους ὀνομαζομένους.

33 του|τω: του|τωι ed. pr. 34–36 suppl. ed. pr. **F46** codd. Photii = g z 1 Μακροκεφάλους Phot. (Μακροκέφαλοι z post corr.) Ἀντιφῶν ... ὁμονοίας om. Epit. Harp. Phot. *Sud.* 2–3 οὗ ... καταλόγῳ om. Epit. Harp. Phot. *Sud.* **F47** codd. = D E Q K M N P Ald. 1 Ἀντιφῶν ... ὁμονοίας huc transp. Bekker: post ὀνομαζομένους (l. 5) Harp.: om. Epit. Harp. Phot. *Sud.* 3 Τρωγλοδύτας: corr. Untersteiner 4 καταλόγου Q (compendia habent M P): καταλόγῳ cet. codd. 4–5 κατουδαίους Epit. Harp.: καττουδαίους Phot. *Sud.*: κατὰ τοῦ δέους Harp.

this, those who are benefited are not wronged, but those who are harmed are . . .

45–71: ΠΕΡΙ ΟΜΟΝΟΙΑΣ

F45 **Shadowfeet**: Antiphon in *On Concord.* It is a Libyan tribe.

F46 **Longheads**: Antiphon in *On Concord.* There is a tribe with this name, which Hesiod mentions in the third book of the *Catalog of Women.*

F47 **Dwelling under the earth**: Antiphon in *On Concord.* He may mean the Trogodytes mentioned by Scylax in the *Periplus*, and those called Subterraneans by Hesiod in the third book of the *Catalog of Women.*

F48 Photius, *Lexicon* s.v. θεαιδέστατον (θ 48, 2.286 Theodoridis); cf. *Anecdota Graeca* s.v. (263 Bekker), *Etymologicum magnum* s.v. θεαιδέστατος (444 Gaisford), *Suda* s.v. θεαιδέστατον (θ 91, 2.689 Adler)

θεειδέστατον· θεοῦ ἰδέαν ἔχον. εἶπε δὲ Ἀντιφῶν ἐν τῷ Περὶ ὁμονοίας οὕτως· **ἄνθρωπος, ὅς φησι μὲν πάντων θηρίων θεειδέστατον γενέσθαι.**

Cf. also Eustathius, *Commentarii ad Homeri Iliadem* 1.597.9–13 van der Valk = Aelius Dionysius, s.v. θεειδέστατον (θ 6, 123 Erbse) ὁ δὲ γράψας ἐν στοιχειακῇ τάξει λέξεων λέγεσθαι θεαιδέστατον διὰ τῆς αι διφθόγγου προπαραληγούσης τὸν θεοῦ ἰδέαν ἔχοντα, καὶ παραθεὶς χρῆσιν Ἀντιφῶντος τὸ **ἄνθρωπος, ὅς φησι πάντων θηρίων θεαιδέστατος γενέσθαι** καινὸν μέν τι γράφει, πιστεύεται δὲ ὡς λόγου πολλοῦ ἄξιος.

F49 Stobaeus, 4.22^{b}.66; cf. 3.6.45 (4.521–23; 3.296 Wachsmuth–Hense)

φέρε δὴ προελθέτω ὁ βίος εἰς τὸ πρόσθεν καὶ γάμων καὶ γυναικὸς ἐπιθυμησάτω. αὕτη ἡ ἡμέρα, αὕτη ἡ νὺξ καινοῦ δαίμονος ἄρχει, καινοῦ πότμου. μέγας γὰρ ἀγὼν γάμος ἀνθρώπῳ. εἰ γὰρ τύχοι μὴ ἐπιτηδεία γενομένη, τί χρὴ τῇ συμφορᾷ χρῆσθαι; χαλεπαὶ μὲν ἐκπομπαί, τοὺς φίλους ἐχθροὺς ποιῆσαι, ἴσα φρονοῦντας ἴσα πνέοντας, ἀξιώ-

F48 codd. = g z 1 θεαιδέστατον (vel –ος) codd. ubique: θεειδέστατον Sylburg ἔχων *Et. Anecd.* (cf. τὸν ... ἔχοντα apud Eustath.) 1–3 εἶπε ... γενέσθαι om. *Anecd.* 1 Ἀντιφὼν g z 2 μὲν *Sud.*: om. Phot. *Et.* 3 θεειδέστατον Diels post Sauppe: θεαιδέστατος Phot. *Et. Sud.* γενέσθαι] γέγονε *Et.* **F49** codd. = S M A Tr. ecloga cum lemm. Ἀντιφῶντος (per compendium S) S M A 1 προελθέτω S M A: προσελθέτω Tr. πρόσθε S 1–2 καὶ γυναικὸς del. Herwerden 4 τύχη A ἐπιτηδεία ἡ ἀγομένη Meineke: ἐπιτηδεία ἡ γαμουμένη Sauppe: ἐπιτήδεια γενόμενα Blass: ἐπιτηδείαν ἀγόμενος Wilamowitz 5 ἐκπομπαὶ ⟨καὶ⟩ τοὺς φίλους Jacobs 6 ἴσα φρονεῖν ἴσα βαίνειν vel ἴσα φρονοῦντας ἴσα βαίνοντας Sauppe

F48 "Most godlike": having the appearance of a god. In *On Concord* Antiphon said: **man, who claims to be the most godlike of all creatures**.

The man who wrote in an alphabetical glossary that one with the appearance of a god is called "most godlike" (with the diphthong "ai" in the antepenultimate syllable), and who cited as evidence a passage from Antiphon (**man, who claims to be the most godlike of all creatures**), is writing something new. But he is believed because he is deserving of great consideration.

F49 Now then, let life go forward and desire a wedding, wedlock, and a wife. This day, this night begins a new destiny, a new fate. Marriage is a great contest for a man. For if a wife should chance to be unsuitable, how is he to deal with the misfortune? Divorce is difficult: to make enemies of relatives who think the same and breathe the same as

σαντα καὶ ἀξιωθέντα· χαλεπὸν δὲ κεκτῆσθαι κτῆμα τοιοῦτον, δοκοῦντα ἡδονὰς κτᾶσθαι λύπας ἄγεσθαι. φέρε δή, μὴ τὰ παλίγκοτα λέγωμεν, λεγέσθω τὰ πάντων ἐπιτηδειότατα. τί γὰρ ἥδιον ἀνθρώπῳ γυναικὸς καταθυμίας; τί δὲ γλυκύτερον ἄλλως τε καὶ νέῳ; ἐν τῷ αὐτῷ δέ γε τούτῳ, ἔνθα τὸ ἡδύ, ἔνεστι πλησίον που καὶ τὸ λυπηρόν· αἱ γὰρ ἡδοναὶ οὐκ ἐπὶ σφῶν αὐτῶν ἐμπορεύονται, ἀλλ' ἀκολουθοῦσιν αὐταῖς λῦπαι καὶ πόνοι. ἐπεὶ καὶ ὀλυμπιονῖκαι καὶ πυθιονῖκαι καὶ οἱ τοιοῦτοι ἀγῶνες καὶ σοφίαι καὶ πᾶσαι ἡδοναὶ ἐκ μεγάλων λυπημάτων ἐθέλουσι παραγίγνεσθαι· τιμαὶ γάρ, ἆθλα – δελέατα ἃ ὁ θεὸς ἔδωκεν ἀνθρώποις – μεγάλων πόνων καὶ ἱδρώτων εἰς ἀνάγκας καθιστᾶσιν. ἐγὼ γάρ, εἴ μοι γένοιτο σῶμα ἕτερον τοιοῦτον οἷον ἐγὼ ἐμαυτῷ, οὐκ ἂν δυναίμην ζῆν, οὕτως ἐμαυτῷ πολλὰ πράγματα παρέχων ὑπέρ τε τῆς ὑγιείας τοῦ σώματος ὑπέρ τε τοῦ καθ' ἡμέραν βίου ἐς τὴν ξυλλογὴν ὑπέρ τε δόξης καὶ σωφροσύνης καὶ εὐκλείας καὶ τοῦ εὖ ἀκούειν. τί οὖν, εἴ μοι γένοιτο σῶμα ἕτερον τοιοῦτον, ὅ γέ μοι οὕτως ἐπιμελὲς εἴη; οὔκουν δῆλον, ὅτι γυνὴ ἀνδρί, ἐὰν ᾖ καταθυμία, οὐδὲν ἐλάττους τὰς φιλότητας

6–7 πνέοντας ⟨ζῆν⟩ ἀξιώσαντα Diels ἐξιώσαντα Tr.: ἐξώσαντα καὶ ἐξωσθέντα Jacobs 7 καὶ ἐκτῆσθαι Diels 8 δοκοῦν τε Diels ἄδεσθαι A post corr. 8–9 φέρε δὲ Sauppe 9 λεγέσθω] γενέσθω Blass 11 τί δὲ A: τί δαὶ S M ἄλλω A ante corr.: ς add. corr. νέα A: νεάζοντι Meineke 12–14 ἔνθα τὸ ἡδύ ... λῦπαι καὶ πόνοι = Stob. 3.6.45 12 ἡδύ ἐστι Stob. 3.6.45 13–14 ἐκ σφῶν αὐτῶν ἐκπορεύονται Stob. 3.6.45 17 παραγίνεσθαι S M A γὰρ S M A ante corr.: καὶ suprascr. add. A post corr. (nullius auctoritatis secundum Hense) post ἆθλα lacunam statuit Hense ἃ δελέατα Meineke 17–18 τιμαὶ γὰρ ἃς ἄθλων δελέατα ὁ θεὸς Valckenaer 19 καθιστῶσιν S M A: corr. Sauppe 19–20 εἴ μοι ... ἐμαυτῷ del. Sauppe 20 τοιοῦτον ⟨ἐπιμελὲς ὂν⟩ οἷον Diels: τοιοῦτον ⟨μέλημα ὂν⟩ οἷον Hense οἷον ἔχω Weidner: οἷον ἔχω τὸ ἐμαυτοῦ Blass ἐμαυτῷ del. Wilamowitz 21 ⟨μὴ⟩ οὕτως Sauppe 22 ὑγείας S M A 22–23 ἐς τὴν ξυλλογὴν del. Sauppe 23 καὶ σωφροσύνης καὶ εὐκλείας del. Wilamowitz 23–24 καὶ τοῦ εὖ ἀκούειν del. Meineke: ἐς τὸ εὖ ἀκούειν Diels 24 τί αν A εἴ μοι] εἰ γυνὴ Diels: εἰ δή μοι Bignone 25 μοι Gesner: μ cum λι suprascr. S: μ' M Tr.: μὴ A οὔκουν scripsi: οὐκ οὖν codd.

he does, after deeming them worthy and being deemed worthy himself by them. But it is difficult also to own such a possession, to bring home pains when he thought he was acquiring pleasures.

Very well, let us not speak of what is adverse; let the most suitable things of all be spoken of. What is more pleasant for a man than a woman after his own heart? And what is sweeter, especially for a young man? Yet in this very place where the pleasant is, the painful too is somewhere near by. For pleasures do not travel by themselves; rather, pains and toils accompany them. Victories at Olympia and at Pythia and in other such contests, skills, and all pleasures are wont to arise from great pains. For honors, prizes – traps that god gives to men – place them under the constraint of great toil and sweat. If I were to have a second person like the one I am for myself, I would not be able to live, so many troubles do I cause myself for the sake of bodily health, for the sake of daily livelihood (for its collection), and for the sake of honor, prudence, glory, and reputation. What, then, if I were to have a second such person, who would be an object of such care? Is it not clear that if a wife is according to her husband's heart, she causes him no fewer pleasures and pains than he

παρέχεται καὶ τὰς ὀδύνας ἣ αὐτὸς αὑτῷ ὑπέρ τε τῆς ὑγιείας δισσῶν σωμάτων ὑπέρ τε τοῦ βίου τῆς συλλογῆς [καὶ] ὑπέρ τε τῆς σωφροσύνης καὶ τῆς εὐκλείας; φέρε δὴ καὶ παῖδες γενέσθωσαν· φροντίδων ἤδη πάντα πλέα καὶ ἐξοίχεται τὸ νεοτήσιον σκίρτημα ἐκ τῆς γνώμης καὶ ⟨τὸ⟩ πρόσωπον οὐκέτι τὸ αὐτό.

F50 Stobaeus, 4.34.63 (5.844 Wachsmuth–Hense)

τὸ ζῆν ἔοικε φρουρᾷ ἐφημέρῳ, τό τε μῆκος τοῦ βίου ἡμέρᾳ μιᾷ, ὡς ἔπος εἰπεῖν, ᾗ ἀναβλέψαντες πρὸς τὸ φῶς παρεγγυῶμεν τοῖς ἐπιγιγνομένοις ἑτέροις.

F51 Stobaeus, 4.34.56 (5.841 Wachsmuth–Hense)

εὐκατηγόρητος πᾶς ὁ βίος θαυμαστῶς, ὦ μακάριε, καὶ οὐδὲν ἔχων περιττὸν οὐδὲ μέγα καὶ σεμνόν, ἀλλὰ πάντα σμικρὰ καὶ ἀσθενῆ καὶ ὀλιγοχρόνια καὶ ἀναμεμειγμένα λύπαις μεγάλαις.

F52 Harpocration, s.v. ἀναθέσθαι (α 111, 21 Keaney); cf. Photius, *Lexicon* s.v. (α 1472, 1.152 Theodoridis), *Suda* s.v. (α 1872, 1.168 Adler)

ἀναθέσθαι· Ἀντιφῶν ἐν τῷ Περὶ ὁμονοίας· **ἀναθέσθαι δὲ ὥσπερ πεττὸν τὸν βίον οὐκ ἔστιν** ἀντὶ τοῦ ἄνωθεν βιῶναι μετανοήσαντας ἐπὶ τῷ προτέρῳ βίῳ.

27 ὀδύνας Tr.: ὠδῖνας S M A αὐτῶ M 28 ὑγείας S M A 29 καὶ del. Sauppe 31 τὸ pr.] τὸν M τὸ alt. add. Sauppe **F50** codd. = S M A Tr. ecloga cum lemm. Ἀντιφῶντος S M A 1 ἔοικεν M 1–2 τό τε μῆκος . . . μιᾷ del. Sauppe 2 ἡμέρα (vel -ᾳ) S M A: μοίρᾳ Diels μία M ᾗ Gaisford: ἣ S A: ἢ M: ἣν Tr. **F51** codd. = S M A Tr. ecloga cum lemm. Ἀντιφάνους (per compendium S) S M A: cum lemm. Ἀντιφῶντος Tr. 1 θαυμαστὸν ὦ μακάριε vel θαυμαστῶς ὡς ὦ μακάριε Sauppe: θαυμαστῶς ὡς [μακάριε] Blass: ⟨καὶ ὁ⟩ θαυμαστῶς ὡς μακάριος Diels: θαυμαστῶς del. Meineke 1–2 οὐδὲν ἔχων καὶ Sauppe: καὶ οὐδὲν ἔχει vel [καὶ] οὐδὲν ἔχων Wilamowitz: καὶ del. Kranz 2 πάντα] ταῦτα neglegenter Gaisford 3 μικρὰ S M A Tr. ἀναμεμιγμένα S M A Tr. **F52** 1 ἐν τῷ Epit. Harp. Phot. *Sud.*: om. Harp. ὁμονοίας] προνοίας Epit. Harp. Phot. *Sud.* post ὁμονοίας add. φησιν Epit. Harp. Phot. *Sud.* δὲ om. Epit. Harp. Phot. *Sud.* 3 ἐπὶ] ἐν *Sud.*

causes himself, for the sake of the health of two bodies, for the sake of the collection of their livelihood, and for the sake of prudence and glory?

Now then, let children too be born: all is now full of cares, and the youthful leap is gone from the mind, the face is no longer the same.

F50 Living is like a daily watch, and the length of life like practically one day, on which, after looking up at the light, we hand over to the others who come next.

F51 The whole of life, my friend, is amazingly easy to blame, since it has nothing outstanding or great and impressive, but everything small, weak, short-lived, and mixed up with great pains.

F52 **It is not possible to revoke one's life like a move in a board game** for "to live over again, repenting of one's former life." Antiphon in *On Concord.*

F53 Stobaeus, 3.10.39 (3.418 Wachsmuth–Hense)

οἱ δὲ ἐργαζόμενοι μὲν καὶ φειδόμενοι καὶ ταλαιπωροῦντες καὶ προστιθέντες ἥδονται οἷα δή τις ἂν εἰκάσειεν ἥδεσθαι· ἀφαιροῦντες δὲ καὶ χρώμενοι ἀλγοῦσιν ὥσπερ ἀπὸ τῶν σαρκῶν ἀφαιρούμενοι.

F53A Stobaeus, 3.16.20 (3.485 Wachsmuth–Hense)

εἰσί τινες οἳ τὸν παρόντα μὲν βίον οὐ ζῶσιν, ἀλλὰ παρασκευάζονται πολλῇ σπουδῇ ὡς ἕτερόν τινα βίον βιωσόμενοι, οὐ τὸν παρόντα· καὶ ἐν τούτῳ παραλειπόμενος ὁ χρόνος οἴχεται.

F54 Stobaeus, 3.16.30; cf. 4.40.19 (3.488–89; 5.924 Wachsmuth–Hense); cf. also Harpocration, s.v. ἀχαριστεῖν (α 283, 54 Keaney)

ἔστι δέ τις λόγος, ὡς ἄρα ἰδὼν ἀνὴρ ἄνδρα ἕτερον ἀργύριον ἀναιρούμενον πολὺ ἐδεῖτό οἱ δανεῖσαι ἐπὶ τόκῳ· ὁ δ᾽ οὐκ ἠθέλησεν, ἀλλ᾽ ἦν οἷος ἀπιστεῖν τε καὶ μὴ ὠφελεῖν μηδένα· φέρων δ᾽ ἀπέθετο ὅποι δή· καί τις καταμαθὼν τοῦτο ποιοῦντα ὑφείλετο· ὑστέρῳ δὲ χρόνῳ ἐλθὼν οὐχ εὕρισκε τὰ χρήματα ὁ καταθέμενος. περιαλγῶν οὖν τῇ συμφορᾷ τά τε ἄλλα καὶ ὅτι οὐκ ἔχρησε τῷ δεομένῳ, ὃ ἂν αὐτῷ καὶ σῷον ἦν καὶ ἕτερον προσέφερεν, ἀπαντήσας δὲ

F53 codd. = S M A ecloga cum lemm. Ἀντιφῶντος S M A 1 μὲν suprascr. S **F53A** codd. = S M A Tr. Mac. et corp. Par. ecloga cum lemm. Ἀντιφῶντος S M^{d}: sine lemm. A Mac.: iteratur (lemm. τοῦ αὐτοῦ, *sc.* Δημόνακτος) corp. Par. 351 1–3 εἰσί τινες ... βιωσόμενοι om. A 1 παρόντα μὲν S M^{d} Mac.: μὲν παρόντα corp. Par. 2 τινα om. corp. Par. 3–4 καὶ ἐν τούτῳ ... οἴχεται om. corp. Par. 3 παραλειπόμενος (per compendium S) S M^{d} A Mac.: περιλειπόμενος Tr. 4 οἴχεται S M^{d} Mac. A post corr.: εἴχεται A ante corr. **F54** codd. = S M A Br et gnomol. Par. ecloga cum lemm. Ἀντιφῶντος S M^{d} A: sine lemm. Br: iteratur (lemm. Ἀντιφῶντος) gnomol. Par. 288 3 μὴ om. S 4 ὅποι Blass: ποι vel ποῖ S M^{d} A Br 6 ηὕρισκε Blass 8 δὲ del. Sauppe: δὴ Meineke

F53 Whereas others feel in working, living thriftily, toiling, and adding to their savings the sort of pleasure one would conjecture them to feel. But they are pained at drawing down and using their savings, as though they were taking from their own flesh.

F53A There are some people who do not live the life at hand, but prepare with great earnestness like people who are going to live some other life, not the present one. Meanwhile, time is neglected and lost.

F54 The story goes that a man, upon seeing another removing money, begged him earnestly for a loan at interest. But the other refused, and was the kind of man who is mistrustful and helps no one. He took the money and hid it somewhere or other. Someone observed him doing this and stole the money. Afterwards, the man who had hidden the money came and was unable to find it. Now, greatly pained at his misfortune – particularly because he had not lent the money (which would be safe and earning interest for him) to the man who at the time asked him for a loan –

τῷ ἀνδρὶ τῷ τότε δανειζομένῳ ἀπωλοφύρετο τὴν συμφοράν, ὅτι ἐξήμαρτε καὶ ὅτι οἱ μεταμέλει οὐ χαρισαμένῳ, ἀλλ' ἀχαριστήσαντι, ὡς πάντως οἱ ἀπολόμενον τὸ ἀργύριον. ὁ δ' αὐτὸν ἐκέλευε μὴ φροντίζειν, ἀλλὰ νομίζειν αὑτῷ εἶναι καὶ μὴ ἀπολωλέναι καταθέμενον λίθον εἰς τὸ αὐτὸ χώριον· Πάντως γὰρ οὐδ' ὅτε ἦν σοι ἐχρῶ αὐτῷ, ὅθεν μηδὲ νῦν νόμιζε στέρεσθαι μηδενός· ὅτῳ γάρ τις μὴ ἐχρήσατο μηδὲ χρήσεται, ὄντος ἢ μὴ ὄντος αὐτῷ οὐδὲν οὔτε πλέον οὔτε ἔλασσον βλάπτεται. ὅταν γὰρ ὁ θεὸς μὴ παντελῶς βούληται ἀγαθὰ διδόναι ἀνδρί, χρημάτων πλοῦτον παρασχών, τοῦ φρονεῖν ⟨δὲ⟩ καλῶς πένητα ποιήσας, τὸ ἕτερον ἀφελόμενος ἑκατέρων ἀπεστέρησεν.

F55 Photius, *Lexicon* s.v. ἵνα (ι 133, 2.326 Theodoridis); cf. *Suda* s.v. (ι 360, 2.635 Adler)

ἵνα· ὅπου. Ἀντιφῶν ἐν τῷ Περὶ τῆς ὁμονοίας· **ὀκνεῖν, ἵνα οὐδὲν ἔργον ὀκνεῖν.**

F56 *Suda* s.v. ὀκνῶ (ο 116, 3.514 Adler)

ὀκνῶ· φοβοῦμαι ... καὶ οἱ ῥήτορες οὐκ ἐπὶ δειλίας καὶ ῥᾳθυμίας ἐχρήσαντο τῷ ὀνόματι, ἀλλ' ἐπὶ τοῦ φόβου καὶ

9 ἀπωλοφύρετο S A post corr.: ἀνωλοφύρετο M[d] Br A ante corr. gnomol. Par. 9–10 ἐπὶ τῇ συμφορᾷ gnomol. Par 10 μεταμέλει M[d]: μεταμέλλει S A χρησαμένῳ Br 11 ἀχαριστήσαντι] ἀχαριστεῖν ἀντὶ τοῦ μὴ χαρίζεσθαι. οὕτως Ἀντιφῶν Harp. (cf. *Anecdota Graeca* 174 Bachmann; *Anecdota Graeca Oxoniensia* 2.491; *Suda* α 4675, 1.437) ὡς Blass: καὶ S M A οἱ ἀπολόμενον Gesner: οἱ ἀπολλόμενον S: οι (οἱ Br) ἀπολούμενον M[d] Br: σοι ἀπολυόμενον A ante corr.: οἱ ἀπωλόμενον A post corr. 13 αὑτῷ Sauppe: αὐτὸ S: αὐτῶ M[d] A Br 15 ὅτω S M[d]: οὕτω A 16 χρήσεται ex χρήσαιται S ut vid. 17 ἔλασσον S M[d]: ἔλαττον A Br βλέπεται Bücheler: ἔχει (dubitanter) Nauck 17–20 ὅταν γὰρ ... ἀπεστέρησεν = Stob. 4.40.19 17–18 ὅταν ... βούληται S M[d] A Br: τῶ (ὅτῳ Sauppe) ... βούλεται Stob. 4.40.19 18 τἀγαθὰ Cobet 19 φρονεῖν ⟨δὲ⟩ καλῶς Sauppe: φρονεῖν καλῶς S M[d] A Br: καλῶς φρονεῖν (φθονεῖν A ante corr.) Stob. 4.40.19: καλῶς φρονεῖν ⟨δὲ⟩ Diels post Hense 20 ἀμφοτέρων Stob. 4.40.19 **F55** 1 ὀκνεῖν ἵνα *Sud.*: ὀκνεῖν om. Phot. **F56** codd. = A G F V M ed. pr. 1 καὶ ... οὐκ om. A 2 τὸ ὄνομα V

he met the latter and bewailed his misfortune, saying he had made a mistake and regretted that he had not obliged but acted ungraciously, since at all events the money had gotten lost on him. The other bade him not to worry, but to put a stone down in the same place and imagine that he still had the money and that it had not been lost. "You made no use whatsoever of it when you had it, so do not imagine that you are deprived of anything now. For when someone has not used a thing and will not use it, he is harmed no more if he does not have it, and no less if he does have it." For whenever god does not altogether want to give good things to a man, by providing him monetary wealth, but making him poor in good sense, he deprives him of both things by taking away one.

F55 To hesitate where [*hina*] **there is no use in hesitating**. Antiphon in *On Concord.*

F56 The rhetors used the word "hesitate" not for cowardice and laziness, but for fear and

τοῦ φοβεῖσθαι. Ἀντιφῶν· **κακὸς δ' ἂν εἰ ἀποῦσι μὲν καὶ μέλλουσι τοῖς κινδύνοις τῇ γλώττῃ θρασύνεται καὶ τῷ θέλειν ἐπείγειν, τὸ δὲ ἔργον ἂν παρῇ, ὀκνεῖν.**

F57 Stobaeus, 3.8.18 (3.344 Wachsmuth–Hense)

νόσος δειλοῖσιν ἑορτή· οὐ γὰρ ἐκπορεύονται ἐπὶ πρᾶξιν.

F58 Stobaeus, 3.20.66 (3.553–54 Wachsmuth–Hense)

ὅστις δὲ ἰὼν ἐπὶ τὸν πλησίον κακῶς ποιήσων δειμαίνει, μὴ ἃ θέλει ποιῆσαι, ἁμαρτὼν τούτων, ἃ μὴ θέλει ἀπενέγκηται, σωφρονέστερος. ἐν ᾧ γὰρ δειμαίνει, μέλλει· ἐν ᾧ δὲ μέλλει, πολλάκις ὁ διὰ μέσου χρόνος ἀπέστρεψε τὸν νοῦν τῶν θελημάτων· καὶ ἐν μὲν τῷ γεγενῆσθαι οὐκ ἔνεστιν, ἐν δὲ τῷ μέλλειν ἐνδέχεται ⟨μὴ⟩ γενέσθαι. ὅστις δὲ δράσειν μὲν οἴεται τοὺς πέλας κακῶς, πείσεσθαι δ' οὔ, οὐ σωφρονεῖ. ἐλπίδες δ' οὐ πανταχοῦ ἀγαθόν· πολλοὺς γὰρ τοιαῦται ἐλπίδες κατέβαλον εἰς ἀνηκέστους συμφοράς, ἃ δ' ἐδόκουν τοὺς πέλας ποιήσειν, παθόντες ταῦτα ἀνεφάνησαν αὐτοί. σωφροσύνην δὲ ἀνδρὸς οὐκ ἂν ἄλλου ὀρθότερόν τις κρίνειεν ἢ ὅστις τοῦ θυμοῦ ταῖς παραχρῆμα ἡδοναῖς ἐμφράσσει αὐτὸς ἑαυτὸν κρατεῖν τε καὶ νι-

2–3 τοῦ φοβεῖσθαι καὶ τοῦ φόβου F 3–5 Ἀντιφῶν ... ὀκνεῖν om. F V 3 κακῶς ed. pr.: κακῶν G. Hermann ἂν εἰ] ἀεὶ Gaisford: οὖν ἐν G. Hermann: ἂν εἴη Sauppe: ἂν ⟨εἴη⟩ εἰ Diels ⟨ἐπ'⟩ ἀποῦσι Sauppe 4 θρασύνεσθαι G. Hermann 5 ἐπείγει Blass ὀκνεῖ Küster **F57** codd. = S M A Voss et Apostol. ecloga cum lemm. Ἀντιφῶντος S M A: cum lemm. Ἀντιφάνους Voss (compendio male explicato): iteratur (lemm. Ἀντιφάνους) Apostol., cent. 12, 14i (2.546) **F58** codd. = S M A Tr. ecloga cum lemm. Ἀντιφῶντος S: om. M A 5 νοῦν Sauppe: νόων S: νόον Tr. 5–6 οὐκ ἔνεστι ⟨μὴ γενέσθαι⟩ Sauppe: post οὐκ ἔνεστι lacunam statuit Blass 6 ⟨μὴ⟩ Bücheler: ⟨καὶ τὸ μὴ⟩ Diels 7–8 δὲ οὔ, οὐ S (coniecerat Jacobs): δι' ἃ οὐ Tr.: δὲ μηδέν, οὐ Gesner: δὲ μή, οὐ Gaisford 10 τοὺς Meineke: τοῖς S 11 ἂν ἐφάνησαν (dubitanter) Diels ἄλλου E. Jacoby: ἄλλος S: ἄλλο Sauppe: ἄλλως Bücheler 12–13 τὰς παραχρῆμα ἡδονὰς ἐμφράσσων [αὐτὸς ἑαυτὸν] Sauppe

being afraid. Antiphon: **if he is confident about absent and future dangers with his tongue and with willingness to press hard, he would be cowardly to hesitate, if the task is at hand**.

F57 Sickness is a holiday for cowards: they do not go out to action.

F58 When going against another to do him harm, the man who fears that he will fail at what he wishes to do, and obtain what he does not wish, is more prudent. For while he fears, he hesitates; and while he hesitates, often the intervening time deters his mind from what it wishes. Not-happening is impossible in the case of having-already-happened, but possible in the case of delaying. But whoever thinks that he will harm others while avoiding suffering himself is not prudent. Hopes are not in every case a good thing: such hopes have thrown many into irremediable misfortune; and it turned out that what they thought they would do to others, they suffered themselves instead. Temperance would be attributed to no one more correctly than to whoever blocks himself to the immediate pleasures of his heart, and is able to overcome

κἂν ἠδυνήθη αὐτὸς ἑαυτόν. ὃς δὲ θέλει χαρίσασθαι τῷ θυμῷ παραχρῆμα, θέλει τὰ κακίω ἀντὶ τῶν ἀμεινόνων.

F59 Stobaeus, 3.5.57 (3.278–79 Wachsmuth–Hense)

ὅστις δὲ τῶν αἰσχρῶν ἢ τῶν κακῶν μήτε ἐπεθύμησε μήτε ἥψατο, οὐκ ἔστι σώφρων· οὐ γὰρ ἔσθ' ὅτου κρατήσας αὐτὸς ἑαυτὸν κόσμιον παρέχεται.

F60 Stobaeus, 2.31.39 (2.208 Wachsmuth–Hense)

πρῶτον, οἶμαι, τῶν ἐν ἀνθρώποις ἐστὶ παίδευσις· ὅταν γάρ τις πράγματος κἂν ὁτουοῦν τὴν ἀρχὴν ὀρθῶς ποιήσηται, εἰκὸς καὶ τὴν τελευτὴν ὀρθῶς γίγνεσθαι· καὶ γὰρ τῇ γῇ οἷον ἄν τις τὸ σπέρμα ἐναρόσῃ, τοιαῦτα καὶ τὰ ἔκφορα δεῖ προσδοκᾶν· καὶ ἐν νέῳ σώματι ὅταν τις τὴν παίδευσιν γενναίαν ἐναρόσῃ, ζῇ τοῦτο καὶ θάλλει διὰ παντὸς τοῦ βίου, καὶ αὐτὸ οὔτε ὄμβρος οὔτε ἀνομβρία ἀφαιρεῖται.

F61 Stobaeus, 2.31.40 (2.208 Wachsmuth–Hense)

ἀναρχίας δ' οὐδὲν κάκιον ἀνθρώποις· ταῦτα γινώσκοντες οἱ πρόσθεν ἄνθρωποι ἀπὸ τῆς ἀρχῆς εἴθιζον τοὺς παῖδας ἄρχεσθαι καὶ τὸ κελευόμενον ποιεῖν, ἵνα μὴ ἐξανδρούμενοι εἰς μεγάλην μεταβολὴν ἰόντες ἐκπλήσσοιντο.

F62 Stobaeus, 2.31.41 (2.209 Wachsmuth–Hense)

ὅτῳ τις ἂν τὸ πλεῖστον τῆς ἡμέρας συνῇ, τοιοῦτον ἀνάγκη γενέσθαι καὶ αὐτὸν τοὺς τρόπους.

14–15 τῷ θυμῷ παραχρῆμα, θέλει vel τῷ παραχρῆμα θυμῷ Blass: τῷ θυμῷ, παραχρῆμα θέλει Sauppe: παραχρῆμα del. Hense **F59** codd. = L M A Tr. et [Max.] ecloga cum lemm. Ἀντιφῶντος M A Tr.: sine lemm. L: iteratur (lemm. *Antiphontis*) [Max.] 3 1 ὥστις L rubr. δὲ om. A ἢ τῶν κακῶν om. Tr. μήτ' ἐπεθύμησε L 2 ὅτου] ὅπου Sauppe 3 παρέσχετο Blass **F60** cod. = L ecloga cum lemm. Ἀντιφῶντος L 1 ἀνθρώποις Pflugk: οὐρανοῖς L 3 ποιήσται (ται suprascr.) L **F61** cod. = L ecloga cum lemm. τοῦ αὐτοῦ (*sc.* Ἀντιφῶντος; post 2.31.39 = F60) L 2 ἀρχῆς] πρώτης Meineke **F62** cod. = L ecloga sine lemm. (post 2.31.40 = F61) L 1 ὅτῳ scripsi: (ὅ)τω L: οἵῳ Wachsmuth

and conquer himself. But whoever wishes to gratify his heart immediately, wishes what is worse instead of what is better.

F59 If someone neither desires nor has contact with shameful or bad things, he is not temperate. For there is nothing which he makes himself orderly and well-behaved by overcoming.

F60 The most important thing in the world, I think, is education. For whenever you begin any matter whatsoever in the right way, the end too is likely to turn out right: whatever sort of seed you plant in the earth, this is the sort of crop you should expect. And whenever you plant in a young body an education that is good, the end-product lives and blossoms through the whole of life, and neither rain nor drought can destroy it.

F61 Nothing is worse for human beings than the absence of rule. Recognizing this, the men of the past used to habituate their children from the beginning to being ruled and to doing what they were told, so they would not be thrown into disturbance when they came into a great change upon reaching maturity.

F62 One necessarily becomes similar in character to the person with whom one spends the greatest part of the day.

F63 Harpocration, s.v. διάθεσις (δ 42, 74 Keaney); cf. Photius, *Lexicon* s.v. (δ 319, 1.398 Theodoridis), *Anecdota Graeca Oxoniensia* s.v. (2.492 Cramer), *Suda* s.v. (δ 558, 2.56 Adler)

διάθεσις· ... ἀντὶ δὲ τοῦ διοίκησις ὁ αὐτὸς [*sc.* Ἀντιφῶν] ἐν τῷ Περὶ ὁμονοίας· **ἀλλὰ εἰδότες τὴν διάθεσιν ἀκούουσιν.**

F64 Φιλοσόφων λόγοι 62 (11 Schenkl) = *Excerpta Vindobonensia* 44 (4.293 Meineke)

αἱ νέαι φιλίαι ἀναγκαῖαι μέν, αἱ δὲ παλαιαὶ ἀναγκαιότεραι.

F65 *Suda* s.v. θωπεία (θ 434, 2.723 Adler)

θωπεία· κολακεία ... Ἀντιφῶν ἐν τῷ Περὶ ὁμονοίας· **πολλοὶ δ' ἔχοντες φίλους οὐ γινώσκουσιν, ἀλλ' ἑταίρους ποιοῦνται θῶπας πλούτου καὶ τύχης κόλακας.**

F66 Clement of Alexandria, *Stromata* 6.2.19.7 (1.438 Stählin–Früchtel)

Ἀντιφῶν ὁ ῥήτωρ λέγει· **γηροτροφία γὰρ προσέοικεν παιδοτροφίᾳ.**

F67 Harpocration, s.v. ἀθεώρητος (α 43, 9 Keaney); cf. *Anecdota Graeca* s.v. (37 Bachmann), Photius, *Lexicon* s.v. (α 461, 1.53 Theodoridis), *Anecdota Graeca Oxoniensia* s.v. (2.488 Cramer), *Suda* s.v. ἀθεωρητί (α 717, 1.68 Adler)

F63 1 ἀντὶ δὲ] Ἀντιφῶν δὲ ἀντὶ Epit. Harp. Phot. *Anecd. Oxon. Sud.* 1–3 ὁ αὐτὸς ... ἀκούουσιν om. Epit. Harp. Phot. *Anecd. Oxon. Sud.* **F64** codd. = Par. Pal. et Exc. Vind. flor. Vind. ecloga cum lemm. Ἀντιφάνους Par. 53 Exc. Vind.: sine lemm. Pal. 52: iteratur flor. Vind. 50: Ἀντιφῶντος (dubitanter) Meineke 1 παλαιαὶ] πολλαὶ flor. Vind. **F65** codd. = A² G I T F V M 3 θῶκας G M **F66** cod. = L 1 γηρωτροφία L

F63 "Arrangement" [*diathesis*] for "administration," Antiphon in *On Concord*: **but they listen, knowing the arrangement**.

F64 New friendships are necessary, old ones more so.

F65 Antiphon in *On Concord*: **many do not recognize that they have friends, but make flatterers of wealth and adulators of fortune their companions**.

F66 Antiphon the orator says: **for care of the elderly is like the rearing of children**.

ἀθεώρητος· ἀντὶ τοῦ ἀθέατος παρ' Ἀντιφῶντι ἐν τῷ Περὶ ὁμονοίας.

F67A Harpocration, s.v. ἀνδρεία (α 131, 25 Keaney); cf. Photius, *Lexicon* s.v. (α 1754, 1.174 Theodoridis), *Suda* s.v. (α 2164, 1.195 Adler)

ἀνδρεία· ἡ τῶν ἀνδρῶν ἡλικία. Ἀντιφῶν ἐν τῷ Περὶ ὁμονοίας.

F68 Harpocration, s.v. αὐλιζόμενοι (α 265, 51 Keaney); cf. *Anecdota Graeca* s.v. (164 Bachmann), Photius, *Lexicon* s.v. (α 3178, 1.293 Theodoridis), *Anecdota Graeca Oxoniensia* s.v. (2.491 Cramer), *Suda* s.v. αὐλίζεται (α 4441, 1.414 Alder)

αὐλιζόμενοι· ἀντὶ τοῦ κοιμώμενοι. Ἀντιφῶν Περὶ ὁμονοίας.

F69 Harpocration, s.v. βαλβῖσιν (β 1, 55 Keaney); cf. Photius, *Lexicon* s.v. (β 41, 1.324 Theodoridis), *Etymologicum magnum* s.v. βαλβίς (186 Gaisford), *Suda* s.v. (β 69, 1.450–51 Adler)

βαλβῖσιν· Ἀντιφῶν Περὶ ὁμονοίας ἀντὶ τοῦ ταῖς ἀρχαῖς.

F70 Harpocration, s.v. εὐηνιώτατα (ε 156, 116 Keaney); cf. Photius, *Lexicon* s.v. (ε 2175, 2.207 Theodoridis), *Suda* s.v. (ε 3473, 2.448 Adler), *Etymologicum magnum* s.v. εὐήνιον (390 Gaisford)

εὐηνιώτατα· Ἀντιφῶν ἐν τῷ Περὶ ὁμονοίας. εὐήνιος ὁ πρᾶος καὶ μέτριος καὶ μὴ ταραχώδης· ἡ μεταφορὰ ἀπὸ τῶν ἵππων.

F67 1 ἀντὶ τοῦ om. *Anecd. Oxon. Sud.* 1–2 παρ' Ἀντιφῶντι . . . ὁμονοίας om. Epit. Harp. *Anecd.* Phot. *Anecd. Oxon. Sud.* **F67A** 1 ἐν τῷ Epit. Harp. Phot. *Sud.*: om. Harp. **F68** 1 ante ἀντὶ transp. Ἀντιφῶν (Περὶ ὁμονοίας omissis) Epit. Harp. *Anecd.* Phot. *Anecd. Oxon. Sud.* **F69** 1 βαλβῖσιν Epit. Harp. Phot. *Et. Sud.*: βαλβὶς ἡ ἀρχή Harp. Ἀντιφῶν . . . ὁμονοίας om. Epit. Harp. Phot. *Et. Sud.* ἀντὶ τοῦ ταῖς ἀρχαῖς Epit. Harp. Phot. *Et. Sud.*: om. Harp. **F70** 1 εὐηνιώτατα om. *Et.* Ἀντιφῶν . . . ὁμονοίας om. Epit. Harp. Phot. *Sud. Et.* εὔηνος Epit. Harp. Phot. *Sud. Et.* ὁ Epit. Harp. Phot. *Sud. Et.*: ἐστι Harp. 2 ἡ μεταφορὰ ἀπὸ] ἡ μεταφορὰ δὲ ἀπὸ Epit. Harp.: ἀπὸ μεταφορᾶς *Et.*

F67 Unseen (**unseeing**) for "invisible" ("not seeing"), in Antiphon in *On Concord*.

F67A Manhood: the time of life of men. Antiphon in *On Concord*.

F68 Passing the night for "sleeping." Antiphon, *On Concord*.

F69 Starting-posts for "beginnings." Antiphon, *On Concord*.

F70 Most obedient to the rein, Antiphon in *On Concord*. "Obedient to the rein" is one who is gentle, moderate, and not troublesome. The metaphor is from horses.

Cf. also *Anecdota Graeca* s.v. εὐηνιώτατα (257 Bekker); *Etymologicum magnum* s.v. εὐήνιον (390 Gaisford) **εὐηνιώτατα·** τὰ εὖ ἔχοντα, ἀπὸ μεταφορᾶς τῶν ἵππων, αἳ θέουσαι ἡνία ἄγουσιν.

F71 Harpocration, s.v. φηλώματα (φ 12, 260 Keaney); cf. Photius, *Lexicon* s.v. (2.645 Porson), *Etymologicum magnum* s.v. (791 Gaisford), *Suda* s.v. (φ 267, 4.718 Adler)

φηλώματα· Ἀντιφῶν ἐν τῷ Περὶ ὁμονοίας ἐξαπάτας· φηλοῦν γὰρ τὸ ἐξαπατᾶν.

72–77: ΠΟΛΙΤΙΚΟΣ

F72 *Anecdota Graeca* s.v. ἀπειθαρχία (78 Bekker)

ἀπειθαρχία· Ἀντιφῶν Πολιτικῷ.

F73 Athenaeus, 10 423A (2.420 Kaibel)

καταριστᾶν δὲ εἴρηκεν ἐν τῷ Πολιτικῷ Ἀντιφῶν οὕτως· **ὅτε δή τις πράγματα τὰ ἑαυτοῦ ἢ τὰ τῶν φίλων κατηρίστηκεν.**

F74 Harpocration, s.v. εὐσύμβολος (ε 168, 118 Keaney); cf. Photius, *Lexicon* s.v. (ε 2345, 2.222 Theodoridis), *Etymologicum magnum* s.v. (398 Gaisford), *Suda* s.v. εὐσύμβουλος (ε 3758, 2.474 Adler)

6 μεταφορᾶς om. *Et.* 7 τὰ ἡνία *Et.* **F71** cod. Photii = g 1 φιλώματα Phot. g (corr. Porson) Ἀντιφῶν ... ὁμονοίας om. Epit. Harp. Phot. *Et.* *Sud.* ἐξαπατήματα *Et.* post ἐξαπάτας add. οὕτως Ἀντιφῶν *Sud.* 2 φιλοῦν Phot. g (corr. Porson) φηλοῦν ... ἐξαπατᾶν om. *Sud.* ἀπατᾶν *Et.* post ἐξαπατᾶν add. οὕτως Ἀντιφῶν Epit. Harp. Phot. **F73** cod. = A 2 ὅτε δή Kaibel: ὅτ' ἄν A: ὅτι δή Meineke: alii alia πράγματα] χρήματα Meineke ἢ τὰ] καὶ τὰ C. Müller **F74** cod. Photii = z

F71 **Bamboozlings** for "deceits," Antiphon in *On Concord*. For to bamboozle is to deceive.

72–77: ΠΟΛΙΤΙΚΟΣ

F72 **Disobedience to authority**, Antiphon in *Politicus*.

F73 Antiphon said "squander on lunches" in *Politicus*, as follows: **now that** (**since**) **one has squandered his own possessions, or those of his friends, on lunches**.

εὐσύμβολος· ἀντὶ τοῦ ῥᾳδίως καὶ εὖ συμβάλλων, τουτέστιν ἀγαθὸς συμβάλλειν. Ἀντιφῶν Πολιτικῷ.

F75 Harpocration, s.v. ἡμιολιασμός (η 12, 124 Keaney); cf. Photius, *Lexicon* s.v. (η 170, 2.267 Theodoridis), *Suda* s.v. (η 341, 2.570 Adler)

ἡμιολιασμός· Ἀντιφῶν Πολιτικῷ· **διπλασιασμοῦ καὶ ἡμιολιασμοῦ** ἀντὶ τοῦ τὸ ἡμιόλιον δοῦναι ἐν τοῖς λογισμοῖς.

Cf. also Pollux, 4.164 (1.249 Bethe) διπλασιασμὸν δ' Ἀντιφῶν εἶπεν.

F76 Priscian, *Institutiones* 18.230 (3.321–22 Hertz)

Illi 'καταμελεῖν τούτων' καὶ 'ταῦτα.' Ἀντιφῶν Πολιτικῷ: **μήτε φιλοπότην κληθῆναι καὶ δοκεῖν τὰ πράγματα καταμελεῖν ὑπὸ οἴνου ἡσσώμενον.**

F77 Plutarch, *Antonius* 28

ἀναλίσκειν καὶ καθηδυπαθεῖν τὸ πολυτελέστατον, ὡς Ἀντιφῶν εἶπεν, ἀνάλωμα, τὸν χρόνον.

1 εὐσύμβουλος Epit. Harp. Phot. z (corr. Theodoridis) *Et.* codd. (corr. Sylburg) *Sud.* συμβάλων *Sud.* 2 συμβαλλεῖν Epit. Harp.: συμβαλεῖν Phot. z (corr. Theodoridis) ἐν τῷ Πολιτικῷ Epit. Harp. Phot. *Et. Sud.* **F75** 1–2 Πολιτικῷ . . . ἡμιολιασμοῦ om. Epit. Harp. Phot. *Sud.* 2 ἡμιολιασμοῦ Schneider: ἡμιόλιστον Harp. τὸ ἡμιόλιον vel τὸ ⟨διπλάσιον καὶ τὸ⟩ ἡμιόλιον Sauppe: τῶν ἡμιολίων Harp.: τὰ ἡμιόλια Epit. Harp. Phot. *Sud.* δοῦναι Epit. Harp. Phot. *Sud.*: om. Harp.: θεῖναι Sauppe 2–3 ἐν τοῖς λογισμοῖς om. Epit. Harp. Phot. *Sud.* codd. = F S A C B 4–5 διπλασιασμὸν . . . εἶπεν om. B C 4 διπλάσια F S **F76** *codd.* = *R V M O D N* 1 Illi] Graeci *(per compendia) D N* ταιτα *M* πωλιτικωι *M*: ιτολιτικωι *V*: πολιτικοι *O* 2 φιλοιτοτην *V R* κανθηναι *V*: κανθ . ηναι *R*: κανηεναι *M* δεκειν *M* ιτραγματα *V R* 2–3 καταμηλειν *M* 3 υιτο *V R* ησσωμηνων *M*

F74 **Good at calculating** for "calculating easily and well," that is, good at calculating. Antiphon in *Politicus*.

F75 **Doubling** and **multiplication by one and one-half** for "making half as much again" in calculations. Antiphon in *Politicus*.

F76 Greeks say "neglect *touton*" and "*tauta*." Antiphon in *Politicus*: **nor to be called fond of drinking and be reputed to neglect one's affairs, yielding to wine**.

F77 To use up and squander time, the most costly expenditure, as Antiphon said.

78–81B: DREAM-BOOK

F78 Artemidorus, *Onirocritica* 2.14 (131 Pack)

οἱ δὲ μαλακοὶ τῶν ἰχθύων μόνοις τοῖς πανούργοις συμφέρουσι· καὶ γὰρ αὐτοὶ μεταβάλλοντες τὰ χρώματα καὶ ὁμοιούμενοι τοῖς τόποις ἐν οἷς ἂν γένωνται λανθάνουσι. τοῖς δὲ λοιποῖς ἐμπόδια καὶ κατοχὰς σημαίνουσι διὰ τὸ καθεκτικὸν καὶ ἰξῶδες, καὶ ἐν ταῖς πράξεσιν ἀτονίας πολλὰς προαγορεύουσι διὰ τὸ μὴ ὀστέα ἔχειν· ἰσχὺς γὰρ σώματος ὀστέον. εἰσὶ δὲ οἵδε· πολύπους τευθὶς ἀκαλήφη ναύπλιος ἑλεδώνη πορφυρίων σηπία. αὕτη δὲ μόνη καὶ τοὺς ἀποδρᾶναι πειρωμένους ὠφελεῖ διὰ τὸν θόλον, ᾧ χρωμένη πολλάκις φεύγει. μέμνηται δὲ τούτου τοῦ ὀνείρου καὶ Ἀντιφῶν ὁ Ἀθηναῖος.

F79 Cicero, *De divinatione* 1.39

sed omittamus oracula, veniamus ad somnia. de quibus disputans Chrysippus multis et minutis somniis colligendis facit idem quod Antipater ea conquirens, quae Antiphontis interpretatione explicata declarant illa quidem acumen interpretis, sed exemplis grandioribus decuit uti.

Cf. ibid. 1.116 hic magna quaedam exoritur neque ea naturalis sed artificiosa somniorum [Antiphontis] interpretatio eodemque modo et oraculorum et vaticinationum. [sunt enim explanatores, ut grammatici poetarum.]

F78 codd. = L V 1 μόνοι L πανούργοις] πανουργεῖν τι ἐπιχειροῦσι V 2 αὐτοὶ del. Hercher 3 ὁμοιούμενα L 5 καθεκτικὸν αὐτῶν L: καθεττικὸν V: corr. Hercher 6 μὴ om. V 6–7 ἰσχὺς . . . εἰσὶ δὲ om. L 7 οἵδε] ἣ δὲ L 8 ναύπλιος L V: ναυτίλος Jacobs ἑλεδώνη Bursian: ἀληνῶν L: om. V σιπία V: σηπεα L: corr. Rigault 9 ἀποδιδράσκειν L πειρωμένους] βουλομένους V: προῃρημένους Hercher δόλον V 10 δὲ om. V 10–11 τοῦ ὀνείρου τούτου V **F79** *codd. = A V B Ald.* 3 idem *V post corr.*: isdem *A B V ante corr.* 7 Antiphontis *Ald.*: antiphonis *A V B*: *del. Baiter* 9 sunt . . . poetarum *del. Kayser*: enim *et* ut . . . poetarum *del. Christ*: *alii alia*

78–81B: DREAM-BOOK

F78 Soft fish are advantageous for criminals alone, for they escape notice by changing their colors and becoming like whatever places they are in. For other people, however, they signify impediments and delays because of their stickiness and ability to hold on, and portend much slackness in business undertakings on account of their not having bones. (For bone is the body's strength.) The following are soft fish: octopus, squid, sea-anemone, nautilus, musk-octopus, purple polyp, cuttlefish. The last one alone benefits as well those who are trying to escape, because of its ink, which it often uses to run away. Antiphon of Athens also mentions this dream.

F79 But let us leave off oracles and move on to dreams. When treating of them, Chrysippus does the same thing as Antipater, collecting many frivolous dreams and seeking out those which declare the interpreter's cleverness when explained with Antiphon's method of interpretation. But he should have used more impressive examples.

Here arises a certain important method of interpreting dreams (and likewise oracles and prophecies) – not a natural but an artificial method.

F80(a) Cicero, *De divinatione* 2.144

quid, ipsorum interpretum coniecturae nonne magis ingenia declarant eorum quam vim consensumque naturae? cursor ad Olympia proficisci cogitans visus est in somnis curru quadrigarum vehi. mane ad coniectorem. at ille 'vinces' inquit; 'id enim celeritas significat et vis equorum.' post idem ad Antiphontem. is autem 'vincare' inquit 'necesse est; an non intellegis quattuor ante te cucurrisse?' ecce alius cursor – atque horum somniorum et talium plenus est Chrysippi liber, plenus Antipatri – sed ad cursorem redeo: ad interpretem detulit aquilam se in somnis visum esse factum. at ille 'vicisti; ista enim avis volat nulla vehementius.' huic eidem Antipho 'baro' inquit 'victum te esse non vides? ista enim avis insectans alias avis et agitans semper ipsa postrema est.'

F80(b) Diogenes of Oenoanda, fr. 24 (= NF 122) (186–87 Smith)

[ἐχρήσα]-

I

[το δ' ἐντ]αῦθα φυσι-
[κὸς δια]λεκτικοῦ
[λόγοι]ς, ἐπιχειρῶν
[τὴν π]ερὶ τῶν ὀνεί-
[ρων μ]ạντευτικὴν
[καὶ τὸ] π̣ᾶν αὐτοῖς

F80(a) *codd.* = *A B Erlang. Asc.* 6 anthiphontem *B* 8 talium ⟨interpretationum⟩ *Diels* 9 chriseppe *A*: chrisippi *B* 11 avis *A B*: avi *Asc.* 12 eidem *Lambinus*: equidem *A B post corr.*: est quidem *B ante corr.*: quidem *Erlang.*: aeque idem *H. Schöne*: aeque fidens *Allen* anticho *B* 13 vides] dives *B ante corr.* avis *alt. del. Sauppe* **F80(b)**1 Sedley = D. Sedley *apud* Smith (1984), 47–48 1 (et praecedentia) [ἐχρήσατο δ'] Smith: [φαίνεται] Sedley 1 [ἐντ]αῦθα Smith 2–3 suppl. Sedley 3 ante ἐπιχειρῶν spatium minimum 4 [τὴν π]ερὶ Smith: [καὶ π]ερὶ Sedley 5 suppl. Smith 6 [καὶ τὸ] Smith: [οὐ τὸ] Sedley

F80(a) Is it not true that the interpretations of the dream-interpreters reveal their own cleverness rather than a natural power and connection? A runner planning to set out for the Olympic games dreamed he was riding in a four-horse chariot. The next morning he went to a dream-interpreter, who said: "You will be victorious; for the speed and power of the horses signify this." Afterwards the same man went to Antiphon, who said: "You will necessarily be defeated; or do you not understand that four ran in front of you?" Here is another runner – Chrysippus' book is full of these and such-like dreams, and Antipater's too – but back to the runner. He reported to an interpreter that he dreamed he had become an eagle. The interpreter said: "You have won, for no bird flies with greater force than that one." To this same man Antiphon said: "Stupid! Do you not see that you have been defeated? For that bird itself is always last, chasing and driving others before it."

F80(b) Here a natural philosopher (?) [used the arguments] of a dialectician, putting his hand to the art of dream-divination,

[πιστεύ]ων. *v* ἐφυ-
[spatium c. 11 litt.] γὰρ
- - - - - - - - - - - - -
- - - - - - - - - - - - -
- - - - - - - - - - - - -
[ὁ γὰρ Ἀντιφῶν, φησί,]
[προεῖπεν, ἐπερωτη]-
[θεὶς ὑπὸ δρομέως ἤ]-

II

δη μέλλοντος [Ὀ]λυμ-
πίασιν ἀγωνιεῖσθαι,
ὅτι λελείψεται. *v* ὁ μὲν
γάρ, φησίν, ἀετὸν ἔφη
δόξαι διώκειν ἐν τοῖς
ὀνείροις, *v* ἐπερωτῶν
τὸν Ἀντιφῶντα· *v* ὁ δ᾽ αὐ-
[τ]όθεν κ̣ε̣λ̣ [spatium c. 4 litt.] Ο̣υ̣ . . ΙΙ
- - - - - - - - - - - - -
- - - - - - - - - - - - -
- - - - - - - - - - - - -
- - - - - - - - - - - - -
- - - - - - - - - - - - -
[- - - - - - - - - - ἐπε]-

III

ρ̣ω̣[τηθέντα οὐκ] ἄν-
τικρυς εἰπεῖν τῷ
δρομεῖ τὸν θεὸν
ὅτι λελείψῃ, *v* καὶ
τὸν ἀετὸν μηδὲν
ὀχλεῖν. εἰ μή τι δι᾽

7 [πιστεύ]ων Smith: [βεβαι]ῶν Sedley 7–8 ἐφυ[σιολόγει μὲν] Sedley: ἐφυ[λάττετο μὲν] (dubitanter) Smith 12–14 suppl. (exempli grat.) Smith **F80(b)II** 1 suppl. Smith 8 suppl. Smith κ̣ε̣-λ̣-[εύσας] vel κ̣ε̣λ̣[εύει] Smith 14 suppl. Smith **F80(b)III** 1 suppl. Smith 6 ante εἰ spatium minimum

[trusting] them entirely. For ... [Antiphon, he says, predicted, when consulted by a runner who] was about to compete at Olympia, that he would be outdistanced ... For when consulting Antiphon, he says, the runner said that in his dreams he thought an eagle was giving chase (thought he was chasing an eagle). And Antiphon ... [when consulted] said at once that the god had not told the runner at all that "You will be outdistanced" ... and that the eagle does not cause any anxiety. If the runner

Ἀντιφῶντα παρέ-
[δ]ẹịξεν αὐṭόν, ἵν' ε-
9–14 desunt

IV

I[
μ[
εἰς ụII
πρὸς γạ̀[ρ
πραγμα[
ὡς μαρ̣[τυροῦσιν ὄ]-
ν[ε]ιρ̣[οι
8–14 desunt

F81 Seneca, *Controversiae* 2.1.33 (79 Håkanson)

Otho Iunius pater solebat difficiles controversias belle dicere, eas in quibus inter silentium et ⟨apertam⟩ actionem medio temperamento opus erat. edidit quidem quattuor libros colorum, quos belle Gallio noster Antiphontis libros vocabat: tantum in illis somniorum est.

F81A Melampus, Περὶ παλμῶν μαντική 18–19 (22–23 Diels)

ὀφθαλμὸς δεξιὸς ἐὰν ἅλληται, κατὰ Φημονόην καὶ Αἰγυπτίους καὶ Ἀντιφῶντα ἐχθροὺς ὑποχειρίους ἕξει· ἄγει

8 suppl. Smith ante ἵν' spatium minimum 8–9 ἕ[χῃ] Smith **F80(b)IV** 3 εἰς ụ̔π̣[οψίαν] vel ụ̔π̣[οψίας] Smith 4 suppl. Smith 4–5 [ταῦτα τὰ] πράγμα[τα] vel [τούτοις τὰ] πράγμα[τα] vel [τούτοις τὸ] πρᾶγμα vel [τούτοις τοῖς] πράγμα[σι] Smith 6 μαρ[τυροῦσιν] vel μαρ̣[τυρεῖ] Smith 6–7 [ὄ]ν[ε]ιρ̣[οι] vel [ὄ]ν[ε]ιρ̣[ος] vel [ὄ]ν[ε]ίρ̣[ατα] vel [ὀ]ν[ε]ιρ̣[οκρίτης] vel [ὀ]ν[ε]ιρ̣[οκρίται] Smith **F81** *codd.* = *A B V* 1 oto *A B V* sollebas *V ante corr.* 2 ⟨apertam⟩ actionem *Håkanson (coll. Con. 2.1.39)*: detectionem *Gertz* 3 opus erat] operat *V* 4 liberos *A B* quo *A B* bello *A* anthipontis *A B V* liberos *A B* 5 tantis *V ante corr.* in illis] millis *A ante corr.* soniorum *B* **F81A** codd. = B R N 1 post Φημονόην add. καὶ Μελάμποδα B N 2 ἀνάγει Triller: ἄξει vel ἐπανάξει Diels (coll. Artemid. 2.36)

had not shown him up, by the aid of Antiphon, in order ... as dreams testify ... (translation after Smith [1993], 378–79).

F81 Junius Otho senior used to declaim difficult *controversiae* well – those in which a blend midway between silence and an open manner of speaking was needed. He published four books of "colors," well-named by our friend Gallio "books of Antiphon," so many dreams do they contain.

F81A If the right eye twitches, you will have your enemies under control, according to Phemonoe and Egyptians and Antiphon;

δὲ καὶ ἀποδήμους. ὀφθαλμοῦ δεξιοῦ τὸ ἄνω βλέφαρον ἐὰν ἅλληται, ἐπίκτησιν πάντως δηλοῖ, κατὰ δὲ Ἀντιφῶντα πρᾶξιν καὶ ὑγείαν, δούλῳ ἐπιβουλήν, χήρᾳ ἀποδημίαν.

F81B Fulgentius, *Mitologiae* I.14 (24 Helm) [fabula de lauro]

at vero amica Apollinis ob hac re vocitata est, quia illi qui de somniorum interpretatione scripserunt ut Antiphon, Filocorus [= *FGrHist* 328 F 179] et Artemon et Serapion Ascalonites promittant in libris suis quod laurum si dormientibus ad caput posueris, vera somnia esse visuros.

2–3 ἄγει ... ἀποδήμους] *et peregrinationes* N 5 ὑγείαν R N: ὑγρὰν B
F81B *codd.* = *R T H M D E G Bern* 1 apollini *R M* ab hac *R M D*: ob hac *T*: ob hanc *H E G* rem *R H E G* 2 interpretatione somniorum *E G* 2–3 philocrus *G*: filocrus *cet. codd.*: philochorus *Scriverius*: *corr. Helm* 3 sarapion *Bern* 4 in *om. H* quod *om. R E G* 5 visuros esse *T*

and it also brings travelers. If the upper lid of the right eye twitches, it signifies gain generally, and according to Antiphon success and health; for a slave it signifies a plot, and for a widow, travel abroad.

F81B The laurel was called Apollo's friend for this reason, that those who have written about the interpretation of dreams – like Antiphon, Philochorus, Artemon, and Serapion of Ascalon – promise in their books that if you lay laurel beside the head of sleepers, they will see true dreams.

COMMENTARY

COMMENTARY

T1

Memorabilia 1.6, which consists of three separate encounters between Socrates and Antiphon, belongs to a series of reports and conversations (extending from 1.4 to 2.1) which have as their purpose to show that Socrates both encouraged his companions to virtue and helped them to attain it (cf. Erbse [1961], 270–71, 273; Gigon [1953], 151–52). Antiphon's aim in all three encounters is to win over Socrates' followers to himself by showing Socrates up as an incompetent teacher. Xenophon indicates this in his introduction to the first encounter (T1, ll. 2–3: βουλόμενος τοὺς συνουσιαστὰς αὐτοῦ παρελέσθαι), and Gigon (1946), 135–36 is clearly mistaken in contending that the motif of detaching Socrates' followers is "completely forgotten after a few lines." It must therefore be assumed (*pace* Dodds [1954]) that they are present at all three encounters, although this is made explicit only in the case of the first (T1, l. 4: παρόντων αὐτῶν). Cf. Döring (1895), 133; Morrison (1953), 5. Schmid (1940), 159 and Avery (1982), 154 with n. 1 emphasized greed (φιλοχρηματία) as the motivation behind Antiphon's attacks; but this is at best subordinate to the motive of professional rivalry. Since the whole of *Memorabilia* 1.6 is an attack on Socrates' credibility as a teacher, each of Antiphon's criticisms must be understood specifically in this light (cf. below).

The disputes between Antiphon and Socrates are not attested in any source independent of Xenophon, and it is doubtful whether they ever actually took place. Like the Platonic dialogues and other works of Socratic literature, the events narrated in the *Memorabilia* were probably not intended by their author to be taken for reproductions of actual encounters between the historical Socrates and his contemporaries (cf. Erbse [1961], 287 n. 1; Momigliano [1971], 46–47, 52–54). Xenophon claims to have been a silent participant in the encounters between Antiphon and Socrates (cf. T1, l. 94: ἐμοὶ μὲν δὴ ταῦτα ἀκούοντι κτλ.). But of course this proves nothing (cf. Maier [1913], 21; Breitenbach [1967], 1779–80; Guthrie [1971b], 25 n. 2). What source (or sources) Xenophon depended on here is completely unknown. Dümmler (1889), 81 suggested a Cynic source, which Joël (1893–1901), 2.629–73, Altwegg (1908), 6–7, and others identified as Antisthenes; Dittmar (1912), 195–210, esp. 209–10 suggested Aeschines of Sphettus' dialogue Καλλίας. But there is simply no evidence.

The significance of Xenophon's evidence for the problem of the identity of Antiphon is discussed in section 1 of the Introduction. Here it is necessary to consider what light (if any) Xenophon's portrait sheds on Antiphon's thought and writings. Antiphon's crude greed (φιλαργυρία) and undisguised hostility are easily recognizable as stock traits of the typical sophistic opponent of Socrates. As such, they tend to support the view of Wilamowitz (1931–32), 2.217 n. 1 and Gigon (1953), 165 that Xenophon's Antiphon is merely a type, devoid of real individuality. More difficult to judge is the unmistakable hedonism of the Xenophontic Antiphon (cf. e.g. T1, ll. 59–60: ἔοικας, ὦ Ἀντιφῶν, τὴν εὐδαιμονίαν οἰομένῳ τρυφὴν καὶ πολυτέλειαν εἶναι). Gigon (1953), 165 noted that this characteristic serves Xenophon's dramatic (and, it should be added, apologetic) purposes, as Antiphon's vices of τρυφή and πολυτέλεια are made the foil to Socrates' virtues of ἐγκράτεια and καρτερία. Yet it is by no means impossible that Antiphon's hedonism reflects (perhaps in an exaggerated and hence distorted fashion) the type of outlook reflected in passages such as F44(a)v.13–22 (cf. Nestle [1942], 379; Morrison [1953], 4–5; commentary ad loc.). Bignone (1938), 126 connected Antiphon's point about students imitating their teachers (T1, ll. 13–16) with F62 of Περὶ ὁμονοίας, which expresses a related idea. But the idea was a commonplace, and the resemblance is unlikely to be more than coincidental (cf. commentary on F62). More interesting is the attempt by Jaeger (1939–45), 2.379 n. 130 and Untersteiner (1962), 17, 43 to connect Socrates' profession of *Bedürfnislosigkeit* or freedom from needs (T1, ll. 60–63) with F10 of Περὶ ἀληθείας (ἀδέητος, applied to god?). On this interpretation, Socrates' profession amounts to an ironic reversal of Antiphon's thought. For the adjective ἀδέητος in F10 means "lacking nothing because having everything," while Socrates reinterprets "needlessness" to mean having few desires, *Bedürfnislosigkeit* (cf. Zeller [1922], 155 n. 6; Döring [1895], 135). Not only is the ideal of *Bedürfnislosigkeit* a favorite of Xenophon's, however (cf. *Agesilaos* 11.11), it also constitutes the appropriate response to Antiphon's critique of Socrates' impoverished lifestyle. Moreover, it is uncertain whether "god" is the subject of F10 – as Jaeger's and Untersteiner's interpretation requires (cf. commentary on F10). For these reasons, an allusion to F10 seems doubtful.

1 τὸν σοφιστήν: for the epithet σοφιστής cf. *Suda* s.v. Ἀντιφῶν = T3, ll. 1–2; scholium on Aristotle, *Posterior Analytics* 75b40 = F13(l), l. 3; Simplicius, *In Aristotelis Physica* 273.36 = F15(f), l. 2; Introduction, section 1.

5 εὐδαιμονεστέρους: Antiphon is perhaps playing ironically on two senses of εὐδαιμονία, "material prosperity" and "happiness." Alternatively (as David Sedley suggests to me), his remarks may simply betray his own materialistic assumptions about the nature of happiness.

6–7 τἀναντία τῆς φιλοσοφίας ἀπολελαυκέναι: cf. the curiously similar passage in Plato, *Apology* 31B: καὶ εἰ μέν τι ἀπὸ τούτων ἀπέλαυον καὶ μισθὸν λαμβάνων ταῦτα παρεκελευόμην κτλ.

7–11 ζῇς γοῦν . . . ἀχίτων διατελεῖς: Antiphon's brief description of Socrates' lifestyle is reminiscent of the depiction of Socrates in Attic comedy. Cf. Eupolis, fr. 386; Amipsias, fr. 9; Aristophanes, *Clouds* 103–4, 363. For Socrates' δίαιτα cf. *Memorabilia* 1.2.1, 5; 1.3.5–8; Breitenbach (1967), 1784.

13 ἐλευθεριώτερον: Antiphon is made to express the exact opposite of Socrates' view. Cf. *Memorabilia* 1.2.6 (τούτου [*sc.* pay for teaching] δ' ἀπεχόμενος ἐνόμιζεν ἐλευθερίας ἐπιμελεῖσθαι· τοὺς δὲ λαμβάνοντας τῆς ὁμιλίας μισθὸν ἀνδραποδιστὰς ἑαυτῶν ἀπεκάλει διὰ τὸ ἀναγκαῖον αὐτοῖς εἶναι διαλέγεσθαι παρ' ὧν [ἂν] λάβοιεν τὸν μισθόν); and the lines from an otherwise unknown work on Socrates preserved in a Hibeh papyrus: ἔτ[ι] εἰ Σωκράτει χρήματ[α λα]μβάνοντι ἐξῆν ἐλευθ[έρ]ω[ς] ζῆν καὶ μὴ ἐπι[πόν]ως διαιτ[ᾶσθ]α[ι]· μ[ό]ν[ον γὰρ] πλοῦτον κ[αὶ] χρήμ[ατα] εἰς τὰ ἐκ [τ]ῆς τύχης [ἀκλ]ηρήματα . . . [ἐπι]κούρους, [ὡσ]αύτως δὲ [εἰς] τὰς νόσους . . . καὶ εἰς τὴν τοῦ γή[ρως] ἀσθένειαν (Gallo [1980], 186–87, fr. (b), 4.19–29). Cf. further *Memorabilia* 1.6.5 = T1, ll. 20–23; Breitenbach (1967), 1793.

75–76 Ὦ Ἀντιφῶν, παρ' ἡμῖν κτλ.: Blass (1889), 9 and Dodds (1951), 119 n. 100, (1954) interpreted the phrase παρ' ἡμῖν to mean "among us Athenians," and inferred that Xenophon's Antiphon was not an Athenian. The phrase can be understood in other ways (cf. Joël [1893–1901], 2.639 n. 1; Gigon [1953], 160; Morrison [1953], 5; Narcy [1989], 239–40). But even if it is interpreted as Blass and Dodds suggested, their inference as to Antiphon's nationality does not follow. For Socrates may speak as one Athenian to another, reminding Antiphon of attitudes which he (as an Athenian) ought to share.

90–93 καὶ τοὺς θησαυροὺς . . . ἐκλεγόμεθα: this passage is unique in the extant Socratic literature. Dümmler (1889), 82, and many other commentators refer the words τῶν πάλαι σοφῶν to philosophers. Accepting this interpretation, Burnet (1924), 163–64 and Taylor (1928), 20–22 argued that the passage provides evidence of an earlier phase in Socrates' career during which he concerned himself with the speculations of Presocratic natural philosophy. But as Zeller (1922), 133 n. 4 rightly pointed out, ἀγαθόν refers to what is morally useful. For this reason, τῶν πάλαι σοφῶν more likely refers to poets than Presocratic philosophers (cf. Döring [1895], 136). The passage should perhaps be connected with Polycrates' charge that Socrates misused famous poets for immoral ends (cf. Xenophon, *Memorabilia* 1.2.56–59; Zeller [1922], 133 n. 4; Gigon [1953], 163; Breitenbach [1967], 1789–90).

97–102 καὶ πάλιν κτλ.: Gigon (1953), 33, 164–65; Breitenbach (1967), 1794–95, and other commentators have misunderstood the connection between this final conversation (which Nestle [1940], 47 with n. 45 thought was inspired by Plato, *Apology* 31cff. and *Gorgias* 521D) and the preceding ones. It is not the specific content of Antiphon's attack which furnishes the link but rather his continued aim of discrediting Socrates as a teacher. By pointing out the (alleged) incompatibility between Socrates' teaching and practice in the area of politics (πῶς ἄλλους μὲν ... αὐτὸς δ' οὐ πράττει), Antiphon tries to cast doubt on Socrates' knowledge of the subject (εἴπερ ἐπίσταται), and hence his fitness to teach it. Cf. Morrison (1953), 5; Döring (1895), 133. On the commonplace character of Antiphon's criticism cf. Introduction, section 1.

T2(a)

The treatise entitled *De ideis* by Hermogenes of Tarsus is concerned with the "ideas" of style (ἰδέαι or εἴδη).[1] (On Hermogenes' theory of ideas cf. Kroll [1940], 1125–28; Hagedorn [1964]; Kennedy [1972], 619–33; Lindberg [1977], 8–129, 200–62; Patillon [1988], 103–278.) After a general introduction, Hermogenes proceeds to a long and detailed discussion of the individual ideas of style. Next he offers idealized models for different types of discourse, and then discusses discourse which falls short of the ideal (ἁπλῶς λόγος). In a section on political discourse which falls short of the ideal (ἁπλῶς πολιτικὸς λόγος), Hermogenes briefly analyzes the styles of the ten canonical Attic orators (excepting Demosthenes, who represents the ideal), as well as of the sophists Antiphon and Critias. Hermogenes prefaces his analysis of the works current under the name of Antiphon with a brief discussion of the identity of their author(s). The significance of this discussion for the problem of the Antiphons is considered in section 1 of the Introduction. It must be emphasized that the discussion on identity is motivated solely by the stylistic differences which Hermogenes perceives within the *corpus Antiphonteum*, differences so great as to constrain him to separate analyses of the speeches of the Rhamnusian and of the works attributed to "the

[1] Patillon (1988), 8–19 contended that the author of *De ideis* (whom he calls Hermogenes "the rhetor") should be distinguished from the better-known Hermogenes of Tarsus, the "sophist" profiled by Philostratus in *Vitae sophistarum*.

other" Antiphon. The prosopographical problem for Hermogenes is completely subordinate to the problem of stylistic analysis.

Hermogenes' judgment on the style of the sophist Antiphon is largely negative. This results primarily from his treatment of Antiphon as a representative of political discourse (πολιτικὸς λόγος), a genre that demands ideas of style such as clarity (σαφήνεια), sincerity (ἀλήθεια), character (ἦθος), and the ideas subordinate to them (cf. *De ideis* 381.6–9, 395.17–23; translations of Hermogenes' technical terms are adopted from Lindberg [1977], 10–11). But these are precisely the ideas that Antiphon's discourse lacks. His works are characterized instead by magnitude (μέγεθος), beauty (ἐπιμέλεια), and subordinate ideas such as dignity (σεμνότης), asperity (τραχύτης), and amplitude (περιβολή). Such ideas are appropriate in political discourse only to a limited extent (cf. *De ideis* 381.9–382.7). The above-mentioned ideas are manifested in Antiphon's discourse throughout most of the "categories" or constituent elements into which Hermogenes divides all discourse: thought (ἔννοια), figures of thought (μέθοδος), and λέξις. This last category (by an extension of meaning) includes figures of speech (σχήματα); cola (κῶλα); composition (συνθήκη); and cadence (ἀνάπαυσις). On the categories cf. Lindberg (1977), 30–39; Hagedorn (1964), 19–20.

In the the category of thought (ἔννοια), for example, Antiphon's discourse is characterized as σεμνός and ὑπέρογκος, adjectives related to magnitude (μέγεθος) and its subordinate ideas (cf. *De ideis* 396.19–20). To illustrate what he means by dignified thoughts (σεμναὶ ἔννοιαι), Hermogenes instances discussions of natural phenomena (δεύτεραι δὲ μετ' ἐκείνας σεμναὶ αἱ περὶ τῶν θείων ὡς ὄντως πραγμάτων, οἷον ὡρῶν φύσεις εἰ ἐξετάζοι τις, ὅπως τε καὶ καθ' ἃς αἰτίας γίνονται, καὶ τὴν τοῦ παντὸς περιφορὰν καὶ φύσιν ἢ κινήσεις γῆς ἢ θαλάττης εἰ ζητοίη τις ὅπως γίνονται, ἢ σκηπτῶν φορὰς ἢ ὅλως τοιαῦτα (*De ideis* 243.22–244.1) and of ethical topics (τρίτη δὲ σεμνότητος ἐννοιῶν τάξις, εἰ περὶ πραγμάτων ἃ δὴ φύσει μέν ἐστι θεῖα, τὸ πλεῖστον δ' ἐν ἀνθρώποις θεωρεῖται λέγοι τις, οἷον εἰ περὶ ψυχῆς, ὅτι ἀθάνατος, ἢ περὶ δικαιοσύνης ἢ σωφροσύνης ἢ τῶν τοιούτων διεξίοιμεν ἢ περὶ τοῦ βίου παντὸς ἢ τί νόμος ἢ τί φύσις ἢ τὰ τοιαῦτα (*De ideis* 245.3–9). The remains of Antiphon's writings offer numerous examples of each (cf. F26–29, F32, F44(a)–(c), F49, F58, F59). Furthermore, it is important how these subjects are treated. If natural phenomena are simply described (κατ' ἔκφρασιν), the discourse is political (πολιτικός) as well as dignified (σεμνός). But if their causes are investigated (κατὰ τὰς αἰτίας), then the discourse is dignified only but not political (cf. *De ideis* 244.1–15). Both Antiphon's subject-matter and the way in which it is treated make for magnitude (μέγεθος). His "thoughts" (ἔννοιαι) are the exact opposite of the commonplace or simple (καθαρός) thoughts which create the clarity (σαφήνεια) necessary in political discourse.

In the category of μέθοδος or figures of thought, according to Hermogenes, Antiphon employs ἀπόφανσις or categorical assertion, which produces magnitude (μέγεθος) and its subordinate idea dignity (σεμνότης; cf. *De ideis* 246.10ff. with Lindberg [1977], 69). Examples of such categorical assertion are found in F2, F10, F52, F59, and throughout the papyrus fragments of Περὶ ἀληθείας. (In F60, by contrast, the qualification οἶμαι softens the categorical assertion; cf. *De ideis* 250.17–19.) Antiphon's λέξις or diction is described by Hermogenes as harsh (τραχύτης is a subordinate idea to μέγεθος). One type of harsh diction is constituted by figurative language, ἡ τετραμμένη (cf. *De ideis* 258.7–18, 248.9ff. with Lindberg [1977], 211–12). Hermogenes castigates all the older sophists and their pupils for excessive use of figurative language, which is excusable in poetry but not in political discourse (cf. *De ideis* 248.25–249.12). The fragments of Περὶ ὁμονοίας, which is written in the characteristic style of sophistic ἐπίδειξις, furnish many examples of the kind of figurative language Hermogenes objects to (cf. Introduction, section IV). Also relevant here is Antiphon's (occasional) use of substantival periphrases in place of verbs – a stylistic device which creates σεμνὴ λέξις (cf. *De ideis* 249.12–250.5; F44(a)II.23–26, V.27–33, with commentary). In the categories of figures of speech (σχήματα) and composition (συνθήκη),[2] Antiphon's discourse displays to excess the idea of beauty, ἐπιμέλεια or κάλλος (cf. Lindberg [1977], 75 with n. 2, 273–74; Hagedorn [1964], 53 interpreted these terms differently). Hermogenes finds the very same fault in Critias (cf. *De ideis* 402.7–10: ἐπιμελὴς δὲ ὢν οὐ μετρίως ὅμως οὐχ ἁπλῶς χρῆται τῷ τοιούτῳ κόσμῳ οὐδὲ κατὰ τὸν Ἀντιφῶντα προσκόρως κτλ.). In respect to composition (συνθήκη), Hermogenes may have had in mind Antiphon's frequent use of quasi-poetic rhythms (cf. *De ideis* 308.13ff.; F49, ll. 2–3, F57, F44(a)I.20–23, all with commentary). Numerous examples of various kinds of figures of speech (σχήματα) are found in the fragments of Περὶ ὁμονοίας (cf. commentary on F45–71 *passim*).

As a result of the preponderance of ideas related to magnitude (μέγεθος) in the categories of thought (ἔννοια), figures of thought

[2] On the meaning of συνθήκη cf. Kustas (1973), 14 n. 2: "Hermogenes understands two things by συνθήκη: (1) relation of the last syllable of one word to the beginning of the next, e.g. hiatus, though purely rhythmical considerations are also involved; and (2) general sequence of long and short syllables."

(μέθοδος), and diction (λέξις) – and of ideas of beauty (ἐπιμέλεια or κάλλος) in the categories of figures of speech (σχήματα) and composition (συνθήκη) – Antiphon's discourse lacks character (ἦθος) and sincerity (ἀλήθεια). (On these terms cf. Lindberg [1977], 9–82, 222–25, 236–38, 263–65; Hagedorn [1964], 57–70.) The grandeur and artfulness of his writing deprive it of the appearance of sincerity and spontaneity which is essential to political discourse. Because Antiphon's discourse is deficient in the ideas appropriate to political discourse (σαφήνεια, ἦθος, and ἀλήθεια; cf. *De ideis* 381.6–9, 395.17–23) and rich in those that are inappropriate to it (μέγεθος and ἐπιμέλεια), Hermogenes reasonably concludes that Antiphon lacks true δεινότης, which is defined as the correct and appropriate (εἰς δέον καὶ κατὰ καιρόν) use of all the other ideas. (On Hermogenes' conception of δεινότης cf. *De ideis* 368.23–369.9; Lindberg [1977], 103–11; Hagedorn [1964], 33–41.) His discourse exhibits instead the apparent but unreal δεινότης that arises primarily from λέξις (in the broad sense) and is characteristic of the older sophists and their pupils (ὁ [*sc.* λόγος] τῶν σοφιστῶν, λέγω τῶν περὶ Πῶλον καὶ Γοργίαν καὶ Μένωνα), who cloak shallow and commonplace thoughts in impressive and beautiful language (cf. *De ideis* 372.24ff., 377.10ff.; Lindberg [1977], 105–8). It is apparent that Hermogenes' negative judgment on the sophist Antiphon results in large part from his misclassification as a representative (like the Rhamnusian) of the genre of political discourse (πολιτικὸς λόγος). In the terms of Hermogenes' classification, it would have been fairer to treat him (with Plato, Aeschines of Sphettus, and other philosophers) as a representative of the genre of panegyric discourse (πανηγυρικὸς λόγος; cf. *De ideis* 403.20ff.). Here, the dominance of a few ideas such as magnitude (μέγεθος) and beauty (ἐπιμέλεια or κάλλος) would not have been judged a defect, but appropriate to the genre (cf. *De ideis* 403.22–404.2).

2–3 Δίδυμος ὁ γραμματικός: it is not known where Didymus expounded his views on Antiphon. Schmidt (1854), 310, followed by Susemihl (1891–92), 2.203 n. 309, conjectured a separate commentary on the Rhamnusian; but this was rejected by Cohn (1903), 458–59. As Schmidt himself admitted, there is no evidence that Didymus wrote such a work (though of course he may have).

3 ἀπὸ ἱστορίας: Wooten (1987), 122 translates "history," which is not impossible (*pace* Gagarin [1990], 36 n. 31). But more likely ἱστορία here means "inquiry" or "investigation" (so Gagarin). Patillon (1997), 498 translates: "ce qu'on nous rapporte."

3–4 πλείους μὲν γεγόνασιν Ἀντιφῶντες: Antiphon was in fact a very common name. For Attica, see Fraser and Matthews (1994), 40, s.v. Ἀντιφῶν; cf. Davies (1971), 327: "the forest of Antiphons in the late fifth century [*sc.* at Athens] is unlikely ever to be satisfactorily and completely mapped."

4 δύο δὲ οἱ σοφιστεύσαντες: the precise sense of σοφιστεύσαντες here is uncertain. Maximus Planudes (Walz [1832–36], 5.560) interpreted it to mean "head a rhetorical school": οἱ σοφιστεύσαντες· οἱ διδασκαλείων ῥητορικῶν προστάντες. The same sense is found in Photius, *Bibliotheca* 102a (2.121) = Caecilius, fr. 123: οὗτος μὲν οὖν ὁ ῥήτωρ [*sc.* Isocrates] σοφιστεύειν μᾶλλον ἢ τῶν κοινῶν προστατεῖν ὥσπερ οἱ ἄλλοι ἐννέα ῥήτορες ... εἵλετο. (The antithetical parallelism between σοφιστεύειν and τῶν κοινῶν προστατεῖν shows the sense.) In later antiquity, the Rhamnusian was thought to have headed a rhetorical school (cf. Plutarch, *De gloria Atheniensium* 350C); and Hermogenes may have believed the same of the sophist Antiphon. Wooten (1987), 122 translates more generally: "were engaged in rhetorical pursuits." In any case, σοφιστεύσαντες here almost certainly does not mean simply "be a sophist." For Hermogenes treats σοφιστής and related terms as strongly pejorative (cf. *De ideis* 248.21–249.4, 377.10ff.; Brandstätter [1894], 249–52); and his analysis of the Rhamnusian (at least) shows that Hermogenes did not consider *him* a "sophist" in this sense.

6 οὗπερ οἱ φονικοὶ φέρονται λόγοι κτλ.: Caecilius of Calacte (fr. 100) distinguished thirty-five genuine, and twenty-five spurious, speeches in the *corpus Antiphonteum* (cf. Blass [1887–98], 1.96). All of the extant speeches concern homicide (cf. Blass [1887–98], 1.96). Examples of the δημηγορικοί are the fragmentary speeches Περὶ τοῦ Λινδίων φόρου (frr. 25–33) and Περὶ τοῦ Σαμοθρᾴκων φόρου (frr. 49–56); cf. Blass (1887–98), 1.91–92.

7–8 ἕτερος δὲ ... γενέσθαι: Hermogenes' form of expression (ὁ ... λεγόμενος γενέσθαι) implies that the identification of the author of Περὶ ἀληθείας etc. with Antiphon the dream-interpreter does not rest on his own authority. Like other elements in the passage, it may go back to Didymus (so Jacoby, *FGrHist* IIIB 1.261, on 328 T 7). For the epithet τερατοσκόπος cf. *Suda* s.v. Ἀντιφῶν = T3; Diogenes Laertius, 2.46 = T5, with commentary; Introduction, section I.

9–10 [καὶ οἱ δημηγορικοὶ] καὶ ὁ Πολιτικός: on the textual problem here and the division of works cf. Introduction, section II. Morrison (1961), 55 suggested that the words καὶ οἱ δημηγορικοὶ have taken the place of the title of Antiphon's dream-book as the result of textual corruption. This is highly unlikely, paleographically and otherwise.

10 ἐγὼ δὲ ἕνεκα: the emphatic "I" with which Hermogenes introduces his stylistic arguments for and against Didymus' distinction tells against the suggestion of Drerup (1901), 300 that his doubts about the distinction go back to Didymus.

10–11 τοῦ διαφόρου τῶν ... ἰδεῶν: not "the difference of genre among these works" (Morrison [1972], 115), but "the difference of style in these works" (cf. Lindberg [1977], 9). Cf. l. 19, where τῷ εἴδει probably also means "style," and l. 21, where εἴδεσι could mean "genres" but more likely again means "styles." Cf. Lindberg (1977), 9.

12–14 πολὺ γὰρ ... τοὺς λοιπούς: according to some commentators, Hermogenes means that the style of Περὶ ἀληθείας is different from that of all the other works in the *corpus Antiphonteum* (those of "the other" Antiphon as well as those of the Rhamnusian). But the phrase τῶν ἐπιγραφομένων τῆς Ἀληθείας λόγων here – like τῶν τῆς Ἀληθείας λόγων in ll. 19–20 and οἱ τῆς Ἀληθείας λεγόμενοι λόγοι in ll. 25–26 – is probably just an abbreviated way of referring to all the works of the sophist Antiphon. In exactly the same way, Hermogenes identifies the Rhamnusian by reference to the φονικοὶ λόγοι alone (cf. l. 18 οἱ φονικοί and *De ideis* 400.22–23: ὁ τοίνυν Ῥαμνούσιος Ἀντιφῶν, οὗπερ οἱ φονικοὶ φέρονται). Cf. Sauppe (1896), 511; Buresch (1886), 88; Blass (1887–98), 1.96 n. 1. There is no reason to think that Hermogenes was familiar with Περὶ ἀληθείας alone (as Sauppe [1896], 511 and others have suggested) or that his analysis of the sophist Antiphon's style is based solely on this work.

14 ἕνεκα δὲ τοῦ καὶ παρὰ Πλάτωνι: Hermogenes is thinking of *Menexenus* 236A, where (like other commentators ancient and modern) he detects an allusion to Thucydides, who "praised Athenians in front of Athenians" in Pericles' funeral oration. This interpretation of the *Menexenus* passage is likely to have arisen only after Caecilius of Calacte inferred that Thucydides was Antiphon of Rhamnus' pupil (cf. below). Sauppe (1896), 512 went so far as to suggest that it was Caecilius who first interpreted the *Menexenus* in this way; but this is pure speculation.

15–17 Θουκυδίδην γὰρ ... πολλῶν λεγόντων: cf. Marcellinus, *Vita Thucydidis* 22 (= Caecilius, fr. 99a); *Vita Anonymi* 2; [Tryphon] in Walz (1832–36), 8.750; *Suda* s.v. Θουκυδίδης (θ 414, 2.721), etc. All of these depend ultimately on Caecilius of Calacte, who first deduced the relationship from the way in which Thucydides praises the Rhamnusian. Cf. [Plut.], *Vitae X or.* 832E (= Caecilius, fr. 99): Καικίλιος δ' ἐν τῷ περὶ αὐτοῦ [*sc.* Antiphon of Rhamnus] συντάγματι Θουκυδίδου τοῦ συγγραφέως μαθητὴν[3] τεκμαίρεται γεγονέναι ἐξ ὧν ἐπαινεῖται παρ' αὐτῷ ὁ Ἀντιφῶν. Against Caecilius cf. Wilamowitz (1877), 332–35; Dover

[3] So the manuscripts. Since this inverts the relationship as given in most other sources, Cuvigny (1981), 45 and other editors adopt Wyttenbach's καθηγητὴν. Yet Photius, *Bibliotheca* 486a (8.42), whose source is [Plut.], also read μαθητὴν (cf. Henry [1959–77], 8.42 n. 3). The transmitted text should perhaps be kept and the mistake ascribed to confusion on the part of [Plut.] (so Buresch [1886], 86 n. 3).

(1950), 59; Andrewes in Gomme et al. (1981), 173–74. Buresch (1886), 86–89 theorized that Thucydides was actually the pupil of the *sophist* Antiphon; but this is without foundation.

17–20 καὶ τὸν μὲν Ῥαμνούσιον . . . Ἀληθείας λόγων: construction of this passage is difficult. With the transmitted text, it seems best to take ἐκεῖνον in the μέν-clause as predicate, with ὄντα (in indirect statement after εἰδὼς) understood: "knowing that Antiphon of Rhamnus is the one to whom the homicide speeches belong." The δέ-clause then will be parallel: "but knowing on the other hand that Thucydides is far separated etc." So Patillon (1997), 498 ("je sais que l'Antiphon de Rhamnunte est l'auteur des discours sur des affaires de meurtre et que le style de Thucydide en est fort éloigné etc."). Alternatively (as Michael Reeve suggests to me), something may have fallen out.

18–20 τὸν Θουκυδίδην . . . Ἀληθείας λόγων: Bignone (1938), 191; Croiset (1883), 160, and others express surprise at Hermogenes' judgment. Other ancient critics noted an affinity between the styles of the Rhamnusian and Thucydides. Cf. Dionysius of Halicarnassus, *De compositione verborum* 10, 22 (but contrast *De Thucydide* 5); [Tryphon] in Walz (1832–36), 3.206. On the whole subject cf. Both (1875).

20 πάλιν οὐ πείθομαι: because of the stylistic differences among the works ascribed to Antiphon, Hermogenes finds it credible that Antiphon of Rhamnus and "the other" Antiphon are really two people. Yet according to Plato and many others, Thucydides was the pupil of the Rhamnusian. Thucydides' style, however, resembles that of Περὶ ἀληθείας. Therefore his teacher must have been the author of Περὶ ἀληθείας (on the assumption that the styles of teacher and pupil will be similar). Therefore the author of Περὶ ἀληθείας must be Antiphon of Rhamnus, whose student Thucydides is said to have been. Cf. Sauppe (1896), 512; Croiset (1917), 18 and others misunderstand the argument. It is important to note that Hermogenes counters one (separatist) argument from style with another (unitarian) argument from style.

20–24 οὐ μὴν ἀλλ' . . . διελθεῖν: it is significant that Hermogenes does not find it inconceivable (as have some modern commentators) that one man should have employed such different styles as are found in the *corpus Antiphonteum.*

25–26 οὗπερ . . . λεγόμενοι λόγοι: Hermogenes seems here to combine two different expressions, "the discourses of *Truth*" (οἱ λόγοι τῆς Ἀληθείας, the latter either a possessive or a defining genitive) and "the discourses called *Truth*" (οἱ ἡ Ἀλήθεια λεγόμενοι λόγοι). David Sedley suggests "to whom the discourses said to be those of *Truth* belong." But the hint of doubt this seems to create about the provenance of the λόγοι in question is unmotivated by anything else Hermogenes says.

26–36 πολιτικὸς μὲν ἥκιστα . . . οὐ μὴν οὔσης γε ὡς ἀληθῶς: for an attempt to relate the details of Hermogenes' analysis to the remains of the sophist Antiphon's works cf. introductory note above.

27 τοῖς τε ἄλλοις: by process of elimination, this most likely refers to the category of thought. For in the remainder of the discussion, Hermogenes treats the other categories of figures of thought (ll. 27–29), λέξις (ll. 29–30), figures of speech (ll. 30–32), and composition (ll. 32–33).

T2(b)

On Philostratus' description of the style of Περὶ ὁμονοίας cf. Introduction, section IV.

T3

All three of these notices derive probably from Hesychius of Miletus, the sixth-century biographer whose *Onomatologus* (in abridged form) was an important source for the *Suda*. Cf. Flach (1882), 17; *Suda* s.v. Ἡσύχιος Μιλήσιος (η 611, 2.594); Schultz (1913); Adler (1928–38), I.XXI. It is impossible to determine whether the distinction drawn here between the sophist Antiphon and the Rhamnusian was based on information available to Hesychius, or is merely the result of confusion on his part or that of the epitomist – as the distinction of Antiphon the diviner (τερατοσκόπος) from the author of the dream-book (ὀνειροκρίτης) certainly is (cf. Flach [1882], 17 n.).

1 Ἀθηναῖος: on the nationality of the sophist Antiphon cf. Introduction, section I.

τερατοσκόπος: for this epithet cf. Hermogenes, *De ideis* 400.3 = T2(a), l. 7; Diogenes Laertius, 2.46 = T5, with commentary; Introduction, section I.

ἐποποιός: Antiphon the epic poet is otherwise unknown. Buresch (1886), 74 n. 1 suspected a confused reference to Antiphon the tragic poet, a suggestion which would gain credence if ἐποποιός could mean "verse-maker," "poet." LSJ s.v. so interpreted the word in Lucian, *Iuppiter Tragoedus* 6; but it is clear from the context that ἐποποιός there means "composer of hexameters" (that is, epic poet). Untersteiner suspected textual corruption, and proposed to read ἐποπτὴς τἀληθοῦς (*vel sim.*); but this is fanciful. There may some confusion here with Herodotus' relative Panyasis the epic poet, who is identified in the *Suda* (π 248, 4.24–25) as a τερατοσκόπος καὶ ποιητὴς ἐπῶν, and/or with Panyasis the Younger, who according to the *Suda* (π 249, 4.25) wrote a two-volume work on dreams (cf. Del Corno [1969], 34–36, 121–22).

1–2 σοφιστής: for this epithet cf. Xenophon, *Memorabilia* 1.6.1 = T1, l. 1; scholium on Aristotle, *Posterior Analytics* 75b40 = F13(l), l. 3; Simplicius, *In Aristotelis Physica* 273.36 = F15(f), l. 2; Introduction, section 1.

2 Λογομάγειρος: Blass (1889a), 5 and Luria (1924b), 326–27 explained this nickname as an allusion to the sophist Antiphon's fondness for poetic and compound words or for neologisms. It seems more likely that there is some confusion here, and that the epithet λογομάγειρος (like Νέστωρ; cf. below) refers to Antiphon of Rhamnus' well-known logographical activity. This would be even more likely if the epithet derives from comedy (as Aly [1929], 110 and others have suggested). In that case, λογομάγειρος might refer "ad orationem nimia diligentia concoctam et a veritate remotam" (Jacoby [1908], 52 n. 104, who compared the epithet λογοδαίδαλος in Plato, *Phaedrus* 266E). As Geffcken (1934), 79 n. 49 pointed out, the metaphor in λογομάγειρος recalls Plato's famous comparison of ῥητορική and ὀψοποιητική (*Gorgias* 463A–C, 464B–465E).

5–6 λέγεται . . . διδάσκαλος: cf. Introduction, section 1; T2(a), ll. 15–17 with commentary.

7 Νέστωρ: cf. [Plut.], *Vitae X or.* 832E; Philostratus, *Vitae sophistarum* 498 = T6(d), l. 2; Photius, *Bibliotheca* 486a (8.42). Plato (*Phaedrus* 261B–C) applies the same nickname to Gorgias.

T4

The context of this testimonium is a discussion of the meaning of the phrase λυγινὸς στέφανος in Anacreon, fr. 352. After Cynulcus (Theodorus) questions Ulpian about the meaning of Anacreon's words and the latter is unable to answer, Democritus intervenes with a long disquisition in explanation of the problematic verses (cf. *Dipnosophistae* 15 671D–673D). Democritus claims that after he had discovered the correct explanation, Hephaestion plagiarized his discovery and published a treatise of his own on the problem. Citing another example of Hephaestion's plagiarism, Democritus alleges that he took all the material for his treatise "On the Antiphon in Xenophon's *Memorabilia*" from a monograph by Adrastus on Theophrastus' Περὶ ἠθῶν and Aristotle's *Nicomachean Ethics.*

On the significance of this passage for the problem of the identity of Antiphon cf. Introduction, section 1. Despite the hesitation of Zeller (1923), 805 n. 2, 809–10, the Adrastus (Casaubon's certain correction for the manuscript's impossible ἄδραντον) in question is almost certainly the famous Aristotelian commentator Adrastus of Aphrodisias. Cf. Moraux (1973–84), 2.294–332, especially 2.323–30 for Adrastus' monograph on Aristotle and Theophrastus. Hephaestion is probably the famous metrist (though other identifications are conceivable). Cf. Moraux (1973–84), 2.295 with nn. 7–8. It is not clear what occasioned Adrastus to discuss the poet Antiphon (and the character Plexippus from his tragedy *Meleager*) in a monograph on Peripatetic ethical treatises. Aristotle refers to the poet Antiphon several times in the *Rhetoric* (twice in connection with the *Meleager*), but never mentions him in the *Nicomachean Ethics*. (But Antiphon the poet is referred to in *Ethica Eudemia* 1239a37.) Adrastus' interests were wide-ranging, however, and he must have found some occasion to discuss Antiphon (cf. Introduction, section 1). The allegation that Hephaestion plagiarized *all* the material for his monograph (οὐδὲν ἴδιον προσεξευρών) from Adrastus' discussion of the *poet* Antiphon has led some commentators to conjecture that Hephaestion or Adrastus or both identified Xenophon's Antiphon with the poet. So Altwegg (1908), 11; Aly (1929), 112; Untersteiner (1962), 26; cf. Sauppe (1896), 509. But the allegation may be exaggerated or false. (On accusations of plagiarism in antiquity cf. Stemplinger [1912]; K. Ziegler [1950].) And even if it is true, it hardly follows that either Adrastus or Hephaestion identified the sophist Antiphon with the homonymous tragic poet. It is perfectly conceivable that in the course of a lengthy discussion of the person of the poet Antiphon (καὶ πλεῖστα ὅσα καὶ περὶ αὐτοῦ τοῦ Ἀντιφῶντος εἰπόντος), Adrastus would have commented on his identity *vis-à-vis* other personages of the same name, and so provided Hephaestion with material for his own monograph on Xenophon's Antiphon. Cf. Introduction, section 1.

T5

This testimonium derives from the third book of Aristotle's lost work on poets, entitled Περὶ ποιητῶν or Περὶ ποιητικῆς. (On this work cf. Laurenti [1987], 211–300; Janko [1987], 56–65, 175–95.) Both titles are well attested, so there is no need to emend the text (as Castelvetro and others have done). Cf. Haslam (1972), 19; Laurenti (1987), 238–39; Janko (1991), 50–51, 58. To judge from Diogenes, Aristotle mentioned the rivalry between Antiphon and Socrates in the context of a catalog of rivalries involving famous poets, wise men, philosophers, and statesmen (cf. Laurenti [1987], 234–35 nn. 39–50, 273–74, with details on the various personages mentioned in the passage). Although it also offered discussions of a historical or theoretical character, Aristotle's work seems to have contained many anecdotal elements of the kind exemplified by this passage (cf. Laurenti [1987], 239, 280–82; Janko [1991], 51–53).

Aristotle almost certainly had in mind the disputes depicted by Xenophon in *Memorabilia* 1.6 = T1. The author of [Plut.], *Vitae X or.* 832c (or his source) thought so as well, for the claim that Antiphon disputed with Socrates οὐ φιλονείκως ἀλλ' ἐλεγκτικῶς is surely a conscious correction of Aristotle's characterization of the dispute (ἐφιλονείκει). And [Plut.] refers explicitly to the *Memorabilia*. It is not certain, however, whether Aristotle refers directly to Xenophon or to an earlier Socratic source on which Xenophon depended. Joël (1893–1901), 2.638; Altwegg (1908), 7–8; Gigon (1953), 152, and others argued for the latter alternative, primarily on the grounds that Aristotle mentions Antiphon alongside Antilochus of Lemnos (who does not appear in Xenophon) and identifies him as a diviner (τερατοσκόπος) rather than sophist (as does Xenophon). (Roeper [1848], 55 preferred to delete τερατοσκόπος, since he identified Xenophon's Antiphon with the Rhamnusian.) But neither of these considerations is compelling. In the first place, there is no reason to think that Socrates' dispute with Antilochus derives from the same source and context as the dispute with Antiphon. Secondly, the epithet τερατοσκόπος need not go back to Aristotle (as nearly all commentators have assumed), but may derive from Diogenes or his source. Cf. Bignone (1938), 163. (If the epithet does go back to Aristotle, however, then the identification of the sophist Antiphon with the author of the dream-book would be confirmed beyond all doubt; cf. Introduction, section 1.) Lastly, Aristotle's characterization of the dispute between Antiphon and Socrates as contentious argument (ἐφιλονείκει) well suits the tone of the encounters in the *Memorabilia* (cf. Morrison [1961], 58).

On this testimonium's importance as evidence of uncertainty in later antiquity about the identity of Xenophon's Antiphon cf. Introduction, section 1. Sauppe (1896), 510 suggested that Aristotle may have mentioned the sophist Antiphon in a work on poets in order to distinguish him from the homonymous tragic poet. But this ignores the anecdotal character of the reference.

T6

The relations among the various sources that constitute this testimonium are not entirely clear. Photius (6(c)) obviously depends on [Plut.] (6(a)). Blass (1887–98), 1.93 thought that the anonymous *Vita Antiphontis* (6(b)) and Philostratus (6(d)) likewise depend entirely on [Plut.]. Yet both of them (and especially Philostratus) differ in details from [Plut.]. Perhaps therefore they derive (independently) from a common source shared with [Plut.], or even from a different source. Cf. Buresch (1886),

73 n. 3, 76; Cuvigny (1981), 27 with n. 2, 31 n. 1; Gagarin (1990), 39 n. 43.

That the alleged τέχνη ἀλυπίας refers to an oral "technique" of removing grief rather than to a written work is argued in section II of the Introduction. Most modern commentators have accepted the story of Antiphon's grief-clinic at face value. Cf. Sauppe (1896), 513; Joël (1893–1901), 2.649; Kassel (1958), 9; Guthrie (1971a), 290–91; Furley (1992), and others. Some even go so far as to scrutinize the fragments of his writings for traces of a doctrine of ἀλυπία (cf. Nestle [1942], 379 with n. 40; Diano [1961], 118–24; Furley [1992]). Bignone (1938), 83, 123, 221–26 proposed to ascribe to Antiphon the anti-hedonist theory expounded in Plato, *Philebus* 44B–D, where he detected echoes of the alleged doctrine of ἀλυπία as well as of Antiphon's supposed pessimism. But there is no reason to credit Antiphon with a theory like that expounded by the enemies of Philebus, which defines pleasure in purely negative fashion as the mere cessation of pain (λύπη). (On this passage of the *Philebus* cf. Tarán [1981], 79–80.) However, despite the credulity of commentators, who have perhaps been unduly influenced by the example of psychotherapy or modern cognitive therapies, the story of the grief-clinic is more likely than not the fantasy of a comic poet or a fictitious anecdote concocted by a Hellenistic writer. Cf. Altwegg (1908), 40, 92; Morrison (1961), 57–58, (1972), 108. Whether the story has any basis in Antiphon's life or thought, for example as a reflection of themes from Περὶ ὁμονοίας (as Altwegg suggested) or of his predilection for "comfortable living" (as Morrison supposed), is very doubtful. (On the unreliability of ancient biographical anecdotes in general cf. Tarán [1981], 3–4, with references and examples.) Indeed, it seems more likely than not that the anecdote originally envisaged Antiphon of Rhamnus rather than the sophist Antiphon (as is usually assumed). [Plut.] appears to connect the story with Antiphon the tragic poet (cf. [Plut.], *Vitae X or.* 833C: ἔτι δ' ὢν πρὸς τῇ ποιήσει τέχνην ἀλυπίας συνεστήσατο κτλ.). But he confuses this Antiphon with the Rhamnusian and with the sophist (on the unreliability of [Plut.] cf. Introduction, section I with nn. 4–5). The context in Philostratus, however, clearly attaches the story of the grief-clinic to Antiphon of Rhamnus (cf. *Vita sophistarum* 498). More important, the motivation for the anecdote appears to have been the Rhamnusian's reputation for eloquence and persuasiveness. This appears clearly from Philostratus' introduction to the story (T6(d), ll. 1–2): πιθανώτατος δὲ ὁ Ἀντιφῶν γενόμενος καὶ προσρηθεὶς Νέστωρ ἐπὶ τῷ περὶ παντὸς εἰπὼν ἂν πεῖσαι. Cf. Altwegg (1908), 92, who compared the Platonic Gorgias' boast that a skilled rhetorician is more able to persuade a sick patient to accept treatment than any doctor (*Gorgias*

456B) – a motif which Altwegg suggested may have been transferred to Antiphon by an admirer. Furthermore, the more famous Rhamnusian seems a far likelier target of comic fantasy or Hellenistic anecdote than the lesser-known sophist Antiphon.

T7

The context of this passage is Lucian's visit to the island and city of dreams (*Verae historiae* 2, 32–35). Antiphon's appearance here as spokesman or interpreter (προφητεύων) for the oracle (μαντεῖον) of dreams no doubt reflects his fame as a dream-interpreter. Lucian's reference to the temple of Truth (Ἀλήθεια) could be understood (as some commentators have suggested) as an allusion to Περὶ ἀληθείας, in which case Lucian will have identified the sophist Antiphon with the dream-interpreter. But the distinction between true and false dreams is a commonplace going back to the very passage of the *Odyssey* (19.560–67) that provides the basis of Lucian's whole description. Cf. *Verae historiae* 2, 32 with *Odyssey* 19.565 (ἐλεφαίρονται) and 19.567 (ἔτυμα κραίνουσι). (On the topical character of Lucian's description cf. Anderson [1976], 25 with n. 21.) It is unnecessary therefore to read an allusion to Περὶ ἀληθείας into this passage, and Antiphon's name can be understood as purely decorative.

T8–9

Clement (*Stromata* 7.4.24.4 = T8) relates his anecdote about Antiphon in the course of discussing the superstitiousness (δεισιδαιμονία) of the Greeks, who believe that their gods are easily angered and so consider everything that happens a portent or sign of trouble. Cf. *Stromata* 7.4.24.1 (εἰκότως τοίνυν δεισιδαίμονες περὶ τοὺς εὐοργήτους γινόμενοι πάντα σημεῖα ἡγοῦνται εἶναι τὰ συμβαίνοντα καὶ κακῶν αἴτια). Such is the attitude of the unnamed man in the anecdote, who treats a sow's devouring of her sucklings as an evil omen. (For οἰωνίζομαι = "regard as an omen" cf. LSJ, s.v. II.2.) Antiphon, by contrast, views the event merely as a natural result of the sow's hunger, and his ironic response constitutes an implicit rejection of his interlocutor's superstitious attitude. Clement's source for the anecdote is unknown. Conceivably it could derive (directly or indirectly) from Antiphon's dream-book.

T9 is preserved in two alphabetically arranged collections of χρεῖαι, the *Gnomologium Vindobonense*, published by C. Wachsmuth; and the larger and more comprehensive *Gnomologium Vaticanum*, edited by L. Sternbach. (On the genre of χρεία cf. Schmid and Stählin [1920–24],

1.54–55.) Diels (*FVS* 2.337 n.) and others have called attention to the fact that Antiphon's definition of divination as εἰκασμός recalls Euripides, fr. 963 (μάντις δ' ἄριστος, ὅστις εἰκάζει καλῶς). For this and other reasons the authenticity of the saying is suspect (though Nestle [1942], 389 drew the opposite conclusion). In any case, neither this definition nor Antiphon's interpretation of the sow's behavior in T8 reveals him as an opponent of divination (as Nestle [1942], 389 wrongly inferred). *Pace* Nestle, the term εἰκασμός is neither pejorative in connotation nor dismissive of divination. On the contrary, it points to an essential aspect of dream-interpretation and other forms of divination: the discovery of analogies or resemblances between the divination-sign and the real-life situation signified (cf. Goebel [1910], 387; Luria [1927b], 465; and especially van Lieshout [1980], 207–11, with references). Cf. the substantive εἰκαστής = "diviner" (Thucydides, 1.138; Gregory of Nazianzus, *or.* 5.23, 35.692 Migne – the latter a reminiscence of the Euripides fragment). (The text printed here as T9 is followed in the *Gnomologium Vindobonense* by the statement, derived ultimately from [Plut.], *Vitae X or.* 833C, that Antiphon composed tragedies by himself and with the tyrant Dionysius. This is absent from the *Gnomologium Vaticanum* and has been omitted here.)

T10

This passage of Philodemus' *De poëmatis* derives from the very end of *P.Herc.* 994 (= Treatise A), which has been edited most recently by Sbordone (1976), 1–113. *P.Herc.* 994 belongs to a group of fragments which also includes *P.Herc.* 1081b, 1074b, 1676, and 1677. Together these fragments form a single roll (cf. Dorandi [1992], 31–32, 36; Janko [1995], 82–83, with references) representing either the second book (so Janko [1995], 75, 82–83) or the third (so Greenberg [1990], 267, 268–70; Dorandi [1992], 39, 44) of Philodemus' treatise.

The immediate context of the passage (col. XXXVI.11ff.) is a discussion of a euphonic theory of smooth (λεῖα) and rough (τραχεῖα) styles, advocated by an unnamed opponent of Philodemus. Cf. Sbordone (1976), XXX–XXXI; Greenberg (1990), 204–6. (On ancient theories of euphony cf. in general Sbordone [1955]; Rispoli [1986], [1987].) As far as Antiphon is concerned, this testimonium raises two interrelated questions. The first concerns the identity of the work of "Antiphon" to which Philodemus alludes. One possibility (favored by Gomperz [1891], 49 n. 3) is Glaucus of Rhegium's Περὶ τῶν ἀρχαίων ποιητῶν καὶ μουσικῶν, which some in antiquity ascribed to "Antiphon" (cf. [Plut.], *Vitae X or.* 833D; Jacoby [1910]; Introduction, section II). The origin and basis of this ascription are completely unknown; furthermore, it is uncertain precisely which Antiphon is intended (cf. Introduction, section ii). In any case, nothing we know about Glaucus' work suggests that it dealt with theoretical issues of literary style (such as euphony). It is much more likely that Philodemus' reference is to the rhetorical handbook (Τέχναι ῥητορικαί) current in antiquity under the name of Antiphon (so Diels, *FVS* 2.369 n.; cf. F3 with commentary). A passage of Galen plausibly ascribed to this work suggests that it dealt with the subject of word-formation. Cf. Antiphon of Rhamnus, fr. 76 (= *AS* B X 9): ὅτι δὲ καὶ αὐτὸς ἕκαστος τῶν περὶ λόγους ἐχόντων ἠξίου ποιεῖν ὀνόματα καινὰ δηλοῖ μὲν καὶ Ἀντιφῶν ἱκανῶς, ὅς γε ὅπως αὐτὰ ποιητέον ἐκδιδάσκει. Consideration of the euphonic qualities of individual letters would fit comfortably into the context of a discussion of word-formation. The second (and more important) issue raised by this testimonium concerns the problem of the identity of Antiphon. Altwegg (1908), 8 and Untersteiner (1962), 167 interpreted Philodemus' concluding remark (εἴτ' οὖν ῥητορικὸς εἴτε καὶ φιλόσοφος ἠβούλετ' εἶναι) as evidence that he (mistakenly) confused the sophist Antiphon and the Rhamnusian. Indeed, these scholars suggested that this is the earliest attestation of the confusion. On the other side, commentators such as Gagarin (1990), 33 with n. 23; Decleva Caizzi (1984), 97 with n. 13; and Cassin (1985), 68 n. 3 interpreted Philodemus' evidence as ancient support for the unitarian position. It is doubtful, however, whether Philodemus' remark has anything to do with the problem of Antiphon. It is more plausibly interpreted simply as a sarcastic judgment on what Philodemus considers the philosophical pretensions (εἴτε καὶ φιλόσοφος ἠβούλετ' εἶναι) of the author whose work he alludes to.

T11(a)–(b)

Pseudo-Callisthenes' anecdote about Antiphon the diviner (T11(a)) was probably inspired by a famous legendary incident from the life of Philip of Macedon recounted in detail by Plutarch (*Alexander* 2.6–3.4) and mentioned by many other ancient writers (cf. Pease [1920–23], 2.565). According to the legend, Philip saw a snake lying in bed beside his wife Olympias; the snake was alleged to be none other than the god Ammon and was thought to have fathered Alexander (cf. Braun [1952]; Hamilton [1969], 4–7). The use of Antiphon's name here is purely decorative; no value whatsoever attaches to the anecdote as evidence for the chronology of Antiphon the diviner (cf. Del Corno [1969], 132 with n. 8; Introduction, section i; and below on T11(b)). It should be noted that Antiphon's name appears only in the α-recension of the Alexander-romance; in other recensions the seer summoned by Philip is left unnamed. (On the various recensions of the *Historia Alexandri* cf. Kroll [1919], 1707–9, 1720–23, [1926], III–XIV.) It is worth remarking in this connection that the figure of Aristander of Telmessus, the actual court-diviner of Philip and of Alexander, was systematically displaced in the Alexander-romance. (On Aristander cf. Berve [1926], 1.90–92, 2.62–63; Del Corno [1969], 7–23, 105–8.) His place was taken by other famous seers, historical (such as Antiphon) or legendary (such as Melampus), or by unnamed diviners. Cf. Del Corno (1969), 105 n. 3, with references.

John Tzetzes' scholium on Hermogenes (T11(b)) was published by van Spaan (1773) on the authority of David Ruhnken. It derives from a work of Tzetzes on the Hermogenic rhetorical corpus partially extant in several manuscripts (for details cf. Wendel [1948], 1989–90). The work is neither an epitome nor a collection of scholia (as Walz and Cramer, respectively, designated the portions of it they published), but rather a collection of λογισμοί – that is, reports and critical comments on Hermogenes' rhetorical system (cf. Wendel [1948], 1990). Tzetzes' notion that Antiphon the diviner was a contemporary of Alexander depends in all likelihood on the anecdote in the Alexander-romance (T11(a)), a work with which he was certainly acquainted (cf. *Chiliades* 1.327). It is entirely without evidential value.

T12

In *De anima* 45–49, Tertullian deals with the subject of dreams. He explains that they result from an ecstatic force or power (*ecstasis*) which takes hold of the soul while the body sleeps (cf. *De anima* 45.1–3). After setting out various opinions regarding the existence of revelatory dreams, Tertullian recounts fourteen noteworthy examples of prophetic dreams (*De anima* 46.1–9). These serve to refute the Epicurean denial of dream-divination. Immediately following this is the catalog or list of dream-interpreters that constitutes this testimonium. Tertullian's source for the list is undoubtedly Hermippus of Beirut, whom he cites by name at *De anima* 46.11 (cf. Waszink [1947], 44*–45*, 488). (On Hermippus, who wrote a work on dreams in five volumes, cf. Heibges [1912]; Del Corno [1969], 61–65, 142–43.) On the various authorities on dream-interpretation mentioned by Tertullian cf. Hopfner (1937), 2237–40; Waszink (1947), 495–96. The evidence for them is collected in Del Corno (1969), 24–29, 110–14 (Artemon of Miletus); 67, 145–47 (Strato of Lampsacus); 83, 165–66 (Philochorus); 60, 140–41 ("Epicharmus"); 40, 125 (Serapion); 76–77, 158–60 (Cratippus of Pergamum); 31, 117–18 (Dionysius of Rhodes, who is perhaps to be identified with Dionysius of Heliopolis). On the possible relationship between this passage and Fulgentius, *Mitologiae* 1.14 (= F81B) cf. commentary on F81B.

F1–44: ΠΕΡΙ ΑΛΗΘΕΙΑΣ

F1

This fragment is quoted by Galen to illustrate the use of the word γνώμη in the sense of "mind," "faculty of thought." It is seriously corrupt as transmitted in the only primary witness (cod. Parisinus gr. 1849; cod. Marcianus gr. 279 derives from P). The most plausible of the many restorations proposed is that of Hermann Diels, whose text (as printed in the fourth and subsequent editions of *FVS*) is adopted here, with two changes. In l. 5, Diels suggested both αὐτῶν and αὐτῷ, but printed the latter; the former is preferred here (cf. below). Also in l. 5, Diels inserted the participle ⟨ὂν⟩, which is not accepted into the text here (again cf. below). In earlier editions of *FVS* Diels printed a somewhat different text, in which Galen's introductory formula οὕτω λέγων (as Diels later reconstructed it) is transformed into the opening words of the fragment (ἐν τῷ προτέρῳ τῆς Ἀληθείας· ἓν τῷ λόγῳ πᾶν· τάδε γνοὺς κτλ.). Wilamowitz (*apud FVS* 2.337 n.) proposed a restoration not very different from those of Diels (ταῦτα δὲ γνοὺς εἴσεται οὐδὲν αὐτῶν οὔτε ὧν ὄψει ὁρᾷ μακρότατα οὔτε κτλ.).

In an interpretation that has exercised enormous influence, Diels (*FVS* 2.337 n.) proposed to understand Antiphon's fragmentary utterance against the background of the Eleatic doctrine of Being. In l. 5, Diels inserted the participle ⟨ὂν⟩ (whose omission could be explained by haplography), thereby producing an indirect-statement construction dependent on εἴσ⟨ῃ⟩. In the indirect statement, Diels construed ἕν τι οὐδέν as the subject and ὄν as existential, translating: "nichts einzelnes existiert." Kranz (*FVS* 2.338) construed similarly but slightly differently, taking οὐδέν as the subject and ἕν τι as predicate ("nichts ... etwas Einzelnes ist"). But on either construction, the basic sense is the same: the assertion that nothing single exists, which Diels identified as a restatement of the (supposed) Eleatic doctrine that all things are one. Diels' Eleaticizing interpretation is adopted (in one form or another) by Goebel (1910), 381; Nestle in Zeller and Nestle (1920), 1327 n. 2; Joël (1921), 716 with n. 4; Stenzel (1924), 37; Aly (1929), 141; Cherniss (1977), 291 n. 35; Zeppi (1962), 147–48; Wiesner (1994), 239–40 (who detected a reminiscence of Melissus, *FVS* 30 B 8.3), and many others. (Diels and his followers interpret other fragments of Περὶ ἀληθείας in similar fashion; cf. commentary on F4, F5, and F10.)

Despite its great popularity, there are serious objections against the Eleaticizing interpretation. In the first place, Diels's insertion of ⟨ὂν⟩ is unnecessary, since the sentence can be construed perfectly well without it (cf. below). Even if the insertion is retained, the sense which Diels ("nichts einzelnes"), Kranz ("nichts ... etwas Einzelnes"), and their followers attach to the words ἕν τι οὐδέν is not the most plausible one. The phrase is more naturally interpreted as signifying "not one single thing," "nothing." Cf. LSJ, s.v. οὐδείς B; Herodotus, 1.32; Thucydides, 2.51; Plato, *Republic* 488A, *Laws* 747B; Demosthenes, *or.* 21.12; Sauppe (1896), 516. This point was seen clearly by Schmid (1940), 160 n. 2, who interpreted the fragment accordingly as an expression of extreme epistemological scepticism, knowledge being attainable neither through the mind nor through the senses. But such scepticism is not easy to reconcile with the dogmatic tone and doctrines found in other fragments of Περὶ ἀληθείας. (David Sedley recalls the case of Democritus, whose pessimistic remarks about the possibility of knowledge did not prevent him from expounding dogmatic theses. On Schmid's interpretation, however, F1 would go far beyond Democritus, who admitted a genuine [γνησίη] knowledge alongside the bastard [σκοτίη] variety; cf. *FVS* 68 B 9, 11 with Cherniss [1935], 81–83.) Even if Diels's interpretation of ἕν τι οὐδέν is accepted, it is unnecessary to follow him in detecting the influence of Eleatic philosophy. For one thing, the fundamental thesis of Parmenides is *not* that "all things are one" (as Diels and others would have it, following Plato), but rather that there is only being. (Cf. Tarán [1965], 188–94, 269–78.) Reinhardt (1916), 248 n. 1 offered an idiosyncratic interpretation of the relationship of the fragment to Eleatic philosophy. On his restoration (ταὐτὸ δὲ γνοὺς ἴσον τε οὐδὲν αὐτῷ οὔτε ὧν ὄψει ὁρᾷ [μακρότατα] οὔτε ὧν γνώμῃ γινώσκει ὁ μακρότατα γινώσκων), the opening words of the fragment would express the idea that everything is in constant flux and nothing stays the same ("es gibt in der Welt kein ταὐτόν und ἴσον, alles ist in beständigem Wechsel"). Reinhardt notoriously contended that this idea belonged to Parmenides' explanation of the sensible world in the Δόξα. His interpretation of F1 falls together with his interpretation of Parmenides (against which cf. Tarán [1965], 207–9).

Breaking with the Eleaticizing interpretation, a number of commentators have sought to understand the fragment in opposition to the doctrines of others among Antiphon's precedessors and contemporaries. Bignone (1938), 216–21, for example, proposed to relate the fragment to Protagoras. He restored the opening words of the fragment as οὗ τάδε γνώσει, and referred the pronoun οὗ to Protagoras. Bignone suggested that F1 restates Protagoras' supposed doctrine of infinite divisibility for the purpose of refuting it. But both the restoration and the interpretation are open to seemingly fatal objections. In the first place, it is not easy to see why Galen would have quoted the words οὖ τάδε γνώσει at all, syntactically and semantically unconnected as they are (in Bignone's reconstruction) with the sentence whose usage he is interested in. Cf. Burkert (1964), 143. Secondly, direct citation of the kind presupposed in Bignone's interpretation would be highly unusual in Presocratic literature, which otherwise knows only indirect or general polemic (again cf. Burkert [1964], 144 with n. 9). Thirdly, the words ἕν τε οὐδέν by themselves can hardly mean (as Bignone supposed) "nothing is one and indivisible." Lastly, there is no reason at all to follow Bignone in supposing either that Protagoras defended or that Antiphon rejected a doctrine of infinite divisibility. Antiphon's quadrature attempt proves nothing in this regard (cf. commentary on F13); and Protagoras' Περὶ τοῦ ὄντος (*pace* Bignone) almost certainly had nothing to do with the problem of infinite divisibility (cf. Porphyry *apud* Eusebius = *FVS* 80 B 2). Bignone's interpretation of Protagoras' objection to the geometers (Aristotle, *Metaphysics* 997b32ff. = *FVS* 80 B 7) as a defense of infinite divisibility is simply mistaken. Untersteiner (1962), 35, (1954), 235 with nn. 3–4 = (1967), 57 with nn. 3–4 for his part adopted Bignone's text but interpreted it (rather differently) as a polemical restatement of Gorgias' alleged denial of the unity of being and knowledge. Untersteiner's ascription of such a doctrine to Gorgias and his notion that Antiphon combated it are alike purely arbitrary (cf. Kerferd [1965], 32–33; Introduction, section VII). And in any case, the objections brought against Bignone's restoration and interpretation of the words οὖ τάδε γνώσει are equally valid against Untersteiner. Gomperz (1912), 66–67 proposed a slightly different text (ταῦτα δὲ γνώσεις· ἕν τι οὐδὲν αὐτῷ κτλ.) and supposed an allusion to Empedocles' doctrine of the cosmic cycle. More specifically, Gomperz suggested that Antiphon refers to the portion of the cycle when the roots are completely mixed by Love and nothing unitary (ἕν τι οὐδέν) exists any longer besides or outside ("ausser") the Sphere (= αὐτῷ). Cf. *FVS* 31 B 17.1–13. Once again, however, it is hard to see why Galen would have quoted the words ταῦτα δὲ γνώσεις; and even harder to extract the notion of "unity" from ἕν τι οὐδέν (cf. above). Furthermore, Gomperz's interpretation seems to rest on a misunderstanding of Empedocles' doctrine. For even in the Sphere, the roots remain distinct constituents and do not become a single homogeneous body (as Gomperz appears to think). Cf. Cherniss (1935), 50–51. Indicative of the arbitrary character of Gomperz's interpretation is his admission that the fragment may refer instead to the opposite portion of the cycle, when the roots are completely separated by Strife. In a letter to Diels (cf. *FVS* 2.338 n.; 2.340 n.), A. Diès proposed a restoration of the fragment which would connect it with Anaxagoras (ὁ νοῦς εἷς· ἕν τε οὐδὲν ⟨ἄλλο⟩ αὐτῶν κτλ.). Diès suggested that this is a paraphrase of Anaxagoras' famous description of νοῦς: ἀλλὰ μόνος αὐτὸς ἐπ' ἑωυτοῦ ἐστιν (*FVS* 59 B 12). Diès' text and interpretation were adopted by Momigliano (1969), 137. It is doubtful, however, whether εἷς by itself can convey the sense Diès and Momigliano ascribe to it. Moreover, the insertion of ⟨ἄλλο⟩ is paleographically implausible. (On Antiphon and Anaxagoras cf. commentary on F2 and F10.) Building on Diès' restoration, Morrison (1963), 35–40 proposed to read ἓν τῷ λέγοντι οὐδέ γε νοῦς εἷς, ἕν τε οὐδὲν αὐτῷ κτλ. Morrison understood νοῦς (differently from Diès and Momigliano) as the "meaning" or "sense" of words and related F1 to the problem of names and things. On his view, the fragment asserts one of the central tenets of Περὶ ἀληθείας: that no single meaning (οὐδέ γε νοῦς εἷς) or permanent reality attaches to the words we speak (ἓν τῷ λέγοντι). (Cf. Morrison [1963], [1972], 212–13; Introduction, section III; commentary on F13 and F15.) Morrison's restoration involves several arbitrary alterations of the paradosis (for example, τοῦ τάδε γνοὺς εἰς becomes οὐδέ γε νοῦς εἷς). Furthermore, his explanation of the crucial phrase οὐδέ γε νοῦς εἷς as "no single meaning" runs into the very same difficulty previously discussed in connection with Diels' and others' interpretations of the phrase ἕν τι οὐδέν (cf. above). Even if correctly restored, οὐδέ γε νοῦς εἷς more likely would signify "not even one meaning," "absolutely no meaning."

Older commentators generally interpreted the fragment in nominalist terms, as a denial of the Socratic–Platonic doctrine of unitary abstract concepts separate from particulars (for example μακρότης, "length"). So Bernays (1854), 255 n. 2; Sauppe (1896), 516–17. (Sauppe read ταῦτα δὲ γνώσει, ἕν τε οὐδὲν τὸ αὐτό· οὔτε οὖν ὄψει ὁρᾷ ὁ ὁρῶν μακρότητα οὔτε οὖν γνώμῃ γιγνώσκει ὁ γιγνώσκων; Bernays suggested ἑνί τε λόγῳ, ταυταδὶ νοῦς εἴσεται, ἕν τε οὐδὲν αὐτῷ· οὔτε οὖν ὄψει ὁρᾷ μακρότητα οὔτε ἂν γνώμῃ γιγνώσκοι ὁ μακρότητα γιγνώσκων.) Wolff (1856), 59 n. 1; Gomperz (1901), 434–35 = (1922), 360–61, and Zumpos (1965–66) interpreted in similar fashion. The exact opposite idea was extracted from the fragment by Croiset (1883), 145–48, who restored ταῦτα δὲ γνοὺς αἰσθάνεται οὐδὲν αὐτῶν· οὔκουν ὄψει ὁρᾷ μακρότητα, οὐδ' ἐὰν γνώμῃ γιγνώσκῃ, ὁ μακρότητα γιγνώσκων. Croiset interpreted this to mean that abstract qualities such as μακρότης can be known by the mind or reason, even though they are imperceptible to the senses. Both the nominalist type of interpretation and its opposite, however, seem anachronistic for a fifth-century thinker like

Antiphon. (The whole notion of abstract qualities is probably not earlier than Plato; cf. *Theaetetus* 182A–B with Cherniss [1935], 361–62.)

Diels' restoration remains the most plausible from a paleographical standpoint, and furthermore yields intelligible Greek. Nevertheless, serious difficulties remain. In l. 5, Diels' ⟨ὂν⟩ is unnecessary and is better omitted. In that case, ἕν τι οὐδέν will be the direct object of εἴσ⟨ῃ⟩, and the sense will be: "you will know none" (*sc.* of the things that can be seen or thought). The philosophical import of this statement, however, remains obscure. Again in l. 5, Diels suggested αὐτῶν as well as αὐτῷ. He printed the latter, suggesting that it refers to the λόγος or reason (cf. Diels [1922], 2.292 n.). But this seems unlikely (for one thing, λόγος in the sense indicated is unattested for Antiphon, who would perhaps have used γνώμη instead). αὐτῶν produces better grammar as well as better sense, functioning as a partitive genitive with ἕν τι οὐδέν and serving as antecedent to the relatives ὧν ... ὧν (ll. 5–6), which are attracted into its case. An additional problem is presented by the pronoun ταῦτα in l. 4. If it refers to the same things as αὐτῶν (that is, to what can be seen or thought), then why does Antiphon deny that one who has come to know (γνούς) "these things" has any knowledge of them (εἴσ⟨ῃ⟩ ἕν τι οὐδὲν αὐτῶν)? But if ταῦτα does not refer to the same things as αὐτῶν, then its reference is totally obscure. The possibility that Galen has quoted the fragment in incomplete form should be reckoned with. His purpose in citing Antiphon is to illustrate the contrast between reason (γνώμη) and the senses (αἰσθήσεις) and to exemplify the use of γνώμη to designate "mind" or the faculty of thought. Both of these purposes are fully satisfied by the latter half of the quotation (ll. 5–7: οὔτε ὧν ὄψει ὁρᾷ ... ὁ μακρότατα γιγνώσκων), which illustrates both of the things Galen wanted to show. It may be that Galen has omitted something at the beginning of the quotation, something essential to deciphering Antiphon's meaning but superfluous to his own purposes.

4 ταῦτα: on the reference of this pronoun cf. introductory note above.

5 εἴσ⟨ῃ⟩: this is most likely an impersonal address to the reader. Cf. F29A, ll. 4–5 and F51, l. 1, with commentary.

ὄψει: cf. commentary on F7. In F44(b)III.7–8, ὄψις seems to refer to the "visual ray" (cf. commentary ad loc.).

6 γνώμῃ: for γνώμη in the sense of "mind," "faculty of thought" cf. F2–3 with commentary; Critias, *FVS* 88 B 6, 19, 39–40 (the last two fragments quoted by Galen immediately before F1); Snell (1924), 35–36; Huart (1973), 24 n. 2, 33–89. γνώμη appears in a different sense in F49, l. 31 (cf. commentary ad loc.). In F44(a)III.15 (from Περὶ ἀληθείας) as well as F58, l. 5 (from Περὶ ὁμονοίας), Antiphon employs νοῦς rather than γνώμη to designate "mind." (The relation between the two in his psychology is obscure.) The fact that Antiphon opposed mind to the senses implies that he distinguished thought from sensation, just as other Presocratics did (cf. Cherniss [1935], 79–83, 292 n. 10, 299 n. 32, 313 n. 87, 374).

6–7 γιγνώσκει . . . γιγνώσκων: γιγνώσκω and γνώμη are often (as here) paired with the sense of sight. Cf. Melissus, *FVS* 30 B 8.3 (ὥστε συμβαίνει μήτε ὁρᾶν μήτε τὰ ὄντα γινώσκειν); [Hippocrates], *De arte* 2 (ἅ γε εἴη καὶ ὀφθαλμοῖσιν ἰδεῖν καὶ γνώμῃ νοῆσαι ὡς ἔστιν. ἀλλ' ὅπως μὴ οὐκ ᾖ τοῦτο τοιοῦτον· ἀλλὰ τὰ μὲν ἐόντα αἰεὶ ὁρᾶταί τε καὶ γινώσκεται, τὰ δὲ μὴ ἐόντα οὔτε ὁρᾶται οὔτε γινώσκεται), 11 (τῇ τῆς γνώμης ὄψει); [Hippocrates], *De victu* 1.21; Thucydides, 7.75 (τῇ τε ὄψει ἑκάστῳ ἀλγεινὰ καὶ τῇ γνώμῃ αἰσθέσθαι); Snell (1924), 20–39. On the meaning of γιγνώσκω in early Greek cf. Huffman (1993), 116–17.

Diels and Kranz (*FVS* 2.338–39) printed the entire second chapter of the pseudo-Hippocratic *De arte* as a sort of appendix to F1, apparently in the belief that it expresses the opposite of the Eleatic notions Diels and others have read into F1. Untersteiner (1962), 36–39; Morrison (1972), 213, and others have followed suit. *De arte* 2 does not appear to have anything to do with F1, however, and there is no justification for printing it alongside the fragment. (For different parallels between *De arte* and Antiphon cf. commentary on F2; F7; F15; and F44(a)II.30ff.)

F2

Galen quotes this fragment immediately after F1. The contrast drawn here between mind and body recalls the contrast of mind and the senses in F1. Yet it does not look as if the two fragments were originally contiguous (the γάρ in l. 1 does not shed light on the question). Therefore, the common assumption on the part of commentators that F2 derives from the same (apparently epistemological) context as F1 is far from certain. It could instead derive from a medical context (cf. F29A and F33–39, with commentary; Introduction, section III). The opposition between mind and body is a frequent theme in the Hippocratic corpus. Cf. *De vetere medicina* 10; *De aëre aquis et locis* 6; *De victu* 1.4; *De flatibus* 1; Snell (1924), 35–36. Furthermore, as Cherniss (1977), 115 n. 10 pointed out, Antiphon's notion of the primacy of mind over body in matters of health and disease finds a close parallel in the pseudo-Hippocratic *De arte* 7: οἱ μὲν [*sc.* ἰητροὶ] γὰρ ὑγιαινούσῃ γνώμῃ μεθ' ὑγιαίνοντος σώματος ἐγχειρέουσι . . . οἱ δὲ [*sc.* κάμνοντες] οὔτε ἃ κάμνουσιν οὔτε δι' ἃ κάμνουσιν εἰδότες οὐδ' ὅτι ἐκ τῶν παρεόντων ἔσται οὐδ' ὅτι ἐκ τῶν τούτοισιν ὁμοίων γίνεται ἐπιτάσσονται ... θέλοντες τὰ πρὸς τὴν νοῦσον ἤδη μᾶλλον ἢ τὰ πρὸς τὴν ὑγιείην προσδέχεσθαι, οὐκ ἀποθανεῖν ἐρῶντες ἀλλὰ καρτερεῖν ἀδυνατέοντες. In this passage, the mental disposition of the sick (that is, their ignorance) is accounted partly responsible for their unwillingness to endure the cure prescribed by their doctors, who (by contrast) operate with a healthy mind and a healthy body. This passage is also presumptive evidence against Stenzel's and Untersteiner's view that the words καὶ νόσον (l. 2) are otiose.

Zeppi (1962), 145 contended that the term γνώμη in this fragment stands for rhetoric, which Antiphon either simply identified with medicine or at least ranked on the same level as medicine. Bignone (1938), 134–35 read into the fragment a contrast between intellect (which is capable of harm as well as help) and natural instinct in accordance with the norms of nature (which is exclusively pleasurable and beneficial). According to Untersteiner (1962), 38, (1954), 241 = (1967), 2.64, the fragment deals with the order within man (the microcosm), just as F24A concerns the order in the world at large (the macrocosm). Untersteiner furthermore would read into the fragment the notion of concord, ὁμόνοια (cf. Ryffel [1949], 44). None of these odd interpretations is supported by the slightest evidence.

F3

The context of this fragment is completely unknown. Diano (1961), 123–24 connected the phrase ἀπαρασκεύῳ γνώμῃ with the idea of meditation in advance on future misfortunes (*praemeditatio futurorum malorum*), a commonplace theme in the later genre of consolation literature. He inferred accordingly that Antiphon dealt in Περὶ ἀληθείας with the art of avoiding grief, the so-called τέχνη ἀλυπίας. Cf. *contra* Introduction, sections II and IV; commentary on T6. Buresch (1886), 85–86; Nestle (1942), 390, and others proposed to attribute to the sophist Antiphon the rhetorical handbook (Τέχναι ῥητορικαί) current in antiquity under the name of Antiphon (cf. Antiphon of Rhamnus, frr. 71–76 = *AS* B X 5–12). They pointed out that the handbook seems to have dealt with the subject of word-formation (cf. Antiphon of Rhamnus, frr. 73, 75–76 = *AS* B X 9–11; commentary on T10), while the sophist Antiphon used many neologisms (cf. Blass [1887–98], 1.127). Other commentators have ascribed it to the Rhamnusian (cf. Spengel [1828], 116; Jacoby [1908], 52–53; Diels and Kranz, *FVS* 2.339 n.; Untersteiner [1962], 39). The argument about which Antiphon the handbook should be attributed to would be moot if (as Pollux suggests and as seems likely) the work in fact is spurious (cf. Norden [1918], vol. I "Nachträge," 7; but contrast the different view taken earlier in Norden [1918], 1.72 n. 2). Nestle (1942), 390 suggested (implausibly) that ancient doubts about the work's authenticity pertained solely to the *Rhamnusian's* authorship, and thus left open the possibility of its belonging to the sophist Antiphon. There is no reason to think that the discrepancy in usage noted by Pollux is responsible for the doubts about the handbook's authenticity. (Against the attempts of Spengel [1828], 115–16 to discredit Pollux's testimony cf. Blass [1887–98], 1.114.)

For γνώμη in the sense of "mind," "faculty of thought" cf. F1–2, with commentary.

F4–5

Diels (*FVS* 2.337 n.); Joël (1921), 716 with n. 4; Zeppi (1962), 147, and other commentators interpreted these fragments in terms of the Eleatic doctrine on the unreliability of sense-perception (cf. Parmenides, *FVS* 28 B 7; Melissus, *FVS* 30 B 8; Tarán [1965], 76–80). Untersteiner (1962), 40, (1954), 235 with n. 5 = (1967), 2.58 with n. 5 contended that Antiphon here restates Gorgias' supposed denial of the validity of all "experiences" (cf. Introduction, section VII; commentary on F1). Even if Diels and others were right in thinking that these fragments dealt with the fallibility of sense-perception, there would be no need to posit influence from the Eleatics, since other Presocratics besides them admitted the unreliability of the senses. (Cf. Anaxagoras, *FVS* 59 B 21; Democritus, *FVS* 68 B 11, 125; [Hippocrates], *De arte* 11; Bignone [1938], 218; Guthrie [1971a], 287 n. 5.) Diano (1961), 118–19 proposed to link these fragments (like F3) with the theme of *praemeditatio futurorum malorum* and the alleged τέχνη ἀλυπίας (cf. commentary on F3).

F4

ἄοπτα: this adjective seems to appear elsewhere only in Cyril of Alexandria (references in Lampe, s.v.) and Gregory of Nyssa, *Apologia in hexaemeron* 44.69 Migne.

F5

ἀπαθῆ: the specific sense ("not experienced") which Antiphon gives to the common adjective ἀπαθής seems to be without parallel (cf. LSJ, s.v.). To judge from Harpocration's explanatory gloss, the adjective modified πάθη (so Sauppe [1896], 517 and others). If so, the type of figure exemplified is paralleled in Aeschylus, *Prometheus* 808 (ἀπόλεμος

πόλεμος), *Persae* 680 (νᾶες ἄναες). Cf. Untersteiner (1962), 40. Precisely what sort of πάθη Antiphon had in mind is unclear. πάθος has a wide field of application, ranging from the medical (= disease; ubiquitous in the Hippocratic corpus) to the astronomical (= celestial phenomenon; cf. Plato, *Hippias maior* 285C, *Phaedo* 96C; Aristotle, *Metaphysics* 986a5; LSJ, s.v. III.2) to the generic "experience." Any of these senses could conceivably have found a place in Περὶ ἀληθείας.

F6–8

These three texts (from Pollux) were first printed among the fragments of Περὶ ἀληθείας by Diels, and subsequent editors have followed his lead. (Sauppe [1896], 520 had so assigned F8, though not the others.) Yet the complete absence of source-citations leaves it doubtful whether any of the words διοπτεύειν, εἴσοπτοι, τὸ ὀψόμενον, τῇ ὄψει, ὀδμάς, and εὐοδμίαν belongs to Περὶ ἀληθείας or other works of the sophist Antiphon. (ἄοπτα, quoted in F7, belongs to F4.) The mere fact that these terms have to do with sense-perception (like ἀπαθῆ and ἄοπτα in F4–5) is, of course, no guarantee of their attribution. Diels thought that the words τῇ ὄψει (F7) derive from F1. But ὄψις in that fragment is anarthrous, whereas Pollux cites it with the article. Funghi (1984), 5 referred τῇ ὄψει instead to F44(c)III.7–8. There, however, the noun appears in the genitive case, not the dative which Pollux quotes. Besides, ὄψις there probably does not mean "eyes," as Pollux interprets the word (cf. commentary ad loc.). As Blass (1881), 149 n. long ago pointed out, Pollux's citation of ὄψις almost certainly derives from Antiphon of Rhamnus, fr. 36 (οἱ γὰρ ἄνθρωποι ἅττα ἂν ὁρῶσι τῇ ὄψει πιστότερα ἡγοῦνται ἢ οἷς εἰς ἀφανὲς ἥκει ὁ ἔλεγχος τῆς ἀληθείας). Despite Diels and others, Blass (1881), 148–49 was completely justified in printing these texts from Pollux among his "Fragmenta ambigua" (= frr. 161, 174, 173).

F6

εἴσοπτοι: εἴσοπτος (ἔσοπτος) is primarily an Ionic word; it seems to be attested elsewhere only in Simonides (fr. 579) and Herodotus (2.138). Cf. LSJ, s.v.

F7

τὸ ὀψόμενον: J. Kühn in Lederlin and Hemsterhuis (1706), I.181 n. 10; Untersteiner (1962), 41, and Burkert (1972), 260 n. 107 all propose to give ὀψόμενον a passive sense here. But despite the difficulties created by the article and by the neuter gender, ὀψόμενον more likely is active (as the future middle forms of this verb usually are). Cf. LSJ, s.v. ὁράω II; Kühner–Gerth 1.116; Huffman (1993), 118–19.

F8

2–3 ἔστι δὲ ποιητικά ... Αἰολικά: cf. Phrynichus, *Eclogae* 62 (65); *Anecdota Graeca* 110 (Bekker), and other ancient and medieval authorities cited by Aly (1929), 155 n. 157 and Fischer (1974), 65 note. Cf. also LSJ, s.vv. εὐοσμία, ὀσμή. Phrynichus in this context refers to Xenophon for the form ὀδμή (παρανομεῖ οὖν Ξενοφῶν εἰς τὴν πάτριον διάλεκτον λέγων ὀδμή). Aly suggested that this is a mistake for Antiphon, since manuscripts of Xenophon offer only ὀσμή (with the single exception of cod. Vindobonensis phil. gr. 109 in *Symposium* 2.3). As Breitenbach (1967), 1898 pointed out, however, the absence of ὀδμή from our manuscripts of Xenophon may be the result of Atticist criticism.

3–4 ὀδμὰς καὶ εὐοδμίαν: despite the variants offered in some manuscripts, Pollux certainly wrote ὀδμάς and εὐοδμίαν, for these spellings are the very reason he cites the words (cf. Aly [1929], 155 n. 157). Although ὀδμή appears in Democritus in the sense of ὄσφρησις, "sense of smell" (cf. *FVS* 68 B 11; LSJ, s.v. ὀσμή II), the plural here suggests the ordinary meaning "odors," "smells."

F9

This testimonium almost certainly pertains to the sophist Antiphon, and in particular to Περὶ ἀληθείας (so Sauppe [1896], 519, followed by almost all subsequent commentators). The lemma Ἀντιφάνης offered by the manuscripts of Stobaeus is a simple mistake for Ἀντιφῶν (as Meineke [1839–57], I.XLI already saw). For the frequent confusion of the two names cf. commentary on F51. Sorabji (1983), 95 inexplicably supposed that the "Antiphon (or Antiphanes)" in question here is an otherwise unknown Peripatetic philosopher of uncertain date. But the attribution to the sophist Antiphon can hardly be doubted (cf. Dunn [1996]).

As far as Critolaus is concerned, the conception of time as a measure (that is, of motion) represents standard Peripatetic doctrine. Cf. Aristotle, *Physics* 219b1–2 (ὅταν δὲ τὸ πρότερον καὶ ὕστερον, τότε λέγομεν· τοῦτο γάρ ἐστιν ὁ χρόνος, ἀριθμὸς κινήσεως κατὰ τὸ πρότερον καὶ ὕστερον). Aëtius' attribution to Critolaus of the notion that time is a "thought" is explicable in light of Aristotle's argument that time would not exist without soul and intellect. Cf. *Physics* 223a21–29; Wehrli (1959), 66; Sorabji (1983), 89–94; Dunn (1996), 68. The significance of the denial that time is a substance is unclear. Following Olivier (1895), Untersteiner (1962), 42 suggested that Critolaus may have defended the Peripatetics against the accusation of making time a substance (cf. Aristotle, *De caelo* 279a14–16); or opposed the Peripatetic conception of time to that of Stoics, who regarded time as a substance. The Stoics, however, agreed with Aristotle in considering time as a measure of motion. Cf. Chrysippus, frr. 509–10 = fr. 51A–B Long–Sedley; Posidonius, fr. 98; Long and Sedley (1987), 1.306–7; Kidd (1988), 1.396–97. Proclus even goes so far as to accuse them of reducing time to a mere thought (cf. *In Timaeum* 271D = Chrysippus, fr. 521 = fr. 51F Long–Sedley; Long and Sedley [1987], 1.307). But Chrysippus did believe that intervals of time such as day, night, and month (though not time *per se*) are bodies. Cf. Plutarch, *De communibus notitiis* 1084C–D = Chrysippus, fr. 665 = fr. 51G Long–Sedley; Long and Sedley (1987), 1.308.

Antiphon can plausibly be credited with the idea that time is a measure, as the association of time with change and measurement is securely attested in Presocratic thought. Cf. Diogenes Laertius, 8.84; Hippolytus, *Refutatio* 1.6.1; Cherniss (1935), 217 n. 279. But despite Goebel (1910), 382; Luria (1933), 164; Nestle (1942), 373 with n. 9; Guthrie (1971a), 292, and others, Aëtius' ascription to Antiphon of the doctrine that time is a thought seems anachronistic. Dunn (1996), 69 suggested he may have argued "that time has no existence apart from an individual's recognition of temporally marked events." But the suggestion does nothing to make Aëtius' ascription more plausible. If it is rejected, then the attempt of Wolff (1856), 59 n. 1 to interpret F9 (like F1) along nominalist lines falls to the ground. No evidence supports the fantastic interpretation of Untersteiner (1962), 42, (1954), 235–36 = (1967), 2.58, who explained this testimonium as a statement of the consequences that follow for the concept of time from Gorgias' supposed denial of the predicates "eternity" and "generation" to Being. (Cf. Introduction, section VII; commentary on F1 and F4–5.)

F10

The main difficulty presented by this fragment is the uncertainty regarding its subject. The vast majority of critics supply "god" (θεός) as subject. So van Spaan (1773), 827; Sauppe (1896), 515; Wilamowitz (1895), 2.277; Diels and Kranz (*FVS* 2.340 n.); Jacoby (1908), 32; Norden (1913), 13–14; Joël (1921), 695 with n. 3 (but cf. below); Nestle in Zeller and Nestle (1920), 1445 n. 2 (where "Fr. 20" is a misprint); Aly (1929),

141; Bignone (1938), 122–23; Nestle (1942), 373; Schmid (1940), 160 n. 3; Mondolfo (1956), 293 with n. 1; Untersteiner (1962), 42–43, (1954), 236 = (1967), 2.58; Guthrie (1971a), 230 with n. 3(c). In favor of this view is the traditional (even commonplace) character of the notion that the gods need nothing. Cf. Xenophanes, *FVS* 21 A 32 (ἀποφαίνεται δὲ καὶ περὶ θεῶν ὡς οὐδεμιᾶς ἡγεμονίας ἐν αὐτοῖς οὔσης· οὐ γὰρ ὅσιον δεσπόζεσθαί τινα τῶν θεῶν· ἐπιδεῖσθαί τε μηδενὸς αὐτῶν μηδένα μηδ' ὅλως); Euripides, *Heracles* 1345–46 (δεῖται γὰρ ὁ θεός, εἴπερ ἔστ' ὀρθῶς θεός, οὐδενός, probably echoing Xenophanes; cf. Bond [1981], 400); Xenophon, *Memorabilia* 1.6.10 = T1, ll. 60–62; Norden (1913), 13–14, with further references. The major stumbling-block is the predicate ἄπειρος, which sounds somewhat strange applied to god. In order to get round this difficulty, van Spaan proposed εὔπορος and Sauppe ἄπηρος; but neither proposal carries the least conviction. The notion of an infinite god is credited to Xenophanes by both Cicero (*De natura deorum* 1.11.28 = *FVS* 21 A 34) and Nicolaus of Damascus (*FVS* 21 A 31). These reports are perhaps to be explained in terms of the "Eleaticization" of Xenophanes in the doxographical tradition. Cf. Mansfeld (1987), especially 303–5 = (1990b), 147–73, especially 164–66; Jaeger (1947), 51–54. But in any case, they cannot be taken seriously as evidence for the notion of an infinite god in Presocratic thought (cf. Cherniss [1935], 201 n. 228). Nestle (1942), 373 suggested that Antiphon borrowed the predicate ἄπειρος from Melissus' description of Being (cf. *FVS* 30 B 2–7) and applied it to god (cf. Aly [1929], 141). Mondolfo (1956), 293 with n. 1 contended that ἄπειρος here does not mean "infinite" but "absolutely complete" (a sense for which there is no other evidence). Untersteiner (1954), 236 n. 13 = (1967), 2.58 n. 13 argued that the clause οὐδὲ προσδέχεται οὐδενός τι explains the epithet ἄπειρος as the clause οὐδενὸς δεῖται explains ἀδέητος (in chiastic arrangement). He concluded from this analysis that ἄπειρος (applied to god) has the double sense of "infinite" and "inexperienced" (cf. Plato, *Timaeus* 55D). Untersteiner's interpretation was misrepresented by Guthrie (1971a), 230–31 n. 3(d), who mistakenly claimed that Untersteiner understood ἄπειρος in the (unparalleled) sense of "untried." (Guthrie seems to have been misled by K. Freeman's mistranslation of Untersteiner's "inesperto" as "untried" rather than "without experience"; cf. below.) The motivation behind Untersteiner's interpretation is his extravagant notion that the fragment restates Gorgias' concept of an infinite, contradictory, and therefore non-existent God. (Cf. Introduction, section VII; commentary on F1, F4–5, and F9.)

Dümmler (1901), 177 n. 1 took a different approach to the problem of the fragment's subject. Arguing that ἄπειρος would aptly describe the world or universe, he proposed κόσμος as subject. (So also Goebel [1910], 381–82; cf. Bignone [1938], 218 n. 1, but contrast the different view taken in 122–23.) Dümmler further suggested that the fragment contains a polemic against what he described as Anaxagoras' concept of a "half other-worldly" (halbausserweltlichen) νοῦς. If κόσμος were the subject, however, both the predicate ἀδέητος and the clause οὐδὲ προσδέχεται οὐδενός τι would be difficult to explain. Plato attributed the qualities of self-sufficiency and freedom from needs to the cosmos (cf. *Timaeus* 33C–34B), as did Chysippus after him (cf. Plutarch, *De Stoicorum repugnantiis* 1052D = Chrysippus, fr. 604; Cherniss [1976], 567 n. *c*). But this is explicable in light of their conception of the world as a divine living being – a notion there is no reason to credit Antiphon with. An additional objection to understanding κόσμος as subject is suggested to me by David Sedley, who argues that a world bounded by a heaven (κόσμος) could hardly have been called infinite (ἄπειρος). But perhaps κόσμος in the sense of "universe" could have been so designated (cf. Aristotle, *De caelo* 280a21: ἡ δὲ τοῦ ὅλου σύστασίς ἐστι κόσμος καὶ οὐρανός).

Besides god and the world, commentators have proposed a wide variety of other candidates for subject of the fragment. A. Diès (*apud FVS* 2.340 n.) and Momigliano (1969), 137 understood νοῦς as subject, supposing a reference to Anaxagoras. (Cf. *FVS* 59 B 12: τὰ μὲν ἄλλα παντὸς μοῖραν μετέχει, νοῦς δέ ἐστιν ἄπειρον καὶ αὐτοκρατὲς καὶ μέμεικται οὐδενὶ χρήματι, ἀλλὰ μόνος αὐτὸς ἐπ' ἑωυτοῦ ἐστιν.) But the predicate ἀδέητος presents an apparently insuperable objection to this interpretation. For according to the explanation in the *Suda*, the subject of the fragment is "without needs" (ἀδέητος) in the sense of possessing everything (πάντα ἔχων). Anaxagoras' νοῦς, by contrast, is the one entity in the world that has no portion or share of anything else. Burkert (1964), 144 n. 10 suggested nature (φύσις) as subject, comparing Euripides, fr. 910 (ὄλβιος ὅστις τῆς ἱστορίας ἔσχε μάθησιν ... ἀθανάτου καθορῶν φύσεως κόσμον ἀγήρων). Zeppi (1962), 147–48 proposed the Eleatic being (οὐσία?). As adjectives of two terminations, ἄπειρος and ἀδέητος could modify a feminine noun such as φύσις (or οὐσία). But for what it is worth, the explanation in the *Suda* seems to presuppose a masculine subject (ὁ μηδενὸς δεόμενος ... ἔχων). The same objection applies against the theory of Romeyer-Dherbey (1985), 101–2 that the subject is the so-called ἀρρύθμιστον (cf. Introduction, section III; commentary on F15). To designate the metaphysical entity he considered the cornerstone of Antiphon's philosophy, Romeyer-Dherbey normally employs the neuter form ἀρρύθμιστον as a substantive adjective. In the case of this fragment, however, in order (presumably) to satisfy the need for noun–adjective agreement, he uses the masculine form ἀρρύθμιστος, without explanation and without indication of what noun is to be understood with it. Joël (1893–1901), 2.672 and Luria (1927b), 1070 n. 1 understood ἄπειρος as "inexperienced" and interpreted the fragment (differently from other commentators) as a statement about human ethics rather than theology, cosmology, or metaphysics. As subject Joël supplied "the man of few needs" (cf. Plato, *Gorgias* 492E; Xenophon, *Memorabilia* 1.6.1–10 = T1, ll. 1–63); Luria, "the wretched savage" (den elenden Wilden). Luria neglected to provide any details about the identity of this enigmatic figure, whose possible role in the context of Περὶ ἀληθείας is difficult to fathom. Joël's suggestion seems to be ruled out by the explanation in the *Suda*, which indicates that the subject of the fragment is without needs (ἀδέητος) in the sense of possessing everything (πάντα ἔχων) rather than in the sense of having few desires (*Bedürfnislosigkeit*; cf. above and commentary on T1).

It is impossible in the present state of the evidence to decide for certain what the subject of this fragment is. God (θεός) and the world (κόσμος, or perhaps οὐρανός) remain the likeliest candidates. The objections to each have been rehearsed above. But the arguments are inconclusive, and a better suggestion has yet to appear. In the circumstances, the attempts of Goebel (1910), 381–82; Gomperz (1912), 65–66; Bignone (1938), 77; Diels (*FVS* 2.337 n.); Aly (1929), 141; Nestle (1942), 373; Diès (*apud FVS* 2.340 n.), and others to relate the fragment to the doctrines of the Eleatics, Empedocles, Anaxagoras, Protagoras, etc. seem even more dubious than usual.

2 διὰ τοῦτο: "for this reason." The characteristics defined by the adjectives ἀδέητος and ἄπειρος seem to be consequent on some previously mentioned characteristic or state of affairs.

2–3 οὐδὲ προσδέχεται οὐδενός τι: despite Untersteiner (cf. above), this clause is most naturally understood as explaining ἀδέητος. οὐδενός may be masculine or neuter.

3 ἀδέητος: Antiphon may have coined this word (as Buresch [1886], 85 and Jacoby [1908], 52 suggested). It seems to appear elsewhere only in Ptolemy, *Tetrabiblus* 159, where the sense is different (cf. LSJ, s.v.). An epic form ἀδεύητον, of unknown provenance, is cited by Hesychius (α 1075, 1.40): ἀδεύητον· χαλεπόν. ἢ ⟨οὗ⟩ οὐκ ἄν τις ἐπιδεηθείη.

F11

This fragment likely is related to F10. For δέησις in the sense of "need," "want" cf. Aristotle, *Politics* 1257a27 (and other passages cited by LSJ, s.v. II).

F12

In *Contra Celsum* 4.23–30, Origen responds to Celsus' attack on the Judeo-Christian belief that human beings possess a special relationship with God and a privileged place in the order of creation. (Cf. Borret [1967–76], 5.73–75; Daniélou [1955], 111–13; Chadwick [1966], 106–7.) In the course of his polemic, Celsus related a fable in which he compared Jews and Christians by turns to a company of bats (cf. *Odyssey* 24.6–8; Plato, *Republic* 387A); to ants emerging from an ant-hole; to frogs in council around a marsh (cf. *Phaedo* 109B, and the Jewish *sanhedrin*); and to worms holding an assembly in a muddy corner (cf. the Christian ἐκκλησία). Cf. *Contra Celsum* 4.23; Borret (1967–76), 2.238 n. 1. Origen responds that it is wrong in principle to compare human beings with such lowly creatures on account of their supposed physical or spiritual inferiority (cf. *Contra Celsum* 4.24–25). Likewise, it is wrong to compare Christians and Jews in particular to such creatures on account of the supposed inferiority of their doctrines (cf. *Contra Celsum* 4.26ff.).

Most commentators accept Origen's claim that Antiphon denied divine providence at face value. Cf. van Spaan (1773), 826–27; Norden (1893), 435; Gomperz (1912), 67–68; Bignone (1938), 124–25; Stenzel (1924), 39; Schmid (1940), 160; Nestle (1942), 373; Guthrie (1971a), 230–31; Untersteiner (1962), 44–45, (1954), 242–43 with n. 74 = (1967), 2.65–66 with n. 74. Norden (1893), 435 explained the denial in terms of Antiphon's supposed pessimism, as evidence for which he cited F50 and F51. But Norden overlooked the fact that these fragments derive (in all likelihood) from Περὶ ὁμονοίας rather than Περὶ ἀληθείας (to which Origen refers). The denial is more often connected with F10, on the theory that it is but a short step from the assertion of divine self-sufficiency to the denial of divine providence – as Epicurean theology seems to show (cf. Lucretius, 1.44–49 = 2.645–51). So van Spaan (1773), 827; Dümmler (1901), 177 n. 1; Bignone (1938), 124–25; Borret (1967–76), 4.220 n. 2. Origen in fact attacks the Epicureans often for their denial of divine providence, a concept which plays an important role in his theology (cf. *Contra Celsum* 1.21, 2.13, 3.75, 5.61; Daniélou [1955], 74–75, 205–6). Other commentators have rejected Origen's claim as a mere inference, whether from Antiphon's mechanistic physics (so Gomperz [1901], 585–86 n. = [1922], 490 n.; cf. Sauppe [1896], 515) or from his disregard of the possibility of divine detection and punishment of secret wrongdoing (so Guthrie [1971a], 231; cf. F44(a)II.3–10). Diels (*FVS* 2.340 n.) simply branded Origen's claim a "christliche Folgerung," without further explanation.

The complete absence of corroborating evidence (verbatim or doxographical) justifies a sceptical attitude towards Origen's claim. F10 in no way demonstrates that Antiphon denied divine providence (even if "god" is the subject). Belief in divine self-sufficiency is by no means incompatible with belief in divine providence – as the examples of the Xenophontic Socrates (cf. *Memorabilia* 1.4, 1.6.10 = T1, ll. 60–63) and Plato show. But Origen might well have read such a denial into F10 or some other statement of Antiphon's. Dümmler (1901), 177 n. 1 theorized that Antiphon identified god and the world and so rejected providence (πρόνοια) as too anthropocentric a term to designate the immanent purposiveness of the cosmos. But there is no evidence that Antiphon identified god and the world. Even more fanciful is the theory of Joël (1893–1901), 2.654, who suggested that Origen's report goes back to a dialogue of Antisthenes in which Antiphon appeared as a *dramatis persona* who denied divine providence in a dispute with Socrates.

10–13 κἂν Δημοσθένης τις κτλ.: the construction here is difficult. Chadwick (1965), 200–1 took ὁ ῥήτωρ and ἄλλος as subjects, translating: "Even if an orator was a Demosthenes and yet committed sin as he did and the actions which he did as a result of evil; or even if another is thought to be an Antiphon etc." Borret (1967–76), 2.243 more plausibly construed τις as the subject, Δημοσθένης ὁ ῥήτωρ and Ἀντιφῶν as predicates, and ἄλλος with ῥήτωρ, translating: "Que l'on soit un Démosthène, l'orateur, avec sa lâcheté et les actions qu'elle lui inspira, ou un Antiphon, autre orateur renommé etc." Untersteiner (1962), 45 and Morrison (1972), 215 translate differently again.

12 κακίας ... ἀπὸ κακίας: for ancient accusations against Demosthenes cf. [Plut.], *Vitae X or.* 847D–F; Aulus Gellius, *Noctes Atticae* 1.5.1, 1.8.3–6; Athenaeus, *Dipnosophistae* 13 592E–593A, and other texts cited by Borret (1967–76), 2.242 n. 1 and Chadwick (1965), 201 n. 1.

13 ἄλλος ῥήτωρ: Norden (1893), 435 with n. 2 proposed τοῦ ῥήτορος (a genitive of comparison after ἄλλος), thus manufacturing a reference to the problem of the identity of Antiphon. But the structure of the sentence supports the transmitted text. Moreover, it is highly unlikely that Origen would refer in so terse and oblique a fashion to a distinction not widely familiar in his day (even if he was aware of it).

14 ἀναιρῶν: ἀναιρέω is a *terminus technicus* for "doing away with" philosophical or religious doctrines. Cf. LSJ and Lampe, s.v.; Aëtius, 1.3.3 (Diels [1879], 278), 1.23.7 (Diels [1879], 320); Origen, *Contra Celsum* 2.13; etc.

F13

The quadrature of the circle – that is, the construction of a square equal in area to a given circle with the sole means of a ruler and compass – was one of the most widely canvassed problems in ancient Greek mathematics. (Cf. Rudio [1907], 83–125; Heath [1921], 1.173, 183–200, 218–32; commentary on F13(c), l. 1.) Antiphon's quadrature attempt can confidently be assigned to Περὶ ἀληθείας, although this is nowhere explicitly attested (so Sauppe [1850], 148, [1896], 519, followed by all later commentators). But whether it derives from the first book (as Sauppe and Diels supposed) or from the second is uncertain.

Aristotle mentions Antiphon's quadrature attempt twice, but only briefly and without providing any details. In his investigation of the principles (ἀρχαί) of physical science at the commencement of the *Physics*, Aristotle argues that consideration of the Eleatic thesis of the unity and immobility of being does not belong to the subject of physics. For if being is only one, there can be no physical principle at all, since an ἀρχή must be the principle of something else – which contradicts the alleged unity of being. Since it is not the task of any particular science to refute those who do away with its principles, it is not the task of physics to consider the Eleatic thesis. Similarly, it is not the task of the geometer to refute Antiphon's quadrature attempt, which does away with the principles of geometry. (On the argument cf. Cherniss [1935], 154–55.) In the *Sophistici elenchi*, Aristotle compares the relationship between eristic and dialectic arguments to that between the drawer of false diagrams (ὁ ψευδογράφος) and the geometer. Eristic argument reasons falsely (παραλογίζεται) from the same principles as dialectic argument, just as the drawer of false diagrams argues from the principles of geometry. The drawer of false diagrams is not eristic, however, inasmuch as he argues from geometrical principles. For this reason, Hippocrates' quadrature of the circle, or that by lunes, is not eristic (cf. *Sophistici elenchi* 171b12–16). But the quadrature of Bryson is eristic, since it is based on principles not peculiar to geometry (cf. *Sophistici elenchi* 171b16–18; *Posterior Analytics* 75b37ff.). After mentioning Bryson's quadrature, Aristotle adds "or as Antiphon attempted to square the circle," thus seeming to range Antiphon's quadrature attempt with that of Bryson. Aristotle's exact reasoning is uncertain; most likely he means that Antiphon's quadrature attempt is eristic because it does not accord with geometric principles (cf. Heath [1949], 48, 50).

All of our information about the details of Antiphon's quadrature attempt derives from later writers, in particular the Aristotelian commentators Simplicius (F13(c)), Themistius (F13(c)), and Philoponus (F13(d)). Although their accounts are generally similar, there are some important differences among them. All three commentators agree that Antiphon began by inscribing a regular polygon in a circle, then constructed isosceles triangles upon the sides of the polygon, and subsequently repeated this process until an inscribed polygon was produced whose sides coincided with the circumference of the circle. Since it is possible to construct a square equal in area to any given polygon, the circle will in this fashion have been squared. According to Themistius, Antiphon began from an inscribed equilateral triangle, whereas Philoponus has him begin from an inscribed square. Simplicius states more generally that Antiphon began from one of the polygons that can be inscribed in a circle. Simplicius then chooses an inscribed square as the starting-point for his exposition of the quadrature attempt. The three commentators also disagree about the geometric principle (or principles) which the quadrature attempt violated. According to Themistius, Antiphon violated the hypothesis of infinite divisibility (τὴν ἐπ' ἄπειρον τομήν); according to Philoponus, the principle that a straight line never coincides with an arc of a circle (μηδέποτε ἐφαρμόζειν εὐθεῖαν περιφερείᾳ). Simplicius discusses the question at some length. He reports Alexander's opinion that the quadrature attempt violates the geometrical assumption that a circle and straight line touch at a point (ὑποτίθεται μὲν ὁ γεωμέτρης κτλ.). Simplicius rejects this opinion on the grounds that the "assumption" in question is in fact demonstrated by Euclid (cf. *Elements* 3.16 and commentary on F13(e), l. 44). In evident confusion, Simplicius suggests it would be better to say that the principle violated is the impossibility of a straight line coinciding with an arc of a circle. He further points out that the area between the inscribed polygon and the circumference of the circle will never be exhausted; otherwise, the principle of infinite divisibility of magnitudes is violated. Simplicius adds that according to Eudemus, it is precisely this principle which Antiphon's quadrature attempt violated.

It is clear that Simplicius drew his information about Antiphon's quadrature attempt from Eudemus' *History of Geometry* as well as from the lost commentary of Alexander on the *Physics* (cf. Diels [1882], 54 n.; Rudio [1907], II, 31 n. 1, 104–5). Tannery at one time argued that Eudemus' *History* was no longer extant in the time of Simplicius, who accordingly had no direct access to it. Tannery hypothesized that Simplicius knew the *History* only indirectly, through Alexander and through a certain Sporus whom Tannery and others identify with the Porus of Nicea mentioned by Eutocius, author of a work entitled Κηρία (cf. Tannery [1882] = [1912], 168–77 and *apud* Diels [1882], XXVI–XXVII; commentary on F13(f), l. 11). Wehrli (1969), 116, who speaks of "das durch Alexander vermittelte Referat über Antiphon," seems to take a similar view. Later, Tannery changed his mind and suggested that Simplicius derived his information on Antiphon from Eudemus' commentary on Aristotle's *Physics* (not the *History of Geometry*) as well as from Alexander (cf. Tannery [1887], 115). None of the arguments put forward by Tannery carries any weight, and it is perfectly obvious that for his information on Antiphon Simplicius was able to draw directly on Eudemus' *History of Geometry* as well as on Alexander's lost commentary on the *Physics* (cf. Heiberg [1884], 345; Heath [1922], 1.35). Where Themistius and Philoponus derived their information on the quadrature attempt from is not clear. If (as Simplicius claims) Eudemus identified the infinite divisibility of magnitudes as the geometrical principle violated by Antiphon, then Themistius may depend on Eudemus. Philoponus' source, by contrast, may have been Alexander. For Philoponus identifies Antiphon as having violated the principle that a straight line will never coincide with the circumference of a circle, which is essentially equivalent to the principle Alexander identified him as having violated (cf. Rudio [1907], 107 n. 4; commentary on F13(e), l. 44). The disagreement among Aristotle's commentators concerning the inscribed figure from which Antiphon began his quadrature points toward the same conclusions. Simplicius' words (F13(e), ll. 13–14: ἔστω δὲ εἰ τύχοι τετράγωνον τὸ ἐγγεγραμμένον) leave no doubt that the choice of an inscribed square as the basis for his exposition is entirely his own (cf. Heiberg [1884], 336; Rudio [1907], 27 n. 1, [1902], 12 n. 23). The discrepancy between him and Themistius on this point is most easily explained on the assumption that they depend on a common source that did not specify which inscribed figure Antiphon began from. So Rudio (1907), 105, (1902), 12 n. 23, who rightly rejected the absurd suggestion of Bretschneider (1870), 125 and Cantor (1900–7), 1.190 that Antiphon undertook the quadrature twice – beginning once from a square and the second time from a triangle – in order to assure himself of the correctness of his procedure. (Cantor subsequently retracted this view in later editions of his *Vorlesungen*.) In all likelihood, therefore, the common source of Simplicius and Themistius was Eudemus' *History of Geometry*. This inference is reinforced by the close verbal similarities in their respective reports of the concluding step of the quadrature attempt (cf. commentary on F13(e), ll. 30–31). The wording of Philoponus' report at this point is quite different, which suggests that Simplicius and Themistius shared a source not utilized by Philoponus (cf. Rudio [1907], 104–5, [1902], 13 n. 25). In addition, Philoponus makes several confused or mistaken remarks on mathematics which may indicate either that his source was inferior to that of Simplicius and Themistius, or that he did not follow it very closely, or both (cf. Rudio [1907], 106 nn. 1–2, 107 nn. 1–2, 4; commentary on F13(d), ll. 7–8, 12).

Regrettably, the reports of Aristotle's commentators leave a number of questions about Antiphon's quadrature attempt unanswered. First is the question of the inscribed figure Antiphon began from (cf. above).

Heiberg (1884), 336 argued that Themistius is right about Antiphon's use of a triangle and that Simplicius depended on an incomplete account. Heath (1921), 1.221 took a similar view. But there is no reason to prefer Themistius' account on this point to that of Simplicius. Their common source (most likely Eudemus' *History of Geometry*, as argued above) seems not to have specified which polygonal figure Antiphon began from (so Rudio [1907], 105, who mistakenly attributes this view to Heiberg). This may have been merely an omission on Eudemus' part (Simplicius, *In Aristotelis Physica* 60.29–30 remarks on his concise manner of writing: διὰ τὸν ὑπομνηματικὸν τρόπον τοῦ Εὐδήμου κατὰ τὸ ἀρχαϊκὸν ἔθος συντόμους ἐκθεμένου τὰς ἀποδόσεις). Or perhaps Antiphon himself framed the quadrature attempt in general terms, without specifying a specific polygon. A second problem concerns the geometrical principle (or principles) Aristotle thought the quadrature attempt violated. Here Eudemus is likely to be right: Aristotle probably objected to Antiphon's supposed violation of the principle of infinite divisibility of geometric magnitudes (So Heath [1921], 1.222, [1949], 96; for a different view cf. Hoppe [1911], 116–17.)

Beyond these matters of detail, there remain the broader questions of precisely what Antiphon was trying to accomplish with his quadrature attempt, and how it fitted into the larger argument of Περὶ ἀληθείας as a whole. Aristotle himself dismisses the attempt as merely eristic, and his commentators' claim that Antiphon believed the inscribed polygon would eventually coincide with the circumference of the circle seems to justify such an evaluation. Most modern commentators have taken this claim at face value. In default of first-hand evidence, however, legitimate doubt remains as to whether Antiphon actually claimed or believed this (cf. von Fritz [1955], 93 n. 174). It is at least conceivable that the quadrature attempt was intended rather as an approximation-construction. (Cf. Tannery [1878], 180 = [1912], 47–48; Rudio [1902], 13 n. 26, [1907], 1, 11; Zeuthen [1913], 26–28.) There is no reason, however, to credit Zeuthen's suggestion that Antiphon calculated the areas of the successively obtained inscribed polygons (or his judgment that the value of the quadrature attempt depends on how far such calculations were carried). Even if Aristotle's commentators are right about Antiphon's having believed that the polygon would coincide with the circumference of the circle, it does not follow that he conceived the circle as composed of atomic magnitudes or espoused a theory of mathematical atomism, as many modern commentators have supposed (cf. Allman [1889] 56, 81–82; Tannery [1887], 125; Bignone [1938], 219–20; Nestle [1942], 375 with n. 18; Luria [1933], 127–28; Mondolfo [1956], 256–57; Wicksteed in Wicksteed and Cornford [1957], 100; Untersteiner

[1962], 48, [1954], 236 = [1967], 2.58–59; Knorr [1986], 27–28). It is not impossible that he did so, but the quadrature attempt by itself falls well short of proof (cf. Sorabji [1983], 353). Luria (1933), 128, 141, 183 adduced evidence in support of Antiphon's supposed mathematical atomism from an unpublished Hebrew treatise on the quadrature of the circle by the fifteenth-century Jewish scholar Alphonso. Luria claimed that Antiphon is quoted in this work as speaking of "jene Teilchen, aus welchen sowohl die Gerade wie der Kreisumfang bestehen" – a clear statement of mathematical atomism. Luria, however, did not even attempt to explain where Alphonso derived his supposed quotations of Antiphon from. Another passage cited by Luria seems to indicate that Alphonso was familiar with Simplicius' report. But neither Simplicius nor any other ancient or medieval source (known to me) contains anything like what Luria cited from Alphonso. (Significantly, no source offers any *direct* quotation from the quadrature attempt such as Luria claimed for Alphonso.) It is impossible to take Luria's information seriously as evidence of Antiphon's supposed mathematical atomism.

The place of the quadrature attempt in the argument of Περὶ ἀληθείας as a whole is completely unknown. Nevertheless, commentators have attempted to fit it into their diverse reconstructions of the work. For Bignone (1938), 219–20 and Untersteiner (1962), 48, (1954), 236 = (1967), 2.58–59, it formed part of Antiphon's alleged polemic against (respectively) Protagoras and Gorgias. In complete contradiction to Bignone, Michel (1950), 664–65 and Kerferd (1970), 171 argued (from different viewpoints) that the quadrature attempt proceeded from mathematical assumptions similar to those motivating Protagoras' objection to the geometers (cf. commentary on F1). Aly (1929), 146–47 connected the quadrature attempt with Antiphon's search for the underlying essence of things, Morrison (1963), 45 n. 2, (1972), 212 with the relation of names and things. Romeyer-Dherbey (1985), 100–1 read into it his theory of the ἀρρύθμιστον. No evidence supports any of these conjectures.

Whatever Antiphon sought to accomplish with his quadrature attempt, to dismiss it as merely eristic (as do Aristotle and his commentators, Zeller in Zeller and Nestle [1920], 1372 with n. 3, and Rufini [1926], 30–33) is surely unjustified. On the contrary, as many other commentators have rightly recognized, it constitutes an original and significant contribution to mathematics (cf. Hankel [1874], 116–17; Allman [1889], 81–82; Loria [1914], 94–96; Rudio [1902], 13 n. 34, [1907], 11; Heath [1921], 1.219–20, 222–23, [1931], 140–42, [1949], 96–97; Cherniss [1935], 340; von Fritz [1955], 93 n. 174; Wasserstein [1959], 94). With the quadrature attempt, Antiphon seems to have introduced the idea of exhausting a curvilinear figure by means of an inscribed polygon – a procedure subsequently taken up and developed by Eudoxus of Cnidos in his famous method of exhaustion (cf. Euclid, *Elements* 10. 1; 12. 2, 7, 10, 18). That Antiphon himself originated this idea remains uncertain; but there is at least no evidence that he borrowed it from Hippocrates of Chius or some other professional geometer (as Knorr [1986], 28 suggested). Furthermore, the method of inscribed polygons pioneered by Antiphon has been used to calculate the value of π by mathematicians from Archimedes to François Viète (who acknowledged his debt to Antiphon) and Christiaan Huygens. Cf. Smith (1911), 393–95; Cantor (1900–7), 2.594–95, 716–17; Rudio (1892), 33–35, 37–41. The historical importance of Antiphon's quadrature attempt can be summed up in the words of one modern historian of mathematics: "To *Antiphon*, therefore, we trace one of the earliest steps in the invention of the modern calculus" (Smith [1911], 393). Of course, neither Antiphon nor Aristotle nor any other ancient writer could have known that the squaring of the circle is impossible, or why it is so. The impossibility of the quadrature-construction depends on the fact that π is a transcendental number, that is, a number which is not the solution of an algebraic equation with rational co-efficients of the form $C_0 + C_1x + C_2x^2 + \cdots + C_nx^n = 0$. Such a number "cannot be found by means of the ordinary algebraic operations, and therefore cannot be constructed geometrically by the use of the instruments of elementary geometry" (Smith [1911], 416). The transcendental nature of π, though long suspected, was not finally demonstrated until the late nineteenth century by Lindemann (1882), 213–25. (Cf. Smith [1911]; Klein [1955], 1–12, 49–60, 68–80; Hobson [1913], 47–51 and *passim*; Rudio [1892], 6–8, 61–69.)

F13(a)

2–3 τὸν τετραγωνισμὸν . . . τμημάτων: on the problems raised by the term τμῆμα and on the "quadrature by segments" (probably that of Hippocrates of Chios) cf. Heiberg (1884), 344; Rudio (1907), 22–23; Heath (1921), 1.184–85, 198–99, (1949), 33–34, 94–95; Ross (1936), 463–66.

F13(b)

8 ὁ δὲ Βρύσωνος ἐριστικός: on Bryson's quadrature attempt cf. Heath (1921), 1.223–25, (1949), 47–50; Heiberg (1884) 336–37; Rudio (1907), 108–10; Wasserstein (1959), 95–100; commentary on F13(d).

F13(c)

13–14 τοῦ εἰς τὸν κύκλον ἐγγραφομένου, * ἀπόδειξιν:** cod. Parisinus gr. 1891 (= L) fills in the lacuna here (unsatisfactorily) with a passage inspired by Simplicius, *In Aristotelis Physica* 58.16 (cf. Schenkl's note ad loc.).

16–17 ἕτερον ἰσοσκελὲς συνιστὰς πρὸς τῇ περιφερείᾳ: συνίστασθαι is *vox propria* for constructing, on a given base line, two straight lines that meet to form a triangle. Cf. LSJ, s.v. III.4; Heath (1922), I.259, 289.

F13(d)

4 τέμω δὲ τὰ τμήματα κτλ.: Simplicius' account is more detailed and precise at this point than that of Philoponus (cf. F13(c), ll. 14–18: ἔπειτα ἑκάστην τῶν τοῦ τετραγώνου πλευρῶν . . . τοῦ κύκλου).

7–8 τὰ περιέχοντα τὰς γωνίας τμήματα: πλευράς (sides of the inscribed octagon) might have been expected here instead of γωνίας (cf. Rudio [1907], 106 n. 1, 107 n. 1). But there are no variants.

10–11 ἐπὶ πολύ: for the temporal sense cf. LSJ, s.v. πολύς IV.4b.

12 μικρὰς πάνυ ἔχον τὰς γωνίας: as Rudio (1907), 106 n. 2, 107 n. 2 pointed out, Philoponus' manner of expression is again confused: the polygon has small *sides* but *large* angles. Rudio (1907), 107 with n. 2, 170 (s.v. σμικρός) suggested he meant that the angles are "flat" or "insignificant."

12–13 ἃς αἱ περιέχουσαι εὐθεῖαι . . . τῷ κύκλῳ: Rudio (1907), 107 translated: "die [*sc.* die Ecke] durch die einschliessenden Geraden, da sie sehr klein sind, mit dem Kreise werden zur Deckung gebracht werden." This is not exact, since ἐφαρμόσουσι is intransitive and the subject is αἱ περιέχουσαι εὐθεῖαι.

17–19 ἀρχὴ γάρ . . . περιφερείᾳ: comparison of this passage with Simplicius' account (cf. F13(c), ll. 44–45: ἄμεινον οὖν λέγειν ἀρχὴν εἶναι τὸ ἀδύνατον εἶναι εὐθεῖαν ἐφαρμόσαι περιφερείᾳ) suggests that Philoponus did not know Eudemus' exposition, and that his source may instead have been Alexander. Cf. Rudio (1907), 107 n. 4 and introductory note above.

35ff.: despite Lacey (1993), 20 n. 89, there is no reason to think that the argument Philoponus here ascribes to Antiphon is anything other than a confused reminiscence of Bryson's quadrature attempt. Antiphon's name here is clearly just a mistake (cf. Wasserstein [1959], 96 n. 1). At *In Aristotelis Analytica posteriora* 111.31–112.2, Philoponus reports Ammonius' claim that Proclus criticized Alexander for making the opposite mistake of assimilating Bryson's quadrature to that of Antiphon.

F13(e)

1 πολλῶν ζητούντων: the names of several of Antiphon's contemporaries are connected with the problem of squaring the circle. Anaxagoras is reported by Plutarch (*De exilio* 607F = *FVS* 59 A 38) to have "drawn" a quadrature (cf. Rudio [1907], 91–93; Heath [1921], 1.173; Aly [1929], 143). Against the attempt of Frank (1923), 47–48 with n. 100 to credit Anaxagoras with a quadrature by the method of exhaustion cf. Luria (1933), 111 n. 19. Aristophanes (*Birds* 1001–5) depicts the astronomer Meton effecting a comic "squaring" of the circle (cf. Rudio [1907], 90–91; Knorr [1986], 26; Dunbar [1995], 550–51, 555–58). Proclus (*In Euclidem* 272.7–10, 356.10–12) ascribes the discovery of a quadratrix curve to "Hippias" (cf. Heath [1921], 1.225–30). Although many modern commentators have identified this Hippias with the famous sophist from Elis, the objections to the identification are overwhelming (cf. Cherniss [1977], 116 n. 11, with references; Knorr [1986], 80–83). Therefore it is probably pointless to speculate (as Aly [1929], 146 and others have done) about the relation between the quadratures of Antiphon and Hippias.

3 Ἱπποκράτης ὁ Χῖος: for Hippocrates and his quadratures of lunes cf. Simplicius, *In Aristotelis Physica* 55–69; Rudio (1907); Heath (1921), 1.182–200; Ross (1936), 463–66; Bulmer-Thomas (1972); Knorr (1986), 28–39.

12–14 ἐνέγραψέ τι χωρίον . . . τὸ ἐγγεγραμμένον: cf. introductory note above.

15–16 ἀπὸ τῆς τομῆς: here and in the phrase ἀπο τῆς τομῆς ἐπὶ τὴν περιφέρειαν (ll. 23–24) below, τομή refers to the "point of division" on the side of the inscribed square (cf. Rudio [1907], 176, "Wörterverzeichnis" s.v. τομή). But in the phrase ἀπὸ τῆς τομῆς (ἐπεζεύγνυεν) in l. 18, the same word refers to the "point of intersection" of the arc with the straight lines drawn from the side of the inscribed polygon.

16 ἐπὶ τὰς περιφερείας: for περιφέρεια = "arc" cf. Rudio (1907), 167–68, "Wörterverzeichnis" s.v.; LSJ, s.v. 1.2.

18–19 ἐπὶ τὰ πέρατα τῶν γραμμῶν: πέρατα here are "end-points" (cf. Rudio [1907], 166, "Wörterverzeichnis" s.v.) – a sense not recognized in LSJ.

27–28 κατὰ τὸν αὐτὸν πάλιν λόγον: Rudio (1907), 29 interpreted λόγος here as "Verhältnis" (ratio). But the phrase probably means the same thing as κατὰ τὴν αὐτὴν μέθοδον (ll. 21–22) above, "in the same way" (so Rudio [1902], 13).

29–30 καὶ ἐπιζευγνὺς εὐθείας: *sc.* from the points of intersection on the arcs to the end-points of the sides of the inscribed polygon.

Simplicius here omits the step of drawing straight lines to the arcs from the points of division on the sides of the inscribed polygon (cf. ll. 15–16: ἀπὸ τῆς τομῆς ἐπὶ τὰς περιφερείας πρὸς ὀρθὰς ἦγε γραμμάς; ll. 23–24: ἀπὸ τῆς τομῆς ἐπὶ τὴν περιφέρειαν πρὸς ὀρθὰς ἄγων).

30–31 καὶ τοῦτο ἀεὶ ποιῶν ᾤετο: ποιῶν ὥστε (the reading of all manuscripts) can hardly stand, since the sentence would lack a main verb. Torstrik suggested τοῦτο ἀεὶ ἐποίει; but this leaves the preceding καὶ unmotivated. Usener suspected a lacuna. Diels conjectured (but did not venture to print) ᾤετο. His conjecture was endorsed by Tannery (*apud* Diels [1882], xxvi) and is confirmed (as Rudio [1902], 13 n. 25, [1907], 28 n. 2, 104 pointed out) by the parallel passage in Themistius (F13(c), ll. 17–18: καὶ τοῦτο ἐφεξῆς ποιῶν ᾤετο). The corruptions involved are easy ones in capitals. The close verbal agreement here between Simplicius and Themistius suggests that they follow a common source (most likely Eudemus; cf. introductory note above).

31 ποτέ: it is unclear whether this adverb goes with δαπανωμένου or ἐγγραφήσεσθαι or with the sentence as a whole.

δαπανωμένου τοῦ ἐπιπέδου: this claim is the basis for the charge that Antiphon violated the principle of infinite divisibility of magnitudes (cf. introductory note above). Wasserstein (1959), 93 with n. 1 called attention to the present tense of the participle, translating appropriately "with the progressive exhaustion of the area."

33 διὰ σμικρότητα ἐφαρμόσουσι: this claim is the basis for the charge that Antiphon violated the geometrical "hypothesis" that a circle and a straight line touch at a single point (cf. introductory note above).

35 ἐν τοῖς Στοιχείοις: cf. Euclid, *Elements* 2.4.

36–37 διὰ τὸ ἴσον . . . αὐτῷ: τὸ ὑποκεῖσθαι here is an articular infinitive; τὸ πολύγωνον ἐφαρμόζον αὐτῷ is its accusative subject; ἴσον is a predicate adjective agreeing with τὸ πολύγωνον; and τῷ κύκλῳ is dative after ἴσον: "on account of the fact that the polygon coinciding with it is assumed to be equal to the circle." (ὄν or εἶναι must be supplied in thought with ὑποκεῖσθαι.) So correctly Rudio (1907), 29 (contrast Rudio [1902], 13) and Untersteiner (1962), 51 (who, however, makes "circle" the logical subject). For ὑπόκειμαι = "be assumed," "taken for granted" cf. LSJ, s.v. II.2. The assumption in question is reminiscent of the fourth of Euclid's common notions or axioms (κοιναὶ ἔννοιαι): καὶ τὰ ἐφαρμόζοντα ἐπ' ἄλληλα ἴσα ἀλλήλοις ἐστίν (on the authenticity of this cf. Heath [1922], I.224–25).

39 ἡ συναγωγή: either "conclusion" ("Schlussfolgerung," Rudio [1907], 29) or (less likely) "demonstration" ("Beweisführung," Rudio [1902], 12).

40 οὐχ ὡς ὁ Ἀλέξανδρός φησιν κτλ.: on Simplicius' objection cf. below. Wasserstein (1959), 94–95 argued that Alexander's criticism is irrelevant to a quadrature attempt by means of inscribed polygons alone, since the point of contact between an inscribed polygon and a circle is always a vertex and never a line. He therefore suggested that Antiphon may have employed circumscribed as well as inscribed polygons, since the point of contact between a circle and a circumscribed polygon lies on the polygon's *side*. No evidence supports this hypothesis, which is in fact unnecessary. (On Philoponus, *In Aristotelis Physica* 206.20–25 cf. commentary on F13(d), ll. 35ff.) Alexander's objection is perfectly intelligible as directed against the belief (ascribed to Antiphon by Aristotle's commentators) that an inscribed polygon of sufficiently many sides would coincide with the circumference of a circle. The nature of the contact between a straight line and a circle seems to have been discussed by Democritus in his work entitled Περὶ διαφορῆς γνώμης [γνώμονος Cobet: γωνίας Hicks and Heath] ἢ περὶ ψαύσιος κύκλου καὶ σφαίρης (cf. Diogenes Laertius, 9.47 = *FVS* 68 B 11; Kranz, *FVS* 2.141 n.; Heath [1922], 2.40). Relevant also is Protagoras' objection to the geometers (Aristotle, *Metaphysics* 997b32ff. = *FVS* 80 B 7).

44 ἐν τῷ τρίτῳ βιβλίῳ: τῷ τρίτῳ is Diels' plausible correction for the manuscripts' τῶ ιγ or τῷ ὀγδόῳ. Diels (1882), 55 n. thought that Simplicius was referring to *Elements* 3.16; Rudio (1907), 29 n. 2 cited *Elements* 3.2 as well. The proposition that a circle and a straight line external to it touch at a single point (the proof of which depends in fact on both 3.16 and 3.2) appears in manuscripts of Euclid as a corollary to *Elements* 3.16, where Heiberg omitted it as an addition of Theon's. Simplicius may have read it in his text of Euclid, but not Alexander in his.

ἄμεινον οὖν λέγειν κτλ.: as Tannery (*apud* Diels [1882], XXVI) pointed out, Simplicius is confused here. The principle (ἀρχή) he suggests is simply a more precisely formulated version of the one suggested by Alexander, which he has just criticized. Rudio (1902), 13 n. 31, (1907), 28–30 and Schmidt (1903), 120–21 proposed to rescue Simplicius by altering the text so as to read ἄμεινον οὖν λέγειν ἀρχὴν εἶναι ἀδύνατον τὸ εὐθεῖαν κτλ., with ἀρχήν understood as an adverb: "it is better therefore to say that it is absolutely (ἀρχήν) impossible that a straight line should coincide etc." This requires not one but two textual changes (deletion of the first εἶναι; transposition of τό and ἀδύνατον), and furthermore assumes an awkward repetition of ἀρχήν in a different sense than it bears just above in the phrase ὡς ἀρχήν (l. 42). Worst of all, on Rudio's and Schmidt's interpretation the whole sentence becomes otiose. For after noting that the proposition identified as an assumption by Alexander is in fact proved by Euclid, Simplicius need not have said anything more.

47 κατὰ σημεῖον: Tannery's insertion of ἕν is possible (cf. l. 46 κατὰ ἓν σημεῖον), but hardly necessary (cf. Rudio [1902], 13 n. 32).

F13(f)

This passage derives from the prologue to Eutocius' commentary on Archimedes' *Measurement of the Circle.* As Mansfeld (1998), 46 points out, Eutocius' brief historical overview is appropriate to the context of his discussion of authorial intention in the work.

10 τὴν Εὐδήμου Γεωμετρικὴν ἱστορίαν: on Eudemus' *History of Geometry* as a source of information on Antiphon's quadrature attempt cf. introductory note above.

11 τῶν Ἀριστοτελικῶν μετασχόντας κηρίων: Tannery at one time suggested that this refers to a work of Sporus of Nicea entitled Ἀριστοτέλικα κηρία (κηρία = *electa*; cf. Diels [1882], XXVII). Cf. Eutocius, 3.76.1, 258.25; introductory note above. Heiberg (1884), 345–46, (1910–15), 229 n. 2 more plausibly suggested a metaphorical reference (cf. μετασχόντας) to Aristotle's *Sophistici elenchi* (so also Mansfeld [1998], 46).

F13(g)

Both Michael Psellus and Michael of Ephesus have been suggested as author of the commentary on the *Sophistici elenchi* (falsely ascribed to Alexander) from which this passage derives (cf. Wallies [1898], v with nn. 2–5). More recently, Ebbesen has argued that this commentary, which he designates "Pseudo-Alexander–1," is the latest of several versions of a commentary on the *Sophistici elenchi* by Michael of Ephesus (cf. Ebbesen [1981], 1.268–85, 3.12–63). The fact that the commentator not only confuses Antiphon's quadrature attempt with Hippocrates' quadrature of lunes, but also asserts that Antiphon's attempt preserves the principles of geometry, shows that he had no accurate information about or understanding of it.

F13(h)–(i)

The passage printed here as F13(h) derives from a commentary which Ebbesen designated "Pseudo-Alexander–2" and identified as the earliest version of Michael of Ephesus' commentary on the *Sophistici elenchi* (cf. Ebbesen [1981], 1.268–85, 3.12–63). Ebbesen (1981), 2.235 quoted the passage in his notes on "Alexander" (cf. on F13(k)). Additional excerpts from this commentary are printed in Ebbesen (1981), 2.153–99 and Wallies (1898), XVIII–XXI.

F13(i) is a scholium on *Sophistici elenchi* 171b14–15 that appears in two fourteenth-century manuscripts (cod. gr. 42 of the Bibliotheca Angelica in Rome and cod. Marcianus gr. 203 = 746; cf. Ebbesen [1981], 3.288, 291). The origin of the scholium is uncertain. Ebbesen speculated that it might derive from an independent commentary (now lost) on the *Sophistici elenchi* dating from the thirteenth or fourteenth century, a commentary he designated "Commentarium V." Alternatively, "Commentarium V" may be simply a branch of the "Pseudo-Alexander–2" tradition independent of other extant witnesses. In the latter case, this scholium, differing as it does from both "Pseudo-Alexander–1" (F13(g)) and "Pseudo-Alexander–2" (F13(h)), would derive from another, unknown source. Cf. Ebbesen (1981), 1.290–300, 3.17–18.

Whatever their origins, neither F13(h) nor F13(i) provides any reliable information on Antiphon's quadrature attempt. Both proffer the view (found also in F13(g)) that it is based on geometrical principles, which contradicts Aristotle's express opinion to the contrary.

F13(j)

F13(j) consists of three separate passages. The first two derive from what Ebbesen has identified as a Latin translation of a lost Greek commentary on the *Sophistici elenchi* erroneously ascribed by medieval western scholars to Alexander of Aphrodisias. (The attribution of the third passage is uncertain; cf. below.) The author of the Latin translation, according to Ebbesen, was James of Venice, on whom cf. Minio-Paluello (1972), 164–77, 189–228, 241–49, 565–86 and Ebbesen (1981), 1.286–89. As for the lost Greek original, Ebbesen suggested that it could have been composed in the period 850–1100 and translated by James in the second quarter of the thirteenth century. Alternatively, it may have been fabricated by James himself, who may have collected under the name "Alexander" Greek scholia culled from several different sources. Cf. Ebbesen (1981), 1.286–89. The Latin fragments are collected in Ebbesen (1981), 2.331–538. Whatever the origin and nature of this commentary, it obviously offers no reliable information on Antiphon's quadrature attempt.

1.2–3 ex propriis: for the claim that Antiphon's quadrature attempt respects the principles of geometry cf. F13(g), F13(h), F13(i), all with commentary. On the close affinities between "Alexander" and the several versions of Michael of Ephesus' commentary on the *Sophistici elenchi* cf. Ebbesen (1981), 1.286–88.

3–5 et tamen ... ex communibus: evidently the anonymous author used a manuscript of "Alexander" that had marginal figures illustrating a quadrature attempt. As Ebbesen (1981), 3. 235 noted, it is uncertain whether these figures go back to the Greek original of "Alexander" or are a western addition, and equally uncertain whether they were intended to illustrate Antiphon's quadrature attempt or that of Bryson. (The author himself seems to suppose the former, for he notes that the figures contradict the claim of "Alexander" that Antiphon's quadrature attempt follows the principles of geometry.) The manuscript of the Anonymus Laudianus' commentary (fol. 7 *verso*) itself has two marginal figures here, which may be similar to those the author found in his copy of "Alexander." They are reproduced in Ebbesen (1981), 3.235.

2.8–9 dicit Alexander ... consimiles: Ebbesen (1981), 3.235 confessed that he was unable to cite any Greek text similar to this scholium. But for the comparison between the quadrature attempts of Antiphon and Bryson cf. commentary on F13(d), ll. 35ff.

3.11–13: this scholium was printed by Ebbesen (1981), 2.533 among the doubtful fragments of "Alexander." The identity of the author of the "Glossulae" mentioned is uncertain (cf. Ebbesen [1981], 3.258).

F13(k)

These passages derive from an anonymous paraphrase of the *Sophistici elenchi*, the author of which is probably Sophonias (cf. Hayduck [1884], v; Ebbesen [1981], 2.333 with nn. 1–6). It is obvious that the author had no accurate knowledge of Antiphon's quadrature attempt. Not only does he seem to confuse it with Hippocrates' quadrature of lunes, he also asserts (contradicting Aristotle) that it respects the principles of geometry. His account closely resembles the final version of Michael of Ephesus' commentary on the *Sophistici elenchi* (cf. F13(g) with commentary), which may have been his source (cf. Tarán [1981], 245; Ebbesen [1981], 2.335–39).

9–10 ὁ μέντοι Ἀντιφῶν: codd. M and N read Ἱπποκράτης, which is correct from a factual standpoint. But the parallel passage *In Sophisticos elenchos paraphrasis* 30.36 confirms the reading Ἀντιφῶν (cf. Hayduck's note ad loc.).

F13(l)

This scholium on *Posterior Analytics* 75b40 is preserved in cod. Ambrosianus 490 and was printed by Waitz (1844–46), 1.50. It is remarkable for the fact that Antiphon is designated as "the sophist" (ὁ σοφιστής).

5–7 διὰ τῆς διχοτομίας . . . τῶν πλευρῶν: Sauppe (1896), 520, who first called attention to this text in connection with Antiphon, believed that the scholiast mistakenly attributed to Antiphon a procedure which belongs in fact to Hippocrates. More likely he refers to Antiphon's quadrature attempt in abbreviated fashion by singling out one step in the procedure (cf. F13(e), ll. 14–15: ἑκάστην τῶν τοῦ τετραγώνου πλευρῶν δίχα τέμνων).

F14

The meaning of this fragment is rendered obscure by the lack of context and by uncertainty about the subject of the single sentence which constitutes it. Aly (1929), 141; Nestle (1942), 374–75 with n. 16, and Untersteiner (1962), 51–52, (1954), 239 with nn. 37–39 = (1967), 62 with nn. 37–39 supplied φύσις as subject, understood ἀφορμῆς as "material" or "matter," and interpreted the fragment as an expression of materialism (cf. F15 with commentary). Romeyer-Dherbey (1985), 101 understood the fragment in similar fashion, but with reference to the so-called ἀρρύθμιστον (cf. Introduction, section III; commentary on F10 and F15). These interpretations presuppose that Antiphon used the noun φύσις (which they supply as subject) in the sense of "universal nature." This is of course possible; but it goes against the usage of the papyrus fragments (where φύσις seems to refer to individual human nature or to birth; cf. commentary on F44(a), F44(b), and F15). The really decisive objection to the materialist interpretation, however, is that it seems to saddle Antiphon with patent nonsense. For what are the "many fine things" (πολλὰ καὶ καλά) nature would arrange badly if it were deprived of any matter or material to arrange in the first place? The proposal of Burkert (1964), 144 n. 10 to supply τέχνη as subject is open to the same objection. Other commentators interpret the fragment in terms of psychology or ethics. Supplying γνώμη as subject, Croiset (1883), 149 suggested that the fragment affirms the mind's need for sense-data as the indispensable starting-point (ἀφορμῆς) in the process of cognition. But it is difficult to see what διαθεῖτο might mean in such a context. Momigliano (1969), 136–37 similarly suggested as subject γνώμη, διάνοια, or even διάθεσις (which he inferred from F24A

is equivalent in sense to γνώμη or διάνοια). ἀφορμῆς Momigliano understood as "means of sustenance," without which the human mind (γνώμη, διάνοια, or διάθεσις) would administer many good things badly. Momigliano's interpretation leaves the verb διαθεῖτο (again) without any real explanation. Blass (1889a), 12; Diels (1922), 2.295 n., and Bignone (1938), 93 n. 1 all understood ἀφορμῆς as "material resources" or "capital." (For this sense cf. LSJ, s.v. 3–4.) Blass supposed a political context, suggesting ἡ τῶν στρατηγῶν ἀρχή (*vel sim.*) as subject; Bignone conjectured that Antiphon urged the rich to supply seed-capital to the poor. Joël (1893–1901), 2.672 understood ἀφορμῆς similarly, but interpreted the fragment as an expression of Antiphon's materialistic ethics (which provoked Antisthenes to a defence of the Cynic ideal of *Bedürfnislosigkeit*).

It is easy enough to construct a completely different type of interpretation from the foregoing, one that would situate the fragment in a rhetorical or literary (rather than physical, psychological, or ethical) context. In the language of Antiphon's contemporaries, ἀφορμή often designates the factual basis of a discourse, a speaker's "brief" or "case." Cf. Euripides, *Heracles* 236–37, *Hecuba* 1239, *Phoenissae* 199, *Bacchae* 266–67; Antiphanes, fr. 256; Anaximenes, *Ars rhetorica* 2.3, 38.2; Dodds (1960), 103; Bond (1981), 125. Cf. also the work entitled Ἀφορμαὶ ῥητορικαί ascribed to Thrasymachus (*FVS* 85 A 1 = *AS* B IX 1). διαθεῖτο could refer to the recitation or delivery of a discourse (cf. LSJ, s.v. B.6); or alternatively perhaps to its arrangement or composition (cf. Harpocration, s.v. διάθεσις, δ 42; Plutarch, *Lucullus* 1: ὡς συνταξομένῳ καὶ διαθήσοντι τὴν ἱστορίαν ἄμεινον; F63 with commentary). The sense of the fragment might then be that a successful speech or discourse needs a well-conceived "brief" or subject-matter. In addition to its technical rhetorical sense, however, ἀφορμή can signify a basis or starting-point in a wide variety of different contexts. Cf. Euripides, *Ion* 474; Andocides, *or.* 1.109; [Hippocrates], *De affectionibus interioribus* 51; Aristotle, *De caelo* 292a15–16; Demosthenes, *or.* 1.23, 2.22; Eusebius, *Praeparatio evangelica* 14.19.8 = Metrodorus of Chios, *FVS* 70 B 1; Wilamowitz (1895), 2.60–61; Sandys (1897), 150. In view of the lack of context and other difficulties presented by the fragment, interpretation is likely to remain guesswork.

F15

At the beginning of the second book of the *Physics*, Aristotle defines nature (φύσις) as the principle of motion and rest in those things in which it is essentially and primarily, not accidentally, present (cf. *Physics*

192b8ff.). He then reports the view of certain thinkers who (he claims) identify the nature of naturally existing objects with the matter of which they are made (*Physics* 193a9–28 = F15(b)).[4] He cites Antiphon as adducing in support of this view the argument that if one were to bury a bed and the rotting wood were to send up a shoot, the shoot would not be a bed but wood. In the same way, Aristotle continues, if wood and bronze stand in a similar relationship (respectively) to earth and water as a bed and a statue do to wood and bronze, then earth and water will be the nature (respectively) of wood and bronze. For this reason, Aristotle adds, some people identify one or more of the four elements fire, earth, air, and water as the nature and substance of existing things. (Aristotle has in mind the Presocratics generally; cf. Simplicius, *In Aristotelis Physica* 274.21–25 = F15(f), ll. 30–35.) In response to such views, Aristotle offers three arguments designed to show that the nature of naturally existing objects should be identified with their form more than with their matter (cf. *Physics* 193a30–b18; Cherniss [1935], 242–46). First, that which is only potentially flesh or bone does not have its "nature" until it receives the form by which it is defined (and a thing is more properly said to be what it is when it exists actually than when it exists only potentially). Secondly, the fact that a man is born from a man demonstrates (along the lines of Antiphon's own argument, which is here alluded to) that form is nature also. Thirdly, things attain their nature by a process of growth, which progresses towards the form. Aristotle offers a very similar account of the use of φύσις to designate the matter of naturally existing objects in *Metaphysics* 1014b26–35 (= F15(b)). Cf. Ross (1924), 1.296.

Although the main outlines of Aristotle's argument in *Physics* 193a9–28 are plain enough, several problems of detail stand in need of clarification. The first is the meaning of the term πρῶτον in the summary statement of the materialist conception of nature, τὸ πρῶτον ἐνυπάρχον ἑκάστῳ, ἀρρύθμιστον ⟨ὂν⟩ καθ' ἑαυτό (*Physics* 193a10–11 = F15(b), ll. 2–3). Simplicius, *In Aristotelis Physica* 273.20–34 saw here a reference to prime matter, the absolutely formless (καθ' αὑτὸ ἀρρύθμιστον) substrate of the simple bodies earth, air, fire, and water. And in his commentary on the *Metaphysics*, Alexander interpreted the words πρώτου ἐνυπάρχοντος in the parallel passage *Metaphysics* 1014b17–18 in the same way (cf. F15(c), ll. 5–7). But Alexander's inter-

[4] On the basis of this and similar passages, John Burnet argued that the Presocratics employed φύσις to designate the various primary substances of which they conceived all things to be made. Cf. Burnet (1930), 10–12, 363–64; Lovejoy (1909). His argument was refuted by Heidel (1910) = (1980), 79–133 and Beardslee (1918), 65–67, 93–95, 100–1.

pretation of the *Metaphysics* passage is most likely mistaken (cf. Ross [1924], 1.296); and Simplicius' interpretation should be rejected as well. In the first place, it does not accord with the immediately following examples of bronze and wood as the nature (respectively) of a statue and a bed. Furthermore, in *Metaphysics* 1069a27–28 Aristotle argues that the ancients (that is, the Presocratics) did not regard individual things like fire and earth (τὰ καθ' ἕκαστα) as substance (οὐσία), but body in general. Cf. Hamelin (1931), 44; Ross (1936), 502; Wagner (1972), 449–50. The real meaning of πρῶτον appears clearly from *Metaphysics* 1015a7–10 (the relevance of which is misunderstood by Ross [1936], 502): φύσις δὲ ἥ τε πρώτη ὕλη (καὶ αὕτη διχῶς, ἢ ἡ πρὸς αὐτὸ πρώτη ἢ ἡ ὅλως πρώτη, οἷον τῶν χαλκῶν ἔργων πρὸς αὐτὰ μὲν πρῶτος ὁ χαλκός, ὅλως δ' ἴσως ὕδωρ, εἰ πάντα τὰ τηκτὰ ὕδωρ) κτλ. In this passage, the πρώτη ὕλη of bronze implements is said to be *either* their immediate constituent (bronze) *or* bronze's immediate constituent (water); prime matter does not appear at all. The argument in the *Physics* proceeds in the same way, from bronze and wood as the nature (respectively) of statue and bed to the simple bodies earth, air, fire, and water. πρῶτον, then, should be understood in the sense of "proximate" (so Ross and Hamelin; cf. Philoponus, *In Aristotelis Physica* 212.5–10).

A second difficulty involves Aristotle's use of artifacts like bed and statue as examples in a discussion of the nature and essence of *naturally* existing entities. Precisely the same difficulty arises in the parallel passage *Metaphysics* 1014b26–35 (= F15(c)). There, the scribe of cod. Laurentianus 87.12 resolved the difficulty by reading τῶν μὴ φύσει ὄντων at 1014b27 – doubtless by conjecture (cf. Ross [1924], 1.297). Jaeger proposed to get round the difficulty in the *Metaphysics* passage by construing τῶν φύσει ὄντων with ἐξ οὗ πρώτου rather than with τι (cf. his critical apparatus ad loc.). But the construction is very strained, and the problem would still remain in the *Physics* passage. It is true that Aristotle sometimes uses the term φύσις more broadly to signify the "essential character" of things other than natural entities in the strict sense. Cf. *Politics* 1252b32 (of a house); *Poetics* 1449a15 (of tragedy); *Physics* 218a31 (of time). The reason for this is given at *Metaphysics* 1015a11–13: μεταφορᾷ δ' ἤδη καὶ ὅλως πᾶσα οὐσία φύσις λέγεται διὰ ταύτην, ὅτι καὶ ἡ φύσις οὐσία τίς ἐστιν. Cf. Bonitz (1870), 838a43ff.; Beardslee (1918), 102. Moreover, Aristotle often uses artifacts to illustrate the distinction between form and matter (cf. Waterlow [1982], 71–72). Nevertheless, "bed" is used immediately prior to the passage under discussion as an example of a *non-natural* object (cf. *Physics* 192b16ff.); and so its appearance soon after in a discussion of naturally existing entities is (to say the least) surprising. Ross (1936), 502–3, (1924), 1.297

contended that bed and statue qualify as examples of natural entities (φύσει ὄντα) – *qua* wood and bronze. (Cf. *Physics* 192b17–20 with Simplicius, *In Aristotelis Physica* 265.26–30.) This may be right, but is really irrelevant to the discussion in *Physics* 193a9ff. Untersteiner (1962), 54, (1954), 239 n. 43 = (1967), 62 n. 43 suggested that Aristotle has reproduced Antiphon's own terminology, employing τὰ φύσει ὄντα in the sense of what Untersteiner called "experiences." But there is no evidence whatsoever for such a sense (here or elsewhere). Georgiadis (1984), 108 contended that the phrase τὰ φύσει ὄντα designates things "whose existence is anchored in *physis* in the ontological sense" of "essential reality," rather than entities possessing an internal source of movement and rest (as ordinarily in Aristotle). Georgiadis failed to explain what sort of things these are; and his interpretation ignores the plain meaning of the Aristotelian technical terminology (cf. commentary on F15(b), l. 1). The whole problem would be avoided if οἷον (F15(b), l. 3) could be interpreted as introducing comparisons or analogies rather than examples, as Wagner (1972), 450 and Wicksteed (in Wicksteed and Cornford [1957], 111) seemed to interpret, and as Bonitz interpreted οἷον in the parallel passage *Metaphysics* 1014b29 (= F15(b)). Cf. Bonitz (1849), 2.229 ("Quum autem rerum naturalium, τῶν φύσει ὄντων, elementa φύσιν appellari dicat, res per artem effectas ἀνδριάντα, σκεύη etc. modo comparationis loco ad notionem illustrandam adhibet"); Bonitz (1870), 501b55–502a1. In the *Metaphysics* passage, this interpretation might be right (n.b. τοῦτον γὰρ τὸν τρόπον καὶ τῶν φύσει ὄντων τὰ στοιχεῖά φασιν εἶναι φύσιν κτλ.). In the case of the *Physics*, however, it would upset the logical articulation of the whole passage. For example, F15(b), ll. 4–13 (the report of Antiphon's views) would then have to be understood as merely explicating the analogy rather than expounding the main idea (the identification of nature with matter).[5] Bonitz's inter-

[5] Thomas Aquinas seems to have interpreted οἷον as introducing a comparison, and furthermore to have supposed that Antiphon himself argued by analogy from the case of artificial objects to that of naturally existing entities. Cf. Aquinas, *In Physica expositio* 149 [1], 78–79. The ancient physical philosophers whose opinions Aristotle reports, Thomas explains, had not yet conceived of prime matter. Instead, they posited some sensible body as the material substrate of things and thought that natural forms supervene on matter as on something already actually existing, precisely as artificial forms do ("omnes formae advenirent materiae tanquam in actu existenti, ut contingit in artificialibus"). In this way, they treated natural and artificial forms similarly ("similem opinionem accipiebant de formis naturalibus, sicut de formis artificialibus").

pretation of οἷον in the *Metaphysics* passage could be adopted and the exposition in *Physics* 193a9–28 explained as a confused abridgment of the discussion in the *Metaphysics*. Bonitz (1849), 2.230–31 himself, however, offered convincing arguments for the reverse conclusion on the relative merits of the two passages. Ross (1936), 502–3 seems right to reject the interpretation of οἷον in the *Physics* passage as introducing comparisons or analogies. Guthrie (1946), 70–72 argued that bed and statue are Antiphon's own examples, retained by Aristotle in order to show up the confusion inherent in Antiphon's use of artifacts in a discussion of the meaning of nature (φύσις). The bed is unquestionably Antiphon's example; the statue is another matter (cf. below). But Guthrie's diagnosis of fallacy in Antiphon's argument is misguided. Guthrie maintained that if a bed was to be considered *qua* natural object, then the fact of its being a bed should have been ignored and the argument amended so as to run: "if one were to bury a *piece of wood*, and it took root and grew, what came up would be wood." Reformulated in this fashion, Guthrie concluded, the argument would demonstrate Aristotle's contention that form is nature rather than Antiphon's claim that matter is nature. But there is no reason to think that Antiphon used bed as an example of a "natural object" in anything like Aristotle's sense of the term. Guthrie's argument ignores the likelihood that Antiphon did not conceive "nature" as Aristotle does nor restrict the term φύσις to the case of "naturally existing entities" as Aristotle defines them. If he did not, then there need be no fallacy in his use of an artifact in an argument about φύσις. Guthrie's interpretation is open to the further objection that Aristotle would hardly have retained what he regarded as confused or erroneous examples without signaling more clearly his purpose in doing so. (For a different criticism of Guthrie cf. Georgiadis [1984], 110–13.) Romeyer-Dherbey (1985), 98–99 suggested that Antiphon used the example of a bed because the form of a fabricated object is even more "weak and fleeting" than that of a natural one. Even if this were right, it would not touch the problem of why Aristotle retains Antiphon's example. The curious appearance of bed and statue as examples in the context of a debate about naturally existing entities was probably occasioned by the dialectical imperatives of Aristotle's own argument. For his discussion of the meaning of "nature" in *Physics* 193a9–b18, Aristotle required partisans of the view that matter is nature. He claimed to find these in the Presocratics generally and Antiphon in particular. Desiring to cite Antiphon's argument about the buried bed as proof that some people identify nature with matter, Aristotle was led to introduce the example of the bed into a discussion where it does not in strict logic belong.

A third difficulty raised by the passage concerns the precise extent or scope of the report of Antiphon's views. Aristotle's citation of Antiphon begins with a ὅτι-clause reporting a conditional sentence, the apodosis of which is expressed in the accusative and infinitive construction of indirect discourse (F15(b), ll. 4–6: σημεῖον δέ φησιν ... ἀλλὰ ξύλον; cf. commentary ad loc.). Appended to this are antithetical μέν- and δέ-clauses which offer an explanation of why the buried bed would produce wood (and not another bed) in terms of a distinction between accidental and essential properties (F15(b), ll. 6–9: ὡς τὸ μὲν ... πάσχουσα συνεχῶς). This much at least is ascribed to Antiphon (explicitly or otherwise) by all modern commentators. But Sauppe (1896), 515–16 thought that the report of Antiphon's views extended further, to include the following sentence as well (F15(b), ll. 9–13: εἰ δὲ καὶ ... αὐτῶν). Untersteiner (1967), 56–57 considered this "certainly possible," and Cherniss (1935), 242–43 treated the whole passage F15(b), ll. 4–13 as a unified argument of Antiphon's (cf. Ross [1936], 349). Like the preceding sentence, F15(b), ll. 9–13 is cast in the form of a condition, with the apodosis in the accusative and infinitive construction of indirect discourse. If the indirect statement here depends on φησιν in F15(b), l. 4, then there can be no doubt but that this sentence continues the report of Antiphon's views. But if it depends instead on δοκεῖ in F15(b), l. 1 (as Cornford in Wicksteed and Cornford [1957], 111 n. *c* construed), then the decision is uncertain. If grammar is unable to settle the question, consideration of the contents suggests that F15(b), ll. 9–13 does *not* report the views of Antiphon. In this passage, the reasoning applied previously to the relation between bed and statue and their immediate material constituents (wood and bronze) is applied in turn to the relation between bronze and gold, bones and wood and their material constituents (water and earth). Gold and bones make their first appearance in the argument here, and the identification of water and earth as their material constituents seems to depend on Plato's *Timaeus* (cf. commentary ad loc.). These facts suggest that F15(b), ll. 9–13 represents Aristotle's own development of the materialist thesis. The suggestion receives support from the observation that Antiphon's whole argument depends essentially on the behavior of the bed when buried – that is, on the notion of spontaneous growth (cf. below). It is difficult to see how the reasoning that underlies the example of the buried bed could be extended to the case of a statue, or of bronze, or gold, or bones. It is much more likely that these are Aristotle's own examples, introduced for the purpose of generalizing the materialist thesis he extracts from Antiphon's argument about the buried bed. Furthermore, it is significant (and hardly accidental) that the argument of F15(b), ll. 9–13 forms an essential bridge between the materialist view articulated in F15(b), ll. 1–4, and the somewhat different position outlined in F15(b), ll. 13–20. In the former passage, the nature of entities is identified with their *proximate* material constituent; in the latter, the simple bodies earth, air, fire, and water are said to constitute the nature of entities and "the whole of substance." The argument of F15(b), ll. 9–13 paves the way for the latter position, proceeding down the chain of material constituents from wood, bronze, and gold to the simple bodies earth and water. Waterlow (1982), 56–58 recognized this transitional function of F15(b), ll. 9–13, but contended that the argument of the passage fails in its purpose, since it leads to the conclusion that the simple bodies do not themselves have a nature (for they are not composed of anything) and so cannot be the nature and substance of everything else. The obvious solution to the difficulty raised by Waterlow is the concept of prime matter, the absolutely formless material substrate of the simple bodies. Following Charlton (1970), 78–79, 129–145 and others, however, Waterlow (1982), 55 n. 7 banished the notion of prime matter from the *Physics*. In any case, Waterlow greatly exaggerated the incompatibility between the distinct yet obviously related materialist positions articulated (respectively) in F15(b), ll. 1–4 and ll. 13–20. It was to bind them together that Aristotle (not Antiphon) constructed the argument of F15(b), ll. 9–13.

According to Aristotle and his commentators, the example of the buried bed was intended to show that the nature of entities should be identified with their matter. Aristotle's interpretation has been accepted by Nestle (1942), 374–75; Untersteiner (1954), 239–40 with nn. 45, 47 = (1967), 2.62 with nn. 45, 47, and many other commentators. Nevertheless, there are reasons to believe that it may mistake the original import of Antiphon's reasoning. In the first place, Aristotle's general claim that the Presocratics (Antiphon included) identified nature with matter should be treated with caution. As Cherniss (1935), 243–45, 359–61 long ago pointed out, this claim is only the logical consequence of Aristotle's own doctrine that nature may be identified with either the material or formal causes (cf. *Physics* 193a28–31, 194a12ff., 199a30–31; *De partibus animalium* 640a30–32, 640b28, 641a25–32; Mansion [1945], 101–3, 105; Beardslee [1918], 103–4) taken together with his firm belief that the Presocratics in general recognized only the material cause and material principles (cf. *Metaphysics* 983b6–984a16, 988a18–32; Cherniss [1935], 218–46, 359–61). If the Presocratics recognized only material causes, then they must have identified nature with matter – precisely as Antiphon is claimed to have done. In the second place, the reasoning imputed to Antiphon in F15(b), ll. 6–9 may be suspected of distorting his views in the direction of Aristotle's own philosophical concepts and categories. For despite the appearance of individual terms which can be linked more or less plausibly with Antiphon (νόμος, διάθεσις, τέχνη; cf. below and commentary on F15(b), l. 7), the controlling concepts and terminology of the passage are indubitably Aristotelian. These are: the opposition of essence and accident (F15(b), ll. 6–8: κατὰ συμβεβηκός ... τὴν δ' οὐσίαν); and the conception of wood as a material substrate of alteration persisting through change (F15(b), ll. 8–9: ἣ καὶ διαμένει ταῦτα πάσχουσα συνεχῶς; cf. ll. 17–18: τὰ δὲ ἄλλα πάντα ... διαθέσεις). The latter is only one example of Aristotle's persistent tendency to identify the material principles of the Presocratics with his own prime matter and interpret them as substrates of alteration. (Cf. *Metaphysics* 983b9–10, 17–18, 1014b26–27, 31–32; Cherniss [1935], 53ff., 219–20, 370–72.) The net result of Aristotle's interpretation is to read into Antiphon's argument a clearer distinction between form and matter, substrate and attribute than is plausible to ascribe to any Presocratic. This is unwittingly revealed by the anachronistic conclusions of commentators such as Stenzel (1924), 39 and Aly (1929), 141. The former inferred from Antiphon's argument in its Aristotelian guise that discussion of the problem of form and matter must have begun at a very early date ("recht früh schon eine Diskussion des Form-Stoffproblems eingesetzt haben muss") – a discussion hardly conceivable before Plato. The latter concluded that Antiphon's views on the nature of the bed are closely related to Aristotle's own doctrine of essence or formal cause ("in engster Verbindung mit dem Aristotelischen Substanzbegriff des τὸ τί ἦν εἶναι"). (Against Aly's interpretation cf. Untersteiner [1954], 240 n. 47 = [1967], 2.62 n. 47.)

There is no good reason to ascribe to Antiphon more than is immediately entailed by the example of the buried bed (cf. Lacey [1993], 21 n. 100). The chief point of his thought-experiment (as Wiesner [1994], 241 aptly called it) is the distinction and contrast drawn between the bed's nature (φύσις), which is wood, and its conventional arrangement as a bed (διάθεσις κατὰ νόμον). The example of the buried bed illustrates in graphic terms the opposition of φύσις and νόμος, nature and convention, the essential and the adventitious. So Dümmler (1889), 84–85; Diels (1917), 84–85; Bignone (1938), 72, 125–26; Stenzel (1924), 39; Wiesner (1994), 241. The papyrus fragments of Περὶ ἀληθείας offer several suggestive parallels to the line of reasoning embodied in the buried-bed argument. In F44(a)I.25, for example, law and convention are said to be "added" or "imposed" (ἐπίθετα) upon nature, much as the bed's disposition or arrangement is imposed upon the wood (cf. Stenzel [1924], 39; Bignone [1938], 125 n. 2). And in F44(a)I.23–34, nature is characterized as "grown" (φύντα) and contrasted in this respect with law and convention, which are the product of agreement rather than of growth (ὁμολογηθέντα, οὐ φύντα). This emphasis on growth or spontaneity accords closely with the reasoning underlying the buried-bed argument, which identifies φύσις with what grows naturally or spontaneously (the wood), in contrast to the arrangement which is imposed by human convention (κατὰ νόμον) and is accidental (κατὰ συμβεβηκός, in Aristotle's terminology) rather than spontaneous and organic. As Cherniss (1977), 115 n. 10 pointed out, Antiphon's treatment of *growth* as the characteristic indication of φύσις (in contrast to νόμος) finds a close parallel in the Hippocratic *De arte* 2 (τὰ μὲν γὰρ ὀνόματα φύσεως νομοθετήματά ἐστιν, τὰ δὲ εἴδεα οὐ νομοθετήματα, ἀλλὰ βλαστήματα). It is reasonable to assume that the example of the buried bed was intended to demonstrate the superiority of φύσις, with its dynamic and spontaneous character, to human convention (νόμος) and art (τέχνη). (The antithesis of τέχνη and φύσις is not attested elsewhere in the fragments; but cf. [Hippocrates], *De arte* 13, *De victu* 1.6; Antiphon the poet, fr. 4; Beardslee [1918], 70, 98–99; Heinimann [1945], 105 with n. 48; Shorey [1909], 185–201 = [1980], 1.2–18.) This interpretation has the advantage of avoiding the anachronism involved in Aristotle's reading. Furthermore, it places Antiphon's argument squarely in the context of the fifth-century debate on the relative merits of nature and convention (which the papyrus fragments show to have been an important theme of Περὶ ἀληθείας). A variant of this interpretation was defended by Wagner (1972), 450 and Georgiadis (1984), who identified nature with "reality:" what is real in the bed is the wood. This is undoubtedly a common connotation of φύσις in fifth-century literature (cf. Beardslee [1918], 68–70; Heinimann [1945], 92–95, 106–9). It is not certainly attested for Antiphon, however, since F44(a)II.54–56 falls short of proving that he identified φύσις and ἀλήθεια, nature and reality (cf. commentary ad loc.). If the buried-bed argument is understood along the lines suggested, it is not hard to see how Aristotle, from the standpoint of his own concerns, concepts, and terminology, could have reinterpreted Antiphon's opposition of nature and conventional arrangement as a distinction between form and matter. In doing so, he imports into Antiphon's argument not only the identification of nature with matter he attributes to the Presocratics generally, but also one of the central doctrines of his own philosophy.

What further import (if any) the buried-bed argument may have had in the scheme of Περὶ ἀληθείας is uncertain. Morrison (1963), 44–45, (1972), 212 and Aly (1929), 141–42, 146–47 connected it (respectively) with the problem of names and the search for the underlying essence of things. But there is no more support for these commentators' interpretations here than anywhere else (cf. Introduction, section III; commentary on F1 and F13). Romeyer-Dherbey (1985), 96–105 turned the buried-bed argument into an opposition between shape or figure (ῥυθμός) and the metaphysical entity he called the ἀρρύθμιστον or that which is "free from structure." Romeyer-Dherbey made this entity (which he compared to Anaximander's ἄπειρον) the cornerstone of Antiphon's whole philosophy and interpreted in its light many fragments from Περὶ ὁμονοίας as well from Περὶ ἀληθείας. Romeyer-Dherbey's theory of the ἀρρύθμιστον (for which he seems indebted to Heidegger) goes far beyond the evidence, however, and involves him in many forced and implausible interpretations of individual fragments. (It is indicative of the character of his exposition that Romeyer-Dherbey [1985], 114 with n. 104 took [Hippocrates], *De arte* 2 as a verbatim fragment of Antiphon; cf. commentary on F1.)

F15(a)

Harpocration's quotation evidently derives from the protasis of a future-less-vivid condition, a mode of expression reflected in Aristotle's paraphrase (cf. F15(a), ll. 4–6: εἴ τις κατορύξειε κλίνην καὶ λάβοι ... οὐκ ἂν γενέσθαι). Sauppe (1896), 515 offered a reconstruction of Antiphon's original wording based on Harpocration's quotation, Aristotle's paraphrase, and several passages from Theophrastus' *De causis plantarum* (1.3.3; 5.4.5): εἴ τις κατορύξειε κλίνην καὶ ἡ σηπεδὼν τοῦ ξύλου ἔμβιος γένοιτο, οὐκ ἂν γένοιτο κλίνη ἀλλὰ ξύλον. Diels and Kranz as well as Untersteiner ventured (without justification) to print this as though it were Antiphon's.

1 ἡ σηπεδών: cf. commentary on F15(b).

2 ἔμβιος γένοιτο: this could mean simply "become alive." But the same phrase means "germinate" in Theophrastus, *De causis plantarum* 5.4.5 (λέγω δὲ λανθανούσης, εἰ ἐπιπέσοι σπέρμα καὶ ἔμβιον γένοιτο σῆψιν ἔχοντος γεώδη τινὰ τοῦ δένδρου); and that is probably the sense here as well (so LSJ, s.v. ἔμβιος I.1).

F15(b)

1 ἡ φύσις καὶ ἡ οὐσία: "nature" and "essence" are synonymous, and the καί explicative (cf. Mansion [1945], 102 n. 22; Wagner [1972], 449; Georgiadis [1984], 108). This reflects standard Aristotelian doctrine (cf. *Metaphysics* 1014b35ff. with Cherniss [1935], 243 n. 114; *Metaphysics* 983a27, 1017b21–22, 25–26 with Mansion [1945], 102 with n. 23). According to Georgiadis (1984), 108, φύσις here denotes essential reality (οὐσία) rather than an internal principle of movement and rest (the regular Aristotelian technical sense). But the distinction is illusory, for there is no difference between these (cf. *Metaphysics* 1015a17–19 with Ross [1924], 1.298; Simplicius, *In Aristotelis Physica* 273.15–17; Philoponus, *In Aristotelis Physica* 212.10–27).

ἐνίοις: this could be a genuine plural referring to Antiphon and others; or a so-called allusive plural referring to Antiphon alone. (On the allusive plural in Aristotle cf. Cherniss [1977], 427 n. 2.)

2–3 τὸ πρῶτον ἐνυπάρχον ἑκάστῳ, ἀρρύθμιστον ⟨ὂν⟩ καθ' ἑαυτό: that is, their proximate material constituent or matter. Cf. *Physics* 193a29 (ἡ πρώτη ἑκάστῳ ὑποκειμένη ὕλη) and introductory note above. With ἀρρύθμιστον may be compared the atomists' use of ῥυσμός in the sense of "shape" (cf. Aristotle, *Metaphysics* 985b16ff. and other passages collected in *FVS* 67 A 6). Ross' insertion of ⟨ὂν⟩ is supported by grammar as well as by ἀρρυθμίστου ὄντος in the parallel passage *Metaphysics* 1014b27–28 (= F15(b)); cf. Ross (1936), 502. The omission is easily explained (haplography).

3–4 οἷον . . . χαλκός: cf. introductory note above.

4 σημεῖον δέ φησιν κτλ.: ὅτι = "the fact that," and εἶναι must be supplied in thought after φησιν. For the construction cf. *Physics* 221b5; *Posterior Analytics* 74b18; *Historia animalium* 570b28; *Meteorology* 372b28; Bonitz (1870), 677b17ff. The accusative and infinitive construction in the apodosis (οὐκ ἂν γενέσθαι κτλ.) is probably due to confusion induced by φησιν. Cf. Ross (1936), 481 (on *Physics* 187a7), with the reference to Kühner–Gerth 2.357–58, Anmerkung 3.

5 ἡ σηπεδών: for putrefaction as a condition of generation cf. [Hippocrates], *De carnibus* 3; Plato, *Phaedo* 96B with Burnet (1911), 100–1; Aristotle, *Historia animalium* 556b25–26; Theophrastus, *De causis plantarum* 5.4.5–6; Dümmler (1889), 230; Ross (1936), 503. Despite Nestle (1942), 375 with n. 19, there is no reason at all to credit Antiphon with the theory that living beings first arose from mud (cf. Democritus, *FVS* 68 A 139, B 5; Empedocles, *FVS* 31 B 81; Diogenes Laertius, 9.32).

ἀνεῖναι: ἀφεῖναι was read by Themistius (cf. F15(d), l. 6) and is offered by several manuscripts of Simplicius (cf. the critical apparatus to F15(f), l. 6). But ἀνεῖναι (the reading of all manuscripts of the *Physics*) is preferable. The phenomenon of spontaneously sprouting pieces of wood (τὰ αὐτόματα διαβλαστάνοντα ξύλα) is discussed in Theophrastus, *De causis plantarum* 1.1.3, 5.4.3, *Historia plantarum* 2.1.2. Although it is regarded by some as a portent and a marvel (Theophrastus explains), the phenomenon is susceptible of rational explanation. Owing to their density (πυκνότης), certain types of wood such as ἐλαία, μύρρινος, and κότινος (cf. Einarson and Link [1990], 42 n. 1) retain their moisture (ὑγρότης) and vital principle (ζωτικὴ ἀρχή) even after they have been cut. As a result, they sprout readily whenever they are able to obtain some external moisture (ἔξωθεν ἰκμάς), for example when they are buried (κατορυττόμενα). Diels (1917), 84 n. 5 offered a modern scientific explanation.

6–9 ὡς τὸ μὲν . . . συνεχῶς: ὑπάρχον and οὖσαν are most likely circumstantial participles agreeing with κλίνην and ξύλον (respectively), but attracted into the genders of τὸ μέν and τὴν δ' οὐσίαν (respectively). ὡς is adverbial. Philoponus (F15(e), ll. 17–18) paraphrases the passage with a genitive absolute. On the content cf. introductory note above.

7 τὴν κατὰ νόμον διάθεσιν: for νόμον Themistius (F15(d), ll. 8–9) read ῥυθμόν, a variant known also to Philoponus (cf. *In Aristotelis Physica* 213.6–8) and Simplicius (cf. *In Aristotelis Physica* 275.3–5). It is not attested in the direct tradition, and was probably suggested by ἀρρύθμιστον. Both Simplicius (F15(f), ll. 8–10) and Philoponus (*In Aristotelis Physica* 213.6, 9–11) explain νόμον in terms of the "norms" or "conventions" of the art or craft of carpentry. Diels (1917), 85 and Wiesner (1994), 241 contended, probably rightly, that this incidental mention of νόμος in the context of a discussion about the meaning of φύσις points toward a borrowing from Antiphon. It is less certain whether Antiphon's use of the term διάθεσις (cf. F14, F24A, F63, with commentary) has any connection with its appearance here.

7–8 καὶ τὴν τέχνην: these words are usually taken in parallel with νόμον, in dependence on κατά: "the arrangement in accordance with convention and art." So Untersteiner (1962), 55–56; Romeyer-Dherbey (1985), 98; Georgiadis (1984), 108, and others. But the word-order is odd, and the article (τήν) unexpected. It is tempting to construe them instead as parallel to διάθεσιν. So (apparently) Morrison (1972), 217, who translated "craftsmanship." This sense, or better "artistic form," is not attested for τέχνη in lexica. But it seems to be implied by Simplicius, *In Aristotelis Physica* 276.9–10 (θαυμαστὴν γὰρ τέχνην τοῦ ἀνδριάντος τὴν μορφὴν αὐτοῦ λέγομεν) as well as by Philoponus, *In Aristotelis Physica* 209.5–6 (ἀλλ' ὅταν ἀπολάβῃ τὸ τῆς κλίνης εἶδος, τότε λέγεται ἔχειν τὴν τῆς κλίνης τέχνην). Charlton (1970), 24 and Georgiadis (1984), 108 both translated "artistry."

10–12 οἷον ὁ μὲν χαλκὸς . . . ὁτιοῦν: for the derivation of bronze and gold from water, and bones from earth, cf. Plato, *Timaeus* 59B–C, 64C, 73E (cf. introductory note above). As Ross (1936), 503 pointed out, Aristotle's own view is that whatever can be solidified and melted is made of water, or of water and earth (cf. *Meteorology* 382b31).

13–20 διόπερ . . . ἀπειράκις: Aristotle has in mind the Presocratics generally. Simplicius in his commentary on the passage (F15(f), ll. 32–35) mentions Thales, Anaximenes, Heraclitus, Parmenides, and Empedocles. (For yet others who may be intended cf. Ross [1936], 503.) The remark about earth (cf. *Metaphysics* 1014b33 = F15(b)) is puzzling, since Aristotle elsewhere denies that any of the material monists posited earth as principle (though he describes this as a popular view which was held also by Hesiod). Cf. *Metaphysics* 989a5ff., *De anima* 405b8; Cherniss (1935), 29 with n. 50. Mansfeld (1987), 294 = (1990b), 155 suggested that earth's appearance here (and presumably also in *Metaphysics* 1014b33, which he does not mention) is "an involuntary echo of a pre-Aristotelian list of monists," which presented Xenophanes as a proponent of earth as principle and which is the ultimate source of the later doxographical tradition on this issue (cf. *FVS* 21 A 36; Mansfeld [1987], 289–94 = [1990b], 150–55). Simplicius (F15(f), ll. 35–36) offers a different, and simpler, explanation: γῆν δὲ μόνην οὐδεὶς εἶπεν, ἀλλὰ τῇ συνεκδρομῇ τῶν ἄλλων καὶ ταύτην τέθεικεν ὁ Ἀριστοτέλης.

F15(c)–(f)

Unfortunately, none of Aristotle's commentators supplements his report with any additional information about Antiphon's buried-bed argument. Alexander (F15(c)) mentions the argument briefly in his commentary on *Metaphysics* 1014b17–18 (ἕνα δὲ ἐξ οὗ φύεται πρώτου τὸ φυόμενον ἐνυπάρχοντος), a passage he mistakenly interprets as referring to prime matter (τὸ δὲ πρῶτον τῷ ἐνυπάρχον προσκείμενον τὴν πρώτην ὕλην δηλοῖ, οὐ τὴν ἑκάστου προσεχῆ). In fact it refers to the seed, the starting-point of growth (so Ross [1924], 1.296, following Bonitz). *Metaphysics* 1014b26–35 (= F15(b)) on the other hand Alexander interprets correctly, as referring to the proximate material substrate (cf. *In Aristotelis Metaphysica* 358.36ff.). It would have been more appropriate to mention the buried-bed argument here; but Alexander only briefly alludes to it, and without naming Antiphon. Cf. *In Aristotelis Metaphysica* 359.2–3: οὕτω τὸ ξύλον τῆς κλίνης ὕλη (μένει γὰρ ξύλον καὶ κλίνη γενόμενον) καὶ ὁ χαλκὸς τοῦ ἀνδριάντος. Themistius (F15(d)) and Philoponus (F15(e)) merely paraphrase and repeat the main points of Aristotle's discussion, adding nothing new. The same holds for Simplicius (F15(f)), although his initial remarks may perhaps reflect Antiphon's original emphasis on the dynamic character of φύσις. (Cf. F15(f), ll. 1–3: σημεῖον δὲ τοῦ τὸ ὑποκείμενον ἀλλ' οὐχὶ τὸ εἶδος εἶναι τὴν φύσιν ὁ Ἀντιφῶν ὁ σοφιστὴς ἐποιεῖτο τὸ φύσιν μὲν εἶναι τὴν φύουσαν κτλ.)

F15(g)–(h)

Sauppe (1850), 148 first seems to have called attention to these texts in connection with Antiphon. It is noteworthy that Proclus (F15(g)) distinguishes what he takes to be Antiphon's conception of nature from the materialistic theory mentioned by Plato in *Laws* 892C (καὶ τὴν φύσιν ὀνομάζειν ταῦτα αὐτά, in reference to the simple bodies). Some modern commentators, by contrast, have contended that *Laws* 888D–889E is a précis or résumé of the doctrine of Antiphon (cf. Introduction, section VII). The little work entitled Ἀπορίαι καὶ λύσεις (printed in Waitz [1844–46], I.15ff.) bears the name of John Italus, but is evidently by an anonymous pupil of his. The author is obviously indebted to Proclus for his information on Antiphon.

F16

The attribution of this fragment to Περὶ ἀληθείας and the sophist Antiphon is completely uncertain. The sense of "reach," "extend" attributed to ἀφήκω here is not recognized by LSJ, s.v. But cf. [Hippocrates], *De ossium natura* 9.9: καὶ αἱ μέν αὐτέων [*sc.* φλεβῶν] ἀπὸ τῆς κεφαλῆς ὄπισθεν διὰ τοῦ αὐχένος, ἔξωθεν παρὰ τὴν ῥάχιν ἔνθεν καὶ ἔνθεν ἐς τὰ ἰσχία ἀφικνέεται καὶ ἐς τὰ σκέλεα· ἔπειτα διὰ τῶν κνημέων ἐπὶ τῶν σφυρῶν τὰ ἔξω καὶ ἐς τοὺς πόδας ἀφήκει. In this passage, ἀφήκει seems to mean "reach," "extend" (perhaps by analogy with ἀφικνέεται). In fact, in the parallel passage *De natura hominis* 11 διήκει appears in place of ἀφήκει.

F17

In what context Antiphon mentioned the subject of sex in the first book of Περὶ ἀληθείας is not known. Cf. perhaps F21 and F20.

F18

The context of this fragment is unknown. Passages such as Herodotus, 5.92.ζ and Aeschines, *or.* 3.192 confirm the interpretation of Antiphon's ἀναποδιζόμενα as equivalent to ἐξεταζόμενα (so LSJ, s.v.).

F19

The differing explanations of Antiphon's ἀνήκει offered by lexicographers are at first sight puzzling. In Aelius Dionysius and the later sources that depend on him (F19(b)), the citation from Antiphon is followed immediately by a citation from the comic poet Amipsias: Ἀμειψίας δὲ ἀνήκω ἀντὶ τοῦ ἀναβέβηκα (καὶ προελήλυθα add. *Anecdota Graeca*) ἔφη (= fr. 30). This evidence suggests that something is amiss with the text of Harpocration as it now stands, and that the explanation ἢ οἷον ἀνεβιβάσθη καὶ προελήλυθεν may originally have pertained to another citation (perhaps from Amipsias). If so, then only the first explanation (ἀντὶ ἁπλοῦ τοῦ ἥκει) would apply to Antiphon, and Harpocration's interpretation (ἀνήκει = ἥκει) would essentially agree with that of Aelius Dionysius and dependent sources (ἀνήκει = καθήκει). Sauppe (1850), 148 n., however, preferred what he called Harpocration's "careful" explanation.

F20

The sense in which Antiphon used the term ἐπάλλαξις is uncertain. LSJ, s.v. interpret it as "interweaving," "dovetailing." In support of this interpretation could be cited passages such as Aristotle, *Meteorology* 387a13 (of the corpuscular structure of viscous substances); Plutarch, *Coniugalia praecepta* 140E (of links in a chain); Polybius, *Historiae* 18.18.12 (of stakes forming a palisade), and [Aristotle], *De MXG* 974a26–27 (= *FVS* 30 A 5). Simplicius reports that ἐπάλλαξις was used by the Atomists to designate the interlinking of atoms to form sensible bodies. Cf. *In Aristotelis De caelo* 295.14–16 (*FVS* 68 A 37 = Aristotle, fr. 208: τοῦ δὲ συμμένειν τὰς οὐσίας μετ' ἀλλήλων μέχρι τινὸς αἰτιᾶται τὰς ἐπαλλαγὰς καὶ τὰς ἀντιλήψεις τῶν σωμάτων); ibid. 609.24–25 (τὴν δὲ συμπλοκὴν Ἀβδηρῖται ἐπάλλαξιν ἐκάλουν, ὥσπερ Δημόκριτος). But Harpocration's explanation (ἀντὶ τοῦ συναλλαγὰς ἢ μίξεις) points rather to the sense "dealings," "commerce" (cf. LSJ, s.vv. συναλλαγή 2, μῖξις II), or perhaps sexual "intercourse" (cf. LSJ, s.vv. συναλλάσσω, συναλλαγή 2; F17; and perhaps F21). Without a context, it is difficult to determine the specific sense in which Antiphon employed ἐπαλλάξεις.

F21

The verb ὀριγνάομαι means "aim at," "desire" (cf. LSJ, s.v.). The aorist passive infinitive form ὀριγνηθῆναι seems to be attested elsewhere only in Isocrates, *Epistulae* 6.9. Cf. F17, and perhaps F20.

F22

The noun ἀειεστώ (employed by Antiphon in the accusative case) is attested only here. (Jacoby [1908], 52 and Untersteiner [1962], 59 suggested, perhaps rightly, that Antiphon coined it himself.) Harpocration offers two different explanations: "eternity" (ἀϊδιότητα) and "being always in the same condition" (τὸ ἐπὶ τῶν αὐτῶν ἀεὶ ἑστάναι). Bignone (1938), 137 with n. 2 and Untersteiner (1962), 59, (1954), 240–41 with n. 53 = (1967), 2.63 with n. 53 preferred the latter, believing that Antiphon applied ἀειεστώ to the eternal equilibrium of the ordered world. But this interpretation seems to rest on the false etymology which derives ἀειεστώ from ἑστάναι and ἀεί. (Hesychius offers a similar false etymology for εὐεστώ, ε 6809, 2.224 = Democritus, *FVS* 68 B 140: εὐεστώ ... καὶ εὐδαιμονία· ἀπὸ τοῦ εὖ ἑστάναι τὸν οἶκον.) In fact, ἀειεστώ is formed from ἀεί and -εστω (from ἐστι). Cf. Hesychius, ε 6809 (2.224): εὐεστώ· εὐθηνία· ἀπὸ τοῦ εὖ εἶναι; Chantraine (1933), 116–17. Antiphon, of course, need not have accepted or even been aware of the correct etymology. Nevertheless, Harpocration's first explanation seems preferable, not only on etymological grounds but also because it better accords with the explanation offered by Hesychius, "eternal being" (αἰώνιον οὐσίαν).

The context of this fragment is uncertain. Deriving as it does from the second book of Περὶ ἀληθείας, in which Antiphon discussed the origin and present state of the world (cf. F23–25, with commentary), a cosmological context is possible. Vlastos (1945–46), 583 n. 30 contended that Antiphon's use of ἀειεστώ "almost certainly" reveals the influence of Democritus, who used εὐεστώ to designate tranquillity of mind (εὐθυμία), the goal (τέλος) of human life (cf. *FVS* 68 A 1, 167, B 2c, 4, and 140, quoted above). But compounds in -εστώ are not uncommon in fifth-century literature (cf. Herodotus, 1.85, 6.128, 9.85; Aeschylus, *Septem* 187, *Agamemnon* 647, 929; Schwyzer [1939–53], 1.478). Moreover, the notion of "eternal being" fits squarely into the realm of Presocratic speculation on the nature of reality (cf. Huffman [1993], 130–31 on Philolaus, *FVS* 44 B 6), and there is no need to posit specifically Democritean influence here.

F23

This fragment, from the second book of Περὶ ἀληθείας, shows that Antiphon discussed the present state of the world as well as its origin, cosmology as well as cosmogony (cf. F24–25 with commentary). This is typical of Presocratic speculation on the cosmos (cf. Heidel [1910], 86 n. 32 = [1980], 86 n. 32, [1921], 263 = [1980], 263). Sauppe (1896), 514, 517 conjectured that the fragment derives from the very beginning of the second book. The phrase περὶ τῆς νῦν κρατούσης διαστάσεως does have a programmatic ring, but Sauppe's conjecture remains just that.

διάστασις, which refers literally to "separation," occurs only here in the sense of "orderly arrangement" of the world (διακόσμησις). But the cosmogonic model implied by this term – a process of segregation or separation from an original mixture – is the one that underlies Presocratic theorizing on the origin of the universe from Anaximander on. Cf. Aristotle, *Physics* 187a20–23, *Metaphysics* 1069b22; Empedocles, *FVS* 31 B 8 (note that Plutarch paraphrases Empedocles' term διάλλαξις with διάστασιν), 17; Anaxagoras, *FVS* 59 B 1, 4, 9, 12, 13; Leucippus, *FVS* 67 A 1 (2.70.28–71.2); Heidel (1906a), 344–47 = (1980), 344–47, (1912), 229–32 = (1980), 229–32; Cherniss (1935), 375–79, (1951), 324–26 = (1977), 67–69. Antiphon's bold application of an action noun (in -σις) denoting the process of separation to the world-order itself which results from that process implies that he too adopted such a model (cf. F24–F25, with commentary). Gomperz (1901), 585 n. = (1922), 490 n. and Bignone (1938), 152–53 detected the influence of Empedocles and Protagoras (respectively) in this fragment, on inadequate grounds.

1 νῦν κρατούσης: on the implication of νῦν cf. introductory note above. κρατέω (= "hold sway, prevail") is one of Antiphon's favorite verbs. Cf. F29, l. 10 (also from Περὶ ἀληθείας); F58, l. 13, F59, l. 2 (both from Περὶ ὁμονοίας). The concept of "prevalence" (κρατεῖν, ἐπικρατεῖν) is ubiquitous in early Greek philosophy and medicine. It is applied to the prevailing of one cosmic element over others (cf. Empedocles, *FVS* 31 A 38, 41, B 17.27–29, 26.1; Diogenes of Apollonia, *FVS* 64 B 5; Archelaus, *FVS* 60 A 1; [Hippocrates], *De victu* 10 = *FVS* 22 C 1, an imitation of Heraclitus); of mind over matter (cf. Anaxagoras, *FVS* 59 B 12); and of opposites, humors, and seed or sperm in the body (cf. Lonie [1981], 129–30, with references). The idea appears already in Anaximander (cf. *FVS* 12 B 1; Heidel [1912], 233–34 = [1980], 233–34); according to Vlastos (1947) and others, it was adopted from the sphere of society and politics. With characteristic linguistic innovation, Antiphon transfers the application of κρατεῖν from the individual element or entity which prevails to the prevailing "world-order" itself (cf. the remarks on διάστασις in introductory note above).

F24

Although this fragment is transmitted without a book-title, it almost certainly derives from Περὶ ἀληθείας, most likely from the second book (cf. Sauppe [1850], 152 n.; Blass [1881], 146 n. doubted the ascription, without justification). From Harpocration's explanation it can be inferred that Antiphon applied the adjective ἀδιάστατον to the original disordered state which existed before the beginning of the cosmogonic process (cf. F23 and F25, with commentary). Which noun it modified is uncertain; perhaps μεῖγμα/μῖγμα (cf. Aristotle, *Physics* 187a23, *Metaphysics* 1012a28, 1069b22; LSJ, s.v. μῖγμα) or τὸ πᾶν (cf. Empedocles, *FVS* 31 B 13–14, 17.32).

Photius' second entry s.v. ἀδιάστατον (α 359, 1.42) first came to light in 1907, with Reitzenstein's publication of the α-glosses from cod. Berolinensis gr. oct. 22 (cf. Reitzenstein [1907], 31). The attribution to Xenophon seems to be corrupt, since the phrase καὶ τὸ οἰκοδόμημα ἀδιάστατον does not appear in the extant *corpus Xenophonteum*. Eduard Schwartz conjectured Ἀντιφῶν (for Ξενοφῶν), and Diels accordingly included this text as part of *FVS* 87 B 24. He was followed (though hesitantly) by Kranz in later editions of *FVS* (cf. *FVS* 2.343 n.), as well as by Untersteiner and others. The meaning of ἀδιάστατον in this quotation is obscure; but it obviously has nothing to do with the cosmological sense Antiphon gave the word. Schwartz's conjecture is completely unjustified, and there is no reason to connect this text with Antiphon.

F24A

The portion of the *Suda*'s entry s.vv. διάθεσις καὶ διατίθεσθαι concerned with Antiphon cites three different uses of the noun διάθεσις, only the last of which is accompanied by a book-title. Diels and Kranz printed the entire passage (ll. 1–5: Ἀντιφῶν . . . διακοσμήσεως) as *FVS* 87 B 24a, and Untersteiner followed suit. But Kranz translated only the last citation (διάθεσις ἐπὶ τῆς διακοσμήσεως). Momigliano (1969), 135–39; Untersteiner (1954), 240–41 = (1967), 2.63–64, and Zeppi (1958), 362 = (1962), 126 attributed the first citation (ἐπὶ γνώμης ἢ διανοίας) as well as the last to the sophist Antiphon. They inferred that he posited a single rational organizing principle operative both in human beings (where it is called γνώμη; cf. F2) and in the world at large (where it is called διακόσμησις). Sauppe (1850), 148–49 n. contended that the book-citation ἐν τῷ β′ τῆς Ἀληθείας belongs with the second citation (ἐπὶ τοῦ διαθεῖναι λόγον κτλ.) rather than with the third. He therefore punctuated with a full stop after Ἀληθείας in l. 4, and assigned only the second usage to Περὶ ἀληθείας. The words ὁ αὐτὸς κέχρηται . . . διακοσμήσεως Sauppe explained as a misplaced gloss on F23 (διάστασις). This last suggestion at least is refuted by the evidence of Hesychius, which shows that the gloss applies in fact to διάθεσις. Sauppe ascribed the same view on the articulation of the passage to L. Küster, who in fact punctuates with a full stop after ἐξαγγεῖλαί τι and takes the words ἐν τῷ β′ κτλ. with what follows (cf. Küster [1705], 1.553). Sauppe further invoked the authority of the scholium of "Ulpian" on Demosthenes, *or.*

2.16 (113a, 68). But the attribution to Ulpian is doubtful (cf. Gudeman [1921], 700); and in any case, Antiphon is not even mentioned in this scholium. The mistaken notion that he is stems apparently from the edition of Demosthenes by Lambin and Morel (1570), in which Morel enlarged the genuine scholium with paraphrases derived from the *Suda* and (mis)punctuated the passage in the same way as Sauppe suggested. (Cf. Dindorf [1851], 8.94–95; Dilts [1983], XVII.) Sauppe also offered an argument from word-order, but this is without force.

Of the three usages of διάθεσις attributed to "Antiphon" in the *Suda*, only the last can be assigned with confidence to Περὶ ἀληθείας and the sophist Antiphon, since it alone is accompanied by a book-title. The origin of the others remains uncertain. Antiphon's use of διάθεσις (in the accusative case, according to Hesychius) in the sense of "orderly arrangement" of the world is without an exact parallel. But Aristotle comes very close to this sense when he applies the word to the alternate states of the world in the cyclical cosmologies of Heraclitus and Empedocles (cf. *De caelo* 280a11–13; Cherniss [1935], 181 n. 162). Untersteiner (1955), LXXXV n. 234, (1962), 61 cited as parallels Theophrastus, *De sensu* 4 (Diels [1879], 500) and [Aristotle], *De MXG* 977b32–33. But his interpretation of the meaning of διάθεσις in these passages is purely arbitrary. It is uncertain how διάθεσις is related to διάστασις, which Antiphon seems to have used in the same sense (cf. F23 with commentary). Zeppi (1958), 362 = (1962), 126 and Untersteiner (1962), 61 detected Anaxagorean influence in Antiphon's references to the subject of the formation of the world (διακόσμησις); but this topic was the common concern of many Presocratics. For Antiphon's use of related terms cf. F23 (cited above); F14 (διαθεῖτο); F24 (ἀδιάστατον); and F63 (διάθεσις, from Περὶ ὁμονοίας), all with commentary.

F25

The δῖνος or δίνη (vortex or eddy) is a familiar feature of Presocratic cosmologies. Cf. Empedocles, *FVS* 31 A 30, 49, B 35.3–4; Anaxagoras, *FVS* 59 A 12, 57, B 9, 12, 13; Leucippus and Democritus, *FVS* 67 A 1, 68 A 1, 83; Aristophanes, *Clouds* 380–81, 828, 1471; Plato, *Phaedo* 99B; [Plato], *Epinomis* 983C with Tarán (1975), 275–76; Aristotle, *De caelo* 295a7ff.; Heidel (1906b), 279–82 = (1980), 279–82; Burnet (1930), 61–62; Ferguson (1971); Tigner (1974); Furley (1987), 22–23, 72–74, 91–94, 140–42, 146–47. The very popularity of the vortex in Presocratic speculation undermines the attempts of Dümmler (1889), 85; Luria (1926d), 265, (1928b), 220 n. 4; Nestle (1942), 374 with n. 15, and others to detect Democritean influence here or to interpret Aristophanes' references to the vortex in *Clouds* as allusions to Antiphon. Exactly how Antiphon used the vortex (to explain the start of the cosmogonic process, for example, or the motion of the heavenly bodies) is not known. Cf. Untersteiner (1954), 242 n. 68 = (1967), 2.65 n. 68.

F26

Aëtius' report most likely refers to views expressed in the second book of Περὶ ἀληθείας (so Sauppe [1896], 517, and all subsequent commentators). Antiphon's explanation of the sun as fire that feeds on the moist air surrounding the earth appears to be borrowed from Heraclitus. Cf. Aristotle, *Meteorology* 354b33–355a21; Aëtius, II.17.4 (Diels [1879], 346), II.28.6 (Diels [1879], 359); Diogenes Laertius, 9.9; Cherniss (1935), 134 n. 542; Kirk (1954), 270; Mondolfo in Mondolfo and Tarán (1972), 219. That the *Meteorology* passage cited refers exclusively to Heraclitus and his followers is argued by Cherniss (1935), 133–34 with nn. 541–42; Marcovich (1978), 221–22, and others. But Kirk (1954), 264–79 and others contend that Aristotle has in mind a larger group of Presocratics (including, of course, Heraclitus). However this may be, the evidence of Heraclitean borrowing in F28 suggests that it is Heraclitus to whom Antiphon is indebted for his theory of the sun. As Aëtius indicates (ἀνατολὰς δὲ καὶ δύσεις ποιούμενον κτλ.), Antiphon used the theory to explain the sun's diurnal movements. Whether he also used it to explain solstices and the phenomenon of the seasons (as Mondolfo in Mondolfo and Tarán [1972], 219 seems to assume) is uncertain. (For Heraclitus' explanation of solstices cf. Aristotle, *Meteorology* 354b34ff. with the differing interpretations of Cherniss [1935], 133–34 on one side, and Kirk [1954], 266 and Marcovich [1978], 222 with n. 6 on the other.)

1 ἐπινεμόμενον: Untersteiner (1962), 63 translated "diffondentesi" (cf. LSJ, s.v. II.2); but the sense is rather "feeds on." Cf. Kirk (1954), 266, 270; Mondolfo in Mondolfo and Tarán (1972), 219; LSJ, s.v. II.2c.

3–4 τοῦ δὲ ὑπονοτιζομένου . . . ἀντέχεσθαι: Dicks (1970), 90 misinterpreted this to mean that the sun's risings and settings are caused by "the recurrent failure of its burning owing to the opposing effect of moisture." But ἀντέχεσθαι here means rather "cling" or "adhere to" (cf. LSJ, s.v. III.2).

F27

This testimonium also can confidently be referred to the second book of Περὶ ἀληθείας (so Sauppe [1896], 517, and all subsequent commentators). The first part of Aëtius' report is straightforward: Antiphon thought that the moon shines by its own light. In this view he follows Presocratics such as Anaximander (cf. Aëtius, II.28.1, Diels [1879], 358 = *FVS* 12 A 22); Xenophanes (cf. Aëtius, II.28.1, Diels [1879], 358 = *FVS* 21 A 43); and Heraclitus (cf. Aëtius, II.28.6, Diels [1879], 359 = *FVS* 22 A 12; Diogenes Laertius, 9.10–11 = *FVS* 22 A 1, and below). The alternative (and correct) view that the moon receives its illumination from the sun is ascribed to Parmenides (cf. Aëtius, II.26.2, Diels [1879], 357 = *FVS* 28 A 42; Aëtius, II.28.5, Diels [1879], 358; *FVS* 28 B 14–15; Tarán [1965], 245 n. 40; Dicks [1970], 51–52); the Pythagoreans (cf. Aëtius, II.28.5, Diels [1879], 358; *FVS* 58 B 1a; Diogenes Laertius, 8.27 = *FVS* 58 B 1; but contrast Aëtius, II.29.4, Diels [1879], 360 = *FVS* 58 B 36); Empedocles (cf. Aëtius, II.28.5, Diels [1879], 358 = *FVS* 31 A 60; *FVS* 31 B 43, 45, 47; Dicks [1970], 53–54); Anaxagoras (cf. Plato, *Cratylus* 409A–B = *FVS* 59 A 76; Plutarch, *De facie in orbe lunae* 929B = *FVS* 59 B 18; Aëtius, II.28.5, Diels [1879], 358 = *FVS* 59 A 77; Hippolytus, *Refutatio* 1.8.8 = *FVS* 59 A 42); and Democritus (cf. Plutarch, *De facie in orbe lunae* 929C = *FVS* 68 A 89a). The fact that Antiphon espoused an outmoded theory of the moon's illumination is taken by some commentators as evidence of the superficial character of his science (so Zeller in Zeller and Nestle [1920], 1373; cf. Nestle [1942], 374). But the theory continued to receive support long after Antiphon; it is ascribed to Aristotle (cf. Aëtius, II.28.2, Diels [1879], 358) as well as to Berossus (cf. Aëtius, II.28.1, Diels [1879], 358; Cleomedes, *Caelestia* 2.4, 67). A compromise explained the moon's illumination as resulting from the mixture (σύγκρασις) of its own light with that of the sun (cf. Cleomedes, *Caelestia* 2.4, 68; Plutarch, *De facie in orbe lunae* 929B–C, E). This theory was embraced by Cleomedes and is ascribed to Posidonius by Cherniss (1957), 101 n. *h* (but see the doubts expressed by Kidd [1988], 1.474–78). Its ascription to Anaximenes and Parmenides by O'Brien (1968), 122–24 has little plausibility.

The remainder of Aëtius' report is not as clear. τὸ δὲ ἀποκρυπτόμενον κτλ. was interpreted by Cherniss (1957), 131 n. *b*; Mras (1954–56), 2.403 n., and Untersteiner (1962), 63 as an explanation of the lunar phases. But this is difficult or impossible to reconcile with the explanation of eclipses attributed to Antiphon in F28, for the moon's bowl-like shape accounts for its phases as well as for eclipses. (Cf. Heraclitus, *FVS* 22 A 1; Kirk [1954], 276; commentary on F28.) This same objection applies against Gundel (1933), 87, who suggested that this portion of Aëtius' report provides an explanation for the dark or hidden side of the moon. Moreover, according to Aëtius the phenomenon in question occurs in the case of other heavenly bodies (τὰ ἄλλα ἄστρα) besides the moon. (Other planets in the solar system display phases; but they are invisible to the naked eye and could not have been detected by ancient observers.) In all likelihood, the words τὸ δὲ ἀποκρυπτόμενον κτλ. are meant to offer an explanation as to why the moon fails to appear brightly in the daytime sky, even though it has its own light. The reason for this is that its light is hidden and dimmed by the stronger light of the sun. Other heavenly bodies (τὰ ἄλλα ἄστρα), which are similarly hidden in daylight, suffer the same fate. So O'Brien (1968), 126 with nn. 67, 71; cf. Gilbert (1907), 700 ("[Antiphon] das geringe Licht von Mond und Sternen auf die alles beherrschende Macht des Sonneslichtes zurückführte"). Anaxagoras and Democritus offered a rather similar explanation to account for the appearance of the Milky Way. Cf. Aristotle, *Meteorology* 345a5–31 = *FVS* 59 A 80, 68 A 91; Aëtius, III.1.5–6 (Diels [1879], 365); Diogenes Laertius, 2.9 = *FVS* 59 A 1; Hippolytus, *Refutatio* 1.8.10 = *FVS* 59 A 42; Cherniss (1935), 330; O'Brien (1968), 126.

1–2 τὸ δὲ ἀποκρυπτόμενον: φέγγος must be understood from ἰδιοφεγγῆ (or ἰδίῳ φέγγει) in the preceding clause.

2–3 ὑπὸ τῆς . . . ἀμαυροῦσθαι: for the principle involved cf. Cleomedes, *Caelestia* 2.3 (67): πᾶν γὰρ πύρινον σῶμα λαμπρότερον μὲν ἐν σκιᾷ, ἀμαυρότερον δὲ ὑπὸ τὰς αὐγὰς τοῦ ἡλίου φαίνεται; Plutarch, *De facie in orbe lunae* 933C–D with Cherniss (1957), 129 n. *f*, 130 n. *a*, 131 n. *b*; O'Brien (1968), 126 n. 67. Dio of Prusa uses the principle in a rhetorical argument urging concord between the quarreling cities of Prusa and Apamea in *or.* 40.38, where Bignone (1938), 137 would detect the influence of Antiphon. But this ignores the commonplace character of the principle.

3 τοῦ ἰσχυροτέρου: Diels and Kranz printed ἰσχυροτέρου πυρός (the reading of most manuscripts of [Plut.], of Eusebius, and that implied by the Arabic translation). But Sauppe (1896), 517 was probably right to attribute both πυρός and φωτός (the reading of cod. m of [Plut.]) to the interpretative zeal ("interpretandi studio") of scribes (cf. Untersteiner [1962], 63). Neither is necessary, since φέγγους is easily understood from the context (cf. above).

F28

The attribution of this testimonium to Antiphon depends solely on the authority of Stobaeus (the names of both Antiphon and Alcmaeon are absent from [Plut.]), but can hardly be doubted. Antiphon seems to have adopted his theory of the sun from Heraclitus (cf. F26 with commentary), and the explanation of lunar eclipses (and the lunar phases) credited to him here was probably borrowed from Heraclitus as well. Cf. Diogenes Laertius, 9.9–10 = *FVS* 22 A 1; Aëtius, II.27.2, 28.6 (Diels [1879], 358–59) = *FVS* 22 A 12; Kirk (1954), 270–79; Marcovich (1978),

234–35. (That Antiphon was indebted to Alcmaeon rather than Heraclitus is much less likely; cf. Mondolfo in Mondolfo and Tarán [1972], 219.) Frank (1923), 188 n. 1 proposed to attribute to Heraclitus only the purely mythical conception of a heavenly boat. The "mathematical" explanation of lunar eclipses (and phases) by means of the turning bowl Frank believed originated with Antiphon, from whom later doxographers transferred it to Heraclitus and Alcmaeon. But there is no reason to deny Heraclitus the lunar theory ascribed to him in the accounts of Diogenes and Aëtius, which probably go back to Theophrastus (cf. Kirk [1954], 269–70). On the mythical antecedents of the theory cf. Mondolfo in Zeller and Mondolfo (1961), 206–7; Marcovich (1978), 234–35 (who is sceptical of the thesis of mythological influence).

2 καὶ τὰς περικλίσεις: περίκλισις (attested only here) denotes "sideways sloping" or "inclination." Cf. LSJ, s.v.; Mondolfo in Mondolfo and Tarán (1972), 219. The movements of the moon's bowl referred to here were probably intended to explain the lunar phases as well as lunar eclipses (cf. Diels, *FVS* 1.146 n.; Mondolfo in Mondolfo and Tarán [1972], 125 n. 167). Cf. Diogenes Laertius, 9.10 (ἐκλείπειν τε ἥλιον καὶ σελήνην ἄνω στρεφομένων τῶν σκαφῶν· τούς τε κατὰ μῆνα τῆς σελήνης σχηματισμοὺς γίνεσθαι στρεφομένης †ἐν αὐτῇ† [ὡσαύτως Marcovich] κατὰ μικρὸν τῆς σκάφης); Kirk (1954), 276; Marcovich (1978), 235. The evidence of Diogenes seems to refute Diels' suggestion that the words καὶ τὰς περικλίσεις (which are lacking in [Plut.]) pertain to Alcmaeon and/or Antiphon rather than to Heraclitus. The interpretation of καὶ τὰς περικλίσεις adopted here underlies Ruestow's (unnecessary) conjecture καὶ ⟨σχηματίζεσθαι κατὰ⟩ τὰς περικλίσεις.

F29

This fragment is quoted by Galen in his commentary on the third book of the Hippocratic *Epidemics*. The immediate context is a discussion of the meaning of the word κατείλλουσαι in *Epidemics* 3.33 (φωναί τε πολλοῖς ἐπεσήμαινον κακούμεναι καὶ κατείλλουσαι, πρῶτον μὲν τοῖσι φθινώδεσιν ἀρχομένοισιν, ἀτὰρ καὶ τοῖσι καυσώδεσι καὶ τοῖσι φρενετικοῖσιν; cf. Galen, *In Hippocratis Epidemiarum librum* III 126.10–130.15). Galen rejects the connection with ἰλλαίνειν proposed by certain exegetes, preferring to derive the verb instead from εἴλλομαι, for the use of which he cites Plato (*Timaeus* 40B, 76B; cf. below) as well as this fragment from the second book of Περὶ ἀληθείας.

Despite the doubts expressed by Zeller in Zeller and Nestle (1920), 1373 n. 1, the fragment almost certainly describes the formation of hail. Ancient meteorological theories agreed in identifying hail as ice or frozen water, but offered differing accounts of the process by which it is formed. Cf. Aëtius, III.4 (Diels [1879], 370–71); Plato, *Timaeus* 59D–E; Aristotle, *Meteorology* 347b28–349a12; [Aristotle], *De mundo* 394b1; Seneca, *Naturales quaestiones* IVb.3.1–2; Gilbert (1907), 503–8; Kidd (1988), 1.510–14; and the texts cited below. According to Antiphon, hail is formed during violent rainstorms (ὄμβροι) when rain water is condensed and compacted or frozen by the force of contrary winds. Other ancient authorities connected hail with frozen rain (cf. Arius Didymus, fr. 35, Diels [1879], 468 = Chrysippus, fr. 701; Anonymus II, *Isagoga in Arati Phaenomena* 8, 127; Kidd [1988], 1.514). But the mechanism of hail formation described by Antiphon seems to be without an exact parallel elsewhere. Bignone (1920), 136 n. 4 compared it with the second theory of hail proposed in Epicurus, *Epistola ad Pythoclem* 106. But the similarities he detected depend entirely on textual alterations introduced by Usener that are (to say the least) unnecessary (cf. Bailey [1926], 312). The best parallel is furnished by the process of rain-formation described in [Hippocrates], *De aëre aquis et locis* 8: ἕως μὲν οὖν διεσκεδασμένον ᾖ [*sc.* τὸ λαμπρότατον καὶ κουφότατον ὄμβριον] καὶ μήπω συνεστήκῃ, φέρεται μετέωρον. ὁκόταν δέ κου ἀθροισθῇ καὶ συστραφῇ ἐς τὸ αὐτὸ ὑπὸ ἀνέμων ἀλλήλοισιν ἐναντιωθέντων ἐξαίφνης, τότε καταρρήγνυται, ᾗ ἂν τύχῃ πλεῖστον συστραφέν. Here, as in Antiphon's explanation of hail, atmospheric moisture collects (ἀθροισθῇ; cf. τῶν ξυμπιπτόντων) and is compacted or compressed (συστραφῇ; cf. συστρέφεται, συνεστράφη) by the force of contrary winds (ἀνέμων ἀλλήλοισιν ἐναντιωθέντων; cf. πνεύματα ὑπεναντία ἀλλήλοις). In the Hippocratic theory, the compressed moisture coalesces into drops of rain; in Antiphon's theory it freezes and becomes hail.

Stylistically, this fragment is remarkable for its careful articulation (ὅταν ~ τότε; ὅτι ~ τοῦτο) as well as rhetorical ornamentation in the form of chiasmus (συστρέφεται ... πυκνοῦται ... ἐπυκνώθη ... συνεστράφη) and hendiadys (ὑπό τε τοῦ πνεύματος ... καὶ ὑπὸ τῆς βίας; cf. below).

8 συστρέφεται: cf. [Aristotle], *De mundo* 394b1 (χάλαζα γίνεται νιφετοῦ συστραφέντος καὶ βρῖθος ἐκ πιλήματος εἰς καταφορὰν ταχυτέραν λαβόντος); [Hippocrates], *De aëre aquis et locis* 8 (quoted above).

9 πυκνοῦται: = "is condensed" or "frozen." Cf. LSJ, s.v. I.2, with references.

κατὰ πολλά: this could mean "in many places" (Kranz, *FVS* 2.344; Morrison [1972], 223) but more likely means "many [*sc.* drops] at a time." Cf. LSJ, s.v. κατά B.II. Untersteiner's "per la maggior parte" does not give as good a sense.

9–10 ὅτι δ' ἂν τῶν ξυμπιπτόντων †κρατήσῃ†: text and interpretation are uncertain. κρατήσῃ (the reading of all manuscripts) is evidently corrupt. Sauppe's conjecture κρατηθῇ (adopted by Blass, Diels and Kranz, and Untersteiner) would seem to mean "whichever of the drops falling together is overcome." The corruption postulated (C for Θ) is an easy enough one in capitals. But τῶν ξυμπιπτόντων construed as a partitive genitive with ὅτι seems awkward; and ξυμπίπτω would more naturally be applied to the violent winds (cf. LSJ, s.v., with the reference to *Odyssey* 5.295). Wenkebach (1936), 129 n. suggested κρυστήνῃ, an active form used intransitively (cf. Kühner–Blass 2.263). This verb seems to be attested only in Nicander, *Alexipharmaca* 314, where the middle-passive form κρυσταίνεται refers to congealing blood. No obvious solution to the textual problem presents itself.

10 ἐπυκνώθη καὶ συνεστράφη: these seem to be gnomic aorists.

11 εἰλλόμενον: Wenkebach's orthography is followed here (Diels and Kranz and others printed εἰλούμενον). On the orthography and meaning of the verbs εἴλω, εἴλλω (εἵλλω), εἰλέω (εἱλέω), and ἴλλω cf. Buttmann (1836), 253–71; Kühner–Blass 2.412–13; Solmsen (1901), 224–44, and especially Burdach (1922). Timpanaro-Cardini (1955), 28 argued that εἴλλομαι regularly connotes motion contrary to natural tendency. In this passage, she contended, the verb does not designate condensation or compression but rather the backwards movement impressed by wind upon rain-water, which allows it to condense instead of falling. Her only evidence comes from several passages of Plato's *Timaeus*, none of which supports her interpretation. In *Timaeus* 40B, the correct reading is most likely ἰλλομένην rather than εἰλλομένην (cf. Cherniss [1944], 552–58, [1959–60], 223–24; Tarán [1975], 99–101). In *Timaeus* 76B and 86E, εἴλλομαι has its regular sense of "compress" or "confine." Galen interprets εἰλλόμενον here in exactly the same way, paraphrasing it with the expressions κατακλειόμενον ("confined") and συνειλούμενον εἰς ἑαυτό ("compressed into itself"). This makes excellent sense in the context and is unquestionably right.

ὑπὸ τῆς βίας: ὑπό τε τοῦ πνεύματος . . . καὶ ὑπὸ τῆς βίας is a hendiadys for "violent wind" (cf. Sider [1981], 88).

F29A

This fragment consists of three separate passages from Περὶ ἀληθείας quoted by Galen in the first book of his treatise *On Medical Names*. The Greek original of this treatise, which consisted of five books, is lost; the work survives only in an Arabic translation of book 1, published by Meyerhof and Schacht in 1931. The Arabic version was produced in the ninth century by Hubaish ibn al-Hasan, the nephew and pupil of the great translator Hunayn ibn Ishaq. (On Hunayn cf. Anawati and Iskandar [1978]; Strohmaier [1971]; Bergsträsser [1913]. On Hubaish cf. Anawati and Iskandar [1978], 237–38.) It was made not directly from the Greek (of which Hubaish seems to have been ignorant) but from a Syriac translation of the first three books of *On Medical Names* produced earlier by Hunayn (cf. *On Medical Names* 8.3–8, 32.13–15; Bergsträsser [1925], 38, 47). The Arabic translation is extant in a single Leiden manuscript (Or. 585 (VI) Warner; cf. Meyerhof and Schacht [1931], 3–4).

In the first book of *On Medical Names*, Galen sets out his views on the proper use of medical terminology (for a detailed summary cf. Meyerhof [1926]). He deprecates excessive preoccupation with medical names and faults those who begin their teaching of medicine with names instead of the things to which they refer (cf. Deichgräber *apud* Meyerhof and Schacht [1931], 14 n. 5). Galen sharply criticizes certain medical men (whom he nicknames "sophists") for their failure to pay heed to etymology or traditional usage when establishing the meaning of medical terms. He exemplifies the practice of such "sophists" through a discussion of the word πυρετός (fever). Contradicting Erasistratus and his followers (cf. *On Medical Names* 35.4ff. with Deichgräber's notes), Galen affirms that etymology (πῦρ) and usage alike demonstrate that πυρετός refers to fiery heat in the body (cf. Pellegrin [1988]). In support of this contention, Galen cites a range of ancient authorities including Aristophanes, Hippocrates, Plato, and (for evidence from the "rhetors") Antiphon.

It is clear from the way in which Galen introduces his quotations from Antiphon that all three derive from the second book of Περὶ ἀληθείας (F29A, ll. 24, 28–29). All three deal with the aetiology of disease and invoke a humoral pathology based on the internal flux of bile or gall (this is explicit in the first two and probable in the third; cf. below). Humoral pathologies of this sort were well established by the later fifth century, in medical as well as in popular thought (cf. Grensemann [1975], 198; Lonie [1981], 58–59). They appear in works of the Hippocratic corpus such as *De aëre aquis et locis*, *De morbo sacro*, and *De morbis* II 12–75 which are approximately contemporary with Περὶ ἀληθείας (cf. Lesky [1971], 550–51; Jouanna [1974], 511–12, [1983], 11–12) and in Herodotus (cf. 4.187; Jouanna [1974], 511 n. 3; Heinimann [1945], 180). (On Hippocratic humoral theory cf. Jouanna [1974], 26–126, 136–47; Schöner [1964], 15–58; Lonie [1965], 24–29, [1981], 54–62; Fredrich [1899], 33–50; Hornstein [1911], 62–74.) Interest in humoral theories is attested for Presocratic philosophers as well. According to Aristotle, *De partibus animalium* 677a5–19 (= *FVS* 59 A 105), Anaxagoras and his followers explained acute diseases as resulting from the internal movements of bile (cf. Diels, *FVS* 2.30 n.; Cherniss [1935], 265 with n. 186). Lanza (1966), 176 and Vegetti (1965), 195–96 contended that Aristotle's reference is to the Hippocratic *De locis in homine* rather than to Anaxagoras himself; but this is unconvincing. Democritus also may have discussed the subject of humoral pathology (cf. *FVS* 68 A 159, quoted in commentary on ll. 32–33 below).

The first fragment quoted by Galen begins by referring back to an earlier discussion of a pathological condition said to be caused by bile in the hands and feet (cf. ll. 4–8). Unfortunately, the disease in question is not named. But the mention of hands and feet, and the pathological function assigned to bile, taken together strongly suggest arthritis or gout, which is mentioned explicitly in the third quotation (cf. below). The fragment goes on to discuss the effects produced by bile when it reaches the flesh, where it is said to cause corruption, swelling, and chronic fever when present in large quantities (cf. ll. 8–16). The second, much shorter quotation repeats the idea that bile in the flesh causes fever (cf. ll. 26–28). According to standard Hippocratic doctrine, any accumulation of humor can cause heating and fever (cf. *De morbis* IV 48; Lonie [1981], 327; Jouanna [1974], 243 n. 3). But the connection between bile and fever is especially close. Cf. *De natura hominis* 15 (οἱ πλεῖστοι τῶν πυρετῶν γίνονται ἀπὸ χολῆς); *De morbis* II 40–43; Lonie (1981), 284, with further references. The third fragment is quoted by Galen to demonstrate that Antiphon, like other ancient writers, refers to inflammation (φλεγμονή) as fever (cf. ll. 39–45). Yet fever is not mentioned in the fragment, which seems rather to deal with a joint disease that is said to arise when a painful inflammation becomes chronic (cf. Meyerhof and Schacht [1931], 34 n. 8, and below). This happens when the vessels become overloaded and open up. Just what the vessels become overloaded with is uncertain, however, since the subject of the introductory clause is not expressed. The likeliest possibilities are blood and bile, either of which can function as a pathological agent according to Hippocratic medical theory. For an excess of blood causing disease cf. *De morbis* II 17–18; *De affectionibus interioribus* 4(5); Jouanna (1974), 141, 222 n. 3, 244 with n. 2. For diseases caused by bile and/or phlegm in the vessels cf. *De affectionibus interioribus* 18; *De morbis* II 41; Anaxagoras, *FVS* 59 A 105 (cf. above); Jouanna (1974), 143 n. 2, 246 with n. 2. It is impossible to be certain, but the pathological function of bile in the first two quotations greatly strengthens the case for it as the agent of disease here. Whether bile or blood, it is noteworthy that the pathological agent here seems to operate by a purely *quantitative* mechanism: too much of it causes the vessels to overflow. In the second fragment, by contrast, the chronic fever is said to result from a *qualitative* change (corruption) induced in the flesh by bile. This characteristic distinguishes Antiphon's aetiology of the joint disease from the aetiology of gout given in *De affectionibus* 31, which invokes a qualitative mechanism (corruption of blood in the vessels by bile and phlegm). *De affectionibus* 30 offers yet another aetiology of a joint disease, more precisely rheumatic fever or Bouilland's disease (cf. Grmek [1983], 130 with n. 147 = [1989], 83 with n. 150). This aetiology also seems to differ from Antiphon's (*pace* Deichgräber *apud* Meyerhof and Schacht [1931], 34 n. 6), since it involves two humors (bile and phlegm) rather than one and furthermore makes no mention of vessels.

There is no good reason to think that Galen cites the three fragments from Περὶ ἀληθείας in their original order. The past-tense verbs in the first sentence of the first fragment (ll. 4–8) indicate that Antiphon there is recapitulating an earlier discussion. The mention of bile in the hands and feet strongly suggests that the expression "these ... things" (ll. 4–5) refers to gout or arthritis, the aetiology of which is discussed in the third fragment (with present-tense verbs). The possibility suggests itself that the third fragment originally preceded the first, and formed part of the discussion to which Antiphon there alludes. On the other hand, Galen indicates that the third fragment followed the second (cf. ll. 28–29). So the second fragment also may have preceded the first. (The use of tenses seems consistent with this, for the second fragment employs present-tense verbs to refer to fever produced by bile in the flesh – a condition which the first fragment refers to with past-tense verbs.) The original order of the three quotations may therefore have been: second – third – first.

1–2 rhetors: this need not imply that Galen identified the sophist Antiphon with the Rhamnusian (cf. the remarks on the *corpus Antiphonteum* in Introduction, section 1).

4–5 as I told you: on the past-tense verbs in this quotation cf. introductory note above. The use of the first person, attested only here in the fragments of Περὶ ἀληθείας, is a conventional feature of Ionian scientific prose-style. Cf. Heraclitus, *FVS* 22 B 1, 49, 50, 55, 101; Anaxagoras, *FVS* 59 B 4; Diogenes of Apollonia, *FVS* 64 B 1, 2, 5, 8; Protagoras, *FVS* 80 B 4; Hippias, *FVS* 86 B 6; *Dialexeis* 1.2; Aly (1929), 58–60; Jouanna (1974), 252–53. The second-person address should probably be understood as an impersonal address to the reader. Cf. εἴσ⟨η⟩ (restored in F1, l. 5), ὦ μακάριε (F51, l. 1, from Περὶ ὁμονοίας), both with commentary.

8–9 For when it advances etc.: the narrative device employed here (brief recapitulation followed by a more detailed exposition of the point recapitulated) can be paralleled in the Hippocratic corpus. Cf. *De morbis* IV 51–52; Lonie (1981), 337–38, 345–46.

10 corruption: cf. (e.g.) *De affectionibus* 22. The concept of corruption of tissue is already prominent in what Grensemann has identified as the oldest stratum of the Hippocratic corpus, the so-called A–I stratum of the gynecological treatises. Cf. Grensemann (1987), 67–68, 72.

11 swells up: for swelling caused by an accumulation of humor cf. *De affectionibus interioribus* 48; *De morbis* I 15; *De morbis* II 1; Fredrich (1899), 40.

The unnatural warmth etc.: a distinction seems to be drawn here between the origin of the unnatural warmth, occasioned by corruption and swelling of the flesh ("from this place," but the phrase is unexpected), and its deterioration into a condition of chronic fever, caused by the continuing presence of bile. But the distinction seems strained, since the corruption and swelling are themselves caused by bile. For heat and fever caused by swelling cf. *De morbis* II 10 (καὶ ἐπὴν [*sc.* ὁ γαργαρεὼν] φλεγμήνῃ, θερμαίνεται); *De locis in homine* 27 (πυρετοὶ διὰ τόδε γίνονται, ὅταν τοῦ σώματος ὑπερφλεγμήναντος αἱ σάρκες συνοιδήσωσι); Fredrich (1899), 40.

12–13 becomes engrained: Meyerhof and Schacht (1931), 34 translated "Kontinuierlichwerden." At first sight this might suggest the type of fever called συνεχής (Plato, *Timaeus* 86A) or σύνοχος (*De natura hominis* 15); cf. LSJ, s.vv. Professor Fritz Zimmermann informs me, however, that the Arabic original is ambiguous and may be corrupt. In addition, the fever discussed by Antiphon is chronic, whereas "continuous fever" is reckoned by the author of *De natura hominis* to be the shortest-lived of the four major kinds of fever.

20 *therme*: the Arabic merely transliterates the Greek. Meyerhof and Schacht (1931), 34 n. 5 suggested that πυρετός might have been expected here for θέρμη. But Galen's whole purpose in quoting Antiphon is to prove that by "fever" the ancients understood unnatural heat (cf. ll. 1–3). And the first quotation is apposite precisely because "fevers" (l. 8; presumably πυρετοί) and "unnatural warmth" (ll. 11, 16; presumably θέρμη) seem to be equated in it. θέρμη and πυρετός are frequent synonyms in the Hippocratic corpus (though occasionally they are distinguished, as in *De morbis* II 48–49).

20–21 so as to say . . . a warmth: nothing like this is said in the fragment (at least as Galen quotes it).

26–27 every bit of it: according to Professor Zimmermann, the Arabic here is ambiguous as to singular or plural: either "every bit of it" (*sc.* bile) or "any one of them" (*sc.* kinds of bile; cf. Kühner–Gerth 1.15). Ancient physicians recognized many varieties of bile, distinguished by color, taste, and pathological effect. Cf. *De affectionibus inter-*

ioribus 20 (περὶ τοῦ φλέγματος τὰς αὐτὰς γνώμας ἔχω, ἃς καὶ χολῆς· ἰδέας πολλὰς εἶναι); Plato, *Timaeus* 83A–C; Fredrich (1899), 43–44; Schöner (1964), 49; Lonie (1981), 117, 373.

31 a designation other than that etc.: the word "fever" does not appear here (cf. above), and Galen may be suspected of tendentiousness in his claim that Antiphon equated φλεγμονή and fever (cf. Meyerhof and Schacht [1931], 34 n. 8). For the relation of inflammation, swelling, and fever cf. above.

32 *phlegmone*: here as in ll. 35, 41, and 42, the Arabic simply transliterates the Greek.

32–33 two names . . . burning: φλεγμονή ~ φλέγω. Cf. Soranus, *Gynaecia* 3.17 = Democritus, *FVS* 68 A 159: ἡ φλεγμονὴ κέκληται μὲν ἀπὸ τοῦ φλέγειν καὶ οὐχ, ὡς ὁ Δημόκριτος εἴρηκεν, ἀπὸ τοῦ αἴτιον εἶναι τὸ φλέγμα. Cf. also Prodicus, *FVS* 84 B 4; Philolaus, *FVS* 44 A 27.

39 when more gets into etc.: this probably refers to bile or blood (cf. introductory note above).

vessels: in Hippocratic medical theory, these are hollow vessels which carry blood, other fluids, or air. Cf. Fredrich (1899), 67–70.

41 through them: according to Professor Zimmermann, the Arabic term employed here (*bi-hā*) is again ambiguous as to singular or plural: either "through them" (*sc.* the vessels) or "through it" (bile or blood, presumably). The same ambiguity recurs in l. 42.

***phlegmone*:** for inflammation arising from an excess of humor cf. above.

43 pain: for the pain caused by arthritis and gout cf. *De affectionibus* 30 (ὀδύνη ὀξείη), 31 (νοῦσος ἐπίπονος).

44–45 arthritis (gout): the Arabic term for the joint disease (*niqris*) apparently can refer to gout or to arthritis. (The German "Gicht," which Meyerhof and Schacht used to render *niqris*, is similarly ambiguous.) Gout (ποδάγρα) and the several varieties of arthritis (rheumatic fever, rheumatoid arthritis, and osteoarthritis) are of course distinct diseases, and were recognized as such by the Hippocratic doctors (cf. *De affectionibus* 30–31; *De morbis* I 3). But in later times they were confused, as by Galen. Cf. Delpeuch (1900); Ruiz Moreno (1941); Byl (1987); Lopez Ferez (1987). It remains uncertain whether Antiphon referred to gout (ποδάγρα) or (as Deichgräber *apud* Meyerhof and Schacht [1931], 34 n. 6 supposed) to arthritis (ἀρθρῖτις).

F30–31

These two fragments deal with seismic phenomena and are evidently closely related. F30 is attributed explicitly by Harpocration to the second book of Περὶ ἀληθείας, and F31 can confidently be assigned to the same source.

F31 obviously deals with earthquakes, and Capelle (1924), 366 postulated that F30 concerns the same topic. He supplied τὸ πῦρ as subject (as did Sauppe [1896], 518) and credited Antiphon with a so-called volcanic theory, which explains earthquakes as resulting from subterranean fire that burns the earth below its surface and thereby causes collapse. Most ancient theorizing on the subject, by contrast, identified moving air (πνεῦμα) or water as the cause of earthquakes. Cf. Aristotle, *Meteorology* 365a14–369a10; Aëtius, III.15 (Diels [1879], 379–81); Seneca, *Naturales quaestiones* 6; [Aristotle], *De mundo* 395b30–396a16; Diogenes Laertius, 7.154; Ammianus Marcellinus, 17.7.9–14; Gilbert (1907), 293–324; Capelle (1924); Kidd (1988), 1.116–18, 2.816–20. Capelle doubted that this volcanic theory could have originated with Antiphon, since the latter was a sophist and furthermore an Athenian (whose native land experienced only weak quakes), and suggested Empedocles instead as its author. But despite Capelle, Gilbert (1907), 304, and others, there is no evidence that Empedocles offered any explanation of earthquakes. As Bollack (1965–69), 3.1.227 rightly observed *à propos* of Empedocles, *FVS* 31 A 68, "Le feu souterrain se manifeste, non pas dans les éruptions volcaniques, sur lesquelles nous n'avons aucun témoignage, mais dans les sources chaudes" (cf. *FVS* 31 A 69, B 52). Equally, there is no reason to identify the theory Capelle reconstructed for Antiphon with the seismic theory reported in Seneca, *Naturales quaestiones* 6.9.2 (as Capelle suggested). Anaxagoras' theory of earthquakes involved αἰθήρ or fire (cf. Aristotle, *Meteorology* 365a19–35; Cherniss [1935], 207–8); but the mechanism he postulated is obviously different from that described in F30.

One difficulty with Capelle's interpretation of both fragments in terms of a volcanic theory is the seemingly different explanations they offer for the wrinkling of the earth's crust. According to F30, wrinkling results from the earth's being burned and melted or fused together (συντῆκον). In F31, by contrast, the lexicographers' explanation of Antiphon's γρυπανίζειν mentions vibration or shaking (παλλομένην) rather than fire. This explanation could be wrong or incomplete. But it is at least as likely that the two fragments are describing different geological phenomena. F31 refers unmistakably to earthquakes; cf. the class of quakes called παλματίαι in [Aristotle], *De mundo* 396a8–11 and *tremor* in Seneca, *Naturales quaestiones* 6.21.2 (cf. Kidd [1988], 2.817–18). Instead of an earthquake, F30 may describe a volcanic lava-flow which melts the earth's surface and thereby wrinkles it (γρυπάνιον). Volcanic and seismic phenomena are closely related in ancient (as in modern) seismology. Cf. [Aristotle], *De mundo* 395b18–26; Strabo, 1.3.16 = Posidonius, fr. 231; Kidd (1988), 2.811, 821–22; Gilbert (1907), 322–23, with further references. Theophrastus wrote a treatise on the lava-flow from Aetna entitled Περὶ ῥύακος τοῦ ἐν Σικελίᾳ (cf. Diogenes Laertius, 5.49; Regenbogen [1940b], 1422). The two fragments might therefore derive from an account of geological features of the earth's surface produced by earthquakes and volcanoes – a subject of considerable interest to ancient scientists and geographers (cf. Gilbert [1907], 321–22; Capelle [1924], 371–72).

F30

1–2 καῖον . . . συντῆκον: if the neuter forms attested in Harpocration are correct (as is likely), τὸ πῦρ should probably be understood as subject. If the masculine forms attested in the Epitome of Harpocration and derivative sources are right, the subject could be ὁ φλόξ or ὁ ῥύαξ. (For the latter cf. Thucydides, 3.116; Plato, *Phaedo* 111E, 113B; Lycurgus, *In Leocratem* 23.95; Theophrastus, *De lapidibus* 22; Diodorus, *Bibliotheca* 5.6; Appian, *Bellum civile* 5.117; [Aristotle], *Mirabilia* 833a17, 21; Athenaeus, *Dipnosophistae* 11 507B; LSJ, s.v. ῥύαξ 2; Gilbert [1907], 323 n. 1.)

2 γρυπάνιον: Capelle (1924), 366 seems to have understood this as a noun, translating "Krümmung, Wölbung." But the word is certainly an adjective, formed as if from *γρυπανον and meaning "wrinkled." Cf. LSJ, s.v.; Frisk (1960–72), 1.329–30; Hesychius, γ 954 (1.392): γρυπάλιον· γερόντιον. ἢ γρυπάνιον. Stenzel (1924), 40 wrongly inferred from this entry in Hesychius that Antiphon's γρυπάνιον is equivalent to γερόντιον and designates "das vom Alter Runzelige."

F31

1 γρυπανίζειν: this verb does not seem to be attested elsewhere. Cf. the related words γρυπάνιον (F30); γρυπαίνειν (Harpocration, s.v. γρυπάνιον, γ 18); γρυμπάνειν (Hesychius, γ 949, 1.392); γρύπτειν (Harpocration, s.v. γρυπάνιον, γ 18; Hesychius, γ 959, 1.392; LSJ, s.v.), and γρυποῦσθαι (cf. below).

2 ⟨γ⟩ρυποῦσθαι: ῥυποῦσθαι (the reading of z, the only manuscript) makes no sense in the context and is obviously corrupt. ῥυσοῦσθαι (the reading of the *Etymologicum magnum*, adopted by Sauppe, Blass, Diels and Kranz, and Untersteiner) looks like an attempt to make sense of it. Theodoridis' convincing correction ⟨γ⟩ρυποῦσθαι is supported by Harpocration, s.v. γρυπάνιον (γ 18): γρυπαίνειν ἐστί, φησί [*sc.* Διονύσιος ὁ τοῦ Τρύφωνος], τὸ γρυποῦσθαι.

F32

This testimonium (which most likely pertains to the second book of Περὶ ἀληθείας) is concerned with the problem of the origin and salinity of the sea. For the various Presocratic theories on this subject cf. Aristotle, *Meteorology* 353a32–359b26; Aëtius, III.16.1–5 (Diels [1879], 381–82); Cherniss (1935), 131–33, 135–39; Gilbert (1907), 399–415; and below. Unfortunately, the details of Antiphon's theory are obscured by textual difficulties.

For his edition of Aëtius in *Doxographi Graeci*, Diels (1879), 381–82 was content to print the text of [Plut.] substantially as it is transmitted, as did Untersteiner (1962), 66–68. Later, in his edition of the Presocratics, Diels proposed extensive additions which amount to a wholesale rewriting of Aëtius' notice: Ἀντιφῶν ἱδρῶτα τοῦ ⟨πρώτου ὑγροῦ ἐξατμισθέντος ὑπὸ τοῦ⟩ θερμοῦ, ἐξ οὗ τὸ περιλειφθὲν ὑγρὸν ἀπεκρίθη ⟨καὶ θάλασσα ἐπωνομάσθη⟩ τῷ καθεψηθῆναι παραλυκίσασα κτλ. (*FVS* 2.344–45). Diels' additions are far too extensive to command confidence. Furthermore, as emended by Diels the notice seems to credit Antiphon with a theory like that ascribed to Anaximander and Diogenes of Apollonia, who explained the sea as a remnant of the original liquid condition of the earth which has been reduced by evaporation. (Cf. Aristotle, *Meteorology* 353b6–11, 355a21–25; Alexander, *In Aristotelis Meteorologica* 67.3–14 = Theophrastus, Φυσικῶν δόξαι fr. 23, Diels [1879], 494–95; Aëtius, III.16.1, Diels [1879], 381; *FVS* 12 A 27, 64 A 17; Gilbert [1907], 405–6; Cherniss [1935], 131 with n. 529, 135 with n. 544, 137–38 with n. 555.) But this type of theory is quite distinct from the rather different conception of the sea as sweat, and is treated so by Aristotle (cf. *Meteorology* 353b11–13, 357b18–21) as well as by Alexander (cf. *In Aristotelis Meteorologica* 67.14–17). That Antiphon would have combined these different theories seems unlikely. For these reasons, Diels' additions should be rejected. Nevertheless, the text as transmitted is at least problematic, and probably corrupt. In the first place, the words ἱδρῶτα τοῦ θερμοῦ yield no satisfactory meaning (Diels [1879], 382 n. justifiably pronounced them hardly sound, "vix sanum"). Translations such as "durch die Hitze bewirkte" (Zeller in Zeller and Nestle [1920], 1373 n. 1), "provocato dal caldo" (Untersteiner [1962], 67–69), and "resulting from" (Morrison [1972], 223) assign to the bare genitive τοῦ θερμοῦ an instrumental sense that is (to say the least) doubtful. (Daiber [1980], 187 offered a similar translation of the Arabic version of [Plut.], but it is unclear what the underlying Greek was.) Secondly, the metaphor of sea as sweat seems to require some mention of earth (cf. Zeller's paraphrase "Ausschwitzung des Erdkörpers" in Zeller and Nestle [1920], 1373 n. 1, and the remarks on Empedocles below). So perhaps τῆς γῆς or the like has dropped out. In the third place, παραλυκίσασα is corrupt itself or else is evidence of corruption earlier in the sentence, since there is no feminine noun for it to agree with (cf. below).

Despite the textual difficulties, it is a reasonable hypothesis that Antiphon's account of the origin and salinity of the sea resembled that of Empedocles, who likewise called the sea sweat (cf. Gilbert [1907], 406 n. 1). According to Empedocles, the sea was originally formed when particles of moisture present in the earth were expressed by the heat of the sun; its salinity is accounted for by particles of salt which were expressed together with the moisture. (Cf. Aristotle, *Meteorology* 353b11–13, 357a24–26; Aëtius, III.16.3, Diels [1879], 381; *FVS* 31 A 66, B 55; Gilbert [1907], 406–7; Cherniss [1935], 131 with n. 530, 138–39.) Similar "filtration" theories were espoused by Anaxagoras and Metrodorus of Chios, though without the metaphor of sweat. (Cf. Alexander, *In Aristotelis Meteorologica* 67.17–22 = Theophrastus, Φυσικῶν δόξαι fr. 23, Diels [1879], 495; Aëtius, III.16.2, 5, Diels [1879], 381–82; *FVS* 59 A 90, 70 A 19; Gilbert [1907], 408–9; Cherniss [1935], 132 n. 533.) Aëtius' further information that the sweat or sea "became salty by boiling" (τῷ καθεψηθῆναι †παραλυκίσασα†) is puzzling, since the sea's salinity appears to be adequately explained by its being a kind of sweat (cf. Aristotle, *Meteorology* 353b11–13). A rather similar difficulty arises with Anaxagoras' theory of the sea (cf. Aëtius, III.16.2, Diels [1879], 381). Gilbert (1907), 409–10 proposed to solve the problem there by postulating a two-step process, whereby particles of water mingled with salt are first expelled from the earth by the sun's heat to form the sea, and the lighter, fresh-water component of sea water is subsequently evaporated, allowing the salt content to manifest itself more clearly. If this explanation is right, Antiphon's theory may have been similar, and therefore indebted perhaps to Anaxagoras as well as to Empedocles (cf. Zeller in Zeller and Nestle [1920], 1373 n. 1).

1 ἱδρῶτα: for the metaphor of sweat cf. (in addition to Empedocles' theory, discussed above) Aëtius, IV.1.6 (Diels [1879], 385): Ἔφορος ὁ ἱστοριογράφος κατὰ θέρος φησὶν ἀναχαλᾶσθαι τὴν ὅλην Αἴγυπτον καὶ οἱονεὶ ἐξιδροῦν τὸ πολὺ νᾶμα. Aristotle also uses the metaphor, despite his criticism of Empedocles over it (cf. *Meteorology* 350a1–2; Cherniss [1935], 138 n. 557).

†τοῦ θερμοῦ†: on the textual problem see introductory note above.

περιληφθέν: περιληφθὲν (the reading of codd. A E α of [Plut.])

is required by the sense; περιλειφθέν (the reading of codd. M m, of *P. Antin.*, and of Eusebius) may be merely the result of iotacism. "The contained moisture" refers (presumably) to the water originally contained in the earth that is expelled to make the sea.

2 τῷ καθεψηθῆναι: according to Diodorus Siculus (*Bibliotheca* 1.40), boiling "sweetens" the water of the Nile ἅτε φύσει τοῦ πυρώδους πᾶν τὸ ὑγρὸν ἀπογλυκαίνοντος. Cf. Xenophon, *De re equestri* 9.6 (both passages cited by LSJ, s.v. καθέψω). But Antiphon evidently follows the common Presocratic idea that the lighter, fresh-water component of sea water is evaporated by the heat of the sun, rendering the remaining liquid saltier. (Cf. Aristotle, *Meteorology* 354b26–30, 355a32–34; Gilbert [1907], 404, 409–10, 411–12; Cherniss [1935], 138.)

†παραλυκίσασα†: Mras (1956), 2.420 n. and Untersteiner (1962), 69 defended παραλυκίσασα (the reading of codd. M m of [Plut.] as well as of Eusebius; παρακυλίσασα, the reading of codd. A E α, is a *vox nihili*). They suggested that it agrees with θάλασσα understood as the implied subject; but this is clearly impossible as the sentence stands. Either παραλυκίσασα is corrupt or something has fallen out. The most plausible solution seems to be παραλυκίσαν, a marginal correction by the second corrector of cod. Voss. (Diels [1879], 38–39 seems to ascribe this correction to Guillaume Budé.) παραλυκίζειν (from παρα- and *ἁλυκίζω, from ἁλυκός) is not attested elsewhere, but may have been coined by Antiphon.

2–3 ὅπερ . . . συμβαίνει: cf. Aristotle, *Meteorology* 357a28–32.

F33

This citation, from the second book of Περὶ ἀληθείας, may derive from a medical context (cf. Introduction, section III; F34–39 with commentary). The term φορίνη normally is used of the hide of animals, especially pigs. Cf. Pollux, 6.55 (τὸ δὲ δέρμα τοῦ χοίρου φορίνην καλοῦσι); Herodas, 4.16; Athenaeus, *Dipnosophistae* 9 381C, 13 585E; LSJ, s.v. It is applied to human beings elsewhere only in Aristomenes, fr. 10 (quoted by Harpocration immediately after the citation from Antiphon) and Plutarch, *Quomodo adulator* 57A. In Plutarch the tone is humorous and/or derogatory; and the same may be suspected in Aristomenes (though nothing is known of the context). Whether φορίνη had similar overtones in Antiphon it is impossible to say. Cf. Latin *corium* and English "hide." A similar phenomenon is seen in the Greek ῥύγχος (cited by Headlam in Headlam and Knox [1922], 179, 248), which properly denotes the snout of a pig or other animal but is applied also to the human face (cf. English "snout").

F34–39

Most of these fragments are preserved exclusively by Pollux. (F38 is cited also in Photius, and probably in Hesychius as well.) They appear to derive from an embryological or other medical context in the second book of Περὶ ἀληθείας (cf. Introduction, section III). This is all but certain in the case of F39, which is cited explicitly from Περὶ ἀληθείας (though without a book-number); and very likely for F36–38, which are technical terms from embryology and anatomy. The situation is less certain with F34–35, which are not as obviously connected with medicine or embryology, and are cited without a book-title (cf. commentary ad locc.). Van Spaan (1773), 829–30 and Sauppe (1896), 519 theorized that F34–37 derive from a medical work entitled Σύνοψις τῶν κατ' ἄνθρωπον, by an otherwise unknown physician named Antiphon. The existence of this work they inferred from a scholium on Pollux, 2.224 (Bethe [1900–37], 1.151 n.): ἐντωυθα σύνοψις [ἐνταῦθα σύνοψις Blass: ἐν τῷ θ' συνόψεως Meineke] τῶν κατ' ἄνθρωπον. (Cf. also Meineke [1839–57], 3.299.) As Blass (1881), 150 n. rightly saw, however, the scholium refers to Pollux's own catalog (σύνοψις) of terminology dealing with the human body. "Antiphon the doctor" and his Σύνοψις are merely a figment.

F34

καρόω usually means "stun" or "stupefy." From the context in Pollux, LSJ, s.v. inferred that Antiphon applied the verb to the effects of wine. Cf. Anaxandrides, fr. 3; Aristotle, fr. 106 (ὁ μὲν γὰρ οἶνος καρηβαρικός, ὁ δὲ κρίθινος καρωτικός); Athenaeus, *Dipnosophistae* I 33A; John Chrysostom, *De resurrectione* 50.435 Migne; etc. If this is right, the sense would be "make drowsy" or "sleepy." Diels (*FVS* 2.345 n.) interpreted in similar fashion, but suggested that the fragment might belong to Πολιτικός rather than Περὶ ἀληθείας (cf. F76 with commentary).

F35

ἐναιμῶδες seems not to be attested elsewhere. If it derives from an embryological context in Περὶ ἀληθείας, it may have modified (e.g.) χόριον (cf. F36).

F36

χόριον ordinarily refers to the outermost fetal membrane. But as the fragment itself makes clear, Antiphon applied it to the whole group of fetal membranes – a usage found also in the Hippocratic corpus (cf. *De natura pueri* 16; Lonie [1981], 176). This despite the fact that Empedocles seems already to have named (and so presumably distinguished) the ἀμνίον (cf. *FVS* 31 B 70; but see the reservations of Bollack [1965–69], 3.2.435). In light of its frequency in Hippocratic gynecological treatises, Lonie (1981), 176 suggested that χόριον was a technical term from midwifery, which Antiphon "is introducing ... to the lay public."

F37

ἐπίπλοος (ἐπίπλους) is the *omentum maius*, a membrane that is attached to the stomach and covers the transverse colon and small intestine. Both masculine and neuter forms of the noun are attested. The neuter is regular in the Hippocratic corpus, Aristotle, and most later authors. For the masculine cf. Herodotus, 2.47; Rufus of Ephesus, *De partibus corporis humani* 53; Athenaeus, *Dipnosophistae* 3 106E–F; *Anecdota Graeca Oxoniensia* 3.107; and Galen as cited below. (For variant spellings of the noun cf. LSJ, s.v. ἐπίπλοον.) It is surprising that Antiphon used both masculine and neuter forms in the same work (that the word is cited from more than one work of the *corpus Antiphonteum* seems unlikely). Yet Galen did the same: cf. *De usu partium* 3.286 (τὸ καλούμενον ἐπίπλοον), 3.336 (τὰ κατὰ τὸν ἐπίπλουν ἀγγεῖα), 3.372 (αἱ κατὰ τὸν ἐπίπλουν φλέβες).

F38

It is likely (if not certain) that Hesychius' entry refers to Antiphon. ἄμβλωμα means "aborted fetus" (ἔκτρωμα, as Hesychius glosses it). Cf. Gregory of Nyssa, *In inscriptiones Psalmorum* 2.15 (44.596 Migne); Eustratius, *In Analytica posteriora* 185.13; Eustathius, *Commentarii ad Iliadem* 1.134.17; etc. (LSJ, s.v. refer to Aretaeus, *De curatione acutorum morborum* 1.6; but the correct reading there is ἄμβλωσις.)

F39

LSJ, s.v. interpret ἀνάπηρος as "maimed," "mutilated." The related terms πηρόω and πήρωσις can refer to congenital deformities as well as to mutilation (cf. [Hippocrates], *De semine* 10–11; Lonie [1981], 145). ἀνάπηρος, then, could mean "deformed," "malformed" (a sense not recognized in LSJ) and refer to birth defects. Cf. Plato, *Republic* 460C; Aristotle, *De generatione animalium* 743a30, 769b29, 775a4, *Historia animalium* 585b29; Dionysius of Halicarnassus, *Antiquitates Romanae* 2.15.2; Plutarch, *Publicola* 21; Dio of Prusa, *or.* 10.11. If so, then this fragment also would belong to an embryological context in Περὶ ἀληθείας.

The explanation of ἀνάπηρος offered by Pollux, 2.60–61 (ἀνάπηρος δ' ἐστὶν ὁ πᾶν τὸ σῶμα πεπηρωμένος) is not supported by the evidence for the use of the word. Contrast Photius, *Lexicon* s.v. (α 1595, 1.162): ἀνάπηρον· οὐδὲν πλέον σημαίνει τοῦ πηρός.

F40

This fragment seems to have been first attributed to Περὶ ἀληθείας by Sauppe (1896), 520. Nothing about its content or the way in which it is cited by Pollux supports the attribution, however, and its provenance remains quite uncertain.

βάψις (from βάπτω) occurs elsewhere only in a fragment of "Perictione" quoted by Stobaeus, where it refers to the dyeing of clothes: ἠμφιάσθαι ⟨δ'⟩ εἵματα ἀπεικότα λίην καὶ ποικίλα ἀπὸ θαλασσίης βάψιος τοῦ κόχλου ἢ ἄλλης χρόης πολυτελέος μωρίη πολλή (4.28.19, 5.690 = Thesleff [1965], 143). Used here in connection with bronze and iron, however, its sense is uncertain. LSJ, s.v. and others suggest that it refers to "quenching," the dipping of heated steel into cold water or oil, which forms part of the well-known process of tempering or hardening iron or steel. Cf. *Odyssey* 9.391–93; Blümner (1875–87), 4.344–48; Pachler (1885); Rommel (1929), 2128–29. In that case, however, Pollux's reference to χαλκοῦ is problematic, since there is no such thing as tempering of bronze (the claims of certain ancient and modern authorities to the contrary notwithstanding). Cf. Blümner (1875–87), 4.333–37; Forbes (1972), 43 (but contrast 159–60, where he seems to adopt the opposite view); and below. Others interpret Antiphon's βάψις in reference to the coloring of metal (so Blümner [1875–87], 4.334 n. 1, with references to older commentators who interpreted in this fashion; Thomson in Headlam and Thomson [1966], 2.54). As indicated above, the only other known occurrence of βάψις refers in fact to coloring (albeit of clothes). More relevant perhaps is Aeschylus, *Agamemnon* 612 (χαλκοῦ βαφάς), which Rose (1958), 47–48 and others have interpreted (not without plausibility) as referring to the coloring of metal (cf. Fraenkel [1950], 2.304–5, with references). Blümner and Thomson contended that the context in Pollux supports a similar interpretation of Antiphon's βάψις; but Fraenkel noted the weakness of this argument. Nevertheless, the possibility that Antiphon referred to the coloring of metal should not be ruled out. Ancient literary references to the coloring of bronze, though often discounted by modern commentators, receive support from a growing body of scientific evidence for the practice of artificial patination and painting of bronze objects, in both the classical and later periods. Cf. Born (1990), 183–94, with references. Yet if Antiphon's βάψις is interpreted in this way, then Pollux's mention of iron alongside bronze becomes difficult, for no such coloring of iron is conceivable.

The possibility that Antiphon employed βάψις in reference to both the quenching of iron and the coloring of bronze can be dismissed. It is possible, however, that the words χαλκοῦ καὶ σιδήρου do not derive from him at all (as is usually assumed). They might instead have been added by Pollux, in order to indicate that the original context was a metallurgical one. In that case, Antiphon will have used βάψις in the sense of "quenching," whether literally or metaphorically. (For metaphors from quenching cf. Aristotle, *Politics* 1334a8; Plutarch, *Alexander* 32; Blümner [1875–87], 4.345 n. 4; Rommel [1929], 2128.) Pollux might have added χαλκοῦ with the above-cited passage of *Agamemnon* in mind, or because he shared the widespread late-antique belief in a lost art of tempering bronze. (Cf. Plutarch, *De Pythiae oraculis* 395B; scholium on Hesiod, *Works and Days* 143–51, 58.13–17; Eustathius, *Commentarii ad Iliadem* 1.146.16–18, 661.17; Pausanias, 2.3.3; Blümner [1875–87], 4.333–34; Schröder [1990], 117–18.) But without more evidence, it is impossible to reach any firm conclusions about Antiphon's use of βάψις.

F41

Sauppe (1896), 520 first seems to have attributed this fragment to Περὶ ἀληθείας. Pollux cites it without a book-title, however, and its provenance remains conjectural. βιομήχανος ("good at getting a living") appears elsewhere only in Aristotle, who applies it twice to birds. Cf. *Historia animalium* 616b11, 17–18; Bonitz (1870), 137a37–38; LSJ, s.v.

F42

Pollux cites ταλάντωσις explicitly from Antiphon. The citations of the word in Hesychius, Bachmann's *Anecdota*, Photius, and the *Suda* (= F42(b)) may also refer to him, or they could refer to Basil, *Homiliae in hexaemeron* 6.11 (29.144 Migne), who uses the dative form ταλαντώσει (as in Hesychius). In any case, it is quite uncertain whether this fragment belongs to Περὶ ἀληθείας and the sophist Antiphon (as Sauppe [1896], 520 first suggested). ταλάντωσις seems to occur elsewhere only in Aristotle, *Meteorology* 354a11; Alexander, *In Aristotelis Meteorologica* 69.30; and the passage of Basil cited above. In all of these passages it signifies the oscillation or ebb and flow of the sea in straits. Cf. LSJ, s.v. 2, and the related verb ταλαντεύεσθαι (Aristotle, *Meteorology* 354a8). Antiphon appears to have used the word differently, in the sense of "weighing" or "balancing" (so LSJ, s.v.; cf. s.v. ταλαντεύω 2).

F43

The attribution of this fragment to Περὶ ἀληθείας is guaranteed by Hesychius, but it is uncertain which book it derives from. If the lexicographers' interpretation is correct, Antiphon's ἄβιος provides an example of the so-called alpha-intensivum (α-ἐπιτατικόν). Cf. *Iliad* 11.155, which became the *locus classicus* for this usage (probably by a misinterpretation; cf. LSJ, s.v. ἄξυλος); Schwyzer (1939–53), 1.433; West (1990), 121, 309 (who tries to cast doubt on several apparent examples in Aeschylus). Antiphon may have been influenced by the above-mentioned passage of the *Iliad*, and/or by the Homeric proper name Ἄβιοι (*Iliad* 13.6), which some in antiquity interpreted to mean "powerful" (πολύβιος) or "long-lived" (μακρόβιος). Cf. scholia AT *Iliad* N 6*d* (3.395–96); *Anecdota Graeca* s.v. ἄβιος (6 Bachmann) = Photius, *Lexicon* s.v. (α 37, 1.11); Eustathius, *Commentarii ad Iliadem* 3.426.6.

F44

F44 comprises three substantial fragments from Περὶ ἀληθείας preserved on papyri from Oxyrhynchus. *P.Oxy.* 1364 (published first by Grenfell and Hunt [1915] and re-edited in Decleva Caizzi and Bastianini [1989]) consists of two fragments of continuous text and eleven small, unconnected scraps. (For the latter, not included here, cf. Grenfell and Hunt [1915], 100–1.) The larger of the two fragments (fr. 1 = F44(a)) contains six columns of thirty-three lines and one of thirty-four (as it appears; but the text is very fragmentary). The smaller (fr. 2 = F44(b)) is now supplemented by *P.Oxy.* 3647 (first published by Funghi [1984]), which supplies line-ends in the second column (II.4–11) and the upper portions of two additional columns (which in the case of this fragment seem to consist of thirty-four lines each). *P.Oxy.* 1364 + 3647 is plausibly dated on paleographical grounds to the early third century AD (cf. Grenfell and Hunt [1915], 92; Decleva Caizzi and Bastianini [1989], 181). The text is furnished with marks of punctuation, accentuation, breathing, elision, and quantity as well as with corrections, supplied by the hand of a (probably contemporary) corrector. The lines of the papyrus do not present a uniform length, ranging from eight to fifteen letters (three to seven syllables). At the ends of lines, the scribe sometimes condensed the letter-size to fit letters in or (conversely) used the *diple*-sign to fill up space. (For further details on the physical characteristics of the papyrus and the handwriting cf. Grenfell and Hunt [1915], 92; Ohly [1928], 62–63; Funghi [1984], 1; Decleva Caizzi and Bastianini [1989], 180–82.)

The attribution of *P.Oxy.* 1364 + 3647 to Περὶ ἀληθείας is guaranteed by the fortunate coincidence (first noticed by Wilamowitz) of F44(a) I.18–20 with a citation in Harpocration (s.v. ἄγοι, α 7: Ἀντιφῶν δ' ἐν τῷ Περὶ ἀληθείας φησίν· τοὺς νόμους μεγάλους ἄγοι, ἀντὶ τοῦ ἡγοῖτο). Unfortunately, however, Harpocration does not indicate which book of Περὶ ἀληθείας his citation derives from. Most commentators assign both fr. 1 (= F44(a)) and fr. 2 (= F44(b)) to the first book, on grounds of subject-matter (so Grenfell and Hunt [1915], 93; Philippson [1918], 122; Stenzel [1924], 39; Aly [1929], 116–17; Schmid [1940], 160 n. 8, 162; Untersteiner [1954], 249 n. 127 = [1967], 2.72 n. 127). They call attention to the fact that, whereas all of the fragments explicitly attributed to the second book deal with scientific or medical subjects, a few fragments of possibly ethical content (F2, F17, F21) are cited from book 1. Furthermore, the opposition of law and nature, which plays so important a role in the argument of F44(a) and F44(b), appears also in F15, which is explicitly attributed to book 1. Such considerations are persuasive but not decisive, and those commentators (including Kuiper [1920], 24 n. 1; Mewaldt [1929], 79 with n. 14) who assign these fragments to the second book of Περὶ ἀληθείας could be right (cf. Decleva Caizzi and Bastianini [1989], 182). The relative position at least of fr. 1 (= F44(a)) within its roll or book (whether the first or the second) can be established with greater certainty. For the stichometrical sign Δ in the margin at F44(a) VI.24 most likely indicates the 400th so-called normal line (one consisting of 15–16 syllables; cf. Ohly [1928], 1–30, 75). On the assumption that one such normal line is equal to approximately three lines of *P.Oxy.* 1364 + 3647, it can be estimated that at least one thousand lines (some 30 columns) of text preceded the beginning of fr. 1 (= F44(a)). This fragment (at least) seems therefore to derive from the middle portion of the roll or book which contained it. (Grenfell and Hunt [1915], 93 reached a different conclusion; but they ignored the factor of the normal line.)

The relative order of the two fragments is also uncertain. Funghi (1984), 1 (followed by Decleva Caizzi and Bastianini [1989], 180, 183) contended that fr. 2 (= F44(b)) originally preceded fr. 1 (= F44(a)). She pointed out that the former fragment is dirtier than the latter and not as well preserved, and so may have come from nearer the outside of the roll. At the same time, Funghi believed that the two fragments were separated by not much more than three columns, the minimum interval according to the indications of *kollesis* (cf. Funghi [1984], 1; Decleva Caizzi and Bastianini [1989], 180). As evidence of their original proximity, Funghi adduced the striking resemblance between the lists of natural functions in F44(a)II.30–III.18 and F44(b)II.27–III.12. But this hardly proves her point. If Funghi's estimate of the distance separating the two fragments is even approximately right, then her explanation for the inferior state of preservation of fr. 2 can hardly stand (see the remarks above on the relative position of fr. 1 within its roll, and cf. Luginbill [1997], 170 n. 29). Funghi further suggested that Antiphon's argument would progress most naturally if it passed from the treatment of nature (which is primary) in fr. 2 to the consideration of law and custom (which is secondary) in fr. 1. There is no doubt that Antiphon regarded φύσις as primary and νόμος as secondary; but Funghi's suggestion assumes more than is known about the logic and course of his argument. Untersteiner (1962), 91–92, (1954), 249 n. 127 = (1967), 2.72 n. 127 advocated a very different order. He contended that fr. 2 supplies the conclusion to the argument developed in *P.Oxy.* 1797 (= F44(c)), and so would place the latter fragment between fr. 1 (= F44(a)) and fr. 2 (= F44(b)). Untersteiner further suggested (arbitrarily and without evidence) that fr. 2 may have concluded the first book of Περὶ ἀληθείας and at the same time presaged the theme of Περὶ ὁμονοίας. *P.Oxy.* 1797 (= F44(c)) and fr. 1 (= F44(a)) both deal with the subject of legal justice; and there are other, more remote connections between the two (cf. commentary on F44(c)). Nonetheless, Untersteiner's proposed arrangement (like Funghi's) rests on assumptions about the course of Antiphon's argument that are no better than guesses. In the present state of the evidence, it seems best to refrain from conclusions about the relative order of fr. 1 (= F44(a)) and fr. 2 (= F44(b)). For the sake of convenience, the two fragments are printed and discussed here in the order first assigned them by Grenfell and Hunt (1915), which Diels and Kranz in *FVS* and even Untersteiner (1962) followed. (Decleva Caizzi and Bastianini [1989] follow Funghi and place fr. 2 before fr. 1.)

P.Oxy. 1797 (= F44(c)) was originally published by Grenfell and Hunt (1922) and re-edited in Decleva Caizzi and Bastianini (1989). It consists of two columns of writing, each containing thirty-eight lines. The lines range in length from eleven to eighteen letters. (A second fragment, consisting only of the letters τους νομ̣[, does not certainly belong to the same roll and is not considered here; cf. Grenfell and Hunt [1922], 122; Decleva Caizzi and Bastianini [1989], 214.) The writing is plausibly assigned to the first half of the third century AD and is similar (though not identical) to that of *P.Oxy.* 1364 + 3647. Accents, breathings, diaereses, marks of quantity, high and medial dots, and a pair of *paragraphi* have been added, most likely by a second hand. Grenfell and Hunt (1922), 119 suggested that this may be the same hand as the one which made analogous additions in *P.Oxy.* 1364 + 3647. But despite the affirmations of Untersteiner (1954), 249 n. 127 = (1967), 2.72 n. 127, this remains uncertain. Except for the addition of an *iota mutum* at I.18, there are no interlinear variants or corrections. (On the marginal symbol at II.18 cf. commentary ad loc.)

Although *P.Oxy.* 1797 belonged to the same find as *P.Oxy.* 1364 + 3647, the differences in handwriting and in the length and width of columns make it unlikely that the two derive from the same roll. As a result, the external evidence (from Harpocration) that guarantees the ascription of F44(a) and F44(b) does not cover this fragment. Nevertheless, Grenfell and Hunt's original attribution of the fragment to the sophist Antiphon in general, and to Περὶ ἀληθείας in particular, has never been questioned. It is supported by considerations of both style and content (cf. Grenfell and Hunt [1922], 119; Decleva Caizzi and Bastianini [1989], 214). Like F44(a), this fragment offers a critical examination of conventional notions about just conduct and of the relation of justice to individual self-interest. Its style (like that of F44(a) and F44(b)) is marked by the use of short clauses, antithetical parallelism, and rhythm. Grenfell and Hunt (1922) suggested that the fragment might derive from Antiphon's Περὶ ὁμονοίας or Πολιτικός rather than from Περὶ ἀληθείας. But the fragments plausibly attributed to Περὶ ὁμονοίας differ radically from F44(c) in style as well as in content (cf. Bignone [1938], 99–100). And the little that is known about Πολιτικός does not commend the attribution to it of F44(c). Bignone (1938), 100 (but contrast 126–27) suggested that *P.Oxy.* 1797 and *P.Oxy.* 1364 + 3647 may have belonged to different copies of Περὶ ἀληθείας. The suggestion is attractive, but unfortunately unverifiable. Which book of Περὶ ἀληθείας F44(c) belonged to is uncertain, as is its relative position *vis-à-vis* F44(a) and F44(b). Grenfell and Hunt (1922), 119–20 suggested that it came later in the same roll or book as the other fragments. Untersteiner (1962), 91, 95–96, (1954), 248–49 with n. 127 = (1967), 2.78 with n. 127 located it between F44(a) and F44(b), the latter of which (he suggested) formed the end of book I of Περὶ ἀληθείας (cf. above). Diels and Kranz (*FVS* 2.353) and Bignone (1938), 126–27 (but contrast 100) assigned F44(c) to a different book than F44(a) and F44(b). But none of these suggestions is supported by any real evidence. As Bignone (1938), 110–11 and Untersteiner both noted, the subject-matter of F44(c) bears comparison with the criticism of judicial procedure in columns VI–VII of F44(a). But the contexts are sufficiently different to justify caution in drawing any conclusion about the relative positions of the two fragments.

F44(a)

The argument of this fragment, in the first instance, concerns the relative merits of law and nature as standards of advantageous conduct for the individual. More broadly, the fragment deals with the general relationship of opposition obtaining between the two: the celebrated antithesis of νόμος and φύσις. (On the origin and history of the antithesis cf. Beardslee [1918], 68–81, Heinimann [1945]; for an attempt to put Antiphon's discussion in its historical context cf. Introduction, section VII.) The expressions οἱ νόμοι, τὰ νόμιμα and τὰ τῶν νόμων – which are used interchangeably throughout F44(a) – must be taken in a broad sense, as referring to written laws as well as to customs, conventions, and unwritten norms of conduct. (Cf. von Arnim [1916], 7–8; Heinimann [1945], 139–40; Barnes [1982], 513; Ostwald [1990], 297; Decleva Caizzi and Bastianini [1989], 183, 203.) All attempts to restrict the focus of Antiphon's discussion to written law primarily (so Moulton [1972], 333 and *passim*; de Romilly [1971], 80 n. 9) are refuted by passages such as II.30–III.18 and IV.32–V.13, which indubitably envisage unwritten as well as written norms of conduct. The other term of the antithesis, φύσις, appears everywhere in this fragment with the article (contrast F44(b), II.10 with commentary). Passages such as II.30–III.18, III.25–IV.1, and IV.8–24 show that it refers primarily to individual human nature. Cf. Heinimann (1945), 133; Kerferd (1956–57), 32; Havelock (1957), 277; Barnes (1982), 513; Nill (1985), 59 with n. 27; Ostwald (1990), 298–99; Luginbill (1997), 177 n. 53. Comparable is the use of φύσις in the context of the buried bed argument to refer to wood as the essential nature of an individual bed, in contradistinction to the conventional shape imposed on it (cf. commentary on F15; Dillon [1984], 129–30 sensed a confusion of different senses of φύσις). Whether (as David Sedley suggests) φύσις took on a wider sense in the argument of Περὶ ἀληθείας, designating the natural order of things generally as contrasted with all human attempts to impose artificial order on the world, is possible but uncertain. No single passage in the fragments requires such an interpretation; and φύσις in the sense of "universal nature" appears but infrequently in extant texts from the late fifth century (cf. Beardslee [1918], 4–5 and *passim*). If Antiphon applied φύσις primarily to the nature(s) of individual things like people and beds, this was in accord with the general usage of his time. Heinimann (1945), 127–28, 138–39, and *passim* contended that Antiphon's conception of (human) nature was derived chiefly from the sphere of medical thought. Influence from this quarter is possible, even likely, in light of his evident interest in medicine (cf. F29A, F33–F39 with commentary; Introduction, section III). But Antiphon's conception of human nature is more than merely biological (cf. Nill [1985], 71–72); and the evidence of Thucydides, tragedy, and other contemporary literature reveals a broad range of reflection on human nature and its characteristics which could have influenced his thinking on this subject. Luginbill (1997), 174–83 argued that Antiphon's use of the νόμος–φύσις antithesis reveals no preference for nature (which he in fact regarded ambivalently as "a dark and powerful force" of at best mixed potential) but is merely a convenient tool to subvert the Athenian democratic equation of justice with obedience to existing laws. This argument ignores (among other things) the generally positive terms in which φύσις is evaluated (*vis-à-vis* νόμος) in the fragment, as well as the conclusion in IV.18–24 that true or real advantages are those which help *nature.*

I.5–II.23 Starting from the conventional conception of justice as obedience to the laws of the city (cf. commentary on I.6–11), Antiphon argues that the most advantageous way for an individual to deal with justice is to obey the laws in the presence of witnesses, but disregard them in their absence. This is so because transgression of the laws entails harm only when it is observed and so exposes the transgressor to the sanctions of the justice system (II.7–8 αἰσχύνης καὶ ζημίας). Violations against nature, by contrast, are punished automatically. For now, the argument simply assumes (1) that behavior in accordance with the laws is disadvantageous for the individual, while behavior contrary to the laws is advantageous; and (2) that behavior in accordance with nature is advantageous. (That behavior *contrary* to nature is disadvantageous follows from the fact of its automatic punishment, as well as from the fact that it entails more pain than is necessary and less pleasure than is possible; cf. IV.1–V.24.) No real argument for the second assumption is offered anywhere in the fragment as extant (unless the discussion in IV.1–24 on the "free" advantages laid down by nature qualifies as such); Antiphon may have regarded it as self-evident. But the remainder of the fragment from II.23 forward constitutes an extended demonstration of the first assumption, as Antiphon argues that most legal prescriptions are in conflict with nature, and thus disadvantageous for the individual. It has often been supposed that Antiphon's larger purpose is to expose the inadequacy of the conventional equation of justice with legal obedience (δίκαιον = νόμιμον), and so clear the ground for an alternative, and superior, conception of justice. So Diels (1917), 87–89; Philippson (1918), 123; Bignone (1938), 74–76, 79–81, 109–10; Pfister (1925), 202–3; Altheim (1926), 263; Regenbogen (1940a), 98–99; Lana (1951), 318; Untersteiner (1962), 73, (1954), 243 = (1967), 2.69; Pohlenz (1966), 69; Niceforo (1972), 405, 409. (Cf. Democritus, *FVS* 68 B 181.) Many of these commentators conceive of this alternative form of justice in relation to φύσις or nature. But Luginbill (1997), 170–74 and *passim* argued that Antiphon's purpose was to refute the prevailing Athenian democratic equation of justice with law (δίκαιον with νόμιμον) in order to make room for a conception of justice more in line with his own oligarchic sympathies. The argument of the fragment, however, provides absolutely no support for the notion that Antiphon rejected the definition of justice in 1.6–11 as a definition or wished to propose an alternative one. On this (crucial) point cf. Furley (1981); Introduction, section VII; and commentary on F44(c).

I

5–6 Decleva Caizzi and Bastianini (1989), 192, 203 proposed to join the small scrap fr. 5 (Grenfell–Hunt) with the end of l. 5, and so to restore νόμι[μον]. They suggested that Antiphon alludes to the conventional equation of δίκαιον and νόμιμον, from which the definition of justice in ll. 6–11 would follow. This is possible but uncertain. Since the definition is not Antiphon's own (cf. below), Körte's proposal τίθημι ὅτι (Körte [1924], 153) is most unlikely.

6–11 δικαιοσύνη . . . παραβαίνειν: a thoroughly commonplace conception of justice. Cf. Lysias, *or.* 2.19; Xenophon, *Memorabilia* 4.4.12–13; Plato, *Republic* 359A; Diels (1917), 86; Barnes (1982), 516 n. 6, with further parallels. Luginbill (1997), 170–74 understood it specifically as the Athenian democratic conception, which equated justice with obedience to the prevailing laws of the δῆμος. But the passages cited and other evidence show that it is unwarranted to interpret the conception of justice in question in such narrow terms. According to Bignone (1938), 73–78, this was the definition of justice defended by Protagoras, whose view Antiphon is here attempting to reduce to absurdity (cf. the equation of δίκαιον with δόξα τῆς πόλεως in Plato, *Theaetetus* 167A–B, 172A). Bignone's interpretation has been embraced by Regenbogen (1940a), 99, 101–2; Funghi (1984), 4; Decleva Caizzi and Bastianini (1989), 203, and others. Pohlenz (1966), 69 n. 75 and La Face (1969), 31–32 rejected it, while Untersteiner (1962), 74, (1954), 246 n. 100 = (1967), 2.69 n. 100 tried to steer a middle course. Even if this conception of justice is rightly ascribed to Protagoras (which La Face [1969], 28 n. 9 justifiably doubted), there is no reason whatsoever to think that Antiphon had him specifically in mind. More important, the whole notion that Antiphon intended to discredit the conception of justice in question is most likely mistaken (cf. above).

7 δ' οὖν τά: Grenfell and Hunt's πά]ντα was rightly rejected by

Schöne (1920–24), 139–40, who proposed δ' ἦν (the "philosophic" imperfect). Diels' οὖ|ν (a favorite particle of Antiphon's; cf. commentary on I.12–16) seems too short for the space (cf. Decleva Caizzi and Bastianini [1989], 199). δ' οὖν (Decleva Caizzi and Bastianini) may be resumptive, but can hardly be inferential (as Decleva Caizzi and Bastianini seem to suppose).

8 νόμιμα: *pace* Havelock (1957), 270, the use of νόμιμα here and at II.3–4 below hardly implies that Antiphon had in mind customs more than written laws (cf. introductory note above and commentary on II.30–31).

12–16 χρῷτ' ἂν ... δικαιοσύνῃ: these lines state the proposition which the argument in I.23–II.23 will support. οὖν may be inferential (so Kerferd [1956–57], 27; cf. II.3) or progressive (cf. III.18). Since Antiphon envisages the violation of laws when witnesses are absent, the phrase χρῆσθαι δικαιοσύνῃ here can hardly mean "conduct oneself justly," as it does in Herodotus, 2.151 and Xenophon, *Memorabilia* 1.2.24 (cf. Redard [1953], 22). The sense is rather "use," "practice," or "employ" justice. Cf. Plato, *Gorgias* 483D (ἐπεὶ ποίῳ δικαίῳ χρώμενος Ξέρξης ἐπὶ τὴν Ἑλλάδα ἐστράτευσεν κτλ.); LSJ, s.v. χράω (B) C.II; Redard (1953), 19–25. To ignore its requirements when unobserved by witnesses is certainly one way of "practicing" justice, and the difficulties raised about the phrase by Kerferd (1956–57), 27 are hypercritical. Cf. Furley (1981), 83; Guthrie (1971a), 108 with n. 4 (his translation, "manipulating," is, however, too strong).

13–15 μάλιστα ἑαυτῷ ξυμφερόντως: this means "with the greatest advantage possible" rather than "with perfect self-advantage." For as Kerferd (1956–57), 28 pointed out, someone who obeys the laws in the presence of witnesses will avoid legal sanctions but suffer the harm (II.18 τὸ κακόν) which results automatically from violating nature. Thus (as Kerferd put it) "the individual who is being watched is in an impossible situation, because whatever he does he is bound to suffer." Kerferd finds this problematic; but Antiphon nowhere claims that it is possible to act with perfect self-advantage, given the existence of laws which are mostly inimical to nature (cf. II.26–30). All his argument requires for consistency is that the harm which results from violating nature when the presence of witnesses compels legal obedience should be *less* than the damage (II.7–8 αἰσχύνη καὶ ζημία) which would result from transgressing the laws in such a situation. Wiesner (1994), 231 n. 33 also ignored the calculus of relative advantage when he argued that to obey the laws and violate nature in the presence of witnesses is not at all so advantageous, since it means avoiding the lesser ("geringeren") harm through human opinion (διὰ δόξαν) while incurring the genuine ("echten") harm δι' ἀλήθειαν. But there is no reason to assume that the harm which results from transgressing laws is always the lesser; where it is, Antiphon's argument would dictate following nature, despite the presence of witnesses.

18–20 τοὺς νόμους μεγάλους ἄγοι: for ἄγω = "regard," "consider" cf. Herodotus, 7.150; Sophocles, *Oedipus Tyrannus* 775; Cratinus, frr. 119, 347; LSJ, s.v. v; Kock (1880–88), 1.50; Jacoby (1908), 49; Aly (1929), 155 n. 157. The words τοὺς νόμους μεγάλους ἄγω are quoted in a late scholium on Euripides, *Hecuba* 386 (cf. Kock [1880–88], 3.536; the scholium is not included in Schwartz's edition) and were printed by Kock (1880–88) as com. adesp. fr. 726. But Kassel and Austin rightly consider this a paraphrase of Antiphon (cf. *PCG* 8.511).

20–22 μονούμενος δὲ μαρτύρων: in the satyric drama *Sisyphus*, Critias (or Euripides; cf. Dihle [1977]) suggested that belief in gods was invented precisely for the purpose of deterring crime in the absence of witnesses (cf. *FVS* 88 B 25). Cf. Xenophon, *Memorabilia* 1.4.19; Guthrie (1971a), 244. As Grenfell and Hunt noted, the words μονούμενος δὲ ... τῆς φύσεως form an iambic trimeter (φύσεως scanned as a disyllable). Moulton (1972), 332 suggested that this might be accidental (cf. Aristotle's remarks in *Rhetoric* 1408b33–35 and *Poetics* 1449a24–27 on iambic rhythms in everyday speech and prose). But the occurrence of similar passages in other fragments suggests a deliberate stylistic device. Cf. IV.14, VI.17–20; F44(b)II.7–9; F49, ll. 2–4; F57; F62; Grenfell and Hunt (1915), 102; Jacoby (1908), 65–66; Bignone (1938), 190 n. 2, 195–96.

22–23 τὰ τῆς φύσεως: commentators customarily supply substantives such as "precepts," "norms," "Forderungen," "disposizioni," etc. with this phrase. Decleva Caizzi and Bastianini (1989), 204 suggested that Antiphon deliberately eschewed the expression "law of nature," in order to avoid any ambiguity between "nature" and a type of law which might (because of its universal validity) be confused with religious norms. There is no reason, however, to think that the (paradoxical) expression νόμος τῆς φύσεως ever occurred to him; it appears first in *Gorgias* 483E and was probably coined by Plato himself (cf. Dodds [1959], 268). No substantive need be understood with the phrase, which is probably just a periphrasis for φύσις, as the parallelism with τοὺς νόμους suggests: "nature" as contrasted with "laws." Cf. Plato, *Gorgias* 483A (ἐὰν μέν τις κατὰ νόμον λέγῃ, κατὰ φύσιν ὑπερωτῶν, ἐὰν δὲ τὰ τῆς φύσεως, τὰ τοῦ νόμου), where the periphrasis τὰ τῆς φύσεως alternates with φύσιν exactly as τὰ τοῦ νόμου does with νόμον (cf. I.23–24 τὰ τῶν νόμων). For τὰ τῆς φύσεως = φύσις cf. further Plato, *Phaedrus* 279A with Cherniss (1977), 178; *Laws* 655E. For the general type of periphrasis involved cf. Demosthenes, *or.* 9.45 (ἐκ δὲ τούτων εἰκότως τὰ τῶν Ἑλλήνων ἦν τῷ βαρβάρῳ φόβερ', οὐχ ὁ βάρβαρος τοῖς Ἕλλησιν). Heinimann (1945), 123–24 suggested that this periphrasis was forced on Antiphon by the double meaning of νόμος, the plural of which (in the sense of "laws and customs") required as its antithesis a periphrasis such as τὰ τῆς φύσεως. But there seems to be no reason why Antiphon could not have opposed φύσις *tout court* to νόμοι, just as Euripides does in fr. 920 (ἡ φύσις ἐβούλεθ', ᾗ νόμων οὐδὲν μέλει; on this text cf. Heinimann [1945], 132–33).

23 τὰ μὲν γὰρ κτλ.: as γάρ indicates, the argument or proof for the proposition stated in I.12–23 begins here.

23–24 τὰ . . . τῶν νόμων: as Heinimann (1945), 124 pointed out, this periphrasis was probably suggested by τὰ τῆς φύσεως above, and adopted for the sake of rhetorical parallelism. For τὰ τῶν νόμων = οἱ νόμοι cf. Plato, *Laws* 634D, 820E, 963A.

25 ἐπίθετα: Gernet (1923), 176 n. (hesitantly) and Luria (1927*a*), 1067 with n. 3 (confidently) suggested ξύνθετα, which Decleva Caizzi and Bastianini (1989), 199 consider too long for the space. It also has the disadvantage of anticipating the point made below in I.27–31, and furthermore does not offer as good a contrast with ἀναγκαῖα as Grenfell and Hunt's ἐπίθετα. The latter does not exactly mean "arbitrary," "willkürlich" (Kranz, *FVS* 2.347) or "occasionale" (Untersteiner [1962], 77, but note the correct interpretation at 76–77), but rather "imposed" or "added" upon nature – with the implication that what is additional is unnecessary and undesirable. Cf. Aristotle, *Nicomachean Ethics* 1118b9 (ἴδιοι and ἐπίθετοι desires contrasted with those which are κοιναί); Menander, fr. 620 (evils ἐπίθετα τῇ φύσει contrasted with those which are given by nature itself and so ἀναγκαίων); LSJ, s.v. ἐπίθετος; Schmid (1940), 160 with n. 11; Decleva Caizzi and Bastianini (1989), 201, 204–5. The adjectives ἐπίκτητος and ἔπακτος have a similar connotation (as Heinimann [1945], 31 with n. 32, 147 n. 74 pointed out).

26–27 ἀναγκαῖα: that is, essential and unavoidable. In Aristophanes, *Clouds* 1075 the phrase "necessities of nature" (αἱ τῆς φύσεως ἀνάγκαι) refers to sexual drives; in Isocrates, *or.* 4.84 the same phrase refers to the natural necessity of death (cf. Beardslee [1918], 21 n. 4). For the association of nature with necessity cf. F44(b)II.18ff.; Heinimann (1945), 125–26, 130–32, 135; Beardslee (1918), 21 n. 4; Guthrie (1971a), 99–101.

29–30 ὁμολογηθέντα: Diels (1917), 87; Altheim (1926), 266; Aly (1929), 133–34; Nestle (1942), 376 n. 24; Heinimann (1945), 139; Kahn (1981), 95 with nn. 3, 5, 102 n. 17, and others saw a social-contract theory here, with the aorist participles ὁμολογηθέντα and ὁμολογήσαντας (II.5–6) expressing (in Altheim's words) "die Übereinkunft als einmaliges historisches Faktum." But τοὺς ὁμολογήσαντας at least can hardly refer to the parties to an original compact or agreement; and it is unnecessary to read a social-contract doctrine into Antiphon's words. Cf. Menzel (1922), 59. The idea that laws are merely the product of human agreement (rather than, for example, a gift from the gods) was a commonplace of sophistic thought. Cf. Xenophon, *Memorabilia* 4.4.13; Plato, *Republic* 358E–359A; Guthrie (1971a), 135–41.

29–II.1 ὁμολογηθέντα οὐ φύντα ... φύντα οὐχ ὁμολογηθέντα: note the chiastic arrangement. LSJ, s.v. φύω B.II.6 take φύντα here in the absolute sense, "are natural." Since Antiphon envisages human nature in particular, some trace of the sense "be born" (cf. LSJ, s.v. φύω B.2) may also be present. Decleva Caizzi (1986), 68 and Decleva Caizzi and Bastianini (1989), 205 detected an ironic allusion to this passage in Plato, *Menexenus* 239A (ἡ ἰσογονία ἡμᾶς ἡ κατὰ φύσιν ἰσονομίαν ἀναγκάζει ζητεῖν κατὰ νόμον). But the contexts of the two passages are quite different, and it is difficult to discern the similarity Decleva Caizzi detected.

II

1–3 [[ουχ ομολογηθεντα]]: these words are obviously a dittography and were deleted already by the corrector.

3–5 τὰ οὖν νόμιμα παραβαίνων ἐὰν λάθῃ: οὖν is probably inferential. With the hyperbaton here cf. II.10–12; IV.1–3. For ἐάν the papyrus offers ᾗ ἄν, which Grenfell and Hunt (1915), 96, 101 translated (impossibly) "whenever." David Sedley suggests to me that the paradosis could mean "to whatever extent" (cf. Empedocles, *FVS* 31 B 17.12; LSJ, s.v. ᾗ II.3). But ᾗ ἄν in this sense would seem to require a correlative term such as ταύτῃ with ἀπήλλακται κτλ. below. Furthermore, the parallel clauses μὴ λαθών and ἐάν τι κτλ. strongly suggest a conditional clause here. Diels and Kranz and Decleva Caizzi and Bastianini accepted Wilamowitz's εἰὰν, a form attested in fourth-century Attic inscriptions but apparently not in literature (cf. LSJ, s.v. ἐάν). Antiphon elsewhere consistently employs ἐάν, which it seems best to restore here. From the standpoint of traditional Greek morality, it is remarkable that the argument completely ignores the possibility of divine detection and punishment of hidden transgressions. Contrast Critias (or Euripides), *FVS* 88 B 25.9–40; cf. Dover (1974), 257–58.

7–8 καὶ αἰσχύνης καὶ ζημίας: as Dillon (1984), 128–29 rightly emphasized, αἰσχύνη refers to social disgrace or shame rather than to internalized guilt or conscience, which is completely absent from Antiphon's calculations. Contrast Democritus, *FVS* 68 B 264, 262 (on conscience in Greek popular morality cf. Dover [1974], 220–23). Diels

(1917), 89; Heinimann (1945), 139 (comparing Thucydides, 2.37); Decleva Caizzi and Bastianini (1989), 205, and Wiesner (1994), 231 refer αἰσχύνη to the transgression of unwritten laws. But it is unnecessary to restrict the scope of Antiphon's words in this way: punishment inflicted by the legal system also entails shame and disgrace (cf. Guthrie [1971a], 138 n. 2).

10–12 τῶν δὲ τῇ φύσει ξυμφύτων: the phrase is vague, but must have the same reference as τὰ τῆς φύσεως above. τῇ φύσει is not a modal or causal dative (as Diels [1917], 88, Kranz, *FVS* 2.347, and Aly [1929], 134 seem to interpret, translating "von Natur" or "natürlich") nor a dative of reference. Rather it is governed by ξυμφύτων: "mit der Natur verwachsen" (Schmidt [1924], 13). Cf. Fraenkel (1950), 2.91–92.

13–14 παρὰ τὸ δυνατὸν βιάζηται: Aly (1929), 134; Kerferd (1956–57), 27–28, and others interpret παρὰ as "contrary to" and infer that it is impossible to violate nature. But Antiphon is hardly thinking of inviolable laws of nature. Most likely the prepositional phrase means "beyond what is possible" (*sc.* without incurring harm or damage). So Decleva Caizzi and Bastianini (1989), 205–6; Heinimann (1945), 135 n. 39, with references; Moulton (1972), 335–36; Nill (1985), 55 n. 20. βιάζηται is probably conative (cf. Plato, *Protagoras* 337D, quoted below on II.26–30).

17–18 οὐδὲν ἔλαττον τὸ κακόν: for the notion of automatic punishment cf. Xenophon, *Memorabilia* 4.4.21–24 and Menzel (1922), 61, who noted the similarities as well as the fundamental difference of outlook between the two passages.

21–23 δόξαν . . . ἀλήθειαν: δόξα and ἀλήθεια refer in the first instance to "what people think" and "the truth" (respectively). Cf. Furley (1981), 83: "a lawbreaker is punished if he is believed by other men to be a lawbreaker, whereas one who flouts nature suffers for it just because it is true that he flouts nature." But it is hard not to see here a general contrast between appearance and reality, which is a commonplace of Greek literature and thought. Cf. Simonides, fr. 598; Aeschylus, *Septem* 592; Antiphon of Rhamnus, *or.* 3.β.2; Democritus, *FVS* 68 B 7; Plato, *Apology* 21C; Antisthenes, fr. 58; Isocrates, *or.* 15.18; Heinimann (1945), 43–58. Nill (1985), 56 inferred from this passage that on Antiphon's view, "*nomos*-transgressing agents do not suffer *true* loss if they are caught and punished." But this grossly overinterprets the terminology. Precisely because the contrast of appearance and reality was a commonplace, there is no need to see specifically Eleatic influence here (as Heinimann [1945], 133, 139, 152; Untersteiner [1962], 79–80, and others have). Cf. Niceforo (1972), 396; Furley (1981), 83. On the supposed identification of nature and reality, φύσις and ἀλήθεια, cf. commentary on IV.18–19.

23–30 This passage effects a transition to the broader discussion of the relation of law and nature, which occupies most of the remainder of the fragment. But despite Heinimann (1945), 135 and Nill (1985), 54, the conflict of law and nature emphatically asserted here is already implicit in the argument of I.12–23. For Antiphon's claim that an individual's best advantage lies in obeying the law in the presence of witnesses, but nature in their absence, would be pointless if law and nature did not (at least sometimes) conflict. Kerferd (1956–57), 28–30, (1981), 115–17 deduced from this passage that F44(a) throughout does not present Antiphon's own views as much as develop apparent conflicts and contradictions generated by the antithesis of law and nature. His deduction receives no support from the text, however, and is completely unwarranted. Cf. Moulton (1972), 330 n. 2; Saunders (1977–78), 216 n. 7; Nill (1985), 54 n. 17, 73; Dillon (1984), 128.

24–25 πάντων ἕνεκα τούτων: before correction, the papyrus offered τῶνδε ἕνεκα τούτων. This reading was adopted by Diels (1916), 933, Diels and Kranz in *FVS*, and Untersteiner (1962) together with Diels' arbitrary addition πάν[τως]; and by Decleva Caizzi and Bastianini (1989), 194, 206 without it. Anaphoric οὗτος and prospective ὅδε are often paired in the fashion presupposed by this reading. Nevertheless, the collocation τῶνδε ἕνεκα τούτων ἡ σκέψις (where τῶνδε must be construed with ἕνεκα and τούτων with ἡ σκέψις) seems intolerably awkward, particularly so since the phrases πάντων ἕνεκα τούτων and τούτων ἕνεκα πάντων are well attested. (Cf. Plato, *Republic* 526C, 417B; Xenophon, *Cyropaedia* 3.3.27; Anonymus Iamblichi, 4.4.) πάντων ἕνεκα τούτων (the text intended by the corrector) is for these reasons far preferable. (David Sedley, however, considers it a mere banalization.) πάντων τούτων could refer back to the preceding discussion ("for the sake of all these things" or "because of all these things"); so Kerferd (1956–57), 28–29. In that case, however, the relationship between πάντων ἕνεκα τούτων and the following ὅτι-clause (which also has a causal sense) is obscure. It seems at least as likely that πάντων τούτων points forward to the ὅτι-clause, just as the similar phrase αὐτῶν δὲ τούτων ἕνεκα does in Antiphon of Rhamnus, *or.* 5.88, 6.6. With the clause as a whole cf. Plato, *Laws* 894B: σχεδόν, ὠγαθέ, ἐκείναιν ὧν ἕνεκα πᾶσα ἡμῖν ἐστιν ἡ σκέψις τὰ νῦν. For the periphrastic ἔστι σκέψις cf. V.27–33 with commentary.

26–30 τὰ πολλὰ ... κεῖται: cf. Plato, *Gorgias* 482E (ὡς τὰ πολλὰ δὲ ταῦτα ἐναντί' ἀλλήλοις ἐστίν, ἥ τε φύσις καὶ ὁ νόμος), *Protagoras*

337D (ὁ δὲ νόμος, τύραννος ὢν τῶν ἀνδρῶν, πολλὰ παρὰ τὴν φύσιν βιάζεται). Philippson (1918), 123 and Moulton (1972), 334 try to soften the assertion by translating τὰ πολλά as "many" (cf. V.15 πόλλ') rather than "most." But this ignores the article, and accords ill with the tenor of the following passage. Wiesner (1994), 232–33 inferred from the qualification "most" that some laws at least are not at odds but in accord with nature (cf. commentary on III.25–32 and Introduction, section 1). Perhaps; but Antiphon pays no apparent attention to such laws, and it seems impossible to say anything about them. With πολεμίως κεῖται cf. Plato, *Laws* 634E (συμφωνεῖν ὡς πάντα [*sc.* τὰ τῶν νόμων] καλῶς κεῖται θέντων θεῶν); Demosthenes, *or.* 20.134 (ὅσα Λεπτίνης ἐρεῖ περὶ τοῦ νόμου διδάσκων ὑμᾶς ὡς καλῶς κεῖται), 23.82 (σκέψασθε γὰρ ὡς νομίμως καὶ σφόδρ' ἀνθρωπίνως [*sc.* ὁ νόμος] κεῖται); V.16–17 (πολέμια τῇ φύσει). Heinimann (1945), 140 (cf. 123–24) plausibly suggested that νόμος in the phrase τῶν κατὰ νόμον δικαίων connotes prevailing opinion (the "philosophischer Nomosbegriff") as well as particular laws and customs.

II.30–III.18 Here begins the explanation and justification for the general proposition stated in II.26–30. νόμος and φύσις are inimical because the manifold injunctions of νόμος restrict the individual's free exercise of his nature. (Cf. Heinimann [1945], 135–36; Nill [1985], 59.) Stenzel (1924), 36; Heinimann (1945), 136 with n. 40; Decleva Caizzi and Bastianini (1989), 206, and others suppose that a conception of natural activities or functions of the human organs underlies the argument here. Cf. Antiphon of Rhamnus, *or.* 4.δ.2: εἰ μὲν γὰρ ὥσπερ βλέπειν μὲν τοῖν ὀφθαλμοῖν, ἀκούειν δὲ τοῖς ὠσίν, οὕτω κατὰ φύσιν ἦν ὑβρίζειν μὲν τοὺς νέους, σωφρονεῖν δὲ τοὺς γέροντας, οὐδὲν ἂν τῆς ὑμετέρας κρίσεως ἔδει κτλ. This is probably right (cf. F44(b)II.27ff.), though the passage can be understood without such an idea. Fränkel (1975), 77 n. 5 (followed by Untersteiner [1962], 81) explained the passage as an antiquated survival of the Homeric and archaic conception of man as a congeries of organs, each of which "appertains directly to the person, can deploy an energy of its own, and yet represents the person as a whole." This interpretation is almost certainly mistaken. The catalog of organs should rather be understood as an example of the rhetorical figure of *amplificatio*, which serves here to underline the all-embracing character of the control imposed by νόμος. Cf. Barnes (1982), 514; Decleva Caizzi and Bastianini (1989), 206; F44(b)II.27–III.11 with commentary. Commentators who adduce this passage as evidence that Antiphon conceived nature in narrowly biological terms (so Havelock [1957], 257–59; C. Segal *apud* Moulton [1972], 333 n. 12; D'Agostini [1975], 556–57 and *passim*) unjustifiably ignore the rhetorical aspect.

(Against their interpretation cf. Nill [1985], 59 n. 27, 71–72 with n. 66.) Luginbill (1997), 180–82, 184 interpreted the passage differently, as part of a larger argument (extending from I.12 to IV.24) designed to show that Athenian democratic νόμος is incapable of restraining an unjust man bent on wrongdoing. On this view, the catalog of organs is not intended to illustrate the excessive restrictions imposed by the laws on nature, but rather the *insufficient* restraint exercised by νόμος on the forces of base human nature (which Antiphon viewed in negative terms). Luginbill's interpretation mistakes both the tone and the purpose of the passage, and is scarcely reconcilable with the subsequent argument on life, death, and the advantages and disadvantages from which they come (III.25–IV.24).

30–32 νενομοθέτηται γὰρ κτλ.: for γάρ introducing an example that serves to both explain and prove a proposition cf. F44(b)II.29 and Denniston (1954), 66–67. νομοθετέω can refer to written laws (cf. Lysias, *or.* 15.9; Plato, *Republic* 417B, *Laws* 872C; Aristotle, *Politics* 1268b24) as well as to unwritten rules, customs, and conventions (cf. Plato, *Symposium* 182B, *Laws* 709A, 780B; [Plato], *Epinomis* 982B with Tarán [1975], 269; Xenophon, *Memorabilia* 4.4.25; Aristotle, *Posterior Analytics* 83a14; Plutarch, *Galba* 18.2, *De communibus notitiis* 1063C; Sextus, *Adversus mathematicos* 8.125–26; Lucian, *Rhetorum praeceptor* 17). There is no reason to restrict its reference here to one or the other, as Moulton (1972), 336 and Heinimann (1945), 140 with n. 54 (from opposite points of view) suggested. For ἐπί with verbal expressions denoting the establishment of laws cf. LSJ, s.v. B.I.1C.

32–33 τοῖς ὀφθαλμοῖς: for the sequence of organs Heinimann (1945), 136 n. 40 compared [Hippocrates], *De morbo sacro* 16 (οἱ δὲ ὀφθαλμοὶ καὶ τὰ οὔατα καὶ ἡ γλῶσσα καὶ αἱ χεῖρες καὶ οἱ πόδες οἷα ἂν ὁ ἐγκέφαλος γινώσκῃ, τοιαῦτα πρήσσουσι). Cf. also Parmenides, *FVS* 28 B 7.4–5 (eye, ear, tongue); Dio of Prusa, *or.* 3.104–6 (eyes, ears, tongue, hands); Diogenes Laertius, 3.99 (ἐάν τις ὀφθαλμοῖς ὁρᾷ καὶ τοῖς ὠσὶν ἀκούῃ καὶ τῇ ῥινὶ καὶ τῷ στόματι αἰσθάνηται κτλ.); and the lists of senses/sensibilia in Democritus, *FVS* 68 B 11 (ὄψις, ἀκοή, ὀδμή, γεῦσις, ψαῦσις) and Aristotle, *De sensu* 439a7 (cf. Cherniss [1977], 470 with n. 2).

III

II.33–III.2 ἃ δεῖ αὐτοὺς ὁρᾶν καὶ ἃ οὐ δεῖ: for the twofold character of legal commands (positive and negative) cf. Xenophon, *Memorabilia* 4.4.13 (ἅ τε δεῖ ποιεῖν καὶ ὧν ἀπέχεσθαι); Plutarch, *De Stoicorum repugnantiis* 1037D; Lucian, *Anacharsis* 22; Cassius Dio, *Historiae Romanae* 53.10.2. Decleva Caizzi plausibly suggested that δεῖ here denotes not only what is necessary but also what is suitable or advantageous, and that it is precisely the notion that justice and advantage coincide in law which Antiphon rejects (cf. Decleva Caizzi [1985], 193; Decleva Caizzi and Bastianini [1989], 207; commentary on IV.1–22). If this suggestion is right, the passage presents a notable example of the semantic convergence of δεῖ and χρή, on which cf. Redard (1953), 55–61; Barrett (1964), 164–65, 179; commentary on IV.1–22. (Michael Reeve suggests to me that ἃ δεῖ κτλ. might mean "what it is all right" to do. But δεῖ surely carries a stronger sense of need or obligation; and it is doubtful whether Antiphon would have reacted so strenuously to legal injunctions as weak as this.)

2–3 καὶ ἐπὶ τοῖς ὠσίν: following a suggestion of Diels (1917), 90, Decleva Caizzi argued that Antiphon here envisages primarily (if not exclusively) religious laws and customs, for example the restrictions on seeing, hearing, and speaking imposed on participants in the Eleusinian mysteries, and prohibitions on entering certain sacred spaces (cf. Decleva Caizzi [1969], 75, [1985], 192, 194–95; Decleva Caizzi and Bastianini [1989], 206–7). But there seems to be no reason to single out religious laws in particular; and Decleva Caizzi's argument is largely motivated by the desire to discover in the papyrus fragments of Περὶ ἀληθείας an attitude toward religion similar to that which she detected in Antiphon of Rhamnus' *Tetralogies*.

5–6 καὶ ἐπὶ τῇ γλώττῃ: Moulton (1972), 338 referred to restrictions on speech in the law-courts; Decleva Caizzi (1985), 194 and Decleva Caizzi and Bastianini (1989), 207, to laws against slander (on which cf. MacDowell [1978], 126–29; Halliwell [1991]). Other possibilities include the prohibition against speaking in the assembly and law-courts imposed on the disenfranchised (ἄτιμοι), on prostitutes, and on those who mistreated parents, failed to perform military service, or squandered their patrimony (cf. MacDowell [1978], 74, 126, 174); and the laws against lying in the agora (cf. Harpocration, s.vv. κατὰ τὴν ἀγορὰν ἀψευδεῖν, κ 24; MacDowell [1978], 139, 157) and misleading the people in speech before the assembly, council, or law-courts (cf. MacDowell [1978], 179–81).

8–9 καὶ ἐπὶ ταῖς χερσίν: on the hand as the characteristic organ of action cf. Fraenkel (1950), 3.639. On the several types of violent assault and theft prohibited in Athenian law cf. MacDowell (1978), 123–24, 129–32, 147–49. Perhaps also in view are the laws forbidding idleness and requiring all citizens to earn a living (cf. Herodotus, 2.177; Lysias, fr. 10; MacDowell [1978], 155).

11–12 καὶ ἐπὶ τοῖς ποσίν: besides the obvious case of trespass, Antiphon may have had in mind the (quasi-religious) exclusion of murderers from various sacred and civic spaces and activities, εἴργεσθαι τῶν νομίμων (cf. Antiphon of Rhamnus, *or.* 6.34; Aristotle, Ἀθηναίων πολιτεία 57.3; MacDowell [1978], 111–13, 121–22); and/or the exclusion of exiles from Attica and the various pan-Hellenic religious festivals and games (cf. MacDowell [1978], 120, 176–79).

15 καὶ ἐπὶ τῷ νῷ: Decleva Caizzi (1985), 195 thought of prohibitions on incest. One could also think of laws against adultery and strictures (written or non-written) on homosexual activity (cf. Plato, *Symposium* 182B–185C; Dover [1964]). The appetitive function (ἐπιθυμεῖν) here ascribed to νοῦς might seem surprising, at least from the standpoint of Platonic and Aristotelian psychology. But already in Homer, the νόος is the locus of emotions such as fear, anger, and joy as well as of intellectual functions. Cf. *Iliad* 3.63, 9.553–54; *Odyssey* 8.78; LSJ, s.v. I.3; von Fritz (1943), 83–85, 87–88; Padel (1992), 32 with n. 77. And in ordinary language, the association of desire with νοῦς in the wider sense of "mind" is unproblematic. Cf. Plato, *Republic* 358B (ἐμοὶ δὲ οὔπω κατὰ νοῦν ἡ ἀπόδειξις γέγονεν περὶ ἑκατέρου· ἐπιθυμῶ γὰρ ἀκοῦσαι κτλ.); Demosthenes, *or.* 18.68 (καὶ μὴν οὐδὲ τοῦτό γε οὐδεὶς ἂν εἰπεῖν τολμήσαι, ὡς τῷ μὲν ἐν Πέλλῃ τραφέντι . . . τοσαύτην μεγαλοψυχίαν προσῆκεν ἐγγενέσθαι ὥστε τῆς τῶν Ἑλλήνων ἀρχῆς ἐπιθυμῆσαι καὶ τοῦτο εἰς τὸν νοῦν ἐμβαλέσθαι κτλ.). In F58, ll. 4–5 (from Περὶ ὁμονοίας), νοῦς is said to have wishes or intentions, θελήματα (cf. Dihle [1982], 30). The relation between νοῦς and γνώμη (F1–3, F24A, with commentary) in Antiphon's psychology is uncertain (cf. Decleva Caizzi [1985], 195).

17–18 καὶ ὧν μή: οὐ δεῖ and δεῖ μή are equally possible (cf. Smyth [1956], 616).

18–25 The interpretation of this passage is difficult. Since law and nature were said earlier to be inimical (II.26–30), it is surprising to hear now that what the law prohibits is no friendlier to nature than what it encourages. We might reasonably have expected the reverse assertion: that what is *encouraged* by law is no friendlier to nature than what is prohibited, or (to put it another way) that what is prohibited is no *less* friendly than what is encouraged. Cf. Grenfell and Hunt (1915), 102; Furley (1981), 84 n. 4; Decleva Caizzi (1985), 193 n. 6; Decleva Caizzi and Bastianini (1989), 207–8. One solution to the apparent difficulty would be to treat the sentence as a question (so Theander [1920], 3, reading [ἔστι]ν οὖν; cf. Xenophon, *Oeconomicus* 19.1) or as an imaginary objection (so Barnes [1982], 514–15, reading μὲ]ν οὖν; cf. Denniston [1954], 478–79). Another is to alter the text so as to obtain the expected sense. Thus H. Gomperz proposed to transpose ἢ before ἀφ' ὧν in III.21 (an impossible word-order), while Gernet (1923), 177 n. suggested that ἀφ' ὧν ἀποτρέπουσιν and ἐφ' ἃ προτρέπουσιν have traded places (cf. Stenzel [1924], 35). Decleva Caizzi achieved essentially the same result with her supplement [ἧττο]ν οὖν οὐδὲν ... φιλιώτερα = "no less dear" (cf. Decleva Caizzi [1985], 193 n. 6; Decleva Caizzi and Bastianini [1989], 207–8). ἧττον with a comparative adjective is attested, though rarely. Cf. Plato, *Laws* 854D; Dionysius of Halicarnassus, *Antiquitates Romanae* 3.43; [Plutarch], fr. inc. 149; [Aristotle], *Problemata* 957b8; Kühner–Gerth 1.26; LSJ, s.v. ἥσσων III. In all but one of these passages, however, the comparative adjective with which ἧττον is joined follows upon an earlier comparative, and could conceivably be a mere slip on the part of author or copyist. (The only exception is the fragment doubtfully ascribed to Plutarch, which is transmitted without context.) Furley (1981), 84 with n. 4 and Morrison (1972), 219 avoided the difficulty by interpreting ἤ as "or," but this leaves the comparatives φιλιώτερα and οἰκειότερα without any point of reference. Diels (1917), 91; Heinimann (1945), 136 with n. 41, and Moulton (1972), 337 interpreted the passage to mean that the law's positive and negative demands – its commands and prohibitions – are equally inimical to nature. This interpretation makes good sense in the context; unfortunately, none of these commentators explained how it could be extracted from the Greek. Perhaps it can be if the clauses ἀφ' ὧν οἱ νόμο[ι ἀ]ποτρέπουσι and ἐφ' ἃ [προτρέ]πουσ[ιν] are interpreted as referring to the legal commands and prohibitions themselves rather than the actions commanded and prohibited; in other words, as equivalent to the abstract nouns ἀποτροπαί and προτροπαί. This might be explained as a kind of metonymy (concrete for abstract), or as an example of verbal expressions used in place of nouns. In any case, this interpretation seems to make the best sense of the transmitted text and to be preferable to the alternatives. (For a different attempt to make sense of the passage cf. Saunders [1977–78], 221.) This passage may be the kind of thing Hermogenes had in mind when he said of Antiphon's style: καὶ περιβάλλει δὲ χωρὶς εὐκρινείας· διὸ καὶ συγχεῖ τὸν λόγον καὶ ἔστιν ἀσαφὴς τὰ πολλά (F2(a), ll. 30–32).

18 ἔστιν οὖν: οὖν is probably transitional; cf. I.12 and Denniston (1954), 426.

20–21 φιλιώτερα οὐδ' οἰκειότερα: if φιλιώτερα is meant to contrast with πολεμίως τῇ φύσει κεῖται (II.29–30), it is probably active in sense, "friendly." (For φίλιος and πόλεμιος contrasted cf. LSJ, s.v. φίλιος I.) οἰκειότερα could mean "friendly" and be a mere synonym of φιλιώτερα (cf. LSJ, s.v. II.2). But more likely it signifies that legal commands have no intrinsic connection with nature and so are not "binding" on it. Cf. Plato, *Republic* 538C with Shorey (1930–35), 2.225 n. *d*, (1929) = (1980),

1.442–43. This use of οἰκεῖος may perhaps show the germ of the Stoic doctrine of οἰκείωσις.

24–25 προτρέπουσιν: Decleva Caizzi and Bastianini (1989), 208 defended Schöne's ἐπιτρέπουσιν, on grounds of symmetry of expression (ἀφ' ὧν ἀποτρέπουσι ~ ἐφ' ἃ ἐπιτρέπουσιν) as well as because προτρέπω does not occur elsewhere in the *corpus Antiphonteum*, while ἐπιτρέπω does (cf. VI.10–11; Antiphon of Rhamnus, *or.* 4.γ.5, 5.8). ἐπιτρέπουσιν, however, does not mean "indirizzano" (as they translate) but "allow," "permit," a sense which is inappropriate here (cf. VI.10–11; LSJ, s.v. II). For προτρέπω ἐπί cf. Plato, *Euthydemus* 307A, *Laws* 699E, 711B; Xenophon, *Memorabilia* 1.4.1, 3.3.15; Isocrates, *or.* 5.17, 129, 7.46, 9.77, 15.84; Aeschines, *or.* 1.138; Anaximenes, *Ars rhetorica* 34.1; LSJ, s.v. προτρέπω II.

25–32 The mention of life and death comes in a little abruptly here, but is most easily understood as serving a transitional function. On the one hand, life and death offer a contrast with what precedes: unlike legal injunctions, which are not akin (οἰκεῖα) to nature but imposed on it (νενομοθέτηται ἐπί; cf. II.25 ἐπίθετα), living and dying really do "belong to" nature. (Cf. Furley [1981], 89.) On the other hand, the mention of life and death allows Antiphon to introduce the subject of advantages and their opposite, from which life and death are said to come. Some commentators infer from this passage that nature (in Kerferd's words) "is a source both of things advantageous and things disadvantageous." Cf. Kerferd (1956–57), 31–32; Moulton (1972), 337–38; Guthrie (1971a), 109 n. 1; Dillon (1984), 130; Decleva Caizzi and Bastianini (1989), 208–9. But this mistakes the force of the genitive τῆς φύσεως; for living and dying obviously do not "come from" nature in the sense required by this interpretation. (Nor are they "determined by" it, as Ostwald [1990], 300 would have it.) Guthrie's invocation of "natural" disasters such as earthquakes and floods is completely irrelevant (and not only because φύσις here refers primarily to human nature). It is not from nature that living and dying come but (as Antiphon says explicitly) from what is advantageous and what is not (cf. below on the force of ἀπό in III.30, 33). Living and dying are simply what human beings do, and in this sense are said to "belong to" human nature. Cf. Nill (1985), 60–61 with n. 33, who argues convincingly (against Kerferd and Moulton) that the character of Antiphon's ethical doctrine is essentially unaffected by the question whether disadvantage as well as advantage comes from nature. According to Wiesner (1994), 232–33, the argument here presupposes the existence of a natural drive to preserve life, which anyone who causes the death of another acts against. Wiesner inferred that laws which prohibit homicide are in accord with nature and fall into the category of legal rules not contrary to nature (cf. commentary on II.26–30). Wiesner's argument is motivated by the desire to find some common ground between the papyrus fragments of Περὶ ἀληθείας and the speeches of Antiphon of Rhamnus. But there is no real evidence that the author of Περὶ ἀληθείας felt any differently about homicide laws than about νόμοι of other kinds (cf. Introduction, section 1).

25–26 τὸ δὲ ζῆν κτλ.: the causal connection implied in Grenfell's and Hunt's γὰρ (adopted by the majority of editors and defended most recently by Decleva Caizzi and Bastianini [1989], 208) is hard to discern. (But cf. Denniston [1954], 61–62 on the loose use of γάρ.) Living and dying are more naturally understood as forming a *contrast* with legal injunctions; accordingly I propose τὸ δέ. Diels's δ' αὖ (adopted in *FVS*) would also mark the contrast; but αὖ is otherwise unattested in the sophist Antiphon. τὸ ζῆν and τὸ ἀποθανεῖν should be given their full sense as verbal nouns: "living" and "dying."

26–27 ἐστι τῆς φύσεως: for the force of the (predicate) genitive after verbs of being and becoming cf. Kühner–Gerth 1.371ff.

29 αὐτῇ: Grenfell and Hunt's αὐτοῖς (*sc.* ἀνθρώποις; cf. III.23 τοὺς ἀνθρώπους) has been universally adopted. Since the subsequent discussion centers on what is beneficial to *nature* (cf. IV.11–12 ὀνίνησιν τὴν φύσιν), however, it seems better to read αὐτῇ (*sc.* φύσει).

30–31 ἀπὸ τῶν ξυμφερόντων: Havelock (1957), 275; Moulton (1972), 337; Morrison (1972), 219 with n. 110, and Guthrie (1971a), 109 with n. 1 give a partitive sense to ἀπό here and in III.33 (cf. LSJ, s.v. I.6; Kühner–Gerth 1.457). But as Furley (1981), 89 pointed out, this spoils the argument and turns the reference to living and dying into a casual aside. ἀπό rather indicates source (cf. LSJ, s.v. III.5; Kühner–Gerth 1.458): living and dying come from, depend on, what is advantageous and what is not. As μή shows, τῶν ξυμφερόντων and τῶν μὴ ξυμφερόντων are generic, "whatever things are (are not) advantageous" (cf. Kühner–Gerth 2.201–2, Anmerkung 4).

32 τὸ δὲ ἀποθανεῖν κτλ.: since the subsequent discussion leaves aside the topic of dying and disadvantages and centers on advantages, these words could be seen as a mere rhetorical contrast (so Stenzel [1924], 36–37). But dying and disadvantages belong to the antithetical structure of the argument, which is no mere rhetorical ornament but (here as elsewhere) an integral part of Antiphon's thought-process (so Heinimann [1945], 137; cf. Furley [1981], 89). There is no reason to read into this passage an allusion to capital punishment (Diels [1917], 91) or the conventional belief that it is good to die for one's country (Moulton [1972], 337; Dillon [1984], 130).

IV

1–24 Focusing now on the subject of advantages, Antiphon distinguishes those established (κείμενα) by law and convention from those established by nature. The former are declared to be bonds on nature, the latter are free (IV.1–8). Being bonds, the advantages established by law give pain; and what gives pain does not benefit nature and is not advantageous (IV.8–14). For real advantages must not harm but help (IV.18–22). The advantages established by law, therefore, are not really advantages (IV.14–18). For detailed analysis of the argument cf. Heinimann (1945), 136–38; Nill (1985), 59–60 (its import is completely mistaken by Reesor [1987], 212–14 and Ostwald [1990], 300). Moulton (1972), 337 spoke of the topic of advantages being "reintroduced" here, but in fact it has never been lost sight of. The notion of ξυμφέρον is inextricably bound up with justice, law, and legal prescriptions that purport to define what is and is not advantageous, what should and should not be done. Cf. Xenophon, *Memorabilia* 1.1.3–4: οὗτοί τε γὰρ [*sc.* those who practice μαντική] ὑπολαμβάνουσιν οὐ τοὺς ὄρνιθας οὐδὲ τοὺς ἀπαντῶντας εἰδέναι τὰ συμφέροντα τοῖς μαντευομένοις, ἀλλὰ τοὺς θεοὺς διὰ τούτων αὐτὰ σημαίνειν, κἀκεῖνος [*sc.* Socrates] δὲ οὕτως ἐνόμιζεν. ἀλλ' οἱ μὲν πλεῖστοί φασιν ὑπό τε τῶν ὀρνίθων καὶ τῶν ἀπαντώντων ἀποτρέπεσθαί τε καὶ προτρέπεσθαι· Σωκράτης δ' ὥσπερ ἐγίγνωσκεν, οὕτως ἔλεγε· τὸ δαιμόνιον γὰρ ἔφη σημαίνειν, καὶ πολλοῖς τῶν συνόντων προηγόρευε τὰ μὲν ποιεῖν, τὰ δὲ μὴ ποιεῖν. Cf. further Decleva Caizzi and Bastianini (1989), 209; commentary on II.33–III.2.

1–2 τὰ δὲ ξυμφέροντα: for the hyperbaton cf. II.3–4, 10–12.

3–5 τὰ μὲν ὑπὸ τῶν νόμων κείμενα: ὑπό (Grenfell and Hunt's correction for ἀπό) is confirmed by IV.7. κείμενα (Grenfell and Hunt) is preferable to κεκελευσμένα (Diels) or κεκριμένα (von Arnim); it is equivalent to the (perfect) passive of τίθημι (as ὑπό shows) and means "laid down," "established." (Cf. LSJ, s.v. κεῖμαι IV.3.) It is mistaken to infer from these words that Antiphon recognized genuine advantages established by law (so Altheim [1926], 262–63; Moulton [1972], 337; Saunders [1977–78], 222–23 with n. 27; Ostwald [1990], 300, and others). The whole argument of the passage shows rather that what is laid down *as* advantageous by law and convention is not really such. Cf. Furley (1981), 85 with n. 5; Luria (1926b), 343 n. 2.

5 δεσμοί: either δεσμὰ (Grenfell and Hunt, and most subsequent editors) or δεσμοὶ is possible here. Cf. LSJ, s.v. δεσμός. Decleva Caizzi and Bastianini (1989), 209 preferred the latter, suspecting a (polemical) allusion to the idea of laws as bonds of civic union (cf. Plato, *Protagoras*

322C, *Laws* 793B). With greater plausibility, Dodds (1959), 268–69 suggested that Callicles' portrait of the chained prisoner may echo Antiphon's description of laws as bonds (cf. Plato, *Gorgias* 483E–484A; Introduction, section VII).

7–8 τὰ δ' ὑπὸ . . . ἐλεύθερα: Ostwald (1990), 297 n. 15 denied that κείμενα is to be understood here with τὰ ὑπὸ τῆς φύσεως; but ὑπό would then be inexplicable. Cf. Furley (1981), 85 n. 5. Moulton (1972), 339 found it paradoxical that the advantages established by nature are here called free, while at I.25–27 nature (τὰ τῆς φύσεως) is said to be necesary (ἀναγκαῖα). But the qualification "free" alludes to the fact that these advantages are determined by human nature itself, not imposed on it from without, as are the "advantages" established by law (cf. I.25 ἐπίθετα). It may also allude (as Wiesner [1994], 232 suggested) to the idea that the advantages established by nature do not place restrictions on man, as do those established by law (cf. II.30–III.18).

8–10 οὔκουν . . . γε: οὔκουν here is not a connective with inferential force (as Schmidt [1924], 13; Saunders [1977–78], 217, and others take it) but rather an emphatic negative. Together with the following γε, it serves as the negative form of γοῦν, introducing a "part proof" for the preceding assertion that the advantages established by law are bonds and not true advantages. Cf. Denniston (1954), 422–24, 451–52.

9–10 τὰ ἀλγύνοντα: cf. V.18 ἀλγύνεσθαι. ἀλγύνειν appears mostly in tragedy and late prose, but cf. (with LSJ, s.v.) Democritus, *FVS* 68 B 223; Xenophon, *Apology* 8. Diels (1917), 93 referred ἀλγύνοντα and εὐφραίνοντα to bodily pain and pleasure, λυποῦντα and ἥδοντα (IV.16–18) to psychic. But the evidence of usage does not support such a distinction. Cf. Heinimann (1945), 138 with n. 45, whose own claim that ἀλγύνοντα designates (in contrast with λυποῦντα) "den unmittelbar empfundenen Schmerz, auf den die Physis reagiert," is equally unfounded. The variation between these pairs is probably simply rhetorical (so Saunders [1977–78], 222; Heinimann [1945], 138, who needlessly invokes the influence of Prodicus).

10–11 ὀρθῷ γε λόγῳ: like the adverb ὀρθῶς, this expression is equivalent to ἀληθῶς or τῷ ἀληθεῖ and means "truly," "really." Cf. Herodotus, 1.120, 2.17 with Stein (1893–1908), 1.1.145, 1.2.22; Sophocles, *Antigone* 99 with Jebb (1900), 27; LSJ, s.v. ὀρθός III.2. Despite Untersteiner (1962), 84; Decleva Caizzi and Bastianini (1989), 210, and others, it is unnecessary to read philosophical or sophistic overtones into this expression.

11–12 ὀνίνησιν τὴν φύσιν: Stenzel (1924), 37 and Heinimann (1945), 138 n. 46 claimed that ὀνίνημι connotes a subjective feeling of pleasure, in contrast to the more objective ξυμφέρω. But cf. commentary on IV.15–16 below.

14–15 οὔκουν ἂν οὐδέ: οὖν has inferential connective force, and οὐδέ looks back to the negative in the preceding clause: "not, then, advantageous, either." Cf. Denniston (1954), 439, 441, who cites Euripides, *Medea* 890 as the oldest known example of this usage; Demosthenes, *or.* 18.281. The potential optative (ἂν εἴη) marks this clause as an inference from the fact stated (in the indicative) in the preceding clause (cf. Heinimann [1945], 138 n. 47; Saunders [1977–78], 222).

15–16 ξυμφέροντ': Heinimann (1945), 137 with n. 44 detected a distinction between what is advantageous (ξυμφέροντ') and what helps nature (ὀνίνησιν τὴν φύσιν), pointing to the position of ξυμφέροντ' as evidence. But the conclusion stated in IV.14–18 does not follow unless τὰ λυποῦντα are identical with τὰ ἀλγύνοντα, and "be advantageous" is synonymous with "help nature." Cf. Saunders (1977–78), 222. Although it is the predicate, ξυμφέροντ' is put first for emphasis as well as to produce a chiasmus (τὰ ἀλγύνοντα . . . ὀνίνησιν τὴν φύσιν . . . ξυμφέροντ' . . . τὰ λυποῦντα).

16 τὰ λυποῦντα: the argument tacitly assumes that the advantages established by law are painful (being bonds on nature); and so τὰ λυποῦντα (like τὰ ἀλγύνοντα in IV.9–10 above) is the logical equivalent of τὰ ὑπὸ τῶν νόμων ξυμφέροντα. Cf. Heinimann (1945), 137; Saunders (1977–78), 222; Barnes (1982), 515. Heinimann (1945), 137 n. 43 called attention to the use of λυπεῖν as a technical term in Hippocratic medicine; but this is of doubtful relevance here. For the thought cf. Democritus, *FVS* 68 B 188 (ὅρος συμφόρων καὶ ἀσυμφόρων τέρψις καὶ ἀτερπίη); V.17–24 with commentary.

17 μᾶλλον ἤ: Saunders (1977–78), 222–23 would read into the comparative a tacit acknowledgment that the advantages established by law *do* help nature, only not more so than those established by nature itself. The precise degree of benefit is not at issue, however, and the argument of the passage as a whole suffices to show that the advantages established by law do not (in Antiphon's view) help nature at all.

17–18 τὰ ἥδοντα: active forms of ἥδομαι are mostly confined to late authors. But cf. Anacreon, fr. 131; [Plato], *Axiochus* 366A (*bis*); LSJ, s.v. ἥδομαι II. Pollux (3.98) labels ἥδω an Ionicism, and Bignone (1938), 189 n. 2 argued that τὸ ἧδον was a technical term of Ionian philosophy. But Aly (1929), 155 n. 157 inferred from their imitation in late authors that the active forms of ἥδω belonged to the older Attic dialect.

18–19 τῷ ἀληθεῖ: there is no reason to think that this phrase (a dative of manner or adverbial dative) is equivalent to τῇ φύσει, as

Stenzel (1924), 37; Heinimann (1945), 139; Untersteiner (1967), 85, and others have supposed. Rather, it is close in sense to ὀρθῷ γε λόγῳ in IV.10–11 above (cf. Moulton [1972], 339; Decleva Caizzi and Bastianini [1989], 210).

20–22 βλάπτειν ... ὠφελεῖν: for the pair βλάπτειν/ὠφελεῖν cf. F44(c)II.30–35. The logic of the argument requires that ὠφελεῖν correspond to "help nature" (ὀνίνησι τὴν φύσιν) and "be advantageous" (ξυμφέροντ' ἂν εἴη); βλάπτειν, to "give pain" (τὰ ἀλγύνοντα, τὰ λυποῦντα) and (by implication) "be disadvantageous." It is therefore mistaken to try to insert a wedge between advantage on the one hand and pleasure and pain on the other, as Ostwald does in claiming that "a thing is not to be counted advantageous *per se* because of the pain or pleasure it brings: what is truly advantageous are things which bring us no harm but benefit" (Ostwald [1990], 300). Decleva Caizzi and Bastianini (1989), 210 implausibly assign βλάπτειν and ὠφελεῖν the technical senses they bear in Hippocratic medical texts.

22–24 τὰ τοίνυν τῇ φύσει ξυμφέροντα: τοίνυν can hardly be adversative, as Aly (1929), 135 and Untersteiner (1962), 85 translated. Here, it may mark the transition from a general proposition to a particular application of it: "real advantages should help, not harm. Now, the things advantageous to nature do this ..." (*vel sim.*). Cf. Denniston (1954), 576–77; Decleva Caizzi and Bastianini (1989), 210; Heinimann (1945), 138. Ostwald (1990), 300 suggested (hardly rightly) that with τοίνυν, the discussion turned to a consideration of "pain inherent in what is advantageous to us in terms of nature." Stenzel (1924), 37; von Arnim (1916), 6; Aly (1929), 135; Untersteiner (1962), 85–86; Morrison (1972), 219; Barnes (1982), 510, 514 n. 4, and others interpret τῇ φύσει here as a modal dative: "by nature" or "according to nature." Antiphon may use anarthrous φύσει in this way in F44(b)II.10, 17 (cf. commentary ad locc.); but the presence of the article seems to rule out this interpretation here. In light of ὀνίνησιν τὴν φύσιν in IV.11–12 above, it is much more plausible to interpret τῇ φύσει ξυμφέροντα as "advantageous *to* nature." So Kerferd (1956–57), 32; Decleva Caizzi and Bastianini (1989), 210; and the translations of Grenfell and Hunt (1915), 102, Diels (1917), 92, Schmidt (1924), 13, Saunders (1977–78), 217, and others.

25–33(32) Grenfell and Hunt (1915), 97, 102 thought that two lines had been lost after IV.24. But as Decleva Caizzi and Bastianini (1989), 200 pointed out, this would produce a column of thirty-two lines, whereas all other columns in this fragment have at least thirty-three lines. Unfortunately, the scrap of papyrus containing IV.28(27)–33(32) is no longer extant. It is therefore impossible to confirm the readings in these lines reported by Grenfell and Hunt, or to pass critical judgment on the restoration of IV.31(30)–32(31) proposed by Heinimann (1945), 138 n. 48. Cf. Decleva Caizzi and Bastianini (1989), 180, 200, 210. Evidently, the list of examples of conduct inimical to nature partially extant in V.1–13 began somewhere here.

V

IV.32(31)–V.24 The fragmentary condition of the end of column IV makes it difficult to be sure precisely how this passage connects with what has gone before. But the general course of the discussion, as well as the close parallels between V.17–24 (ἀλγύνεσθαι/ἥδεσθαι/κακῶς πάσχειν) and IV.9–22 (ἀλγύνοντα/ἥδοντα/βλάπτειν) on the one hand, and V.15–17 (πόλλ' ... πολέμια τῇ φύσει) and II.26–30 (τὰ πολλὰ πολεμίως τῇ φύσει) on the other, suggest a continuation of the argument that law and nature are inimical and action in accordance with law disadvantageous for the individual. Following the lead of Greene (1944), 238, Kerferd (1956–57), 29–30 argued that the kind of behavior exemplified in IV.32(31)–V.13 goes far beyond the requirements of law, and so represents a third standard of conduct distinct from both law and nature, the standard of the "Golden Rule" (cf. Ostwald [1990], 300–1). But actual Athenian legislation relevant to the first two examples mentioned shows that the conduct in question does *not* go beyond the requirements of the law (cf. below). Furthermore, the term νόμος (in Antiphon's usage) covers conventional moral attitudes as well as written laws; and it is certain that all three examples concern conduct that would be considered upright (δίκαιος) by conventional standards of morality. Cf. Moulton (1972), 342; Guthrie (1971a), 109 n. 3; Furley (1981), 85; Nill (1985), 62 n. 38; Decleva Caizzi (1985), 196; Decleva Caizzi and Bastianini (1989), 210–11. One feature common to all three examples is that the νόμος-abiding agents (to adopt the convenient terminology of Nill [1985]) are victimized precisely as a result of their νόμος-abiding behavior. Nill (1985), 62–63 accordingly argued that Antiphon distinguished two categories of agents who act in ways inimical to nature: (1) those who fail to pursue their own advantage at the expense of others; and (2) those who are victimized by the aggression of others. But it is far from clear that Antiphon conceived of these as two separate categories (the καί in V.13 does not support such a view; cf. below). Nill's second category can equally well be regarded as a subset of his first, for the victims in IV.32(31)–V.13 also exemplify how νόμος-abiding agents fail to pursue their own interest at the expense of others (for example, by taking the initiative against others, maltreating parents, etc.).

iv.33(32)–v.3 οἵτινες . . . δρᾶν: as Nill (1985), 61 n. 37 rightly argued, Antiphon has in mind those who fail to initiate action against *potential aggressors* (not against others in general). Far from going beyond the requirements of νόμος, such behavior is in perfect accord with both positive law and conventional morality, which sanctioned self-defense and retaliation (ἀμύνεσθαι) but forbade the initiation of aggression. Cf. Antiphon of Rhamnus, *or.* 4.β.2 (quoted below), 4.δ.7 (τῷ μὲν γὰρ ἄρξαντι πανταχοῦ μεγάλα ἐπιτίμια ἐπίκειται, τῷ δὲ ἀμυνομένῳ οὐδαμοῦ οὐδὲν ἐπιτίμιον γέγραπται); Demosthenes, *or.* 23.50, 59.15; Thucydides, 7.68; Paoli (1933), 195–200; Dover (1974), 182–84. Those who initiated aggression (ὃς ἂν ἄρξῃ χειρῶν ἀδίκων πρότερος: Demosthenes, *or.* 47.40, 47) were subject to the δίκη αἰκείας. Cf. Lipsius, Meier and Schömann (1905–15), 643–45; MacDowell (1978), 123. ἀμύνομαι denotes not only self-defense, but more broadly "permissible reaction," which included retaliation. Cf. LSJ, s.v. B.II; Antiphon of Rhamnus, *or.* 4.β.2 (τὸν γὰρ ἄρξαντα τῆς πληγῆς, εἰ μὲν σιδήρῳ ἢ λίθῳ ἢ ξύλῳ ἠμυνάμην αὐτόν . . . ταῖς δὲ χερσὶ τυπτόμενος ὑπ' αὐτοῦ, ταῖς χερσὶν ἅπερ ἔπασχον ἀντιδρῶν) and *passim*; Thucydides, 1.96 (ἀμύνεσθαι ὧν ἔπαθον); Paoli (1933), 196–97; Decleva Caizzi (1969), 244. δρᾶν implies violent aggression; cf. Euripides, *Heracles* 215, 540, 858 with Bond (1981), 121, 202–3, 289–90, who gives further references. For the opposition of παθεῖν and δρᾶν cf. F58 (from Περὶ ὁμονοίας).

4–8 οἵτινες . . . ποιῶσιν: the obligations of sons to parents (and grandparents) were a matter of both legal requirement and conventional expectation (cf. Aeschylus, *Suppliants* 707; Xenophon, *Memorabilia* 4.4.20; Dover [1974], 273–74). Those who struck their parents, refused to house and support them in old age, or failed to provide them proper burial after death were liable under Athenian law to prosecution on the charge of κάκωσις γονέων. Cf. Lipsius, Meier and Schömann (1905–15), 343–44; MacDowell (1978), 92. The first two obligations (though not the last) were waived in the case of illegitimacy, or if parents prostituted their sons or failed to teach them a trade or craft. But it is doubtful that Antiphon has any of these exceptional circumstances in mind in referring to parental maltreatment of children (καὶ κακοὺς ὄντας εἰς αὐτούς), as Aly (1929), 136 and Moulton (1972), 340 with n. 29 suggested. More likely he envisages the normal inequality obtaining in father–son relationships, which is succinctly described by Plato, *Crito* 50E (ἢ πρὸς μὲν ἄρα σοι [*sc.* Socrates] τὸν πατέρα οὐκ ἐξ ἴσου ἦν τὸ δίκαιον καὶ πρὸς δεσπότην, εἴ σοι ὢν ἐτύγχανεν, ὥστε ἅπερ πάσχοις ταῦτα καὶ ἀντιποιεῖν, οὔτε κακῶς ἀκούοντα ἀντιλέγειν οὔτε τυπτόμενον ἀντιτύπτειν οὔτε ἄλλα τοιαῦτα πολλά) and turned on its head in comic fantasies of sons beating their fathers (cf. Aristophanes, *Birds*

757–59, 1347–52, *Clouds* 1405–46; Dunbar [1995], 652–53; Dodds [1959], 258).[6] Cf. Decleva Caizzi (1985), 197; Decleva Caizzi and Bastianini (1989), 211. τοὺς γειναμένους could mean "fathers," but more likely means "parents" (cf. Herodotus, 1.120; LSJ, s.v. γείνομαι II; Aly [1929], 155 n. 157). καί could be a connective with adversative force, joining γειναμένους and ὄντας ("those who bore them and yet are bad to them"); cf. Denniston (1954), 292–93. But more likely it is adverbial, with ὄντας having concessive/temporal or concessive/conditional force ("even when" or "if" they are bad). In v.7, all editors print αὐτοὺς; but the reflexive seems to be required. Cf. F44(c)I.28 with commentary.

8–13 καὶ οἱ κατόμνυσθαι . . . κατομνύμενοι: this example relates to the practice of oath-challenges, πρόκλησις εἰς ὅρκον. Cf. Aristotle, *Rhetoric* 1377a9–b3; Lipsius, Meier and Schömann (1905–15), 895–900; Bonner and Smith (1930–38), 2.146–48, 158–62; Plescia (1970), 43–47; MacDowell (1978), 247; Mirhady (1991). In the situation here evisaged, a νόμος-abiding agent, challenged by an opponent to tender an oath, does so without swearing one himself. (Whether he declines an oath tendered him by the opponent, or fails to issue a counter-challenge to the opponent to tender him one, is not said.) Such a course of action is envisaged by Aristotle, *Rhetoric* 1377a9–10, 31–32, but would have been unusual in Athenian practice, for it puts the νόμος-abiding agent at a considerable disadvantage. Cf. Lipsius, Meier and Schömann (1905–15), 898–99 with n. 137; Plescia (1970), 44; Bonner and Smith (1930–38), 2.158–59. Nill (1985), 62 envisaged a somewhat different scenario: a νόμος-abiding agent, injured by an aggressor, tenders the latter an oath in the (false) expectation that he will tell the truth and so convict himself. This scenario is possible, but less likely than the one outlined above, since it assigns the aggressor a more passive role in the oath-challenge process. At first sight, the oath-challenge example seems to stand out from the others as a clear case of behavior that goes beyond the requirements of either written law or conventional ethical expectation. But Aristotle's moral and religious arguments (*Rhetoric* 1377a15–21, 25–26) in support of tendering an oath, and in defense of not swearing one, may demonstrate otherwise.

9–10 κατόμνυσθαι διδόντες: this phrase is equivalent to the more

[6] Luria (1926d), (1927b), 1070–71; Nestle (1942), 381 with n. 44; Decleva Caizzi (1985), 197; Decleva Caizzi and Bastianini (1989), 211, and others detect Antiphon's influence in Aristophanes' treatment of father–son relationships (particularly in *Clouds*). But the topic was a commonplace. Cf. Heinimann (1945), 141; Moulton (1972), 340–41; Introduction, section III.

usual ὅρκον διδόναι, "tender an oath." It refers here to the νόμος-abiding agent's acceptance of his opponent's offer to swear an oath (cf. Lipsius, Meier and Schömann [1905–15], 895 n. 123). For κατόμνυμαι in the sense of "swear an oath" cf. Aristotle, *Rhetoric* 1377a16 with Cope and Sandys (1877), 1.287–88. The verb here does *not* mean "accuse with an oath" or "swear an accusation against," as von Arnim (1916), 6; Bignone (1938), 179 n. 3, and Untersteiner (1962), 87 interpreted. οἱ διδόντες . . . κατομνύμενοι has generic force (as the μή indicates), and so this participial clause (which lacks a main verb) is functionally equivalent to the preceding general relative clauses introduced by οἵτινες ἄν.

13 καὶ τούτων: Kerferd (1956–57), 30; Nill (1985), 63 n. 41, and Decleva Caizzi and Bastianini (1989), 202 interpret καί adverbially. But this produces an asyndeton which is unmotivated (contrast v.17, with commentary). καί is best taken as a connective, and so supports neither Kerferd's theory of a third standard of conduct nor Nill's analysis of two types of νόμος-abiding agent (cf. above).

13–15 τούτων τῶν εἰρημένων πόλλ': either "many aspects of the behaviors mentioned" (so Havelock [1957], 282–83; Moulton [1972], 339; Decleva Caizzi and Bastianini [1989], 202, and apparently Kranz, *FVS* 2.350) or "many of the behaviors mentioned." On the former interpretation, all of the behaviors mentioned are (in some way) inimical to nature, whereas the latter interpretation implies that some are not.

16–17 πολέμια τῇ φύσει: cf. II.26–30. Aly (1929), 136 spoke of a "framing" technique here ("Einrahmung"); Decleva Caizzi and Bastianini (1989), 211 speak of "ring-composition."

17–18 ἔνι γε αὐτοῖς: the scribe originally wrote γε, which was subsequently altered to τε. If the interlinear ν is rightly read (cf. Grenfell and Hunt [1915], 103), the corrector wished to read τ' ἐν, which is adopted by Diels (1916), Diels and Kranz in *FVS*, Untersteiner (1962), and Decleva Caizzi and Bastianini (1989). Grenfell and Hunt (1915) and Gernet (1923), 178, however, printed γε αὐτοῖς. τε as a sentence-connective is not elsewhere attested in the sophist Antiphon. (But τε connects clauses in F50, l. 1, F58, ll. 13; cf. Jacoby [1908], 50.) According to Kühner–Gerth 1.443, Anmerkung 1, repetition of ἐν after ἔνι when the latter has a figurative rather than literal sense (as here) would not be expected; but F58, ll. 5–6 (ἐν μὲν τῷ γεγενῆσθαι οὐκ ἔνεστιν κτλ.) shows that Antiphon did not always respect this usage. In any case, γε is more idiomatic: it serves here as a quasi-connective, softening the (explanatory) asyndeton, and is nearly equivalent to γοῦν. Cf. Denniston (1954), 144–45 and IV.8–14, a passage which functions very similarly to v.17–24, offering "part-proof" for a preceding assertion.

18–24 ἀλγύνεσθαι . . . μὴ πάσχειν: these lines unmistakably echo IV.8–22. The behavior exemplified in IV.32(31)–V.13 is inimical to nature because it causes more pain than is necessary and less pleasure than is possible. Alhough some commentators demur, it is hard to avoid the label "hedonism" here. Cf. Gomperz (1927), 63; Havelock (1957), 281–82; Nill (1985), 60 n. 29; Wiesner (1994), 232 (but contrast Diels [1917], 93; Reesor [1987], 214; Ostwald [1990], 299–300). Decleva Caizzi and Bastianini (1989), 211 refer ἀλγύνεσθαι to the refusal to initiate aggression (IV.32(33)–V.3); ἥδεσθαι to the treatment of parents (V.4–8); and κακῶς πάσχειν to the refusal to swear an oath (V.8–13). This is overly subtle: there is no reason to limit the application of Antiphon's words in this way. On the comparative forms ἧττω, ἐλάττω, and πλείω (accusative neuter plurals used adverbially) cf. Rosenkranz (1930), 151, who cites parallels from Thucydides and the pseudo-Xenophontean Ἀθηναίων πολιτεία. Such forms are unattested in Antiphon of Rhamnus (who prefers comparative adverbs in -ως), and very rare in the Attic orators generally (cf. Rosenkrantz [1930], 151).

V.25–VI.25 A new stage of the argument begins here. So far, Antiphon has contended that the most advantageous course of action for an individual is to disobey the laws in the absence of witnesses (I.6–II.23), since laws are inimical to nature and behavior in accordance with them incurs pain and disadvantage (II.26–V.24). Now, he offers an *argumentum ex contrario* in support of the same contention by considering the circumstances in which obedience to the laws might be advantageous (cf. Niceforo [1972], 408). It could be so if the system of legal justice were able to prevent aggression in the first place, or at least guarantee retribution afterwards for a victim who has suffered aggression. (Cf. [Demosthenes], *or.* 25.17: δυοῖν γὰρ ὄντοιν, ὦ ἄνδρες Ἀθηναῖοι, ὧν ἕνεκα πάντες τίθενται οἱ νόμοι, τοῦ τε μηδένα μηδὲν ὃ μὴ δίκαιόν ἐστι ποιεῖν, καὶ τοῦ τοὺς παραβαίνοντας ταῦτα κολαζομένους βελτίους τοὺς ἄλλους ποιεῖν κτλ.) Antiphon demonstrates, however, that the system of legal justice can in fact do neither, from which it follows that obedience to the laws is not in an individual's best interests (cf. Niceforo [1972], 408). For a full and careful analysis of the argument cf. Nill (1985), 62–65. Other commentators have interpreted the passage quite differently, as an ethically-minded critique of the workings of the Athenian judicial system, in which Antiphon expresses his sympathy for victims of aggression. So Havelock (1957), 286; Dillon (1984), 130–31, and especially Moulton (1972), 340–43, 352–57, 361–66. Such an interpretation ignores the larger context of the passage, however, and completely mistakes its function as an *argumentum ex contrario.* Cf. Menzel (1922), 63–64. Saunders (1977–78), 224 suggested that Antiphon seriously envisaged the possibility of a new legal system which would work more efficiently than the existing one. But this too ignores the *ex-contrario* character of the argument. That Antiphon considered it impossible for any legal system to satisfy the conditions he lays down by always and everywhere successfully preventing or at least punishing aggression is unambiguously indicated by the contrafactual character of the condition in v.25–vi.3. Cf. Nill (1985), 64; Diels (1917), 95.

25 μὲν οὖν: a transitional formula, with the μέν looking forward to δέ in vi.4. Cf. F44(c)i.30; Denniston (1954), 470–73.

26–27 τοῖς τοιαῦτα προσιεμένοις: the papyrus offers προϊεμαι here and in v.31, but προσίεμαι in vi.5. Grenfell and Hunt and most subsequent editors print προσίεμαι in all three places, while Gernet (1923), 178 with n. 1 and Morrison (1972), 220 with n. 112 adopted προϊεμαι. Gernet translated "font des concessions," supposing a commercial metaphor (for προΐημι = "lend" cf. LSJ, s.v. B.II.9), while Morrison rendered "surrender." Neither of these senses suits the context, however, and προσίεμαι is almost certainly the correct reading in all three passages. As David Sedley suggests to me, the scribe probably mistook προσίεμαι for the commoner προϊεμαι, and then simply repeated the error at v.31. Aly (1929), 135 interpreted προσίεμαι here to mean "etwas geschehen lassen," but this can hardly be right: one element of the desired ἐπικούρησις is precisely the prevention of suffering for potential victims of aggression (cf. vi.9–18). Most likely it means "accept" or "submit to" the laws. Cf. LSJ, s.v. προσίημι II.2b; Herodotus, 1.135 (ξεινικὰ δὲ νόμαια Πέρσαι προσίενται ἀνδρῶν μάλιστα); Xenophon, *Memorabilia* 2.8.5; Plutarch, *De recta ratione audiendi* 46E. Cf. also vi.2–3: τὸ τοῖς νόμοις πείθεσθαι. Kerferd (1956–57), 29–30 argued that προσίεμαι denotes "the deliberate adoption of a particular standard" of conduct *in addition to* (προσ) the requirements of the law, and so supports his notion of a third standard of conduct in addition to law and nature (cf. commentary on iv.32(31)–v.24). But the prepositional prefix in προσίεμαι certainly does not denote "in addition" (Kerferd's reference to Herodotus, 1.135, quoted above, proves nothing). As for τοιαῦτα, Nill (1985), 63 has cogently demonstrated that the logic of the argument rules out the possibility of referring it specifically to the restraints which the νόμος-abiding agents in iv.32(31)–v.13 submit to. (Aly [1929], 135; Kerferd [1956–57], 29–30; Untersteiner [1962], 87; Moulton [1972], 341; Ostwald [1990], 301, and others seem to interpret in this way.) Rather, τοιαῦτα seems to refer generally to *any* "νόμος-imposed restraints which prevent agents from injuring others" (Nill [1985], 63).

27–33 ἐπικούρησις ἐγίγνετο ... ἐλάττωσις: for the periphrasis cf. ii.23–26 (ἔστι σκέψις); vii.13–14 (γίγνεται νίκη, if rightly supplemented); commentary on T2(a). For ἐπικούρησις ("help" or "protection") cf. Euripides, *Andromache* 28; Plato, *Laws* 919B; Appian, *Bellum civile* 1.4.33. ἐλάττωσις does not mean "defeat" (as LSJ, s.v. II interpret) but "loss," "detriment." Cf. Polybius, *Historiae* 4.47.3 (τὴν τῶν πέλας ἐλάττωσιν paired with τὴν σφετέραν βλάβην), 5.11.4 (τοῖς ἐχθροῖς ἐλάττωσιν contrasted with τοῖς ἰδίοις πράγμασιν ἐπικουρίαν); *ThGL* s.v., 4.672. The type of help and loss or detriment Antiphon has in mind is explained in VI.3ff.

VI

1–2 οὐκ ἀνωφελὲς ἂν ἦν: the corrector may have deleted the initial ν in VI.2 and added one at the end of VI.1 because he objected to the line-division in the middle of ἄν (so Grenfell and Hunt [1915], 103). Or (as Richard Janko suggests to me) the ν may have been repeated by dittography. ἀνωφελές (Grenfell and Hunt) is adopted by Gernet (1923), Decleva Caizzi and Bastianini (1989), and others, while Diels and Kranz in *FVS* and Untersteiner (1962) print Diels' ἀνόνητον. The verb ὠφελεῖν appears at IV.21–22 as well as in F44(c)II.31, 33–34, while ὀνίνημι occurs at IV.11. There seems little to choose between them. Moulton (1972), 341 claimed that "ἐπικούρησις would put the man of restraint on a *truly* equal footing with the man of aggression," but this distorts Antiphon's meaning. On what is really implied by ἀνωφελές cf. Nill (1985), 65.

2–3 τὸ τοῖς νόμοις: Grenfell and Hunt (1915) printed τοῖς νόμοις, but suggested τὸ τοῖς νόμοις in their notes. The former would produce a rather short line, but in light of other such lines in this papyrus cannot be considered impossible (cf. I.24, II.27, V.12, V.24). The articular infinitive, however, seems more likely (cf. τὸ ζῆν and τὸ ἀποθανεῖν in III.25–32).

3 πείθεσθαι· νῦν: Diels (1916) proposed πεῖσμα νῦν, which is adopted by Diels and Kranz in *FVS*, Untersteiner (1962), and Decleva Caizzi and Bastianini (1989). Diels and Kranz as well as Untersteiner interpreted πεῖσμα as "obedience." But the substantive πεῖσμα that derives from πείθω (and which is otherwise attested only in late authors) means rather "confidence" or "conviction" (cf. LSJ, s.v. πεῖσμα (B)) – a less than satisfactory sense in the context. Decleva Caizzi (1985), 198 with n. 28 and Decleva Caizzi and Bastianini (1989), 202, 212 understood πεῖσμα as the common noun "cable," "rope" and proposed to read τὸ ἐν τοῖς νόμοις πεῖσμα, "il vincolo che è nelle leggi." This πεῖσμα is sometimes used in a metaphorical sense (cf. LSJ, s.v. πεῖσμα (A)); and the advantages established by the laws are labeled δεσμοί in iv.5. But the phrase is awkward and the sense inappropriate to the context, which seems to demand some reference to obedience or submission to laws (cf. προσιεμένοις). Grenfell's and Hunt's πείθεσθαι is far preferable, though it produces a longer than normal line (cf. iii.23). Aly (1929), 136 suggested that the scribe may have written πειθαι, by haplography.

3–4 νῦν δὲ φαίνεται: for the omission of the supplementary participle ὄν cf. Kühner–Gerth 2.66–67; contrast F44(c)ii.14, 30.

4–5 τοῖς προσιεμένοις: cf. commentary on v.26–27.

6–7 τὸ ἐκ νόμου δίκαιον: most commentators translate simply "legal justice" (*vel sim.*). But Schmidt (1924), 13 ("das vom Gesetz ausgehende Recht") and Kranz (*FVS* 2.350: "das aus dem Gesetz stammende Recht") interpreted the preposition as denoting origin. More likely ἐκ means "in accordance with," as Morrison (1972), 220 translated ("justice according to the law"). Cf. LSJ, s.v. iii.7 and the formula ἐκ τῶν νόμων, "in accordance with the laws" (Aeschines, *or.* 1.45, 188; Hyperides, *In Demosthenem* fr. vii, col. 24.21–22, *Pro Lycophrone* 12, fr. v, col. 10.16–17; Dionysius of Halicarnassus, *Antiquitates Romanae* 10.43.2). τῶν κατὰ νόμον δικαίων in ii.27–28 has a similar sense. The phrase τὸ ἐκ νόμου δίκαιον suggested to Wiesner (1994), 233 and Untersteiner (1962), 88 that Antiphon recognized another kind of justice, that founded on nature. Cf. *contra* Furley (1981), 86.

8–9 ἐπικουρεῖν: cf. v.27–28 ἐπικούρησις.

9–25 ὅ γε πρῶτον . . . ἢ τῷ δεδρακότι: the articulation of this passage is difficult. At first sight, vi.9–18 seem to state one way (πρῶτον μὲν κτλ.) in which the law fails to help victims of aggression, and vi.18–25 a second (εἵς τε κτλ.). (For πρῶτον μέν . . . τε equivalent in sense to πρῶτον μέν . . . ἔπειτα δέ cf. Denniston [1954], 374 n. 2.) The καί in vi.14, however, shows that the preceding lines (vi.9–13) express one complete thought: "legal justice permits aggression." (For the sequence πρῶτον μέν . . . καί cf. Denniston [1954], 374.) vi.14–25 then introduce a second point: "legal justice does not guarantee retribution for victims." What seems to create confusion is Antiphon's choice of a paratactic mode of expression, wherein vi.14–18 (οὔτε . . . δρᾶσαι) is simply juxtaposed (τε) to vi.19–24, in place of a more familiar (and expected) hypotactic formulation, which would have subordinated one to the other. For the construction cf. Euripides, *Hippolytus* 302–3 (οὔτε γὰρ τότε | λόγοις ἐτέγγεθ' ἥδε νῦν τ' οὐ πείθεται) with the comments of Barrett (1964), 216. For the sequence οὔτε . . . τε . . . οὐ cf. Kühner–Gerth 2.288; Denniston (1954), 508–9; Euripides, *Hippolytus* 302–3 (quoted above). This interpretation accounts for the apparent redundancy in vi.14–18, and also helps to explain the imperfect διεκώλυε in vi.15 (cf.

commentary ad loc.). Wiesner (1994), 236 with n. 44 also proposed to coordinate ll. 19–24 with ll. 14–18 rather than with ll. 9–13, but he explained πρῶτον (= "im ersten Fall") in VI.9–10 as a reference back to the first category of νόμος-abiding agents mentioned in IV.32–V.3. But this seems unlikely: the discussion has now moved on to the *ex-contrario* argument against legal obedience in general (VI.2–3 τὸ τοῖς νόμοις πείθεσθαι).

9 ὅ γε: here as often, γε with the relative pronoun = *quippe qui*.

14–15 ἐνταῦθα: as the (imperfect) tense of διεκώλυε indicates, ἐνταῦθα means "at the time" *sc.* of the aggression. So von Arnim (1916), 7; Kranz (*FVS* 2.351); Moulton (1972), 341; cf. LSJ, s.v. II. Diels (1917), 95 translated "in diesem Falle," while Decleva Caizzi and Bastianini (1989), 202, 212 render "in questo senso" (cf. LSJ, s.v. IV).

15 διεκώλυε: this is best explained as an example of the so-called modal usage, in which the time of thinking about an action is transferred to the action itself. The imperfect will then refer to VI.9–13 above: "neither (as we saw) does it prevent etc." Cf. F44(c)I.11 with commentary. The wording here seems to be influenced by the formula ὁ νόμος κωλύει, which is often used of legal prohibitions (cf. Isaeus, *or.* 10.10 with Wyse [1904], 658–59). For the thought, Moulton (1972), 365 aptly compared the remarks of Diodotus in Thucydides, 3.45: ἁπλῶς τε ἀδύνατον καὶ πολλῆς εὐηθείας, ὅστις οἴεται τῆς ἀνθρωπείας φύσεως ὁρμωμένης προθύμως τι πρᾶξαι ἀποτροπήν τινα ἔχειν ἢ νόμων ἰσχύι ἢ ἄλλῳ τῳ δεινῷ.

17 οὐδέ: Diels (1916), 935; Diels and Kranz in *FVS*; Untersteiner (1962), and Decleva Caizzi and Bastianini (1989) all emend to οὔτε. But then the position of οὔτε in VI.14 is very awkward, construed as it must be with τὸν πάσχοντα rather than with ἐνταῦθα.

19–21 εἴς τε τὴν τιμωρίαν ἀναφερόμενον: ἀναφέρω εἰς commonly means "refer" or "appeal to" (cf. LSJ, s.v. ἀναφέρω 6b). Herodotus, 1.157, 7.149 has ἀναφέρω ἔς τινα περί τινος, "refer to someone in connection with." But here it seems that ἀναφερόμενον (the subject of which is τὸ ἐκ νόμου δίκαιον) must be taken in isolation from the preposition, and with a passive sense: "when legal justice is appealed to." The prepositional phrase εἰς τὴν τιμωρίαν then will express purpose (cf. LSJ, s.v. εἰς V.2). The translation of Morrison (1972), 220 seems to come closest to the truth: "When justice is brought in to assist in punishment . . ." τιμωρία connotes retribution exacted to satisfy the victim; cf. Aristotle, *Rhetoric* 1369b11–14 (διὰ θυμὸν δὲ καὶ ὀργὴν τὰ τιμωρητικά. διαφέρει δὲ τιμωρία καὶ κόλασις· ἡ μὲν γὰρ κόλασις τοῦ πάσχοντος ἕνεκά ἐστιν, ἡ δὲ τιμωρία τοῦ ποιοῦντος, ἵνα ἀποπληρωθῇ).

21–25 οὐδὲν ἰδιώτερον . . . τῷ δεδρακότι: ἰδιώτερον is best taken as an adverb, with ἐπί denoting "in the power of" (cf. LSJ, s.v. ἐπί B.I.1g) and ἐστι understood: "justice is in the power of the victim no more peculiarly than in that of the aggressor." If this interpretation is right, the comparative adverb-form ἰδιώτερον is attested here first (next in Anonymus Londinensis, 20.17: ἰδιώτερον παθολογεῖ).

25–33 None of the many attempts to restore this fragmentary passage can be considered satisfactory. In VI.25–30, Diels (1916), 935 tentatively ("versuchsweise") proposed πεῖ[σ]αι γὰρ ἄ[ν ἕ]λοιτο [το]ὺς τ[ιμω]ρ[ήσοντ]ας, ὡς ἔπαθεν, [καὶ] δύνασθαι αἰτ[ιάσ]ει δίκην [ἑλεῖ]ν, which he translated: "Er würde wohl wünschen, die Strafrichter zu überzeugen, dass er die Beleidigung erlitten, und die Möglichkeit zu erlangen, durch seine Anklage den Prozess zu gewinnen" (Diels [1917], 95). To mention only the most obvious difficulties with Diels' proposal: ἕλοιτο ἄν can hardly mean "he would wish"; the repetition of ἑλεῖν in two different senses is awkward; and the ε in αἰτ[ιάσ]ει (VI.29) does not appear to fit the sole surviving (vertical) trace (cf. Decleva Caizzi and Bastianini [1989], 201). Schmidt (1918), 96 modified Diels' proposal by writing δ[εῖ] αὐτό[ν] for ἄ[ν ἕ]λοιτο in VI.25–26 – an alteration adopted by nearly all subsequent editors and commentators. The same suggestion was made independently by Bignone (1938), 58–61, who, however, reconstructed the following lines in very different fashion: [καὶ] δύνασθαι, ἅ γ[ε ἐρ]εῖ, δίκην [ἕξει]ν. Despite Bignone's attempt to justify the futures ἐρεῖ and ἕξειν by reference to τιμωρήσοντας (itself quite uncertain), they are really pointless here, as is the γε (and ἐρεῖ does not fit the trace; cf. above). Furthermore, δίκην ἕξειν would mean "obtain justice" rather than "essere vittorioso," as Bignone translated (cf. LSJ, s.v. δίκη IV.3 and commentary below). In VI.29, Diels and Kranz in *FVS* accepted Regenbogen's ἀπ[αιτ]εῖ, which Kranz translated "wünscht" – an otherwise unparalleled sense. In any case, δύνασθαι ἀπαιτεῖ ἑλεῖν ("demands to be able to win") is intolerably awkward, and ἀπαιτεῖ does not fit the trace (cf. above). The reconstruction and interpretation of the passage proposed by Kuiper (1920), 23 with n. 2 (πεῖσαι γὰρ δεῖ αὐτὸν τοὺς τιμωροῦντας ὡς ἔπαθέν τι δύνασθαι ἀνθ' οὗ χρὴ δίκην λαβεῖν = "Want hij moet zelf de straffers kunnen overtuigen dat hij geleden heeft waarvoor het behoorlijk is dat hij recht verkrijgt") makes πεῖσαι dependent on δύνασθαι, and the latter on δεῖ – a seemingly intolerable word-order. Besides, ἀνθ' οὗ χρὴ in VI.29 does not fit the traces (cf. above). Decleva Caizzi (1985), 198–201 and Decleva Caizzi and Bastianini (1989), 197, 213 adopted the widely-accepted restoration of VI.25–28 (πεῖσαι γὰρ αὐτὸν τοὺς τιμωρήσοντας ὡς ἔπαθεν), but in VI.28–30 proposed [ἢ] δύνασθαι ἀπ[άτ]ῃ δίκην [ἔχει]ν, which they translated: "oppure che sia in grado di ottenere giustizia con l'inganno." While unobjectionable from the viewpoints of grammar and paleography, this proposal does violence to the logic of the argument. For it is difficult to see how the ability to obtain satisfaction (δίκην ἔχειν; cf. LSJ, s.v. δίκη IV.3) by means of deception (ἀπάτῃ) constitutes an *alternative* (ἤ) to the victim's need to convince those who will exact vengeance (τοὺς τιμωροῦντας) that he has in fact suffered (ὡς ἔπαθεν). In support of their proposal, Decleva Caizzi and Bastianini refer to passages such as Thucydides, 3.43 and Plato, *Phaedrus* 272D–E, where it is claimed that even speakers who have the truth on their side resort to deception when plausible falsehood is more persuasive than truth. If Antiphon's hypothetical victim resorted to deception, however, it would be precisely for the purpose of proving that he has suffered, not as an alternative (ἤ) to doing so. Therefore, VI.28–30 cannot in good logic present an alternative to VI.25–30; and the supplements [ἤ] and ἀπ[άτ]ῃ proposed by Decleva Caizzi and Bastianini lose all plausibility. In sum, no convincing restoration of VI.25–30 has yet appeared. Nevertheless, the words ὡς ἔπαθεν (VI.27–28) taken together with VI.30–33 suggest that Antiphon here offered support for the claim (VI.19–25) that legal justice is no more particularly in the power of the victim than of the aggressor. For (VI.25 γάρ) the possibility of exacting vengeance (τιμωρία) depends on the victim's ability to prove that he has suffered (ὡς ἔπαθεν) – something which the aggressor can deny (VI.30–33).

30–31 ταῦτα: Diels and Kranz in *FVS*, Untersteiner (1962), and Decleva Caizzi and Bastianini (1989) all read ταὐτά. Untersteiner interpreted this as an adverb ("nello stesso modo"), Diels and Kranz as a pronoun, the subject of καταλείπεται. (ἀρνεῖσθαι they construed with Diels' conjectural supplement ἑλομένῳ in VII.1.) Decleva Caizzi and Bastianini more plausibly construed ταὐτά as the object of ἀρνεῖσθαι, with καταλείπεται understood impersonally (cf. LSJ, s.v. καταλείπω III). However, ταῦτα (rather than ταὐτά) should probably be read.

VII

5–13 The argument of this passage is obscure. G. Murray (*apud* Grenfell and Hunt [1915], 103) suggested that in VII.6–10, Antiphon made the point that the severity of the retribution exacted from an aggressor depends on an accuser's persuasiveness. But as Bignone (1938), 62–63 rightly objected, the word τιμωρία does not appear in the extant text, and the subject of retribution is introduced purely by conjecture. Adopting a suggestion of Diels (1916), 935, Bignone himself argued that Antiphon raised the issue of "counter-accusations," which put the advantage inherent in being an accuser at the disposal of the aggressor, who can counter-accuse the victim who has accused him (cf. Bignone [1938], 63–64). Bignone's interpretation was accepted by Untersteiner (1962), 89–90 and La Face (1969), 70–71. Precisely what Bignone meant by "counter-accusation," however, is unclear. In Lysias, *or.* 6.42 (cited by Bignone), the term ἀντικατηγορεῖν does not refer to a formal counter-indictment (as Bignone and his followers seem to think), the proper terms for which are ἀντιπροσκαλεῖσθαι and ἀντιγραφή (cf. Lipsius, Meier and Schömann [1905–15], 860 with nn. 48–49). ἀντικατηγορεῖν refers rather to an argumentative strategy whereby defendants counterattack their accusers with (informal) countercharges instead of replying to the charges raised against them. See Lipsius, Meier and Schömann (1905–15), 860 n. 49; Lysias, *or.* 6.42; Isocrates, *or.* 12.22; Gorgias, *Palamedes* 27, and especially Aeschines, *or.* 1.178–79, who deplores the practice as ἀδικώτατον. Bignone's interpretation is in any case open to the same objection he raised against Murray: the absence of any mention of counter-accusations in the extant text. Decleva Caizzi (1985), 201–3 and Decleva Caizzi and Bastianini (1989), 213 offered a new reading and reconstruction of vii.5–9. On their interpretation, the passage refers to the limited amount of time (regulated by the clepsydra) granted to litigants to make speeches. The fact that this amount was exactly the same (ὅσηπερ) for accuser and defendant alike (cf. MacDowell [1978], 249) constitutes yet another way in which the legal process fails to accord any special advantage to the victims of aggression. While not impossible, this interpretation depends on very uncertain readings of the traces preserved in vii.5–6. Moreover, ὅσηπερ can just as well be taken with πειθώ in vii.10 as with κατηγορία (as Decleva Caizzi and Bastianini take it). Construed this way, the words suggest an interpretation like that of Diels (1917), 96, who conjectured that Antiphon pointed out how a successful outcome at trial depends (for accuser and accused alike) more on the ability to persuade than on the truth or facts of a case. However this passage is interpreted, the whole course of the argument in columns vi–vii belies Joël's view that Antiphon immorally "stellt die Beredsamkeit ebenso dem Gewalttäter wie dem Unrechtleidenden zur Verfügung" (Joël [1921], 673 with n. 1, 698, 728).

13ff. The traces of the remainder of this column are too scanty to yield any sense. Pollux (2.109) cites from "Antiphon" (without a book-title) the rare word ἀγλωττίαν, which Luria (1924b), 329 proposed to restore in vii.18 (δ' ἐς ἀγλωττίαν). But the papyrus fragments of Περὶ ἀληθείας consistently offer εἰς rather than ἐς (cf. v.7, vi.19; F44(b)ii.29, iii.5; F44(c)i.7). The motivation behind Luria's proposal was his desire to identify Antiphon as the source of what he took to be a polemic against slavery in Euripides' *Alexandros*, where ἀγλωσσία happens also to be attested (fr. 34.2 Snell = 56.2 Nauck; cf. Luria [1924b], [1929a]). Luria's theory of Euripidean dependence on Antiphon was rejected by Wilamowitz (1927), 288–90 and Lefke (1936), 75, 89–90, and is now refuted by the new evidence of *P.Oxy.* 3647. Cf. Hall (1989), 218–19 and commentary on F44(b).

F44(b)

Older interpreters generally read into this fragment an egalitarian-spirited argument attacking the artificiality of distinctions customarily drawn between the rich and the poor, high-born and low-born, slave and free. But this type of interpretation has now been demolished by the evidence of the new papyrus (*P.Oxy.* 3647), which eliminates the textual supplements on which alone it rested. Cf. Decleva Caizzi (1986), 61–62; Hall (1989), 218–20, and commentary below. Even before the appearance of the new papyrus, a few cautious commentators had drawn attention to the conjectural character of the egalitarian interpretation and the evidence supporting it (so Moulton [1972], 344–45; Isnardi Parente [1975], 17–18; Avery [1982], 148–49; cf. Decleva Caizzi [1986], 61 n. 3). Luria's attempt to detect the influence of Antiphon in Euripides' *Alexandros* (cf. commentary on F44(a)VII.13ff.) and the efforts of Bignone (1938), 68–71 to expose inconsistencies between F44(a) and F44(b) both take their starting-point from the egalitarian interpretation, and so fall together with it.

Unfortunately, the new evidence fails to provide a direct answer to the question concerning the reference of the words τοὺς δέ in II.3, and thus the precise nature of the contrast drawn in the crucial passage II.1–6. Nevertheless, it has long been recognized that the fragment as a whole (like F44(a)) is concerned with the antithesis of νόμος and φύσις (cf. Diels [1917], 97–98; Wilamowitz [1927], 288). It is plausible, therefore, to refer τοὺς δέ to νόμοι (so Funghi [1984], 4; Luppe [1986], 121). This suggestion receives some confirmation from the active-voice forms of the verb σέβειν, which governs τοὺς δέ (cf. below); and perhaps also from the fragmentary words τούς (or τοῖς) νομ in IV.8 (cf. Decleva Caizzi and Bastianini [1989], 188 and commentary ad loc.). As an alternative to νόμοι, Decleva Caizzi (1986a), 62–63, (1986b), 293–94 and Decleva Caizzi and Bastianini (1989), 187–88 suggested a reference to the gods (θεοί). Cf. Thucydides, 2.53.4 (θεῶν τε φόβος ἢ ἀνθρώπων νόμος οὐδεὶς ἀπεῖργε, τὸ μὲν κρίνοντες ἐν ὁμοίῳ καὶ σέβειν καὶ μή κτλ.). It is certain that Antiphon and his contemporaries recognized differing religious practices as one factor differentiating Greeks from barbarians (cf. Herodotus, 8.144; Hall [1989], 181–84). But it is doubtful whether he would have singled out religion as the *primary* such factor, worthy of being counterposed to the natural similarities which unite all human beings. Decleva Caizzi (1986a), 63 and Decleva Caizzi and Bastianini (1989), 188 further suggested that in the end it makes little or no difference whether τοὺς δέ refers specifically to laws or to gods, since for Antiphon religion belonged to the domain of νόμος. If this means that he considered religious *practices* a matter of custom and convention, the point may be granted. But these commentators' reference to *Laws* 889E suggests they meant rather that Antiphon believed the gods to *exist* only in conventional opinion, not in reality. This view, however, there is no reason whatsoever to ascribe to him. (On *Laws* 888D–890A as a précis of Antiphon's doctrine cf. Introduction, section VII.) If νόμους is understood with τοὺς δέ, the argument of the fragment can be plausibly reconstructed along the following lines (cf. Funghi [1984], 4). By knowing and observing their own laws and customs but not those of others (II.1–6), human beings end up establishing arbitrary distinctions among themselves which have no basis in nature (II.7–15) – such as that between Greeks and barbarians. For all human beings exercise the same natural functions in the same way (II.15–24, 27ff.); and in these, there can be no differentiation between Greek and foreigner (II.24–27). Understood in this way, Antiphon's argument opposes the common (physical) nature shared by all human beings to the varying laws by allegiance to which people divide themselves into artificial categories like Greek and barbarian. As in the buried-bed argument (F15) and the argument of F44(a), φύσις here is identified with what is primary and essential, νόμος with what is secondary and adventitious (cf. Diels [1917], 98, and commentary on F15 and F44(a)I.25–II.1). Interpreting φύσις in the sense of universal nature, Funghi (1984), 4–5 detected a contrast between the "laws of φύσις" and "human νόμος." But the whole notion of a "law of nature" is probably anachronistic for Antiphon (cf. commentary on F44(a)I.22–23). Furthermore, it is obvious from II.27ff. that φύσις in this fragment refers to *human* nature, not universal nature or the natural order of things as a whole. For these reasons, Funghi's claim that "for Antiphon the criterion of truth is not man, but φύσις and its realities" sets up a false contrast. The "realities" of nature for Antiphon are none other than those of (physical) human nature. The contrast drawn here between the artificial distinctions created by νόμος and a common human nature recalls the argument of the sophist Hippias in Plato, *Protagoras* 337C–D: Ὦ ἄνδρες, ἔφη, οἱ παρόντες, ἡγοῦμαι ἐγὼ ὑμᾶς συγγενεῖς τε καὶ οἰκείους καὶ πολίτας ἅπαντας εἶναι – φύσει, οὐ νόμῳ· τὸ γὰρ ὅμοιον τῷ ὁμοίῳ φύσει συγγενές ἐστιν, ὁ δὲ νόμος, τύραννος ὢν τῶν ἀνθρώπων, πολλὰ τὴν φύσιν βιάζεται κτλ. (cf. Introduction, section VII). The exact opposite view is expounded by the anonymous author of [Demosthenes], *or.* 25.15, who identifies nature as that which divides men, since it is different in each individual (κατ' ἄνδρ' ἴδιον τοῦ ἔχοντος). Laws, by contrast, being common and the same for all (κοινὸν καὶ ταὐτὸ πᾶσιν), unite what nature divides (cf. Heinimann [1945], 150–52).

Funghi (1984), 4–5 (followed by Decleva Caizzi [1986b], 296 and Decleva Caizzi and Bastianini [1989], 192) proposed to situate the argument of this fragment in the larger context of an historical–anthropological account of the development of human civilization. (On ancient theories of cultural development or *Kulturentstehungslehren* cf. Uxkull-Gyllenband [1924]; Spoerri [1959]; Cole [1967], with the review of Graeser [1969].) More specifically, Funghi argued that Antiphon espoused a developmental schema similar to that found in John Tzetzes' commentary on Hesiod's *Works and Days*, which describes the earliest stages of human existence as characterized by relationships of mutual affection or φιλαλληλία (cf. *FVS* 68 B 5; Spoerri [1957]; Cole [1967], 21–23, 207–8). Starting from this idealized view of the original human condition, Funghi suggested, Antiphon proceeded to sketch a process of progressive decline, as various human communities separated in space diverged and became alienated from one another through the adoption of differing local, contingent laws in place of the universal, necessary ordinances of nature. It is noteworthy that Heinimann (1945), 113–14 postulated a very similar account as the background to Archelaus' supposed views on the conventional, rather than natural, foundation of justice (τὸ δίκαιον εἶναι καὶ τὸ αἰσχρὸν οὐ φύσει, ἀλλὰ νόμῳ: Diogenes Laertius, 2.16 = *FVS* 60 A 1). Plato discusses the effects of spatial and social isolation in early human communities in somewhat similar terms in *Laws* 681B: ἑκάστην τῶν σμικρῶν [*sc.* οἰκήσεων] παρεῖναι κατὰ γένος ἔχουσαν τόν τε πρεσβύτατον ἄρχοντα καὶ αὐτῆς ἔθη ἄττα ἴδια διὰ τὸ χωρὶς ἀλλήλων οἰκεῖν (cf. 681C, quoted below). In the account of the development of civilization from which this passage derives (*Laws* 681A–D), however, Plato posits precisely the reverse of the process envisaged by Funghi. For he locates the origin of law-giving (ἀρχῇ δὴ νομοθεσίας) in the community's perceived need to replace the divergent νόμιμα of individual families with common laws adopted by and for the community as a whole. Whether Funghi's reconstruction of the larger context of F44(b) is accepted or not, her notion that Antiphon's views were developed in conscious opposition to a Protagorean theory of the gradual ascent of human civilization from an original animal state of nature is without foundation. In the first place, there is (to say the least) legitimate doubt as to whether the myth in Plato's *Protagoras* faithfully reproduces the position of the historical Protagoras (cf. the authorities cited in Cherniss [1959–60], 151–52). But even if it does, there is no reason to single out Protagoras as Antiphon's particular target, since theories of human progress were commonplace in the fifth century (cf. Guthrie [1971a], 60–84, and the references given above). Funghi's theory that Antiphon offered an account of the development of civilization is not without plausibility and might be right. But the only concrete evidence for it is the single past-tense verb συνεχώρησαν – a possible (but by no means certain) supplement in IV.5–6. An equally plausible intellectual context for the argument of the fragment is supplied by fifth-century ethnological relativism, which emphasized the almost bewildering diversity of laws and customs to be found among different peoples. Cf. *Dialexeis* 2.9–18, 26; Xenophon, *Memorabilia* 4.4.19–24; Heinimann (1945), 78–82, 119–20; Aly (1929), 118–22; Hall (1989), 185–86, 189–90; Diels (1917), 98. In a passage which became the *locus classicus* for this topic, Herodotus (3.38) enunciates the truth that each and every group of people considers its own laws and customs to be the best (οὕτω νομίζουσι πολλόν τι καλλίστους τοὺς ἑωυτῶν νόμους ἕκαστοι εἶναι), and illustrates it with the anecdote about Darius' experiment concerning burial customs. As Heinimann (1945), 80–81 rightly emphasized, the purpose of this anecdote is not to devalue νόμοι or demonstrate their unnatural character, but rather to prove their (limited) validity for the group which practices them. Beginning from the same starting-point – the undeniable diversity of laws and customs among human beings – Antiphon arrives at the opposite conclusion. On his reckoning, the chauvinistic partiality each group shows towards its own νόμοι is responsible for unnatural (and therefore false) distinctions such as that between Greeks and foreigners.

While the notion that Antiphon rejected class-distinctions has been put out of court by the evidence of the new papyrus, the cosmopolitan implications of his argument are still open to debate. Some commentators would credit him with a full-blown theory of the unity, equality, and even brotherhood of all mankind. So Diels (1917), 96–98; Bignone (1938), 69–70, 79, 86–87; Nestle (1942), 377, 380–81; Merlan (1950), 163–64; Havelock (1957), 256–58; Untersteiner (1962), 92–93, (1954), 251–52 = (1967), 75–76; Guthrie (1971a), 152–53 with n. 5. Others stress what they regard as the predominantly *biological* emphasis of his argument and are sceptical of its supposed cosmopolitan implications. So Tarn (1933), 124 n. 6; Levinson (1953), 144–46; Schütrumpf (1972), 20–21; Isnardi Parente (1975), 18; D'Agostini (1975), 556–57 with nn. 28–29; Decleva Caizzi (1986a), 65–66; Decleva Caizzi and Bastianini (1989),

189–90. Certainly the fragment provides no evidence that Antiphon drew equalitarian or humanitarian conclusions from his demonstration of the natural similarity of all human beings. Yet it is equally misleading to interpret this similarity in purely biological terms, as Tarn, Schütrumpf, Decleva Caizzi, and Hall (1989), 220–21 seem inclined to do. For to do so is to ignore the implicit judgment Antiphon's argument passes on the attitude of cultural and moral superiority which characterized much contemporary Greek thinking about foreigners. If the distinction between Greek and foreigner can be reduced to differences of νόμοι, and νόμος represents what is secondary and adventitious, then there is little or no room left for assertions of cultural superiority. It seems hard to deny the label of "cosmopolitan" to an argument which affirms the natural similarity of all human beings, while simultaneously devaluing the importance of cultural differences among them. Cf. Isnardi Parente (1975), 18 n. 31. Schütrumpf (1972), 21–22 objected that Antiphon's cosmopolitanism is theoretical rather than practical. But whether true or not, this is really irrelevant to the question at hand. F44(b) deserves a place alongside passages such as Sophocles, fr. 591 (ἓν φῦλον ἀνθρώπων . . . οὐδεὶς ἔξοχος ἄλλος ἔβλαστεν ἄλλου κτλ.) as evidence for an embryonic form of cosmopolitanism in the later fifth century. Cf. Mewaldt (1926), 180; Cherniss (1977), 462.

Luginbill (1997), 183–86 contested the view that the fragment offers an attack on artificial distinctions such as that between Greeks and foreigners in a spirit of cosmopolitanism. Interpreting βεβαρβαρώμεθα in II.9–10 in a pejorative sense, Luginbill suggested that Antiphon is describing the plight of aristocrats in contemporary democratic Athens. Just as Greeks retain cultural superiority over barbarians in spite of shared physical similarities, so important differences in education and personal virtue exist in Athenian society between those who are qualified to rule and those who are not, in spite of the leveling effect of base φύσις. By ignoring such distinctions, Athenians have sunk to the level of barbarians in their relations with one another. This novel interpretation is open to a number of objections. In the first place, βεβαρβαρώμεθα almost certainly cannot bear the negative sense Luginbill ascribes to it (cf. commentary on II.8–10). Secondly, the first person plural "we" used throughout the fragment must refer to all human beings, not merely to Athenians. Thirdly, Luginbill deals inadequately with the crucial passage II.1–6, which he suggested voices the complaint that aristocratic virtues and accomplishments no longer receive the respect they deserve. But Luginbill failed to explain how this sense is to be gotten from the Greek (his proposal to read τοὺς δὲ [ἐκ κα]λοῦ οἴκ[ου ὄν]των in II.3–4 is incoherent; cf. Luginbill [1997], 186 n. 76). Luginbill (1997), 184–85 recognized that Antiphon's use of common physical characteristics as the basis of a positive appeal against artificial distinctions in this fragment is incompatible with his interpretation of the parallel passage F44(a)II.30–III.18 (cf. commentary ad loc.), and indeed the entire argument of F44(a). For if nature and natural functions are evaluated in positive terms here, this would obviously contradict Luginbill's theory that Antiphon's view of nature was "essentially negative." The insight is apt.

I

1–34 No coherent sense can be extracted from these scraps of lines. With Schöne's conjecture τεκμαίρε[σθαι δέ] in I.10–11 cf. II.15–16 σκοπεῖν δὲ παρέχει, with commentary. On the deletion of]υς in I.33, and the apparently related marginal note, cf. Grenfell and Hunt (1915), 103.

II

1–6 On the argument of these lines cf. introductory note above. For the correlation between differences in νόμοι and the notion of barbarian cf. Xenophon, *Anabasis* 5.4.34 (τούτους [*sc.* the Molussini] ἔλεγον οἱ στρατευσάμενοι βαρβαρωτάτους διελθεῖν καὶ πλεῖστον τῶν Ἑλληνικῶν νόμων κεχωρισμένους) and Montaigne: "chacun appelle barbarie ce qui n'est pas de son usage. Comme de vrai il semble que nous n'avons autre mire de la vérité et de la raison que l'exemple et idée des opinions et usances du pays où nous sommes" (*Essais* 31, "Des Cannibales").

1 -ρων: the older supplements of Grenfell and Hunt, Wilamowitz, Schmidt, and Bignone imported into the passage the subject of social or economic class-distinctions. The proposal of Mazzarino (1966), I.317 n. 281 manufactured an allusion to Pericles' citizenship law of 451/0 BC. All have been definitively ruled out by the evidence of the new papyrus. More recently, Luppe (1986), 121 suggested τῶν ἡμετέρων, Decleva Caizzi (1986a), 63 n. 6 and Decleva Caizzi and Bastianini (1989), 188 τῶν πατέρων. It is not clear what substantive is to be understood with ἡμετέρων (ἀνθρώπων?); for the latter cf. Diodorus Siculus, *Bibliotheca* I.23.5 (τὰ τῶν πατέρων νόμιμα); Plutarch, *De defectu oraculorum* 416C (κατὰ νόμον πατέρων); Alexander of Aetolia, *Anthologia Palatina* 7.709 (πατέρων νόμος). In view of the strict antithetic parallelism employed throughout F44(a) and visible in this fragment as well (cf. e.g. I.1–2, 5–6: ἐπιστάμεθά τε καὶ σέβομεν . . . οὔτε ἐπιστάμεθα οὔτε σέβομεν), neither ἡμετέρων nor πατέρων seems to offer an adequate contrast to τῶν τηλοῦ οἰκούντων. Much more satisfactory from this point of view is Funghi's attractive proposal τῶν ἐγγυτέρων (cf. Funghi [1984], 4). LSJ, s.v. ἐγγύτερος cite no example of this form of the comparative adjective earlier than Procopius of Gaza; but in fact it occurs in Aristotle, *Physics* 197a24, fr. 94; Theophrastus, *De causis plantarum* 5.1.9; Tyrtaeus, fr. 2.11 (a text unknown to LSJ). Funghi alternatively suggested οἰκειοτέρων; but this proposal raises the question of what Antiphon would have understood by degrees of "kinship," given his emphatic assertion of the natural similarity of all human beings. Another alternative might be ἐγχώρων, "natives." In contrast to the common ἐγχώριος, this form of the adjective is attested elsewhere only in tragedy. (Cf. Aeschylus, *Suppliants* 976; Sophocles, *Philoctetes* 693, *Oedipus at Colonus* 125, fr. 937, quoted below; Lycophron, *Alexandra* 267, 509, 719, 859, 927, 949.) Antiphon often uses poetic vocabulary, however, and ἐγχώρων would in this respect match the equally poetic τηλοῦ. It would furthermore provide an appropriate contrast with τῶν τηλοῦ οἰκούντων. Cf. Sophocles, fr. 937 (= Menander, *Sententiae* 518): νόμοις ἕπεσθαι τοῖσιν ἐγχώροις καλόν.

1–2 ἐπιστάμεθά τε καὶ σέβομεν: the line-endings provided by the new papyrus in II.5–6 confirm this restoration, against Grenfell's and Hunt's ἐπαιδούμεθά τε καὶ σεβόμεθα, formerly universally adopted. For ἐπίστασθαι νόμους cf. Aeschines, *or.* 1.39 (τοὺς νόμους ἐπιστάμενος τοὺς τῆς πόλεως); Aristotle, *Nicomachean Ethics* 1113b34 (τοὺς ἀγνοοῦντάς τι τῶν ἐν τοῖς νόμοις, ἃ δεῖ ἐπίστασθαι); *Dialexeis* 8.10 (δεῖ δὲ αὐτὸν καὶ τὼς νόμως ἐπίστασθαι πάντας). σέβειν in the active voice (as here) means "observe" or "practice" rather than "respect" (Funghi [1984], 4) or "venerate" (Decleva Caizzi [1986a], 62–63; Decleva Caizzi and Bastianini [1989], 187–88). Cf. Fraenkel (1950), 3.761–62, with references. For its application to laws and customs cf. Euripides, *Iphigenia in Tauris* 1189 (τὸν νόμον ἀνάγκη τὸν προκείμενον σέβειν), *Helen* 1270 (τόδ' Ἑλλὰς νόμιμον ἐκ τίνος σέβει;), *Phoenissae* 294 (τὸν οἴκοθεν νόμον σέβουσ'), fr. 433 (ἔγωγε φημὶ καὶ νόμον γε μὴ σέβειν | ἐν τοῖσι δεινοῖς τῶν ἀναγκαίων πλέον); trag. adesp. fr. 181 (σέβοντα τοὺς θεῶν νόμους). On juxtaposed τε καὶ cf. Denniston (1954), 512, who notes its absence from the speeches of Antiphon of Rhamnus.

7–15 Because people know and observe only their own laws and customs and disregard those of others, they become like foreigners to one another. It is only νόμοι which differentiate people into groups like "Greek" and "foreigner." By nature, everyone is perfectly adapted to be either.

7 ἐν τούτῳ οὖν: τούτῳ refers to the whole preceding sentence and the behavior described in it. ἐν τούτῳ is one of Antiphon's favorite phrases (cf. F44(c)I.30–31, II.32–33; F49, ll. 11–12; F53A, l. 3). οὖν (supplied by the new papyrus) may be progressive or inferential.

8–10 πρὸς ἀλλήλους βεβαρβαρώμεθα: these words have often been taken in a pejorative sense, "behave like uncivilized barbarians toward one another." So Kuiper (1920), 49 with n. 1; Bignone (1938), 69; Mewaldt (1926), 179; Luria (1929a), 494 n. 1; Merlan (1950), 164 with n. 15; Untersteiner (1962), 94; Guthrie (1971a), 153; Dreher (1983), 76–79. But this is to saddle Antiphon with the gross contradiction of embracing a distinction (that between Greeks and foreigners) whose validity he proceeds immediately to deny (cf. II.10ff.). Other commentators recognize the difficulty but try to get round it while maintaining the pejorative interpretation. Kranz (1951), 230 = (1967), 405, for example, suggested that Antiphon unthinkingly adopted the ordinary pejorative sense of βαρβαρόω and so was led into unconscious contradiction. Guthrie (1971a), 153 with n. 4 supposed a deliberate, "sophistic" play on two different senses of βαρβαρόω (factual and pejorative). Dreher (1983), 78 with n. 45 tried to smooth out the logic of the passage by interpreting ἐπεί in II.10 in the (unparalleled) sense of "while." Kerferd (1981a), 158–59 sought the key to Antiphon's argument in the twelfth chapter of the Hippocratic *De aëre aquis et locis*, where the contrasting characteristics of the inhabitants of Europe and Asia are ascribed to differences of climate and environment. Kerferd suggested that like the Hippocratic author, Antiphon acknowledged the biological similarity of all human beings at birth, yet affirmed the importance of subsequent cultural influences – influences which result in a divergent development into intelligent, superior Greeks on the one hand, and inferior barbarians on the other, whose stupidity is imitated by those Greeks who behave in the manner indicated in II.1–6. Antiphon, however, denies any natural basis for the conventional distinction between Greek and barbarian; and his attitude (as Furley [1981], 90 rightly noted) is essentially at odds with that of the author of *De aëre aquis et locis*. Decleva Caizzi (1986a), 63–69, (1986b), 294–95 and Decleva Caizzi and Bastianini (1989), 188–89 interpreted Antiphon's use of βαρβαρόω in light of the Persian custom described by Herodotus, 1.134, who reports that Persians (and Medes) esteem and honor foreign peoples in direct proportion to their geographical proximity. On this interpretation, Antiphon will have alluded to this custom in order to remind his fellow Greeks that their conventional attitude of superiority to foreigners amounted to an unwitting adoption of a typical "barbarian" behavior. The text gives absolutely no indication that Antiphon had this custom in mind, however, and the allusions to his ideas which Decleva Caizzi sought to detect in the *Menexenus* are far too uncertain to support her interpretation of βαρβαρόω here (cf. Introduction, section I; commentary on F44(a)I.29–II.I). The use of the first person plural "we" throughout the fragment constitutes a decisive stumbling-block to the interpretations of Decleva Caizzi and all others who understand βεβαρβαρώμεθα in a pejorative sense. For "we" clearly must refer throughout to all human beings, Greeks and foreigners alike; II.I–6 therefore describes behavior that is not exclusively or primarily Greek (as the pejorative interpretations of βαρβαρόω assume), but rather characteristic of all human beings. Since Antiphon rejects the distinction between Greek and foreigner as a purely conventional imposition upon nature, βεβαρβαρώμεθα here must have a strictly neutral sense: "we have become" or "we have made ourselves" "foreigners" to one another or in one another's eyes (*sc.* by the behavior described in II.I–6). So Wilamowitz (1927), 289; Funghi (1984), 4. (Cf. Furley [1981], 89–90, whose interpretation is not entirely clear.)

10–15 ἐπεὶ φύσει γε . . . εἶναι: this clause is customarily translated as if ὁμοίως were the predicate, with καὶ βάρβαροι καὶ Ἕλληνες taken in apposition to the subject πάντες. So Diels (1917), 97; Kranz (*FVS* 2.352–53); Bignone (1938), 69, 170 (but contrast the more careful translation at 58); Gernet (1923), 178; Nestle (1942), 377; Merlan (1950), 164; Lana (1951), 319; Moulton (1972), 344; Morrison (1972), 220; Saunders (1977–78), 218; Dreher (1983), 78 n. 45; Furley (1981), 89 (though their translations differ in other details). As an adverb, however, ὁμοίως cannot function as a predicate adjective in this way with πεφύκαμεν εἶναι understood as the copula (cf. Tarán [1977], 663–64, with references). ὁμοίως could be construed with εἶναι if the latter were given existential force. (So apparently Funghi [1984], 4: "we come to exist in a similar way.") But the resulting sense does not really suit the context. Alternatively, ὁμοίως could serve as a predicate with πεφύκαμεν alone (cf. LSJ, s.v. φύω B.II, with references); but this leaves εἶναι without any grammatical function. Holwerda (1955), 75 construed εἶναι as a limiting infinitive with καὶ βάρβαροι καὶ Ἕλληνες, with the resulting sense of ὅσοι ἐσμὲν βάρβαροι καὶ ὅσοι ἐσμὲν Ἕλληνες. But it is very difficult to parallel such a use of absolute or limitative εἶναι. The word-order strongly suggests that ὁμοίως qualifies πάντες ("all alike"), with καὶ βάρβαροι καὶ Ἕλληνες forming the predicate. εἶναι (copulative, not existential) depends on πεφύκαμεν, the combination signifying "naturally disposed to be" (cf. LSJ, s.v. φύω B.II.2; Kühner–Gerth 2.10–11). Grenfell and Hunt (1915), 103; Mewaldt (1926), 180; Kerferd (1981a), 158; Decleva Caizzi (1986a), 65–66, and Decleva Caizzi and Bastianini (1989), 189–90 all construe the clause in this fashion.

10 φύσει γε: Decleva Caizzi and Bastianini (1989), 189 understood γε as emphatic, comparing F44(a)IV.10. But γε in that passage is certainly limitative (cf. commentary ad loc.), as it probably is here also, "what we are by nature, at any rate" being contrasted with what we have become as a result of the behavior described in II.1–6. So Funghi (1984), 4, who translates "For by nature, at least." For the redundant φύσει πεφύκαμεν cf. Sophocles, *Philoctetes* 79–80 (ἔξοιδα, παῖ, φύσει σε μὴ πεφυκότα | τοιαῦτα φωνεῖν μηδὲ τεχνᾶσθαι κακά); [Hippocrates], *De aëre aquis et locis* 16, *De flatibus* 14; Euripides, *Bacchae* 896; Lysias, *or.* 2.29; Plato, *Cratylus* 383A, *Philebus* 14C; Xenophon, *Cyropaedia* 5.1.24; Aristotle, *De caelo* 296b27. It is noteworthy that φύσις is anarthrous here and in II.17 (the only occurrences of the noun in this fragment). In F44(a), by contrast, φύσις has the article everywhere it appears. Kerferd (1956–57), 32 suggested that anarthrous φύσει here means "birth," a sense which is possible in this context but seemingly impossible in II.17. "By nature" (that is, human nature; cf. Beardslee [1918], 21, 36, 39, 45, and *passim*) seems to make the best sense in both passages. Heinimann (1945), 142 n. 62 rightly noted that the modal-dative formula νόμῳ–φύσει is completely absent from the sophist Antiphon; but he overlooked both instances of φύσει in this fragment.

13–14 καὶ βάρβαροι καὶ Ἕλληνες: for καὶ ... καί used where English idiom demands "either ... or" cf. Lysias, *or.*12.26 (ἐπειδὴ δέ σοὶ ἐγένετο καὶ σῶσαι Πολέμαρχον καὶ μή) with Adams (1905), 80–81; Plato, *Laws* 647A with England (1921), 1.262.

15–23 The precise sense of this passage, which has yet to be restored in a convincing fashion, is uncertain. Its subject seems to be the natural necessities (τῶν φύσει ἀναγκαι[) which are common to all human beings (πᾶσιν ἀν[θρώ]ποις), and in respect of which no one is differentiated as Greek or foreigner. Cf. II.24–27.

15–16 σκοπεῖν δὲ παρέχει: for παρέχει used impersonally with an infinitive in the sense of "it is possible" cf. LSJ, s.v. παρέχω A.III.2; Kühner–Gerth 1.34, and I.10–11 above. Lana (1951), 319 construed πᾶσιν ἀνθρώποις in II.19–20 with σκοπεῖν παρέχει: "A tutti gli uomini e dato indagare ecc." But the word-order shows that πᾶσιν ἀνθρώποις goes rather with ἀναγκαι[. Both Furley (1981), 89 ("It is possible to see that whatever belongs to the things of nature is both necessary etc.") and Decleva Caizzi and Bastianini (1989), 187 ("È possibile vedere che le cose appartenenti all' ambito della natura sono necessarie ecc.") seem to construe σκοπεῖν here as introducing indirect statement. The verb can introduce a ὅτι-clause, as well as interrogative and other kinds of subordinate clauses (cf. LSJ, s.v.). But the type of indirect-statement construction presupposed in these commentators' translations is without parallel.

16–20 τὰ τῶν φύσει . . . ἀνθρώποις: Grenfell and Hunt (1915) proposed (and others have adopted) τὰ τῶν φύσει [ὄντων] ἀναγκαί[ων], which they construed as the direct object of σκοπεῖν. But ὄντων is decidedly otiose (cf. Aeschines, *or.* 1.138: τῶν ἐκ φύσεως ἀναγκαίων). τῶν φύσει alone would produce a very short line; but cf. II.28, 34, III.2. With or without ὄντων, the real difficulty is the very awkward periphrasis τὰ τῶν φύσει ἀναγκαίων, which Saunders (1977–78), 218 alone of all commentators known to me even attempts to translate ("the matters of the things that are by nature given . . ."). The periphrases τὰ τῆς φύσεως and τὰ τῶν νόμων in F44(a)I.22–32 are perhaps comparable. Funghi (1984), 5 proposed τὰ τῶν φύσει [ὄντων], ἀναγκαῖα, which she translated: "It is possible to examine (the rules) which exist by nature: they are necessary for all human beings . . ." But it is hard to separate ἀναγκαῖα τοῖς ἀνθρώποις from σκοπεῖν δὲ παρέχει κτλ. as an independent clause in this way. (And τὰ τῶν φύσει ὄντων are hardly "rules.") Decleva Caizzi and Bastianini (1989), 185 adopted Funghi's text but construed it differently, omitting the comma after ὄντων and understanding ἀναγκαῖα as a predicate adjective, seemingly in an indirect-statement construction after σκοπεῖν. This, however, seems impossible (cf. above).

20–24 None of the restorations that have been suggested inspires conviction. Bignone (1938), 65 proposed to reconstruct the passage on the basis of Theophrastus, fr. 531 (2.350–53), which according to Bignone and Mewaldt (1926), 181–82 reproduces the thought of Antiphon. This fragment is preserved in Porphyry, *De abstinentia* 3.25.1–3 and seems to derive either from Περὶ εὐσεβείας or from Περὶ ζῴων φρονήσεως καὶ ἤθους (cf. Pötscher [1964], 95–99). In the fragment, Theophrastus explains that all human beings are related and akin to one another (οἰκείους τε καὶ συγγενεῖς), either because they have common ancestors or because they share the same food (τροφῆς), customs (ἠθῶν), and race (ταὐτοῦ γένους). In the same way, human beings are akin (συγγενεῖς) to all other animals as well, since all share the same physical principles such as skin, flesh, and bodily fluids, and (more important) all have souls that are naturally alike. For all have similar desires and angry impulses (ταῖς ἐπιθυμίαις καὶ ταῖς ὀργαῖς), reasoning (λογισμοῖς) and perceptions (αἰσθήσεσιν), and share a kinship of emotions (τῶν παθῶν οἰκειότης; translation after Fortenbaugh et al. [1992]). There is some similarity here with the argument from common emotions and perceptual functions in II.33–III.8 below. On the other hand, Theophrastus' point about the kinship of men with animals is foreign to Antiphon's argument. For this and other reasons, it seems best to reserve judgment on the relationship between F44(b) and this fragment of Theophrastus (on which cf. further Schütrumpf [1972], 23). In any case, the resemblances do not suffice to support Bignone's reconstruction of II.20–24.

24–27 These lines amount to a restatement in negative form of what was said in positive terms in II.10–15: no human being is naturally differentiated as a Greek or foreigner.

24 τοις: the papyrus offers what appears to be a mark of punctuation after τοις, a low dot unique in *P.Oxy.* 1364 + 3647 (cf. Grenfell and Hunt [1915], 92). Diels (1916), 936 rejected this punctuation, comparing what he thought was the equally mistaken punctuation in F44(a)VI.29 (but that is probably just an accidental ink-trace; cf. Decleva Caizzi and Bastianini [1989], 200). He has been followed by Diels and Kranz in *FVS*, Untersteiner (1962), and Decleva Caizzi and Bastianini (1989). Funghi (1984), 2, however, punctuated with a comma after τοις. Retention of a full stop or colon after τοις would produce asyndeton in the following clause (the δέ originally written in II.26, but subsequently expunged, would give an impossible word-order and is certainly wrong). But the asyndeton could be defended as explanatory (cf. Kühner–Gerth 2.342–43). Funghi's punctuation avoids the asyndeton, but requires that the preceding words be taken as a subordinate clause.

24–27 βάρβαρος . . . Ἕλλην: Diels (1917), 97–98; Schmidt (1924), 13; Kranz (*FVS* 2.353); Lana (1951), 319; Barnes (1982), 511, and others construe βάρβαρος and Ἕλλην in apposition to the subject οὐδείς. But considerations of sense as well as of word-order suggest that these words form the predicate (after ἀφώρισται). Cf. Aristotle, *Historia animalium* 504b13–14 (τῶν δ' ἐνύδρων ζῴων τὸ τῶν ἰχθύων γένος ἓν ἀπὸ τῶν ἄλλων ἀφώρισται, πολλὰς περιέχον ἰδέας). So Grenfell and Hunt (1915), 103; Untersteiner (1962), 95; Guthrie (1971a), 153; Funghi (1984), 5; Decleva Caizzi and Bastianini (1989), 187, and others. Lana (1951), 319 n. 2 proposed to read ⟨ὑφ'⟩ ἡμῶν, which he translated: "noi non poniamo differenza fra alcun barbaro e Greco." This is unnecessary, and the agent with the perfect passive ἀφώρισται would more naturally be expressed with the dative.

II.27–III.12 In structure as well as in function, this long sentence closely resembles F44(a)II.30–III.18 (cf. Luginbill [1997], 184 n. 74). In the latter passage, Antiphon illustrates his contention that most of what is just according to νόμος is inimical to nature by a long enumeration (in short, parallel clauses) of the restrictions imposed upon individuals, anatomized into their component bodily organs and functions – eyes, ears, tongue, hands, feet, and mind. Here, the claim that no one is marked out by nature as a Greek or foreigner is substantiated through an enumeration (in short, parallel clauses) of the functions and activities in respect of which all people are similar – breathing, laughing, crying, hearing, seeing, working, and walking. Funghi (1984), 1 inferred from these obvious similarities that the two passages originally stood in close proximity; but the inference hardly follows (cf. introductory note on F44). For the notion that what is natural is the same for all cf. Xenophon, *Cyropaedia* 8.7.13: πιστοὺς δὲ μὴ νόμιζε φύσει φύεσθαι ἀνθρώπους· πᾶσι γὰρ ἂν οἱ αὐτοὶ πιστοὶ φαίνοιντο, ὥσπερ καὶ τἆλλα τὰ πεφυκότα πᾶσι τὰ αὐτὰ φαίνεται.

27–33 ἀναπνέομέν τε γὰρ ... ῥῖνας: for γάρ introducing an instance which exemplifies a proposition cf. Denniston (1954), 66–67; F44(a)II.32 with commentary. Translations such as "breathe the air" (Grenfell and Hunt [1915], 103; Funghi [1984], 5) are inexact, for the prepositional phrase εἰς τὸν ἀέρα shows that ἀναπνέομεν here means "exhale." (This rules out Schöne's proposal [ἐκπνέομε]ν in II.33–34.) ἀναπνέω normally means "inhale" (cf. LSJ, s.v. II; Empedocles, *FVS* 31 B 100; Plato, *Phaedo* 112B; Aristotle, *Historia animalium* 487a29, *De respiratione* 472b19) or generally "breathe," "respire" (cf. Aristotle, *Historia animalium* 589b7, *De respiratione* 471a19, *De anima* 421a6; Theophrastus, *De sensibus* 44, Diels [1879], 511). In poetry, however, the verb is sometimes used with a cognate accusative in the sense "breathe out." Cf. LSJ, s.v. III; Pindar, *Olymp.* 8.36 (λάβρον ἀμπνεῦσαι καπνόν), fr. 70b.15–16 (ὁ παγκρατὴς κεραυνὸς ἀμπνέων πῦρ); Pherecrates, fr. 138.1 (ἀναπνέων δ' ὑάκινθον); Apollonius of Rhodes, *Argonautica* 3.231 (πυρὸς δεινὸν σέλας ἀμπνείεσκον). Cf. also ἀναπνοή, "exhalation." From κατὰ τὸ στόμα κτλ. it appears that Antiphon did not share the transpiration-theory espoused by Empedocles (cf. *FVS* 31 B 100); Plato (cf. *Timaeus* 77E–79E, esp. 79D–E: δυοῖν δὲ τοῖν διεξόδοιν οὔσαιν, τῆς μὲν κατὰ τὸ σῶμα ἔξω, τῆς δὲ αὖ κατὰ τὸ στόμα καὶ τὰς ῥῖνας); Philistion (cf. Anonymus Londinensis, 20.45–47: οὐ γὰρ μόνον κατὰ τὸ στόμα καὶ τοὺς μυκτῆρας ἡ ἀναπνοὴ γίνεται, ἀλλ' καὶ καθ' ὅλον τὸ σῶμα), and others. These lines reminded Kassel (1958), 65 of the (later) *topos* of the "common air" breathed by all (cf. Menander *apud* [Plut.], *Consolatio ad Apollonium* 103C; [Aristotle], *De audibilibus* 800a16; Marcus Antoninus, 9.8.1, etc.). Decleva Caizzi and Bastianini (1989), 191 noted that the Hippocratic *De aëre aquis et locis* attributes differences among peoples to differences in the air they breathe.

33–III.3 καὶ γελῶμεν ... λυπούμενοι: the new papyrus confirms (after a fashion) the old conjecture of Bignone (1938), 65 and Theander (1920), 7, who speculated that after the physical characteristics mentioned in II.27–33, Antiphon proceeded to discuss psychic qualities or mental faculties. (On the possible connection between this passage and the fragment of Theophrastus preserved in Porphyry, *De abstinentia* 3.25

cf. commentary on II.20–24.) In II.33–III.1, Funghi (1984), 5 suggested καὶ γελῶμεν χαίροντες τῷ νῷ ἤ, which Decleva Caizzi and Bastianini (1989) adopted. But ἤ is odd, the defense of it offered by Decleva Caizzi and Bastianini (1989), 191 notwithstanding. Furthermore, τῷ νῷ (to which Decleva Caizzi and Bastianini [1989], 187 give an improbable locative sense, "nell' animo") would be out of position in comparison with the instrumental datives τῇ ἀκοῇ, τῇ αὐγῇ, ταῖς χερσίν, and τοῖς ποσίν in the succeeding clauses which parallel this one. Luppe's proposal καὶ γελῶμεν χαίροντες καί is far superior and is certainly to be preferred (cf. Luppe [1986], 121). For the natural character of laughter and weeping Decleva Caizzi and Bastianini (1989), 191 compared [Hippocrates], *De morbo sacro* 14, where γέλωτες and κλαυθμοί are said to arise from the brain. [Alexander], *Problemata* 1.31 and Gregory of Nyssa, *De hominis opificio* 12 (44.160 Migne) offer a physiological explanation of laughter and weeping in terms of pores. Whether this passage reflects the importance Antiphon attached to pleasure and pain (as Decleva Caizzi and Bastianini suggested) is uncertain.

III

3–6 καὶ τῇ ἀκοῇ . . . εἰσδεχόμεθα: cf. Aristotle, *Topics* 105b8–9 (ἀκούομέν τε γὰρ εἰσδεχόμενοί τι, οὐκ ἐκπέμποντες); Xenophon, *Memorabilia* 1.4.6 (τὸ δὲ τὴν ἀκοὴν δέχεσθαι μὲν πάσας φωνάς, ἐμπίμπλασθαι δὲ μήποτε); Plutarch, *De genio Socratis* 588E (πληγῇ γὰρ ἡ φωνὴ προσέοικε τῆς ψυχῆς δι' ὤτων βίᾳ τὸν λόγον εἰσδεχομένης). For ἀκοή in the sense of "organ of hearing" cf. Aristotle, *De anima* 419b8, 420a4, 425a5 with Ross (1961), 249; Theophrastus, *De sensibus* 9 (Diels [1879], 501) = Empedocles, *FVS* 31 A 86; LSJ, s.v. II.3. It is impossible to tell, from the little that is said here, what theory of hearing (if any) Antiphon espoused.

6–8 καὶ τῇ αὐγῇ . . . ὁρῶμεν: the ancient theory of sight by means of visual rays seems to be presupposed here. The theory is attributed to Archytas (cf. Apuleius, *Apologia* 15 = *FVS* 47 A 25; Cherniss [1935], 317 n. 106), and was adopted in modified form by Plato (cf. *Timaeus* 45B–46A, 67C–68D with Cornford [1937], 152–53, 276–78; *Theaetetus* 156 with Cornford [1935], 48–50). Plato employs the concept and terminology of the visual ray casually and without much explanation; apparently he felt able to take his audience's familiarity with them for granted. So there seems to be no insuperable difficulty in crediting Antiphon with the theory, which was widely accepted both in antiquity and in the middle ages, by philosophers and scientists as well as in popular belief. Cf. Dihle (1983). (Aristotle's attempt to ascribe the theory to Empedocles, however, must be rejected; cf. Bignone [1916], 249 n. 2 and Cherniss [1935], 317 n. 106.) It is tempting at first glance to refer αὐγῇ to the visual ray itself (cf. Plato, *Timaeus* 46C) and ὄψεως to the eye or vision. Funghi (1984), 5 in fact suggested that Pollux, 2.57 = F7 (Ἀντιφῶν δὲ ... εἶπε καὶ τῇ ὄψει οἷον τοῖς ὀφθαλμοῖς) refers to this very passage. But ὄψις here is in the genitive case, not the dative which Pollux quotes (cf. commentary on F7). Furthermore, if ὄψεως designated the eye or sight, then μετά would have to be given an unusual (though not quite unparalleled) instrumental sense (cf. LSJ, s.v. A.III). The instrumental datives τῇ ἀκοῇ, ταῖς χερσίν, and τοῖς ποσίν in the parallel clauses suggest that it is αὐγῇ (rather than ὄψεως) which refers to the bodily organ or function. For these reasons, it is preferable to understand αὐγῇ as "eye." Cf. LSJ, s.v. 5, who refer to the Homeric *Hymn to Mercury* 361, Euripides, *Andromache* 1180, *Rhesus* 737 (all of which have the plural αὐγαί), as well as to Plato, *Republic* 540A (τὴν τῆς ψυχῆς αὐγήν). Cf. further αὐγάζω, "see"; Latin *lumina* = "eyes"; Dihle (1983), 88. ὄψεως then (as often) will designate the visual ray. Cf. Plato, *Theaetetus* 156E, *Timaeus* 45C (τὸ τῆς ὄψεως ῥεῦμα), 46B, 67C; Aristotle, *De anima* 435a6, *Meteorology* 343a13, 370a19, 373b7; Theophrastus, *De sensibus* 5 (Diels [1879], 500); Aëtius, III.2.1 (Diels [1879], 366), III.5.5 (Diels [1879], 372); LSJ, s.v. IIC; Martin (1841), 2.157; Beare (1906), 25 n. 3, 66 n. 1, 84 n. 1, 91. And μετά will have its ordinary sense of "by aid of" (cf. LSJ, s.v. A.II), designating the visual ray as the conjunct means or instrument of vision.

8–10 καὶ ταῖς χερσὶν ἐργαζόμεθα: for ἐργάζομαι in reference to manual labor cf. LSJ, s.v. For the phrase ἐργάζομαι χερσίν cf. Dio of Prusa, *or.* 3.106; Libanius, *or.* 11.267; 1 *Epistula ad Corinthios* 4.12.

10–12 καὶ τοῖς ποσὶν βαδίζομεν: Funghi's supplement βαδίζομεν produces a longer than average line, but seems to be supported by the final ink-trace in III.11 as well as by the acute accent which survives above the lacuna. For walking as a natural activity cf. Xenophon, *Cyropaedia* 2.3.10: οὐ γὰρ μόνον φύσει ἦν, ὥσπερ τὸ βαδίζειν καὶ τρέχειν, ἀλλὰ καὶ ἡδὺ πρὸς τῷ πεφυκέναι τοῦτο (*sc.* playing with sabres) ἐδόκει μοι εἶναι.

IV

1–9 The first three lines of this column are all but lost. In IV.4–6, Funghi (1984), 3 suggested κατὰ τὸ ἀρέ[σκον συν]εχώρησ[αν] ἕκαστοι, which is adopted by Decleva Caizzi and Bastianini (1989). The phrase κατὰ τὸ ἀρέσκον is attested elsewhere only in late authors. (Cf. Origen, *Contra Celsum* 1.13, 2.9; Iamblichus, *In Nicomachi Arithmeticam* 10; Simplicius, *In Aristotelis De caelo* 392.22, etc.) Presumably it would mean "in accordance with what pleases them" or "in accordance with their views." As parallels, Decleva Caizzi and Bastianini (1989), 192 referred to participial expressions such as τὸ θυμούμενον τῆς γνώμης and τὸ λειπόμενον τοῦ βίου (Antiphon of Rhamnus, *or.* 2.γ.3; 3.β.10); but these are different. συνεχώρησαν (if correctly restored) might mean "agree" or "concede" and refer to the process by which various different human communities (ἕκαστοι) established their own peculiar νόμοι through voluntary agreement. So Funghi (1984), 4–5; Decleva Caizzi (1986b), 296; Decleva Caizzi and Bastianini (1989), 192. Cf. F44(a)I.28–31 (καὶ τὰ μὲν τῶν νόμων ὁμολογηθέντα οὐ φύντα); Plato, *Laws* 889E (ὅπῃ ἕκαστοι ἑαυτοῖσι συνωμολόγησαν νομοθετούμενοι), *Laws* 681C (καὶ μὴν τούς γε αὑτῶν νόμους ἀρέσκειν ἑκάστοις ἀναγκαῖόν που, τοὺς δὲ τῶν ἄλλων ὑστέρους); Porphyry, *De abstinentia* 1.8 (οὐδὲν γὰρ ἐξ ἀρχῆς βιαίως κατέστη νόμιμον οὔτε μετὰ γραφῆς οὔτε ἄνευ γραφῆς τῶν διαμενόντων νῦν καὶ διαδίδοσθαι πεφυκότων, ἀλλὰ συγχωρησάντων αὐτῷ [καὶ] τῶν χρησομένων). This interpretation may receive some support from the very fragmentary passage IV.8–9, where Decleva Caizzi and Bastianini (1989), 186 proposed to restore καὶ τοὺς νόμους ἔθεντο. But the suprascript word there can equally well be read as τοῖς (cf. Funghi [1984], 5). εχωρη[is certainly suggestive; but the fragmentary state of the text leaves it doubtful whether there is any more justification for speaking of a social contract doctrine here than in F44(a)I.28–II.1 (cf. commentary ad loc.).

F44(c)

F44(c) offers a closely-reasoned argument in support of the contention that conventional (νομίζεται: I.5) notions of just conduct are inconsistent, even contradictory. Cf. Crönert (1922), 424; Regenbogen (1940a), 100–1; Nestle (1942), 379; Furley (1981), 87–88; Barnes (1982), 515; Dillon (1984), 131–32, and below. More specifically, Antiphon tries to demonstrate that bearing true witness, judging, and arbitrating – activities conventionally regarded as both just and useful (cf. I.3–9) – are in fact neither, since they are incompatible with a conventional formula of just conduct which forbids wrongdoing as well as the suffering of wrong (cf. I.10–15 and II.17–25, with commentary). (Aly [1929], 137–40 contended that Antiphon was concerned with the unwritten law commanding truthfulness and with the problem of justifiable deceit; but this mistakes the target of his argument.) The case of bearing witness or testifying occupies the largest part of the extant discussion (I.3–II.25). Bearing true witness, it is argued, not only harms and so wrongs the man testified against (I.23–35), it also exposes the witness to reciprocal harm in the form of hatred and reprisal at the hands of the man testified against (I.35–II.12). These consequences are manifestly inconsistent with the aforesaid formula of just conduct, which forbids wrongdoing and the suffering of wrong. It follows that either the activity of bearing witness or the formula of just conduct or both must be wrong and unjust (II.17–25). The same conclusion is then declared to hold for the activities of judging and arbitrating, which produce winners and losers in judicial processes and thereby cause harm and injustice to the losers (II.25–36). Besides demonstrating that the specific activities of testifying, judging, and arbitrating are wrong or unjust, the argument shows more generally that conventional ideas about justice are inconsistent or even contradictory, inasmuch as they affirm contradictory claims about what is right and just.

A very different interpretation of the import of Antiphon's argument has received widespread support among commentators who contend that the formula of just conduct in I.12–15 and II.19–25 represents Antiphon's own ideal of justice. So Luria (1924a), 382, (1927a); Pfister (1925), 203–4; Altheim (1926), 267; Mewaldt (1926), 179; La Face (1969), 44–50; Momigliano (1969), 141–42; Havelock (1957), 260–64; Guthrie (1971a), 110 n. 2, 112. Some of these interpreters take the further step of identifying the formula with "natural justice" (τὸ φύσει δίκαιον), an identification for which there is absolutely no evidence. (The name and notion of nature, φύσις, is notably absent from the fragment.) I.12–15 and II.19–25 enunciate a thoroughly conventional conception of justice (cf. commentary on II.19–21), but one which there is no reason whatsoever to ascribe to Antiphon. As Kerferd (1956–57), 31 pointed out, the text offers no indication that the conception of justice embodied in the formula is somehow to be preferred to the activities (testifying, judging, and arbitrating) with which it is shown to be inconsistent. On the contrary, in II.24–25 it is suggested that *both* are unjust – a possibility Antiphon would hardly have raised had he accepted the formula as his own ideal of justice (cf. Furley [1981], 87–88). Luria (1927a), 81–83 tried to get round this difficulty by speculating that in a continuation of the argument no longer extant, Antiphon proceeded to demonstrate the opposite conclusion, that both could not be *unjust*. But to all appearances, the argument on testifying comes to an end when the discussion turns in II.25ff. to judging and arbitrating, with no room left for other conclusions than those already articulated in II.22–25. (Against Luria cf. also La Face [1969], 38–39.) A variation on the interpretation mentioned previously was defended by Bignone (1938), 104–9, 112–19, Untersteiner (1962), 97–100, (1954), 250–51 = (1967), 2.74–75, and Moulton

(1972), 347–49, all of whom contended that I.12–15 and II.19–21 formulate two *different* conceptions of justice, only the latter of which represents Antiphon's own ideal. (Nill [1985], 67–73 agreed that there are two conceptions of justice in the fragment, but ascribed neither to Antiphon.) In the view of these commentators, the formula in II.19–21 involves an unconditional ban on harming others, whereas that in I.12–15 forbids aggression (τὸ μὴ ἀδικεῖν μηδένα) but permits retaliation for a wrong suffered (μὴ ἀδικούμενον αὐτόν). Indeed, Bignone (1938), 106–7, 112–18 and others regard the latter formula as simply a polemical rewording (with ἀδικεῖν substituted for βλάπτειν) of the conventional principle that it is right to help friends and harm enemies. Cf. Paoli (1933), 198; Aly (1929), 139; Isnardi Parente (1975), 13. (On this principle of popular Greek ethics cf. Plato, *Republic* 332D with Tarán [1985], 104 n. 87; Dover [1974], 180–84; Slings [1999], 193 with n. 348.) The formula in I.12–15, however, can be understood without any reference to the issue of retaliation (cf. commentary ad loc.). Moreover, to interpret it as justifying retaliation (even implicitly) is to undermine Antiphon's argument, which repeatedly insists that the witness who wrongs the man testified against (ὁ καταμαρτυρούμενος) is himself *wronged* in turn (cf. I.20–21 αὐτὸν ἀδικεῖσθαι; I.35–36 αὐτὸς δ' ἀδικεῖται; II.14–16 τἀδικήματα ... ἃ αὐτὸς ἀδικεῖται). But the retaliatory actions of the man testified against would not be wrong or unjust if retaliation were justified (except in so far as "harming," βλάπτειν, and "wronging," ἀδικεῖν, are simply equated). The really decisive objection to the notion that I.12–15 and II.19–21 articulate different conceptions of justice, however, is Regenbogen's cogent demonstration that the entire argument of the fragment collapses unless the two passages refer to one and the same principle of just conduct, which is shown to be incompatible with testifying. Cf. Regenbogen (1940a), 101. This consideration definitively rules out all attempts (including that of Kerferd [1956–57], 31) to distinguish the formula in II.19–21 from that in I.12–15.

Like F44(a), this fragment is concerned with the relationship between law and conventional notions of justice on the one hand, and the advantage and disadvantage of the individual on the other. But the attack on conventional justice is even sharper and more pointed here than in F44(a). In the latter fragment, Antiphon tries to show that an individual's best interests are served by ignoring conventional justice (defined as obedience to the laws) when unobserved by witnesses. But the argument does not directly attack the notion of justice itself, as Antiphon does here by attempting to demonstrate that conventional ideas about just conduct are inconsistent, even contradictory. Another obvious difference lies in the (striking) absence from this fragment of the antithesis of law and nature, which is fundamental to the arguments of F44(a) as well as F44(b). What significance these differences have for the nature and purpose of Antiphon's discussion of justice, law, and nature as a whole is impossible to determine without more evidence.

I

1–3 τοῦ δικαίου . . . δοκουν-: Grenfell's and Hunt's proposal τοῦ δικαίου σπουδαίου δοκοῦντος gains support from Plato, *Republic* 333E (οὐκ ἂν οὖν, ὦ φίλε, πάνυ γέ τι σπουδαῖον εἴη ἡ δικαιοσύνη), *Laws* 889D; Xenophon, *Memorabilia* 4.4.14; Aristotle, *Nicomachean Ethics* 1137b4 (ἣ γὰρ τὸ δίκαιον οὐ σπουδαῖον). Cf. Aly (1929), 137–38. The objections to it raised by Luria (1924a), 382 depend on misinterpretation of the Greek and may be dismissed. As Aly pointed out, however, τοῦ δικαίου σπουδαίου δοκοῦντος can neither begin nor end a sentence (at the very least, a connecting particle or conjunction is wanted). The text remains uncertain (cf. Decleva Caizzi and Bastianini [1989], 218).

3–9 Antiphon seems here to envisage the common Athenian practice of supporting the litigation of one's friends and allies with testimony. Cf. Demosthenes, *or.* 54.35 (καὶ ταῦτα τὰ λαμπρὰ καὶ νεανικά ἐστιν αὐτῶν, Οὐ γὰρ ἡμεῖς μαρτυρήσομεν ἀλλήλοις; οὐ γὰρ ταῦθ' ἑταίρων ἐστὶ καὶ φίλων;), 21.112, 139; Lycurgus, fr. 93 (δεῖ ⟨τοῖς Sauppe⟩ φίλοις καὶ τοῖς οἰκείοις βοηθεῖν ἄχρι τοῦ μὴ ἐπιορκεῖν); Dover (1974), 304. Athenian law also compelled testimony under pain of fine or prosecution (cf. Lipsius, Meier and Schömann [1905–15], 784–85, 876–79; Bonner and Smith [1930–38], 2.138–43; MacDowell [1978], 243–44); but this does not seem to be at issue here. Such testimony is conventionally regarded as both just and useful. (The coupling of justice with advantage is traditional: cf. Plato, *Republic* 332Eff.; Tarán [1985], 104 with n. 88; Decleva Caizzi and Bastianini [1989], 219; Heinimann [1945], 116, 149; Dover [1974], 309–10.) But Antiphon's argument will try to show that it is in fact neither. Cf. Moulton (1972), 347; Saunders (1977–78), 224–25; Nill (1985), 67.

4 ἀλλήλοις: Grenfell and Hunt (1922) and subsequent editors print ἐν ἀλλήλοις; H. Fränkel suggested ἐπ' ἀλλήλοις. The former, though variously translated, could only mean "among" or "in the presence of" or "in respect to" one another (cf. LSJ, s.v. ἐν I.5, 7). But none of these senses is really appropriate here. Fränkel's ἐπ' ἀλλήλοις could perhaps mean "for one another" (as Kranz, *FVS* 2.353 seems to take it). But ἐπί with the dative denoting a person is relatively uncommon (cf. MacDowell [1990], 262, but also LSJ, s.v. B.IC). The same sense (which suits the context very well) is better obtained with the bare dative ἀλλήλοις. Cf. LSJ, s.v. μαρτυρέω 2; Mewaldt (1926), 179 ("Wenn man also ... *für jemand* eintritt, zum Beispiel mit einer Zeugenaussage").

τἀληθῆ: τἀληθῆ is an internal accusative ("bear true witness"), rather than a direct object as Grenfell and Hunt (1922), 121 translate ("testify to the truth"). Cf. LSJ, s.v. μαρτυρέω I.3, and below.

5 νομίζεται: the antithesis of law and nature is absent from this fragment (cf. introductory note above). But the subject of νόμος in the sense of conventional attitudes and norms of conduct is central to the discussion.

7 οὐδὲν ἧττον: Aly (1929), 138 (whom Untersteiner [1962], 96 seems to follow) suggested that οὐδὲν ἧττον compares testifying with some other, now lost example of just and useful conduct. More likely it compares the predicates δίκαιον and χρήσιμον: "no less useful than just." Cf. Moulton (1972), 347.

8 τῶν ἀνθρώπων: cf. F44(a)I.13 (ἄνθρωπος), III.23 (τοὺς ἀνθρώπους); F44(b)I.5 (ἀνθρώποις), II.19–20 (πᾶσιν ἀνθρώποις).

10–15 The conventional notion (νομίζεται) that testifying is just and useful is contradicted by the (equally conventional) notion that it is just to do no wrong and not be wronged onself.

10 τοίνυν: the adversative sense ("however," "yet," "und doch," "tuttavia") given to this particle by Grenfell and Hunt (1922), Kranz in *FVS*, Decleva Caizzi and Bastianini (1989), and many other translators and commentators is impossible. τοίνυν instead is transitional: "well," "now." Cf. F44(a)IV.22; Denniston (1954), 574. As Denniston (1954), 568–69 noted, τοίνυν is essentially an Attic and colloquial particle, rare in Antiphon of Rhamnus and rarer still in sophistic declamation.

11 ἔσται: this is best understood as an example of the so-called modal usage, in which the time of thinking about an action is transferred to the action itself: "will be found to be." Cf. F44(a)VI.15 with commentary; Plato, *Meno* 78E (οὐκ ἔσται ἀρετή), 98C (ὠφελίμη ἔσται), *Gorgias* 475B (ἤτοι λύπῃ ἢ κακῷ ὑπερβάλλον αἴσχιον ἔσται); Thompson (1901), 135, 143; Bluck (1961), 315; Goodwin (1890), 19. *Pace* Bignone (1938), 101 n. 3 and Regenbogen (1940a), 101, the future tense does not by itself prove that Antiphon rejects the premiss (I.12–15) from which this clause follows as the conclusion.

12 εἴπερ: since the formula of just conduct in I.12–15 does not represent Antiphon's own ideal of justice (cf. introductory note above), καὶ γάρ (Grenfell and Hunt), ἐπείπερ (Wilamowitz), and ὥσπερ (Diels) are all ruled out on grounds of sense. (ἐπείπερ also seems too long for the space; cf. Decleva Caizzi and Bastianini [1989], 220.) Even though he rejected the interpretation identifying the formula as Antiphon's own ideal of justice, Furley (1981), 107 inexplicably contended that it makes no difference what conjunction is read. In this, he claimed to agree with Guthrie (1971a), 110 n. 2; but the latter accepted the formula as Antiphon's own ideal. εἴπερ is almost certainly right. It was suggested first by Diels (1922), vol. 2 "Nachträge," XXXVII n., and later (apparently independently) by Bignone (1938), 101 n. 3. Its tone here (as often) is sceptical (= *si modo*; cf. Thompson [1901], 258–64; Denniston [1954], 488 n. 1).

12–14 τὸ μὴ ἀδικεῖν . . . αὐτόν: for arguments in support of the identification of this formula of just conduct (rather than "definition of justice," as it is often called) with that in II.19–21 cf. introductory note above. If the two are identified, then μὴ ἀδικούμενον αὐτόν should be interpreted as expressing simply an attendant circumstance, rather than a condition or a cause ("while not being wronged oneself"). Cf. Moulton (1972), 349 n. 44, who suggested this interpretation without adopting it. The negative μή does not indicate that the participle is conditional, but is used because of the articular infinitive. Cf. Plato, *Apology* 29A (τὸ γάρ τοι θάνατον δεδιέναι, ὦ ἄνδρες, οὐδὲν ἄλλο ἐστὶν ἢ δοκεῖν σοφὸν εἶναι μὴ ὄντα), *Republic* 361A (ἐσχάτη γὰρ ἀδικία δοκεῖν δίκαιον εἶναι μὴ ὄντα); Aristophanes, *Wealth* 552 (πτωχοῦ μὲν γὰρ βίος, ὃν σὺ λέγεις, ζῆν ἐστιν μηδὲν ἔχοντα).

15–21 A man who bears even true witness against another necessarily (ἀνάγκη) wrongs him, and is himself wronged in turn. The whole argument (as has often been noted) depends on an apparently equivocal use of ἀδικεῖν in the double sense of "treat unjustly" and "harm." Cf. II.35–36 (οἱ δὲ βλαπτόμενοι ἀδικοῦνται); Bignone (1938), 116–17; Saunders (1977–78), 224 n. 28; Nill (1985), 67–68 with n. 52. (Barnes [1982], 515 denied that there is any equivocation, but offered no justification for his view.) As Furley (1981), 86 pointed out, however, the adverbial qualifier πως (I.19) seems to indicate that Antiphon was not unaware of the paradoxical nature of his claim that a truthful witness "wrongs" the man whom he testifies against. Furthermore, the equivocation is sanctioned by Greek usage, since ἀδικεῖν is often employed as a near-synonym of βλάπτειν or κακῶς ποιεῖν. (Cf. Dover [1974], 181–82, with references.) Havelock (1957), 260–61, 265–67 regarded the equivocation as a natural consequence of what he (misleadingly) called Antiphon's "utilitarianism." But equating the good with what is beneficial or advantageous for individuals need not entail identifying "harm" with "treat unjustly." Bignone (1938), 116 with n. 2 and others refer in this context to the apparent equation of "harm" and "wrong" in Plato, *Crito* 49C (τὸ γάρ που κακῶς ποιεῖν ἀνθρώπους τοῦ ἀδικεῖν οὐδὲν διαφέρει). But Plato certainly would not have agreed with Antiphon that bearing true witness against another constitutes κακῶς ποιεῖν – as the legislation concerning testimony in *Laws* 936E–937A clearly demonstrates (cf. *Gorgias* 480A–481B).

17–18 κἂν ἀληθῆ μαρτυρῇ: Blass (1889b), 20–22 argued for a distinction between the expressions μαρτυρεῖν τἀληθῆ and μαρτυρεῖν ἀληθῆ. In the latter, he contended, ἀληθῆ has predicative force and emphasizes the truth of the testimony, so that μαρτυρεῖν ἀληθῆ is equivalent in sense to μαρτυρεῖν μαρτυρίαν ἣ ἀληθής ἐστιν. Blass' distinction seems to be borne out here, where the truth of the witness's testimony is emphasized in the concession. Cf. commentary on I.38–II.2 τἀληθῆ μαρτυρήσας.

19 ἄλλον πως: ἄλλον (Grenfell and Hunt) balances αὐτόν in I.20.

20–21 αὐτὸν ἀδικεῖσθαι: in the lacuna preceding these words, Grenfell and Hunt's εἰκὸς δέ is ruled out on grounds of sense, since the vengeance inflicted upon the witness by the man testified against is viewed as inevitable, not merely likely. Cf. I.15–16 ἀνάγκη; I.35–II.12; and for the inevitability of retribution for wrong done, F58 with commentary. Either καὶ ἅμα (Diels), or ἅμα δὲ καί (Wilamowitz), or εἶτα δέ (Decleva Caizzi and Bastianini) would give an acceptable sense.

21–22 No satisfactory restoration of these lines has yet been proposed. In I.21–22, Grenfell and Hunt (1922) proposed εἰς ὕστερον, Diels ὕστερον. But in I.35ff., Antiphon employs the *present* tense in describing the wrongs suffered by the witness at the hands of the man testified against. The same consideration argues against Diels' proposal ὧ]ν ἕνε[κα εἶπεν in I.22, while Grenfell and Hunt's ἕνε[στι γε can be ruled out for the same reason as their similar proposal εἰκὸς δέ in I.20 (cf. commentary on I.20–21). Decleva Caizzi and Bastianini (1989) print Funghi's proposal μίσει οὖν ἐνεχόμενος. (This is perhaps a misprint for ἐνεχόμενον: an accusative is surely needed here in the indirect statement construction after ἀνάγκη; cf. I.20 αὐτόν.) But this involves a seemingly impossible postponement of οὖν (cf. Denniston [1954], 427; Decleva Caizzi's reference to Aristophanes, *Birds* 1405 is irrelevant). In I.22, the mark after the first ν is probably an accidental ink-trace rather than a mark of punctuation (as Grenfell and Hunt suggested). Cf. Decleva Caizzi and Bastianini (1989), 217.

23–30 Because of the witness's testimony, the man testified against is convicted (ἁλίσκεται) and either fined or executed (ἀπόλλυσιν ἢ χρήματα ἢ αὐτόν).

23 ἐν ᾧ: Grenfell and Hunt's ἐν ᾧ is very plausible, but its sense is uncertain. Translations such as "insofar as" (Grenfell and Hunt, and many others), "insofern" (Schmidt [1924], 15), and "dadurch nämlich, dass" (Kranz, *FVS* 2.354) give this prepositional phrase a causal sense which is attested in the New Testament, but rare or non-existent in classical Greek. Perhaps the closest parallel is Plato, *Republic* 455B: ἆρα οὕτως ἔλεγες τὸν μὲν εὐφυῆ πρός τι εἶναι, τὸν δὲ ἀφυῆ, ἐν ᾧ ὁ μὲν ῥαδίως τι μανθάνοι, ὁ δὲ χαλεπῶς κτλ., which Shorey (1930–35), 1.445 renders: "Was this the basis of your distinction between the man naturally gifted for anything and the one not so gifted – that the one learned easily etc." ἐν ᾧ in this passage seems to bear a sense very like that required here. Moreover, it seems correlated with the preceding οὕτως, just as ἐν ᾧ here seems correlated with πως in I.19, the clause as a whole explaining precisely how the witness "wrongs" the man testified against. Decleva and Bastianini (1989), 220 proposed to take ἐν ᾧ proleptically with ἐν μὲν οὖν τούτῳ in I.31–32, translating "in quanto . . . in questo." This would make one period of I.23–35 (ἀδικεῖ), with αὐτὸς δ' ἀδικεῖται in I.35–36 introducing a new stage of the argument. But Antiphon of Rhamnus, *or.* 5.83, which they cite as a parallel, hardly supports such a construction (Thalheim, Gernet, and others mark a lacuna between κατηγοροῦσι and τούτων μάρτυρες). And μὲν οὖν, which is surely transitional rather than retrospective (as they suggest), is decisive evidence against it. (On transitional μὲν οὖν cf. Denniston [1954], 470–73.)

23–24 τὰ ὑπ' ἐκείνου: ἐκείνου (proposed by Grenfell and Hunt [1922] and adopted by Decleva Caizzi and Bastianini [1989]) seems slightly awkward in view of τοῦτον in I.29 below. But αὐτοῦ (Diels and Kranz in *FVS*; Untersteiner [1962]) appears too short for the space (but cf. perhaps I.9, 13, 14, 17; II.1).

28 ἢ αὐτόν: Grenfell and Hunt proposed αὐτὸν ⟨τὸν βίον⟩. But as Crönert (1922), 424 pointed out, Xenophon, *Memorabilia* 2.6.38 (ἔχεις τινα ἐλπίδα μὴ ἂν σεαυτόν τε καὶ τῆν ναῦν ἀπολέσαι) lends decisive support to αὑτόν. (αὐτόν in Decleva Caizzi and Bastianini [1989], 216 is presumably a misprint.) The contracted form of the reflexive is attested in F54, l. 13 (αὑτῷ), and should probably be written in F44(a)V.7 (cf. commentary ad loc.). Uncontracted forms in ἑαυτ– appear in I.34 below; F44(a)I.14; F58, ll. 13–14 (*bis*); F59, l. 3. Such variation is unobjectionable.

29–30 διὰ τοῦτον ὃν οὐδὲν ἀδικεῖ: cf. commentary on I.33–35.

I.30–II.12 By causing the fine or execution of the man testified against, the witness wrongs (μέν) him, inasmuch as he harms one who has not wronged him. And he himself in turn (δέ) is wronged by the man testified against, who enters into a life-long relationship of enmity with him.

30–31 ἐν μὲν οὖν τούτῳ: for transitional μὲν οὖν cf. I.23 and F44(a)V.25, both with commentary. For the phrase ἐν τούτῳ cf. II.32–33; F44(b)II.7 with commentary.

33 ὅτι: = "seeing that." Cf. LSJ, s.v. ὅτι B.2.

33–34 οὐκ ἀδικοῦντα ἑαυτόν: at first glance, these words may appear to lend support to the view that the formula of just conduct in I.12–15 permits retaliatory wrongdoing (cf. introductory note above). But the immediately following lines argue otherwise. For if it is just to retaliate for a wrong received, then the claim that the witness is *wronged* by the man testified against falls to the ground (cf. introductory note above). The emphasis here placed on the innocence of the man testified against *vis-à-vis* the witness is probably intended to reinforce the claim that the witness's actions toward him constitute "wrongdoing."

37–38 ὅτι μισεῖται: for the enmity aroused by injustice, Pfister (1925), 202 aptly compared Plato, *Republic* 351D (ἆρα εἰ τοῦτο ἔργον ἀδικίας, μῖσος ἐμποιεῖν ὅπου ἂν ἐνῇ κτλ.). For the readiness with which Athenians entered into relations of enmity, and the frankness with which they acknowledged them, cf. Dover (1974), 181. Havelock (1957), 262 ignored this facet of Athenian life and character when he complained that Antiphon's description of the reactions of the witness and the man testified against "obviously inflates them out of all proportion to the usual facts."

II

I.38–II.2 τἀληθῆ μαρτυρήσας: according to the distinction drawn by Blass (1889b), τἀληθῆ μαρτυρήσας emphasizes the fact of bearing true witness rather than the truth of the testimony given. (Cf. commentary on I.17–18.) In light of this, it is probably mistaken to give concessive force to the participle μαρτυρήσας, as Grenfell and Hunt (1922), Kranz in *FVS*, Untersteiner (1962), and others do. The man testified against hates the witness *because* he testifies, not in spite of the fact that his testimony is true. Cf. the translations of Havelock (1957), 261; Morrison (1972), 221; Saunders (1977–78), 219; Barnes (1982), 512, and Decleva Caizzi and Bastianini (1989), 218.

3 τῷ μίσει: *sc.* ἀδικεῖται. Neuter nouns of the type represented by μῖσος commonly designate a state or condition rather than a force or activity; hence "state of enmity." Cf. Redard (1953), 74–75.

4–5 τὸν αἰῶνα πάντα: for αἰών = "lifetime" cf. Fraenkel (1950), 2.62–63, 278. For the phrase cf. Cratinus, fr. 1.5 (αἰῶνα πάντα); [Hippocrates], *De diaeta in morbis acutis* 3 (ἅπαντα τὸν αἰῶνα), *De fracturis* 11 (τὸν αἰῶνα πάντα). In Demosthenes, *or.* 18.204 and Isocrates, *or.* 4.46, 6.109, the same phrase means "all time" rather than "entire life." Contrast πᾶς ὁ βίος (F51, l. 1), διὰ παντὸς τοῦ βίου (F60, l. 7), both from Περὶ ὁμονοίας.

9–11 τοιοῦτος . . . δρᾶν: for τοιοῦτος . . . οἷος followed by an infinitive cf. LSJ, s.v. οἷος III. For the violent connotations of δρᾶν cf. commentary on F44(a)V.3. καὶ λέγειν καὶ δρᾶν is probably a polar expression, signifying "in every way he can."

12–17 By reiterating the point that testifying results in the witness both inflicting and suffering wrong or injustice, this passage prepares for the conclusion of the argument in II.17–25.

12–13 καίτοι: this is perhaps best explained as an example of the so-called logical use of καίτοι, with an underlying argumentative or combative tone: "but these are *injustices.*" Cf. Denniston (1954), 561, quoting R. W. Chapman's description of Isocrates' apparently very similar use of the particle.

13–15 ταῦτα . . . τἀδικήματα: both the word-order and the litotes add emphasis: "*no small injustices.*"

17–25 The consequences of testifying, and so testifying itself, are irreconcilable with the formula of just conduct. It is logically necessary (ἀνάγκη) that either testifying or the formula or both are unjust rather than just (as originally supposed; cf. I.3–15). Conventional notions of what is right or just (δίκαιον) are thereby shown to be inconsistent, even contradictory.

17–18 οὐ γὰρ οἷόν τε: as γάρ indicates, the following lines support the claim that the consequences of testifying constitute wrongs or injustices (ἀδικήματα). The symbol ·/· in the left-hand margin at II.18 has been interpreted as referring to the accentuation of ταῦτά, or as indicating a correction to the text of II.19–21 (cf. Regenbogen [1940a], 101, and below). More likely (as Richard Janko pointed out to me) it is an abbreviation for ἐστι, indicating the missing copula to be supplied in thought with οἷόν τε. For similar signs in other papyri cf. Bilabel (1923), 2294–96.

18 ταῦτά: ταῦτά is Grenfell's and Hunt's certain correction for the papyrus's τὰυτα (that is, ταὐτά). Cf. F44(a)VI.30. It refers to ἀδικήματα, the wrongs or injustices inflicted as well as suffered by the witness (cf. Aly [1929], 140; Regenbogen [1940a], 101).

19–21 τὸ μηδὲν . . . ἀδικεῖσθαι: that this formula must be identical in sense with the formula of just conduct in I.12–15 is shown in the introductory note above. *Pace* Regenbogen (1940a), 101; Kranz (*FVS* 2.355 n.), and others, there is no reason to suspect the text here. (On the marginal symbol at II.18 see commentary on II.17–18.) "To do no wrong to others and suffer none oneself" represents a thoroughly conventional conception of justice. Cf. Plato, *Republic* 359A (τοῖς μὴ δυναμένοις τὸ μὲν ἐκφεύγειν [*sc.* ἀδικεῖσθαι] τὸ δὲ αἱρεῖν [*sc.* ἀδικεῖν] δοκεῖ λυσιτελεῖν συνθέσθαι ἀλλήλοις μήτ' ἀδικεῖν μήτ' ἀδικεῖσθαι), *Symposium* 196B

("Ερως οὔτ' ἀδικεῖ οὔτ' ἀδικεῖται οὔτε ὑπὸ θεοῦ οὔτε θεόν, οὔτε ὑπ' ἀνθρώπου οὔτε ἄνθρωπον, said in praise of Eros' δικαιοσύνη, 196c); Epicurus, *Ratae sententiae* XXXIII (οὐκ ἦν τι καθ' ἑαυτὸ δικαιοσύνη, ἀλλ' ἐν ταῖς μετ' ἀλλήλων συστροφαῖς καθ' ὁπηλίκους δή ποτε ἀεὶ τόπους συνθήκη τις ὑπὲρ τοῦ μὴ βλάπτειν ἢ βλάπτεσθαι; cf. ibid. XXXI–XXXII); Lucretius, *De rerum natura* 5.1019–20 (*tunc et amicitiem coeperunt iungere aventes | finitimi inter se nec laedere nec violari*); Furley (1981), 88; Decleva Caizzi and Bastianini (1989), 221. Regenbogen (1940a), 101 and others object that an individual cannot *choose* not to be wronged; but the evidence cited shows that the objection is not cogent.

22 ἀνάγκη ἐστίν: cf. I.15–16 ἀνάγκη.

23 τὰ ἕτερα αὐτῶν: that is, either testifying and its consequences or the formula of just conduct. Cf. Regenbogen (1940a), 101. For the plural ἕτερα cf. Kühner–Gerth 1.67–68; Wyse (1904), 205–6.

24–25 ἢ ἀμφότερα ἄδικα: ἀμφότερα refers to testifying and its consequences and the formula of just conduct, not the wrongs suffered by the witness and those suffered by the man testified against (as Bignone [1938], 118–19 seems to interpret). Cf. Regenbogen (1940a), 101. Havelock (1957), 263–64 contended that Antiphon's use of the terms δίκαιον and ἄδικον proves that he held a normative theory of justice. But the appearance of these terms in the argument is entirely conditioned by the conventional beliefs (I.5 νομίζεται) under examination and proves nothing about a putative theory of justice. Cf. Furley (1981), 87–88.

25–36 After showing that bearing true witness is unjust, Antiphon applies the same argument (in abbreviated form) to other varieties of judicial activity as well (II.26 καί). Judging (δικάζειν), deciding (κρίνειν), and arbitrating (διαιτᾶν) are all manifestly unjust (οὐ δίκαια), since they produce winners and losers, the latter of which are harmed and so wronged. Whether the argument on testifying etc. formed part of a larger critique of the Athenian judicial system (as this passage might suggest) seems impossible to determine on present evidence. Cf. F44(a)VI–VII.

26–27 τὸ δικάζειν καὶ τὸ κρίνειν: qualified as it is by the clause ὅπως ἂν περαίνηται, the verb δικάζειν here can hardly mean "condemn" (as Grenfell and Hunt [1922] and others have interpreted). Untersteiner (1962) and Decleva Caizzi and Bastianini (1989) translate "processare," but this sense requires the middle voice (cf. LSJ, s.v. δικάζειν II). Most likely δικάζειν means "sit in judgment" (*sc.* as a δικαστής or juror), "judge." κρίνειν, if it is not a mere synonym of δικάζειν, may signify "decide," "judge" in a more general sense. Cf. Untersteiner (1962), 100–1; Decleva Caizzi and Bastianini (1989), 222.

28–29 ὅπως ἂν περαίνηται: Kranz (*FVS* 2.355); Havelock (1957), 264; Morrison (1972), 221; Saunders (1977–78), 219, and Nill (1985), 67 take this clause with διαιτᾶν, in the sense of "arbitrate to a conclusion." Rather it means "howsoever they [*sc.* the activities of judging, deciding, and arbitrating] are concluded." So rightly Grenfell and Hunt (1922), 121; Untersteiner (1962), 101, and others.

31–32 ὠφελοῦν ... βλάπτει: for the pair βλάπτειν/ὠφελεῖν cf. F44(a)IV.18–22. There is no reason to follow Decleva Caizzi and Bastianini (1989), 222 in detecting an allusion here to the popular principle that it is right to help friends and harm enemies.

32–33 ἐν δὲ τούτῳ: cf. I.30–31; F44(b)II.7 with commentary.

35–36 οἱ δὲ βλαπτόμενοι ἀδικοῦνται: Havelock (1957), 265 suggested that Antiphon here is "advancing a new criterion." But the equation of harming (βλάπτειν) and wronging (ἀδικεῖν) made explicit here is presupposed throughout the whole discussion (cf. introductory note above).

F45–71: ΠΕΡΙ ΟΜΟΝΟΙΑΣ

F45–47

Each of these fragments consists of a single word or phrase designating a mythical or fabulous people, the Shadowfeet (Σκιάποδες), Longheads (Μακροκέφαλοι), and Subterraneans (ὑπὸ τὴν γῆν οἰκοῦντες). The context in which Antiphon mentioned these peoples is completely unknown. Despite the complete lack of supporting evidence, commentators have not hesitated to relate these fragments, in various ways, to the supposed theme of civic concord (cf. Introduction, section IV). Sauppe (1896), 521, for example, suggested that Antiphon tried to show how nature itself commends concord by bestowing a unique physical form on each population. Other commentators interpret the fabulous peoples as idealized exemplars of Antiphon's social ideals. So Dümmler (1901), 206; Croiset (1883), 152; Krämer (1915), 56–58; Bignone (1938), 86, 153; Aly (1929), 150; Momigliano (1969), 135; Untersteiner (1962), 112–14. (On the idealization of primitive or far-off peoples in ancient thought cf. Lovejoy and Boas [1935], 287–367.) Others again interpret them in the exact opposite fashion, as paradigms of primitive incivility. So Diels (*FVS* 2.357 n.); Wilamowitz (1893), 1.173 n. 77, (1959), 1.62. Jacoby (1908), 29–30 combined this interpretation with the theme of civic concord by suggesting that the fabulous peoples were introduced as admonitory examples of what life would be like in the absence of concord. Nestle (1942), 382 with n. 50 struggled to reconcile the opposing interpretations of Antiphon's fabulous peoples, though previously, in reviews of the monographs by Jacoby (1908) and Altwegg (1908), the same scholar had expressed his despair of reaching any firm conclusions owing to the lack of evidence (Nestle [1909a], 121, [1909b], 213; cf. Guthrie [1971a], 288 n. 1). Morrison (1972), 226–27 sought the clue to Antiphon's meaning in the Hippocratic *De aëre aquis et locis*, which explains how the Longheads (Μακροκέφαλοι) came to possess as a natural characteristic a physical deformity that was acquired originally through custom. In the same vein, Morrison suggested, Antiphon introduced the Longheads and the others in an educational context, as proof that nature can be remade through habit and that "by doing good actions we become good men."

There is no compelling reason to connect Antiphon's mention of fabulous peoples with the idea of civic concord, which may or may not have been a theme of Περὶ ὁμονοίας (cf. Introduction, section IV). In particular, all interpretations in which the fabulous peoples figure as idealized exemplars of any sort face the seemingly insurmountable obstacle posed by the unmistakable element of monstrosity in their physical characteristics or way of life (cf. below). Altwegg's proposal to link the fabulous peoples to the theme of the misery of human life does more justice to this element (cf. Altwegg [1908], 53–55). It has as an added advantage the fact that this theme is at least attested for Περὶ ὁμονοίας (cf. Introduction, section IV). Nevertheless, it can hardly be more than a guess. Altwegg seems on firmer ground with his suggestion that the fabulous peoples were introduced as counterexamples to the claim made in F48 that man is the most godlike or beautiful (θεειδέστατον) of all creatures. Cf. commentary on F48.

F45

Σκιάποδες: on the Shadowfeet cf. Herrmann (1927); Dunbar (1995), 710–11. They are perhaps to be identified with the Στεγανόποδες mentioned by Alcman (fr. 148). Ancient authorities located them either in India or in Libya. Herrmann (1927); Jacoby, *FGrHist* IA 371 (on I F 325–28); Untersteiner (1962), 114; and Dunbar (1995), 710 all supposed that Antiphon assigned them to Libya. But Harpocration's phrase ἔθνος ἐστὶ Λιβυκόν need not be based on anything he found in Antiphon. How far the Shadowfeet were from being idealized in ancient thought appears from Tertullian's argument that Christians, who were sometimes referred to derogatorily as Σκιάποδες, are really just men like any others (cf. Tertullian, *Apology* 8).

F46

Μακροκέφαλοι: on the Longheads cf. Herrmann (1928). They appear first in Hesiod, fr. 153 (cf. fr. 150 with Merkelbach and West [1967], 74 n.), and are famously mentioned in the Hippocratic *De aëre aquis et locis* 14.

F47

ὑπὸ γῆν οἰκοῦντες: it is uncertain whether Harpocration is right in identifying Antiphon's Subterraneans with the Κατουδαῖοι and/or the Trogodytes. On the Κατουδαῖοι (first mentioned in Hesiod, fr. 150.9, 18) cf. Gisinger (1962). On the various peoples called Trogodytes cf. Jahn (1948). (For the correct spelling, Τρωγο- rather than Τρωγλο-, cf. Jahn [1948], 2497.) The Trogodytes were widely regarded as standing at a low level of civilization.

F48

As Eustathius perhaps already perceived, θεαιδέστατον (the reading of all manuscripts in all sources) is irreconcilable with the explanatory gloss θεοῦ ἰδέαν ἔχον. Dümmler (1889), 80 n. 2; Aly (1929), 152 n. 153, and Nestle (1942), 382 with n. 49 rejected the gloss in favor of θεαιδέστατον, an adjective formed from θεός and αἰδεῖσθαι and signifying "god-fearing." No such adjective is attested, however, and it is hard to see why Antiphon would have bothered to invent it, since θεουδής, with the same sense, was already available. More important, the alleged θεαιδέστατος gives an unsatisfactory sense in the context, since animals are not "god-fearing" at all (so already Sylburg; cf. Erbse [1950], 44; Altwegg [1908], 34). It is much more plausible to assume textual corruption of a single word than to suppose that the original author of the explanatory gloss, probably Aelius Dionysius (cf. Erbse [1950], 44), misunderstood Antiphon's meaning. Cf. Buttmann (1836), 356 n. 4. In all likelihood, therefore, Antiphon used a superlative form of the common adjective θεοειδής, which was correctly explained by the original glossator but subsequently corrupted to θεαιδέστατον at an early (but no longer precisely determinable) stage of the Atticist lexical tradition. Cf. Buttmann (1836), 356 n. 4; Diels (*FVS* 2.357 n.); Guthrie (1971a), 288 n. 1.

The context and meaning of the fragment are uncertain. Dümmler (1889), 80 n. 2 theorized that it was directed against the words of Protagoras in Plato, *Protagoras* 322A (ἐπειδὴ δὲ ὁ ἄνθρωπος θείας μετέσχε μοίρας, πρῶτον μὲν διὰ τὴν τοῦ θεοῦ συγγένειαν ζῴων μόνον θεοὺς ἐνόμισεν κτλ.), which he supposed were an utterance of the historical Protagoras. Nestle (1942), 381–82 assigned it to a "mytho-historical" introduction which he postulated for Περὶ ὁμονοίας. These theories are inextricably linked with their authors' interpretation of θεαιδέστατον, and fall together with it (cf. above). The tone of the fragment is unmistakably ironic and sceptical. Unlike ζῷον, the noun θηρίον is ordinarily applied to human beings only in denigration. Cf. Plato, *Laws* 808D; LSJ, s.v. III; Altwegg (1908), 34; contrast *Laws* 766A (ἄνθρωπος δέ ... θειότατον ἡμερώτατόν τε ζῷον γίγνεσθαι φιλεῖ). And φημί (here as elsewhere) implies doubt about the truth of what is asserted (cf. Mewaldt [1929], 79 n. 16). Evidently, Antiphon looked askance at man's proud claim in the fragment to be the most godlike or beautiful of creatures (cf. Buttmann [1836], 356 n. 4). It is very tempting to follow Altwegg (1908), 34, 55 in supposing that the fabulous peoples mentioned in F45–47 were introduced precisely as counterexamples to this claim (cf. commentary on F45–47).

2–3 πάντων θηρίων: David Sedley suggests construing this as the non-inclusive partitive genitive, thus excluding man from the category of animals (cf. Thucydides, 1.1: [πόλεμον] ἀξιολογώτατον τῶν προγεγενημένων; Kühner–Gerth 1.23–24). But this spoils the irony.

3 θεειδέστατον: this form of the superlative (on which cf. Buttmann [1836], 356 n. 4) is not attested elsewhere; it may have been the reason why lexicographers preserved the citation. Or perhaps θεοειδέστατον should be restored. Cf. Hesychius, θ 268 (2.312): θεοειδεστέρας· θεῖον εἶδος ἢ ὁμοίωμα ⟨ἐχούσης⟩. Here in the quotation, all sources offer the masculine θεαιδέστατος, which Sauppe plausibly emended to the (more idiomatic) neuter form θεαιδέστατον. Cf. Kühner–Gerth 1.63–64. (In the lemma, the sources vary between masculine and neuter forms of both θεαιδέστατος and ἔχων.) Diels later incorporated Sauppe's correction by writing θεειδέστατον.

F49

This is the longest of the fragments from Stobaeus plausibly ascribed to Περὶ ὁμονοίας (cf. Introduction, section IV). It consists of an amalgam of familiar commonplaces clothed in an elaborate poetical style – a combination typical of sophistic epideictic. The main theme is supplied by one horn of the misogynist's dilemma outlined already by Hesiod: the dangers and difficulties of marriage. (Cf. *Theogony* 607–12; Euripides, *Orestes* 602–4, *Medea* 230–43; Posidippus, *Anthologia Palatina* 9.359; Sinko [1938].) Other commonplaces exploited in the fragment include the troubles occasioned by children; the unavoidable mixture of good and evil in human life; the inseparability of pleasure and pain; and the need for great effort to achieve success (cf. further commentary below). The argument of the fragment falls neatly into three main divisions, each introduced by the exhortation φέρε δή. In the first (ll. 1–8), Antiphon considers the advent of marriage and the worst-case scenario of an unsuitable wife and subsequent divorce. The second (ll. 8–29) examines the best-case scenario of a satisfactory marriage, which nevertheless turns out to be a burden. The last and briefest (ll. 29–32) section deals with the arrival of children, who fill life with cares and drive away the joy of youth. The opening words of the fragment (προελθέτω ὁ βίος εἰς τὸ πρόσθεν) point to the context of an examination of the successive stages of human life and their attendant hardships and difficulties (cf. Introduction, section IV; F51 and F66, with commentary). Altwegg (1908), 29, 34–35 plausibly assigned the fragment to the theme of the misery of human life (cf. also F50). On the supposition that Περὶ ὁμονοίας was a dialogue, Bignone (1940) suggested that the pessimistic view of marriage on display here did not represent Antiphon's own opinion and was contradicted in another part of the work (cf. commentary on F51, l. 1). This suggestion is not supported by any evidence, however, and neglects the commonplace character of the sentiments involved. For a possible connection with the ὁμόνοια of the title cf. Introduction, section IV.

Stylistically, the fragment is remarkable for its profusion of rare and/or poetic vocabulary, bold metaphors, sententious utterances (γνῶμαι), and poetic rhythms. Frequent rhetorical questions enliven the tone and relieve the dryness of more argumentative passages (cf. Jacoby [1908], 60). Among extant fragments of Περὶ ὁμονοίας, this one offers the best evidence for the possibility of Gorgianic influence on Antiphon's style (cf. Drerup [1901], 305; Norden [1918], 1.72; Jacoby [1908], 58–65). Undoubtedly, figures of speech closely associated with Gorgianic style such as antithesis, isocolon (ἰσόκωλον), and paromoeosis (παρομοίωσις) are employed in abundance. Cf. Jacoby (1908), 58–65, and the comments of Hermogenes in T2(a), l. 38. (Blass [1887–98], 1.112, 3.2.362 stubbornly disagreed.) As even Jacoby (1908), 65 admitted, however, the overall impression made by the fragment is perceptibly different from that of Gorgias: less artificial, more relaxed in its pursuit of antithetic parallelism, and far less obtrusive in sound-effects. Even here, Gorgianic influence cannot be said to have been demonstrated. Cf. Altwegg (1908), 82; Aly (1929), 154–55; Bignone (1938), 201.

Havelock (1957), 292–94, 419–20 contended that in its original form, this fragment offered a frontal assault on the conventional Greek institution of marriage. Unable to reconcile this preconceived view with the evidence of the text, Havelock argued that the fragment as transmitted contains a few original phrases from Antiphon embedded in a context of later moralizing interpolations borrowed from Euripides, Plato, and Xenophon. Havelock's contention is purely arbitrary.

1 φέρε δή: *pace* Altwegg (1908), 23 and Bignone (1938), 207 n. 1, (1940), 236, these words are not addressed to a person but go with the following imperatives. Cf. Denniston (1954), 217. On the structural function of φέρε δή cf. introductory note above.

προελθέτω ὁ βίος εἰς τὸ πρόσθεν: προελθέτω is a so-called hypothetical imperative, the equivalent of a conditional protasis. Cf. Sophocles, *Antigone* 1168–69 with Jebb (1900), 208; Kühner–Gerth 1.237; Wackernagel (1926–28), 2.280. So also ἐπιθυμησάτω (l. 2). Wilamowitz (1880), 515 and Norden (1918), 1.72 n. 2, 129 n. 1 interpreted προελθέτω εἰς τὸ πρόσθεν as a command to the personified βίος to "come forward," like a character on stage. (Norden spoke of a θεατρικὸν σχῆμα.) But unlike a stage character, βίος does not speak or act (cf. Jacoby [1908], 30). The sense is rather "advance," "go forward" *in time*.

1–2 καὶ γάμων καὶ γυναικός: Herwerden's proposed deletion of καὶ γυναικός is hypercritical (like many similar proposals regarding the text of this fragment). Fullness of expression is characteristic of the style of Περὶ ὁμονοίας; cf. Philostratus, T2(b), ll. 5–7 (καὶ τὰ ἀποτάδην ἑρμηνευόμενα παραπλήσια τῶν πεδίων τοῖς λείοις). γάμων could mean "wedding," but more likely is the so-called poetic plural, which combines the senses "wedding" and "wedlock." Cf. Bers (1984), 31–32. The singular γάμος (l. 3), by contrast, means "marriage," "wedlock."

2 αὕτη ἡ ἡμέρα, αὕτη ἡ νύξ: since γάμων includes the idea of "wedding," this phrase certainly refers to the wedding-day and wedding-night rather than the day on which the desire for marriage first arises (as Altwegg [1908], 23 interpreted). Cf. Sophocles, fr. 583.11–12 (καὶ ταῦτα, ἐπειδὰν εὐφρόνη ζεύξῃ μία, | χρεὼν ἐπαινεῖν καὶ δοκεῖν καλῶς ἔχειν). On the double anaphora with asyndeton in this phrase and the next (καινοῦ δαίμονος κτλ.) cf. Fehling (1969), 210.

2–3 καινοῦ δαίμονος . . . πότμου: the use of δαίμων in a depersonalized sense equivalent to "fate" is poetic and tragic. Cf. Fraenkel (1950), 3.632–33, with references. πότμος, an almost exclusively poetic word which seems not to occur elsewhere in Attic prose, is here synonymous with δαίμων (*pace* Altwegg [1908], 23, who translated "calamitatis"). Cf. LSJ, s.v.; Jacoby (1908), 51. The anapaestic rhythm of the passage καινοῦ δαίμονος . . . ἀνθρώπῳ (ll. 2–4) lends further poetic coloring, and suggested to Gaisford, Herwerden, Nauck, and others a quotation from tragedy. (Nauck printed καινοῦ δαίμονος . . . πότμου as trag. adesp. fr. 542.) Cf. *contra* Jacoby (1908), 65–66; Bignone (1938), 195 n. 2; Gomperz (1912), 63 n. 109a; Untersteiner (1962), 120.

3–4 μέγας γὰρ ... ἀνθρώπῳ: for the metaphorical use of ἀγών cf. Democritus, *FVS* 68 B 275; LSJ, s.v. III.5. For the phrase μέγας ἀγών cf. Euripides, *Hippolytus* 496 with Barrett (1964), 250. This passage is often compared with Euripides, *Medea* 235ff.: κἀν τῷδ' ἀγὼν μέγιστος, ἢ κακὸν λαβεῖν | ἢ χρηστόν. οὐ γὰρ εὐκλεεῖς ἀπαλλαγαὶ | γυναιξίν κτλ. While Altwegg (1908), 66–67 and others make Euripides dependent on Antiphon, Diels (*FVS* 2.357 n.) would reverse the direction of influence. Both ancient authors make the point that marriage is risky and divorce difficult. But while Euripides' Medea envisages at least the possibility of a happy marriage (cf. *Medea* 241–43), the main point of Antiphon's argument is that even a supposedly happy marriage inevitably brings myriad troubles. The commonplace character of the sentiments (cf. introductory note above) and absence of specific verbal borrowing suggest that it is unnecessary to posit any direct connection between the two authors.

4 μὴ ἐπιτηδεία γενομένη: though often emended (cf. the critical apparatus), these words are unobjectionable, as γυνή is easily understood. Cf. Altwegg (1908), 24 n. 2 (Jacoby [1908], 31 n. 70 disagreed). For ἐπιτήδειος applied to a wife cf. Euripides, *Andromache* 205–6.

4–5 τί χρὴ ... χρῆσθαι: this expression is equivalent to the more usual deliberative subjunctive (e.g. Plato, *Lysis* 213C: τί οὖν δὴ χρησώμεθα;). On this use of χράομαι cf. Redard (1953), 30–31.

5 χαλεπαὶ μὲν ἐκπομπαί: ἐκπομπή in the sense of "divorce" seems to occur only here, though the verb ἐκπέμπειν is regular in this sense. Cf. LSJ, s.v. ἐκπέμπω I.4; Jacoby (1908), 55; Wyse (1904), 295. For the use of an abstract noun in place of a verb cf. Jacoby (1908), 57. For the "rhetorical" plural expressing intensification cf. Bers (1984), 25. The omission of the copula (as often in this fragment) produces a sententious effect. Note also the anaphora χαλεπὸν μὲν ... χαλεπὸν δέ.

5–7 τοὺς φίλους ... ἀξιωθέντα: the asyndeton is explanatory (cf. Kühner–Gerth 2.344 (δ)), and Jacobs' ⟨καὶ⟩ unnecessary. This passage is variously interpreted (and emended). Diels (*FVS* 2.358 n.) referred τοὺς φίλους to the husband and wife, comparing Aeschylus, *Agamemnon* 1235–36 (θύουσαν Ἅιδου μητέρ' ἄσπονδόν τ' Ἄρη | φίλοις πνέουσαν). But (to mention only one objection) φίλοις there does not mean "spouse" (cf. Fraenkel [1950], 3.571–72). τοὺς φίλους is best taken as referring to the husband's former in-laws, the family of his former wife. Cf. Euripides, *Iphigenia in Aulis* 839–40. The participles ἀξιώσαντα and ἀξιωθέντα most likely refer to the husband, who at one time "deemed" his former in-laws "worthy" of the bonds of relationship created by marriage, and was himself deemed worthy by them. So Jacoby (1908), 31 with n. 71a (but contrast 57) and Wilamowitz (*apud* Jacoby). For other interpretations cf. Croiset (1883), 158 n. 1; Jacoby (1908), 31–32; Altwegg (1908), 24–25; Diels (*FVS* 2.358 n.); Nestle (1908), 571; Sinko (1938), 178. For the rhetorical figure in ἀξιώσαντα καὶ ἀξιωθέντα cf. Fehling (1969), 266. For ἀξιόω in this context cf. Herodotus, 9.11 (ἀξιεύμενος θυγατρὸς τῆς σῆς). The use of πνέω with a neuter adjective (functioning as an internal accusative) to express mental activity is a poeticism. Cf. LSJ, s.v. v.2; Jacoby (1908), 51; Euripides, *Andromache* 189; Pindar, *Nem.* 7.5. Jacoby (1908), 31 acutely called attention to a remarkable parallel to this passage in Terence, *Hecyra* 211–12, where Laches reproaches Sostrata for driving their daughter-in-law from their son's home: *tum autem ex amicis inimici ut sint nobis adfines facis, | qui illum decrerunt dignum suos quoi liberos committerent.*

7–8 χαλεπὸν δὲ . . . ἄγεσθαι: Diels' καὶ ἐκτῆσθαι is possible but unnecessary (cf. Altwegg [1908], 24 n. 4). For κτάομαι used of "acquiring" a wife (like a possession) cf. Sophocles, fr. 682; Euripides, *Iphigenia in Aulis* 715. The present infinitive ἄγεσθαι is odd paired with the perfect κεκτῆσθαι. Diels' defense of it (*FVS* 2.358 n.) by reference to κτᾶσθαι is misguided, since the latter depends on δοκοῦντα and is not parallel to ἄγεσθαι. Perhaps the rarity of the perfect middle forms of ἄγω (cf. LSJ, s.v.) accounts for the use of the present-tense infinitive here. ἄγεσθαι λύπας plays on the common use of ἄγεσθαι in the sense of "bring home a wife," "marry," for which cf. Magnien (1937), 297–98.

8 δοκοῦντα κτλ.: the asyndeton is explanatory, and Diels' old proposal δοκοῦν τε unnecessary (cf. Altwegg [1908], 24 n. 5).

8–10 φέρε δή . . . ἐπιτηδειότατα: on φέρε δή (for which Sauppe [1896], 524 proposed φέρε δέ) cf. introductory note above and commentary on l. 1. παλίγκοτα is a predominantly poetic word (cf. LSJ, s.v.), which here seems to mean simply "adverse" (cf. Altwegg [1908], 25 n. 4). Blass' γενέσθω (for λεγέσθω) spoils the epanastrophe (cf. Jacoby [1908], 62).

10–11 τί γὰρ ἥδιον . . . νέῳ: for this commonplace cf. Hesiod, *Works and Days* 702–3 with West (1978), 328–29; Semonides, fr. 6; Theognis, 1225; Sophocles, fr. 682; Jacoby (1908), 35–36; Sinko (1938), 164 n. 9. On καταθύμιος (a poetic and Ionic word) cf. LSJ, s.v.; Jacoby (1908), 49; Nestle (1942), 383 n. 54. For its application to a wife cf. Herodotus, 5.39 with Stein (1893–1908), 3.37. Cf. (with Stein and Sinko [1938], 178) the Homeric θυμαρής, likewise applied to wives (*Iliad* 9.336, *Odyssey* 23.232); and Hesiod's phrase ἀρηρυῖαν [*sc.* ἄκοιτιν] πραπίδεσσι (*Theogony* 608, quoted below).

11–13 ἐν τῷ αὐτῷ . . . τὸ λυπηρόν: the crux of Antiphon's argument: even in the best of circumstances, marriage proves to be a burden. On δέ γε introducing a retort cf. Shorey (1919) = (1980), 1.164–73.

For the thought cf. Hesiod, *Theogony* 607–10: ᾧ δ' αὖτε γάμου μετὰ μοῖρα γένηται, | κεδνὴν δ' ἔσχεν ἄκοιτιν, ἀρηρυῖαν πραπίδεσσι, | τῷ δέ τ' ἀπ' αἰῶνος κακὸν ἐσθλῷ ἀντιφερίζει | ἐμμενές. For the (commonplace) notion that a mixture of good and evil is the best human beings can hope to attain cf. *Iliad* 24.527–30; Hesiod, *Works and Days* 179; Bacchylides, 5.53–55 with Maehler (1982), 2.101; West (1966), 334; Sinko (1938), 179.

13–14 αἱ γὰρ ἡδοναὶ . . . πόνοι: for the inseparability of pleasure and pain cf. Plato, *Phaedo* 60B–C; Aesop, *Fabulae* 13.3 (1.21: τῇ γὰρ ἡδονῇ, ὡς ἔοικεν, ἀδελφή ἐστιν ἡ λύπη). ἐπί ("by themselves") is preferable to ἐκ (Stobaeus, 3.6.45), which gives an inferior sense. ἐμπορεύονται means "travel" (cf. LSJ, s.v.), and pleasures are personified here. As the following sentence shows (cf. ἐκ τῶν λυπημάτων . . . παραγίγνεσθαι), ἀκολουθοῦσιν does not mean "follow" but "accompany," "go with." Contrast Plato's more precise ἐπακολουθεῖ, ἐπακολουθοῦν (*Phaedo* 60C). Jacoby (1908), 59 called attention to the chiasmus, which links αἱ γὰρ ἡδοναί with λῦπαι καὶ πόνοι, and ἐμπορεύονται with ἀκολουθοῦσιν.

15 ὀλυμπιονῖκαι . . . ἀγῶνες: as Rattenbury (1938) pointed out, ὀλυμπιονῖκαι and πυθιονῖκαι ("victories at Olympia" and "at Pythia") are anomalous formations unparalleled in classical Greek. (The normal forms would be ὀλυμπιονικίαι and πυθιονικίαι; cf. Pindar, *Nem.* 3.7 ἀεθλονικία.) In Bacchylides, 4.17, the papyrus offers ὀλυμπιονίκας, but Maas' correction ὀλυμπιονικ⟨ί⟩ας is guaranteed by the meter (cf. Maehler [1982], 2.76–77). Rattenbury also objected to the sense: "for to compete is not necessarily to win, and the expression 'victories at Olympia and Delphi and such contests' is almost nonsense." He proposed to interpret ὀλυμπιονῖκαι and πυθιονῖκαι as masculine nouns used adjectivally to modify ἀγῶνες. Cf. Pindar, *Olymp.* 3.3 (ὀλυμπιονίκαν ὕμνον), 7.88 (ὕμνου τεθμὸν ὀλυμπιονίκαν); LSJ, s.v. ὀλυμπιονίκης. But the context seems to require a reference to victories, not merely contests (cf. τιμαὶ γάρ, ἆθλα). It is difficult to avoid construing ὀλυμπιονῖκαι and πυθιονῖκαι here as feminine nouns, despite the anomalous formation. Cf. πυθιονίκη (Heliodorus, *Aethiopica* 4.16, 5.19); Altwegg (1908), 26 n. 1. οἱ τοιοῦτοι ἀγῶνες will then be used loosely for "victories in other such contests," which is defensible as an example of "illogical idiom." Cf. Altwegg (1908), 26 n. 2; Shorey (1916) = (1980), 1.20–49.

16 σοφίαι: Snell (1924), 15 and Untersteiner (1962), 123 interpreted σοφίαι as "Dichteragone," an unparalleled sense. Altwegg (1908), 26 with n. 3 rendered "artes scientiaeque," while Bignone (1938), 197, 203 n. 1 interpreted it as a poetic plural ("eccellenza di sapere"). Given the context, σοφίαι more likely is a real plural referring to the "skills" needed for victory in athletic and other contests. The plural of this noun is rare in the classical period; to the instances cited by LSJ, s.v. add Plato, *Theaetetus* 176C; Aristotle, *Nicomachean Ethics* 1141a31.

καὶ πᾶσαι ἡδοναί: these are not a separate class from what precedes but a summary generalization: "e cosi tutti gli altri piaceri" (Untersteiner [1962], 123).

16–17 ἐκ μεγάλων ... ἐθέλουσι παραγίγνεσθαι: with the terminology employed here cf. Plato, *Phaedo* 60B (τὸ ἅμα μὲν αὐτὼ [ἡδύ and λυπηρόν] μὴ 'θέλειν παραγίγνεσθαι), 60C (παραγένηται). λύπημα is rare (cf. LSJ and *ThGL*, s.v.). Jacoby (1908), 51–52 plausibly suggested that it is used here (for the common λύπη) to create σεμνότης (cf. Aristotle, *Rhetoric* 1404b8).

17–18 τιμαὶ γάρ ... ἀνθρώποις: the asyndeton in τιμαὶ γάρ, ἆθλα is permissible, and there is no reason to posit a lacuna after ἆθλα (as Hense suggested). δελέατα can be construed in apposition to τιμαί and ἆθλα in the main sentence ("– baits, which god gives") or in hyperbaton as a predicate in the relative clause ("which god gives as baits"). ἔδωκεν is a gnomic aorist. Luria (1929b), 247 suspected δελέατα ... ἀνθρώποις of being an interpolation, on the grounds that Antiphon was a materialist who denied providence (cf. F12). But the sentiment is hardly that of a later moralizing interpreter, and it is in any case naive to treat the passage as a serious statement of theology (as Joël [1893–1901], 2.655; Altwegg [1908], 26–27, 86; Untersteiner [1962], 124, and others also do). Cf. Schmid (1940), 165 n. 1. Nor (*pace* Jacoby [1908], 32–33) does any significance attach to the use of the singular θεός (cf. François [1957], 180–81 and *passim*; Untersteiner [1962], 124).

18–19 μεγάλων πόνων ... καθιστᾶσιν: on the word-order cf. Norden (1918), 1.72 n. 2; Jacoby (1908), 60. For the commonplace notion that toil is the indispensable prerequisite of success cf. Hesiod, *Works and Days* 289–90 with the parallels cited by West (1978), 229; Thucydides, 1.123 (πάτριον γὰρ ἡμῖν ἐκ τῶν πόνων τὰς ἀρετὰς κτᾶσθαι); Sophocles, fr. 938 (πολλῶν πόνων δεῖ τῷ καλῶς τιμωμένῳ). For the plural ἱδρώτων cf. Plato, *Phaedrus* 239C with de Vries (1969), 93; Kühner–Gerth 1.15. For the combination "toil and sweat" Jacoby (1908), 56 referred to the aforementioned passage of the *Phaedrus* as well as to Xenophon, *Memorabilia* 2.1.28, *Cyropaedia* 8.8.8.

19 ἐγὼ γὰρ κτλ.: the argument on marriage resumes here, after the general remarks on the inseparability of pain and pleasure. For γάρ introducing a particular example of a general proposition cf. Denniston (1954), 66–67. Altwegg (1908), 61–63, 68–69 and other commentators detect Euripidean influence here (cf. *Alcestis* 238ff., 874ff., *Hippolytus* 252ff.), while others would reverse the direction of influence. But there is no need to posit any direct connection. Cf. Diels, *FVS* 2.359 n.; Jacoby (1908), 35; commentary on ll. 3–4.

19–20 εἴ μοι . . . ἐμαυτῷ: Wilamowitz proposed to delete ἐμαυτῷ, and Meineke the entire clause, while Diels wished to insert ἐπιμελὲς ὂν after τοιοῦτον. Diels' insertion is unnecessary, since τοιοῦτον is sufficiently explained by οὕτως ἐμαυτῷ πολλὰ πράγματα παρέχων κτλ. below. *Pace* Meineke, the clause as a whole seems indispensable to the sense. ἐμαυτῷ may have been mistakenly imported here from l. 21 (οὕτως ἐμαυτῷ). But perhaps it is defensible as a dative of reference (with εἰμί understood). For σῶμα = "person" cf. LSJ, s.v. II.2; Untersteiner (1962), 124–25.

21–24 ὑπέρ τε τῆς ὑγιείας . . . ἀκούειν: in its rhetorical fullness of expression this passage is comparable to F44(a)II.30–III.18 and F44(b)II.27–III.11 (cf. Bignone [1938], 97, 209–10). The various deletions that have been proposed (cf. the critical apparatus) would spoil the effect. Joined as it is with δόξα, εὔκλεια, and τὸ εὖ ἀκούειν, σωφροσύνης here must mean "reputation for σωφροσύνη." Cf. Kühner–Gerth 1.13; Dover (1974), 235.

24–25 τί οὖν . . . ἐπιμελὲς εἴη: Altwegg (1908), 28 n. 3 defended τί ἄν (cod. A); but a connective particle is wanted. For confusion of ἄν and οὖν cf. Plato, *Republic* 450C with Adam (1902), 1.277. For the optative εἴη (by assimilation of moods) cf. Kühner–Gerth 1.255–56.

25 οὔκουν δῆλον κτλ.: previous editors printed οὐκ οὖν *divisim*. But οὔκουν, introducing a lively question, is much more appropriate here. Cf. Denniston (1954), 431–33. For the figure exemplified in the collocation γυνὴ ἀνδρί cf. Kühner–Gerth 2.602.

26 καταθυμία: cf. commentary on ll. 10–11.

26–27 οὐδὲν ἐλάττους . . . ὀδύνας: LSJ, s.v. 4 interpret φιλότητας here as "sexual intercourse," an impossible sense in the context. In Pindar (*Nem.* 8.1, *Pyth.* 4.92) the noun seems to refer to "sexual pleasures," but the meaning here is obviously wider. Paired as it is with ὀδύνας, φιλότητας probably means simply "pleasures" (a sense not recognized in lexica). There is no apparent difference in meaning between παρέχεται here and the active παρέχων in l. 21 (cf. LSJ, s.v. παρέχω B).

27–29 ὑπέρ τε . . . εὐκλείας: cf. ll. 21–24. συλλογῆς seems suspicious after ξυλλογῆς in l. 23; but cf. Rosenkranz (1930), 173 on spelling variations of this sort in Attic authors.

29–30 φέρε δὴ . . . γενέσθωσαν: for φέρε δή cf. introductory note above and commentary on l. 1. Despite Moeris (ἀγόντων· Ἀττικοί, ἀγέτωσαν· Ἕλληνες), imperative forms like γενέσθωσαν are perfectly good Attic. Cf. Rosenkranz (1930), 153; MacDowell (1990), 228.

30 φροντίδων κτλ.: the asyndeton is explanatory. For the troubles occasioned by children cf. Euenus, fr. 6; Sophocles, *Trachiniae* 149–50 with Davies (1991), 92; Euripides, *Medea* 1090–1115, *Alcestis* 882–88, frr. 571, 908; Democritus, *FVS* 68 A 170, B 275–277; Menander, *Epitrepontes* 252–56; Terence, *Adelphi* 866–67 (*nati filii: alia cura*); Artemidorus, *Onirocritica* 1.15.

31–32 ἐξοίχεται ... τὸ αὐτό: γνώμη here is nearly synonymous with ψυχή – an unusual sense (cf. Huart [1973], 24 n. 2). For the metaphorical connotation of σκίρτημα cf. Basil, *Homilia de gratiarum actione* 4 (31.225 Migne): ἡ δὲ χαρὰ οἷον σκίρτημά τί ἐστι τῆς ψυχῆς ἐπαγαλλομένης τοῖς κατὰ γνώμην. As Buresch (1886), 84 with n. 2 noted, this passage seems to be imitated in Clement of Alexandria, *Quis dives salvetur* 8.3 (ἀλλ' εἴ τις ἐν σκιρτήματι νεοτησίῳ καὶ τῷ καύσωνι τῆς ἡλικίας παρέσχηται φρόνημα πέπανον καὶ πρεσβύτερον τοῦ χρόνου, θαυμαστὸς οὗτος ἀγωνιστὴς καὶ διαπρεπὴς καὶ τὴν γνώμην πολιός). Cf. Philostratus, *De gymnastica* 1.46 (δι' ὧν ὥσπερ οἱ κακῶς παιδεύοντες ἀφαιροῦνται τὸν παῖδα τὸ νεοτήσιον σκίρτημα). On adjectives in -ήσιος cf. Chantraine (1933), 41–42.

F50

The key to this fragment is the meaning of the expression φρουρᾷ ἐφημέρῳ. Buresch (1886), 80–82, 131–32 interpreted "brief imprisonment." Referring ἀναβλέψαντες to the dead ("reversi in aethera, scilicet unde orti sumus") and ἐπιγιγνομένοις to those being reborn, he read into the fragment the "Orphic-Pythagorean" doctrine of transmigration and conception of life as an imprisonment. Cf. Plato, *Phaedo* 62B; *Cratylus* 400B. Other commentators understand φρουρᾷ ἐφημέρῳ as a "watch lasting one day," and refer ἀναβλέψαντες κτλ. to the act of looking up at the light of dawn after an all-day and all-night watch. Cf. Jacoby (1908), 38–39; Altwegg (1908), 30–32; Diels (1922), 2.301 n.; Nestle (1942), 384 with n. 58 (but contrast Nestle [1908], 572). Kranz (*FVS* 2.360 n.) tried to have it both ways, suggesting that φρουρᾷ is intentionally ambiguous between "prison" and "watch." Bignone (1938), 206 n. 1 and Untersteiner (1962), 129 also understand φρουρᾷ as "watch," but interpret ἀναβλέψαντες κτλ. in terms of the last look at the sun by those who are dying. (Cf. Sophocles, *Ajax* 856–58, *Antigone* 808–10.) Kassel (1954), 29 n. 84 = (1991), 25 n. 84 seems to interpret ἀναβλέψαντες κτλ. as referring to birth (cf. *Iliad* 16.188; Pindar, *Nem.* 1.35), but offers no further details about his understanding of the fragment.

Fränkel (1946), 142–44 offered an interpretation of the fragment more complete and convincing than any of the foregoing in an appendix to his important article on the meaning of ἐφήμερος in early Greek literature.[7] Fränkel saw in the fragment a combination of two elements: (1) the equation of "seeing the light" with life and of night with death; and (2) the comparison of life to a watch or guard. For the familiar equation of "seeing the light" with life cf. *Iliad* 5.659, 13.425, 18.442; *Odyssey* 10.499; etc. For the comparison of life to a watch cf. Aeschylus, fr. 265 (διαπεφρούρηται βίος); Lucan, *Bellum civile* 1.45–46 (*te* [*sc.* Caesar], *cum statione peracta* | *astra petes serus* etc.). (The former passage is cited by Schmid [1940], 159 n. 4, 164 n. 11, the latter by E. Fraenkel *apud* Radt [1985], 367 note.) The adjective ἐφημέρῳ Fränkel plausibly explained as "daily," "renewed or recurring every day" – an explanation that has the added merit of saving the clause τό τε μῆκος τοῦ βίου ἡμέρᾳ μιᾷ from redundancy. For this sense cf. Heraclitus, *FVS* 22 B 6 (ἐφ' ἡμέρᾳ); Asclepiodotus, *Tactica* 1.4 (πρὸς τὴν ἐφήμερον γυμνασίαν τε καὶ ἄσκησιν); LSJ, s.v. II; Fränkel (1946), 143 = (1968), 37. The comparison of life to a daily watch emphasizes its laboriousness; the comparison of its length to one day expresses its brevity. This fragment most likely belongs to the theme of the misery of human life (cf. Introduction, section IV).

1 τὸ ζῆν: the infinitive should be given its full force as a verbal noun: "living is like (keeping) a watch." τοῦ βίου, by contrast, refers to an individual life which is like one day.

1–2 τό τε μῆκος . . . μιᾷ: Sauppe (1896), 524 proposed to delete the whole clause, so that his emendation ἣν (for ᾗ) could refer to φρουρᾷ. But τε is an unlikely connective for an interpolator to have employed; and the relative is best referred to ἡμέρᾳ (cf. below).

2 ὡς ἔπος εἰπεῖν: this expression means "practically," "almost" and qualifies μιᾷ. Cf. Fränkel (1946), 144 (but contrast Fränkel [1968], 39); Burnet (1924), 148; Dodds (1959), 196.

ᾗ: this is best referred to ἡμέρᾳ μιᾷ, the single day on which we live, keep our watch, and then die. For the bare dative without a preposition cf. Kühner–Gerth 1.445–46.

3 παρεγγυῶμεν: παρεγγυᾶν is the *terminus technicus* for passing on a signal or watchword (cf. LSJ, s.v. II). The object understood with it could be "watchword," or the watch itself (φρουρά), or perhaps even "life." (Michael Reeve suggests to me that if πρός is deleted, τὸ φῶς

[7] In a reprint of this article published in Fränkel (1968), 23–39, the author modified his classification of the different senses of ἐφήμερος, putting Antiphon's usage in the third category and interpreting ἐφημέρῳ as "lasting for one day." But this gives an inferior sense, and Fränkel's earlier interpretation is much to be preferred.

could be construed as object of παρεγγυῶμεν, with a double sense as in the expression "pass on the torch.")

τοῖς ἐπιγιγνομένοις: for ἐπιγίγνομαι = "be born after," "come later" cf. LSJ, s.v. I; Xenophon, *Cyropaedia* 6.1.12 (ἀντὶ δὲ τῶν ἀποθανόντων ἕτεροι ἐφηβήσουσι καὶ ἐπιγενήσονται).

F51

All three primary witnesses to the text of this fragment (codd. SMA) offer the lemma ἀντιφάνους; only the edition of Trincavelli (Tr.) has ἀντιφῶντος. Hense in Wachsmuth and Hense (1884–1912), 5.841 n. tried to cast doubt on the attribution to Antiphon, suggesting that Tr.'s ἀντιφῶντος may have arisen from misinterpretation of a compendium. (In fact S has a compendium here.) Hense compared Stobaeus, 3.21.4, where SMA offer the (correct) lemma ἀντιφάνους, while Tr. again has ἀντιφῶντος, probably from a misunderstood compendium. Hense further conjectured that the citation from Antiphanes to which the lemma ἀντιφάνους originally corresponded has been lost, and together with it the original, correct lemma for this fragment (which he noted seems to be out of place, located as it is among verse quotations). Hense's scepticism about the attribution to Antiphon is rightly rejected by Diels (*FVS* 2.360 n.). Accidentally or not, Tr. is likely to have preserved the truth here, for the attribution to Antiphanes is impossible, while the ascription to Antiphon is supported by the contents of the fragment. Confusion of the two names, moreover, is quite common. (In addition to the passage of Stobaeus cited above, cf. *Suda* s.v. ἀμαρτυρήτους, α 1500 = Antiphon, *FVS* 87 B 93b; F9 and F64, with commentary; Meineke [1839–57], 1.314–17; van Spaan [1773], 828–29.)

The emphatic declaration of the shortcomings of human life looks programmatic, and Bignone (1938), 207 n. 1 and Altwegg (1908), 38 may be right in thinking that this fragment originally came at or near the beginning of Περὶ ὁμονοίας. The fragment is almost certainly to be connected with the theme of the misery of human life, and in particular with the chronological review of the stages of life with their attendant hardships (n.b. πᾶς ὁ βίος, "the whole of life"). Cf. Introduction, section IV; F49 and F66, with commentary; also F50, F52. According to Bignone (1938), 225, the fragment implies that life is so burdensome that the mere avoidance of pain is the greatest good. (Bignone ascribed to Antiphon the anti-hedonist doctrine in Plato, *Philebus* 44B–D, 51A; cf. commentary on T6.) In this way, Bignone tried to connect the fragment with the alleged theme of ἀλυπία and the story of the grief-clinic. Nestle (1942), 379 n. 40 interpreted similarly, and detected a reminiscence of the fragment in Euripides, *Heracles* 502ff. But the grief-clinic is most likely a fiction (cf. Introduction, section II and commentary on T6), and there is no reason at all to credit Antiphon with the doctrine on pleasure and pain Bignone ascribed to him. Luria (1928b), 209–10 contended that the fragment is simply a translation by Antiphon into the Attic dialect of the curiously similar fragment attributed to Democritus in Stobaeus, 4.34.62 (= *FVS* 68 B 285): γινώσκειν χρεὼν ἀνθρωπίνην βιοτὴν ἀφαυρήν τε ἐοῦσαν καὶ ὀλιγοχρόνιον πολλῇσίν τε κηρσὶ συμπεφυρμένην καὶ ἀμηχανίῃσιν, ὅκως ἄν τις μετρίης τε κτήσιος ἐπιμέληται καὶ μετρῆται ἐπὶ τοῖς ἀναγκαίοις ἡ ταλαιπωρία. The resemblances are undeniable (cf. ἀφαυρήν with ἀσθενῆ; ὀλιγοχρόνιον with ὀλιγοχρόνια; πολλῇσίν τε κηρσὶ συμπεφυρμένην with ἀναμεμειγμένα λύπαις μεγάλαις). But the topical assertion of the brevity and difficulty of life seems to be put to different uses in the two fragments. Democritus' purpose is clearly to urge a limit on the acquisition of material possessions; in F51, by contrast, Antiphon does not appear to draw any practical conclusion from the fact that life is easy to criticize (εὐκατηγόρητος) – at least as the fragment stands. A direct connection between the two remains unproven. Cf. Mewaldt (1929), 85 n. 36; Lana (1951), 317; Capizzi in Zeller and Mondolfo (1969), 330 (whose caution is relevant to the further instances of Democritean influence on Antiphon urged by Luria and others). The opening words of this fragment may be imitated in the fragment of Hermolochus (or Hermolaus) quoted by Stobaeus, 4.34.66 (= fr. 447): ἀτέκμαρτος ὁ πᾶς βίος, οὐδὲν ἔχων πιστὸν πλανᾶται συντυχίαις κτλ. (cf. Luria [1929b], 233).

1 εὐκατηγόρητος: this is a rare word, recurring only in Thucydides, 6.77 (a passage quoted by Dionysius of Halicarnassus, *De Thucydide* 48); Polybius, 4.29.3, Plutarch, *Antonius* 58.6, Cassius Dio, *Historiae* 52.13.7 (all three probably in imitation of Thucydides); and Vettius Valens, *Anthologiae* 9.15.36. On compounds in εὐ– in Antiphon and contemporary authors cf. Jacoby (1908), 54–55.

πᾶς ὁ βίος: not "jedes Leben" (Goebel [1910], 385; Gomperz [1912], 61) but "life, the whole of it," "life in its entirety" (cf. Kühner–Gerth 1.633).

θαυμαστῶς, ὦ μακάριε: the various emendations proposed by Sauppe, Diels, Meineke, and Blass to eliminate the vocative should be rejected. Cf. Altwegg (1908), 21; Bignone (1938), 207 n. 1. Sauppe's insertion θαυμαστῶς ⟨ὡς⟩ is unnecessary. For θαυμαστῶς with an adjective cf. Plato, *Laws* 633B–C; [Plato], *Epistulae* 7.332D, 338D; Plutarch, *Marcellus* 29.9. *Pace* Bignone (1938), 207 n. 1, (1940), 235–37, the vocative does not imply that Περὶ ὁμονοίας was a dialogue (cf. Altwegg [1908], 21 with n. 3). Most likely it represents an impersonal address to the reader or listener; comparable examples are found in the Hippocratic corpus, the pseudo-Xenophontean Ἀθηναίων πολιτεία, and Antiphon's own Περὶ ἀληθείας. Cf. F29A with commentary; Wilamowitz (1959), 1.62 n. 3; Aly (1929), 58–59, 60 n. 68, 62; Frisch (1942), 166, 202. Also possible (though less likely) is an address to a dedicatee (cf. Sauppe [1896], 524; Altwegg [1908], 21 with n. 4; Bignone [1938], 207 n. 1). Hense (Wachsmuth and Hense [1884–1912], 5.841 n.), Bignone (1938), 207 n. 1 and Altwegg (1908), 22 detect an ironic undertone in μακάριε (cf. Plato, *Republic* 432D; Dionysius the tyrant, fr. 2: εἰ δ' ἀξιοῖς σοι μηδὲν ἀλγεινόν ποτε †μηδὲν ἔσεσθαι, μακαρίως ἔχεις φρενῶν· θεῶν γὰρ ἕξειν βίοτον, οὐ θνατῶν δοκεῖς). Alternatively, μακάριε may serve to introduce a point of special importance (cf. Plato, *Phaedo* 69A with Rowe [1993], 149).

1–2 καὶ οὐδὲν ἔχων: though frequently emended, the transmitted text is defensible. Either ἐστι can be understood with ἔχων (for the periphrasis cf. Kühner–Gerth 1.38–39, Anmerkung 3; Demosthenes, *or.* 21.119); or καί can be taken adverbially with οὐδέν (= "actually nothing").

F52

This fragment presents a warning that it is impossible to revoke or take back one's life like a bad move in a board game. As Goebel (1910), 385 noted, it is an application of the principle that it is impossible to undo what has already been done (cf. F58, ll. 5–6 with commentary, where the *topos* reappears, again in an ethical context). Most likely the warning was linked with an exhortation (explicit or implied) to use life rightly in the first place. The fragment can thus be connected with others from Περὶ ὁμονοίας on the same theme. Cf. F53A–54 with commentary; Introduction, section IV; Croiset (1883), 150–51; Jacoby (1908), 26, 39; Altwegg (1908), 14–20. It has often been compared with a fragment preserved by Stobaeus, 4.56.39 and attributed to "Socrates": πεττείᾳ τινι ἔοικεν ὁ βίος, καὶ δεῖ ὥσπερ ψῆφόν τινα τίθεσθαι τὸ συμβαῖνον. οὐ γὰρ ἔστιν ἄνωθεν βαλεῖν οὐδὲ ἀναθέσθαι τὴν ψῆφον. Common elements include the metaphorical comparison of life to a board game, and the warning that it is impossible to revoke (ἀναθέσθαι) one's life like a move in such a game. But the fragment of "Socrates" is explicit on a point that is at best implied in F52 as it stands: the necessity of making the best possible use of the life one has. (For τίθεσθαι τὸ συμβαῖνον = "make the best move the throw of the dice permits" cf. LSJ, s.v. τίθημι A.III.2; Aeschylus, *Agamemnon* 32 with Fraenkel [1950], 2.20–21; Plato, *Gorgias* 499C with Dodds [1959], 317, *Republic* 604C; etc.) Nevertheless, this was almost certainly Antiphon's point as well, so the two passages are after all quite close. In the circumstances, however, it does not seem possible to say anything more specific about the relationship (if any) between the two. (For a different view on this subject cf. Altwegg [1908], 88; Untersteiner [1962], 131.)

1–2 ἀναθέσθαι ... τὸν βίον: ἀναθέσθαι means "revoke," "take back" one's life, like a bad move in a board game. Cf. LSJ, s.v. ἀνατίθημι B.II.2; Plato, *Gorgias* 462A with Dodds (1959), 222; *Phaedo* 87A with Burnet (1911), 85; Xenophon, *Memorabilia* 1.2.44; [Plato], *Hipparchus* 229E; Lucian, *Pseudologistes* 29; Dümmler (1889), 172; Diels (1922), 2.301 n. (who ascribes this interpretation to Guillaume Budé); Altwegg (1908), 14–15; Mewaldt (1929), 80 n. 18. Wilamowitz (1893), 1.173 n. 77 interpreted the metaphor differently, as "play a rematch" ("man kann es [*sc.* das Leben] nicht noch einmal leben wie nach einer verlornen eine Revanche-Partie spielen"). Similarly Gomperz (1901), 435 = (1922), 361. Against this interpretation cf. Diels (1922), 2.301 note. Perhaps these commentators were misled by the wording of Harpocration's explanation (ἀντὶ τοῦ ἄνωθεν βιῶναι μετανοήσαντας ἐπὶ τῷ προτέρῳ βίῳ).

F53

This fragment is quoted by Stobaeus in his chapter on "wrongdoing" (ἀδικία), which deals also with the vices of πλεονεξία and φιλαργυρία. The fragment seems in fact to be concerned with greed. Antiphon adopts a patently critical attitude towards the persons described here, who take pleasure (of a sort) in work and the mere accumulation of possessions, but are pained at their use. The fragment should be connected with F53A and F54, which likewise concern the failure to make proper use of material possessions. Cf. Croiset (1883), 151; Altwegg (1908), 17; Jacoby (1908), 26–27. It also fits squarely within the larger theme of making a right use of life in general (cf. F52 with commentary; Introduction, section IV).

1–2 οἱ δὲ ... ἥδονται: as the position of μέν shows, ἐργαζόμενοι, φειδόμενοι, ταλαιπωροῦντες, and προστιθέντες are supplementary participles with ἥδονται, not attributive participles with οἱ δέ (as Untersteiner [1962], 133 translates). Cf. Morrison (1972), 226. οἱ δέ can be interpreted as "others," suggesting the possibility of a preceding μέν-clause which mentioned people whose behavior was different from that portrayed here (cf. Kranz, *FVS* 2.361). Alternatively (as David Sedley suggests to me), it could mean simply "but they."

2 προστιθέντες: cf. Aristotle, *Rhetoric* 1359b28–29: πρὸς τὰ ὑπάρχοντα προστιθέντες πλουσιώτεροι γίγνονται.

οἷα δὴ κτλ.: δή is ironic and contemptuous. Cf. Denniston (1954), 220.

3–4 ὥσπερ ἀπὸ τῶν σαρκῶν: cf. [Plutarch], fr. inc. 119: σφαγή ἐστι τοῦ φιλαργύρου ἡ πρὸς τὸ κέρδος ἐπιθυμία· ὅθεν ἡ τοῦ χρήματος ἀφαίρεσις ὥσπερ αἵματος ἐπιφέρει τὸν θάνατον αὐτῷ.

F53A

This fragment seems to envisage a situation closely analogous to that in F53 (cf. Jacoby [1908], 26–27; Altwegg [1908], 16–17). As the subjects of that fragment are described as incapable of using and enjoying the material resources they labor to accumulate, so the subjects here are said to spend their time preparing for life but never actually living it, like people who are going to live another life. In fact, the two fragments may well describe the very same people. Stobaeus quotes this fragment in his chapter on φειδωλία, "frugality" or "cheapness," a quality which seems to belong to the greedy subjects of F53 as well. A closely parallel fragment of Democritus (*FVS* 68 B 227), which is quoted in the same chapter of Stobaeus as this fragment, points toward the same conclusion: οἱ δὲ φειδωλοὶ τὸν τῆς μελίσσης οἶτον ἔχουσιν ἐργαζόμενοι ὡς ἀεὶ βιωσόμενοι [βλισσόμενοι Bücheler]. In light of what has been said, it is clear that commentators who refer ἕτερόν τινα βίον to life after death and infer that Antiphon denied the existence of an afterlife completely mistake the meaning of the fragment. (So Dümmler [1889], 80, 172; Untersteiner [1962], 133–34, [1954], 243 n. 86 = [1967], 2.66 n. 86; Schmid [1940], 168 with n. 4, and others.) Cf. Jacoby (1908), 26–27; Altwegg (1908), 16. The sentiment expressed here was already a commonplace in the fifth century. In addition to the fragment quoted above, cf. Democritus, *FVS* 68 B 202, 224, and the description of Athenian πολυπραγμοσύνη in Thucydides, 1.70: καὶ ταῦτα μετὰ πόνων πάντα καὶ κινδύνων δι' ὅλου τοῦ αἰῶνος μοχθοῦσι, καὶ ἀπολαύουσιν ἐλάχιστα τῶν ὑπαρχόντων διὰ τὸ αἰεὶ κτᾶσθαι κτλ. (cited by Aly [1929], 170 n. 172). Later it became a particular favorite of Epicurus and his followers. Cf. Epicurus, frr. 490–491, 493; Cicero, *De finibus* 1.48.60; Lucretius, 3.957–58 with Heinze (1897), 180; Buresch (1886), 82–83; Bignone (1938), 86 n. 1; and especially the apparent imitation in Metrodorus, fr. 53: ἑτοιμάζονταί τινες διὰ βίου τὰ πρὸς τὸν βίον ⟨ὡς⟩ βιωσόμενοι μετὰ τὸ λεγόμενον ζῆν οὐ συνορῶντες ὡς πᾶσιν ἡμῖν θανάσιμον ἐγκέχυται τὸ τῆς γενέσεως φάρμακον (cf. Körte [1890], 56).

1 τὸν παρόντα . . . ἀλλά: for ἀλλά after a negative μέν-clause cf. Denniston (1954), 6–7.

2–3 ὡς . . . βιωσόμενοι: ὡς βιωσόμενοι does not express purpose or intention, but a simple comparison: "like people who are going to live a second [ἕτερον] life." Cf. Kühner–Gerth 2.90–91. The individuals in question do not deliberately prepare for another life. Rather, in their failure to make proper use of the (one) life they have at their disposal they behave like people who have a second life ahead of them. Cf. Altwegg (1908), 16. τινα (here as often) is contemptuous (cf. Plato, *Republic* 363D with Adam [1902], 1.79; Altwegg [1908], 16 n. 4).

3 ἐν τούτῳ: this phrase may have a temporal sense ("meanwhile"). Or τούτῳ could refer to the behavior described: "in doing this" (cf. F44(b)II.7 with commentary; LSJ, s.v. ἐν II.3).

παραλειπόμενος: this probably means "neglected" (like an opportunity). Cf. LSJ, s.v. παραλείπω III.2.

F54

This fragment records a fable about a greedy man (ὁ φιλάργυρος). Close analogues in the Aesopic corpus (cf. *Fabulae* 253.1–3, 2.72–74) suggest that Antiphon has largely taken over a traditional tale, with differences in minor details and one important modification (cf. Aly [1929], 75 and below).

Many commentators link this fragment with the alleged theme of civic concord (cf. Introduction, section IV), arguing that the moral of Antiphon's fable is that wealth should be used to help the needy. So Jacoby (1908), 12–14; Krämer (1915), 55–56; Bignone (1938), 84, 92–93; Aly (1929), 150; Nestle (1942), 383, 386; Untersteiner (1962), 134, (1954), 253 n. 167 = (1967), 2.77 n. 167. Cf. Democritus, *FVS* 68 B 255; Isocrates, *Areopagiticus* 31–35, a passage which Untersteiner (1962), 194–96 treats as a direct imitation of Antiphon (cf. Untersteiner [1954], 229 n. 18 = [1967], 2.46 n. 18; Jacoby [1908], 16–17; Bignone [1938], 92–95). But there is no reason to think that this passage of Isocrates has any connection with Antiphon (cf. Regenbogen [1940a], 100; Sinclair [1968], 72 n. 3). Höistad (1948), 109 contended that the fable concerns not civic concord, but rather the harmony of the individual with himself, psychic concord. But neither of the supposed parallels he cites in support of this interpretation (Plato, *Republic* 351E–352A; Chrysippus, fr. 625) has anything to do with psychic concord (cf. Untersteiner [1962], 135). Proponents of the civic-concord interpretation point for support to an innovation which Antiphon has evidently introduced into the traditional fable: the figure of the δανειζόμενος or man wanting to borrow money (cf. Aly [1929], 75). By showing how the greedy man might have furthered his own interests while simultaneously helping the δανειζόμενος, Antiphon (these interpreters claim) seeks to demonstrate how self-interest coincides with the interests of others, and thus how social harmony can be based on a community of interest and advantage. The text of the fragment, however, offers no support for such an interpretation. In the first place, the subject of concord or social harmony is nowhere mentioned or even implied (unlike in the passages of Democritus and Isocrates cited as parallels). Secondly, the emphasis in the story falls not on the benefit the greedy man might have conferred, but on the double loss he himself suffers. The figure of the δανειζόμενος is introduced primarily in order to exacerbate the misfortune of the greedy man, who by lending to the δανειζόμενος could have prevented the theft of his money while gaining interest into the bargain (ὃ ἂν αὐτῷ καὶ σῷον ἦν καὶ ἕτερον προσέφερεν). In addition, the irony and scorn directed at the greedy man are heightened through the narrative device of his "consolation" by the δανειζόμενος. (In the Aesopic fables, by contrast, the consolation is offered by an unidentified τις.)

It is much more plausible to interpret this fragment as a warning against the sort of excessive frugality (φειδωλία) or greed that prevents people from making proper use of their material possessions. So Altwegg (1908), 17–20; La Face (1969), 83–84; Sinko (1938), 180–81, who aptly compares Horace's use of the fable of Ummidius (*Satires* 1.1.95–100). This is the moral of the Aesopic versions of the fable, as their ἐπιμύθια make plain: ὁ μῦθος (λόγος) δηλοῖ, ὅτι οὐδέν (τὸ μηδέν) ἐστιν ἡ κτῆσις, ἐὰν μὴ (καὶ) ἡ χρῆσις παρῇ (προσῇ). (On the term ἐπιμύθιον cf. West [1978], 208.) Cf. Plato, *Euthydemus* 280C–D: δεῖ ἄρα ... μὴ μόνον κεκτῆσθαι τὰ τοιαῦτα ἀγαθὰ [*sc.* πλοῦτον and other goods] τὸν μέλλοντα εὐδαίμονα ἔσεσθαι, ἀλλὰ καὶ χρῆσθαι αὐτοῖς (cited by Jacoby [1908], 39–40). The same theme is attested elsewhere in Περὶ ὁμονοίας (cf. F53–53A, with commentary). The only apparent obstacle to this interpretation is offered by the final sentence of the fragment (ὅταν γὰρ ὁ θεὸς ... ἀπεστέρησεν). If (as Aly [1929], 75 contended) this sentence is functionally equivalent to the ἐπιμύθιον or moral of Aesopic fables, then the moral of Antiphon's story may be the rather different one that man's lot is at best a combination of the good (e.g. wealth) with the bad (e.g. lack of sense). This theme too is attested for Περὶ ὁμονοίας (cf. F49, ll. 11–13 with commentary). Jacoby (1908), 40; Sinko (1938), 181, and others, however, interpret the sentence differently. On their view, it expresses the need for good sense (καλῶς φρονεῖν) to be joined with riches. Sinko acutely drew attention to a parallel thought in Demosthenes, *or.* 23.113: δυοῖν ἀγαθοῖν ὄντοιν πᾶσιν ἀνθρώποις, τοῦ μὲν ἡγουμένου καὶ μεγίστου πάντων, τοῦ εὐτυχεῖν, τοῦ δὲ ἐλάττονος μὲν τούτου, τῶν δὲ ἄλλων μεγίστου, τοῦ καλῶς βουλεύεσθαι, οὐχ ἅμα ἡ κτῆσις παραγίγνεται τοῖς ἀνθρώποις, οὐδὲ ἔχει τῶν εὖ πραττόντων οὐδεὶς ὅρον οὐδὲ τελευτὴν τῆς τοῦ πλεονεκτεῖν ἐπιθυμίας. In light of this passage, it seems probable that the narrator's final reflection on wealth and good sense concerned the danger of greed rather than the mixture of good and evil in human life.

1 ὡς ἄρα: ἄρα could denote realization of the truth of the story presented here (so Denniston [1954], 39). But more likely it is an instance of the so-called referential use (not recognized by Denniston). Cf. Archilochus, fr. 174 (αἶνός τις ἀνθρώπων ὅδε, ὡς ἆρ' ἀλώπηξ καἰετὸς ξυνεωνίην ἔμειξαν); Pindar, *Nem.* 9.6 (ἔστι δέ τις λόγος ἀνθρώπων κτλ.); de Vries (1969), 100, with references.

ἀνὴρ ἄνδρα: for the figure of speech (*parechesis*) cf. Jacoby (1908), 59; Kühner–Gerth 2.602.

1–2 ἀργύριον ἀναιρούμενον: ἀναιρεῖσθαι is the *vox propria* for removal of buried treasure. Cf. Plato, *Laws* 913A–D with the Solonic law quoted there (ἃ μὴ κατέθου, μὴ ἀνέλῃ); Aesop, *Fabulae* 253.1–3 (2.72–73: τὸ χρυσίον (τὸν βῶλον) ἀνείλετο). For the practice of burying money cf. Aristophanes, *Birds* 599–602; Horace, *Satires* 1.1.41–42; Dover (1974), 175. It is unclear whether the greedy man removes his own treasure (for subsequent burial elsewhere) or that of another. The Aesopic fables fail to shed light on the question, since they begin somewhat differently, with the greedy man converting all his possessions into a lump of gold which he then buries. Cf. e.g. *Fabulae* 253.1 (2.72: φιλάργυρός τις τὴν οὐσίαν ἐξαργυρισάμενος βῶλον χρυσοῦν ὠνήσατο καὶ τοῦτον πρὸ τοῦ τείχους κατορύξας κτλ.).

2 πολὺ ἐδεῖτό . . . τόκῳ: on the figure of the δανειζόμενος cf. introductory note above.

4 ὅποι δή: "somewhere or other." Cf. Denniston (1954), 221–22, who notes the absence of this (probably colloquial) usage from "strict Attic composition."

4–5 καί τις . . . ὑφείλετο: in the Aesopic versions of the fable, the thief is a worker in the area where the money is buried (τῶν δὲ περὶ τὸν τόπον ἐργατῶν τις).

5–6 οὐχ εὕρισκε: for the force of the negated imperfect ("tried but could not find") cf. Gildersleeve (1900–11), 1.95.

6 περιαλγῶν οὖν κτλ.: in the Aesopic versions, the greedy man's reaction is more violent and melodramatic: he weeps (κλαίειν) or wails (θρηνεῖν) and pulls out his hair (τίλλειν/σπαράσσειν τὰς τρίχας).

7 οὐκ ἔχρησε: on χράω = "lend" (only in the aorist) cf. Redard (1953), 16, 37–39.

7–8 ὃ ἂν αὐτῷ . . . προσέφερεν: the relative ὅ refers to ἀργύριον, which must be supplied in thought as object of ἔχρησε in the preceding clause. προσφέρω in the sense of "bear interest" seems to be without an exact parallel; but cf. the sense "bring in," "yield" (LSJ, s.v. II; Xenophon, *Vectigalia* 4.15; Demosthenes, *or.* 27.9).

8 ἀπαντήσας δέ: Meineke's δή (adopted by Hense) would convey pathos. Cf. Denniston (1954), 214–16. But δέ is perfectly defensible as an instance of the type of δέ that sometimes follows participial clauses and is analogous to apodotic δέ. Cf. Denniston (1954), 181–82.

9 ἀπωλοφύρετο: cf. Aesop, *Fabulae* 253.2–3 (2.73): οὕτως ὀλοφυρόμενον (ὀλοφυρόμενον οὕτως).

10 ὅτι ἐξήμαρτε: this and the following ὅτι-clause represent indirect statement, dependent on a verb of speaking implied in ἀπωλοφύρετο. Cf. Kühner–Gerth 2.544, Anmerkung 1.

10–11 οὐ χαρισαμένῳ, ἀλλ' ἀχαριστήσαντι: this use of ἀχαριστέω is cited under Antiphon's name (but without a book-title) in Harpocration and derivative lexicographical sources (*Anecdota Graeca* 174 Bachmann; *Anecdota Graeca Oxoniensia* 2.491; *Suda* α 4675, 1.437). Other citations of the verb in lexicographical sources (Photius, *Lexicon* α 3428, 1.314; Hesychius, α 8828, 1.298; *Suda* α 4674, 1.437) refer to Plato, *Symposium* 186C rather than to Antiphon (cf. Theodoridis [1982–98], 1.314 n.). LSJ, s.v. interpret ἀχαριστέω here as "show ingratitude to," but the greedy man owes no gratitude to the δανειζόμενος. The sense is rather "disoblige," the opposite of χαρίζομαι = "oblige." (This is how LSJ translate the verb in *Symposium* 186C.) On the figure of style employed here cf. Kühner–Gerth 2.586; Jacoby (1908), 63; Aly (1929), 75; Fehling (1969), 252. As Jacoby noted, εἶναι καὶ μὴ ἀπολωλέναι (l. 13) is similar (cf. Fehling [1969], 272).

11 ὡς πάντως κτλ.: Blass' emendation ὡς is essential with the accusative absolute construction. Cf. Kühner–Gerth 2.95–96. πάντως means "at all events," "in any case."

12 ὁ δ' αὐτὸν ἐκέλευε κτλ.: the precise extent of the speech of the δανειζόμενος is disputed. Altwegg (1908), 18; Kranz (*FVS* 2.362); Untersteiner (1962), 137; Morrison (1972), 231, and others make it end at l. 15 (στέρεσθαι μηδενός). But the following sentence (introduced by γάρ) serves to clarify the remarks in ll. 14–15, and also echoes their vocabulary. (Cf. ἐχρήσατο μηδὲ χρήσεται with ἐχρῶ; ὄντος ἢ μὴ ὄντος αὐτῷ with ἦν σοι.) His speech probably extends through l. 17 (ἔλασσον βλάπτεται). In that case, the final sentence ὅταν γὰρ ὁ θεὸς κτλ. (ll. 17–20) will represent the comment of the narrator and the ἐπιμύθιον or moral of the fable. (Cf. introductory note above and commentary on ll. 17–20.)

μὴ φροντίζειν, ἀλλὰ νομίζειν: Jacoby (1908), 59 noted the homoeoteleuton and parisosis, and supposed Gorgianic influence. (Cf. e.g. *Helen* 9: καὶ νομίζω καὶ ὀνομάζω.) For a different view cf. Aly (1929), 75 and introductory note on F49.

14 Πάντως γὰρ οὐδ' κτλ.: πάντως οὐδ' = "not at all," "in no way."

For οὐδέ and μηδέ (l. 15) in corresponsion cf. Denniston (1954), 195–96. The abrupt transition here from indirect to direct speech is characteristic of the naive or simple style (λέξις εἰρομένη). Cf. *Iliad* 15.346ff.; Hecataeus of Miletus, *FGrHist* 1 T 20, F 30; [Hippocrates], *De natura pueri* 13.1; Plato, *Protagoras* 322C; [Longinus], *De sublimitate* 27; Kühner–Gerth 2.556–57; Jacoby (1908), 67; Norden (1913), 368, (1918), 1.38; Aly (1929), 75; Lonie (1981), 164.

15–16 μὴ ἐχρήσατο μηδὲ χρήσεται: for the figure cf. Fehling (1969), 265.

17 οὔτε πλέον . . . βλάπτεται: Antiphon means that the greedy man is not harmed by the loss of the money (since he made no use of it when he had it), and would be no better off if he still had it (since he would not use it anyway). Cf. Altwegg (1908), 18 n. 5; Aesop, *Fabulae* 253.3 (2.74): ἀθύμει· οὐδὲ γὰρ ἔχων τὸν χρυσὸν εἶχες. (For a different interpretation cf. Jacoby [1908], 12 n. 23.) But his manner of expression lacks clarity, and calls to mind the comments of Hermogenes, T2(a), ll. 30–32 (καὶ περιβάλλει δὲ χωρὶς εὐκρινείας· διὸ καὶ συγχεῖ τὸν λόγον καὶ ἔστιν ἀσαφὴς τὰ πολλά).

17–20 ὅταν γὰρ ὁ θεὸς . . . ἀπεστέρησεν: ὅταν . . . βούληται (Stobaeus, 3.16.30) is preferable to ὅτῳ . . . βούλεται (Stobaeus, 4.40.19), which was perhaps influenced by ὅτῳ γάρ in the preceding sentence (not quoted in 4.40.19). Joël (1893–1901), 2.655 and Altwegg (1908), 20, 85 interpreted this passage as a serious expression of Antiphon's theology (but cf. commentary on F49, ll. 17–18), while Luria (1929b), 246–47 condemned it as an obvious interpolation. Among other objections, Luria argued that it represents a second, and unwanted, ἐπιμύθιον or moral after ὅτῳ γάρ . . . βλάπτεται (ll. 15–17), and also that its sentiment ill suits a materialist like Antiphon who denied providence (cf. F12). But ὅτῳ γάρ . . . βλάπτεται probably belongs to the speech of the δανειζόμενος (cf. commentary on l. 12); and the theological language is no more to be taken seriously here than in F49, ll. 17–18 (cf. commentary ad loc.). The notion that wealth and poverty are divine gifts (rather than the merited result of human endeavor or the lack thereof) is a commonplace. Cf. Euripides, *Phoenissae* 555–57 (οὔτοι τὰ χρήματ' ἴδια κέκτηνται βροτοί,|τὰ τῶν θεῶν δ' ἔχοντες ἐπιμελούμεθα.|ὅταν δὲ χρῄζωσ', αὔτ' ἀφαιροῦνται πάλιν); Dover (1974), 174–75.

19 τοῦ φρονεῖν ⟨δὲ⟩ καλῶς πένητα: Sauppe's insertion of δέ is essential. Diels and Kranz in *FVS* and Untersteiner (1962) print τοῦ καλῶς φρονεῖν ⟨δὲ⟩. But this involves an improbable postponement of δέ. (Cf. Denniston [1954], 187–89.) In Stobaeus, 3.16.30, the manuscripts offer φρονεῖν καλῶς; in 4.40.19, καλῶς φρονεῖν. Hense in Wachsmuth and Hense (1884–1912), 3.489 n. plausibly suggested that the archetype had τοῦ φρονεῖν δὲ with καλῶς written above the line, which was subsequently inserted in different places. (Jacoby [1908], 40 n. 95 suggested less plausibly that καλῶς is an intrusive gloss which has pushed out δέ.) For the opposite metaphor of that here ("wealth of mind") cf. Hesiod, *Works and Days* 455 (ἀνὴρ φρένας ἀφνειός), likewise in the context of a contrast between intelligence and wealth. (For further parallels cf. West [1978], 273.) For the thought, Jacoby (1908), 40 compared Democritus, *FVS* 68 B 77: δόξα καὶ πλοῦτος ἄνευ ξυνέσιος οὐκ ἀσφαλέα κτήματα.

F55–57

Altwegg (1908), 40–45 contended that all three of these fragments (as well as F58, F59, and F67) derive from a discussion of appropriate and inappropriate forms of hesitation (ὀκνεῖν). Only F55, however, is explicitly ascribed to Περὶ ὁμονοίας. F57 also may belong to it; Altwegg (1908), 41 and Jacoby (1908), 28 suggested that both fragments refer to the same people. But the attribution of F56 to Περὶ ὁμονοίας was doubted even by Diels, who seems to have first suggested it (cf. *FVS* 2.363). Blass (1881), 146 printed F56 among his "fragmenta ambigua," while Sauppe (1850), 151 n. conjectured that it derives from a lost speech of Antiphon of Rhamnus.

F55

For ὀκνεῖν used absolutely in the sense of "shrink," "hesitate" cf. LSJ, s.v. II. The phrase οὐδὲν ἔργον ὀκνεῖν could mean "it is not difficult to hesitate" (cf. LSJ, s.v. ἔργον IV.1c; Plato, *Phaedrus* 269c). But more likely it means "there is no use in hesitating." So Altwegg (1908), 40 ("cum opus non esset"); cf. LSJ, s.v. ἔργον IV.1b. For the thought, cf. perhaps Sophocles, *Electra* 22: ἵν' οὐκέτ' ὀκνεῖν καιρός, ἀλλ' ἔργων ἀκμή.

F56

This fragment presents a number of textual difficulties. In the first place, the sentence as it stands appears to lack a main verb. Some would remedy this situation by restoring (or inserting) εἴη; but the ellipse seems tolerable. (Cf. Kühner–Gerth 1.41–42, Anmerkung 2(d).) Alternatively, εἴη *vel sim.* could be supplied in thought from the context (cf. Altwegg [1908], 40 n. 1). To govern the dative τοῖς κινδύνοις, Sauppe and Hermann wanted to insert a preposition (ἐπ' and ἐν, respectively). This also is unnecessary, since the dative can be governed by θρασύνεται. Cf. Aristophanes, *Clouds* 1349; Aeschylus, *Suppliants* 772. With the phrase τῇ γλώττῃ θρασύνεται cf. Sophocles, fr. 724.2 (οἱ δὲ τῇ γλώσσῃ θρασεῖς). Both ἐπείγειν and ὀκνεῖν have been emended to indicatives. The former, however, is easily construed with the articular infinitive τῷ θέλειν. The construction of the latter is more difficult. As the text stands, ὀκνεῖν is perhaps best taken as an epexegetic infinitive with κακός (but the word-order seems tortured).

The *Suda*'s claim that ὀκνεῖν here refers to fear (φοβεῖσθαι) rather than cowardice appears mistaken, since κακός almost certainly means "cowardly." (For a different view cf. Altwegg [1908], 41, 44.) For the *topos* that actions are superior to words cf. Democritus, *FVS* 68 B 55, 82 (κίβδηλοι καὶ ἀγαθοφανέες οἱ λόγῳ μὲν ἅπαντα, ἔργῳ δὲ οὐδὲν ἔρδοντες); Xenophon, *Memorabilia* 4.4.10; Cherniss (1977), 115 with n. 9. Since the idea is a commonplace, there is no need to see here an allusion to Aeschylus, *Septem* 556–57, as Schmid (1940), 159 n. 4 suggested.

F57

The words νόσος δειλοῖσιν ἑορτή can be scanned as a paroemiac. Their metrical form reveals them as a poetic quotation (Altwegg [1908], 41) or proverb (Diels, *FVS* 2.363 n.) or both, since the two are not mutually exclusive. (Cf. West [1978], 211, [1982], 198.) Bignone (1938), 195 n. 2 rejected this conclusion, on the grounds that Antiphon often employs poetic rhythms exclusive of quotations. But it seems inescapable. Kranz (*FVS* 2.363) translated δειλοῖσιν "Faulen" ("lazy," "idle"). Cf. Theocritus, *Idylls* 15.26 (ἀεργοῖς αἰὲν ἑορτά). δειλός is not otherwise attested in this sense, however, and should instead be given its ordinary meaning of "cowardly." (Cf. LSJ, s.v. I.) πρᾶξις can refer to military action or battle (cf. LSJ, s.v. IIIb); and ἐκπορεύομαι is frequent in military contexts (cf. LSJ, s.v.). Their collocation with δειλοῖσιν is suggestive; but they may just as well be used here in their ordinary, more general senses. For ἑορτή = "holiday" cf. LSJ, s.v.; Thucydides, 1.70; Theocritus, *Idylls* 15.26 (quoted above); Gow (1950), 2.275.

F58

This is the longest of the Stobaeus fragments after F49. Like its longer sibling, this fragment consists of an amalgam of familiar commonplaces. The main theme is provided by the ethical *topos* "the doer will suffer," for which cf. Hesiod, *Works and Days* 265–66 (οἷ τ' αὐτῷ κακὰ τεύχει ἀνὴρ ἄλλῳ κακὰ τεύχων, | ἡ δὲ κακὴ βουλὴ τῷ βουλεύσαντι κακίστη) with the parallels cited by West (1978), 222; Aeschylus, *Aga-*

memnon 1564 with Fraenkel (1950), 3.737, *Choephoroe* 313–14 with Blass (1906), 111; Bacchylides, 18.43–44 with Shorey (1907), 235 (Maehler [1997], 231–32 and others interpret differently); Sophocles, fr. 223b; etc. Joined to it are further commonplaces on the dangers of hope; the impossibility of undoing what has already been done; and the folly of submitting to momentary impulses (cf. commentary below). With the fragment as a whole Grossmann (1950), 120 n. 39 aptly compared Theognis, 585–88: πᾶσίν τοι κίνδυνος ἐπ' ἔργμασιν οὐδέ τις οἶδεν, | πῇ σχήσειν μέλλει πρήγματος ἀρχομένου. | ἀλλ' ὁ μὲν εὐδοκιμεῖν πειρώμενος οὐ προνοήσας | εἰς μεγάλην ἄτην καὶ χαλεπὴν ἔπεσεν. As far as its sententious subject-matter is concerned, this fragment closely resembles others ascribed to Περὶ ὁμονοίας. The style of the fragment, however, presents a different picture. The crabbed syntax and absence of poetic vocabulary and rhetorical ornament set it apart from the showy epideictic manner of fragments such as F49 and F60.

Many commentators have endeavored to interpret the fragment in terms of the supposed theme of civic concord. Cf. Jacoby (1908), 11–12, 14, 21; Mewaldt (1929), 81–82; Nestle (1942), 382; Schmid (1940), 164; Pohlenz (1966), 70; Untersteiner (1962), 140; La Face (1969), 79–80. (For interpretations in terms of "psychic" concord cf. commentary on F59.) Certainly it is not hard to imagine how a warning that aggression against others will rebound upon the aggressor might be made to serve a larger argument in support of civic concord on grounds of self-interest (rather than altruism). But neither the name nor the notion of concord occurs (even implicitly) in the text, and all attempts to interpret the fragment along these lines remain pure speculation (cf. Introduction, section IV). Other commentators suggest a connection with F55 and the theme of hesitation. Cf. Altwegg (1908), 40–47; Bignone (1938), 97 with n. 3; Nestle (1942), 396–97. On this view, the fragment deals with a type of situation where hesitation and delay are salutary and commendable, as F55 concerns misplaced hesitation. Bignone (1938), 96–97 even speculated that this sort of argument by contraries was characteristic of Περὶ ὁμονοίας as well as Περὶ ἀληθείας. For another suggestion about the place of the fragment in the argument of Περὶ ὁμονοίας cf. commentary on F61.

F58 is unique among the remains of Περὶ ὁμονοίας for the scope it offers for comparison with the papyrus fragments of Περὶ ἀληθείας. Even before the publication of the latter, commentators drew attention to this fragment's emphasis on self-interest and to the way in which the virtue of σωφροσύνη is commended not for its own sake nor out of regard for the interests of others, but purely on the basis of self-interest. Cf. Altwegg (1908), 46–47; Jacoby (1908), 11–12; Schmid (1940), 165;

Guthrie (1971a), 259–60. A similar emphasis on the advantage of the individual characterizes the argument of F44(a). (Cf. North [1966], 89–90; La Face [1969], 51–53.) The fragment's warning that wrongdoing rebounds on the wrongdoer recalls the cycle of injustice and hatred that in F44(c) is said to arise inevitably from testifying against another. (Cf. Pfister [1925], 204–5.) One possible difference appears from a comparison of F58 with F44(a)v.1–24. The latter passage argues that failure to take the initiative in aggression results in greater pain than is necessary and less pleasure than is possible. Here, however, aggression is said to result ultimately in harm to the aggressor. But since the larger contexts of these arguments are not known, the discrepancy should not be exaggerated. The hedonistic coloring of the aforesaid passage of Περὶ ἀληθείας (cf. commentary on F44(a)v.18–24) would find a close parallel in this fragment if commentators are correct in detecting here an anticipation or "germ" of the hedonistic calculus. Cf. Joël (1893–1901), 2.658; Gantar (1966), 155–56; Guthrie (1971a), 259–60; Plato, *Protagoras* 356D–357B. Such an interpretation could be supported by reference to Plato, *Phaedo* 68E–69A, where Socrates contends that the popular (εὐήθη) conception of σωφροσύνη as self-control involves an *implicit* calculus of pleasures (τί δέ; οἱ κόσμιοι αὐτῶν οὐ ταὐτὸν τοῦτο πεπόνθασιν, ἀκολασίᾳ τινὶ σώφρονές εἰσιν; ... φοβούμενοι γὰρ ἑτέρων ἡδονῶν στερηθῆναι καὶ ἐπιθυμοῦντες ἐκείνων, ἄλλων ἀπέχονται ὑπ' ἄλλων κρατούμενοι). Antiphon, however, does not say that the man who resists immediate pleasures (ταῖς παραχρῆμα ἡδοναῖς) does so for the sake of some greater pleasure to come; and it is perhaps a mistake to read this idea into his argument. Saunders (1977–78), 226–30 theorized that this fragment enunciates one of the simple empirical rules or maxims of conduct (γνῶμαι) which Antiphon argued in Περὶ ἀληθείας should replace the established laws of the city. Unlike the existing laws, Saunders explained, such rules would operate automatically and ineluctably – as the *lex talionis* is said here to do, and as nature is said to do in F44(a)II.3–23. Saunders' theory depends essentially on his notion that Antiphon wished to replace existing laws with better ones (cf. Saunders [1977–78], 227–28). But this notion is difficult or impossible to reconcile with the *ex-contrario* character of the argument in F44(a)v.25ff. (cf. commentary ad loc.). La Face (1969), 51–54, 76–77 contended that F58 exemplifies the ideal of natural justice Antiphon formulated in F44(c)I.12–15, an ideal rooted in "rationalistic hedonism" rather than altruism. The latter fragment, however, almost certainly does not present Antiphon's own ideal of justice (cf. introductory note on F44(c)). Saunders (1977–78), 228; Aly (1929), 137, and Untersteiner (1962), 141–42 would read into this fragment the idea that wrongdoing is "naturally unjust" (ἄδικον φύσει) because inevitably punished. But nothing of the kind is either stated or implied in the fragment, which (like others attributed to Περὶ ὁμονοίας) never even mentions "nature" (φύσις).

1–3 ὅστις δὲ . . . σωφρονέστερος: the comparative relates the man who hesitates to one who does not think twice about harming others (ὅστις δὲ δράσειν κτλ.: ll. 6–7ff.). Cf. Altwegg (1908), 43. σωφρονέστερος and σωφρονεῖ (l. 8) refer to the virtue of σωφροσύνη in its common denotation of "prudence," "good sense," which involves a sober assessment of precedents as well as possible consequences of actions. Cf. North (1966), 89; Dover (1974), 122. On the possibility of treating σωφροσύνη as a so-called negative virtue denoting abstention from wrongdoing cf. Dover (1974), 67–68.

1 ἰὼν ἐπί: ἔρχεσθαι ἐπί is common in the language of Attic law in the sense "bring a legal action against" (cf. Maetzner [1838], 228); the expression may have originated in a military metaphor (cf. LSJ, s.v. ἔρχομαι B.8; Thucydides, 2.11; etc.). Here the meaning is more general: "go against," "attack."

τὸν πλησίον: "another," as opposed to oneself; τοὺς πέλας (ll. 7, 10) has the same sense. Cf. LSJ, s.vv. πλησίος II.2, πέλας II; Antiphon of Rhamnus, *or.* 1.28; Democritus, *FVS* 68 B 293; Euripides, *Hippolytus* 441 with Barrett (1964), 239, *Heracles* 192 with Wilamowitz (1895), 2.52.

2–3 μὴ ἃ θέλει . . . ἀπενέγκηται: on the highly artificial word-order cf. Jacoby (1908), 60. For μή negating the indicative θέλει cf. Kühner–Gerth 2.185. Stenzel (1924), 41 (fancifully) read into this passage the Socratic doctrine that no one errs willingly.

3 ἐν ᾧ γὰρ δειμαίνει κτλ.: the stylistic device of repeating key words or phrases (δειμαίνει; μέλλει; ἐν ᾧ; ἐλπίδες; αὐτὸς ἑαυτόν; θέλει) at short intervals is employed throughout this fragment. Cf. Jacoby (1908), 61–62, who cites parallels from Melissus and Anaxagoras.

4–5 ἀπέστρεψε . . . θελημάτων: ἀπέστρεψε is a gnomic aorist; for the sense "dissuade from" cf. LSJ, s.v. ἀποστρέφω I.3. θέλημα is common in the Septuagint and in Christian Greek, but in literature of the classical period seems to appear only here and in Aeneas Tacticus, *Poliorcetica* 18.19 (cf. LSJ, s.v.; on the date of Aeneas cf. Whitehead [1990], 6–10).

5–6 καὶ ἐν μὲν τῷ . . . ⟨μὴ⟩ γενέσθαι: Bignone (1938), 82 n. 5, 213 n. 4 defended the transmitted text, supplying τὸ ἀποστρέψαι τὸν νοῦν as subject of οὐκ ἔνεστιν and ἐνδέχεται γενέσθαι: "in the having-happened, averting the mind from its intentions is not possible; but in the being-about-to-happen, averting the mind can happen." This interpretation is not impossible, but it seems better to insert ⟨μὴ⟩ with Bücheler and take ⟨μὴ⟩ γενέσθαι as subject of οὐκ ἔνεστιν and ἐνδέχεται: "in the having-happened, not-happening is not possible; but in the being-about-to-happen, not-happening is possible." For the *topos* "what has been done cannot be undone" cf. Theognis, 583–84; Agathon, fr. 5; Sophocles, *Trachiniae* 742–43 with Jebb (1892), 113 and Davies (1991), 186; Kassel (1958), 91. Croiset (1883), 155–56 compared Antiphon of Rhamnus, *or.* 5.73 (~5.94): ἐν μὲν γὰρ τῷ ἐπισχεῖν ἔστι καὶ τὰ δεινὰ ταῦτα ποιῆσαι ἃ οὗτοι κελεύουσιν· ἐν δὲ τῷ παραχρῆμα οὐκ ἔστιν ἀρχὴν ὀρθῶς βουλεύεσθαι. But the context and application of the *topos* there are rather different.

6–8 ὅστις δὲ ... οὐ σωφρονεῖ: πείσεσθαι δ' οὔ, οὐ σωφρονεῖ, the text proposed long ago by Jacobs, turns out to be the reading of cod. S (cf. Hense in Wachsmuth and Hense [1884–1912], 3.LXXVII). For τοὺς πέλας cf. commentary on l. 1, and for the sense of σωφρονεῖ here cf. commentary on ll. 1–3.

8 ἐλπίδες ... ἀγαθόν: δέ here is equivalent to γάρ, a predominantly poetic usage. Cf. Denniston (1954), 169–70. πανταχοῦ = "in every case," "in all circumstances." For the neuter predicate (ἀγαθόν) in γνῶμαι cf. F60, l. 1 (πρῶτον ... ἐστὶ παίδευσις); Euripides, *Heracles* 1291–92 with Bond (1981), 389. The danger of hope is a familiar commonplace of Greek literature and thought. Cf. Hesiod, *Works and Days* 498–501 with West (1978), 169–70; Bacchylides, 3.75–76, 9.18 with Maehler (1982), 2.54, 155; Thucydides, 5.103 and other passages cited by Nestle (1942), 383 n. 51, 397 with n. 115. (Nestle's inference that Thucydides depends on Antiphon ignores the commonplace character of the sentiment.)

9 τοιαῦται: that is, hopes of harming others without suffering oneself (cf. ll. 6–7).

10 τοὺς πέλας: the dative τοῖς is defensible (cf. Kühner–Gerth 1.324, Anmerkung 6). But Meineke's emendation τοὺς is supported by the example of τὸν πλησίον (l. 1) and τοὺς πέλας (l. 7) above. The corruption may have arisen from a false construction with ἐδόκουν.

11–12 σωφροσύνην δὲ ... κρίνειεν: σωφροσύνη here is used in a different sense than σωφρονέστερος and σωφρονεῖ above, signifying "self-control" rather than "prudence." (Cf. further commentary on F59.) With the transmitted text (ἄλλος), this sentence is a statement about who can best judge σωφροσύνη. Despite Guthrie (1971a), 259 with n. 5 and Kranz (*FVS* 2.364), this sense does not really suit the context. (Cf. Jacoby [1908], 40 n. 95a.) Some commentators retain ἄλλος and extract the required sense by assuming a harsh and improbable brachyology (so Jacoby; Altwegg [1908], 42 n. 7; Untersteiner [1962], 142). The best emendation is ἄλλου, which gives excellent sense and is adopted by Diels and Kranz in *FVS* (but with an improbable translation by Kranz; cf. below) as well as by Mewaldt (1929), 82 n. 28. Diels and Kranz attribute this emendation to E. Jacoby; but as Mewaldt (1929), 82 n. 28 pointed out, it is not to be found in Jacoby (1908). Its source remains a mystery. κρίνω τί τινος signifies "judge something to belong to someone." Cf. Kühner–Gerth 1.374–75. The sentence as a whole means: "to no other man would one more correctly judge σωφροσύνη to belong than to the man who etc." So Mewaldt (1929), 82 n. 28. Kranz (*FVS* 2.364) translated: "Die Besonnenheit eines anderen Mannes kann doch wohl niemand richtiger beurteilen als wer usw." This is difficult to get from the Greek, and furthermore gives an unsatisfactory sense (cf. above). With ὀρθότερον Heinimann (1961), 127 n. 100 compared what he called the "pregnant" use of ὀρθῶς in Melissus, *FVS* 30 B 8; Anaxagoras, *FVS* 59 B 17, and Thrasymachus, *FVS* 85 B 1.

12 τοῦ θυμοῦ: "his heart." Cf. commentary on ll. 14–15.

12–13 ταῖς παραχρῆμα ἡδοναῖς: cf. Plato, *Protagoras* 353D (αὐτῆς τῆς ἡδονῆς τῆς παραχρῆμα), 355B (τὰς παραχρῆμα ἡδονάς), *Philebus* 21C (τῆς τ' ἐν τῷ παραχρῆμα ἡδονῆς); Xenophon, *Memorabilia* 2.1.20 (αἱ μὲν ῥαδιουργίαι καὶ ἐκ τοῦ παραχρῆμα ἡδοναί).

13 ἐμφράσσει αὐτὸς ἑαυτόν: Sauppe proposed to excise αὐτὸς ἑαυτόν here on the ground that it must be construed with κρατεῖν, with which it is superfluous (cf. αὐτὸς ἑαυτόν in l. 14). But clearly it goes rather with ἐμφράσσει; and the repetition of the phrase is in character. Cf. commentary on l. 3 above; Bignone (1938), 202–4, 206 n. 1, 209 with n. 4. Altwegg (1908), 42 n. 7 was rightly troubled by the construction here. The closest parallel seems to be Basil, *Homilia exhortatoria ad sanctum baptisma* 6 (31.437 Migne: εἷς ἐστιν ὁ κωλύων, ὁ ἐμφράσσων ἡμῖν τὰς εἰς σωτηρίαν ὁδούς). On the development of αὐτὸς ἑαυτόν (in which Gildersleeve [1900–11], 1.68 detected a note of "unnaturalness") and similar reflexive formulas in Greek cf. Gantar (1966), 151–63.

13–14 κρατεῖν ... αὐτὸς ἑαυτόν: τε joins ἐμφράσσει and ἠδυνήθη, while καί links κρατεῖν and νικᾶν (cf. Untersteiner [1962], 144). For juxtaposed τε καί not in corresponsion cf. Antiphon of Rhamnus, *or.* 2.β.12 (φιλοθύτην τε [τε N: δὲ A] καὶ νόμιμον ὄντα); Andocides, *or.* 1.108 (τὴν πόλιν ἀνάστατον παραλαβόντες ἱερά τε κατακεκαυμένα τείχη τε καὶ οἰκίας καταπεπτωκυίας), 3.7 (νεωσοίκους τε ᾠκοδομησάμεθα, χιλίους τε καὶ διακοσίους ἱππέας καὶ τοξότας τοσούτους ἑτέρους κατεστήσαμεν); Thucydides, 2.29 (εἰκός τε [τε CG: δὲ ABEFM] καὶ τὸ κῆδος Πανδίονα ξυνάψασθαι τῆς θυγατρὸς κτλ.). With the phraseology and thought here cf. Plato, *Laws* 626E: τὸ νικᾶν αὐτὸν αὑτὸν πασῶν νικῶν πρώτη τε καὶ ἀρίστη.

14–15 ὃς δὲ θέλει ... τῷ θυμῷ: as θέλει shows, θυμῷ refers to the "heart" as the seat of desires and passions (similarly τοῦ θυμοῦ in l. 12).

Cf. Heraclitus, *FVS* 22 B 85; Democritus, *FVS* 68 B 236; Diels (*FVS* I.VIII); Jacoby (1908), 50; Altwegg (1908), 47; Marcovich (1978), 269–71. Sauppe (1896), 522 wrongly interpreted it as "anger," and Stobaeus may have done the same (he quotes this fragment in his chapter on anger, ὀργή). For the phrase χαρίσασθαι τῷ θυμῷ cf. Antiphon of Rhamnus, *or.* 4.γ.2 (τῷ θυμῷ χαρίζεσθαι); Plutarch, *Sertorius* 18.11 (θυμῷ χαρίσασθαι); Sophocles, *Electra* 331; LSJ, s.v. χαρίζομαι I.2; Jacoby (1908), 50.

15 παραχρῆμα, θέλει: this punctuation (first proposed by Blass) obviates the need to alter the text. Cf. Diels, *FVS* 2.364 n.; Bignone (1938), 209 n. 4.

τὰ κακίω . . . ἀμεινόνων: choosing the worse instead of the better is a proverbial mark of stupidity. Cf. Jacoby (1908), 41, who refers to Philo, *De aeternitate mundi* 41 (6.60: οὐδὲ γὰρ γυνή, φασί, τοσσόνδε νόου ἐπιδεύεται ἐσθλοῦ, ὥστε χερείον' ἑλέσθαι ἀμεινοτέρων ⟨παρεόντων⟩) and Theognis, 21 (οὐδέ τις ἀλλάξει κάκιον τοὐσθλοῦ παρέοντος).

F59

This fragment is quoted in a different chapter of Stobaeus (the one on σωφροσύνη) than F58 (quoted in the chapter on ὀργή); but the similarity of subject-matter and style suggests that the two are closely related. (Compare the way in which a quotation from Plato, *Apology* 28A–B is divided between Stobaeus' chapter on courage, 3.7.50, and that on virtue, 3.1.124.) Whether (as Altwegg [1908], 43 suggested) this fragment was originally contiguous with F58, however, is uncertain.

Here as in the latter part of F58, σωφροσύνη is identified with self-control or mastery over passions and desires (cf. commentary on F58, ll. 11–12). This conception of the virtue was widespread in the later fifth and in the fourth centuries. Cf. Plato, *Symposium* 196C (εἶναι γὰρ ὁμολογεῖται σωφροσύνη τὸ κρατεῖν ἡδονῶν καὶ ἐπιθυμιῶν) with Bury (1932), 78, *Phaedo* 68C (οὐκοῦν καὶ ἡ σωφροσύνη, ἣν καὶ οἱ πολλοὶ ὀνομάζουσι σωφροσύνην, τὸ περὶ τὰς ἐπιθυμίας μὴ ἐπτοῆσθαι ἀλλ' ὀλιγώρως ἔχειν καὶ κοσμίως κτλ.), *Republic* 389E; Aristotle, *Rhetoric* 1366b13–15; Pohlenz (1966), 67–68; de Vries (1943); Larson (1951), 398 with n. 5; North (1966), 70, 89–91, and *passim*; Dover (1974), 119, 208. Starting from such a conception of σωφροσύνη, Antiphon infers that the virtue cannot exist without an object of desire over which control must be exercised. Cf. Plato, *Laws* 647C–D, especially 647D (σώφρων δὲ ἄρα τελέως ἔσται μὴ πολλαῖς ἡδοναῖς καὶ ἐπιθυμίαις προτρεπούσαις ἀναισχυντεῖν καὶ ἀδικεῖν διαμεμαχημένος καὶ νενικηκὼς μετὰ λόγου καὶ ἔργου καὶ τέχνης ἔν τε παιδιαῖς καὶ ἐν σπουδαῖς, ἀλλ' ἀπαθὴς ὢν πάντων τῶν τοιούτων;); North (1966), 191; Wilamowitz (1959), 1.525 n. 1. The ethical significance of this straightforward point is greatly exaggerated by commentators such as Diels (1922), 2.303 n.; Bignone (1938), 80–81, 121; Stenzel (1924), 41; Altheim (1926), 269; Untersteiner (1962), 144–45, and Guthrie (1971a), 259 n. 3, some of whom speak of an "autonomous" doctrine of morality or justice in the fragment. (Justice is not even mentioned.) It is equally misguided to read into the fragment the notion of "psychic" concord, as Altwegg (1908), 59; Stenzel (1924), 41; Altheim (1926), 269 n. 2; Höistad (1948), 108–9; Untersteiner (1962), 144, (1954), 254 with n. 172 = (1967), 2.78 with n. 172; North (1966), 89, and others do. It is true that in the *Republic* Plato advances a conception of σωφροσύνη as a kind of concord with oneself, ὁμόνοια πρὸς ἑαυτόν (cf. *Republic* 430D–434C, 441C–444A). But this conception is based on an original and distinctive redefinition of σωφροσύνη as well as of justice, which there is every reason to think is Plato's own invention and no reason to ascribe to Antiphon (cf. Larson [1951]). Stenzel contended that F58 and F59 portray "psychic" concord as arising from the conflict of opposing wills (θελήματα). But this misrepresents the point at issue, which is not the reconciliation of conflicting desires but the mastery of potentially harmful ones. It is revealing in this context to compare these fragments with the passage from Iamblichus' *Epistle on Concord*, which is so often cited as evidence that Περὶ ὁμονοίας dealt with "psychic" concord (cf. Introduction, section IV). Iamblichus (Stobaeus, 2.33.15 = *FVS* 87 B 44a) defines "concord with oneself" exclusively in terms of *intellectual* constancy: ὑφ' ἑνὸς μὲν γάρ τις νοήματος καὶ μιᾶς γνώμης κυβερνώμενος ὁμονοεῖ πρὸς ἑαυτόν, διχογνωμονῶν δὲ πρὸς ἑαυτὸν καὶ ἀνόμοια λογιζόμενος διαστασιάζει· καὶ ὁ μὲν ἐπὶ τῆς ἀεὶ αὐτῆς ἐπιμένων διανοήσεως ὁμοφροσύνης ἐστὶ πλήρης· ὁ δὲ ἄστατος τοῖς λογισμοῖς καὶ ἄλλοτε ὑπ' ἄλλης δόξης φερόμενος ἀστάθμητός ἐστι καὶ πολέμιος πρὸς ἑαυτόν. This has little or nothing in common either with Antiphon's conception of σωφροσύνη as control over passions and desires or with Stenzel's theory of opposing θελήματα.

1–2 ὅστις δὲ . . . σώφρων: the similarity with the opening clause of F58 (ὅστις δὲ . . . σωφρονέστερος) is obvious. ἐπεθύμησε and ἥψατο are probably gnomic aorists; cf. F58, l. 4 (ἀπέστρεψε).

2 ἔσθ' ὅτου: Sauppe's ὅπου (adopted by Hense and Blass) is worse than unnecessary. Cf. Jacoby (1908), 28 n. 60; Diels (1922), 2.303 note. Sauppe's objection to the transmitted text ("neque tamen ea, quae quis concupiscit vel in quae incidit, superare debet, ut temperantiae laudem inveniat, sed seipsum animique cupiditatem vincere oportet," Sauppe [1896], 524) is adequately met by expressions such as κρείττων χρημάτων/γαστρός/κερδῶν. Cf. LSJ, s.v. κρείσσων III.

3 αὐτὸς ἑαυτόν: cf. commentary on F58, l. 13.

κόσμιον παρέχεται: cf. Lysias, *or.* 7.41 (κόσμιον δ' ἐμαυτὸν ... παρασχών); Isocrates, *or.* 18.18 (κόσμιον αὑτὸν παρέσχεν); Isaeus, fr. 30 (ἡγοῦμαι μεγίστην εἶναι τῶν λῃτουργιῶν τὸν καθ' ἡμέραν βίον κόσμιον καὶ σώφρονα παρέχειν); LSJ, s.v. παρέχω II.3. LSJ cite only the active voice of παρέχω in the sense "show oneself such and such." But cf. Gildersleeve (1900–11), 1.68 on the combination of the middle voice with a reflexive pronoun. κόσμιος and σώφρων are practically synonymous and often (as here) associated. Cf. Aristophanes, *Wealth* 563–64; Lysias, *or.* 21.19; Isocrates, *or.* 2.31, 3.38; Isaeus, fr. 30 (quoted above); Plato, *Charmides* 159B, *Gorgias* 504D, 506E–507A, 508A, *Phaedo* 68C, E, 114E, *Politicus* 309E, *Laws* 802E; [Plato], *Definitions* 414E; Aristotle, *Politics* 1277b21–23; Diogenes Laertius, 3.91; Untersteiner (1962), 145; North (1966), 94–95; Gantar (1966), 156 with nn. 81–82.

F60

On the attribution of this fragment, which concerns the importance of education, cf. commentary on F61. The fragment consists entirely of a string of commonplaces clothed in an elaborate style and diction and uninterrupted by even traces of discursive argument like those found in F49 and F58. The main theme and imagery are supplied by the topical comparison of education with agriculture. Cf. [Hippocrates], *Lex* 2 (ὁκοίη γὰρ τῶν ἐν τῇ γῇ φυομένων [ἡ] θεωρίη, τοιήδε καὶ τῆς ἰητρικῆς ἡ μάθησις. ἡ μὲν γὰρ φύσις ἡμέων, ὁκοῖον ἡ χώρη· τὰ δὲ δόγματα τῶν διδασκόντων, ὁκοῖον τὰ σπέρματα· ἡ δὲ παιδομαθίη, τὸ καθ' ὥρην αὐτὰ πεσεῖν εἰς τὴν ἄρουραν κτλ.); Protagoras, *FVS* 80 B 11; Shorey (1909), 189–90 = (1980), 1.6–7; Jacoby (1908), 45–46. The import of this imagery was misunderstood by Untersteiner (1962), 146–47, (1954), 254 with n. 178 = (1967), 2.79 with n. 178, who inferred from it that Antiphon championed nature in the age-old debate on the relative importance of nature and nurture, on which cf. Shorey (1909), 185–97 = (1980), 1.2–14. As Burkert (1964), 142 n. 7 shrewdly pointed out, however, Greek thought associated agriculture with the realm of human skill (τέχνη or νόμος) rather than the sphere of nature (as Untersteiner supposed). Cf. Sophocles, *Antigone* 336–41. Hence it is misguided to use the fragment's agricultural imagery as evidence that Antiphon championed nature against culture and (in the words of Mondolfo [1958], 655) "cerca sempre nella natura il suo modello e la sua norma." Jacoby (1908), 41 had drawn from the fragment precisely the opposite conclusion to that of Untersteiner on the relative merits of nature and nurture, and Luginbill (1997), 177 interpreted in similar fashion. Luginbill equated the young body (σῶμα) in which education is sown with φύσις and inferred that on Antiphon's view, nature can be altered for the better by education. Luginbill, Jacoby (1908), 46, and Bignone (1938), 95–96 all refer in this context to Democritus, *FVS* 68 B 33, where it is claimed that education remakes a man's nature (φυσιοποιεῖ; cf. Euenus, fr. 9). But φύσις is absent from the fragment (as from all the remains of Περὶ ὁμονοίας), and it is very doubtful whether the concept of nature should be imported into the argument.

Altwegg (1908), 48–51 proposed to join this fragment with F61, F62, and F70 to form a disquisition on education within Περὶ ὁμονοίας. Aly (1929), 150 and Schmid (1940), 164 conjectured that the fragment belongs to the chronological examination of the successive stages of human life (cf. Introduction, section IV; F49, F51, F66, all with commentary). Unlike other fragments plausibly assigned to this theme, however, this one does not dwell on hardships or difficulties (of education, in this case) but instead is optimistic in tone. Other commentators attempt (without great success) to relate the fragment to the theme of civic concord. Its place in the argument of Περὶ ὁμονοίας remains uncertain. (Cf. further commentary on F61.)

1 πρῶτον: both the predicate πρῶτον and the subject παίδευσις are placed in positions of emphasis (cf. Altwegg [1908], 49).

οἶμαι: for the use of the first person cf. F29A, ll. 4–5 with commentary. For the qualification softening the categorical assertion (ἀπόφανσις, in the terminology of Hermogenes) cf. introductory note on T2(a).

τῶν ἐν ἀνθρώποις: for this phrase, which is often joined (as here) with a superlative adjective, cf. Plato, *Hippias maior* 301A; Demosthenes, *or.* 53.2; Antiphon of Rhamnus, *or.* 6.7. These and other parallels cited by Maetzner (1838), 252 show that the implications extracted from the phrase by Mewaldt (1929), 82 are imaginary.

1–3 ὅταν γάρ ... γίγνεσθαι: for the quasi-proverbial idea that a good beginning portends a good end cf. Sophocles, fr. 831 (ἔργου δὲ παντός, ἦν τις ἄρχηται καλῶς, | καὶ τὰς τελευτὰς εἰκός ἐσθ' οὕτως ἔχειν) with the comments of Shorey (1918), 98 = (1980), 1.184, (1909), 190 = (1980), 1.7; Pindar, *Pyth.* 1.34–35; Plato, *Republic* 377A–B (ὅτι ἀρχὴ παντὸς ἔργου μέγιστον ἄλλως τε καὶ νέῳ καὶ ἁπαλῷ ὁτῳοῦν), 453A (ἆρ' οὐχ οὕτως ἂν κάλλιστά τις ἀρχόμενος ὡς τὸ εἰκὸς καὶ κάλλιστα τελευτήσειεν). Antiphon's combination of this *topos* with agricultural imagery in the context of education finds a close parallel in Plato, *Laws* 765E: παντὸς γὰρ δὴ φυτοῦ ἡ πρώτη βλάστη καλῶς ὁρμηθεῖσα, πρὸς ἀρετὴν τῆς αὑτοῦ φύσεως κυριωτάτη τέλος ἐπιθεῖναι τὸ πρόσφορον, τῶν τε ἄλλων φυτῶν καὶ τῶν ζῴων ἡμέρων καὶ ἀγρίων [καὶ ἀνθρώπων] (for text and interpretation cf. England [1921], 1.587).

2 πράγματος κἂν ὁτουοῦν: for the elliptical use of ὁτιοῦν ("any matter, whatever it is") cf. Kühner–Gerth 2.410–11; for adverbial καί with an indefinite pronoun cf. Kühner–Gerth 2.254. Repetition of ἄν when it is joined with the subjunctive seems not to be found in post-Homeric Greek (cf. Kühner–Gerth 1.246, 248 Anmerkung 6). Therefore, either κἄν must be understood as purely formulaic, equivalent to a simple καί; or an ellipse must be assumed, with κἂν ὁτουοῦν standing for καὶ ὁτιοῦν ἂν ᾖ (cf. Kühner–Gerth 1.244–45).

2–3 τὴν ἀρχὴν ὀρθῶς ποιήσηται: for the periphrasis ἀρχὴν ποιεῖσθαι cf. Kühner–Gerth 1.106; Gildersleeve (1900–11), 1.69.

3 εἰκὸς ... γίγνεσθαι: for εἰκός cf. the passages from Pindar (ἐοικότα), Sophocles (εἰκός ἐσθ'), and Plato (ὡς τὸ εἰκός) cited in the commentary on ll. 1–3 above.

3–5 καὶ γὰρ τῇ γῇ ... προσδοκᾶν: καί here is correlative with the καί in l. 5 below, and the two sentences together form a paratactic comparison, introduced (here as often) by γάρ. Cf. Altwegg (1908), 49 n. 1; Davies (1991), 89. For the proverbial idea "as you sow, so shall you reap" cf. Hesiod, fr. 286.1 (εἰ κακά τις σπείραι, κακὰ κερδέα κ' ἀμήσειεν); Aristotle, *Rhetoric* 1406b9–10 = Gorgias, *FVS* 82 B 16 (σὺ δὲ ταῦτα αἰσχρῶς μὲν ἔσπειρας, κακῶς δὲ ἐθέρισας); Plato, *Phaedrus* 260C–D with the proverb quoted by Hermias, *In Phaedrum* 220 (ὁ κακὰ σπείρων κακὰ θερίζοι); 2 *Epistula ad Corinthios* 9.6. Both ἐναρόω and ἔκφορα in the peculiar sense of "produce" are attested only here in extant literature. Cf. LSJ, s.vv. They were perhaps coined by Antiphon (so Altwegg [1908], 49 n. 2; cf. Jacoby [1908], 52, 54).

5 καὶ ἐν νέῳ σώματι κτλ.: this sentence forms the second half of the paratactic comparison (cf. commentary on ll. 3–5). For the importance of early education cf. Protagoras, *FVS* 80 B 3 (ἀπὸ νεότητος δὲ ἀρξαμένους δεῖ μανθάνειν); Democritus, *FVS* 68 B 183 (ἔστι που νέων ξύνεσις καὶ γερόντων ἀξυνεσίη· χρόνος γὰρ οὐ διδάσκει φρονεῖν, ἀλλ' ὡραίη τροφὴ καὶ φύσις); Anonymus Iamblichi, 2.1 (αὐτίκα δεῖ νέον τε ἄρξασθαι); [Hippocrates], *Lex* 2 (παιδομαθίη); Shorey (1909), 189 = (1980), 1.6.

6 τὴν παίδευσιν γενναίαν: γενναῖος here is synonymous with ἀγαθός, "good." Cf. Altwegg (1908), 49; Dover (1974), 95.

ζῇ τοῦτο καὶ θάλλει: τοῦτο refers neither to νέῳ σώματι nor (as LSJ, s.v. θάλλω 2 supposed) to παίδευσις, but rather to the end-product (corresponding to τὰ ἔκφορα in the comparison) that results from a good education implanted in a young person. (Similarly αὐτό in l. 7 below.) Cf. Kühner–Gerth 1.35, Anmerkung 1; Shorey (1916), 207 = (1980), 1.22. For the combination ζῇ καὶ θάλλει ("live and flourish") cf. Plato, *Symposium* 203E; Sophocles, *Trachiniae* 235 with Davies (1991),

107. θάλλει has special appropriateness here, in the context of the agricultural comparison.

7 διὰ παντὸς τοῦ βίου: cf. F51, l. 1 (πᾶς ὁ βίος), with commentary. For the lasting effects of education cf. Euripides, *Suppliants* 916–17 (ἃ δ' ἂν μάθῃ τις, ταῦτα σῴζεσθαι φιλεῖ | πρὸς γῆρας. οὕτω παῖδας εὖ παιδεύετε).

7–8 καὶ αὐτὸ οὔτε ὄμβρος οὔτε ἀνομβρία ἀφαιρεῖται: like ἐναρόσῃ in l. 6 above, these words are appropriate to plants rather than to human beings. As such, they exemplify the "fusion of the comparison and the thing compared" common in Greek poetry. Cf. Fraenkel (1950), 2.438; Davies (1991), 64, 91, with references. Jebb (1892), 27 and others detect in this passage a reminiscence of Sophocles, *Trachiniae* 145–46 (καί νιν οὐ θάλπος θεοῦ, | οὐδ' ὄμβρος, οὐδὲ πνευμάτων οὐδὲν κλονεῖ), while Bignone (1938), 200 with n. 1 thinks that Sophocles copied Antiphon. As Stinton (1985), 416 = (1990), 417 pointed out, however, the contexts of the two passages are quite different. Furthermore, the motif οὔτε ὄμβρος οὔτε ἀνομβρία is a *topos* borrowed from descriptions of the *locus amoenus*. (Cf. *Odyssey* 4.566, 6.43–44; Sophocles, *Trachiniae* 146; Davies [1991], 89, 91; Stinton [1985], 410, 416 = [1990], 411, 417.) For these reasons, any resemblance between the two passages is (as Stinton contended) most likely coincidental. Stinton (1985), 410 n. 32, 416 = (1990), 411 n. 32, 417 himself suggested that Antiphon and Sophocles both depend on a common model, in which the topic of child-rearing and the motif of the *locus amoenus* were joined. But Sophocles, *Ajax* 557 and other passages which Stinton cited in support of this contention are much closer to Sophocles than they are to Antiphon.

F61

The majority of commentators agree in assigning this fragment to Antiphon the sophist's Περὶ ὁμονοίας (cf. Introduction, section IV). Luria (1926b), (1928b), 235–36, however, argued that the commendation of obedience and disapproval of ἀναρχία expressed here are irreconcilable with the attitude towards law and obedience found in the papyrus fragments of Περὶ ἀληθείας. Luria therefore proposed to assign this fragment as well as F60 to Πολιτικός, which he followed Wilamowitz in identifying with Antiphon of Rhamnus' Ἀλκιβιάδου λοιδορίαι (cf. Introduction, section V). Luria conceived this work (differently from other commentators) as a theoretical treatise on education rather than a personal invective against Alcibiades; but this is not supported by the extant evidence for the work (exclusive of F60 and F61). Guthrie (1971a), 290 rightly pointed out against Luria's whole construct that disapproval of general social anarchy (if this is what F61 expresses) is by no means incompatible with the attitude that laws may be disregarded when it suits an individual's own interests. In any case, the discrepancy (perhaps more apparent than real) is hardly sufficient to cast doubt on the attribution of this fragment, which can be linked thematically with other fragments plausibly ascribed to Περὶ ὁμονοίας (cf. below).

Stobaeus quotes this fragment immediately after F60, and the two may originally have stood in close proximity. Both deal with education or training and stress the importance of making a good start. The two fragments begin with formally similar *sententiae* (cf. ἀναρχίας δ' οὐδὲν κάκιον ἀνθρώποις here with πρῶτον . . . ἐν ἀνθρώποις . . . παίδευσις in F60). But whereas Antiphon speaks of education or training (παίδευσις) in F60, here he speaks of habituation (εἴθιζον). (Altheim [1926], 269 inferred from this discrepancy that the fragment concerns the compulsion exercised by law, τὸ κελευόμενον ποιεῖν, to which Antiphon opposed education; but cf. below.) Despite the obvious similarities between this fragment and F60, it is nevertheless possible to conceive of a context other than that of education in which F61 would be at home. This would be a discussion of σωφροσύνη or κοσμιότης, one aspect of which is precisely obedience to authority. Cf. Plato, *Republic* 432A–B, 389D (σωφροσύνης δὲ ὡς πλήθει οὐ τὰ τοιάδε μέγιστα, ἀρχόντων μὲν ὑπηκόους εἶναι κτλ.); Democritus, *FVS* 68 B 47 (νόμῳ καὶ ἄρχοντι καὶ τῷ σοφωτέρῳ εἴκειν κόσμιον); Shorey (1892), 361 = (1980), 1.376. The fragment refers specifically to the training or habituation of children (ἀπὸ τῆς ἀρχῆς εἴθιζον τοὺς παῖδας), and young people in particular were notoriously regarded as lacking in σωφροσύνη. (Cf. Antiphon of Rhamnus, *or.* 4.γ.2, δ.2; Schwartz [1951], 55–56; Dover [1974], 102–3.) It is conceivable therefore that this fragment served as a bridge between a discussion about σωφροσύνη (cf. F58 and F59) and a (related) discussion on education (cf. F60; perhaps F62). Cf. Schmid (1940), 164. Many commentators propose to relate the fragment instead to the supposed theme of civic concord. So Wilamowitz (1893), 1.173 n. 77; Jacoby (1908), 19; Krämer (1915), 55; Momigliano (1969), 141–42; Schmid (1940), 165; Ryffel (1949), 44; Untersteiner (1962), 148–49. In support of this interpretation one could refer to passages such as Xenophon, *Memorabilia* 4.4.16, where Socrates defines obedience to the laws as the goal of ὁμόνοια, and the similar definition of concord in [Plato], *Definitions* 413E (ὁμόνοια· ὁμοδοξία ἀρχόντων καὶ ἀρχομένων ὡς δεῖ ἄρχειν καὶ ἄρχεσθαι). But there is no evidence that Antiphon conceived of concord in this way; and the absence of any explicit mention of ὁμόνοια seems to present a decisive stumbling-block to the civic-concord interpretation. (Cf. further Altwegg [1908], 51–52, 57.)

1 ἀναρχίας ... ἀνθρώποις: cf. F60, l. 1 (πρῶτον ... ἐν ἀνθρώποις ... παίδευσις) and introductory note above. The precise sense of ἀναρχίας here is disputed. (Cf. Altwegg [1908], 51–52; Mewaldt [1929], 82 n. 30; Ryffel [1949], 44 n. 132; Sinclair [1968], 72–73; Untersteiner [1962], 148–49.) Most likely it encompasses the political as well as the personal, "anarchy" as well as "disobedience." Altwegg (1908), 51 52 suggested an individual psychological reference, "animi affectuum voluptatumque effrenatam illam licentiam." Krämer (1915), 55 rejected this, on the (unconvincing) ground that ἀναρχία here must have the same sense as in Sophocles' *Antigone* (cf. below). But Altwegg's interpretation seems to gain support from the verb ἐκπλήσσοιντο, and perhaps also from the fragment's possible connection with the subject of σωφροσύνη (cf. introductory note above). Furthermore, this interpretation of ἀναρχίας is easily combined with the others mentioned above. Cf. Plato, *Republic* 560A–E, 575A–B; Plutarch, *De recta ratione audiendi* 37C (ἀναρχία μὲν γάρ, ἣν ἔνιοι τῶν νέων ἐλευθερίαν ἀπαιδευσίᾳ νομίζουσι, χαλεπωτέρους ἐκείνων τῶν ἐν παισὶ διδασκάλων καὶ παιδαγωγῶν δεσπότας ἐφίστησι τὰς ἐπιθυμίας ὥσπερ ἐκ δεσμῶν λυθείσας). Many commentators suppose that the words ἀναρχίας δ' οὐδὲν κάκιον ἀνθρώποις are copied from Sophocles, *Antigone* 672 (ἀναρχίας δὲ μεῖζον οὐκ ἔστιν κακόν). So Altwegg (1908), 76 with n. 3; Diels and Kranz (*FVS* 2.365 n.); Sinclair (1968), 72; Untersteiner (1962), 149. (Bignone [1938], 140 with n. 2 assumed the reverse relationship.) But the words have a proverbial ring (cf. Iamblichus, *De vita Pythagorica* 175, *FVS* 1.469 = Stobaeus, 4.1.40, *FVS* 1.469: καθόλου δὲ ᾤοντο δεῖν ὑπολαμβάνειν μηδὲν εἶναι μεῖζον κακὸν ἀναρχίας), and may represent a pre-existing γνώμη utilized independently by Sophocles and Antiphon.

ταῦτα γινώσκοντες: ταῦτα may refer to recognition of the evil of anarchy, or to some other point now lost. The spelling γιν- is attested also in F65, l. 2 (γινώσκουσιν), while F1, ll. 6, 7 (from Περὶ ἀληθείας) offer γιγν- (γιγνώσκει, γιγνώσκων).

2 οἱ πρόσθεν ἄνθρωποι: Altheim (1926), 269 inferred from this phrase that Antiphon contrasted an old morality based on legal observance with a new ethics in which the external compulsion of νόμος was replaced by the moral autonomy of the individual with his σωφροσύνη (cf. F58). But as Luria (1926b), 343 n. 2 rightly pointed out, ἀναρχίας κτλ. is a general statement, the validity of which is not restricted to the past.

ἀπὸ τῆς ἀρχῆς: for this phrase cf. Demosthenes, *or.* 18.179, 57.56; Plutarch, *Marius* 3.5, *Quomodo adulator* 51D, *De Alexandri magni fortuna* 334C. Meineke's emendation ἀπὸ τῆς πρώτης is unnecessary, and spoils the probable pun on ἀρχή (cf. Diels, *FVS* 2.365 n.).

3–4 ἵνα μὴ ... ἐκπλήσσοιντο: most likely this means "ne aliter vivere (i.e. oboedire) coacti perturbarentur" (Altwegg [1908], 52, who also suggests other, less plausible interpretations).

F62

This fragment is quoted by Stobaeus immediately after F60 and F61, but without a lemma. Diels (in *FVS*) first printed it among the remains of Περὶ ὁμονοίας, and Untersteiner (1962) and others have accepted the attribution. Spengel, however, rewrote the fragment so as to produce iambic trimeters (οἵῳ τις ἂν τὸ πλεῖστον ἡμέρας συνῇ | τοιόνδ' ἀνάγκη καὐτὸν εἶναι τοὺς τρόπους), which he attributed to Menander (cf. Wachsmuth in Wachsmuth and Hense [1884–1912], 2.209 n.). But the thought expressed is a commonplace, which there is no real difficulty in attributing to Antiphon (so Wachsmuth; cf. Altwegg [1908], 50). Cf. Theognis, 35–36; Democritus, *FVS* 68 B 184; Euripides, frr. 609, 812.7–9; Jacoby (1908), 47; Nestle (1942), 384 n. 56; Guthrie (1971a), 250–51. The rhythmic character of the quotation tends to strengthen rather than weaken the case for attribution to Antiphon, since passages of a similar nature are found elsewhere in his works (cf. F44(a)1.20–23, F49, ll. 2–4, F57, all with commentary; Jacoby [1908], 65–66). If this fragment does in fact derive from Περὶ ὁμονοίας, it may have formed part of a discussion of education (so Untersteiner [1962], 150 and Morrison [1972], 227; cf. F60, F61) or friendship (so Jacoby [1908], 29; cf. F64, F65) or both (so Altwegg [1908], 50–51, 53).

1 ὅτῳ: Wachsmuth's emendation οἵῳ is adopted by Diels and Kranz in *FVS*, Untersteiner (1962), and others. It is unnecessary, however, since ὅτῳ is not uncommon even in prose. Cf. Antiphon of Rhamnus, *or.* 5.96; Thucydides, 1.36, 5.103, 6.86, 7.29; Lysias, *or.* 29.4, 32.18; Isocrates, *or.* 3.18, 16.39; Isaeus, *or.* 3.79, 9.29. And the correlation of ὅτῳ with τοιοῦτον (by brachyology) is unobjectionable. Cf. Euripides, fr. 812.9 (τοιοῦτός ἐστιν οἷσπερ ἥδεται ξυνών); Kühner–Gerth 2.413, Anmerkung 12. ὅτῳ is interpreted as masculine by Jacoby (1908), 47; Bignone (1938), 126; Kranz (*FVS* 2.365); Schmid (1940), 164 with n. 8; Untersteiner (1962), 150–51; Morrison (1972), 227, and others. Nestle (1942), 384 with n. 56 suggested that it might instead be neuter, comparing the famous fragment from Euripides' *Antiope* (fr. 183): ἐν τούτῳ ⟨γέ τοι⟩ | λαμπρός θ' ἕκαστος κἀπὶ τοῦτ' ἐπείγεται | νέμων τὸ πλεῖστον ἡμέρας τούτῳ μέρος, | ἵν' αὐτὸς αὑτοῦ τυγχάνει βέλτιστος ὤν (cf. Plato, *Gorgias* 484E–485A with Dodds [1959], 124, 273–74). Goebel (1910), 384 seems to interpret in this way, translating "denn wie das ist, womit usw." But the sense Nestle extracts from the Euripides fragment ("Der Umgang ist auch für die Bildung des Charakters von grösster Wichtigkeit") cannot be gotten from the Greek, and is contradicted by the interpretation put on the fragment in the *Gorgias* (where it is first quoted). Rightly interpreted, it offers no real parallel to F62 at all (*pace* Nestle as well as Dodds [1959], 274). ὅτῳ is almost certainly masculine.

F63

The meaning of this fragment is obscure. Untersteiner (1954), 254 with n. 170 = (1967), 2.78 with n. 170 proposed to give διάθεσιν here the same sense as it has in F24A of Περὶ ἀληθείας, "orderly arrangement" of the world (cf. commentary on F24A). This contradicts Harpocration's explanation and is completely unjustified. Both διάθεσις itself and διοίκησις (the term Harpocration uses to explain it) are employed in different senses in different contexts, however, and it remains uncertain exactly how Harpocration understood the fragment. In a rhetorical context, διάθεσις can refer to the disposition or arrangement of a discourse (cf. LSJ, s.v. 2; Plato, *Phaedrus* 236A). Perhaps it can also refer to the subject or theme. Cf. *Anecdota Graeca* s.v. διάθεσις λόγου (36 Bekker): ἀντὶ τοῦ ὑπόθεσις; LSJ, s.v. διάθεσις 2. Either of these senses would be appropriate here; the difficulty is that διοίκησις seems to be attested in neither. Altwegg (1908), 48 suggests other interpretations, but without more information about the context, the fragment is likely to remain opaque.

F64

This fragment is preserved in the florilegium called Φιλοσόφων λόγοι, edited by Schenkl (1888); in the *Excerpta Vindobonensia*, edited first by F. Ritschl and thereafter by Meineke in his edition of Stobaeus (Meineke [1855–57], 4.290–96); as well as in an unpublished florilegium preserved in cod. Vindobonensis theol. gr. 167. The fragment is attributed to "Antiphanes" in all the sources which offer a lemma, but this attribution can hardly be right. The ascription to Antiphon was first suggested (tentatively) by Meineke (1855–57), 4.L (who, however, left Ἀντιφάνους in his text). Sauppe (1896), 521 independently made the same suggestion, and proposed the attribution to Περὶ ὁμονοίας. Confusion of the names Antiphon and Antiphanes is common enough (cf. F9 and F51, with commentary). Furthermore, the subject-matter of the fragment, friendship, could support the attribution to Περὶ ὁμονοίας (cf. F65 with commentary). Nevertheless, the lemmata in the sources which preserve F64 are of doubtful reliability, particularly so in the case of this fragment (cf. Schenkl [1888], 3–4). The attribution to Antiphon, therefore, remains no more than a possibility. As another possibility, Meineke (1839–57), 3.160 suggested that Ἀντιφάνους could be a corruption of Ἀντισθένους (on the frequent confusion of these names cf. Meineke [1839–57], 1.317–18).

1–2 ἀναγκαῖαι . . . ἀναγκαιότεραι: Bignone (1938), 85 n. 2, (1940), 235 n. 3; Untersteiner (1962), 151–52; Guthrie (1971a), 289, and others interpret ἀναγκαῖος here in the ordinary sense of "necessary." But Altwegg (1908), 48 with n. 153; Nestle (1908), 572–73, (1942), 384; Gernet (1923), 183; Kranz (*FVS* 2.366); Morrison (1972), 231, and others propose to give it the (unparalleled) sense of "close," "strong," "intimate." ἀναγκαῖος can mean "related by blood" (cf. LSJ, s.v. II.5); but there seems to be no evidence for the sense postulated by these commentators. (The passages cited by Nestle [1908], 573 are irrelevant, as is F44(a)I.26–27, which Bignone [1938], 85 n. 2, Untersteiner [1962], 151–52, and others refer to in this context.)

F65

This fragment demonstrates that Antiphon dealt with the subject of friendship in Περὶ ὁμονοίας (to which it is attributed explicitly). F62 and F64, if they belong to Antiphon, could derive from the same context (cf. Altwegg [1908], 47–48, 53, and commentary ad locc.). Some commentators would relate this subject to the supposed theme of civic concord (so Croiset [1883], 152; Jacoby [1908], 29; Krämer [1915], 56). But cf. Introduction, section IV.

2 φίλους . . . ἑταίρους: φίλος implies a more intimate and longer-lasting relationship than ἑταῖρος, with which it is sometimes contrasted (so perhaps here). Cf. Untersteiner (1962), 152–53, with references.

3 θῶπας πλούτου καὶ τύχης κόλακας: θῶπας and κόλακας seem to be synonymous here. On the style, note the chiasmus.

F66

Despite Clement's reference to Ἀντιφῶν ὁ ῥήτωρ, this fragment is plausibly ascribed to the sophist Antiphon's Περὶ ὁμονοίας by Diels and Kranz in *FVS*; Altwegg (1908), 29 with n. 2; Jacoby (1908), 37 with n. 87; Untersteiner (1962), and others. Clement's reference is probably to be explained in terms of the tendency to cite anything included in the *corpus Antiphonteum* as Antiphon of Rhamnus' (cf. Introduction, section I). The fragment fits easily into the chronological review of the successive stages of human life and their attendant hardships. Cf. Introduction, section

IV; F49 and F51, with commentary; Buresch (1886), 79–80; Croiset (1883), 151; Jacoby (1908), 37; Altwegg (1908), 29; Nestle (1942), 383–84; Schmid (1940), 164 n. 1. For the (topical) comparison of care of the elderly with care of children cf. Teles, fr. v (Stobaeus, 4.34.7 = Hense [1909], 50: παρήκμασε καὶ ἔρχεται εἰς γῆρας· πάλιν παιδοτροφίαν ὑπομένει καὶ ἐπιποθεῖ τὴν νεότητα); Sophocles, fr. 487 (Πηλέα τὸν Αἰάκειον οἰκουρὸς μόνη | γεροντανωγῶ κἀναπαιδεύω πάλιν· | πάλιν γὰρ αὖθις παῖς ὁ γηράσκων ἀνήρ). This comparison, of course, is but a variation on the proverbial comparison of old men with children, for which cf. Sophocles, fr. 487 (quoted above); Cratinus, fr. 28; Theopompus, fr. 70; Aristophanes, *Clouds* 1417 with Dover (1968a), 260; Plato, *Laws* 646A; [Plato], *Epinomis* 974A with Tarán (1975), 212, 382; [Plato], *Axiochus* 367B; Kassel (1954), 41 = (1991), 37.

F67

Both ἀθεώρητος and ἀθέατος (with which it is glossed) have an active as well as a passive sense (cf. LSJ, s.vv.). LSJ, s.v. II and Morrison (1972), 232 interpret ἀθεώρητος here in the passive sense, "unseen." (Cf. Diodorus Siculus, *Bibliotheca* 1.31.4, 3.69.2; Heron, *Pneumatica* 2.17; [Aristotle], *De mundo* 399b22.) But Altwegg (1908), 41–42 and Untersteiner (1962), 153 take it in the active sense, "not having examined." (Cf. Aristotle, *De generatione et corruptione* 316a8; Plutarch, *De Pythiae oraculis* 405A.) Without knowledge of the context, it is impossible to decide between these alternatives. Antiphon's predilection for compounds in α-privative is attested also by F3–5, F10, F24, F43, F54 (ἀχαριστεῖν), F60 (ἀνομβρία), and F72.

F67A

ἀνδρεία in the sense of "manhood," "adulthood" seems to occur only here (cf. LSJ, s.v. III). Altwegg (1908), 29–30; Jacoby (1908), 37; Schmid (1940), 164 with n. 1; Untersteiner (1962), 154, and others would connect this fragment with the chronological review of the stages of human life (cf. Introduction, section IV; F49, F51, and F66, with commentary). This is possible, but quite uncertain.

F68

The explanation of αὐλιζόμενοι given in the lexicographical sources which preserve this fragment leaves some doubt about the sense in which Antiphon used the word. Altwegg (1908), 32 with n. 2 and Untersteiner (1962), 154–55 translate (respectively) "excubare," "bivaccanti," that is, encamp or lie out on night-watch. (Altwegg suggested that the fragment may be connected with F50, but this is very uncertain.) Both αὐλίζομαι and κοιμάομαι (with which it is glossed) can bear this sense. Cf. LSJ, s.vv.; Herodotus, 8.9; Thucydides, 4.13, 4.45; Aeschylus, *Agamemnon* 2 with Fraenkel (1950), 2.3; *Anecdota Graeca* s.v. αὐλίζεται (164 Bachmann: σημαίνει δὲ καὶ τὸ φυλάττει, παρεμβάλλει). But κοιμάομαι normally means "sleep," and if Harpocration had interpreted Antiphon's αὐλιζόμενοι in the sense suggested, he would probably not have chosen κοιμάομαι to explain it. αὐλιζόμενοι more likely means "pass the night," "sleep." For this sense cf. *Anecdota Graeca* s.v. αὐλίζεται (164 Bachmann): καὶ ἰδίως τὸ κοιμᾶται. Εὔπολίς [= fr. 347] φησιν· ἐγὼ δ' ἄδειπνος ἑσπέρας ηὐλιζόμην (similarly Photius, α 3173, 1.292; *Suda* α 4441, 1.414; Hesychius, α 8299, 1.280; Phrynichus, *Praeparatio sophistica* 10). Cf. further LSJ, s.v.; Herodotus, 9.37 (τὰς μὲν νύκτας πορευόμενος, τὰς δὲ ἡμέρας καταδύνων ἐς ὕλην καὶ αὐλιζόμενος); Xenophon, *Cyropaedia* 4.6.10 (ἢν αὔριον ἴῃς πρῴ, τῇ ἑτέρᾳ ἂν αὐλίζοιο παρ' ἡμῖν).

F69

It is clear from the Epitome of Harpocration and dependent sources that Antiphon used βαλβίς in the dative plural form βαλβῖσιν. βαλβίς literally signifies "starting-post," but here (as often) it is employed in the extended or metaphorical sense of "start," "beginning." Cf. LSJ, s.v.; Euripides, *Heracles* 867 with Bond (1981), 292, *Medea* 1245 with Page (1938), 166; Aristophanes, *Knights* 1159, *Wasps* 548. Altwegg (1908), 30 suggested that this fragment also belongs to the chronological review of the stages of human life (cf. Introduction, section IV; F49, F51, and F66, with commentary). This is possible, but very uncertain.

F70

This fragment (like F69) presents a metaphor from horses or racing. εὐήνιος signifies "obedient to the rein" (cf. LSJ, s.v.). Applied to human beings (as Harpocration implies it was here), the adjective denotes docility or tractability. Cf. LSJ, s.v.; Plato, *Laws* 730B, 880A; Plutarch, *De liberis educandis* 7F; Jacoby (1908), 56. The (superlative) form εὐηνιώτατα (which seems to occur elsewhere only in Plato, *Republic* 467E) may be an adjective or (as Untersteiner [1962], 155 translated) an adverb. Altwegg (1908), 50, 53 and Untersteiner (1962), 154–55 connect the fragment with the notion of natural gifts or endowments (*indoles*) and the subject of education (cf. F60, F61, and F62, with commentary). This is possible, but quite uncertain.

F71

The noun φήλωμα seems to be attested only here (cf. LSJ, s.v.). Its orthography is uncertain (cf. φῆλος, φηλόω, but also φιλήτης/φηλήτης). Cf. LSJ, s.v. φιλήτης with the Supplement; Chantraine (1964), 135; West (1978), 251; Verdenius (1985), 179. For similar formations in -μα cf. λύπημα, σκίρτημα (F49, ll. 16, 31); θέλημα (F58, l. 5); ἄμβλωμα (F38); Jacoby (1908), 51–52; Chantraine (1933), 175–90.

F72–77: ΠΟΛΙΤΙΚΟΣ

F72

ἀπειθαρχία is a rare word, which seems to occur elsewhere only in *Divisiones Aristoteleae* 41 = Aristotle, fr. 83 Gigon (ἡ δὲ ἐν τῷ πλήθει ἀταξία ἀπειθαρχία καλεῖται) and Cassius Dio, *Historiae Romanae* 14.17 (ὁ δὲ δὴ Ῥοῦφος οὐδὲ ἐν τῷ πρὶν ὀρθῶς φρονῶν τότε δὴ καὶ μᾶλλον ἐπεφύσητο, καὶ κατέχειν ἑαυτόν, ἅτε καὶ τῆς ἀπειθαρχίας ἆθλον τὴν πρὸς τὸν δικτάτορα ἰσομοιρίαν προσλαβών, οὐκ ἐδύνατο). Luria and Nestle, who identify Πολιτικός with Antiphon of Rhamnus' Ἀλκιβιάδου λοιδορίαι (cf. Introduction, section v and commentary on F61), refer this fragment to Alcibiades, who was notorious for the παρανομία of his lifestyle (cf. Thucydides, 6.15; Andocides, *or.* 4.10; Plutarch, *Alcibiades* 16). ἀπειθαρχία and παρανομία are not synonymous, however, and the identification is probably mistaken (cf. Introduction, section v). The context of this fragment remains totally uncertain.

F73

The sense of this fragment is reasonably clear, although its context is unknown and its opening words present a textual problem (see below). Commentators who identify Πολιτικός with Antiphon of Rhamnus' Ἀλκιβιάδου λοιδορίαι refer καταριστᾶν to Alcibiades, who they allege was mocked by comic poets for his habit of drinking early in the day (cf. Introduction, section v). It is far from certain, however, that the fragment refers to any specific individual; ὅτε δή τις (if correctly restored) does not indicate this. Again, though καταριστᾶν itself is quite rare (see below), other compound verbs in κατα- signifying "eat" are commonly used in the metaphorical sense of devouring or consuming property, possessions, etc. Cf. LSJ, s.vv. καταβιβρώσκω (τὰ ὄντα, Hyperides, fr. 249; τὰς οὐσίας, Hegesippus, fr. 1.30); κατεσθίω 2 (τὰ ὄντα, Demosthenes, *or.* 38.27; τὰ πατρῷα, Antiphanes, fr. 236; πατρῴαν οὐσίαν, Anaxippus, fr. 1.32); καταφαγεῖν 2 (κτήματα, *Odyssey* 3.315, etc.; τὴν πατρῴαν οὐσίαν, Aeschines, *or.* 1.96, quoted below); κατέδω (οἶκον, κτῆσιν, *Odyssey* 2.237–38, 19.534; οὐσίαν, Aeschines, *or.* 1.42). Cf. also Isaeus' splendid verb καθιπποτροφέω, "squander a fortune in keeping horses" (*or.* 5.43), which Michael Reeve calls to my attention. καταριστᾶν, then, is hardly so unusual that it must refer unambiguously to a specific individual. The only real reason for thinking that the fragment refers to Alcibiades is the theory (first advanced by Wilamowitz [1876], 295–98) that καταριστᾶν alludes to his habit of early drinking. Drinking is not mentioned or even implied in the fragment, however, and is imported into it only on the assumption that Alcibiades is the subject. Had Antiphon intended a reference to drinking, he could have expressed himself as (for example) Aeschines does in *or.* 1.96: ἐνταῦθα ἤδη ἐτράπετο ἐπὶ τὸ καταφαγεῖν τὴν πατρῴαν οὐσίαν. καὶ οὐ μόνον κατέφαγεν, ἀλλ' εἰ οἷόν τ' ἐστὶν εἰπεῖν, καὶ κατέπιεν (cf. 1.26 ὑπὸ μέθης; LSJ, s.v. καταπίνω II.3). The case for reading an allusion to Alcibiades into this fragment seems in the end to rest on circular reasoning.

2 ὅτε δή τις: text and interpretation are uncertain. ὅταν with an aorist or imperfect indicative is attested in Hellenistic Greek, especially in the Septuagint and the New Testament (cf. LSJ, s.v. 2); but ὅτ' ἄν (the reading of cod. A, the only manuscript) can hardly stand here. Among the various corrections proposed, both Kaibel's ὅτε δή (adopted by Diels and Kranz in *FVS* and Untersteiner [1962]) and Meineke's ὅτι δή (adopted by Wilamowitz and Blass [1881]) are paleographically plausible and restore sense, but with different nuances. With Meineke's proposal, δή would give ironic emphasis to the (presumably) causal ὅτι, implying "that the reason given is inadequate ... or is not the true reason" (Denniston [1954], 231). With Kaibel's text, δή can be taken either with the preceding ὅτε (perhaps with causal and/or contemptuous force; cf. Denniston [1954], 231–32) or with the following τις (= "a certain man," either expressing vagueness or concealing definiteness; cf. Denniston [1954], 212–13). Decision is difficult, but Kaibel's proposal is preferable as being closest to the paradosis.

ἢ τὰ τῶν φίλων: Miller's proposal καί (for τά) is unnecessary.

2–3 κατηρίστηκεν: καταριστᾶν seems to appear elsewhere only in com. adesp. fr. 615 (κατηριστημένα). Cf. introductory note above; καταμελεῖν (F76, ll. 2–3); and perhaps καθηδυπαθεῖν (F77, but the attribution is doubtful; cf. commentary ad loc.). In Antiphon's time, the meal called ἄριστον was taken at midday (cf. Aristophanes, *Birds* 1499, 1602 with Dunbar [1995], 419, 696), so καταριστᾶν means "have lunch" or "brunch." ὅτε with the perfect (as here) is rare; the sense may be temporal ("now that") or causal. Cf. Plato, *Laws* 956B with England (1921), 2.603.

F74

The context of this fragment is unknown. According to LSJ, s.v. II.2, εὐσύμβολος here means "readily contributing one's συμβολή." But this is incompatible with Harpocration's explanation. Nestle (1942), 388 and Untersteiner (1962), 156–57 interpret it as "good at reasoning" ("ein logischer Kopf," "abile nel ragionare"). This sense is otherwise unattested for εὐσύμβολος, although the related verb συμβάλλω can signify "conclude," "conjecture" (cf. LSJ, s.v. III.3). Untersteiner referred to Aeschylus, *Choephoroe* 170, but the adjective there has a passive sense. In light of F75, it is much more plausible to interpret εὐσύμβολος here as "good at calculating" (so Morrison [1972], 233). Cf. συμβάλλω = "compute" (LSJ, s.v. III.2).

F75

ἡμιολιασμός ("multiplication by one and one-half") seems to be attested only here. Cf. ἡμιόλιος, ἡμιολίζω and LSJ, s.vv. As Harpocration indicates, Antiphon used ἡμιολιασμός as well as διπλασιασμός ("doubling") in the context of calculation or arithmetic (ἐν τοῖς λογισμοῖς). Kranz (*FVS* 2.367) offered "in den Argumenten" as an alternative translation; but it is hard to see what ἡμιολιασμοῦ and διπλασιασμοῦ could mean in such a context. This fragment should probably be connected with F74.

F76

Wilamowitz and other commentators refer this fragment to Alcibiades, Goossens (1942) to Cimon (cf. Introduction, section V). Croiset (1883), 153 interpreted it more generally, as a description of the man fit to hold political office, who must not be such as to neglect his duties under the influence of alcohol. All attempts to identify an allusion to a specific individual here must reckon with the fact that accusations of φιλοποσία were common currency in ancient Greek literature. Cf. Herodotus, 2.174 (Amasis); Philostratus, *Vitae sophistarum* 507 (Aeschines); Plutarch, *Phocion* 20 (Phocus, son of Phocion); Diogenes Laertius, 9.110 (Timon of Phlius); and especially the lengthy catalog of φιλοπόται in Athenaeus, *Dipnosophistae* 10 433B–443C, which includes Nestor, Alcaeus, Ion of

Chios, Philip of Macedon, Alexander the Great, Dionysius the Younger, and many others. In an inversion typical of the genre, φιλοποσία is treated in comedy as a virtue (cf. Aristophanes, *Wasps* 77–80, *Frogs* 739–40, *Knights* 91–94; Alexis, fr. 285; Sommerstein [1983], 159; Arnott [1996], 780, with further parallels). Although the context is unknown, this fragment was very likely connected with F73.

1 Illi: that is, speakers of Greek.

2–3 τὰ πράγματα καταμελεῖν: verbs signifying "neglect" normally govern a genitive. But cf. Xenophon, *Hellenica* 6.2.39 (εἴτε ἀντιπάλους νομίζων, οὕτω θρασέως μήτε καταρρᾳθυμῶν μήτε καταμελῶν μηδὲν φαίνεσθαι [ἐβούλετο] κτλ.); Kühner–Gerth 1.366–67. LSJ, s.v. interpret καταμελέω here and in the Xenophon passage just quoted as "ruin by neglect," a sense which is possible here but very unlikely in Xenophon. τὰ πράγματα may refer to public affairs or politics (so Untersteiner [1962], 157; cf. Croiset [1883], 153) or to personal or business affairs ("seine Geschäfte," Kranz, *FVS* 2.367).

3 ὑπὸ οἴνου ἡσσώμενον: for this way of speaking cf. LSJ, s.v. ἡσσάομαι; Dover (1974), 208–9.

F77

Blass (1881), 139, 145 ascribed this fragment to the sophist Antiphon, and Diels printed it among the remains of Πολιτικός in *FVS*. Altwegg (1908), 16 with n. 5 and Croiset (1883), 151 connect it instead with F52 and F53A of Περὶ ὁμονοίας. Even Diels himself considered the attribution suspect, and Kranz (following Wilamowitz) rejected it (cf. *FVS* 2.367 n.).

F78–81B: DREAM-BOOK

F78

In *Onirocritica* 2.14, Artemidorus discusses the symbolic significance of dreams about cephalopods. Because of their ability to camouflage and conceal themselves (cf. Aristotle, *Historia animalium* 622a8–13; Athenaeus, *Dipnosophistae* 7 316F–317A), Artemidorus explains, cephalopods signify advantage, but only for criminals. For all others, they signify hindrances (because of their stickiness and ability to cling) and foretell slackness in business (because they lack bones). The cuttlefish (σηπία), however, presents an exception to this interpretative rule. Owing to its well-known ability to escape predators by secreting a dark, inky fluid (θολός; cf. Aristotle, *Historia animalium* 621b28–622a1; Athenaeus, *Dip-*

nosophistae 7 323D–E; Cicero, *De natura deorum* 2.127; Pease [1955–58], 2.877–78), the cuttlefish possesses an advantageous significance for people (not "pesci," as Untersteiner [1962], 159 translates) who are trying to run away. Evidently, Antiphon mentioned or discussed a dream involving the cuttlefish and pointed out its significance.

F79

In the first book of *De divinatione*, Quintus Cicero expounds the art of divination from the viewpoint of the Stoics, who staunchly defended it (cf. *De divinatione* 1.8ff.; Pease [1920–23], 20 with n. 91). In this fragment, the discussion passes to the subject of dreams. Chrysippus treated dream-divination in a one-volume work dedicated to the subject of dreams (cf. frr. 1196–1206), and perhaps also in his more general, two-volume work on divination (cf. frr. 1183, 1191, 1216; Cicero, *De divinatione* 1.6; Pease [1920–23], 60–61). Antipater of Tarsus discussed dreams in a two-volume work which probably concerned divination (cf. frr. 37–42; Pease [1920–23], 61). Both authors seem to have made use of Antiphon's dream-book (cf. F80(a) with commentary).

In *De divinatione* 1.116, Antiphon's name is betrayed as a gloss by the awkward double genitive construction. Moreover, Cicero is speaking here about dream-interpretation in general, not a specific type of interpretation practiced by a particular dream-interpreter. Cf. Pease (1920–23), 307. Luria (1927b), 460 n. 1 rejected the excision as arbitrary, but offered no argument to support his position. In any case, Luria's attempt to use this passage as evidence for an "artificial" school of dream-interpretation is completely unjustified. (Cf. Latte [1929], 160 with n. 5 = [1968], 223 with n. 5; Introduction, section VI; commentary on F80.) The same hand which inserted Antiphon's name may also have added the words *sunt enim ... poetarum*, which are likewise a gloss, derived from 1.34 (cf. Pease [1920–23], 153, 307).

F80

In *De divinatione* 2.144, Cicero reports two examples of Antiphon's art of dream-interpretation. His report is now supplemented by an important new fragment from Diogenes of Oenoanda's Epicurean inscription (fr. 24 = F80(b)), in which the second of the examples mentioned by Cicero happens to be discussed. These texts from Cicero and Diogenes provide our only substantial information about the contents of Antiphon's dream-book. Cicero reports the cases of two runners, each of whom received diametrically opposed interpretations of his dream, first from an unnamed dream-interpreter and subsequently from Antiphon.[8] In Cicero's account, it is not explicitly stated which interpretations ultimately proved correct, Antiphon's or those of the other, unnamed dream-interpreters. (Cicero's own scepticism towards dream-interpretation may have prevented him from identifying either as right.) But it is hard to avoid the impression that Antiphon's interpretations trump those of the unnamed interpreters. This impression is confirmed (at least for the case of the dream discussed there) by the Diogenes fragment, which shows that Antiphon's interpretation proved to be the correct one (cf. F80(b)III.6–8 with commentary).

Luria (1927b), 1052–53 and Untersteiner (1962), 160–61 interpret this fragment in the light of Luria's theory of two schools or varieties of dream-interpretation, the "natural" and the "artificial" (cf. Introduction, section VI). The explanations offered by the unnamed interpreters, which accord with the surface meanings of the dreams, are taken to be examples of the "natural" variety of dream-interpretation. The explanations offered by Antiphon, which reverse the obvious import of the dreams and depend on the interpreter's clever detection of subtle correspondences and analogies, are taken to exemplify the "artificial" variety. Untersteiner even seemed to believe that the juxtaposition of the opposing interpretations was the work of Cicero himself, who wished thereby to illuminate Antiphon's "artificial" method. (Luria's view on this point is not clear.) As Latte (1929), 160 = (1968), 223 rightly objected, however, Antiphon's interpretations are no more "artificial" than those of the unnamed interpreters (cf. Introduction, section VI). Furthermore, the new evidence from Diogenes demonstrates (if proof were needed) that the juxtaposition of the opposing interpretations antedates Cicero. It could go back to a common (perhaps Stoic) source shared by Cicero and Diogenes; but more likely it stems from Antiphon himself (cf. Introduction, section VI). In that case, the fragment provides support for the idea that Antiphon's dream-book presented opposing interpretations of the same dreams (cf. Introduction, section VI). If so, his purpose was probably not to construct antilogies or illustrate the relativity of all dream-interpretation (as some commentators have sug-

[8] Luria (1927b), 1053 and Untersteiner (1962), 160–61 ascribed to Antiphon the following example as well, that of the pregnant woman (*De divinatione* 2.145). But Antiphon's name is not mentioned (n.b. *at alter ... dixit*), and the example seems to recall a dream attributed to Philip of Macedon. Cf. Plutarch, *Alexander* 2; Tertullian, *De anima* 46.5; Pease (1920–23), 576; Del Corno (1969), 47.

gested), but rather to show off his own ingenuity (cf. Introduction, section VI).

F80(a)

Cicero's parenthetical remark about the books of Chrysippus and Antipater (*atque horum somniorum et talium plenus est Chrysippi liber, plenus Antipatri*) suggests that his knowledge of Antiphon's dream-book was not direct but mediated by a Stoic source. Cf. *De divinatione* 2.145 (*quae est ars coniectoris eludentis ingenio? an ea quae dixi et innumerabilia quae conlecta habent Stoici quicquam significant nisi acumen hominum ex similitudine aliqua coniecturam modo huc, modo illuc ducentium?*). The sceptical attitude toward the art of dream-interpretation manifested here reflects Cicero's rejection of Stoic doctrines on providence, fate, and divination.

2 consensumque naturae: an allusion to the Stoic doctrine of συμπάθεια. Cf. *De natura deorum* 3.28 (*estque in ea* [sc. *natura*] *iste quasi consensus, quam* συμπάθειαν *Graeci vocant*). On συμπάθεια and divination cf. *De divinatione* 2.33–35 = Posidonius, fr. 106; Kidd (1988), 1.423–25.

4 curru quadrigarum: Pease (1920–23), 57 referred to Artemidorus, *Onirocritica* 1.56 (ὥσπερ καὶ ἅρμα τέτρωρον, ὃ καὶ αὐτὸ τὰ μὲν ἄλλα ἐπίσης τῷ κέλητι σημαίνει [*sc.* ἀγαθόν], ἀθλητῶν δὲ τοῖς μὲν τὰ βαρέα ἀθλοῦσιν ἀγαθὸν ἂν εἴη καὶ νικηφόρον, εἰσελάσουσι γάρ· τοῖς δὲ τρέχουσιν ἧττον σημαίνει, οὐ γὰρ ἱκανοὺς εἶναι τοῖς ποσὶ τοῖς ἰδίοις χρῆσθαί φησι τὸ ὄναρ). Antiphon agrees with Artemidorus in assigning the dream an unfavorable meaning for runners.

8 horum . . . talium: Diels' proposal to insert *interpretationum* is misguided. Pease (1920–23), 574 rejected it on the ground that *talium* by itself can refer to "interpretations," or else because the books of Chrysippus and Antipater were not limited to the subject of dreams. But the words in question probably mean simply "these and such-like dreams."

9 Chrysippi . . . Antipatri: cf. F79 with commentary.

10 aquilam: on dreams involving eagles (though not the one related here) cf. Artemidorus, *Onirocritica* 2.20.

11 ista: there is no need to alter the text, since *ista* is easily interpreted as an ablative (cf. Pease [1920–23], 575).

12 huic eidem: the text here is uncertain, but the sense is not in doubt.

F80(b)

This new fragment from Diogenes of Oenoanda's Epicurean inscription was discovered in 1983 and first published by Smith (1984). The letter-size, upper-margin height, and other physical characteristics of the fragment show that it belongs to the treatise on physics (cf. Smith [1984], 45). Its exact context within that treatise, however, is uncertain. Sedley (*apud* Smith [1984], 45 n. 9) suggested an origin in the treatise's section on dreams (cf. frr. 9–10). But more likely it derives from the discussion of oracles and divination (cf. fr. 23). So Smith (1984), 45, (1993), 447, 464; Clay (1990), 2497. It is conceivable (though very unlikely) that frr. 52–53, which are usually assigned to the treatise on ethics, derive instead from the same context in the physics treatise as this fragment (cf. Smith [1984], 45–46, [1993], 501).

Diogenes here contests the validity of dream-divination against an unnamed philosophical opponent, who cited from Antiphon's dream-book the story of the runner and his dream about an eagle. (Cf. Cicero, *De divinatione* 2.144 = F80(a), ll. 7–14.) The subject of the verb φησίν in II.4, and hence the identity of the unnamed philosopher, is uncertain. Following Sedley and Sandbach, Smith (1984), 47–49, (1993), 465 contended that Diogenes' unnamed opponent is Democritus. According to Sedley (*apud* Smith [1984], 48–49), Diogenes here sets up a debate between a dialectician (διαλεκτικός) and a natural philosopher (φυσικός) who propounded a specious argument for the validity of dream-divination by citing the story of Antiphon and the runner. And from the Epicurean standpoint, Sedley pointed out, Democritus was the φυσικός or natural philosopher *par excellence.* In favor of this interpretation is the fact that Diogenes elsewhere attacks Democritus for his views on dreams (cf. frr. 9–10). (For Democritus' views cf. Sextus, *Adversus mathematicos* 9.19, and the passages from Cicero, *De divinatione* collected as *FVS* 68 A 137–38.) Moreover the alternative interpretation, that φυσικός refers to a Stoic philosopher, seems at first sight implausible (cf. Smith [1993], 465). Nevertheless, there are serious objections to identifying the unnamed philosopher as Democritus. One is chronological, and concerns the question of whether Antiphon's dream-book was sufficiently well known at such an early date for Democritus to have referred to it. This is not impossible (cf. Sedley *apud* Smith [1984], 48–49), but may be thought unlikely. Much more important is the fact that direct and extensive citation from Antiphon of the kind implied in Diogenes' report of the unnamed philosopher's argument would be quite exceptional by Presocratic standards, which favored indirect and allusive reference to the views of others. (Cf. Burkert [1964], 144.) Finally, it would be a remarkable coincidence if Diogenes reporting Democritus citing Antiphon just happened to recount the same dream-story as Cicero reporting a Stoic source citing Antiphon. It is surely much easier to suppose that Diogenes drew on the same (Stoic) source as Cicero, whether this was Chrysippus or Antipater or some other authority on dream-interpretation (cf. Clay [1990], 2497–98; Smith [1984], 47). As for the objection that Diogenes would not have referred to a Stoic with the epithet φυσικός, it is worth recalling that the Stoics' defense of divination was intimately connected with their doctrines on providence, fate, and causation – that is, their physical theory. (Cf. Diogenes Laertius, 7.148–49.) It is possible that the epithet φυσικός (if this is what Diogenes wrote) is somehow connected with the integral relationship in Stoic thought between divination and physics.

I

1 δ' ἐνταῦθα: ἐνταῦθα more likely refers forward than backward (so Sedley *apud* Smith [1984], 48). In that case, the "dialectician's argument" (διαλεκτικοῦ λόγοις) in support of divination includes the story cited from Antiphon.

1–2 φυσικός: Clay (1990), 2497–98 suggested that this refers to the "natural" variety of dream-interpretation. But the Greek for "natural" divination (*not* dream-interpretation; cf. introductory note above and Introduction, section VI) is ἄτεχνος, not φυσικός.

3 ἐπιχειρῶν: Smith (1984), 48 called attention to the slight space before this word, indicating a punctuation mark between λόγοις and ἐπιχειρῶν. The latter therefore governs the accusative τὴν ... μαντευτικήν. (Cf. LSJ, s.v. ἐπιχειρέω 3.)

6 αὐτοῖς: Smith (1984), 48 referred this pronoun to dreams (cf. ὀνείρων, ll. 4–5). With Sedley's supplement βεβαιῶν in l. 7, it would refer instead to the arguments (λόγοις) mentioned in l. 3.

II

4–5 ἀετὸν ... διώκειν: for δοκέω in reports of dreams cf. LSJ, s.v. I.1. The Greek here is ambiguous (cf. Smith [1984], 49, with the remarks of Sandbach quoted there). ἀετόν may be the subject of διώκειν ("he dreamed that an eagle was chasing him") or, less likely, the object ("he dreamed that he was chasing an eagle"). According to Cicero, however, the runner dreamed that he had *become* an eagle. The only way to get this sense from Diogenes' Greek is to understand "runner" (δρομεύς) as the implied subject (accusative) of διώκειν and construe ἀετόν as an appositive ("he dreamed that he, as an eagle, chased") – a harsh construction. The translation offered represents the easiest way to construe the Greek, but uncertainty remains.

III

6–8 δι' Ἀντιφῶντα παρέδειξεν: for παραδείκνυμι = "show up," "expose" cf. LSJ, s.v. 3; Plutarch, *Lysander* 30; Smith (1984), 49. If the verb is correctly interpreted here, it proves that Antiphon turned out to be right, and the other, unnamed dream-interpreter (αὐτόν) wrong. (This inference escaped Clay [1990], 2497.) On the significance of this cf. introductory note on F80 above and Introduction, section VI.

F81

Seneca here relates a witty remark of L. Iunius Gallio, the well-known orator and declaimer who was a close friend of the elder Seneca and his sons (the oldest of whom he adopted) as well as of the poet Ovid. (Cf. Ovid, *Epistulae ex Ponto* 4.11; Seneca, *Suasoriae* 3.7; Schanz and Hosius [1935], 349–50; Gerth [1918a]; Fairweather [1981], 277–79.) Gallio referred to the four-volume work on "colors" written by the orator Junius Otho as "books of Antiphon," because of all the dreams Otho included in it. (On Otho cf. Gerth [1918b]; Fairweather [1981], 167–70.) "Color" in this context refers to the interpretation or "spin" put upon the actions of the accused party in a lawsuit or judicial declamation – a usage which derives ultimately from Hermagoras of Temnos. (Cf. Fairweather [1981], 166–78; LSJ, s.v. χρῶμα IV.4.) In *Controversiae* 7.7.15, Seneca cites an example of such a "color" and refers to Otho as a *somniator.* Gallio's remark provides no new information about Antiphon's dream-book, but does illustrate his continuing fame as a dream-interpreter.

F81A

The pseudonymous treatise of "Melampus" from which this fragment derives dates from the Byzantine era. (Cf. Hopfner [1937], 2238; Krumbacher [1897], 630.) The treatise deals with the subject of τὸ παλμικόν (or παλμαστικόν or παλματικόν), divination by twitching, including involuntary movement of various parts of the body, ringing in the ears, and sneezing. (Cf. Bouché-Leclercq [1879–82], 1.160–65; Pease [1911].) Diels (*FVS* 2.368 n.) toyed with the idea that "Melampus" might transmit genuine information on Antiphon derived ultimately from Posidonius, who may have written on this subject (cf. fr. 113 with Kidd [1988], 1.441–42). As Diels himself admitted, however, it is much more likely that Antiphon's name here (like that of Phemonoe) is purely decorative. Cf. Fischer (1899), 3 n. 6; Del Corno (1969), 131–32. Antiphon's name is used similarly in T11(a) and F81B (cf. commentary ad locc.).

F81B

This text is not included in *FVS*. It was cited first by E. Oder (*apud* Susemihl [1891–92], 1.870 n. 173, in connection with Philochorus) and later by Luria (1927b), 1060, and was printed with the remains of the dream-book by Untersteiner (1962), 162–63 and Del Corno (1969), 47. Fulgentius' list of writers on dream-interpretation recalls the similar list in Tertullian, *De anima* 46.10 (= T12). Some commentators think that Fulgentius depends on Tertullian (cf. Waszink [1947], 49*, 495). As Del Corno (1969), 125 pointed out, however, the order of names in the lists is different. In addition, Fulgentius identifies Serapion (who is known only from these two lists) as being from Ascalon, while Tertullian does not.

Oder (*apud* Susemihl [1891–92], 1.870 n. 173) and Hopfner (1937), 2238 supposed that Philochorus derived the recipe for procuring true dreams mentioned here from Antiphon's dream-book. Luria even argued that the use of such magical means of manipulating dream-experience is perfectly consistent with the scientific or rational character of Antiphon's views on dreams as he understood them (cf. Untersteiner [1962], 163). As a learned scholar, professional diviner, and author of a work on divination (Περὶ μαντικῆς), Philochorus probably was acquainted with Antiphon's dream-book (cf. Jacoby, *FGrHist* IIIB 1.261, on 328 T 7). Nevertheless, the recipe in question (as Del Corno [1962], 348 n. 27 pointed out) has more in common with incubation practices than with dream-interpretation. And while the mantic properties of laurel are well known in ancient literature (cf. Parke and Wormell [1956], 26 with n. 34; Steier [1927], 1441–42), the specific use of it mentioned here is attested elsewhere only in the magical papyri (cf. Hopfner [1937], 2238). For these reasons, the attribution of the recipe to Antiphon (or even to Philochorus) is doubtful. Van Lieshout (1980), 227 suggested that Fulgentius' reference derives from the portrayal of Antiphon in comedy, but this is far-fetched. Most likely Antiphon's name here is purely decorative (cf. Del Corno [1969], 132 n. 7).

WORKS CITED

1. ABBREVIATIONS

AS	L. Radermacher, *Artium scriptores: Reste der voraristotelischen Rhetorik* (Sitzungsberichte der Österreichischen Akademie, Philos.-hist. Klasse 227.3), Vienna 1951
CAG	Commentaria in Aristotelem Graeca, Berlin 1882–1909
DSB	C. C. Gillispie et al. (eds.), *Dictionary of Scientific Biography*. 18 vols., New York 1970–90
FGrHist	F. Jacoby, *Die Fragmente der griechischen Historiker*, Berlin and Leiden 1923–58
FVS	H. Diels and W. Kranz, *Die Fragmente der Vorsokratiker*. 6th ed. 3 vols., Berlin 1951–52
GCS	Die griechischen christlichen Schriftsteller der ersten Jahrhunderte
Kühner–Blass	R. Kühner and F. Blass, *Ausführliche Grammatik der griechischen Sprache*, 1. Teil: *Formenlehre*. 3rd. ed. 2 vols., Hanover and Leipzig 1890–92
Kühner–Gerth	R. Kühner and B. Gerth, *Ausführliche Grammatik der griechischen Sprache*, 2. Teil: *Satzlehre*. 3rd ed. 2 vols., Hanover and Leipzig 1898–1904
Lampe	W. G. H. Lampe, *A Patristic Greek Lexicon*, Oxford 1961–68
LSJ	H. G. Liddell, R. Scott and H. S. Jones, *A Greek–English Lexicon*. With a revised Supplement, Oxford 1996
Migne	J. P. Migne (ed.), *Patrologiae cursus completus: Series Graeca*, Paris 1857–66
PA	J. Kirchner, *Prosopographia Attica*. 2 vols., Berlin 1901–3
PCG	R. Kassel and C. Austin, *Poetae comici Graeci*. 9 vols., Berlin and New York 1983–
RE	G. Wissowa, W. Kroll et al., *Real-Encyclopädie der classischen Altertumswissenschaft*, Stuttgart and Munich 1893–1978
ThGL	C. B. Hase, G. and L. Dindorf et al., *Thesaurus Graecae linguae*. 8 vols., Paris 1831–65
VH^2	*Herculanensium voluminum quae supersunt. Collectio altera*. 11 vols., Naples 1862–76

2. EDITIONS

Adler, A. (1928–38) *Suidae Lexicon.* 5 vols., Leipzig
Arnim, H. von (1903–24) *Stoicorum veterum fragmenta.* 4 vols., Leipzig
Ax, W. (1938) *M. Tulli Ciceronis De divinatione etc.*, Leipzig
Bachmann, L. (1828) *Anecdota Graeca* I, Leipzig
Bailey, C. (1926) *Epicurus: The Extant Remains*, Oxford
Barns, J. W. B. and H. Zilliacus (1960) *The Antinoopolis Papyri* II (Greco-Roman Memoirs 37), London
Bekker, I. (1814) *Anecdota Graeca* I, Berlin
Bernardakis, G. N. (1896) *Plutarchi Chaeronensis Moralia* VII: *Plutarchi fragmenta*, Leipzig
Bethe, E. (1900–37) *Pollucis Onomasticon.* 3 vols., Leipzig
Blass, F. (1881) *Antiphontis orationes et fragmenta.* 2nd ed., Leipzig
Borret, M. (1967–76) *Origène: Contre Celse.* 5 vols., Paris
Borries, I. de (1911) *Phrynichi Praeparatio sophistica*, Leipzig
Calderan, R. and M. Rosellini (1993) *Iuli Valeri Res gestae Alexandri Macedonis*, Stuttgart
Cherniss, H. (1957) *Plutarch's Moralia* XII: *De facie in orbe lunae* (Loeb), London
(1976) *Plutarch's Moralia* XIII.2: *Essays on Stoic Topics* (Loeb), London
Cohn, L. et al. (1896–1915) *Philonis Alexandrini opera quae supersunt.* 6 vols., Berlin
Conomis, N. C. (1970) *Lycurgi oratio in Leocratem cum ceterarum Lycurgi orationum fragmentis*, Leipzig
Couvreur, P. (1901) *Hermiae Alexandrini in Platonis Phaedrum scholia*, Paris
Cramer, J. A. (1835–37) *Anecdota Graeca e codd. manuscriptis bibliothecarum Oxoniensium.* 4 vols., Oxford
Cuvigny, M. (and G. Lachenaud) (1981) *Plutarque œuvres morales* tome XII.1: *Vies des dix orateurs etc.*, Paris
Daiber, H. (1980) *Aetius Arabus: Die Vorsokratiker in arabischer Überlieferung*, Wiesbaden
Decleva Caizzi, F. (1966) *Antisthenis fragmenta*, Milan
(1969) *Antiphontis Tetralogiae*, Milan
Decleva Caizzi, F. and G. Bastianini (1989) "Antipho," in *Corpus dei papiri filosofici greci e latini* I.1* (Florence) 176–236
Del Corno, D. (1969) *Graecorum de re onirocritica scriptorum reliquiae*, Milan
Diehl, E. (1903–6) *Procli Diadochi in Platonis Timaeum commentaria.* 3 vols., Leipzig
Diels, H. (1879) *Doxographi Graeci*, Berlin
(1882) *Simplicii in Aristotelis Physicorum libros quattuor priores commentaria* I (CAG 9), Berlin

(1907) *Beiträge zur Zuckungsliteratur des Okzidents und Orients* I: *Die griechischen Zuckungsbücher* (Abhandlungen der Berliner Akademie, Philos.-hist. Klasse 4), Berlin
(1916) "Ein neues Fragment aus Antiphons Buch Über die Wahrheit," *Sitzungsberichte der Berliner Akademie* 38: 931–36
(1922) *Die Fragmente der Vorsokratiker.* 4th ed. 2 vols., Berlin
Dilts, M. R. (1983) *Scholia Demosthenica* I, Leipzig
Dindorf, W. (1851) *Scholia Graeca ex codicibus aucta et emendata* (*Demosthenes* 8–9). 2 vols., Oxford
(1853) *Harpocrationis Lexicon in decem oratores Atticos* I, Oxford
Ebbesen, S. (1981) *Commentators and Commentaries on Aristotle's Sophistici elenchi* (Corpus Latinum commentariorum in Aristotelem Graecorum 7.1–3). 3 vols., Leiden
Edelstein, L. and I. G. Kidd (1989) *Posidonius* I: *The Fragments.* 2nd ed., Cambridge
Einarson, B. and G. K. K. Link (1990) *Theophrastus: De causis plantarum* V–VI (Loeb), London
England, E. B. (1921) *The Laws of Plato.* 2 vols., Manchester
Erbse, H. (1950) *Untersuchungen zu den attizistischen Lexica* (Abhandlungen der deutschen Akademie der Wissenschaften, Philos.-hist. Klasse, 1949.2), Berlin
(1969–88) *Scholia Graeca in Homeri Iliadem* (scholia vetera). 7 vols., Berlin and New York
Fischer, E. (1974) *Die Ekloge des Phrynichos* (Sammlung griechischer und lateinischer Grammatiker 1), Berlin
Flach, J. (1882) *Hesychii Milesii Onomatologi quae supersunt*, Leipzig
Fortenbaugh, W. W. et al. (1992) *Theophrastus of Eresus* (Philosophia Antiqua 54.1–2). 2 vols., Leiden
Funghi, M. S. (1984) edition of *P.Oxy.* 3647, in H. M. Cockle (ed.) *The Oxyrhynchus Papyri* LII (London) 1–5
Gaisford, T. (1848) *Etymologicum magnum*, Oxford
Gallo, I. (1980) *Frammenti biografici da papyri* II: *La biografia dei filosofi*, Rome
Gernet, L. (1923) *Antiphon: Discours*, Paris
Gesner, C. (1546) *Sententiarum sive capitum, theologicorum praecipue, ex sacris & profanis libris tomi tres per Antonium et Maximum monachos olim collecti etc.*, Zurich
Gigon, O. (1987) *Aristotelis opera ex recensione I. Bekkeri … editio altera* III: *Librorum deperditorum fragmenta*, Berlin and New York
Gomperz, T. (1891) "Philodem und die ästhetischen Schriften der herculanischen Bibliothek," *Sitzungsberichte der österreichischen Akademie*, Philos.-hist. Klasse 123: 1–88

Grenfell, B. P. and A. S. Hunt (1915) edition of *P.Oxy.* 1364, in *The Oxyrhynchus Papyri* XI (London) 92–104

(1922) edition of *P.Oxy.* 1797, in *The Oxyrhynchus Papyri* XV (London) 119–22

Håkanson, L. (1989) *L. Annaeus Seneca Maior: Oratorum et rhetorum sententiae divisiones colores*, Leipzig

Hausrath, A. and H. Hunger (1959–70) *Corpus fabularum Aesopicarum* I. 2nd ed. 2 vols., Leipzig

Hayduck, M. (1884) *Anonymi in Aristotelis Sophisticos elenchos paraphrasis* (CAG 23.4), Berlin

(1891) *Alexandri Aphrodisiensis in Aristotelis Metaphysica commentaria* (CAG 1), Berlin

(1899) *Alexandri in Aristotelis Meteorologicorum libros commentaria* (CAG 3.2), Berlin

(1907) *Eustratii in Analyticorum posteriorum librum secundum commentarium* (CAG 21.1), Berlin

Heiberg, J. L. (1894) *Simplicii in Aristotelis De caelo commentaria* (CAG 7), Berlin

(1910–15) *Archimedis opera omnia cum commentariis Eutocii.* 2nd ed. 3 vols., Leipzig

Helm, R. (1898) *Fabii Planciadis Fulgentii opera*, Leipzig

Henry, R. (1959–77) *Photius: Bibliothèque.* 8 vols., Paris

Hense, O. (1909) *Teletis reliquiae.* 2nd ed., Tübingen

Hertz, M. (1855–59) *Prisciani Institutionum grammaticarum libri* XVIII (Grammatici Latini 2–3). 2 vols., Leipzig

Hude, K. (1934) *Xenophontis Commentarii*, Stuttgart

Jaeger, W. (1957) *Aristotelis Metaphysica*, Oxford

Jaekel, S. (1964) *Menandri Sententiae*, Leipzig

Kaibel, G. (1887–90) *Athenaei Naucratitae Dipnosophistarum.* 3 vols., Leipzig

Kannicht, R. and B. Snell (1981) *Tragicorum Graecorum fragmenta* 2, Göttingen

Kayser, C. L. (1870–71) *Flavii Philostrati opera.* 2 vols., Leipzig

Keaney, J. J. (1967) "New fragments of Greek authors in codex Marc. Gr. 444," *Transactions of the American Philological Association* 98: 205–19

(1991) *Harpocration: Lexeis of the Ten Orators*, Amsterdam

Kenyon, F. G. (1906) *Hyperidis orationes et fragmenta*, Oxford

Kock, T. (1880–88) *Comicorum Atticorum fragmenta.* 3 vols., Leipzig

Körte, A. (1890) *Metrodori Epicurei fragmenta* (Jahrbücher für classische Philologie Suppl. 17), Leipzig

Körte, A. and A. Thierfelder (1953) *Menandri quae supersunt* II: *Reliquiae apud veteres scriptores servatae*, Leipzig

Kroll, W. (1926) *Historia Alexandri Magni* I: *Recensio vetusta*, Berlin
Kühn, C. G. (1821–33) *Claudii Galeni opera omnia*. 20 vols., Leipzig
Küster, L. (1705) *Suidae Lexicon Graece & Latine*. 3 vols., Cambridge
Lachenaud, G. (1993) *Plutarque œuvres morales* tome XII.2: *Opinions des philosophes*, Paris
Lambin, D. and G. Morel (1570) Δημοσθένους λόγοι . . . διὰ φιλοπονίας καὶ ἐπιμελείας τοῦ Γουλιέλμου Μορελίου, Paris
Lanata, G. (1963) *La poetica pre-platonica: Testimonianze e frammenti*, Florence
Latte, K. (1953–66) *Hesychii Alexandrini Lexicon* (Α–Ο). 2 vols., Copenhagen
Leutsch, E. L. von and F. G. Schneidewin (1839–51) *Corpus paroemiographorum Graecorum*. 2 vols., Göttingen
Long, A. A. and D. N. Sedley (1987) *The Hellenistic Philosophers*. 2 vols., Cambridge
Long, H. S. (1964) *Diogenis Laertii Vitae philosophorum*. 2 vols., Oxford
Maass, E. (1898) *Commentariorum in Aratum reliquiae*, Berlin
Macleod, M. D. (1972) *Luciani opera* I, Oxford
Maehler, H. (1982) *Die Lieder des Bakchylides* I: *Die Siegeslieder* (Mnemosyne Suppl. 62). 2 vols., Leiden (reprinted 1997)
(1989) *Pindari carmina cum fragmentis* II: *Fragmenta*, Leipzig
(1997) *Die Lieder des Bakchylides* II: *Die Dithyramben und Fragmente* (Mnemosyne Suppl. 167), Leiden
Maggiòlo, P. M. (1965) *S. Thomae Aquinatis in octo libros Physicorum Aristotelis expositio*, Turin
Marchant, E. C. (1921) *Xenophontis opera omnia* II. 2nd. ed., Oxford
Marcovich, M. (1978) *Eraclito: Testimonianze e frammenti*, Florence
Meineke, A. (1839–57) *Fragmenta comicorum Graecorum*. 5 vols., Berlin
(1855–57) *Ioannis Stobaei Florilegium*. 4 vols., Leipzig
Merkelbach, R. and M. L. West (1967) *Fragmenta Hesiodea*, Oxford
Meyerhof, M. and J. Schacht (1931) *Galen Über die medizinischen Namen* (Abhandlungen der Berliner Akademie, Philos.-hist. Klasse, 1931.3), Berlin (cited from the *separata*)
Mras, K. (1954–56) *Die Praeparatio evangelica* (Eusebius Werke 8.1–2; GCS 43.1–2). 2 vols., Berlin
Nauck, A. (1889) *Tragicorum Graecorum fragmenta*. 2nd ed., Leipzig
Ofenloch, E. (1907) *Caecilii Calactini fragmenta*, Leipzig
Pack, R. (1963) *Artemidori Daldiani Onirocriticon libri V*, Leipzig
Page, D. (1962) *Poetae melici Graeci*, Oxford
Pease, A. S. (1920–23) *M. Tulli Ciceronis De divinatione*. 2 vols., Urbana
Pertusi, A. (1955) *Scholia vetera in Hesiodi Opera et dies*, Milan
Pfeiffer, E. (1949–53) *Callimachus*. 2 vols., Oxford

Porson, R. (1822) Φοτίου τοῦ Πατριάρχου Λέξεων Συναγωγή. 2 vols., London
Rabe, H. (1913) *Hermogenis opera* (Rhetores Graeci 6), Leipzig
Radt, S. (1977) *Tragicorum Graecorum fragmenta* 4: *Sophocles*, Göttingen
(1985) *Tragicorum Graecorum fragmenta* 3: *Aeschylus*, Göttingen
Raeder, H. (1904) *Theodoreti Graecarum affectionum curatio*, Leipzig
Reitzenstein, R. (1907) *Der Anfang des Lexicons des Photios*, Leipzig and Berlin
Rose, V. (1886) *Aristotelis qui ferebantur librorum fragmenta*. 3rd ed., Leipzig
Ross, W. D. (1924) *Aristotle's Metaphysics*. 2 vols., Oxford (reprinted with corrections 1953)
(1936) *Aristotle's Physics*, Oxford
(1950) *Aristotelis Physica*, Oxford
(1958) *Aristotelis Topica et Sophistici elenchi*, Oxford
Rudio, F. (1907) *Der Bericht des Simplicius über die Quadraturen des Antiphon und des Hippokrates*, Leipzig
Sauppe, H. (and J. G. Baiter) (1850) *Oratores Attici* II, Zurich
Sbordone, F. (1976) "[Φιλοδήμου Περὶ ποιημάτων] Tractatus tres," in F. Sbordone (ed.) *Ricerche sui papiri ercolanesi* 2, Naples
Schenkl, H. (1888) *Florilegia duo Graeca* (Jahres-Bericht über das K. K. Akademische Gymnasium in Wien), Vienna
(1900) *Themistii in Aristotelis Physica paraphrasis* (CAG 5.2), Berlin
Schmidt, M. (1854) *Didymi Chalcenteri grammatici Alexandrini fragmenta quae supersunt omnia*, Leipzig
(1858–68) *Hesychii Alexandrini Lexicon*. 5 vols., Jena
Schwartz, E. (1887–91) *Scholia in Euripidem*. 2 vols., Berlin
Smith, M. F. (1984) "Diogenes of Oenoanda, new fragments 122–124," *Anatolian Studies* 34: 43–57
(1993) *Diogenes of Oinoanda: The Epicurean Inscription*, Naples
Snell, B. (1937) *Euripides Alexandros und andere Strassburger Papyri mit Fragmenten griechischer Dichter* (Hermes Einzelschriften 5), Berlin
Snell, B. and R. Kannicht (1986) *Tragicorum Graecorum fragmenta* 1. Rev. ed., Göttingen
Snell, B. and H. Maehler (1980) *Pindari carmina cum fragmentis* 1: *Epinicia*. 6th ed., Leipzig
Spengel, L. (1828) ΣΥΝΑΓΩΓΗ ΤΕΧΝΩΝ *sive artium scriptores*, Stuttgart
(1853–56) *Rhetores Graeci*. 3 vols., Leipzig
Stählin, O. and L. Früchtel (1960–70) *Clemens Alexandrinus: Stromata* (Clemens Alexandrinus 2–3; GCS 15, 17). 2nd–3rd ed. 2 vols., Berlin
Sternbach, L. (1888) "De Gnomologio Vaticano inedito II," *Wiener Studien* 10: 1–49

(1893) "Gnomologium Parisinum ineditum. Appendix Vaticana," *Rozprawy Akademii umiejetnosci, Wydzial filologiczny* (*Dissertationes classis philologicae Academiae litterarum Cracoviensis*) 20: 135–218

Thalheim, T. (1903) *Isaei orationes cum deperditarum fragmentis*. 2nd ed., Leipzig

(1913) *Lysiae orationes*. 2nd ed., Leipzig

(1914) *Antiphontis orationes et fragmenta*, Berlin

Theodoridis, C. (1982–98) *Photii patriarchae Lexicon* (Α–Μ). 2 vols., Berlin

Thesleff, H. (1965) *The Pythagorean Texts of the Hellenistic Period* (Acta Academiae Aboensis, Ser. A 30.1), Åbo

Todd, R. (1990) *Cleomedis Caelestia* (ΜΕΤΕΩΡΑ), Leipzig

Untersteiner, M. (and A. Battegazzore) (1962) *Sofisti, Testimonianze e frammenti* IV: *Antifonte, Crizia*, Florence

Usener, H. (1887) *Epicurea*, Leipzig

Valk, M. van der (1971–87) *Eustathii archiepiscopi Thessalonicensis commentarii ad Homeri Iliadem pertinentes*. 4 vols., Leiden

Vitelli, H. (1887) *Ioannis Philoponi in Aristotelis Physicorum libros tres priores commentaria* (CAG 16), Berlin

Wachsmuth, C. (1882) "Die Wiener Apophthegmen-Sammlung," in *Festschrift zur Begrüssung der in Karlsruhe vom 27.–30. September 1882 tagenden* XXXVI. Philologen-Versammlung (Freiburg im Breisgau and Tübingen) 1–36

Wachsmuth, C. and O. Hense (1884–1912) *Ioannis Stobaei Anthologium*. 5 vols., Berlin

Waitz, T. (1844–46) *Aristotelis organon Graece*. 2 vols., Leipzig

Wallies, M. (1898) *Alexandri quod fertur in Aristotelis Sophisticos elenchos commentarium* (CAG 2.3), Berlin

(1909) *Ioannis Philoponi in Aristotelis Analytica posteriora commentaria* (CAG 13.3), Berlin

Walz, C. (1832–36) *Rhetores Graeci*. 9 vols., Stuttgart

Waszink, J. H. (1947) *Q. S. F. Tertulliani De anima*, Amsterdam

Wehrli, F. (1959) *Hieronymos von Rhodos, Kritolaos etc.* (*Die Schule des Aristoteles* 10), Basel

(1969) *Eudemos von Rhodos* (*Die Schule des Aristoteles* 8). 2nd ed., Basel

Wenkebach, E. (1936) *Galeni in Hippocratis Epidemiarum librum* III *commentaria iii* (Corpus medicorum Graecorum 5.10.2.1), Leipzig and Berlin

West, M. L. (1971–72) *Iambi et elegi Graeci*. 2 vols., Oxford

3. GENERAL

Abert, H. (1924) "Lampros (2)," *RE* XII, 1: 587

Adam, J. (1902) *The Republic of Plato*. 2 vols., Cambridge

Adams, C. D. (1905) *Lysias: Selected Speeches*, New York
Allman, G. J. (1889) *Greek Geometry from Thales to Euclid*, Dublin
Altheim, F. (1926) "Staat und Individuum bei Antiphon dem Sophisten," *Klio* 20: 257–69
Altwegg, G. (1908) *De Antiphonte qui dicitur sophista quaestionum particula* I: *De libro* ΠΕΡΙ ΟΜΟΝΟΙΑΣ *scripto*, Basel
Aly, W. (1929) *Formprobleme der frühen griechischen Prosa* (Philologus Suppl. 21.3), Leipzig
Anawati, G. C. and A. Z. Iskandar (1978) "Hunayn Ibn Ishaq," in *DSB* XV, Suppl. I: 230–49
Anderson, G. (1976) *Lucian. Theme and Variation in the Second Sophistic* (Mnemosyne Suppl. 41), Leiden
Appelboom, T. (ed.) (1987) *Art, History and Antiquity of Rheumatic Diseases*, Brussels
Arnim, H. von (1898) *Leben und Werke des Dio von Prusa*, Berlin
(1916) *Gerechtigkeit und Nutzen in der griechischen Aufklärungsphilosophie* (Frankfurter Universitätsreden), Frankfurt
Arnott, W. G. (1996) *Alexis: The Fragments. A Commentary*, Cambridge
Avery, H. (1982) "One Antiphon or two?," *Hermes* 110: 145–58
Barnes, J. (1982) *The Presocratic Philosophers*. Revised ed., London and New York
Barrett, W. S. (1964) *Euripides: Hippolytos*, Oxford
Beardslee, J. W. (1918) *The Use of* ΦΥΣΙΣ *in Fifth-Century Greek Literature*, Chicago
Beare, J. I. (1906) *Greek Theories of Elementary Cognition from Alcmaeon to Aristotle*, Oxford
Bergsträsser, G. (1913) *Hunain ibn Ishak und seine Schule*, Leiden
(1925) *Hunain ibn Ishaq über die syrischen und arabischen Galen-Übersetzungen*, Leipzig
Bernays, J. (1854) "Neue Bruchstücke des Heraklit von Ephesus," *Rheinisches Museum für Philologie* NF 9: 241–69
Bers, V. (1984) *Greek Poetic Syntax*, New Haven
Berve, H. (1926) *Das Alexanderreich auf prosopographischer Grundlage*. 2 vols., Munich
Bignone, E. (1916) *Empedocle*, Turin
(1920) *Epicuro*, Bari
(1938) *Studi sul pensiero antico*, Naples
(1940) "Intorno al trattato *Della Concordia* di Antifonte sophista," *Giornale critico della filosofia italiana* 2. ser. 8: 233–39
Bilabel, F. (1923) "Siglae," *RE* IIA, 2: 2279–315
Blank, D. (1985) "Socrates versus sophists on payment for teaching," *Classical Antiquity* 4: 1–49

Blass, F. (1887–98) *Die Attische Beredsamkeit.* 2nd ed. 3 vols., Leipzig
(1889a) *De Antiphonte sophista Iamblichi auctore*, Kiel
(1889b) "Demosthenische Studien," *Rheinisches Museum für Philologie* NF 44: 1–24
(1906) *Aischylos' Choephoren*, Halle
Bluck, R. S. (1961) *Plato's Meno*, Cambridge
Blum, C. (1936) *Studies in the Dream-Book of Artemidorus*, Uppsala
Blümner, H. (1875–87) *Technologie und Terminologie der Gewerbe und Künste bei Griechen und Römern.* 4 vols., Leipzig
Bollack, J. (1965–69) *Empédocle.* 4 vols., Paris
Bond, G. W. (1981) *Euripides: Heracles*, Oxford
Bonitz, H. (1849) *Aristotelis Metaphysica.* 2 vols., Bonn
(1870) *Index Aristotelicus*, Berlin
Bonner, R. J. and G. Smith (1930–38) *The Administration of Justice from Homer to Aristotle.* 2 vols., Chicago
Born, H. (1990) "Patinated and painted bronzes: exotic technique or ancient tradition?," in *Small Bronze Sculpture from the Ancient World* (Malibu) 179–96
Both, P. (1875) *De Antiphontis et Thucydidis genere dicendi*, Marburg
Bouché-Leclercq, A. (1879–82) *Histoire de la divination dans l'antiquité.* 4 vols., Paris
Brandstätter, K. (1894) "De notionum ΠΟΛΙΤΙΚΟΣ et ΣΟΦΙΣΤΗΣ usu rhetorico," *Leipziger Studien zur classischen Philologie* 15: 129–274
Braun, E. (1952) "Eine Alexanderlegende," *Jahreshefte des österreichischen archäologischen Instituts* 39: 139–45
Breitenbach, H. R. (1967) "Xenophon von Athen (6)," *RE* IXA, 2: 1569–928, 1981–2052
Bretschneider, C. A. (1870) *Die Geometrie und die Geometer vor Euklides*, Leipzig
Brzoska, J. (1897) "Caecilius (2)," *RE* III, 1: 1174–88
Bulmer-Thomas, I. (1972) "Hippocrates of Chios," in *DSB* VI: 410–18
Burdach, K. (1922) "Die Lehre des Platonischen Timaios (40 B) von der kosmischen Stellung der Erde," *Neue Jahrbücher für das klassische Altertum* 25: 254–78
Buresch, C. (1886) "Consolationum a Graecis Romanisque scriptarum historia critica," *Leipziger Studien zur classischen Philologie* 9: 1–170
Burkert, W. (1964) review of Untersteiner (1962), *Göttingische Gelehrte Anzeigen* 216: 141–44
(1972) *Lore and Science in Ancient Pythagoreanism*, tr. E. L. Minar, Cambridge, Mass.
Burnet, J. (1911) *Plato's Phaedo*, Oxford
(1924) *Plato's Euthyphro, Apology of Socrates, and Crito*, Oxford

(1930) *Early Greek Philosophy*. 4th ed., London
Bury, R. B. (1932) *The Symposium of Plato*. 2nd ed., Cambridge
Buttmann, P. (1836) *Lexilogus*, tr. J. R. Fishlake, London
Byl, S. (1987) "Rheumatism and gout in the corpus Hippocraticum," in Appelboom (1987) 62–66, 119–22
Cahen, E. (1910) review of Jacoby (1908), *Revue des études grecques* 23: 79–80
Cantor, M. (1900–7) *Vorlesungen über Geschichte der Mathematik* I–II. 2nd–3rd ed., Leipzig
Capelle, W. (1924) "Erdbebenforschung," *RE* Suppl. IV: 344–74
Cassin, B. (1985) "Histoire d'une identité," *Ecrit du temps* 10: 65–77
Chadwick, H. (1965) *Origen: Contra Celsum*, tr. with introduction & notes, Cambridge
(1966) *Early Christian Thought and the Classical Tradition*, New York
Chantraine, P. (1933) *La formation des noms en grec ancien*, Paris
(1964) review of Untersteiner (1962), *Revue de philologie* 38: 135–36
Charlton, W. (1970) *Aristotle's Physics* I–II, tr. with introduction and notes, Oxford
Cherniss, H. (1935) *Aristotle's Criticism of Presocratic Philosophy*, Baltimore
(1944) *Aristotle's Criticism of Plato and the Academy* I, Baltimore
(1951) "The characteristics and effects of Presocratic philosophy," *Journal of the History of Ideas* 12: 319–45
(1959–60) "Plato (1950–1957)," *Lustrum* 4: 5–308; 5: 321–648
(1977) *Selected Papers*, ed. L. Tarán, Leiden
Clavaud, R. (1982) *Le Ménexène de Platon et la rhétorique de son temps*, Paris
Clay, D. (1990) "The philosophical inscription of Diogenes of Oenoanda: new discoveries 1969–1983," in Haase (1990) 2446–559
Cohn, L. (1903) "Didymos (8)," *RE* V: 445–72
Cole, T. (1967) *Democritus and the Sources of Greek Anthropology* (APA Monographs 25), Cleveland (reprinted with a Postscript, Atlanta 1990)
Cope, E. M. and J. E. Sandys (1877) *The Rhetoric of Aristotle with a Commentary*. 3 vols., Cambridge
Cornford, F. M. (1935) *Plato's Theory of Knowledge*, London
(1937) *Plato's Cosmology*, London
Croiset, A. (1883) "Les fragments d'Antiphon le sophiste," *Annuaire de l'Association pour l'encouragement des études grecques en France* 17: 143–60
(1917) "Les nouveaux fragments d'Antiphon," *Revue des études grecques* 30: 1–19
Crönert, W. (1922) review of Grenfell and Hunt (1922), *Literarisches Zentralblatt für Deutschland* 73: 423
D'Agostini, F. (1975) "Il pensiero giuridico nella sofistica," *Rivista internazionale di filosofia del diritto* 52: 193–216, 547–73

Daniélou, J. (1955) *Origen*, tr. W. Mitchell, New York
Davies, J. K. (1971) *Athenian Propertied Families 600–300* BC, Oxford
Davies, M. (1991) *Sophocles: Trachiniae*, Oxford
Decleva Caizzi, F. (1984) "Le fragment 44 DK d'Antiphon et le problème de son auteur: quelques reconsidérations," in Η ΑΡΧΑΙΑ ΣΟΦΙΣΤΙΚΗ, *The Sophistic Movement* (papers read at the First International Symposium on the Sophistic Movement, 27–29 Sept. 1982) (Athens) 97–107
(1985) "Ricerche su Antifonte," in M. Capasso et al. (eds.) *Studi di filosofia preplatonica* (Naples) 191–208
(1986a) "Il nuovo papiro di Antifonte," in F. Adorno et al. (eds.) *Protagora, Antifonte, Posidonio, Aristotele: saggi su frammenti inediti e nuove testimonianze da papiri* (Florence) 61–69
(1986b) "'Hysteron proteron': la nature et la loi selon Antiphon et Platon," *Revue de métaphysique et de morale* 91: 291–310
Del Corno, D. (1962) "Ricerche sull'onirocritica greca," *Rendiconti dell'Istituto lombardo*, Classe di lettere, scienze morali e storiche 96: 334–66
Delpeuch, A. (1900) *La goutte et le rhumatisme*, Paris
Denniston, J. D. (1954) *The Greek Particles*. 2nd ed., Oxford
Diano, C. (1961) "Euripide auteur de la catharsis tragique," *Numen* 8: 117–41
Dicks, D. R. (1970) *Early Greek Astronomy to Aristotle*, Ithaca
Diels, H. (1917) "Ein antikes System des Naturrechts," *Internationale Monatsschrift* 11: 81–102
Dietrich, R. (1927) "Das Traumbuch Antiphons," *Philologische Wochenschrift* 47: 29
Dihle, A. (1977) "Das Satyrspiel 'Sisyphus,'" *Hermes* 105: 28–42
(1982) *The Theory of Will in Classical Antiquity*, Berkeley and Los Angeles
(1983) "Vom sonnenhaften Auge," in H.-D. Blume and F. Mann (eds.) *Platonismus und Christentum: Festschrift für H. Dörrie* (Münster) 85–91
Dillon, J. (1984) "Euripides and Antiphon on nomos and physis: some remarks," in Η ΑΡΧΑΙΑ ΣΟΦΙΣΤΙΚΗ, *The Sophistic Movement* (papers read at the First International Symposium on the Sophistic Movement, 27–29 Sept. 1982) (Athens) 127–36
Dittmar, H. (1912) *Aeschines von Sphettos* (Philologische Untersuchungen 21), Berlin
Dodds, E. R. (1951) *The Greeks and the Irrational*, Berkeley and Los Angeles
(1954) "The nationality of Antiphon the sophist," *Classical Review* 68: 94–95

(1959) *Plato: Gorgias*, Oxford
(1960) *Euripides: Bacchae*. 2nd ed., Oxford
Dorandi, T. (1992) "Per una ricomposizione dello scritto di Filodemo Sulla poetica," *Zeitschrift für Papyrologie und Epigraphik* 91: 29–46
Döring, A. (1895) *Die Lehre des Sokrates als soziales Reformsystem*, Munich
Dover, K. J. (1950) "The chronology of Antiphon's speeches," *Classical Quarterly* 44: 44–60
(1964) "Eros and Nomos (Plato, *Symposium* 182A–185C)," *Bulletin of the Institute of Classical Studies* 11: 31–42
(1968a) *Aristophanes: Clouds*, Oxford
(1968b) *Lysias and the Corpus Lysiacum*, Berkeley and Los Angeles
(1974) *Greek Popular Morality*, Berkeley and Los Angeles
Dreher, M. (1983) "Die Sophisten – Parteigänger der Demokraten oder der Oligarchen?," *Studi e ricerche dell' Istituto di storia, Facoltà di lettere e filosofia, Università di Firenze* 2: 63–88
Drerup, E. (1901) "Die Anfänge der rhetorischen Kunstprosa," in E. Drerup (ed.) *Untersuchungen zur älteren griechischen Prosalitteratur* (Jahrbücher für classische Philologie Suppl. 27, Leipzig) 219–351
Dümmler, F. (1889) *Akademika: Beiträge zur Literaturgeschichte der sokratischen Schulen*, Giessen
(1901) "Prolegomena zu Platons Staat," in *Kleine Schriften* 1 (Leipzig) 150–228 (originally published Basel 1891)
Dunbar, N. (1995) *Aristophanes: Birds*, Oxford
Dunn, F. M. (1996) "Antiphon on time (B9 D–K)," *American Journal of Philology* 117: 65–69
Edwards, M. J. (1998) "Notes on Pseudo-Plutarch's *Life* of Antiphon," *Classical Quarterly* 48: 82–92
Erbse, H. (1961) "Die Architektonik im Aufbau von Xenophons Memorabilien," *Hermes* 89: 257–87
Fairweather, J. (1981) *The Elder Seneca*, Cambridge
Fehling, D. (1969) *Die Wiederholungsfiguren und ihr Gebrauch bei den Griechen vor Gorgias*, Berlin
Ferguson, J. (1971) "Dinos," *Phronesis* 16: 97–115
Finley, J. H. (1939) "The origins of Thucydides' style," *Harvard Studies in Classical Philology* 50: 35–84.
Fischer, J. (1899) *Ad artis veterum onirocriticae historiam symbola*, Jena
Forbes, R. J. (1972) *Studies in Ancient Technology* IX. 2nd ed., Leiden
Fraenkel, E. (1950) *Aeschylus: Agamemnon*. 3 vols., Oxford
Fränkel, H. (1946) "Man's 'ephemeros' nature according to Pindar and others," *Transactions of the American Philological Association* 77: 131–45
(1968) *Wege und Formen frühgriechischen Denkens*. 3rd ed., Munich

(1975) *Early Greek Poetry and Philosophy*, tr. M. Hadas and J. Willis, Oxford

François, G. (1957) *Le polythéisme et l'emploi au singulier des mots* ΘΕΟΣ, ΔΑΙΜΩΝ *dans la littérature grecque d'Homère à Platon*, Paris

Frank, E. (1923) *Plato und die sogenannten Pythagoreer*, Halle

Fraser, P. M. and E. Matthews (1994) *A Lexicon of Greek Personal Names* II: *Attica*, ed. M. J. Osborne and S. G. Byrne, Oxford

Fredrich, H. (1899) *Hippokratische Untersuchungen* (Philologische Untersuchungen 15), Berlin

Frisch, H. (1942) *The Constitution of the Athenians*, Copenhagen

Frisk, H. (1960–72) *Griechisches etymologisches Wörterbuch*. 3 vols., Heidelberg

Fritz, K. von (1943) "νοῦς, νοεῖν, and their derivatives in the Homeric poems," *Classical Philology* 38: 79–93

(1955) "Die ἀρχαί in der griechischen Mathematik," *Archiv für Begriffsgeschichte* 1: 13–103

Furley, D. J. (1981) "Antiphon's case against justice," in Kerferd (1981b) 81–91

(1987) *The Greek Cosmologists* 1, Cambridge

Furley, W. D. (1992) "Antiphon der Athener: Ein Sophist als Psychotherapeut?," *Rheinisches Museum für Philologie* NF 135: 198–216

Gagarin, M. (1990) "The ancient tradition on the identity of Antiphon," *Greek, Roman, and Byzantine Studies* 31: 27–44

(1997) *Antiphon: The Speeches*, Cambridge

Gantar, K. (1966) "Amicus sibi 1," *Ziva Antika* 16: 135–75

Geffcken, J. (1934) *Griechische Literaturgeschichte* II, Heidelberg

Georgiadis, C. (1984) "Aristotle's criticism of Antiphon in *Physics*, book II, chapter 1," in Η ΑΡΧΑΙΑ ΣΟΦΙΣΤΙΚΗ, *The Sophistic Movement* (papers read at the First International Symposium on the Sophistic Movement, 27–29 Sept. 1982) (Athens) 108–14

Gerth, B. (1918a) "Iunius (77)," *RE* X, 1: 1035–39

(1918b) "Iunius (113)," *RE* X, 1: 1071–73

Gigon, O. (1946) "Xenophontea," *Eranos* 44: 131–52

(1953) *Kommentar zum ersten Buch von Xenophons Memorabilien* (Schweizerische Beiträge zur Altertumswissenschaft 5), Basel

Gilbert, O. (1907) *Die meteorologischen Theorien des griechischen Altertums*, Leipzig

Gildersleeve, B. (1900–11) *Syntax of Classical Greek*. 2 vols., New York

Gisinger, F. (1962) "Κατουδαῖοι," *RE* Suppl. IX: 381

Goebel, K. (1910) *Die vorsokratische Philosophie*, Bonn

Gomme, A. W., K. J. Dover and A. Andrewes (1981) *A Historical Commentary on Thucydides* V, Oxford

Gomperz, H. (1912) *Sophistik und Rhetorik*, Leipzig and Berlin
(1927) *Die Lebensauffassung der griechischen Philosophen*. 3rd ed., Jena
Gomperz, T. (1901) *Greek Thinkers* I, tr. L. Magnus, London
(1922) *Griechische Denker* I. 4th ed., Berlin and Leipzig
Goodwin, W. W. (1890) *Syntax of the Moods and Tenses of the Greek Verb*, Boston
Goossens, R. (1942) "Une allusion à Cimon dans le Πολιτικός d'Antiphon," *L'Antiquité classique* 11: 91–92
Gow, A. S. F. (1950) *Theocritus*. 2 vols., Cambridge
Graeser, A. (1969) review of Cole (1967), *Gnomon* 41: 9–16
Greenberg, N. A. (1990) *The Poetic Theory of Philodemus*, New York and London
Greene, W. C. (1944) *Moira: Fate, Good and Evil in Greek Thought*, Cambridge, Mass.
Grensemann, H. (1975) *Knidische Medizin* I: *Die Testimonien zur ältesten Lehre und Analysen knidischer Schriften im Corpus Hippocraticum* (Ars Medica 4.1), Berlin and New York
(1987) *Knidische Medizin* II: *Versuch einer weiteren Analyse der Schicht A in den pseudo-hippokratischen Schriften De natura muliebri und De muliebribus* I–II (Hermes Einzelschriften 51), Wiesbaden and Stuttgart
Grmek, M. (1983) *Les maladies à l'aube de la civilisation occidentale*, Paris
(1989) *Diseases in the Ancient World*, tr. M. and L. Muellner, Baltimore and London
Grossmann, G. (1950) *Politische Schlagwörter aus der Zeit des Peloponnesischen Krieges*, Zurich
Gudeman, A. (1921) "Scholien," *RE* IIA, I: 625–705
Gulick, C. B. (1941) *Athenaeus: The Deipnosophists* VII (Loeb), London
Gundel, W. (1933) "Mond," *RE* XVI, I: 76–105
Guthrie, W. K. C. (1946) "Notes on some passages in the second book of Aristotle's *Physics*," *Classical Quarterly* 40: 70–76
(1971a) *The Sophists* (= *History of Greek Philosophy* 3.1), Cambridge
(1971b) *Socrates* (= *History of Greek Philosophy* 3.2), Cambridge
Haase, W. (ed.) (1990) *Aufstieg und Niedergang der römischen Welt* 36.4, Berlin and New York
Hagedorn, D. (1964) *Zur Ideenlehre des Hermogenes* (Hypomnemata 8), Göttingen
Hall, E. (1989) *Inventing the Barbarian: Greek Self-Definition through Tragedy*, Oxford
Halliwell, S. (1991) "Comic satire and freedom of speech in classical Athens," *Journal of Hellenic Studies* 111: 48–70
Hamelin, O. (1931) *Aristote: Physique* II. 2nd ed., Paris
Hamilton, J. R. (1969) *Plutarch: Alexander*, Oxford

Hankel, H. (1874) *Zur Geschichte der Mathematik in Altertum und Mittelalter*, Leipzig
Haslam, M. (1972) "Plato, Sophron and the dramatic dialogue," *Bulletin of the Institute of Classical Studies* 19: 17–38
Havelock, E. (1957) *The Liberal Temper in Greek Politics*, New Haven
Headlam, W. and A. D. Knox (1922) *Herodas*, Cambridge
Headlam, W. and G. Thomson (1966) *The Oresteia of Aeschylus*. New ed. 2 vols., Amsterdam and Prague
Heath, T. L. (1921) *A History of Greek Mathematics*. 2 vols., Oxford
(1922) *The Thirteen Books of Euclid's Elements*. 3 vols., Cambridge
(1931) *A Manual of Greek Mathematics*, Oxford
(1949) *Mathematics in Aristotle*, Oxford
Heiberg, J. L. (1884) "Jahresbericht über griechische und römische Mathematik," *Philologus* 43: 321–46, 467–522
Heibges, J. S. (1912) "Hermippos (8)," *RE* VIII, 1: 853–54
Heidel, W. A. (1906a) "Qualitative change in Pre-Socratic philosophy," *Archiv für Geschichte der Philosophie* 12: 333–79
(1906b) "The ΔΙΝΗ in Anaximenes and Anaximander," *Classical Philology* 1: 279–82
(1910) "Περὶ Φύσεως," *Proceedings of the American Academy of Arts and Sciences* 44: 79–133
(1912) "On Anaximander," *Classical Philology* 7: 212–34
(1921) "Anaximander's book, the earliest known geographical treatise," *Proceedings of the American Academy of Arts and Sciences* 56: 239–88
(1980) *Selected Papers*, ed. L. Tarán, New York
Heinimann, F. (1945) *Nomos und Physis: Herkunft und Bedeutung einer Antithese im griechischen Denken des 5. Jahrhunderts* (Schweizerische Beiträge zur Altertumswissenschaft 1), Basel
(1961) "Eine vorplatonische Theorie der τέχνη," *Museum Helveticum* 18: 105–30
Heinze, R. (1897) *T. Lucretius Carus De rerum natura* III, Leipzig
Herrmann, L. (1927) "Skiapodes," *RE* IIIA, 1: 517–18
(1928) "Makrokephaloi," *RE* XIV, 1: 815
Hobson, E. W. (1913) *Squaring the Circle*, Cambridge
Höistad, R. (1948) *Cynic Hero and Cynic King*, Uppsala
Holland, R. F. (1956) "On making sense of a philosophical fragment," *Classical Quarterly* NS 6: 215–20
Holwerda, D. (1955) *Commentatio de vocis quae est* ΦΥΣΙΣ *vi atque usu praesertim in Graecitate Aristotele anteriore*, Groningen
Hommel, H. (1941) "Antiphon Sophist und Rhetor," *Geistige Arbeit* 8: 1–4
Hopfner, T. (1937) "Traumdeutung," *RE* VIA, 2: 2233–45

Hoppe, E. (1911) *Mathematik und Astronomie im klassischen Altertum*, Heidelberg

Hornstein, S. (1911) "Untersuchungen zum hippokratischen Corpus," *Primitiae Czernovicienses* 2: 54–82

Huart, P. (1973) ΓΝΩΜΗ *chez Thucydide et ses contemporains* (Etudes et commentaires 81), Paris

Huffman, C. (1993) *Philolaus of Croton*, Cambridge

Isnardi Parente, M. (1975) "Egualitarismo democratico nella sofistica?," *Rivista critica di storia della filosofia* 30: 3–26

Jacoby, E. (1908) *De Antiphontis sophistae* ΠΕΡΙ ΟΜΟΝΟΙΑΣ *libro*, Berlin

Jacoby, F. (1910) "Glaukos (36)," *RE* VII: 1417–20

Jaeger, W. (1939–45) *Paideia*, tr. G. Highet. 3 vols., Oxford

(1947) *The Theology of the Early Greek Philosophers*, Oxford

Jahn, K. (1948) "Trogodytai," *RE* VIIA, 2: 2497–500

Janko, R. (1987) *Aristotle: Poetics*, Indianapolis

(1991) "Philodemus' *On Poems* and Aristotle's *On Poets*," *Croniche Ercolanesi* 21: 5–64

(1995) "Reconstructing Philodemus' *On Poems*," in D. Obbink (ed.) *Philodemus and Poetry* (Oxford) 69–96

Jebb, R. (1892) *Sophocles: Trachiniae* (*Sophocles: The Plays and Fragments* 5), Cambridge

(1900) *Sophocles: Antigone* (*Sophocles: The Plays and Fragments* 3). 3rd ed., Cambridge

(1905) *Bacchylides: The Poems and Fragments*, Cambridge

Joël, K. (1893–1901) *Der echte und der Xenophontische Sokrates*. 3 vols., Berlin

(1921) *Geschichte der antiken Philosophie* I, Tübingen

Jouanna, J. (1974) *Hippocrate: Pour une archéologie de l'école de Cnide*, Paris

(1983) *Hippocrate* tome X.2: *Maladies* II, Paris

Jowett, B. (1892) *The Dialogues of Plato*. 3rd ed. 5 vols., New York

Kahn, C. (1981) "The origins of social contract theory," in Kerferd (1981b) 92–108

Kalinka, E. (1910) review of Altwegg (1908), *Zeitschrift für österreichische Gymnasien* 61: 123–24

Kassel, R. (1954) *Quomodo quibus locis apud veteres scriptores Graecos infantes atque parvuli pueri inducantur describantur commemorentur*, Meisenheim am Glan

(1958) *Untersuchungen zur griechischen und römischen Konsolationsliteratur* (Zetemata 18), Munich

(1991) *Kleine Schriften*, ed. H.-G. Nesselrath, Berlin and New York

Kennedy, G. (1972) *The Art of Rhetoric in the Roman World*, Princeton

Kerferd, G. B. (1956–57) "The moral and political doctrines of Antiphon the sophist: a reconsideration," *Proceedings of the Cambridge Philological Society* NS 4: 26–32

(1965) review of Untersteiner (1962), *Classical Review* 15: 32–33
(1970) "Antiphon," in *DSB* I: 170–72
(1981a) *The Sophistic Movement*, Cambridge
(ed.) (1981b) *The Sophists and their Legacy* (Hermes Einzelschriften 44), Wiesbaden
Kidd, I. G. (1988) *Posidonius* II: *The Commentary*. 2 vols., Cambridge
Kirk, G. S. (1954) *Heraclitus: The Cosmic Fragments*, Cambridge
Klein, F. (1955) *Famous Problems of Elementary Geometry*, tr. W. W. Beman and D. E. Smith, 2nd ed., in *Famous Problems and Other Monographs* (New York)
Knorr, W. (1986) *The Ancient Tradition of Geometric Problems*, Boston
Körte, A. (1924) "Literarische Texte mit Ausschluss der christlichen," *Archiv für Papyrusforschung* 7: 115–60
Krämer, H. (1915) *Quid valeat* ὁμόνοια *in litteris Graecis*, Göttingen
Kranz, W. (1951) "Das Gesetz des Herzens," *Rheinisches Museum für Philologie* NF 94: 222–41
(1967) *Studien zur antiken Literatur und ihrem Fortwirken*, Heidelberg
Krauss, F. S. and M. Kaiser (1965) *Artemidor von Daldis: Traumbuch*, Basel and Stuttgart
Kroll, W. (1919) "Kallisthenes (2)," *RE* x, 2: 1707–26
(1940) "Rhetorik," *RE* Suppl. VII: 1039–138
Krumbacher, K. (1897) *Geschichte der byzantinischen Litteratur*. 2nd ed., Munich
Kuiper, K. (1920) "Over de jongst-ontdekte fragmenten van den sophist Antiphon," *Mededeelingen der koninklijke Akademie van Wetenschappen*, Afdeeling Letterkunde 53: 19–52
Kustas, G. L. (1973) *Studies in Byzantine Rhetoric*, Thessaloniki
Lacey, A. R. (1993) *Philoponus: On Aristotle, Physics 2*, London
La Face, A. (1969) *Ricerche Antifontee*, Palermo
Lana, I. (1951) "Tracce di dottrine cosmopolitiche in Grecia prima del cinismo," *Rivista di filologia e d'istruzione classica* 29: 193–216, 317–38
Lanza, D. (1966) *Anassagora: Testimonianze e frammenti*, Florence
Larson, C. W. R. (1951) "The Platonic synonyms, ΔΙΚΑΙΟΣΥΝΗ and ΣΩΦΡΟΣΥΝΗ," *American Journal of Philology* 72: 395–414
Latte, K. (1929) review of Luria (1927b), *Gnomon* 5: 155–61
(1968) *Kleine Schriften*, ed. O. Gigon et al., Munich
Laurenti, R. (1987) *Aristotele: I frammenti dei dialoghi* I, Naples
Lederlin, J. H. and T. Hemsterhuis (1706) *Julii Pollucis Onomasticon Graece et Latine*. 2 vols., Amsterdam
Lee, H. D. P. (1936) *Zeno of Elea*, Cambridge
Lefke, C. (1936) *De Euripidis Alexandro*, Münster
Lesky, A. (1971) *Geschichte der griechischen Literatur*. 3rd ed., Bern

Levinson, R. B. (1953) *In Defense of Plato*, Cambridge, Mass.
Lieshout, R. G. A. van (1980) *Greeks on Dreams*, Utrecht
Lindberg, G. (1977) *Studies in Hermogenes and Eustathios*, Lund
Lindemann, F. (1882) "Über die Zahl π," *Mathematische Annalen* 20: 213–25
Lipsius, J. H., M. H. E. Meier and G. F. Schömann (1905–15) *Das Attische Recht und Rechtsverfahren*. 3 vols., Leipzig
Lonie, I. M. (1965) "The Cnidian treatises of the corpus Hippocraticum," *Classical Quarterly* NS 15: 1–30
(1981) *The Hippocratic Treatises "On Generation," "On the Nature of the Child," "Diseases IV"* (Ars Medica 7), Berlin and New York
Lopez Ferez, J. A. (1987) "Rheumatism, arthritis and gout in Galen," in Appelboom (1987) 84–86, 123–24
Loria, G. (1914) *Le scienze esatte nell'antica Grecia*, Milan
Lovejoy, A. O. (1909) "The meaning of φύσις in the Greek physiologers," *Philosophical Review* 18: 369–83
Lovejoy, A. O. and G. Boas (1935) *Primitivism and Related Ideas in Antiquity*, Baltimore
Luginbill, R. D. (1997) "Rethinking Antiphon's Περὶ Ἀληθείας," *Apeiron* 30: 163–87
Luppe, W. (1986) review of Funghi (1984), *Classical Review* NS 36: 121–25
Luria, S. (1924a) "Ein Gegner Homers," Известия Российской Академии Наук (*Bulletin de l'Académie des sciences de Russie*) 6. ser. 18: 373–82
(1924b) "ΑΓΛΩΤΤΙΑ," *Aegyptus* 5: 326–30
(1926a) "Das, was ist, und das, was nicht ist," *Philologische Wochenschrift* 46: 619–20
(1926b) "Eine politische Schrift des Redners Antiphon aus Rhamnus," *Hermes* 61: 343–48
(1926c) "Un criterio ortografico per distinguere l'oratore e il sofista Antifonte," *Rivista di filologia classica* NS 4: 218–22
(1926d) "Väter und Söhne in den neuen literarischen Papyri," *Aegyptus* 7: 243–68
(1927a) "L'argomentazione di Antifonte in Ox. Pap. XV 1797," *Rivista di filologia classica* NS 5: 80–83
(1927b) "Studien zur Geschichte der antiken Traumdeutung," Известия Академии Наук СССР (*Bulletin de l'Académie des sciences de l'URSS*) 1927: 441–66, 1041–72
(1928a) "Bemerkungen zur Geschichte der antiken Traumdeutung," Доклады Академии Наук СССР (*Comptes rendus de l'Académie des sciences de l'URSS*) в 1928: 175–79
(1928b) "Wann hat Demokrit gelebt?," *Archiv für Geschichte der Philosophie* 38: 205–38

(1928c) "Zu *P.Oxy.* III.414," *Classical Quarterly* 22: 176–78
(1929a) "Noch einmal über Antiphon in Euripides' Alexandros," *Hermes* 64: 491–97
(1929b) "Entstellungen des Klassikertextes bei Stobaios," *Rheinisches Museum für Philologie* NF 78: 81–104, 225–48
(1933) "Die Infinitesimaltheorie der antiken Atomisten," *Quellen und Studien zur Geschichte der Mathematik*, Abt. B: Studien 2: 106–85
(1963) "Antiphon der Sophist," *Eos* 53: 63–67
MacDowell, D. M. (1978) *The Law in Classical Athens*, Ithaca
(1990) *Demosthenes: Against Meidias*, Oxford
Maetzner, E. (1838) *Antiphontis orationes* XV, Berlin
Magnien, V. (1937) "Vocabulaire grec reflétant les rites du mariage," in *Mélanges offerts à A. M. Desrousseaux* (Paris) 293–99
Maier, H. (1913) *Sokrates: sein Werk und seine geschichtliche Stellung*, Tübingen
Mansfeld, J. (1987) "Theophrastus and the Xenophanes doxography," *Mnemosyne* 40: 286–312
(1990a) "Doxography and dialectic," in Haase (1990) 3056–229
(1990b) *Studies in the Historiography of Greek Philosophy*, Assen
(1998) *Prolegomena Mathematica: From Apollonius of Perga to Late Neoplatonism* (Philosophia Antiqua 80), Leiden
Mansfeld, J. and D. T. Runia (1997) *Aëtiana: The Method and Intellectual Context of a Doxographer* I (Philosophia Antiqua 73), Leiden
Mansion, A. (1945) *Introduction à la physique aristotélicienne*. 2nd ed., Louvain
Martin, T. H. (1841) *Études sur le Timée de Platon*. 2 vols., Paris
Mazzarino, S. (1966) *Il pensiero storico classico*. 3 vols., Bari
Menzel, A. (1922) *Kallikles: eine Studie zur Geschichte der Lehre vom Rechte des Stärkeren*, Vienna and Leipzig
Méridier, L. (1931) *Platon œuvres complètes* tome V.1: *Ion, Ménexène, Euthydème*, Paris
Merlan, P. (1950) "Alexander the Great or Antiphon the sophist?," *Classical Philology* 45: 161–66
Mewaldt, J. (1926) "Das Weltbürgertum in der Antike," *Die Antike* 2: 177–89
(1929) "Fundament des Staates," in F. Focke et al. (eds.) *Genethliakon Wilhelm Schmid zum siebzigsten Geburtstag* (Tübinger Beiträge zur Altertumswissenschaft 5) (Stuttgart) 69–93
Meyerhof, M. (1926) "La version arabe d'un traité perdu de Galien," *Byzantion* 3: 413–42
Michel, H. (1950) *De Pythagore à Euclide*, Paris
Minio-Paluello, L. (1972) *Opuscula*, Amsterdam
Mirhady, D. C. (1991) "The oath-challenge in Athens," *Classical Quarterly* 41: 78–83

Momigliano, A. (1930) "Sul pensiero di Antifonte il sofista," *Rivista di filologia classica* NS 8: 129–40, reprinted with additions in Momigliano (1969) 135–44
(1969) *Quarto contributo alla storia degli studi classici*, Rome
(1971) *The Development of Greek Biography*, Cambridge, Mass.
Mondolfo, R. (1956) *L'infinito nel pensiero dell'antichità classica*, Florence
(1958) *La comprensione del soggetto umano nell'antichità classica*, Florence
Mondolfo, R. and L. Tarán (1972) *Eraclito: Testimonianze e imitazioni*, Florence
Moraux, P. (1973–84) *Der Aristotelismus bei den Griechen*. 2 vols., Berlin
Morrison, J. S. (1953) "Xenophon, *Memorabilia* 1.6: The encounters of Socrates and Antiphon," *Classical Review* 67: 3–6
(1961) "Antiphon," *Proceedings of the Cambridge Philological Society* NS 7: 49–58
(1963) "The Truth of Antiphon," *Phronesis* 8: 35–49
(1972) "Antiphon," in R. K. Sprague (ed.) *The Older Sophists* (Columbia) 106–240
Moulton, C. (1972) "Antiphon the sophist, *On Truth*," *Transactions of the American Philological Association* 103: 329–66
(1974) "Antiphon the sophist and Democritus," *Museum Helveticum* 31: 129–39
Mourelatos, A. (1970) *The Route of Parmenides*, New Haven
Mühll, P. von der (1948) "Zur Unechtheit der antiphontischen Tetralogien," *Museum Helveticum* 5: 1–5
Nachmanson, E. (1941) *Der griechische Buchtitel. Einige Beobachtungen* (Göteborgs Högskolas Årsskrift XLVII: 19), Göteborg
Narcy, M. (1989) "Antiphon" (209), in R. Goulet (ed.) *Dictionnaire des philosophes antiques* I (Paris) 225–44
Nestle, W. (1901) *Euripides, der Dichter der griechischen Aufklärung*, Stuttgart
(1908) "Bemerkungen zu den Vorsokratikern und Sophisten," *Philologus* 67: 531–81
(1909a) review of Altwegg (1908), *Wochenschrift für klassische Philologie* 29: 120–22
(1909b) review of Jacoby (1908), *Deutsche Literaturzeitung* 30: 212–13
(1938) *Der Friedensgedanke in der antiken Welt* (Philologus Suppl. 31.1), Leipzig
(1940) "Xenophon und die Sophistik," *Philologus* 94: 31–50
(1942) *Vom Mythos zum Logos*. 2nd ed., Stuttgart
Niceforo, M. M. (1972) "La physis come elemento fondamentale nell'etica di Antifonte il sofista," *Studi classici e orientali* 21: 394–409
Nill, M. (1985) *Morality and Self-Interest in Protagoras, Antiphon and Democritus* (Philosophia Antiqua 43), Leiden

Norden, E. (1893) "Beiträge zur Geschichte der griechischen Philosophie," *Jahrbücher für classische Philologie* Suppl. 19: 365–462

(1913) *Agnostos Theos: Untersuchungen zur Formengeschichte religiöser Rede*, Leipzig and Berlin

(1918) *Die antike Kunstprosa*. 3rd ed. 2 vols., Leipzig and Berlin

North, H. (1966) *Sophrosyne: Self-Knowledge and Self-Restraint in Greek Literature*, Ithaca

O'Brien, D. (1968) "Derived light and eclipses in the fifth century," *Journal of Hellenic Studies* 88: 114–27

Ohly, K. (1928) *Stichometrische Untersuchungen* (Beihefte zum Zentralblatt für Bibliothekswesen 61), Leipzig

Olivier, F. (1895) *De Critolao Peripatetico*, Berlin

Ostwald, M. (1990) "*Nomos* and *phusis* in Antiphon's Περὶ Ἀληθείας," in M. Griffith and D. Mastronarde (eds.) *Cabinet of the Muses: Essays on Classical and Comparative Literature in Honor of T. G. Rosenmeyer* (Atlanta) 293–306

Padel, R. (1992) *In and out of the Mind: Greek Images of the Tragic Self*, Princeton

Paehler, R. (1885) *Die Löschung des Stahles bei den Alten*, Wiesbaden

Page, D. L. (1938) *Euripides: Medea*, Oxford

Paoli, U. E. (1933) *Studi sul processo attico*, Padua

Parke, H. W. and D. E. W. Wormell (1956) *The Delphic Oracle* 1: *The History*, Oxford

Patillon, M. (1988) *La théorie du discours chez Hermogène le rhéteur* (Collection d'études anciennes 117), Paris

(1997) *Hermogène: L'art rhétorique*, Paris

Pearson, A. C. (1917) *The Fragments of Sophocles*. 3 vols., Cambridge

Pease, A. S. (1911) "The omen of sneezing," *Classical Philology* 6: 429–43

(1955–58) *M. Tulli Ciceronis De natura deorum*. 2 vols., Cambridge, Mass.

Pellegrin, P. (1988) "L'imaginaire de la fièvre dans la médecine antique," *History and Philosophy of the Life Sciences* 10: 109–20

Pendrick, G. (1987) "Once again Antiphon the sophist and Antiphon of Rhamnus," *Hermes* 115: 47–60

(1993) "The identity of Antiphon reconsidered," *Greek, Roman and Byzantine Studies* 34: 215–28

Pfeiffer, R. (1968) *History of Classical Scholarship* 1, Oxford

Pfister, F. (1925) "Zu den neuen Bruchstücken des Sophisten Antiphon," *Philologische Wochenschrift* 45: 201–5

Philippson, R. (1918) review of Diels (1916), *Berliner Philologische Wochenschrift* 38: 121–26

Plescia, J. (1970) *The Oath and Perjury in Ancient Greece*, Tallahassee

Pohlenz, M. (1913) *Aus Platos Werdezeit*, Berlin

(1966) *Freedom in Greek Life and Thought*, tr. C. Lofmark, Dordrecht and New York

Pötscher, W. (1964) *Theophrastos:* ΠΕΡΙ ΕΥΣΕΒΕΙΑΣ (Philosophia Antiqua 11), Leiden

Rattenbury, R. M. (1938) "ΟΛΥΜΠΙΟΝΙΚΗ," *Classical Review* 1938: 114–15

Redard, G. (1953) *Recherches sur* ΧΡΗ, ΧΡΗΣΘΑΙ (Bibliothèque de l'Ecole des hautes études. Sciences historiques et philologiques 303), Paris

Reesor, M. E. (1987) "The *Truth* of Antiphon the sophist," *Apeiron* 20: 203–18

Regenbogen, O. (1940a) review of Bignone (1938), *Gnomon* 16: 97–105

(1940b) "Theophrastos (3)," *RE* Suppl. VII: 1354–562

Reinhardt, K. (1916) *Parmenides und die Geschichte der griechischen Philosophie*, Bonn

Rispoli, G. M. (1986) "Eufonia ed ermeneutica: origine ed evoluzione di un metodo filologico," *Koinonia* 10: 134–43

(1987) "Eufonia e poetica in testi ercolanesi," in G. Bolognesi and V. Pisani (eds.) *Linguistica e filologia: Atti del* VII *convengo internazionale di linguisti* (Brescia) 461–78

Roeper, G. (1848) "Conjecturen zu Diogenes Laertius," *Philologus* 3: 22–65

Romeyer-Dherbey, G. (1985) *Les sophistes*, Paris

Romilly, J. de (1971) *La loi dans la pensée grecque*, Paris

(1972) "Vocabulaire et propagande ou les premiers emplois du mot ὁμόνοια," in *Mélanges de linguistique et de philologie grecques offerts à Pierre Chantraine* (Paris) 199–209

Rommel H. (1929) "Stahl," *RE* IIIA, 2: 2126–33

Rose, H. J. (1958) *A Commentary on the Surviving Plays of Aeschylus*, Amsterdam

Rosenkranz, B. (1930) "Der lokale Grundton und die persönliche Eigenart in der Sprache des Thukydides und der älteren attischen Redner," *Indogermanische Forschungen* 48: 127–78

Ross, W. D. (1961) *Aristotle: De anima*, Oxford

Rowe, C. J. (1993) *Plato: Phaedo*, Cambridge

Rudio, F. (1892) *Archimedes, Huygens, Lambert, Legendre. Vier Abhandlungen über die Kreismessung*, Leipzig

(1902) "Der Bericht des Simplicius über die Quadraturen des Antiphon und des Hippokrates," *Bibliotheca Mathematica* 3: 7–62

Rufini, E. (1926) *Il "Metodo" di Archimede e le origini dell'analisi infinitesimale nell'antichità*, Rome

Ruiz Moreno, A. (1941) *Las afecciones reumáticas en el corpus Hippocraticum*, Buenos Aires

Ryffel, H. (1949) ΜΕΤΑΒΟΛΗ ΠΟΛΙΤΕΙΩΝ: *Der Wandel der Staatsverfassungen* (Noctes Romanae 2), Bern

Sandys, J. E. (1897) *The First Philippic and the Olynthiacs of Demosthenes*, London

Saunders, T. J. (1977–78) "Antiphon the sophist on natural laws," *Proceedings of the Aristotelian Society* 78: 215–36

Sauppe, H. (1896) "De Antiphonte sophista," in C. Trieber (ed.) *Ausgewaehlte Schriften* (Berlin) 508–26 (originally published Göttingen 1867)

Sbordone, F. (1955) "Filodemo e la teoria dell'eufonia," *Rendiconti dell'Accademia di archeologia, lettere e belle arti di Napoli* NS 30: 25–51

Schanz, M. and C. Hosius (1935) *Geschichte der römischen Literatur* II: *Die römische Literatur in der Zeit der Monarchie bis auf Hadrian*. 4th ed., Munich

Schmalzriedt, E. (1970) ΠΕΡΙ ΦΥΣΕΩΣ. *Zur Frühgeschichte des Buchtitels*, Munich

Schmid, W. (1907) "Ἐπίδειξις," *RE* VI, 1: 53–56

(1940) *Geschichte der griechischen Literatur* I.3.1, Munich

Schmid, W. and O. Stählin (1920–24) *Geschichte der griechischen Literatur* II. 2 vols., Munich

Schmidt, K. F. W. (1918) review of Grenfell and Hunt (1915), *Göttingische Gelehrte Anzeigen* 180: 95–98

(1924) "Die neuen Funde aus des Sophisten Antiphon Schrift περὶ ἀληθείας," *Das Humanistische Gymnasium* 35: 11–15

Schmidt, W. (1903) "Zu dem Berichte des Simplicius über die Möndchen des Hippokrates," *Bibliotheca Mathematica* 4: 118–26

Schöne, H. (1920–24) "Verschiedenes," *Rheinisches Museum für Philologie* NF 73: 137–60

Schöner, E. (1964) *Das Viererschema in der antiken Humoralpathologie* (Sudhoffs Archiv Beihefte 4), Wiesbaden

Schröder, S. (1990) *Plutarchs Schrift De Pythiae oraculis* (Beiträge zur Altertumskunde 8), Stuttgart

Schultz, H. (1912) "Harpokration (5)," *RE* VII, 2: 2412–16

(1913) "Hesychios (10)," *RE* VIII, 2: 1322–27

Schütrumpf, E. (1972) "Kosmopolitismus oder Panhellenismus?," *Hermes* 100: 5–29

Schwartz, E. (1951) *Ethik der Griechen*, Stuttgart

Schwyzer, E. (1939–53) *Griechische Grammatik*. 4 vols., Munich

Seeliger, K. (1924) review of Sigg (1923), *Philologische Wochenschrift* 44: 14–15

Shorey, P. (1892) review of Jowett (1892), *American Journal of Philology* 13: 349–72

(1907) review of Jebb (1905), *Classical Philology* 2: 233–35
(1909) "Φύσις, Μελέτη, Ἐπιστήμη," *Transactions of the American Philological Association* 50: 185–201
(1916) "Illogical idiom," *Transactions of the American Philological Association* 47: 205–34
(1918) review of Pearson (1917), *Classical Philology* 13: 94–99
(1919) "On δέ γε in retort," *Classical Philology* 14: 165–74
(1929) "Plato and the Stoic *OIKEIOSIS* in the Berlin Theaetetus commentary," *Classical Philology* 24: 409–10
(1930–35) *The Republic of Plato* (Loeb). 2 vols., London
(1980) *Selected Papers*, ed. L. Tarán. 2 vols., New York
Sider, D. (1981) *The Fragments of Anaxagoras* (Beiträge zur klassischen Philologie 118), Meisenheim am Glan
Sigg, H. (1923) *Antiphons zweite Tetralogie und die Schuldfrage des Oedipus*, Bern
Sinclair, T. A. (1968) *A History of Greek Political Thought*. 2nd ed., Cleveland
Sinko, T. (1938) "Ad Hesiodi Theogoniam (603–612) et Antiphontis fragmentum de matrimonio," *Eos* 39: 161–82
Slings, S. R. (1981) *A Commentary on the Platonic Clitophon*, Amsterdam
(1999) *Plato: Clitophon*, Cambridge
Smith, D. E. (1911) "The history and transcendence of π," in J. W. A. Young (ed.) *Monographs on Topics of Modern Mathematics* (New York) 387–416
Smyth, H. W. (1956) *Greek Grammar*. Rev. G. M. Messing, Cambridge, Mass.
Snell, B. (1924) *Die Ausdrücke für den Begriff des Wissens in der vorplatonischen Philosophie* (Philologische Untersuchungen 29), Berlin
Solmsen, F. (1901) *Untersuchungen zur griechischen Laut- und Verslehre*, Strassburg
Sommerstein, A. H. (1983) *Aristophanes: Wasps*, Warminster
Sorabji, R. (1983) *Time, Creation and the Continuum*, Ithaca
Spaan, P. van (1773) "Dissertatio historica de Antiphonte, oratore Attico," in J. J. Reiske (ed.) *Oratorum Graecorum . . . quae supersunt monumenta ingenii* VII (Leipzig) 795–830 (originally published Leiden 1765)
Spoerri, W. (1957) "Über die Quellen der Kulturentstehungslehre des Tzetzes," *Museum Helveticum* 14: 183–88
(1959) *Späthellenistische Berichte über Welt, Kultur und Götter* (Schweizerische Beiträge zur Altertumswissenschaft 9), Basel
Steier, A. (1927) "Lorbeer," *RE* XIII, 2: 1431–42
Stein, H. (1893–1908) *Herodotos*. Rev. ed. 5 vols., Berlin

Stemplinger, E. (1912) *Der Plagiat in der griechischen Literatur*, Leipzig and Berlin

Stenzel, J. (1924) "Antiphon (15)," *RE* Suppl. IV: 33–43

Stinton, T. C. W. (1985) "Heracles' homecoming and related topics: the second stasimon of Sophocles' *Trachiniae*," *Papers of the Liverpool Latin Seminar* 5: 403–32

(1990) *Collected Papers*, ed. H. Lloyd-Jones, Oxford

Strohmaier, G. (1971) "Hunayn B. Ishak," in B. Lewis et al. (eds.) *The Encyclopedia of Islam* (Leiden and London) 3.578–81

Susemihl, F. (1877) "Gorgias und die attische Prosa," *Jahrbücher für classische Philologie* 23: 793–99

(1891–92) *Geschichte der griechischen Litteratur in der Alexandrinerzeit*. 2 vols., Leipzig

Tannery, P. (1878) "Hippocrate de Chio et la quadrature des lunules," *Mémoires de la Société des sciences physiques et naturelles de Bordeaux* 2. sér. 2: 179–85

(1882) "Sur les fragments d'Eudème de Rhodes relatifs à l'histoire des mathématiques," *Annales de la Faculté des lettres de Bordeaux* 4: 70–76

(1887) *La géométrie grecque*, Paris

(1912) *Mémoires scientifiques* I, Toulouse and Paris

Tarán, L. (1965) *Parmenides*, Princeton

(1975) *Academica: Plato, Philip of Opus, and the Pseudo-Platonic Epinomis* (Memoirs of the American Philosophical Society 107), Philadelphia

(1977) review of Mourelatos (1970), *Gnomon* 49: 651–66

(1981) *Speusippus of Athens* (Philosophia Antiqua 39), Leiden

(1985) "Platonism and Socratic ignorance," in D. J. O'Meara (ed.) *Platonic Investigations* (Washington) 85–109

Tarn, W. W. (1933) "Alexander the Great and the unity of mankind," *Proceedings of the British Academy* 19: 123–66

Taylor, A. E. (1928) *A Commentary on Plato's Timaeus*, Oxford

Taylor, J. (1772) "Lectiones Lysiacae," in J. J. Reiske (ed.) *Oratorum Graecorum ... quae supersunt monumenta ingenii* VI (Leipzig) 219–334 (originally published London 1739)

Theander, C. (1920) "De fragmentis Antiphontis sophistae novis," *Nordisk Tidsskrift for Filologi* 4. ser. 9: 1–7

Thompson, E. S. (1901) *The Meno of Plato*, London and New York

Thompson, G. W. (1868) *The Phaedrus of Plato*, London

Tigner, S. (1974) "Empedocles' twirled ladle and the vortex-supported earth," *Isis* 65: 433–47

Timpanaro-Cardini, M. (1955) "Sui passi controversi di Platone, *Timeo* 40B, 36C, 36D, *Leges* 822A–C, di Aristotele, *De caelo* 293a15–293b33," *La Parola del passato* 10: 20–40

Töpfer, K. (1902) *Die sogenannten Fragmente des Sophisten Antiphon bei Jamblichos*, Arnau

Ueberweg, F. and K. Praechter (1926) *Grundriss der Geschichte der Philosophie* I: *Die Philosophie des Altertums*. 12th ed., Berlin

Untersteiner, M. (1954) *The Sophists*, tr. K. Freeman, Oxford

(1955) *Senofane: Testimonianze e frammenti*, Florence

(1961) *Sofisti, Testimonianze e frammenti* I: *Protagora e Seniade*. 2nd ed., Florence

(1967) *I sofisti*. 2nd ed. 2 vols., Milan

Uxkull-Gyllenband, W. von (1924) *Griechische Kulturentstehungslehren*, Berlin

Vegetti, M. (1965) "Il 'De locis in homine' tra Anassagora ed Ippocrate," *Rendiconti dell'Istituto lombardo*, Classe di lettere e scienze morali e storiche 99: 192–213

Verdenius, W. J. (1985) *A Commentary on Hesiod: Works and Days*, vv. 1–382 (Mnemosyne Suppl. 86), Leiden

Vlastos, G. (1945–46) "Ethics and physics in Democritus," *Philosophical Review* 54: 578–92; 55: 53–64

(1947) "Equality and justice in early Greek cosmologies," *Classical Philology* 42: 156–78

Vries, G. J. de (1943) "Σωφροσύνη en grec classique," *Mnemosyne* 11: 81–101

(1949) *Spel bij Plato*, Amsterdam

(1969) *A Commentary on the Phaedrus of Plato*, Amsterdam

Wackernagel, J. (1926–28) *Vorlesungen über Syntax*. 2nd ed. 2 vols., Basel

Wagner, H. (1972) *Aristoteles: Physikvorlesung* (*Aristoteles, Werke in deutscher Übersetzung* 11). 2nd ed., Berlin

Wasserstein, A. (1959) "Some early Greek attempts to square the circle," *Phronesis* 4: 92–100

Waterlow, S. (1982) *Nature, Change, and Agency in Aristotle's Physics*, Oxford

Wendel, C. (1948) "Tzetzes (1)," *RE* VIIA, 2: 1959–2010

West, M. L. (1966) *Hesiod: Theogony*, Oxford

(1978) *Hesiod: Works and Days*, Oxford

(1982) *Greek Metre*, Oxford

(1990) *Studies in Aeschylus* (Beiträge zur Altertumskunde 1), Stuttgart

Whitehead, D. (1988) "Athenians in Xenophon's *Hellenica*," *Liverpool Classical Monthly* 13: 145–47

(1990) *Aineias the Tactician: How to Survive under Siege*, Oxford

Wicksteed, P. H. and F. M. Cornford (1957) *Aristotle: The Physics* I (Loeb). Rev. ed., London

Wiesner, J. (1994) "Antiphon, der Sophist und Antiphon, der Redner – ein oder zwei Autoren?," *Wiener Studien* 107: 225–43

Wilamowitz-Moellendorff, U. von (1876) "Memoriae oblitteratae," *Hermes* 11: 291–304
(1877) "Die Thukydideslegende," *Hermes* 12: 326–67
(1880) "Excurse zu Euripides Medeia," *Hermes* 15: 481–523
(1893) *Aristoteles und Athen*. 2 vols., Berlin
(1895) *Euripides: Herakles*. 2nd ed. 2 vols., Berlin
(1919) "Lesefrüchte," *Hermes* 54: 46–74
(1927) "Lesefrüchte," *Hermes* 62: 276–98
(1931–32) *Der Glaube der Hellenen*. 2 vols., Berlin
(1959) *Platon*. 5th ed. 2 vols., Berlin
Wolff, G. (1856) *Porphyrii De philosophia ex oraculis haurienda librorum reliquiae*, Berlin
Wooten, C. W. (1987) *Hermogenes' On Types of Style*, Chapel Hill
Wyse, W. (1904) *The Speeches of Isaeus*, Cambridge
Zeller, E. (1922) *Die Philosophie der Griechen in ihrer geschichtlichen Entwicklung* II.I. 5th ed., Leipzig
(1923) *Die Philosophie der Griechen in ihrer geschichtlichen Entwicklung* III.I. 5th ed., Leipzig
Zeller, E. and R. Mondolfo (1961) *La filosofia dei greci nel suo sviluppo storico* 1.4: *Eraclito*, Florence
(1969) *La filosofia dei greci nel suo sviluppo storico* 1.5: *Empedocle, Atomisti, Anassagora*, ed. A. Capizzi, Florence
Zeller, E. and W. Nestle (1920) *Die Philosophie der Griechen in ihrer geschichtlichen Entwicklung* I.2. 6th ed., Leipzig
Zeppi, S. (1958) "La posizione storica di Antifonte," *Rivista critica di storia della filosofia* 13: 357–71
(1962) *Studi sulla filosofia presocratica*, Florence
Zeuthen, H. G. (1913) *Sur les connaissances géométriques des grecs avant la réforme platonicienne* (Oversigt over det Kongelige Danske Videnskabernes Selskabs Forhandlinger 6), Copenhagen
Ziegler, K. (1950) "Plagiat," *RE* XX, 2: 1956–97
Zumpos, A. N. (1965–66) "Zum sophisten Antiphon," *Živa Antika* 15: 380

INDEXES

(All references are to page numbers)

1. INDEX OF PASSAGES CITED

1. INDEX OF PASSAGES CITED

1. INDEX OF PASSAGES CITED

I. INDEX OF PASSAGES CITED

1. INDEX OF PASSAGES CITED

1. INDEX OF PASSAGES CITED

2. INDEX OF SUBJECTS

2. INDEX OF SUBJECTS

3. INDEX OF GREEK WORDS

3. INDEX OF GREEK WORDS

3. INDEX OF GREEK WORDS

3. INDEX OF GREEK WORDS

Lightning Source UK Ltd.
Milton Keynes UK
UKOW03f1349200417
299519UK00001BA/7/P

9 780521 126120